THE ROUTLEDGE COMPANION TO CINEMA AND GENDER

The Routledge Companion to Cinema and Gender comprises forty-three innovative essays that offer both an overview of and an intervention into the field of cinema and gender.

The contributions in this volume address a variety of geographical and cultural contexts through an analysis of cinema, from the representation of women and Islam in Middle Eastern film, and female audience reception in Nigeria, to changing class and race norms in Bollywood dance sequences. The book includes a special focus on women directors in a global context, examining films and filmmakers from Asia, Africa, Australia, Europe, and North and South America.

Alongside a comprehensive overview of feminist perspectives on genre, this collection also offers discussion on a range of approaches to spectatorship, reception studies, and fandom, as well as transnational approaches to star studies and the relationship between feminist film theory and new media. Other topics include queer and trans* cinema, ecocinema, the post-human, and the methodological dimensions of feminist film history.

This Routledge Companion provides researchers, students, and scholars with an essential guide to the key political, cultural, and theoretical debates surrounding cinema and gender.

Kristin Lené Hole is an Assistant Professor in the School of Film at Portland State University, USA. She is the author of *Towards a Feminist Cinematic Ethics: Claire Denis, Emmanuel Levinas, and Jean-Luc Nancy* (2016) and co-author (with Dijana Jelača) of *Film Feminisms: A Global Introduction* (2019).

Dijana Jelača teaches in the Film Department at Brooklyn College, USA. She is the author of *Dislocated Screen Memory: Narrating Trauma in Post-Yugoslav Cinema* (2016) and co-author (with Kristin Lené Hole) of *Film Feminisms: A Global Introduction* (2019).

E. Ann Kaplan is Distinguished Professor of English and Women's, Gender and Sexuality Studies at Stony Brook University, USA, where she also founded and directed The Humanities Institute. She is Past President of the Society for Cinema and Media Studies. Kaplan's pioneering research on women in film includes *Women in Film: Both Sides of the Camera*, *Motherhood and Representation*, *Looking for the Other*, *and Feminism* *and Film.* Her recent research focuses on trauma: see *Trauma and Cinema* (2004) with Ban Wang; *Trauma Culture: The Politics of Terror and Loss in Media and Literature* (2005); and *Climate Trauma: Foreseeing the Future in Dystopian Film and Fiction* (2015).

Patrice Petro is Dick Wolf Director of the Carsey-Wolf Center, Professor of Film and Media Studies, and Presidential Chair in Media Studies at the University of California, Santa Barbara, USA. She is the author, editor, and co-editor of twelve books, most recently *Idols of Modernity: Movie Stars of the 1920s* (2010), *Teaching Film* (2012), and *After Capitalism: Horizons of Finance, Culture, and Citizenship* (2016).

Contributors: Eylem Atakav, Jacqueline Bobo, Amy Borden, Sumita Chakravarty, Jenny Chamarette, Sally Chivers, Anne Ciecko, Felicity Colman, Lucy Fischer, Jane Gaines, Tejaswini Ganti, Julie Grossman, Anthony Hayt, Margaret Hennefeld, Kristin Lené Hole, Anikó Imre, Priya Jaikumar, Dijana Jelača, E. Ann Kaplan, Erica Levin, Rachel A. Lewis, Katarzyna Marciniak, Russell Meeuf, Mireille Miller-Young, Katherine E. Morrissey, Ikechukwu Obiaya, Claire Pajaczkowska, Celine Parreñas Shimizu, Constance Penley, Jennifer Peterson, Patrice Petro, Sandra Ponzanesi, Veronica Pravadelli, Hilary Radner, Belinda Smaill, J. E. Smyth, Janet Staiger, Eliza Steinbock, Tristan Taormino, Yvonne Tasker, Maureen Turim, Kathleen M. Vernon, Lingzhen Wang, Alexa Weik von Mossner, Patricia White, Debra Zimmerman.

THE ROUTLEDGE COMPANION TO CINEMA AND GENDER

Edited by Kristin Lené Hole, Dijana Jelača,
E. Ann Kaplan, and Patrice Petro

Routledge
Taylor & Francis Group

LONDON AND NEW YORK

First published in paperback 2019

First published 2017
by Routledge
2 Park Square, Milton Park, Abingdon, Oxon OX14 4RN

and by Routledge
52 Vanderbilt Avenue, New York, NY 10017

Routledge is an imprint of the Taylor & Francis Group, an informa business

British Library Cataloguing-in-Publication Data
A catalogue record for this book is available from the British Library

Library of Congress Cataloging-in-Publication Data
Names: Hole, Kristin Lenâe, editor. | Jelaéca, Dijana, 1979- editor. | Kaplan, E. Ann,
editor. | Petro, Patrice, 1957- editor.
Title: The Routledge companion to cinema and gender / edited by Kristin Lenâe Hole,
Dijana Jelaca, E. Ann Kaplan, Patrice Petro.
Description: New York : Routledge, 2017. | Includes index.
Identifiers: LCCN 2016017952 | ISBN 9781138924956 (hardback : alk. paper) |
ISBN 9781315684062 (ebook)
Subjects: LCSH: Sex role in motion pictures
Classification: LCC PN1995.9.S47 R68 2017 | DDC 791.43/653--dc23
LC record available at https://lccn.loc.gov/2016017952

ISBN: 978-1-138-92495-6 (hbk)
ISBN: 978-1-138-39184-0 (pbk)
ISBN: 978-1-315-68406-2 (ebk)

Typeset in Goudy
by Taylor & Francis Books

CONTENTS

Contents

Contents

FIGURES

Figures

CONTRIBUTORS

Eylem Atakav is Senior Lecturer in Film and Television Studies at the University of East Anglia where she teaches courses on women and film; women, Islam and media; and Middle Eastern cinemas. She is the author of *Women and Turkish Cinema: Gender Politics, Cultural Identity and Representation* (2012) and editor of *Directory of World Cinema: Turkey* (2013).

Jacqueline Bobo is Professor of Feminist Studies and affiliated faculty member of Film and Media Studies at the University of California, Santa Barbara. Her books include *Black Women as Cultural Readers* (1995); *Black Women Film and Video Artists* (1998); *Black Feminist Cultural Criticism* (2001); and, *The Black Studies Reader* (2004).

Amy Borden is Assistant Professor of Film at Portland State University. She specializes in silent film history, gender, and classical film theory. She is currently writing about modernity and the theorization of motion pictures in gilded age American magazines. Her work appears in *Cycles, Sequels, Spin-offs, Remakes, and Reboots: Multiplicities in Film & Television* (2016), *Jump Cut*, and *Beyond the Screen: Institutions, Networks and Publics of Early Cinema*.

Sumita S. Chakravarty teaches media and cultural studies at the New School in New York. She is the author of *National Identity in Indian Popular Cinema*. She is currently working on a book on the historical intersections of media and migration.

Jenny Chamarette is Senior Lecturer in Film Studies at Queen Mary, University of London. She is an author of *Phenomenology and the Future of Film: Rethinking Subjectivity beyond French Cinema* (2012) and co-editor of *Guilt and Shame: Essays in French Literature, Thought and Visual Culture* (with Jennifer Higgins, 2010). She is currently working on a monograph entitled *Cinemuseology: Digital Screens, Museum Vitrines and Cultural Politics*.

Sally Chivers is Professor of English Literature at Trent University. Author of *From Old Woman to Older Women: Contemporary Culture and Women's Narratives* and *The Silvering Screen: Old Age and Disability in Cinema*, and co-editor of *The Problem Body: Projecting Disability on Film*, she is currently researching the interplay between aging and disability in the public sphere, with a focus on care narratives in the context of austerity.

Anne Ciecko is Associate Professor in the Department of Communication at the University of Massachusetts Amherst. She has published widely on international women filmmakers and gender representations in world cinema.

Felicity Colman is Professor of Film and Media Arts at the Manchester School of Art, Manchester Metropolitan University. She is the author of *Film Theory: Creating a Cinematic Grammar* (2014), *Deleuze and Cinema* (2011), and editor of *Film, Theory and Philosophy: The Key Thinkers* (2009), and co-editor of *Sensorium: Aesthetics, Art, Life* (2007).

Lucy Fischer is a Distinguished Professor of English and Film Studies at the University of Pittsburg. She is the author of eleven books, including: *Shot/Countershot: Film Tradition and Women's Cinema* (1989), *Imitation of Life* (1991), *Cinematernity: Film, Motherhood, Genre* (1996), *Designing Women: Art Deco, Cinema and the Female Form* (2003), *Stars: The Film Reader* (2004), *Teaching Film* (co-edited with Patrice Petro, 2012), and *Cinema By Design: Art Nouveau and Film History* (forthcoming). She has served as President of the Society for Cinema and Media Studies (2001–3) and in 2008 received its Distinguished Service Award.

Jane Gaines is Professor of Film at Columbia University where she directs the MA in Film and Media Studies. She has written two award-winning books: *Fire and Desire: Mixed-Blood Movies in the Silent Era* (2001), and *Contested Culture: The Image, the Voice, and the Law* (1991). She received an Academy of Motion Picture Arts and Sciences Scholarly Award for her forthcoming book on early cinema, *Pink-Slipped: What Happened to Women in the Silent Motion Picture Industries?*, companion to the Women Film Pioneers Project digital database published by Columbia University Libraries: https://wfpp.cdrs.columbia.edu.

Tejaswini Ganti is Associate Professor in the Department of Anthropology and its Program in Culture and Media at New York University. She is the author of *Producing Bollywood: Inside the Contemporary Hindi Film Industry* (2012) and *Bollywood: A Guidebook to Popular Hindi Cinema* (2004, 2013).

Julie Grossman, Professor of English and Communication and Film Studies at Le Moyne College, has published essays on film, literature, gender, and popular culture. She is author of *Rethinking the Femme Fatale in Film Noir* (2009, 2012) and *Literature, Film, and Their Hideous Progeny* (2015). Her co-authored book on the directing work of Ida Lupino is forthcoming from Rutgers University Press, and she is co-editor of the book series *Adaptation and Visual Culture* (Palgrave Macmillan).

Anthony Hayt earned his PhD in English with a focus in film studies from the University of Oregon in 2014 with the dissertation *Remade in Our Image: Gender, Melodrama, and Conservatism in Post-9/11 Slasher Remakes*. His focus on feminist inflected research encompasses genre theory, auteur studies, remake theory, race studies, and mainstream American film. He is currently co-writing a graphic novel that explores many of these areas in a fictional format.

Margaret Hennefeld is an Assistant Professor of Cultural Studies and Comparative Literature at the University of Minnesota. She is the author of *Specters of Slapstick and Silent Film Comediennes* (forthcoming) and is currently co-editing a volume, *The Abject Objection:*

Theories of Graphic and Comedic Violence, as well as a themed journal issue of *Feminist Media Histories* on "Gender and Comedy."

Kristin Lené Hole teaches in the Film Studies program at Portland State University. Her book is entitled *Towards a Feminist Cinematic Ethics: Claire Denis, Emmanuel Levinas, and Jean-Luc Nancy* (2015). She is currently co-authoring a textbook on feminism and film from a global perspective.

Anikó Imre is Associate Professor and Chair in the Division of Cinema and Media Studies at the School of Cinematic Arts of the University of Southern California. She is the author of *Identity Games: Globalization and the Transformation of Post-Communist Media Cultures* (2009), editor of *East European Cinemas* (2005), *The Blackwell Companion to East European Cinemas* (2012), and co-editor of *Transnational Feminism in Film and Media* (2007), and *Popular Television in the New Europe* (2012). Her monograph *TV Socialism* is forthcoming in 2016 in Duke University Press's Console-ing Passions series.

Priya Jaikumar is Associate Professor in the Department of Cinema and Media Studies at the University of Southern California's School of Cinematic Arts. Jaikumar is the author of *Cinema at the End of Empire: A Politics of Transition in Britain and India* (2006), and several essays and book chapters including "An 'Accurate Imagination': Place, Map and Archive as Spatial Objects of Film History." She is completing a book titled *Where Histories Reside: India as Filmed Space* about theatrical and non-theatrical films shot on location in India.

Dijana Jelača teaches in the Department of Communication and Media Studies at Fordham University. She is the author of *Dislocated Screen Memory: Narrating Trauma in Post-Yugoslav Cinema* (2016). Her work has appeared in *Camera Obscura, Feminist Media Studies, Studies in Eastern European Cinema*, and *Jump Cut*. Together with Kristin Lené Hole, she is currently working on a textbook titled *Film Feminisms: Global Perspectives*.

E. Ann Kaplan is Distinguished Professor of English and Women's, Gender and Sexuality Studies at Stony Brook University. She is Past President of the Society for Cinema and Media Studies. Kaplan's pioneering research on women in film includes *Women & Film: Both Sides of the Camera, Motherhood and Representation, Looking for the Other*, and *Feminism in Film*. Her recent research focuses on trauma: *Trauma and Cinema* (2004), *Trauma Culture: The Politics of Terror and Loss in Media and Literature* (2005), and *Climate Trauma: Foreseeing the Future in Dystopian Film and Fiction* (2015). Kaplan is working on her next book, *The Unconscious of Age: Screening Older Women*.

Erica Levin is an Assistant Professor of Art History at The Ohio State University. Her writing has been published in *World Picture, Millennium Film Journal, Discourse*, and most recently in the collection, *Carolee Schneemann: Unforgivable*. She is currently at work on a book that examines the conditions under which artists who trained as painters turned to filmmaking during the 1960s and in the process began to reckon with the effects of spectacularized political violence on the body politic.

Rachel A. Lewis is an Assistant Professor in the Women and Gender Studies Program at George Mason University. Her research and teaching interests include transnational feminisms, queer theory, media and cultural studies, sexuality, race and immigration, human rights, and transnational sexualities. She has published articles in *Sexualities*, *Feminist Formations*, *Social Justice*, *International Feminist Journal of Politics*, *Journal of Lesbian Studies*, and *Women & Music: A Journal of Gender and Culture*.

Katarzyna Marciniak is Professor of Transnational Studies in the English Department at Ohio University. She is the author of *Alienhood: Citizenship, Exile, and the Logic of Difference* (2006), co-author of *Streets of Crocodiles: Photography, Media, and Postsocialist Landscapes in Poland* (2010), and co-editor of *Transnational Feminism in Film and Media* (2007), *Immigrant Protest: Politics, Aesthetics, and Everyday Dissent* (2014), and *Teaching Transnational Cinema: Politics and Pedagogy* (2016). She is Series Editor of *Global Cinema* from Palgrave.

Russell Meeuf is Assistant Professor of Media Studies at the University of Idaho. He is the author of *John Wayne's World: Transnational Masculinity in the Fifties* (2013), and co-editor of *Transnational Stardom: International Celebrity in Film and Popular Culture* (2013).

Mireille Miller-Young is Associate Professor of Feminist Studies at the University of California, Santa Barbara. Her research explores race, gender, and sexuality in visual culture and sex industries in the United States. Her book *A Taste for Brown Sugar: Black Women in Pornography* (2014) examines African American women's representation and labor in pornographic media.

Katherine E. Morrissey is Visiting Assistant Professor of English at the Rochester Institute of Technology and PhD Candidate in the English Department at the University of Wisconsin–Milwaukee. Her research interests include the representation of female desire in popular culture, production environments for romantic storytelling, and participatory culture. Her work has been published in the *Journal for Popular Romance Studies* and *Transformative Works and Cultures*.

Ikechukwu Obiaya lectures at the School of Media and Communication of the Pan-Atlantic University, in Lagos, Nigeria. His research is based on the Nigerian film industry with particular focus on the National Film and Censors Board as well as audience analysis.

Claire Pajaczkowska, independent filmmaker and lecturer, was Reader in Psychoanalysis and Visual Culture at Middlesex University to 2008 and is Senior Research Tutor at the Royal College of Art, London. She is contributor and co-editor (with Luke White) of *The Sublime Now* (2009), and co-editor (with Catalina Bronstein and Julia Borossa) of *The New Klein-Lacan Dialogues* (2015).

Celine Parreñas Shimizu is Professor of Feminist Studies at the University of California, Santa Barbara. She is an award-winning filmmaker and film scholar. She is the author of *The Hypersexuality of Race: Performing Asian/American Women on Screen and Scene* (2007) and *Straitjacket Sexualities: Unbinding Asian American Manhoods in the Movies* (2012).

Constance Penley is Professor of Film and Media Studies at the University of California, Santa Barbara. She is a founding editor of *Camera Obscura: Feminism, Culture, and Media Studies*. Her books include *The Future of an Illusion: Film, Feminism, and Psychoanalysis*, *NASA/ TREK: Popular Science and Sex in America*, and the forthcoming *Teaching Pornography*. Penley is a recipient of the MacArthur Foundation Digital Media and Learning Award and the Kenneth Burke Society Prize in Rhetorical Criticism.

Jennifer Peterson is the author of *Education in the School of Dreams: Travelogues and Early Nonfiction Film* (Duke University Press, 2013). She has published articles in *Cinema Journal, Camera Obscura, The Moving Image,* the *Getty Research Journal,* and numerous edited book collections. She is currently Associate Professor and Chair of the Department of Communication at Woodbury University in Los Angeles.

Patrice Petro is Professor of Film and Media Studies at the University of California, Santa Barbara, where she also serves as Director of the Carsey-Wolf Center. She is the author, editor, and co-editor of eleven books, including *Teaching Film* (with Lucy Fischer, for the MLA Teaching Series) (2012). She is former Treasurer (2002–5) and two-term President of the Society for Cinema and Media Studies (2007–11). Her most recent project is an edited volume, *After Capitalism* (2016).

Sandra Ponzanesi is Professor of Gender and Postcolonial Studies at the Department of Media and Culture Studies, Utrecht University, the Netherlands. She is the author of *The Postcolonial Cultural Industry* (2014), and *Paradoxes of Postcolonial Culture* (2004), and editor of multiple volumes, among which is *Postcolonial Cinema Studies* (2012).

Veronica Pravadelli is Professor of Film Studies at Roma Tre University where she directs the Center for American Studies (CRISA). She has been Visiting Professor at Brown University. She has written many books and articles on feminist film theory and women's cinema, Hollywood cinema, and Italian post-neorealist film. Her two most recent books are *Classic Hollywood: Lifestyles and Film Styles of American Cinema, 1930–1960* (2015) and *Le donne del cinema: dive, registe, spettatrici* (2014).

Hilary Radner is Professor of Film and Media Studies in the Department of History and Art History, at the University of Otago, New Zealand. Her published works include *Shopping Around: Feminine Culture and the Pursuit of Pleasure* (1995) and *Neo-Feminist Cinema: Girly Films, Chick Flicks and Consumer Culture* (2011), as well as numerous co-edited volumes. She is currently completing a book under contract with Routledge, *The New Woman's Film: From Chick Flicks to Movies for Smart "Femmes."*

Belinda Smaill teaches Film and Screen Studies at Monash University in Melbourne. She is the author of *The Documentary: Politics, Emotion, Culture* (2010), *Regarding Life: Animals and the Documentary Moving Image* (2016), and co-author of *Transnational Australian Cinema: Ethics in the Asian Diasporas* (2013). She has published widely on documentary, women and cinema, and Australian film and television.

J. E. Smyth is an American historian specializing in the history of cinema. Her research focuses on historical filmmaking in Hollywood and in Europe from the silent era to the present. Smyth is the author of *From Here to Eternity* (2015), and her work has appeared in *Cineaste, The Blackwell Companion to American Film History, The Quarterly Review of Film and Video,* and elsewhere. She teaches at the University of Warwick.

Janet Staiger is William P. Hobby Centennial Professor Emeritus in Communication and Women's and Gender Studies at the University of Texas. Among her books are *Media*

Reception Studies (2005), *Blockbuster TV* (2000), *Perverse Spectators* (2000), and *Interpreting Films* (1992).

Eliza Steinbock from the Department of Film and Literary Studies at Leiden University's Centre for the Arts in Society has a critical curiosity for bodies and art. Her writing on sexuality, aesthetics, visual culture, and transgender studies is published in the *Journal of Homosexuality*, *Routledge Companion to Media*, *Sex and Sexuality*, and *TSQ: Transgender Studies Quarterly*.

Tristan Taormino is a feminist author, columnist, sex educator, activist, editor, speaker, radio host, and porn film director. Taormino has authored seven books, including *The Ultimate Guide to Anal Sex for Women* (1997).

Yvonne Tasker is Professor of Film, Television, and Media Studies at the University of East Anglia, UK. Since the publication of her first book, *Spectacular Bodies*, in 1993 she has authored numerous books and essays exploring aspects of gender, sexuality, and race in popular visual culture. Her most recent books are *Gendering the Recession* (co-edited with Diane Negra), published by Duke University Press in 2014, and *Hollywood Action and Adventure Cinema*, published by Wiley-Blackwell in 2015.

Maureen Turim is Professor of English at the University of Florida. She is the author of *Abstraction in Avant-Garde Films* (1985), *Flashbacks in Film: Memory and History* (1989), and *The Films of Oshima: Images of a Japanese Iconoclast* (1998). She has published on a wide range of theoretical, historical, and aesthetic issues in cinema and video, art, cultural studies, feminist and psychoanalytic theory, and comparative literature. Several of these essays have appeared in translation in French and German.

Kathleen M. Vernon is Associate Professor and Chair of the Department of Hispanic Languages and Literature at Stony Brook University. She has published widely on various aspects of Spanish-language cinema and is currently completing a book entitled *Listening to Spanish Cinema*.

Lingzhen Wang is Associate Professor in East Asian Studies at Brown University. She specializes in Chinese literature and cinema, gender studies, and transnational feminist theory. She is the Brown Director of the Brown–Nanjing Joint Program in Gender Studies and the Humanities.

Alexa Weik von Mossner is Assistant Professor of American Studies at the University of Klagenfurt, Austria. She is the author of *Cosmopolitan Minds: Literature, Emotion, and the Transnational Imagination* (2014), the editor of *Moving Environments: Affect, Emotion, Ecology, and Film* (2014), and co-editor of *The Anticipation of Catastrophe: Environmental Risk in North American Literature and Culture* (with Sylvia Mayer, 2014). Her new book, *Affective Ecologies: Environmental Narrative and the Embodied Mind*, is forthcoming with Ohio State University Press.

Patricia White is the Eugene Lang Research Professor of Film and Media Studies at Swarthmore College and the author of *unInvited: Classical Hollywood Cinema and Lesbian Representability* (1999) and *Women's Cinema, World Cinema: Projecting Contemporary Feminisms* (2015). She is co-author with Timothy Corrigan of the widely adopted introductory film textbook *The Film Experience* (4th edn 2014) and co-editor with Corrigan and Meta Mazaj of *Critical Visions in Film Theory* (2011).

Debra Zimmerman has been the Executive Director of Women Make Movies since 1983. Zimmerman has curated numerous films and media exhibitions, most recently as Co-Curator of the Doc Fortnight at MoMA. She is the recipient of the New York Women in Film and Television's Loreen Arbus Changemaker Award, the Athena Award and Hot Doc's 2013 Doc Mogul Award. Zimmerman served as the 2014–15 Blanche, Edith, and Irving Laurie New Jersey Chair in Women's Studies at Douglass College, Rutgers University.

ACKNOWLEDGMENTS

The editors would like to thank Natalie Foster and Sheni Kruger at Routledge for their support on this project.

We would like to extend our deepest thanks to all contributors for helping to make this a strong collection. We have learned so much from your scholarship and your work demonstrates the vitality and breadth of the field.

Kristin and Dijana would specifically like to extend thanks to Patrice and Ann for their mentorship and support throughout this project. It has been a privilege to work as a team.

Thanks also to Claire Lindsay for her administrative assistance in the final hours of preparing the manuscript.

INTRODUCTION

Decentering feminist film studies

Kristin Lené Hole, Dijana Jelača, E. Ann Kaplan, and Patrice Petro

Cinema and gender are concepts with a long and complicated relationship that extends to every aspect of filmmaking—production, representation, exhibition, spectatorship, reception, and distribution. The volume at hand approaches this relationship through the diverse and dynamic field of feminist film studies—from psychoanalytic and semiotic to phenomenological and Deleuzian approaches, and from studies of genre and reception to the practices of digital culture. The relationship between cinema and gender is never static. Rather, it has perpetually shifted in relation to emerging practices, technologies, and recognition of the limitations of prevailing intellectual paradigms at any given moment.

From the early years of cinema, the medium has reflected and constructed ideals of both femininity and masculinity (a fact often forgotten in the feminist paradigm's closer association with femininity). Over the course of the twentieth century, cinema has not only reiterated raced and classed gender norms, but *constructed* them as well. These norms typically took the form of privileging Western geographies and white histories, not least because, since the medium's emergence, Hollywood established itself as the world's dominant film industry. At the same time, even with the dominance of Western geographies and white histories, cinema often served as a venue where provocative challenges to the status quo of gender inequality (as well as its links to race, class and sexuality) were leveled, sometimes in clandestine ways. For instance, a closer inspection of women's roles in 1920s and 1930s Hollywood films reveals a complex spectrum of female agency, exemplified in the figures of Mae West, Lillian Gish, and Marlene Dietrich. Women were active, if often uncredited, participants in film production throughout Hollywood's history. Furthermore, recent efforts by feminist film historians have uncovered a significant number of women film pioneers from around the world, writing women's film histories where previously there were none (for more on these issues, see the essays by Pravadelli, Smyth, Hennefeld, Bobo, and Gaines in this volume). These efforts at uncovering the hidden transcripts of film history should not be taken as implying that women did not experience structural gender-based discrimination in the industry. Quite the contrary, the fact that the film industry is still predominantly white and male speaks to the ongoing importance of the feminist intellectual project at hand.

Reflecting on feminist film theory and history

The origins of feminist film studies are typically located in theoretical work of the 1970s and 1980s, much of which connected with major intellectual currents of the time, such as semiotics, post-structuralism, and psychoanalysis. As many contributions to this volume demonstrate, feminist film scholars' continued engagement with classical feminist film scholarship indicates that its influence is far from over (see, for example, essays by Petro, Fischer, Pajaczkowska, Steinbock, Weik von Mossner, Jelača, and Hole in this volume). There is a tacit recognition here that classical feminist film theory, as endlessly parsed and scrutinized as it has been, still has something insightful to offer as a basis for current and future film scholarship. In other words, its business remains unfinished.

But what do we mean by the oft used but rarely defined term "classical feminist film theory?" Before offering a brief genealogy, it is important to acknowledge that the very focus on "theory" obscures the interconnected nature of theory and practice in early feminist film circles. While women were beginning to write about cinema and gender, they were also advocating alternate modes of representation, creating women's film collectives, holding women's film festivals, and organizing on the ground in order to increase women's access to making and exhibiting films. The field's inauguration in the 1970s (coinciding with Second Wave feminism) is linked to the publication of several important works, such as Marjorie Rosen's *Popcorn Venus: Women, Movies and the American Dream* (1973), Molly Haskell's *From Reverence to Rape: The Treatment of Women in Movies* (1974), and two seminal essays: Claire Johnston's "Women's Cinema as Counter-Cinema" (1973), and Laura Mulvey's "Visual Pleasure and Narrative Cinema" (1975). Writing about the new wave of film scholarship coming out of Great Britain in particular, E. Ann Kaplan notes in 1974 that scholars such as Johnston and Pam Cook are influenced by psychoanalysis and linguistics (or rather, the structuralist and post-structuralist turns), and theorists as varied as Sigmund Freud, Jacques Lacan, Raymond Williams, Christian Metz, and Karl Marx (Kaplan 1974). Moreover, the broader group of film scholars to which Johnston, Cook, and Mulvey belonged was centered around journals such as the *New Left Review* and *Screen*, which later prompted the denomination "*Screen* theory." These approaches have largely eclipsed the more sociologically inflected analyses of the representation of women in the work of Rosen and Haskell. While Rosen and Haskell did the important work of identifying the pervasively negative or controlling images of women in dominant cinema, they may have assumed too simple a connection between representation and the real. The theorists that followed realized that the specifically cinematic formal language of film must also be examined for its "invisible" ideological effects.

In the groundbreaking critique that feminist film scholars were leveling at cinema and existing film scholarship alike, they faced a significant conundrum summarized by Constance Penley in the following question: "How could feminists account for the disruptive effects of femininity in the classical film without falling back on an essentialist notion of 'femininity' or 'Woman' as an eternal and *naturally* subversive element?" (1988: 5). The potential trap, according to Penley, needed to be countered by historicizing the notion of "essence" rather than taking it as an immutable given. In her widely influential essay "Women's Cinema as Counter-Cinema," Claire Johnston focuses on the neo-Marxist understandings of ideology inscribed in any cultural form or work of art, and argues that:

> Any revolutionary strategy must challenge the depiction of reality: it is not enough
> to discuss the oppression of women within the text of the film: the language of the

cinema/depiction of reality must also be interrogated, so that a break between ideology and text is affected.

(1973: 29)

Like Johnston, Laura Mulvey was concerned with diagnosing the mechanisms of studio-era Hollywood cinema while advocating the radicalization of film form. Yet while Johnston argued that some forms of pleasure could be strategically coopted from mainstream cinema, Mulvey's "Visual Pleasure and Narrative Cinema" tacitly dismisses the notion that conventionalized notions of visual pleasure can be a form of feminist subversion. She turns to psychoanalysis to identify voyeurism and fetishism as primary channels of spectatorial identification invited by classic Hollywood cinema. The film apparatus caters to the male gaze so that woman occupies a to-be-looked-at position for the male spectator (one of her case studies was Hitchcock's *Vertigo*, 1958). This seminal essay sparked a seemingly endless debate around spectatorship, identification, sexual difference, and the unconscious. As the reader will undoubtedly notice, Mulvey's work frequently resurfaces on the pages of this volume in many chapters and in relation to many different themes, further attesting to the fact that her insights are still being wrestled with. Mulvey herself reframed her position some years later in "Afterthoughts on 'Visual Pleasure and Narrative Cinema' inspired by *Duel in the Sun*" (1981). Here she conceded that there is a place for the female spectator in mainstream cinema, but that it is a difficult position since it requires a certain level of "trans-sex identification" in the woman's accepting of a male point of view (for a discussion of this apparatus in relation to trans* cinema, see Steinbock, this volume).

In the intervening years, feminist film scholars took the field in many diverging and exciting directions: offering further insights into spectatorship and the film apparatus, women's cinema, semiotics, film history and globalization, race and whiteness, genre, LGBTQ perspectives, critical postcolonial perspectives, feminist Marxism or socialist feminism, audience and reception studies, trauma, and transnational perspectives, among others (we have provided a selective—and by no means comprehensive—bibliography at the end of this introduction).

In recent years, debates around the concept of post-feminism reveal that its meaning is heavily contested. The term is frequently used to perpetuate the notion that feminism has become somehow obsolete (for essays touching on post-feminist representations see Lewis and Radner, this volume). Yet, any notion about the end of feminism as a political project is frequently contradicted by the still existing (and in many ways increasing) global gender inequalities, in film industries and beyond. In the next section, we highlight some current strains of feminist film inquiry and its ongoing influence in film and media studies more broadly.

Feminist film futures

In the twenty-first century, celluloid film has been largely replaced by digital technologies, prompting some to declare the end of cinema as we know it. However, regardless of the shifts in the ways in which films are made, distributed, and consumed, it is unquestionable that, rather than being done away with altogether, cinema as a medium has taken on new forms that draw heavily on its celluloid and analog history and legacy (see, for example, Peterson, Jelača, Levin, and Pajaczkowska in this volume). And while these shifts in technology may be lamented by some critics as the loss of the elusive but unmistakable quality of celluloid screen images, they have in many ways democratized access to filmmaking as a mode of expression, thereby challenging the invisible barriers that dictate who gets to make movies and whose stories are represented in the first place (see Smaill and Zimmerman, this volume). Likewise, new technologies have made it increasingly easier to access and see films, which has been a particularly beneficial development when it comes to the broader context of world cinema, and especially films made by minority women filmmakers from parts of the world less prominently featured in normative film histories. New technologies have also made it possible for industries other than Hollywood to establish themselves more firmly on the global stage of world cinema—notably, Bollywood, Nollywood, and other non-Western film geographies (discussed, for example, in Ponzanesi, Wang, Meeuf, Jaikumar, Ganti, and Obiaya in this volume).

Unsurprisingly, the technological shifts that cinema has encountered in the twenty-first century have influenced (and in some ways shaped) its evolving relationship to gender. Within the study of film itself, feminist approaches have taken diverse and generative iterations. In this introduction, we outline several current trajectories of cinema and gender that seem most germane to our current moment, each related to a theme of decentering. One of them is the transnational turn—as both a project of decentering of the dominant Western perspectives in film studies itself, and an exploration of the ways in which non-Western cinemas have (and have not) provided space for women to articulate their experiences and innovate forms of cinematic storytelling. This shift extends the interventions of feminist film inquiry beyond the hegemony of the West, but also beyond the limitations of the national as a paradigm in film studies, and toward a more nuanced plurality of gender norms as they are inflected by religion, war, class, and ethnicity (see, for example, Ponzanesi, Chakravarty, Atakav, Marciniak, Meeuf, and Imre in this volume). The transnational also prompts a re-investigation of what has been taken as representative of Western film. In this respect, Jacqueline Bobo's essay on Black women filmmakers, and Rachel Lewis's writing on lesbian authorship, in this *Companion* are exemplary of the ways in which decentering the West simultaneously entails dislocating whiteness and heteronormativity in order to make visible other stories and film histories (see also White, this volume).

The second iteration reflects a focus on trans* topics as a way to decenter cis-gendered perspectives and fixed polarities of sexual difference, upon which much of classical feminist theory has rested (see Steinbock, this volume). And just as queer theory in the 1980s and 1990s challenged the perceived heteronormative premises of psychoanalytic feminist film theory, so does the trans* paradigm today continue to challenge an assumption that gender is inextricably bound to a particular body rather than being a fluid and contingent practice (see Borden, this volume).

Despite the radical challenge that the growing awareness of non-cis-gendered identities presents to deeply entrenched notions of sexual difference, the third iteration reveals that the intransigent problem of sex-based inequality persists alongside complex and shifting cultural understandings of gender, the body, and identity. This trajectory decenters still-prevalent male privilege in the film industry as such, most prominently featured as an ongoing debate around the wage gap in Hollywood, which was prominently exposed after the massive Sony studio data hack in 2014. Some of the leaked information revealed that Hollywood's female talent is still persistently paid less than their male counterparts. The revelation prompted an FBI probe, and resulted in Hollywood's most prominent star, Jennifer Lawrence, penning an open letter from a feminist perspective, which critically reflects on Hollywood's ongoing double standards when it comes to gender (Lawrence 2015).

Moreover, the cultural prominence in recent years of the Bechdel test—which purports to measure the depth of a film's representation of its female characters by asking the following question: does it feature at least two prominent female characters who talk to each other about something other than a man?—reflects an increased level of critical public scrutiny when it comes to cinema and gender. It nevertheless remains true that the struggle for equality is far from over, since women remain a minority when it comes to most film industries—both as filmmakers and as subjects whose stories are represented on the screen beyond mere clichés and stereotyping. This is particularly true for women of color, and queer and trans* filmmakers. The recent rise to mainstream critical prominence of filmmakers such as Ava DuVernay, and of films such as *Carol* (Todd Haynes, 2015) and *Tangerine* (Sean S. Baker, 2015) are often exceptions that simply confirm the rule that the vast majority of mainstream cinema remains in the hands of a single, still dominant group (for more on female directors see, for example, Bobo, White, Fischer, Turim, Atakav, Lewis, Ciecko, this volume). This has become particularly evident during the #OscarsSoWhite controversy, sparked over the fact that in 2015 and 2016 all forty Academy Award acting nominations went to white actors. The controversy has instigated a lively debate about race, whiteness and privilege, and prompted the Academy of Motion Picture Arts and Sciences to implement new policies toward diversifying its membership. At the same time, filmmakers such as Alejandro González Iñárritu pointed out that efforts toward greater diversity need to happen at every step of the filmmaking process, and not just in the distribution of awards (Utichi 2016). The debate has also prompted *The New York Times* film critic Manohla Dargis to coin the "DuVernay test" (named after Ava DuVernay, and in reference to the Bechdel test), which would be passed by films "in which African-Americans and other minorities have fully realized lives rather than serve as scenery in white stories" (Dargis 2016). These ongoing, culturally prominent conversations attest to the fact that feminism still has a lot to offer to the future of cinema and vice versa.

Finally, the dynamism of the field of social media, and the intersections between movies, music videos, viral media, videogames, and television series causes two additional modes of decentering: on one hand, film theory must increasingly contend with these post-cinematic avatars (see, Jelača in this volume) and, on the other, the digital decenters the subject herself. As a result, increasing interest in ecocinema, animals, affect, and the post- or non-human is another response to the context of our current moment, and reflected in the latter parts of the volume at hand (see Weik von Mossner's writing on ecocinema, Kaplan's writing on climate trauma, Peterson's discussion of the non-human, and Colman's writing on Deleuzian spectatorship).

About this volume

We envisioned this *Companion* as providing an overview of the field of cinema and gender, while also reflecting a desire to rethink some of the predominant ways in which feminist film theory and filmmaking is historicized, theorized, and taught. The explicitly feminist interpretation of gender as a topic is a conscious methodological choice that reflects the roots of our thinking about gender and/or sex in relation to films and their modes of address.

One of our guiding principles is the assumption that gender is not a category separable from those of sexuality, race, class, ethnicity, and so on. Nor are the above categories stable or fixed in their affective or semiotic meanings. Throughout the volume, an effort was made to offer a global perspective that challenges the equation of gender with women in a reductive way that implies a white, Western, middle-class, heterosexual subject.

The *Companion* is informed by a desire to maintain the political and non-normative impact of feminist inquiry, while also highlighting its proximity and political allegiance to queer and trans* theoretical approaches, critical race theory, and postcolonial studies.

As there already exists a *Routledge Companion to Gender and Media* (2014), we envision this volume as complementary to its aims, but focused more specifically on film *to the extent that cinema can still be studied in isolation from other media forms.* The fact that it is becoming increasingly difficult to do so is well noted. Cinema's increasing convergence with other media forms is something we asked each contributor to consider. The changing media landscape itself prompts interesting inquiries into how specific topics have altered over the past several decades. The aim within each essay is to evaluate and emphasize the importance and ongoing relevance of feminist thought to each of these areas. We encouraged contributors to write critical overviews that politicize how feminism has and must continue to inform how we think about topics such as film history, genres, auteur theory, spectatorship, and transnational production.

The *Companion* is divided into five parts. Each part contains a number of essays that illuminate various dimensions of the topic, and frequently reveal insightful connections across subfields, foci, and methodological approaches. In the beginning of each section is a short introduction that situates the discussion and briefly summarizes the essays that follow. The first part, entitled "What is [feminist] cinema?," rephrases Bazin's canonical question to interrogate a range of topics, from what constitutes a feminist mode of address to postcolonial and queer critiques, to women filmmakers in Islamic contexts and Chinese Socialist cinemas, as well as gender, age, and disability in Hollywood. The second part, "Genres, modes, stars," examines a variety of approaches to stardom and genre, incorporating transnational and queer perspectives and offering contemporary insight on generic figures such as the femme fatale and the action hero, as well as a focus on historically neglected talents such as slapstick comediennes. The third part, "Making movies," focuses on the production side of film, exploring authorship in relation to race and sexuality from Hollywood to postcolonial sites and practices. It also examines the nature of women's contributions historically to Hollywood cinema in silent and studio-era practice. "Spectatorship, reception, projecting identities," the fourth section, focuses on the audience side of the film equation, and looks at paradigms as diverse as psychoanalysis, reception studies, phenomenology, and fandom. Finally, the fifth part is entitled "Thinking cinema's future." This closing section includes topics we found to be among the most pressing in the present, and indicative of some of the most generative paths for future inquiry, including trans* cinema, the post-human, and the post-cinematic. That said, we feel strongly that all the essays in the *Companion* are evidence of the future directions feminist film studies can take and is currently embarking on. What this suggests is that the future of film theory, like its past, will be feminist.

References

Dargis, M. (2016). "Sundance Fights Tide with Films like 'The Birth of a Nation.'" *The New York Times.* January 29: www.nytimes.com/2016/01/30/movies/sundance-fights-tide-with-films-like-the-birth-of-a-nation.html?smprod=nytcore-ipad&smid=nytcore-ipad-share&_r=2 (last accessed March 12, 2016).

Haskell, M. (1974). *From Reverence to Rape: The Treatment of Women in Movies.* Chicago: University of Chicago Press.

Johnston, C. (1973). "Women's Cinema as Counter Cinema" in *Notes on Women's Cinema.* London: Society for Education in Film and Television, pp. 24–31.

Kaplan, E. A. (1974). "Aspects of British Feminist Film Theory: A Critical Evaluation of Texts by Claire Johnston and Pam Cook." *Jump Cut*, 2: 52–5.

Lawrence, J. (2015). "Why do I Make Less than my Male Co-Stars?" *Lenny*. www.lennyletter.com/work/a147/jennifer-lawrence-why-do-i-make-less-than-my-male-costars/ (last accessed March 12, 2016).

Mulvey, L. (1975). "Visual Pleasure and Narrative Cinema." *Screen*, 16(3): 6–18.

Penley, C. (ed.) (1988). *Feminism and Film Theory*. New York: Routledge.

Rosen, M. (1973). *Popcorn Venus: Women, Movies and the American Dream*. New York: Coward, McCann & Geoghegan.

Utichi, J. (2016). "Iñárritu on Oscars Diversity at PGA Nominees Breakfast: The Academy 'Is at the End of the Chain.'" *Deadline*. January 23: http://deadline.com/2016/01/pga-nominees-breakfast-inarritu-talks-diversity-in-hollywood-1201689100/ (last accessed March 12, 2016).

A selected list of further reading

Please see individual essays in the collection for more topic-specific suggestions.

General overviews

Fischer, L. (1989). *Shot/Countershot: Film Tradition and Women's Cinema*. Princeton, NJ: Princeton University Press.

Feminist criticism applied to a large number of films, from Welles and Chabrol to Arzner and von Trotta, and dealing with a range of themes from the actress to female friendship to the lesbian.

Hollinger, K. (2012). *Feminist Film Studies*. London: Routledge.

An overview of some key debates in feminist film studies, such as psychoanalysis and spectatorship. Includes detailed case studies.

Kaplan, E. A. (ed.) (2002). *Feminism and Film*. London: Oxford University Press.

An anthology of major works that includes influential early essays and key debates within feminist film theory.

Kuhn, A. (1994). *Women's Pictures: Feminism and Cinema*. London: Verso.

An influential book that critically surveys the question of what the relationship between feminism and cinema is, could be, or should be.

McCabe, J. (2004). *Feminist Film Studies: Writing the Woman into Cinema*. New York: Columbia University Press.

Succinct history of feminist film theory; considers feminist film studies from a cultural studies point of view.

Mulvey, L. and A. Backman Rogers (eds.) (2015). *Feminisms: Diversity, Difference and Multiplicity in Contemporary Film Cultures*. Amsterdam: Amsterdam University Press.

An edited volume that brings together scholars who survey the history and new developments of feminist film theory.

Thornham, S. (1999). *Feminist Film Theory: A Reader*. New York: NYU Press.

An anthology of important works in feminist film studies.

Spectatorship and the film apparatus

Doane, M. A. (1982). "Film and the Masquerade: Theorising the Female Spectator." *Screen*, 23(3–4): 74–88.

This essay examines several viewing positions available to women spectators and introduces the important concept of femininity as a mask, or masquerade.

Doane, M. A. (1991). "Dark Continents: Epistemologies of Racial and Sexual Difference in Psychoanalysis and the Cinema" in *Femmes Fatales: Feminism, Film Theory, Psychoanalysis*. New York and London: Routledge, pp. 209–48.

This essay offers an examination of the intersections between sexuality and race from a psychoanalytic perspective.

Gledhill, C. (2006). "Pleasurable Negotiations" in *Cultural Theory and Popular Culture: A Reader*. J. Storey (ed.). London: Pearson, pp. 111–23.
Focuses on the ways in which spectatorship is a process of negotiation that does not rely on firm identity politics or subject positions.

Modleski, T. (1988). *The Women Who Knew Too Much: Hitchcock and Feminist Theory*. New York and London: Routledge.
An influential work that focuses on spectatorship and women in a number of Hitchcock's films, including *Rebecca, Rear Window, Vertigo*, and *Frenzy*.

Mulvey, L. (1975). "Visual Pleasure and Narrative Cinema." *Screen*, 16(3): 6–18.
A key essay in psychoanalytic spectatorship theory that introduced influential concepts such as the male gaze, to-be-looked-at-ness, scopophilia, voyeurism, and fetishism to the field of feminist film studies.

Mulvey, L. (1981/1989). "Afterthoughts on 'Visual Pleasure and Narrative Cinema' Inspired by King Vidor's *Duel in the Sun* (1946)" in *Visual and Other Pleasures*. London: Palgrave Macmillan, pp. 29–38.
In this essay, Mulvey offers further thoughts and slight revisions on her theory of the cinematic (male) gaze.

Silverman, K. (1988). *The Acoustic Mirror: The Female Voice in Psychoanalysis and Cinema*. Bloomington: Indiana University Press.
An important book that looks at the role of the voice in cinema.

Studlar, G. (1984). "Masochism and the Perverse Pleasures of the Cinema." *Quarterly Review of Film Studies*, 9(4): 267–82.
This essay made a key intervention into ongoing debates about the gaze, specifically arguing for the masochistic dimensions of spectatorship.

Womens cinema

Blaetz, R. (ed.). (2007). *Women's Experimental Cinema: Critical Frameworks*. Durham: Duke University Press.
This edited volume includes essays on experimental film work by women filmmakers written by a number of influential film theorists, including Mary Ann Doane and Maureen Turim.

Butler, A. (2002). *Women's Cinema: The Contested Screen*. New York: Wallflower Press.
An overview of major scholarship and currents in thinking about female auteurs that takes a transnational approach. Butler also develops the idea of women's cinema as "minor cinema," after Deleuze and Guattari's concept of minor literature.

de Lauretis, T. (1984). *Alice Doesn't: Feminism, Semiotics, Cinema*. Bloomington: Indiana University Press.
An influential book of essays that examine cinema and feminism from the perspective of semiotics, psychoanalysis, anthropology, and visual perception.

de Lauretis, T. (1990). "Guerilla in the Midst: Women's Cinema in the 80s." *Screen*, 31(1):6–25.
An influential essay which argues that "women's cinema" needs to engage current problems on a global scale, but with close attention to local specificities.

Johnston, C. (1973). "Women's Cinema as Counter Cinema" in *Notes on Women's Cinema*. London: Society for Education in Film and Television, pp. 24–31.
Focuses on the production of ideology in cinema, particularly in relation to the construction of women, using a variety of frameworks including structuralism, Marxism, and psychoanalysis.

Kaplan, E. A. (1990). *Women and Film: Both Sides of the Camera*. London: Routledge.
A detailed and influential study of women's roles on both sides of the film camera—as filmmakers, and as objects on the screen. Deals with both Hollywood cinema and the avant-garde.

Martin, F. (2011). *Screens and Veils: Maghrebi Women's Cinema*. Bloomington: Indiana University Press.

This book examines seven films, looking at how Maghrebi women filmmakers negotiate and push back against various national and cultural contexts. She develops the concept of "transvergence" as a way to discuss the aesthetic and cultural strategies of the films and explores the many valences of the gaze as it relates to the *hijab*.

Mayne, J. (1990). *The Woman at the Keyhole: Feminism and Women's Cinema*. Bloomington: Indiana University Press.

Focuses on films by women filmmakers that reconfigure the representation of female desire and women's point of view on the cinematic screen.

Ramanathan, G. (2007). *Feminist Auteurs: Reading Women's Films*. New York: Wallflower Press.

The book takes a global approach that examines the work of many female directors through the lens of feminist film as a genre.

Wang, L. (ed.) (2011). *Chinese Women's Cinema: Transnational Contexts*. New York: Columbia University Press.

A collection of essays that examines female filmmakers from Mainland China, Taiwan, Hong Kong, and the Chinese diaspora with an interdisciplinary and transnational approach.

White, P. (2015). *Women's Cinema/World Cinema: Projecting Contemporary Feminisms*. Durham: Duke University Press.

A study of contemporary women filmmakers (who emerged as internationally recognized authors post-2000) active and influential on the world cinema stage—case studies include Samira Makhmalbaf, Lucrecia Martel, and Jasmila Žbanić.

Film history

Bean, J. and D. Negra (eds.) (2002). *A Feminist Reader in Early Cinema*. Durham: Duke University Press.

A collection of feminist writing on early cinema with topics from female criminality in French serials to actresses in early Chinese cinema to Pola Negri.

Callahan, V. (2010). *Reclaiming the Archive: Feminism and Film History*. Detroit: Wayne State University Press.

A collection of work taking feminist historiographic approaches to film history.

Gaines, J., R. Vatsal, and M. Dall'Asta, (eds.) (ongoing) *Women Film Pioneers Project*. Center for Digital Research and Scholarship, New York, NY: Columbia University Libraries: https://wfpp.cdrs.columbia.edu/ (last accessed July 16, 2016)

An ongoing archive of women's contributions to the development of motion pictures.

Gledhill, C. and J. Knight (eds.) (2015) *Doing Women's Film History: Reframing Cinemas Past and Future*. Champaign Urbana: University of Illinois Press.

A collection of work with global coverage that greatly expands methodological approaches in feminist film historiography.

Lant, A. (ed.) (2006). *Red Velvet Seat: Women's Writings on the First Fifty Years of Cinema*. New York and London: Verso.

Examines the significance of women's contributions to early cinema.

Petro, P. (2002). *Aftershocks of the New: Feminism and Film History*. New Brunswick, NJ: Rutgers University Press.

A collection of Petro's writings that address questions of history and feminist film studies, from the medium of television to Weimar, Germany.

Race and whiteness

Dyer, R. (1997). *White: Essays on Race and Culture*. London: Routledge.

A study of the omnipresent focus on, and representation of, whiteness in Western culture, including cinema.

Foster, G. A. (2003). *Performing Whiteness: Postmodern Re/Constructions in the Cinema*. Albany: SUNY Press.

A book-length study that critically examines the visual supremacy of whiteness in mainstream cinema.

Gaines, J. (1986). "White Privilege and Looking Relations: Race and Gender in Feminist Film Theory." *Screen*, 29(4): 12–27.

An important intervention into spectatorship theory that brings whiteness and race into sharp focus.

hooks, b. (1992). *Black Looks: Race and Representation*. Boston: South End Press.

A critical study of the representation of African Americans in cinema, which examines how white supremacist patriarchy controls racial images as a way to ensure domination.

Williams, L. (2002). *Playing the Race Card: Melodramas of Black and White from Uncle Tom to O. J. Simpson*. Princeton, NJ: Princeton University Press.

This book charts fantasies of race in the US through the melodramatic mode from theater to film and television.

Young, L. (1995). *Fear of the Dark: "Race," Gender and Sexuality in the Cinema*. London: Routledge.

Focuses on the depiction of Black female sexuality and develops a critical approach to its analysis, looking at films from *Sapphire* (1959) to *Mona Lisa* (1987).

Genre

Clover, C. J. (1992). *Men, Women, and Chainsaws: Gender in the Modern Horror Film*. Princeton, NJ: Princeton University Press.

A groundbreaking study of the slasher film and the subjection of women to male violence. Introduces the influential concept of "the final girl."

Creed, B. (1993). *The Monstrous-Feminine: Film, Feminism, Psychoanalysis*. New York: Routledge.

A study of the concept of abject femininity (adopted from Julia Kristeva) with respect to sci-fi and horror genres. Case studies include *Alien*, *Carrie*, and *Psycho*.

Doane, M. A. (1987). *The Desire to Desire: The Woman's Film of the 1940s*. Bloomington: Indiana University Press.

A psychoanalytic study of the representation of women in the "woman's pictures" of the 1940s, and the spectatorial positions they offer women, which result in an "impossible gaze."

Fischer, L. (1996). *Cinematernity: Film, Motherhood, Genre*. Princeton, NJ: Princeton University Press.

Focuses on the representation of motherhood in different cinematic genres that include melodrama, horror, comedy, and thriller.

Gledhill, C. (1987) *Home is Where the Heart Is: Studies in Melodrama and the Woman's Film*. London: BFI.

A collection of important scholarship on melodrama and the woman's film.

Jeffords, S. (1994). *Hard Bodies: Hollywood Masculinity in the Reagan Era*. New Brunswick: Rutgers.

Study examining the links between action—and some more drama-based—films of the Reagan era as they relate to the media representation of Reagan and the geopolitical position of America in the 1980s.

Kaplan, E. A. (1992/2000). *Motherhood and Representation: The Mother in Melodrama and Popular Culture*. New York: Routledge.

Examines representations of motherhood in film and in literature.

Tasker, Y. (1993). *Spectacular Bodies: Gender, Genre, and the Action Cinema*. New York: Routledge.

A book-length study of gender roles in action cinema, including a critical examination of masculinity, as well as female action movie protagonists.

Williams, L. (1989). *Hard Core: Power, Pleasure, and the "Frenzy" of the Visible*. Berkeley: University of California Press.

A groundbreaking study of porn that examines the in/visibility of women's libidinal pleasure within some of the genre's conventions.

Williams, L. (2004) "Film Bodies: Gender, Genre, and Excess." *Film Theory and Criticism: Introductory Readings*. 6th edn. Leo Braudy and Marshall Cohen (eds.). New York: Oxford University Press, pp. 727–41.

An influential essay that focuses on the "gross" bodily genres—horror, melodrama, porn—in order to analyze how bodies become key sites of spectatorial encounter.

LGBTQ perspectives

Aaron, M. (ed.) (2004). *New Queer Cinema: A Critical Reader*. New Brunswick: Rutgers University Press.

A collection of essays on topics relating to queer cinema, including issues of race, reception, and spectatorship.

Halberstam, J. (2005). *In a Queer Time and Place: Transgender Bodies, Subcultural lives*. New York: NYU Press.

An influential work that focuses on transgender topics, and includes illuminating case studies such as the analysis of *Boys Don't Cry*.

Mayne, J. (2000). *Framed: Lesbians, Feminists, and Media Culture*. Minneapolis: University of Minnesota Press.

An examination of the lesbian representation in film and television that includes discussion of lesbian authorship.

Rich, B. R. (2013). *New Queer Cinema: The Director's Cut*. Durham: Duke University Press.

A collection of Rich's writing on the New Queer Cinema, with many discussions of individual films and directors, from Derek Jarman to Gus Van Sant.

Stacey, J. and S. Street (2007). *Queer Screen: A Screen Reader*. London: Routledge.

A collection of important writing on queer cinema topics from the journal *Screen*.

Straayer, C. (1996). *Deviant Eyes, Deviant Bodies: Sexual Re-orientation in Film and Video*. New York: Columbia University Press.

Explores films that construct sites of lesbian intervention, implicitly or overtly. Case studies include *Voyage en Douce*, *Entre Nous*, and *Virgin Machine*.

Villarejo, A. (2003). *Lesbian Rule: Cultural Criticism and the Value of Desire*. Durham: Duke University Press.

Examines the question of lesbian visibility in a variety of cinematic modes, analyzing the possibilities and limits of cultural representations of the lesbian.

White, P. (1999). *unInvited: Classical Hollywood Cinema and Lesbian Representability*. Bloomington: Indiana University Press.

A study of lesbian spectatorship through a psychoanalytic lens. Focuses on studio-era Hollywood films and the possibilities of structuring an apparatus for lesbian desire.

Critical postcolonial and transnational perspectives

Durovicová, N. and K. E. Newman (2009). *World Cinemas, Transnational Perspectives*. New York and London: Routledge.

An edited volume that explores the dynamic interaction between national and transnational cinemas, as well as the uneven flow of images across various borders.

Ezra, E. and T. Rowden (eds.) (2006). *Transnational Cinema: The Film Reader*. London: Routledge.

An anthology of influential works on transnational cinema, including Hamid Naficy's "accented cinema," and Ella Shohat's "post-Third-Worldist" culture.

Kaplan, E. A. (1997). *Looking for the Other: Feminism, Film and the Imperial Gaze*. Routledge.

A study of the imperial and racialized gaze in cinema, focusing on representations of women.

Marciniak, K., A. Imre and A. O'Healy (eds.) (2007). *Transnational Feminism in Film and Media*. New York: Palgrave Macmillan.

An edited volume that highlights the field of transnational film and media studies. In the introduction, editors note that an increasing number of films reflect diasporic, exilic, and accented experiences over stable national cinematic frames.

Ponzanesi, S. and W. Waller (eds.) (2012). *Postcolonial Cinema Studies*. London: Routledge.
An edited volume that merges cinema studies and postcolonial studies in order to probe dynamic departures from colonial formations of power and knowledge.

Shohat, E. (ed.) (2006). *Taboo Memories, Diasporic Voices*. Durham: Duke University Press.
Essays that put forth feminist and (post)colonial cultural critiques. Western cinema is explored as constitutive of the gendered Western gaze.

Shohat, E. and R. Stam (1994). *Unthinking Eurocentrism: Multiculturalism and the Media*. London: Routledge.
An influential intervention into existing Eurocentrism in cinema, Shohat and Stam's volume focuses on the ways in which non-Western spaces are represented in cinema as exotic and as sources of libidinal investment for a white Western subject.

Trinh, T. M. (1991). *When the Moon Waxes Red: Representation, Gender, and Cultural Politics*. New York: Routledge.
A collection of essays that challenges the Western gaze and dominant ways of representing and claiming to know the Other.

Audience and reception studies

Bobo, J. (1995). *Black Women as Cultural Readers*. New York: Columbia University Press.
This book examines the ways in which Black women engage with films, focusing on *The Color Purple* and *Daughters of the Dust*.

Hansen, M. (1991). *Babel and Babylon: Spectatorship in American Silent Film*. Cambridge, MA: Harvard University Press.
Focuses on silent film spectatorship, examining its emergence in relation to changes in the public sphere. Offers a detailed analysis of sexuality, gender, and reception in relation to studies of Valentino's star image and Griffith's *Intolerance* (1916).

Stacey, J. (1994). *Star Gazing: Hollywood Cinema and Female Spectatorship*. London: Routledge.
An empirical case study of women fans of classic Hollywood movie stars, female spectatorship, and the paradoxes of consumerism.

Staiger, J. (2000) *Perverse Spectators: The Practices of Film Reception*. New York: NYU Press.
Discussion of reception studies with specific analyses of major films and directors from *A Clockwork Orange* to *The Silence of the Lambs*.

PART I

What is [feminist] cinema?

In this section, we interrogate the question of what [feminist] cinema is within a range of political, historical, geographical, and cultural contexts. Patrice Petro's opening essay situates the history of feminist film studies with respect to the ongoing scholarly contestations over its impact and relevance. She examines the tension between theory and practice, and between activism and academia. Sandra Ponzanesi and Sumita Chakravarty turn to postcolonial and transnational frameworks in order to chart current and emerging directions of the field. Ponzanesi highlights filmmakers such as Shirin Neshat and Gurinder Chadha, and situates postcolonial theoretical interventions as pivotal for rethinking the concept of cultural difference. Chakravarty focuses on the cinema of migration and particularly on US films such as *Gran Torino* and *Frozen River*, which stage a white protagonist's encounter with (im)migrant Others. Lucy Fischer highlights the work of Mai Zetterling as a way to explore the links between women's cinema and feminist forms of address. Kathleen Vernon and Sally Chivers illuminate some critical, but frequently overlooked, aspects of feminist film inquiry—sound (Vernon) and age and disability (Chivers). Lingzhen Wang and Anikó Imre examine film and feminism in different socialist contexts that may, on closer inspection, offer important counter-examples to Western-centric understandings of both cinema and gender alike, while Amy Borden returns to the radical aspects of queer cinema and queer theory in order to examine them as a practice that disrupts some of the identity-based tendencies of LGBT+ cinema.

Although not meant as a comprehensive overview of feminist cinema, this group of essays aims to give the reader insight into the breadth of the field of feminist film studies, as well as provide an introduction to the concerns that inform the field's past, present, and future trajectories.

1

CLASSICAL FEMINIST FILM THEORY

Then and (mostly) now

Patrice Petro

In an April 2015 interview, University of Groningen student Daniel O'Neill asked Laura Mulvey about what we might now call "classical" feminist film theory—that is, feminist film theory of the 1970s. Specifically, he asks, what has changed since the publication of "Visual Pleasure and Narrative Cinema" in 1975? Mulvey responded by explaining that her now infamous essay was a political intervention and not an academic one. She stated,

> One absolutely crucial change is that feminist film theory is now an academic subject to be studied and taught. "Visual Pleasure and Narrative Cinema" was a political intervention, primarily influenced by the Women's Liberation Movement and, in my specific case, a Women's Liberation study group, in which we read Freud and realised the usefulness of psychoanalytic theory for a feminist project. In addition to this feminist context, the essay could be seen as experimental, within the cultural context of the 1970s avant-garde: its writing, its films, and its ideas.[1]

Indeed, as Mandy Merck has recently described it, "Visual Pleasure" was a manifesto, a call to arms, and part of a larger history of feminist polemics and manifestos, stretching from "Mary Wollstonecraft's *Vindication of the Rights of Women* to Emma Goldman's 'The Tragedy of Women's Emancipation' to Shulamith Firestone's *The Dialectic of Sex* to Mary Daly's *Gyn/Ecology*" (Merck 2007:7).

As Merck points out, "Visual Pleasure" may be (overly) familiar to film and media scholars, but is still less well known within feminist theory more generally. Similarly, Claire Johnston's early writings, including "Women's Cinema as Counter-Cinema" (1973) and "Feminist Politics and Film History" (1975) were likewise written in the mode of the polemic and the manifesto and are even less known today than the ubiquitous "Visual Pleasure" essay, which has been expansively reprinted although repeatedly criticized for its lack of scholarly and theoretical rigor (as a direct result of its engagement with psychoanalysis, not to mention its lack of features traditionally found in scholarly essays, such as footnotes).

In this essay, I explore the standing and status of "classical" feminist film theory in the past and today. I reflect on recent writings and scholarship that trace the history of film studies, especially the history of film theory and its "academic turn" in the 1980s and beyond. Finally, I offer an intervention into the status of feminist film theory within larger accounts of our field.

So to begin. At the 2012 Society for Cinema and Media conference, held in Boston, I attended a workshop entitled "Where is Film Theory Today?" In the course of the discussion, I was surprised to learn that many of the participants believed that film theory "died" in the mid-1990s after a prolonged critique by those who were uneasy about what they saw as its undue influence on the field. David Bordwell, for example, famously coined the phrase "S.L.A.B." theory to describe film theory in the 1970s and 1980s—that is, the theories of Saussure, Lacan, Althusser, and Barthes, and/or Baudrillard—to capture what he believed was a detrimental orthodoxy in the vast majority of scholarship, perhaps especially feminist film scholarship.

Admittedly, I was not only surprised to learn that film theory had been dead for more than fifteen years—I was also perplexed by the funereal tone surrounding discussions of film theory. To be sure, I had read David Rodowick's 2007 essay (although not his book, which was not yet published) entitled "An Elegy for Theory." Here, Rodowick challenges Bordwell's critique of the field and, more specifically, what he sees as Bordwell's attempt to establish film studies as a discipline modeled on cognitivist science and historical poetics, along the lines of the ideals of the natural sciences (2007: 91–109). Rodowick's "elegy," however, is not exactly a lament for film theory's or even the cinema's death (and, tellingly, in the 2007 essay, he has absolutely nothing to say about feminist theory or feminist theorists). Instead, it is more of a reflection on what should constitute a philosophy of the humanities today, and in Rodowick's view, this entails a return to the work of Stanley Cavell and Gilles Deleuze.

In his book that followed, *Elegy for Theory*, published in 2014, Rodowick does mention feminist film theory but mostly relegates it in his account to identity politics and cultural studies. His first mention of feminism in relation to theory, moreover, occurs on page 201 in a book of 265 pages; and here, it is included as part of a longer list, including "formalism, myth criticism, Marxist criticism, psychoanalysis, feminism, queer theory, critical race theory, postcolonial theory, new historicism, cultural studies, media studies, and so on" (2014: 201–2). Even Cavell himself, writing in 1990, emphasized the centrality of feminist film theory to film studies when he wrote: "So since it seems to me generally recognized, and incontestable, that feminist theory is, as a body of work, the most influential in the field of film study, its most powerful force" (1990: 239).[2] How is it, then, that some twenty-five years later, feminist theory is nearly absent from Rodowick's history of film theory and his philosophy of the humanities? What is at stake in this voluntary forgetting of feminist film theory's centrality to film theory more generally?

To be sure, it is not just Rodowick who has sidelined feminist film theory in his account of the field. Indeed, many criticisms have been leveled against feminist film theory specifically in the writings of feminist film scholars, who denounce feminist film theory, not on epistemological grounds but because of its opacity and abstraction, its propensity towards jargon and cliché, and its aloofness from activism and political engagement.[3] In her 1998 book *Chick Flicks*, for example, B. Ruby Rich, characterizes academic film feminism in disparaging terms, claiming that in place of the broad coalitions and contradictory communities that so defined feminist work in the 1970s, feminist film theory in the 1980s and beyond devolved into an academically hierarchical, heterosexist, party-line feminist film theory, with its own conferences, journals, and its own "professionalized, parochial, self-absorbed, and deracinated writing" (1998: 6). As she explained: "What sprang up in the seventies and was institutionalized in the eighties has been stagnating in the nineties, its vigor bypassed by queer culture, on the one hand, multiculturalism on the other, and cultural studies in general" (ibid. 5). There are, of course, a number of unexamined tensions here: between theory and practice as well as between activism and academia. Mulvey herself claims that her "Visual Pleasure" essay was written for polemical, political purposes, and yet it was also, and from the very beginning, central to academic debates, to the institutionalization of film studies, and to the work of many who were at once activists and scholars alike.

More recently, in a 2012 interview to promote her book on *New Queer Cinema*, Rich nevertheless makes the point that gender discrimination in the industry remains rampant and, one assumes, that feminist analysis remains as relevant as ever. When asked why the New Queer Cinema is dominated by male filmmakers, for instance, she explains,

> Why? Because gay men are still men, whereas lesbians are still women. The run up to the Oscars this year resulted for some reason in the "discovery" of how few women have been nominated for the award and how low the numbers of women in the industry [are]—even the independent world. Lesbians though are in even worse positions than heterosexual women in the film biz, since they aren't seen as available bedmates (well, mostly) and since the craft guilds are still so gender-bound. Editing is the great exception because it's close work in dark rooms dedicated to helping the guy look good—a fit job for a woman.[4]

Thus, Rich points out a significant fact: that regardless of a seemingly greater prominence (or cultural recognition) of minority filmmakers and themes, such prominence remains delineated along gender lines.

In view of these remarks, it is important to return to the political and historical context of the 1980s, not because I believe that feminist film theory declined after this date, but because the eighties more broadly figure as a rhetorical turning point in the writings of many critics and theorists who seek to chart historical change. For some theorists, the 1980s were a watershed, especially when considered in relation to technological, cultural, and political change. Indeed, it is now something of commonplace for scholars to locate 1989 as a major historical pivot point, marking the fall of the Berlin Wall, the end of the Cold War, and the acceleration of major technological innovations in communication technologies that have fundamentally altered our relationship to the world. As Siva Vaidhyanathan puts in his book, *The Googlization of Everything: And Why We Should Worry*:

> In 1989, as a young man of twenty-three, I could not have been more optimistic about the prospects for justice and democracy in my country and the rest of the world. … To a naïve young American like me, fascinated by new technology and devoted to the belief that free speech can be deeply and positively transformative, this simple connection between a new technology and stunning historical events was irresistible. Such a techno-optimistic story accorded well with the other views I held at that time: that the Reformation and the Enlightenment were driven, or made necessary, but the emergence of the printing-press in fifteenth-century Europe, and that mass-market pamphlets such as Thomas Paine's *Common Sense* were essential factors in the birth of the American republic. Of course, this view was far too simple an explanation for the sudden (and in many places, temporary) spread of democracy and free speech. Historians of both politics and technology knew the story was more complex.

> *(2011: 122)*

The story is indeed more complex, and when we look to the field of cinema and media studies to trace the recent history of feminist film theory over the last four decades, this techno-optimistic narrative gives way to a different account of a loss of utopian aspirations and transformation. As Mulvey herself has pointed out (in her contribution to a roundtable on feminist film theory, published in 2004 in the feminist journal *Signs*, of which I will have more to say momentarily):

> During the 1980s, events on a world scale marked the point at which the traditions of progressive politics could no longer struggle against the changing balance between left and right. The success of neoliberal economics, the collapse of communism, the globalization of capitalism, the export of industry to nonunionized developing economies, the impoverishment of Africa, and an increase in racism both in Europe and other parts of the world definitively changed the political spectrum. During this period, not only was it impossible to maintain the progressive optimism of the 1970s, it was also hard to privilege the problems of women (especially those of developed economies) and the priorities of film feminism while left politics failed in postcolonial and third-world countries.
>
> *(2004: 1288)*

Mulvey does not locate 1989 as the watershed moment that moved us beyond ideologies and into an era of social justice and democracy; instead, for her, the 1980s were the tipping point of a new era, defined by the expansion of neoliberal economics and the expansion of capitalism on a global scale.

Nevertheless, like Vaidhyanathan, Mulvey also takes up the question of technology and historical change, but in her case, by reflecting on the history of cinema and the emergence of digital forms. "The cinema's one-hundredth birthday in 1995," she explains,

> may have been a temporal marker of purely symbolic importance, but this symbolism coincided with objective, material changes in its conditions of production, distribution, and consumption. The arrival of video and then, more significantly, digital technologies marked a definite end of an era for the way in which celluloid had functioned within the sphere of mass entertainment and within that of radical or avant-garde aesthetics during the greater part of the twentieth century.
>
> *(Mulvey 2004: 1287)*

The relationship between film and feminism came at the very end of that era, Mulvey further explains; moreover, feminist film theory and practice had close links with an even longer tradition of cinephilia. "It was a last wave," she says,

> following the great Third Cinema movements, above all in Latin America, and the European and North American avant-gardes of the 1960s. For these movements, cinema was of central importance as a symptom and symbol of utopian political teleology. Not only could cinema articulate the desire for a better world, its complex way of interpreting and representing could also produce both critique and new ways of seeing. For feminism, this was particularly the case: the cinema doubled as a major means of women's oppression through image and

as a means of liberation through transformation and reinvention of its forms and conventions.

(ibid.)

Mulvey concludes by emphasizing that new digital capacities nonetheless open up a space for new reflections on cinema and film feminism. Refracted through new technologies, film not only provides the raw material for re-forging links across the great divide of the 1980s but also suggests a metaphor for reflecting on the difficulty of time and history. "From this perspective," she writes, "feminist alternative histories, the reconfiguring of storytelling, and the questioning of given patterns provides an invaluable point of departure" (ibid.).

So what are these alternative histories, these new points of departure? Or, to put it differently, how might we begin to trace the spaces and places for feminist film theory today, especially given recent accounts, including Mulvey's own, that argue that film feminism foundered in the 1990s, unable to maintain the progressive optimism, enthusiasm, and political activism that so marked its formation in the 1970s? To be sure, there are many scholars who continue to engage in feminist scholarship and the process of its historiography, and younger scholars (many of them included in this anthology) have shown a renewed interest in feminist film theory as well. Established scholars, too, have endeavored to recall the history of feminist film theory, most notably, for example, E. Ann Kaplan, in her 2001 anthology *Feminism and Film*, which brought together major essays on feminist film theory in an effort to trace that history from the 1970s to the new century. In 2004, moreover, a special issue of the journal *Signs* explicitly aimed to address recent approaches to feminist film theory. Co-edited by Kathleen McHugh and Vivian Sobchack, it was entitled "Beyond the Gaze: Recent Approaches to Film Feminisms." According to the editors, the special issue sought to "provide a forum for the new film and media feminisms emerging now, more than twenty-five years after the 'first wave' of feminist film theory." Invited participants were asked to assess the current state of the discipline as well as how the field of film and media studies has changed over the past decades. The entries in the round table—ten all together, including personal reflections from Lynn Spigel, Annette Kuhn, Mary Ann Doane, E. Ann Kaplan, Laleen Jayamanne, Judith Mayne, Linda Williams, Anna Everett, Laura Mulvey, and myself—represent a broad range of scholars and scholarship; each participant came of age during a slightly different period in history, and each plays a different role in relation to feminism, film, television, and media. Hence, I think this is a useful way to sketch out developments in feminist film theory since the 1970s and beyond.

Importantly, this *Signs* "roundtable" was not really a "roundtable" in the conventional sense at all; the respondents were never actually brought together for a discussion, and so the various reflections are not part of a larger conversation, but rather statements based on individual experiences, here expressed for the first time. It is nonetheless remarkable that at least two of the participants shared very similar views, which surprisingly denigrate feminist film theory *as an orthodoxy* even though it had otherwise been so important to their earlier work. Linda Williams's stance is obvious from the title of her essay, "Why I Did Not Want to Write This Essay." As she explains,

When I was asked to contribute to this roundtable, my first impulse was to duck. Film feminisms are no longer the highest priority of my scholarship. Writing about a field that had once felt very exciting … was, in the case of this essay 'assignment,' beginning to feel like an unwanted duty.

(Williams 2004: 1264)

She continues with the following statement:

> Often I have the same experience teaching film theory in graduate seminars. I find I have more enthusiasm for Hugo Münsterberg than for Laura Mulvey ... I now feel weighed down by the burdens of what feels like orthodox feminist position taking. Looking at my writing over the past ten years, I also find a similar reluctance. I have not written a single thing with the word feminist in the title. Pressed by the editors of this volume to say something, I have decided to examine briefly what might be behind this personal backlash.
>
> *(ibid.)*

In an ironic reversal of Tania Modleski's 1991 book, *Feminism Without Women*, which scrutinizes both the triumph of male feminist perspectives as well as feminist disavowals of "woman" in the name of anti-essentialism, we now have not feminism without women but women without feminism, or rather, major feminist film theorists who no longer identify as such. Williams writes: "Feminist film and media scholarship must now compete with a wide number of other theories, other methods, other objects of study, some of which now seem more vital, more pressing." She concludes her essay abruptly, and rather surprisingly, given what she has said up to this point: "While I understand that political and social realities have led some women to claim to be beyond feminism, for me it will always be the crucial foundation to whatever work I do in film and media" (Williams 2004: 1270). Thus, Williams has moved away from feminism but not entirely beyond it.

I do take Williams at her word that she has indeed never moved beyond feminism, which still informs her recent and important work, especially her work on porn and sexual politics more generally.[5] Indeed, some of the most compelling recent feminist work on film (and media) has been devoted to exploring issues of privacy, policy, sexuality, and technology that had their origins in the 1970s sexual revolution; Williams and Constance Penley have been at the forefront of this work.[6] And yet, Williams' expression of weariness with "orthodox feminist position taking" finds resonance as well in Lynn Spigel's take on feminist television history in the *Signs* issue, where she provides similar insight into her views of feminist film theory, when she offers a personal account of archiving her collection of feminist texts after moving houses, which necessitated that she weed out her vast library. "To save space," she writes,

> I put my old feminist theory books down in the basement. This, for sure, was a meaningful gesture. It meant I no longer really regarded these books as "primary" texts I need for writing but rather as "storage." Still, they are not just dusty remnants but rather a kind of quotidian archive, foundational for everything I write.
>
> *(Spigel 2004: 1209)*

Like Williams, Spigel argues that feminist film theory remains foundational if no longer directly relevant to her work. For her part, Spigel directly locates the problem with feminist film theory in "psychoanalytic film theory's universalizing aspects and blind spots, particularly with regard to issues of race and ethnicity" (ibid. 1211). Although she offers no further detail about these blind spots, the critique she poses here has been offered elsewhere. In an introduction to a special issue on "The Spectatrix" in *Camera Obscura* which they edited in 1989, Mary Ann Doane and Janet Bergstrom ask: "How has feminist film criticism, which was marginal and controversial at the outset, come to be seen so quickly as an orthodoxy, a monolithic enterprise?"[7] To which they answer:

> To some extent, this is undoubtedly linked to its alliance with psychoanalysis, which has always been confronted by the specter of orthodoxy. But it is also a function of feminist film criticism's academic entrenchment. Critical and theoretical texts which conveyed a political and intellectual urgency in the 1970s have become part of a canon which graduate students must master for their oral exams or dissertation projects. ... There is a feeling among many, whether they were veterans of the sixties or not, that feminist film and media theory has been cut off from its original sense of bold innovation and political purpose. It is time to reexamine our priorities and to remember a sense of shared goals in the light of our history over the past fifteen years, in order to renew the sense of vitality that once kept film studies from the self-perpetuating careerism that inevitably invades any academic (publish-or-perish) discipline.
>
> *(1989: 15–16)*

Like Mulvey, Doane, and Bergstrom emphasize the need for film feminism to renew its sense of purpose. They also stress the need for feminists to forge bridges between generations and to reclaim their contested history—a call that has been answered by many feminist scholars over the years. Significantly, moreover, they locate a tendency on the part of scholars and critics to dismiss anything produced from a psychoanalytic framework or an ideological analysis which depends on its insights. Indeed, equating feminism with psychoanalysis and both with "orthodoxy" has become a shorthand way for some scholars to reject them both. And yet, even at the height of psychoanalytic feminist film theory, feminist film scholars explicitly recognized the limitations of the psychoanalytic framework. Writing in 1991, for instance, Mary Ann Doane explained:

> Much of my own work has been shaped by the conviction that psychoanalysis was a particularly appropriate methodology for deciphering the psychical operations of the cinema and its impact upon the spectator. But this belief always existed in an uneasy tension with the simultaneous conviction that psychoanalysis was most significantly about the limits and instability of such knowledge, about the decenteredness of the investigative position itself as the effect of the unconscious.
>
> *(1991: 7)*

Doane goes on to say, "When my work is unproblematically labeled 'psychoanalytic,' there is, I think, a failure to register the wariness in my relation to psychoanalysis which is legible in the earliest essays" (ibid.).

By way of a conclusion, allow me to offer some final thoughts about the spaces and places for feminist film theory today, particularly in view of the many claims that feminist film theory has died or failed, or that feminist film theory is over, or that the cinema itself is at an end. On the one hand, as I have just described, there are major film scholars who formerly identified as feminist that now disavow that label; on the other hand, there are theorists like Jack Halberstam, whose book *Gaga Feminism: Sex, Gender, and the End of Normal* (2012) explicitly aims to reinvent feminism for a new generation, showing how Lady Gaga's sexual politics and performative style opens up new possibilities for sex and gender models in the digital age. Halberstam sees Lady Gaga as an exemplar of a new kind of feminism that privileges gender and sexual fluidity, and his book has been described as "part handbook, part guidebook, and part sex manual ... the first book to take seriously the collapse of heterosexuality and find signposts in the wreckage to a new and different way of doing sex" (ibid. back cover). While I am less certain that heterosexuality has entirely collapsed (although I understand the aspirational nature of the claim), I am interested in the way that Halberstam explains his approach to the topic:

> [A]s someone for whom feminism was formative and foundational as a political discourse, I am stunned at how disinterested people are in feminism now. And when I say "people" I mean young people, popular audiences, intellectuals, and so on. I believe that part of the split between the perceived anachronism of feminism and the perceived coolness of queer theory can be traced back to the sex wars of the 1980s and the homogenizing popular representations of feminism as anti-sex, anti-male, white and essentialist. I'm not interested in returning to those debates so much as opening up our definitions of feminism—rewriting its genealogies, reframing its theoretical contributions, recasting its contemporary political frames.
>
> *(Potter, 5 December 2012)*

In line with other scholars, many of whose work is included in this volume, new trajectories of feminist insight into cinema and its future (from climate trauma and eco-feminism, to post-human and animal studies) have a great deal to gain from feminist theory.

If feminist film theory in the seventies was explicitly political and polemical, as Mulvey and others have claimed, it seems fair to say that feminist film scholarship in the beginning of the twenty-first century is academic and archival in objective and aim. But what is gained and what is lost in this shift in focus—beyond the obvious move from a critique of cinema to an affirmation of its heterogeneity? Why has early cinema, for example, emerged in our own time as the site for explicitly feminist work?[8] Feminist historians have argued that early cinema affords insights into our own global media culture and to the role of women in that culture. They have also demonstrated through archival research that women were given far more roles and agency in the early days of cinema in terms of their involvement in production on multiple levels. Thus, while our own time—marked by the end of the Cold War, the electronic media revolution, and the restructuring of global capital—certainly bears comparison with the development of international media economy in the turn of the last century, the status of women in media production today is actually worse than in the early part of the twentieth century, as women remain marginalized in the industry, discriminated against even within the more progressive terrain of the New Queer Cinema.

There are always generational and personal factors that explain how and why scholars deemphasize the theoretical knowledge that was previously foundational for their thinking, and yet such practices nevertheless carry institutional and disciplinary consequences and risks. In addition to passing on historical gaps to new generations of students and scholars alike, the practice of consigning feminist film theory to the dustbin of history or characterizing it as essentially anti-sex, anti-male, or simply not rigorously theoretical (as Rodowick does) ultimately encourages less critical and, ultimately, less historical and nuanced scholarship.

Given the revisions to the history of film theory that are now being written in our field, it is important to emphasize once again that feminist film history gains nothing from disowning its origins, whether in activism, the academy, or in relation to psychoanalysis. As I have written before, women "film pioneers" can be found in not only the archives, documents, and incomplete prints of early cinema. They exist also in our very midst, in the writings and essays and books of those feminist theorists who, years ago, and still today, engaged in debates about textual analysis, visual pleasure, progressive texts, and ideological formations, all in an effort to insist on the centrality of feminist issues to film theoretical concerns. As Mulvey explained, for many writing in the 1970s, the cinema as a medium seemed uniquely positioned to articulate the desire for a better world. But it was not the cinema alone, but also feminist film theory, which was so positioned, and the desire for a better world still remains, both in film and media and in feminist approaches to them.

Related topics

Sandra Ponzanesi, "Postcolonial and transnational approaches to film and feminism"
Kristin Lené Hole, "Fantasy echoes and the future anterior of cinema and gender"

Notes

1 "Interview with Laura Mulvey and Anna Backman Rogers, co-editor of 'Feminisms,'" Amsterdam University Press (April 24, 2015): http://en.aup.nl/nieuws/191-interview-with-laura-mulvey-and-anna-backman-rogers-co-editors-of-feminisms.html (accessed July 22, 2015).
2 Stanley Cavell, Letter, *Critical Inquiry*, vol. 17, no. 1 (Autumn 1990), 239. It is important to note that Cavell's remarks about feminist film theory (which run to seven pages) were written in response to Tania Modleski's letter to the *Critical Inquiry* editors, in which she takes issue with the press and with Cavell's pair of essays, "Ugly Duckling, Funny Butterfly: Bette Davis and *Now, Voyager*," and "Postscript (1989): To Whom it May Concern," both of which were published in *Critical Inquiry* in its Winter 1990 issue. Modleski (in a single paragraph) criticizes the journal for publishing these essays, because Cavell fails to cite any previous scholarship on the films he discussed. Modleski writes: "Inasmuch as Cavell, despite this specific charge against feminists, fails to *name* them (Doane, Jacobs, LaPlace, and others have written powerful critiques of *Now, Voyager* and other Bette Davis films), and inasmuch as *Critical Inquiry* exempts Cavell from the minimal requirements of scholarship, both parties perpetuate the very condition being analyzed: they participate in a system in which women go unrecognized, their voices unheard, their identities 'unknown.'" It is no small irony that in his companion volume to *Elegy for Theory*, entitled *Philosophy's Artful Conversation* (Harvard University Press, 2015), Rodowick—in the only extended film analysis he provides in either this or his 2014 book—takes up *Now, Voyager* to demonstrate his Cavellian approach to film analysis. And just like Cavell twenty-five years earlier, Rodowick never mentions any feminist work on the film—not Mary Ann Doane, or Lea Jacobs, or Maria LaPlace, or even more recent work by younger scholars, such as Alison McKee (see Alison McKee, *The Woman's Film of the 1940s: Gender, Narrative, and History* (Routledge Press, 2014). Instead, he writes: "In the recent past and still current context of theory, the temptation to apply a critical template that reads these films as narratives of the redomestication of women and the management of heteronormative desire is strong. But this would be too easy." (256).
3 For an extended discussion of this issue, see my chapter, "Film Feminism and Nostalgia for the Seventies," in *Aftershocks of the New: Feminism and Film History* (Rutgers University Press 2002).
4 The 2012 interview from which this quotation was taken is no longer online. For a related interview, see "B. Ruby Rich Discusses Queer Films on the Festival Circuit," www.youtube.com/watch?v=5rlqazJ4iZI (accessed August 15, 2016).
5 See, for instance, Williams's *Hard Core: Power, Pleasure, and the "Frenzy of the Visible"* (University of California Press 1999) as well as her edited volume *Porn Studies* (Duke University Press 2004).
6 See, for instance, Constance Penley, Tristan Taormino, Celine Parrenas Shimizu, and Mireille Miller-Young, eds., *The Feminist Porn Book: The Politics of Producing Pleasure* (The Feminist Press at CUNY, 2013) and Eric Schaefer, ed. *Sex Scene: Media and the Sexual Revolution* (Duke University Press 2014).
7 I have made this argument in *Aftershocks of the New: Feminism and Film History* (2002); see Chapter 9, "Film Feminism and Nostalgia for the Seventies."

8 I have written more extensively about this in my own contribution to the special issue of *Signs*; see, Patrice Petro, "Reflections on Feminist Film Studies, Early and Late," *Signs: Journal of Women in Culture and Society*, special issue on "Film Feminisms," vol. 20, no. 1 (Autumn 2004), 1272–8.

Bibliography

Amsterdam University Press. (April 24, 2015) Interview with Laura Mulvey and Anna Backman Rogers, co-editor of 'Feminisms' (Online) Available from: http://en.aup.nl/nieuws/191-interview-with-laura-mulvey-and-anna-backman-rogers-co-editors-of-feminisms.html (accessed July 22, 2015).

Bergstrom, Janet. (1990) American Feminism and French Film Theory. *Iris*. (10). pp. 183–97.

Bergstrom, Janet and Mary Ann Doane. (1989) The Female Spectator: Contexts and Directions. *Camera Obscura*. 7 (2–3, 20–21). pp. 5–27.

Cavell, Stanley. (1990) Letter. *Critical Inquiry*. 17 (1). pp. 238–44.

Doane, Mary Ann. (1991) *Femmes Fatales: Feminism, Film Theory, Psychoanalysis*. New York: Routledge.

Halberstam, J. Jack. (2012) *Gaga Feminism: Sex, Gender, and the End of Normal*. Boston: Beacon Press.

Johnston, Claire. (1973) Women's Cinema as Counter-Cinema. Reprinted in Thornham, Sue (ed.). (1999) *Feminist Film Theory. A Reader*. Edinburgh: Edinburgh University Press. pp. 31–40.

Johnston, Claire. (1975) Feminist Politics and Film History. *Screen* 16 (3). pp. 115–25.

Kaplan, E. Ann. (2001) *Feminism and Film (Oxford Readings in Feminism)*. Oxford: Oxford University Press.

Merck, Mandy. (2007) Mulvey's Manifesto. *Camera Obscura*. 66 (3). pp. 1–23.

Modleski, Tania. (1991) *Feminism without Women: Culture and Criticism in a "Postfeminist" Age*. New York: Routledge.

Mulvey, Laura. (2004) Looking at the Past from the Present: Rethinking Feminist Film Theory of the 1970s. *Signs: Journal of Women in Culture and Society*. 30 (1). pp. 1286–92.

Petro, Patrice. (2002) *Aftershocks of the New: Feminism and Film History*. New Brunswick: Rutgers University Press.

Potter, Claire. (2012) Gaga Feminism: An Interview with J. Jack Halberstam (Part 1) *The Chronicle of Higher Education*. (Online) December 5, 2012. Available from: http://chronicle.com/blognetwork/tenuredradical/2012/12/gaga-feminism-an-interview-with-j-jack-halberstam-part-i/ (accessed July 22, 2015).

Rich, B. Ruby. (1998) *Chick Flicks: Theories and Memories of the Feminist Film Movement*. Durham: Duke University Press.

Rodowick, David. (2007) An Elegy for Theory. *October*. 122. pp. 91–109.

Rodowick, David. (2014) *Elegy for Theory*. Cambridge: Harvard University Press.

Rodowick, David. (2015) *Philosophy's Artful Conversation*. Cambridge: Harvard University Press.

Spigel, Lynn. (2004) Theorizing the Bachelorette: 'Waves' of Feminist Media Studies. *Signs: Journal of Women in Culture and Society*. 30 (1). pp. 1209–21.

Vaidhyanathan, Siva. (2011) *The Googlization of Everything: And Why We Should Worry*. Berkeley: University of California Press.

Williams, Linda. (2004) Why I Did Not Want to Write This Essay. *Signs: Journal of Women in Culture and Society*. 30 (1). pp. 1264–71.

2

POSTCOLONIAL AND TRANSNATIONAL APPROACHES TO FILM AND FEMINISM

Sandra Ponzanesi

Since the 1990s, feminist film studies has expanded its analytic paradigm to interrogate the representation of race, ethnicity, religion, sexuality, and the nation (Wiegman 1998). This has included a new understanding of the role of audiences, consumption, and participatory culture, and a shift from textual analysis to broader cultural studies perspectives that include the role of institutions, reception, and technology. This is especially due to the contribution of black feminism in the US (see Hollinger 2012), and its critique of psychoanalysis as a Western universalistic framework of patriarchy (see Gaines 1986; Doane 1991; hooks 1992; Young 1996; Kaplan 1997), and the rise of postcolonial studies following the milestone publication of Edward Said's *Orientalism* (1978) and its aftermath.

The development of postcolonial studies strongly impacted the way of analyzing representations of the Other, asking for a rethinking of long-standing tropes and stereotypes about cultural difference, and also the gendering and racialization of otherness. This ushered in methodological interrogations on how visual representations are implicated in the policing of boundaries between East and West, between Europe and the Rest, the self and the other. The postcolonial paradigm is called upon to challenge the implicit and intrinsic Eurocentrism of much media representation and film theory (Shohat & Stam 1994), which implies a colonization of the imagination, where the Other is structurally and ideologically seen as deviant. Eurocentrism shrinks cultural heterogeneity into a single paradigmatic perspective in which Europe, and by extension the West, is seen as a unique source of meaning and ontological reality. Eurocentrism emerged as a discursive justification for European colonial expansions, making the colonizers, and their civilizational ideology, the lens through which the world is seen and value, judgment, and objectivity attributed (Shohat & Stam 1994, 2–3). It justifies imperial practices under the motto of the white man's burden and the need to bring civilization and progress to the rest of the world. Eurocentrism also generated the forging of race theories and race discourses in order to create a clear distinction between colonizers and the colonized. The eugenics of empire emerged by making the colonies the laboratories of the empire and the battleground in which to ventilate and develop white superiority and supremacy.

Empire cinema contributed to specific ways of seeing, making films that legitimated the domination of colonies by the colonial powers. Colonial images of gender, race, and class carried ideological connotations that confirmed imperial epistemologies and racial taxonomies, depicting natives—in documentary or fiction films—as savages, primitive, and outside modernity.

Ella Shohat has written extensively on the crucial role of sexual difference for the culture of empire. In her seminal 1991 article "Gender and the Culture of Empire: Toward a Feminist Ethnography of the Cinema," she discusses how imperial narratives are organized around metaphors of rape, fantasies of rescue, and eroticized geographies. Gender and colonial discourses intersect with Hollywood's exploitation of Asia, Africa, and Latin America as the pretexts for eroticized images of the Other (Shohat 2006a, 47):

> Exoticising and eroticizing the Third World allowed the imperial imaginary to play out its own fantasy of sexual domination. ... Indeed, cinema invented a geographically incoherent Orient, where a simulacrum of coherence was produced through the repetition of visual leitmotifs. Even as cinema itself evolved and changed over a century, The Orient continued to be mechanically reproduced from film to film and from genre to genre.
>
> *(ibid. 49)*

Orientalized representations of the Harem, with belly dancers and dark-haired women, allowed flesh to be shown without risking censorship. Popular culture and cinema extended the Eurocentric assumptions of scientific disciplines such as philology, anthropology, and historiography from the silent era on—from films such as *The Sheik* (George Melford, 1921) to *Lawrence of Arabia* (David Lean, 1962), *Raiders of the Lost Ark* (Stephen Spielberg, 1981), the *Sheltering Sky* (Bernardo Bertolucci, 1990), and *The English Patient* (Anthony Minghella, 1996).

Despite the fact that postcolonial analysis must take into account national and historical specificities, these tropes and stereotypes have stretched and extended to the present day relatively unaltered, signifying an enduring colonial legacy in the realm of visual representation.

Beyond the colonial legacy: Third Cinema, post-Third Worldist cinema, Fourth Cinema, and transcultural cinemas

In her incisive "Post-Third Worldist Culture: Gender, Nation and the Cinema," Shohat examines recent post-Third Worldist feminist film productions in order to see how the reversing of imperial and exoticizing representations takes place. In order to go beyond the binarism of First and Third Worlds, the term "post-Third Worldist" indicates a moving away from this dichotomy towards more intertwined and diasporic formations that signify transnational structures and modes of production. Though the nation is not surpassed or erased in the transnational, post-Thirdist analysis, these approaches propose an engagement with issues of nation, race, and gender, while critiquing national movements and ethnic communities that are exclusive and monocultural.

Post-Third Worldist feminist cinema goes beyond the First World feminist preoccupation with seeking alternative images of women and searching for new cinematic and narrative forms that challenge mainstream films and subvert the notion of "narrative pleasure" based on the "male gaze." Post-Third Worldist feminist films conduct a struggle on two fronts, both aesthetic and political, challenging historiography and proposing formal innovation. Yet post-Third Worldist feminist cinema engages with but also contextualizes the politics of the Third Cinema movement, the militant cinema proposed by Glauber Rocha's "Aesthetic of Hunger" (1965), Octavio Getino and Fernando Solanas's manifesto "Toward a Third Cinema" (1969), and Julio Garcia Espinosa's "For an Imperfect Cinema" (originally written in 1969), all of which championed a kind of "guerilla cinema" that was produced with few means but sought to empower the underprivileged masses and contest the hegemony of Hollywood entertainment and escapism. Third Cinema embraced Fanon's vision of the "wretched of the earth" (1963) and the need to revisit politics and representations from the perspective of the colonized, who look and fight back with a vengeance. The camera assumes the military role of the weapon in order to shoot back the realities and conditions of disenfranchised and marginalized people, which are often neglected in the glossy and polished productions of the First Cinema. It is a cinema that engages with non-professional actors, independence movements, and collective actions that surpass the role of individual heroic narratives and oedipal structures.

Yet, stemming from revolutionary movements, Third Cinema foregrounds universal battles that are by default male, and proposes a priority of national principles, often to the detriment of gender and sexual minority issues, which become co-opted in a so-called united action. Like Shohat's "post-Third Worldist" critical approach, Ranjana Khanna has called attention to the ways in which gender politics and Third Cinema have sometimes missed each other with her concept of a "Fourth cinema," in which women's voices and gazes would not be assimilated in the political program of their male counterparts (Khanna 1998).

In her article *"The Battle of Algiers* and *The Nouba of the Women of Mount Chenoua*: From Third to Fourth Cinema" (1998), Khanna claims that guerilla cinema is inadequate for representing or documenting "the *feminine*, the *excess*, a profound enunciation or crisis in representation, sometimes known as *jouissance*" (14).

The Battle of Algiers

The Battle of Algiers, an Italian–Algerian coproduction made in 1965–6, is an obvious example of this shortcoming. Directed by the Italian Marxist Gillo Pontecorvo, the film was scripted with the collaboration of Third Cinema guru Solanas, after being commissioned by the leader of the Algerian *Front de Libération Nationale*, Yacef Saadi. Made to document the history of the clandestine army and its tactics of resistance, it uses a grainy black-and-white documentary style while putting a disclaimer in the very opening that challenges the realism we are solicited to believe in: "not one foot of newsreel or documentary has been used." The use of a hand-held camera and telephoto lenses, the realization of a negative from the positive images, which conferred a special graininess to the gritty reality, the use of non-professional actors, and the mixing of the French and Arabic languages, are all aspects complying with the immediacy and truthfulness of the documentary style of *cinema verité* or direct cinema. Yet this is set in contrast with the creation of fictional figures such as General Mathieu, a powerful editing style, the use of freeze frames, the crafting of fictional newsreel encompassing images of torture, and the use of the powerful and melodramatic music of Ennio Morricone, which go against the tenets of Third Cinema. The use of "Ali's Theme" as a musical leitmotif (referring to the character Ali La Pointe) and the use of Bach's *St. Matthew Passion* are testimonies to the director's magisterial combination of Third Cinema with avant-garde European cinematic traditions. Pontecorvo managed to combine a "politics of truth" with a "documentary aesthetic" that requires an aestheticization and narrativization of reality in order to reach a more truthful impact than the classic documentary (Harrison 2007).

The film is an ode to people's decolonization struggle. Because of its portrayal of the French military and of torture, it was banned by the French government upon its release and shown only for the first time in 1971 (see Patricia Caillé 2007). The film is still used nowadays by the Pentagon to discuss the strategies and tactics of Islamic rebel groups (Briley 2010).

Khanna critiques the film in her appeal for a Fourth Cinema, as does Djamila Amrane-Minne in the article "Women at War" (2007). Both critics point out the shortcomings in the filmic representations of women's participation in the liberation struggle. *The Battle of Algiers* contains one of the most emblematic scenes of women's active role in the struggle for independence, showing three Algerian women undergoing a true makeover, bleaching their hair, and wearing Western French clothes, in order to pass unobserved at checkpoints between the Kasbah and the French city, while carrying bombs:

> *The Battle of Algiers* sets out to pay tribute to women activists. … However, their contribution to the struggle—unlike those of men and children—is severely under-played. Women appear on screen for a mere fifteen of the film's 121 minutes and, at times, the significance of their role in the war of national liberation is overlooked altogether.
>
> (*Amrane-Minne 2007, 342*)

The Battle of Algiers represents the most difficult period of the resistance and it gave women a vital role to play. Yet Amrane-Minne contends that the role of women in the film is not only short but also merely a supportive one to male militancy. In the film, Amrane-Minne points out, there is a "complete absence of speaking roles for women activists" (2007, 347). This is shown in the film by letting the FLN leader, Djafar, come and look at the three women after their makeover, in order to approve, and see whether they will be fit for the task. Amrane-Minne mentions that not only did women play a more significant role historically, and even partially replace men in the resistance, but there were also famous Algerian women leaders who risked their lives, were tortured, and even sentenced to death, such as Djamila Bouhired and Djamila Boupacha, who were both militants in the FLN. Djamila Bouhired was sentenced to death by guillotine for allegedly bombing a cafe, which killed 11 civilians in July 1957, and Djamila Boupacha was arrested in 1960 for an attempted attack in Algiers and sentenced to death on June 28, 1961. Both cases became notorious for the technique of torture to which the women were submitted during interrogation. Boupacha became a famous case thanks in part to the intervention of Simone de Beauvoir and Gisèle Halimi. Her confessions, which were obtained under torture and rape, changed public opinion in a trial by media of the methods used by the French army in Algeria (Quinan 2014); Bouhired's execution was indefinitely postponed and she was eventually released along with many other Algerian prisoners as the end of the war drew near. Boupacha was given amnesty and freed on April 21, 1962.

Even though *The Battle of Algiers* may have focused on the military strategies used by the liberation movements, choosing a specific theme and telling a partial story of a bigger truth, it is important to notice what remains unspoken, helping to write history. While Amrane-Minne analyzes the role and presence of women at war in cinema, Khanna concentrates on the more fundamental question of the crisis of representation in Third Cinema. *The Battle of Algiers* represents the birth of a nation in documentary style to redress the balance, given the dominance of propagandistic and stereotypical cinema. In the context of Third Cinema, Woman falls out of the system of representation. According to Khanna, this crisis signals a self-reflective moment in representation in which subaltern figures cannot speak (to evoke Spivak (1987)), or report the trauma of memory through words,

> but can enact a space in which "silence" – not speech – is recognized as a symbolic space of political non-representation. A Fourth cinema, which moves beyond the guerrilla cinema where the camera is a weapon, is a revolutionary cinema of the cocoon, where the metaphor of the birth of a nation is not repressed into denial of the feminine, where film could give a voice, silence and image to women in the revolution, where this uncanny could become reified on the screen. Representation which reflects back on itself exists without a renegotiation of imagery, and brings the imagery to crisis.
>
> *(Khanna 1998, 26)*

This would be the example of *The Nouba of the Women of Mont Chenoua* (1979) directed by French-Algerian writer and filmmaker Assia Djebar and discussed by Khanna as an example of Fourth Cinema. Khanna defines Fourth Cinema as a stage of decolonization in cinema, in which the birth of a nation is described from the perspective of the women participating in the moment of decolonization. Fourth Cinema aims to be more inclusive, creating room for the subalterns and women, and therefore overcoming Third Cinema's inability to represent the violence experienced by women in the process of decolonization. It points to Third Cinema's inability to represent the different registers of symbolic violence played out by and upon the bodies of colonized women.

The related notions of post-Third Worldist and Fourth Cinema point to a dissatisfaction with existing analytical frames and the need to reorient cinema so that not only women's perspectives but also other ways of seeing and accounting for difference, otherness, and hybridity are tackled, in both aesthetic and political terms. After Third Cinema, a proliferation of new labels emerged: world cinema, exile cinema, accented cinema, haptic cinema, migrant cinema, diasporic cinema, intercultural cinema, transnational cinema, and border cinema, all attempting to indicate the porous character of a cinema that is no longer linked to national schools and traditions, and signaling the diasporic nature of its subject matter and of new global apparatuses, showing the disaffection with and overcoming of dominant paradigms such as Hollywood, Art Cinema, and Third Cinema, and the emergence of new modes of production that project the local onto the global (Bollywood, Nollywood) in diasporic and diffractive ways.

In *Accented Cinema* Naficy (2001) explores, for example, the characteristic of an "accented cinema" thematically but also stylistically, questioning the notion of belonging and identity, confinement and borders, while exploring language uses (multilingualism, orality, accents, and slangs), and modes of narration (epistolary, autobiographical, e-mailing), in addition to haptic elements that can express a sense of nostalgia and loss, through smell and touch. On this note, the "intercultural cinema" proposed by Laura Marks (2000) is a cinema that questions belonging and identity, but also engages with the phenomenological experience of homelessness and the politics of displacement, stylistically and visually engaging with nostalgia and the feeling of loss through haptic visuality. Transnational cinema as described by Marciniak et al. (2007) focuses on the intricate connection between the local and the global, the domestic and the foreign, questioning the legitimacy of national borders while critiquing the easy rhetoric of connectivity and progress, pointing out the operation of neocolonialism and how it undermines the emerging of new subjectivities across borders.

Postcolonial cinema

Postcolonial cinema has much in common with all these developments that contest ethnic, minority, immigrant, or hyphenated essentialist labels while pointing to more porous and layered dynamics. Yet the focus of postcolonial cinema is on the analysis of contemporary or past asymmetries as dictated by multiple and overlapping histories of conquest and colonialism. Postcolonial cinema is therefore to be understood not as a new genre, or a new rubric, but as an optic through which questions of postcolonial historiography, epistemology, subjectivity, and geography can be addressed (Ponzanesi & Waller 2012, 3). Postcolonial cinema refers to a conceptual space that opens up occluded frames and proposes a new engagement with the visual that is decolonized and de-orientalized, becoming a relational mode of representation, breaking down the *grands récits* and opening the space for specificities that refract larger, often repressed, omitted or deleted, unofficial histories of nations, communities, genders, and subaltern groups.

Feminist examples include Trinh T. Minh-ha, who pointed out in her groundbreaking documentary *Reassemblage* (1982) that she intends "not to speak about/just speak nearby," unlike more conventional ethnographic documentary films, signaling the need not to make the Other the object of interpretation but let cinema as a medium and post-colonialism as an epistemology connect to difference as an empowering and generative source of creativity.

If the postcolonial optic articulated by Trinh is less explicitly polemical than Third Cinema, it is still political and concerned with hegemony and oppression. Even though postcolonial filmmakers engage with the critique of institutions in more oblique ways than the iconic figures of freedom fighters and revolutionary leaders, they still engage with societal issues by questioning and problematizing the cinematic tools, media technologies, and distribution networks, through which we receive images and information:

> Postcolonial cinema, while maintaining engagement with collectives, refocuses on the specificity of the individuals. Protagonists are not present as ego ideals or everypersons, though, but as multi-dimensional figures—often marginalized, subordinated, displaced or deterritorialised—whose subjectivities as well as subject positions are open to the unexpected, the unpredictable, which may enter from somewhere beyond our particular epistemological ken.
>
> *(Ponzanesi & Waller 2012, 7–8)*

The challenge and denaturalization of the colonial episteme is the task of postcolonial film theory, which focuses on the unframing of occluded histories, breaking with universalisms, and learning to navigate more relational modes of knowledge production.

There are various examples of films, filmmakers, and productions that could rightly pertain to the realm of postcolonial cinema and also a series of films that might precede the technical definition of postcolonial cinema but which enter into that optic of critique that interrogates Eurocentrism, the bourgeois paradigm of filmmaking, negotiating with hege-monic structures. Within Indian cinema there are glorious examples that would qualify as predecessors to postcolonial feminist filmmaking: for example, Satyajit Ray's famous *Charulata* (The Lonely Wife, 1964), which is based on a novella by Rabindranath Tagore, *Nastanirh* (The Broken Nest, 1901). The film takes place in the 1870s, in pre-independence India, in the gracious home of a workaholic newspaper editor and his lonely wife, Charulata.

The film exposes the subtle texture of a traditional marriage and the tale of a woman attempting to find her own voice. It depicts the devastating love developing between Charu and the husband's brother Amal, a poet who is summoned to keep his brother's wife occupied and help her with her writing.

The slowness of the film, the sumptuousness of the camera and the delicate handling of ennui, passion, creativity, and loyalty create a real spectacle of banalities and larger feminist and universal themes.

The filming of the wealthy house with its restricted space and compressing walls expresses the loneliness and marginalization of talented women even in upper-class circles, a theme that would be taken up by the Indian feminist filmmaker Aparna Sen, with *Parama* (1984), defined by Sen herself as one of the most feminist of her films. The film is about Parama, a 40-year-old married woman, whose settled and very predictable life turns upside down when she meets an expat photographer, Rahul. He chooses her to pose for a magazine in order to make a photo-essay on "An Indian Housewife." When he asks her the simple question "What do you think, Parama?" her world starts to open up, and she rediscovers herself through his glamorous photos and the unleashing of a passion that will lead to their affair. The affair is more a symptom of her self-discovery, but when Rahul betrays her by publishing her semi-nude photos in the journal without her consent, she has a breakdown and is ostracized by the family. When the family accepts her back, she refuses to feel any sense of guilt and explores other venues of self-realization, such as looking for a job through a friend. Thus Sen adds a clear twist to Ray's ending, which was a stilted reconciliation between husband and wife, showing in *Parama* the uncompromising need for self-realization and growth. Many of these feminist themes have been picked up by Indian filmmakers in the diaspora such as Deepa Mehta, Mira Nair, and Gurinder Chadha, who have all received wide international acclaim. The Indo-Canadian Mehta has produced a successful oeuvre with her *Elements Trilogy*, which addresses issues of lesbianism (*Fire*, 1998), partition (*Earth*, 1998), and widowhood (*Water*, 2005) through a feminist postcolonial lens.

Similarly, Mira Nair has marked her international career in the USA through a critical take on South Asians in the diaspora, and on issues of gender and sexuality at home. Her *Salaam Bombay* (1988), on child prostitution in Bombay, has been accused of orientalism and confirming the stereotypical images of downtrodden Indian women and children. Yet the film's strongest feature is its political denunciation of child prostitution and the use of non-professional actors, which pays homage to the poverty and squalor of urban life for the underclasses. Her subsequent *Mississippi Masala* (1991) deals with the issue of interracial love between blacks and Indians in the US (starring Denzel Washington), and the internationally acclaimed *Monsoon Wedding* (2001) deals with themes of incest, arranged marriages, and diasporic connections, combining a Bollywood-style wedding spectacle with the raw reality of child abuse and family divisions. *Monsoon Wedding* won the Golden Lion in Venice, a rare achievement for women filmmakers.

Kenyan born, British-based Gurinder Chadha is another highly successful transnational and postcolonial feminist filmmaker whose work addresses issues of women's roles in Indian society, the intricacies of interethnic and religious relations, globalization, and the cultural industry. Chadha's early film *Bhaji on the Beach* (1993) is an excellent example of low-budget filming to great effect. Focusing on a community of South Asian women on a leisure trip to the seaside (Blackpool), the film unleashes all the generational, religious, sexual, racial, and gender problems of diasporic life, combining comic and tragic moments with dexterity and verve. Her more successful and well-known *Bend it Like Beckham* (2002) launched Chadha into international fame, with the tale of an Indian girl wanting to become a footballer against all patriarchal and ethnic stereotypes. The film's overwhelming success allowed Chadha to make her own Bollywood blockbuster, *Bride and Prejudice* (2004), starring Miss World 1994, Aishwarya Rai—a tongue-in-cheek adaptation of Jane Austen's novel, where the dynamics of class and gender of the nineteenth century are transferred into a postcolonial response (Ponzanesi 2014).

Recent Indian productions such as *Queen* (Vikas Bahl, 2014) testify to the entrance of feminist and subversive topics such as homosexuality into mainstream Bollywood film-making. It is story of a woman abandoned at the altar by her fiancé who then travels to Europe for her honeymoon alone and discovers herself through a series of hilarious and heart-warming encounters; *Queen* became an instant hit, signaling for many the entry of feminism into Hindi-Bollywood cinema (Borpujari 2015).

Other postcolonial feminist filmmakers around the world can be mentioned, connecting different cinematic traditions, geographical specificities, and feminist concerns. *Measures of Distance* (1988), made by Palestinian video and performance artist Mona Hatoum, displays the fragmented memories of different generations of Palestinian women, mothers in the civil war in Lebanon and daughters dispersed in the West. The voice narrates a tale of geographical distance while communicating great emotional closeness, through the mixture of genres and media, letters, audiotapes, photographs, voice-overs, and past images played in the present, mixing Arabic with English, rendering the reality of multiple generations, geographies, and temporalities. As Shohat writes, *Measures of Distance* also probes issues of sexuality and the female body:

> In Western popular culture, the Arab female body, whether in the art form of the veiled, bare-breasted women who posed for French colonial photographers or the Orientalist harems and belly dancers of Hollywood film, had functioned as a sign of the exotic. But rather than adopt a patriarchal strategy of simply censuring female nudity, Hatoum deploys the diffusively sensuous, almost pointillist images of her mother's nakedness to tell a more complex story with nationalist overtones. She uses diverse strategies to veil the images from voyeuristic scrutiny. ... The superimposed words in Arabic script serve to "envelop" her nudity. "Barring" the body, the script metaphorizes her inaccessibility, visually undercutting the intimacy that is verbally expressed in other registers.
>
> *(2006b, 311–12)*

Fragments of letters, body, and dialogues superimposed create a sense of continuity and fracture between the personal and national, the experience of exile and the past of a country which no longer exists. This particularly aesthetic achievement, which has great political and affective overtones, has been also appropriated, but with very different effects, by Shirin Neshat, an Iranian-American artist, whose photographic series *Women of Allah* (1993–7) superimposed old, poetic texts and scriptures onto faces, hands, bodies, playing between the veiling and unveiling, the profane and the poetic, making the body speak out through unconventional techniques drawing on multiple media forms.

Shirin Neshat received many accolades for her first feature-length film *Women Without Men* (2009), a poetic rendition of four women's stories challenging patriarchy, politics, sexuality, and religion. A photographer by training, Neshat conveys the stunning power of images through an oneiric and surreal visual style, which at times has also been accused of buying into Orientalist representations to win over Western audiences. Yet the road for women filmmakers is not an easy one. In order to find representations by women and about women, it is often necessary to rely on specific festivals or sections of documentary filmmaking.

There is of course a wealth of established and up-and-coming women filmmakers who are contributing to feminist postcolonial cinema in unique ways, sometimes in their struggle as cineastes in a male-dominated world, sometimes through subject matter that focuses on women's representation and the renewal of cinematic language. Euzhan Palcy, from Martinique, is notable for being one of the first black women directors to direct a major Hollywood studio production, with MGM producing *A Dry White Season* (1989), a South African apartheid drama based on André Brink's novel of the same name. The film explored themes of race, gender, and politics from an explicitly feminist perspective. Other up-and-coming directors from the Caribbean include Mary Wells from Jamaica (*Kingston Paradise*, 2013), Mariette Monpierre from Guadeloupe (*Le Bonheur d'Elza*, 2011), and Mitzi Allen from Antigua (*The Sweetest Mango*, 2001).

Moufida Tlatli from Tunisia has also established herself as a prominent African woman in cinema. Her *The Silences of the Palace* (1994) is a painful story of a singer who visits the palace where her mother was once employed as a servant, signaling the last days of French influence in Tunis and the rise of the independence movement. The visit to the palace unleashes many traumatic recollections of her mother's abuse and sexual harassment by the palace owners and her mother's attempt to spare her daughter from the same destiny at her own expense. The film speaks not only to the struggle of the past but also to the struggle of the future where women are not per se liberated from bondage in the new post-independence Tunisia, but are caught up with new militant rhetoric, therefore showing continuity with past oppression but also the transformation into new possibilities for emancipation.

These examples summarize the complexities of categorizing postcolonial feminist filmmaking in either a chronological or a consistent geographical pattern. They demonstrate that the postcolonial as an optic can be applied to the dialogue between the political and the aesthetic in different ways. It is an approach that does not just privilege the issue of women behind the camera, or their representation on screen, but interrogates the visual language used, and the innovations introduced, that can also be used to reflect on productions of the past and how they speak to the present through a postcolonial awareness and deconstructive gaze.

Identifying new visual registers that are not colonizing is important in order to account for how race, ethnicity, class, religion, and sexual desires can be articulated from new vantage points without losing the connection to different filmic traditions and political realities. Postcolonial approaches to film and feminism expand the postcolonial optic to films that are not simply engaging with postcolonial temporalities but deal in more general terms with the understanding of patterns of domination and resistance. The latter are linked to colonial and neocolonial dynamics that need to be read against the grain in order to offer a space for feminist interventions.

Related topics

Priya Jaikumar, "Feminist and non-Western interrogations of film authorship"
Anikó Imre, "Gender, socialism, and European film cultures"
Lingzhen Wang, "Chinese socialist women's cinema: an alternative feminist practice"

Bibliography

Amrane-Minne, D. D. (2007) "Women at War," *Interventions. International Journal of Postcolonial Studies*, 9(3), pp. 340–49.

Borpujari, P. (2015) "India's Wandering Women with Cameras," *Open Democracy*, September 9, 2015 (www.opendemocracy.net/5050/priyanka-borpujari/indias-wandering-women-with-cameras, last accessed September 4, 2015).

Briley, R. (2010) "Terrorism on Screen: Lessons from The Battle of Algiers," *American Historical Association* (https://www.historians.org/publications-and-directories/perspectives-on-history/october-2010/terrorism-on-screen-lessons-from-the-battle-of-algiers, last accessed July 16, 2016).

Caillé, P. (2007) "The Illegitimate Legitimacy of The Battle of Algiers in French Film Culture," *Interventions. International Journal of Postcolonial Studies*, 9(3), pp. 371–88.

Doane, M. A. (1991) "Dark Continents: Epistemologies of Racial and Sexual Difference in Psycho-analysis and the Cinema," in M. A. Doane *Femmes Fatales: Feminism, Film Theory, Psychoanalysis*, New York and London: Routledge, pp. 209–48.

Espinosa, J. G. (1979) "For an Imperfect Cinema," trans. J. Burton, *Jump Cut: A Review of Contemporary Media*, 20, pp. 24–6. (First published in Spanish as Por un Cine imperfecto, Cine Cubano, 14, 1969).

Fanon, F. (1963) *The Wretched of the Earth* (published in French in 1961), preface by J.-P. Sartre, trans. C. Farrington, New York: Grove Weidenfeld.

Gaines, J. (1986) "White Privilege and Looking Relations; Race and Gender in Feminist Film Theory," *Screen*, 29(4), pp. 12–27.

Getino, O. and Solanas, F. (1969) "Toward a Third Cinema" (published in Spanish in 1969), *Cineaste*, 4(3), pp. 1–10.

Harrison, N. (2007) "Pontecorvo's 'Documentary' Aesthetics. The Battle of Algiers and the Battle of Algiers," *Interventions. International Journal of Postcolonial Studies*, 9(3), pp. 389–404.

Hollinger, K. (2012) "Feminist Film Studies and Race," in K. Hollinger, *Feminist Film Studies*, London and New York: Routledge, pp. 190–227.

hooks, b. (1992) *Black Looks: Race and Representation*, Boston: South End Press.

Kaplan, E. A. (1997) *Looking to the Other: Feminism, Film and the Imperial Gaze*, New York: Routledge.

Khanna, R. (1998) "*The Battle of Algiers* and *The Nouba of the Women of Mont Chenoua*: From Third to Fourth Cinema," *Third Text*, 12(43), pp. 13–32.

Marciniak, K., Imre, A. and O'Healy, A. (eds.) (2007) *Transnational Feminism in Film and Media*, New York: Palgrave Macmillan.

Marks, L. (2000) *The Skin of the Film: Intercultural Cinema, Embodiment and the Senses*, Durham: Duke University Press.

Naficy, H. (2001) *An Accented Cinema: Exilic and Diasporic Filmmaking*, Princeton: Princeton University Press.

Ponzanesi, S. (2014) *The Postcolonial Cultural Industry: Icons, Markets, Mythologies*, Houndmills, Basingstoke, Palgrave Macmillan.

Ponzanesi, S. and Waller, W. (2012) *Postcolonial Cinema Studies*, London: Routledge.

Quinan, C. (2014) "Uses and Abuses of Gender and Nationality: Torture and the French–Algerian War," in S. Ponzanesi (ed.) *Gender, Globalization and Violence. Postcolonial Conflict Zones*, New York and London: Routlege, pp. 111–25.

Rocha, G. (1995) "An Aesthetic of Hunger" (published in Portuguese in 1965), trans. R. Johnson and B. Hollyman, in R. Johnson and R. Stam (eds.), *Brazilian Cinema*, New York: Columbia University Press, pp. 68–71.

Said, E. (1978) *Orientalism*, London: Pantheon Books.

Shohat, E. (2006a) "Gender and the Culture of Empire: Toward a Feminist Ethnography of the Cinema," in E. Shohat (ed.) *Taboo Memories, Diasporic Voices*, Durham: Duke University Press, pp. 17–69.

Shohat, E. (2006b) "Post-Third Worldist Culture: Gender, Nation, and the Cinema," in E. Shohat (ed.) *Taboo Memories, Diasporic Voices*, Durham: Duke University Press, pp. 290–330.

Shohat, E. and Stam, R. (1994) *Unthinking Eurocentrism: Multiculturalism and the Media*, London: Routledge.

Spivak, G. C. (1987) *In Other Worlds: Essays in Cultural Politics*, New York: Methuen.

Trinh, T. M. (1992) *Framer Framed*, New York: Routledge.

Wiegman, R. (1998) "Race, Ethnicity and Film," in J. Hillis and P. Church-Gibson (eds.), *Oxford Guide to Film Studies*, Oxford: Oxford University Press, pp.158–68.

Young, L. (1996) *Fear of the Dark: 'Race,' Gender and Sexuality in the Cinema*, London: Routledge.

3

FEMINIST FORMS OF ADDRESS

Mai Zetterling's *Loving Couples*

Lucy Fischer

This essay seeks to examine the relationship between women's cinema and feminist forms of address through a discussion of the early work of Swedish actress/director Mai Zetterling (1925–94)—an important figure in film history who has received scant recent attention. That she has particular relevance to issues of Women and Film is apparent from the fact that the Edinburgh Film Guild titles its biographical entry on her: "Mai Zetterling: Actor, Director, *Feminist*." The Guide states, "Mai Zetterling... was not only one of the first significant female directors of non-documentary feature films, but arguably deserves credit for *being the first director of explicitly feminist films targeted at mainstream audiences*."[1] Before discussing her career, however, it is important to interrogate certain foundational terms as conceived within feminist film studies.

Laying the groundwork

The label "women's cinema" has been used in a variety of ways. For instance, it can mean a film genre directed to a female audience. When referring to the 1940s–50s, scholars speak of the "woman's picture"—generally, melodramas (mostly directed by men) that center on a female protagonist who faces struggles in her domestic life (with conflicts arising around marriage, motherhood, and career). Molly Haskell first examined this mode in *From Reverence to Rape* in 1973, decrying its name and the manner in which it was denigrated. As she noted:

> What more damning comment on the relations between women in America than the very notion of something called the "woman's film?" And what more telling sign of critical and sexual priorities than the low caste it has among highbrows?...
> As a term of critical opprobrium, "woman's film" carries the implication that women, and therefore woman's emotional problems, are of minor significance.
>
> (Haskell 1973, 153–4)

In later years, feminist scholars like Mary Ann Doane embraced the genre and took it (and the problems it surfaced) quite seriously—highlighting the manner in which its female characters had been severed from desire (Doane 1987). In so doing, she examined such forms as the love story and the maternal melodrama. Other critics, like Diane Waldman, concentrated on different instances of the mode—for example, the Gothic (Waldman 1981).

Another (and, for our purposes) stronger sense of the term "women's cinema," however, refers to films *made by women filmmakers*—directing being the craft from which women have largely been excluded. Starting in the 1970s, with the rise of Second Wave feminism, women's film festivals were launched (beginning with one in New York City in 1972). In the decades that followed, some researchers highlighted female directors of the sound era who had been overshadowed by men (e.g. Ida Lupino and Dorothy Arzner in Hollywood, or Leontine Sagan in Germany), while others (through organizations like the Women Film Pioneers Project) unearthed silent film directors that had been ignored (e.g. Lois Weber, Alice Guy-Blaché, Cleo Madison). Recently, with a focus on globalism, attention has also turned to non-Western female directors like Aparna Sen in India, Rakhshan Bani-Etemad in Iran, or Tian-yi Yang in China. Clearly, in examining the films of Mai Zetterling, I am drawing on the latter sense of "women's cinema," and attempting to shed light on an artist heralded in the initial days of film feminist studies but then mostly overlooked.

The second and more complex term that needs to be considered is "feminist address." Here, there will be no monolithic definition, as notions of feminism vary. In fact, in current usage one often speaks of "feminisms" which means that we must also talk of modes of address. Which approach and strand of feminist politics a filmmaker chooses (if any) will be determined by a variety of factors—among them, nationality, race, gender identification, sexual preference, age, and production context. We can, however, distinguish between several levels of address, though they are often inseparable in articulation.

One level involves *subject matter*. Although Dorothy Arzner's film style conformed, in general, to Hollywood conventions, she often took on topics that were important to women and critical of their position in conventional society. So, in *Dance, Girl, Dance* (1940), she critiqued woman as spectacle; in *The Wild Party* (1929), she hinted at the possibility of lesbianism; and in *Christopher Strong* (1933), she examined women in non-traditional occupations. But feminist subject matter need not always center on women; clearly, analyzing masculinity is part of the broader gender equation. Thus, in Susan Bier's *In a Better World* (2010), the focus is on male protagonists—revealing how society sustains and encourages their aggressive behavior. In principle, male filmmakers can also tackle feminist subject matter. In Stephen Frears' *Philomena* (2013), for instance, he confronts the tragedy of an Irish girl who, decades earlier as an unwed mother, was sent to a convent to give birth then forced to sign over the child for adoption at the age of three. So part of a filmmakers' "address" relates to the issues she or he raises (or does not raie) on screen, and their implications for feminist politics.

Another level of address concerns the *audience* to which a film is directed and its consequences. Is a film's target audience primarily male, female, or mixed? Elite or mainstream? Clearly, the works of a director like Susan Seidelman (e.g. *Desperately Seeking Susan* [1985]) were meant for a mainstream audience—and if the spectator gleaned a feminist message from them, so much the better. During the heyday of feminist criticism in the 1970s, however, E. Ann Kaplan coined the term "avant-garde theory film" for works that were experimental, Brechtian, analytical, and (often) didactic in exploring women's issues (1990, 142). Most certainly, these films (e.g. Sally Potter's *Thriller* [1979], Laura Mulvey and Peter Wollen's *Riddles of the Sphinx* [1977]) were aimed at an intellectual, and often female, audience—thus, risking the danger of speaking to the "already convinced." Standing in between these extremes have been feminist "art films"—a form initiated in the 1920s (with works like Germaine Dulac's *The Smiling Madame Beudet* [1923]), extended in the 1960s (with films like Agnés Varda's *Cleo from 5 to 7* [1962]), and continuing today (with movies like Jane Campion's *The Piano* [1993]). While such works veer away from the realm of mass culture, they reach a far wider audience than experimental films, and with them comes a broader message about women and society.

A final level of address concerns *cinematic style and discourse* and the manner in which its employment affects the spectator and the portrayal of figures on screen. Here, of course, the most famous debate reigned around the question of the "gaze"—the look of the camera—either as a conduit for the perspective of the implied narrator, or the eyes of a character. While early on, Mulvey (along with other critics) claimed that the camera, by definition, took a male and often voyeuristic approach, she later modified her position (Mulvey 2009)—a stance echoed by theorists like Kaplan (2000, 119–38) and Teresa de Lauretis (1984). Nonetheless, a ghost haunts the lens of the woman director when aimed at the female body (especially if nude); and she is often asked whether she, too, is objectifying women. Furthermore, her texts are investigated for the manner in which they articulate the gazes of their protagonists—both male and female—questioning how these decisions inflect character portrayal and agency.

Another debate in feminist film studies has revolved around the notion of "counter-cinema"—as first articulated by Claire Johnston (1999, 31–40). Essentially, Johnston argued that, in order for a film to be truly feminist, it needed to oppose the basic tenets of classical form. This led to the assumption that a feminist film must be avant-garde, in the manner of works like Valie Export's *Invisible Adversaries* (1977) or Yvonne Rainer's *The Man who Envied Women* (1985). Again, since then, such stringent prescriptions have been relaxed and it has been acknowledged that feminist films can be made while employing more traditional paradigms.

Other aspects of filmic discourse have been examined for their consequences for a feminist approach. Thus, critics have asked, Whose point of view is the story told from? Is a woman allowed to be the narrative center or is her tale bracketed within a man's story? How is her perspective rendered—through the eyes of others or her own, through depictions of the past or the present, through reality or fantasy? Questions have also surfaced around modes of spectator identification. Initially (as per Mulvey) it was asserted that women viewers identified only with female characters (and this to their peril in mainstream film). In Mulvey's revised theorization (echoed by others), however, identification came to be seen as split and multiple—involving numerous on-screen characters and often a kind of gender "transvestitism." Clearly, such a view presented women filmmakers with a broader palette and loosened the constraints of a more literal approach. All these senses of "women's cinema" and "feminist forms of address" will inform my discussion of the career and works of Mai Zetterling.

Mai Zetterling: from on camera to behind the camera

Zetterling is one of those female film directors who entered the profession after being a screen actress (with beauty almost without exception a prerequisite for the latter position). Thus, she joins the ranks of Ida Lupino, Jodie Foster, Anjelica Huston, Diane Keaton, Jeanne Moreau, and others. Starting as a screen performer, Zetterling had firsthand knowledge of the limited roles available for women, as well as the experience of how women were treated in the industry at large. For this reason it is important to review her move from before to behind the camera.

Zetterling was born in Västerås, Sweden in 1925 to a working class family. She left school early and held several menial jobs, but her professional life began at age 17 with attendance at Dramaten, the Swedish national theater in Stockholm. Her breakthrough came just two years later with an appearance in the film *Torment* (1944) written by Ingmar Bergman (seven years her senior) and directed by Alf Sjöberg. Bergman served as Assistant Director on the project and it was co-produced by renowned auteur, Victor Sjöström; so Zetterling's entry into the profession was in the company of several illustrious figures. In *Torment*, she plays a shop girl, Bertha, who is loved by Jan-Erik, an upper-class student, but is haunted by a prior relationship with a sadistic teacher at Jan-Erik's school. The film "created a sensation and is now considered a landmark of the Swedish cinema," with Zetterling soon proclaimed as "an international star" (Collins 1994).

The next few years saw her involved in international productions. First, she moved to England where, in 1947, she starred in Basil Dearden's film *Frieda*, in the role of a German woman who helps a British airman escape a POW camp. Eventually marrying him and moving to the UK, she faces prejudice there in the post-war era. Zetterling briefly returned to Sweden in 1948 to make *Music in Darkness*, directed by Bergman (who had not yet achieved international success). In it, she plays a servant girl in the home of a wealthy family whose distraught musician son, blinded in the war, develops a relationship with her. Soon thereafter, Zetterling returned to England and appeared in such films as *Quartet* (1948), based on stories by W. Somerset Maugham; *The Romantic Age* (1949), a comedy directed by Edmond T. Gréville; *The Lost People* (1949) about post-war refugees, directed by Muriel Box and Bernard Knowles, co-starring Richard Attenborough; and *Blackmailed* (1951), a thriller directed by Marc Allégret (with screenplay by Roger Vadim), co-starring Dirk Bogarde.

Eventually, she traveled to Hollywood to appear opposite Danny Kaye (a major comic star at the time) in *Knock on Wood* (1954) directed by Melvin Frank and Norman Panama. In it, she plays a psychiatrist who tries to solve the romantic problems of a ventriloquist. As a European, she felt "ill at ease" there: "Hollywood treated its stars rough, not like humans but like monsters, goddesses, heroes. To be admired for your beauty, your sexiness in that crazy public way is both dangerous and disconcerting" (Zetterling 1985, 98, 99). She continues: "I was the wrong kind of property for Hollywood, ill-suited to playing the cutie-pie, the piece of ass" (Ibid. 103). Clearly, Zetterling's feminist consciousness was already raised.

But she was political in a broader sense as well. While in California, she associated with Hollywood Leftists and was reputedly watched by British security agents as a suspected Communist (Pate 2014). While the careers of American radicals were ruined during this period, there was no equivalent of the blacklist in England, so she was able to return there and work in the film and television industries. Thus, she starred in some fourteen films as well as numerous television series, playing against such leading men as Tyrone Power, Richard Widmark, Laurence Harvey, Peter Sellers, Herbert Lom, Keenan Wynn, Stanley Baker, and Dennis Price. She also worked in the theater, playing such parts as Nora in Ibsen's *A Doll's House*—a figure with whom she identified (Ibid. 115–16).

Impatient with the acting roles she was given, Zetterling turned her attention to directing—understanding that this was the seat of power and control in the industry. As she remarked:

> An actress is totally dependent on other people ... although there are good roles in the theater, I had arrived at the point where I had done them all. And acting in films is always a compromise. I decided I wanted to make them myself.
>
> (Canby 1966, 52)

In turning to production, Zetterling first worked for the BBC making short documentaries. *The Polite Invasion* (1960) was shot in Swedish Lapland and portrayed how the "old nomadic Lapp way of life was in danger of disappearing" (Zetterling 1985, 167). *Lords of Little Egypt* (1961) concerned the annual congregation of "gypsies" in the Camargue region of France. *The Prosperity Race* (1962) explored middle-class life in Stockholm and the quest for affluence, getting Zetterling "into serious trouble" with her homeland. As she recalls, "There were savage screams from my country: I was a traitor." Finally, *The Do-It-Yourself Democracy* (1963) took Iceland as its subject. Clearly, her documentaries considered serious contemporary issues and she was not assigned subjects thought to appeal primarily to women.

While working on documentaries, she made a short dramatic film, *The War Game* (1962) which was nominated for a BAFTA award, and won a Silver Lion at Venice. This was an auspicious way to begin a fiction filmmaking career. Already, *The War Game* shows Zetterling's great talent in visual, acoustic, and performative realms. Furthermore, in the manner of Susanne Bier, she tackles issues of gender relevant to women through a critique of masculinity. The film (shot in black and white and running only 15 minutes) depicts two young boys (Ian Ellis and Joseph Robinson) play-fighting in the courtyard of a London housing project. One of the boys (a brunette) has several toy guns, and the film begins with his aiming one at the camera (like the famous shot from *The Great Train Robbery* [1903]).

After pointing it at a sleeping man listening to a radio sports broadcast, he chases the second boy (a blond), who eventually gets hold of one of the guns. The brunette takes an elevator upstairs and the blond follows by stairway and eventually reaches the roof. The boys' fight escalates to the point where the blond is backed up to the edge of the roof, at which point the two boys smile at each other and the blond drops his gun. The film, however, ends on a freeze frame of each boy's hand reaching for the fallen gun as though to imply that the fight continues. On the soundtrack we hear explosive noise which could be gunshots.

Throughout the film, the nameless boys do not speak a single line of dialogue, but the soundtrack is interesting—a mixture of street sounds, radio broadcasts, elevator noise, and nursery music (a reminder, that the boys are only children). Clearly, however, Zetterling underscores the perils of boys' games which lead to adult warfare. While no women appear in the film, a feminist perspective can be read from its critique of masculinity.

Zetterling, filmmaking, and feminist address

> [Zetterling's] filmic statements about the position of women in society are extremely important to the development of a new image of women in film and society, and to the creation of a new belief in women as creative artists.
>
> Linda Thornburg (1974, 13)

Zetterling returned to Sweden to direct her first feature film, *Loving Couples* (1964), based on the work of Agnes von Krusenstjerna, who was considered a woman's novelist. Zetterling co-wrote the screenplay with her second husband David Hughes, with whom she had worked on *The War Game* and would collaborate on future projects. The film was made during the era in which a variety of international "new waves" hit the exhibition and festival circuits, and notions of traditional film (as formulaic light entertainment) were being exploded. Also challenged was conventional film style and such new works allowed for techniques like direct address, jump cuts, elliptical narratives, and plotlessness.

In Sweden, of course, Bergman had, by now, achieved worldwide fame as an auteur who confronted solemn topics previously limited to literature and theater.

Loving Couples was a critical success. Kenneth Tynan in *The Observer* called it "one of the most ambitious debuts since *Citizen Kane*" (Zetterling 1985, 186). Given this reception, it seems all the more regrettable that the film has been forgotten, along with others by Zetterling. *Loving Couples* was not, however, without its controversies. At Cannes, the film was banned due to some sexually explicit scenes.[2] As Zetterling recalls, *Le Monde* called it "Une chronique scandalous" and she was deemed "Swedish and shocking." Furthermore, it was said that "The tough Mai Zetterling ... directs like a man" (Ibid.). Even the film's poster (which pictured silhouettes of people suggestively intertwined) was considered risqué and *Variety* refused to publish it. *Loving Couples* starred a group of first tier Swedish actors who had come to be associated with Bergman (Harriet Andersson, Gunnel Lindblom, and Gunnar Björnstrand) and it was shot by his main cameraman, Sven Nykvist. According to Zetterling: "It was one of the biggest and most costly Swedish productions that had ever been undertaken" (Ibid. 176).

The very subject matter of the film is one that speaks to a feminist address given that it takes on a topic central to women's lives and rarely considered in mainstream film— pregnancy and childbirth. Thus, it is an updated version of a "woman's picture." Of course, Swedish cinema, in general, was known for being more comfortable than its American counterpart with issues of sexuality and the body. (We recall that any depiction of pregnant women had been banned in Hollywood under the infamous 1930s Production Code). In Sweden, the theme had previously been treated by Bergman in *Brink of Life* (1958) and Zetterling's film shows its influence. That Zetterling would tackle such a topic for her first film is not surprising given her own statement. As she notes:

> There are many things I feel haven't been aired on the screen, haven't been looked
> at from a woman's point of view, so naturally I make films about women.
>
> *(Thornburg 1974, 13)*

Loving Couples concerns three women (whose lives intersect) who spend time in a Swedish maternity hospital in the WWI-era. However, in addition to scenes taking place there, the film weaves a complex web of flashbacks in which we learn about each woman's background—her status, position, and relationships with men. These scenes are both melodramatic and satirical and tend to critique bourgeois Swedish society—its sexism, hypocrisies, and oppressions.

Taking on the subject of maternity was not neutral territory for Zetterling who has openly admitted her own conflicts toward childbearing. She says that she hated pregnancy: "The supposedly greatest experience in a woman's life was the worst thing that could have happened to me" (Zetterling 1985, 79). Likewise, she condemns her own performance as a parent: "I feel that I have been an utter failure as a mother ... I lacked all maternal instinct" (Ibid. 123). She even admits to having had an abortion (Ibid. 87). Though the film's negative attitude toward motherhood may have personal roots, it nonetheless represents a corrective to the kind of Pollyanna portrayals that most women face, both on screen and off—depictions that leave them unprepared for the experience.

Significantly, Zetterling describes the film in broad feminist terms, independent of its specific plot details. She writes:

> *Loving Couples* was a film about women and their deeper attitudes to the
> fundamentals of life: birth, and marriage, sexual relations, human feelings,

freedom. It explored the differences between their attitudes of those of men. ...
Women are imprisoned in a world that doesn't belong to them, whose language
they don't speak.

(Ibid. 183)

In this statement, Zetterling seems well "ahead of the curve" of feminist consciousness at the
time, and her mention of women's exclusion from language seems to presage theories later
advanced by French feminist theorists like Luce Irigaray and Hélène Cixous.

The film's three female protagonists have different personalities and come from diverse
backgrounds. What they have in common is their ambivalent attitudes toward pregnancy
and their suffering in a rigid, male-dominated society. The first one we meet is Angela (Gio
Petré), an upper-class woman who was orphaned as a child and raised by Petra (Anita Björk),
a member of her extended family. It is Petra who accompanies Angela to the maternity
hospital, telling her to remember that it is "their" child. This is because Angela (who has had
an affair with Petra's ex-lover) is unwed and has decided that she wants freedom instead of
marriage. She seems entirely content with this decision. Furthermore, she tells the doctor
that she wants to be awake for the birth—not a common stance for the era.

The second woman we encounter is bitter and disgruntled. Adele (Gunnel Lindblom)
was born into a rich family that fell on hard times when her father died. She is now
unhappily married to a farmhand on the estate of a family member. Once in the hospital, she
learns that her baby is stillborn (seemingly a metaphor for her entire life). It is unclear
whether the child is her husband's or that of a former lover who has abandoned her.

The third woman we come upon is Agda (Harriet Andersson), a servant girl who seems
so endlessly cheerful as to be "simple." Indicative of this, she is first seen hopping up and
down the hospital steps, singing and eating candy (like a child). She has been impregnated
by the son of the well-to-do family for which she works; but she has wed the artist Stellan
(Jan Malmsjö) who has been paid off to marry her and save the family's reputation.

Almost everything in Loving Couples is told from the women's point of view. Sometimes
it involves their recollections as presented in flashbacks. For instance, we cut between
present day scenes of Angela in the hospital and retrospective ones of her father's funeral—
the recollection cued in by an extreme facial close-up which dissolves into a memory
(Figure 3.1).

Similarly, we move between Agda in the maternity hospital and scenes of her being
molested as a child by an older man who has treated her to sweets. Here, one of the cuts
between time periods is facilitated by matched shots of Agda eating candy in the hospital
and eating dessert in the bakery with the man—with Zetterling emphasizing his lascivious
expression.

The women's present point of view is also vividly rendered. On a visual level, we often see
low-angle shots taken from the perspective of one of them being wheeled on a gurney; thus
we see images of a skylight, ceiling, light fixtures, etc.

Sometimes, though a shot is not literally from a woman's viewpoint it renders her state of
mind. For example, as Adele is about to be examined by a doctor (Jacob, played by Gunnar
Björnstrand), we see her framed through obstetrical stirrups (Figure 3.2).

Zetterling also creates a sense of the women's acoustic point of view as we hear the
menacing sounds of gurney wheels squeaking (like fingernails on a blackboard), or of babies
screeching. The women also have to endure the insensitive remarks of male physicians.
When Adele is demure about undressing, Jacob brusquely says, "I can't do much unless you
take your pants down." Soon after, he blurts out that her baby is dead. At another moment,

Figure 3.1 Memory and dissolve in *Loving Couples*.

Source: Loving Couples, Mai Zetterling, 1964.

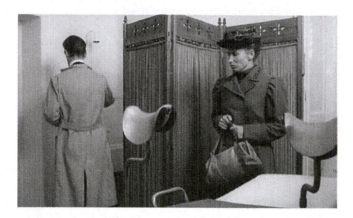

Figure 3.2 A woman's state of mind (*Loving Couples*).

Source: Loving Couples, Mai Zetterling, 1964.

he confesses to Petra his hatred of his job: "The corridors are like prisons. The women are let out, but for us it's a life sentence." Clearly, Zetterling is not interested in presenting a saccharine vision of childbirth and the medical establishment; rather, she portrays it in all its insensitivity and brutality.

The women in *Loving Couples* are aware of their compromised social situation and their fraught relationship with men. The tone of the film is quite cynical and, clearly, the title *Loving Couples* is meant ironically. This skepticism comes out in many lines of dialogue (another tool for assuring a feminist address). At one point, Adele's mother tells her that, "Men always let you down," (a line that Adele later repeats herself); and when, on her wedding night, she informs her husband that she is not a virgin, she says, "It's the only thing you men care about." Finally, having found out that her baby is stillborn, she taunts her husband (who may not be its father) by saying, "Good news for you, it's dead." The other women make similarly barbed comments. Angela says, "We fight to stand on our own feet until a man comes and ruins it all." And Petra mocks convention by stating: "It looks so easy to be womanly and weak, but I can't."

In particular, marriage is portrayed as both ludicrous and repressive—with all marriages in the film being failed, fraudulent, or adulterous. Indicative of this, one woman remarks, "The aim of marriage, like war, is to teach people how to hate each other." Similarly, during the dinner party to celebrate the forced marriage of Agda and Stellan, Adele knocks the bride and groom off the cake and laughs. Finally, when Angela turns 18, she is told that she is "free" but also (incongruously) that her next step will be "holy wedlock." She is then sent to a boarding school to learn "womanly virtues," but the girls there seem intent on sabotaging their conservative Christian education. They dance the "Can Can" (raising their skirts) and giggle as they watch a female dog being humped by a male. (Their scandalized teachers, on the other hand, pour cold water on the canines). Beyond that, one of Angela's teachers is in love with her and is tortured when the girl rejects her advances.

Angela, on the other hand, forms a very close relationship with another student, Stanny (Anja Boman), much to the dismay of their families who are concerned that the women are "too close" (read "lesbians"). Interestingly, there is another character in the drama who is bisexual—Stellan. At his church wedding rehearsal (which Zetterling plays like a farce), not only is Agda present but so is the artist's male lover who walks down the aisle with him as Agda trails behind. The two men even exchange rings. In another scene, taking place in a woman's bedroom, Stellan tries on her feather boa. So, not only does Zetterling critique conventional marriage; she explores the taboo subject of same sex love.

While Zetterling portrays Swedish bourgeois society as static, she underscores the fact (in a dissonant manner) by employing abundant camera movement. Characters often walk toward the camera as it tracks backwards, and it frequently picks up different people at various stages of a shot (a technique that requires complex blocking and planning). There are several tour de force 360-degree pan shots (for instance, at the funeral of Angela's father, around a dinner table, and on a terrace at a midsummer's eve celebration). One particular scene comes to mind for its hyperbolic choice of point of view. After the death of Angela's father, she hides under the table as men discuss her future. She is seen there along with a dog, the men's feet, and the ashes flicked from their cigars. There could be no better way of portraying the girl's powerlessness than this. In general, Zetterling favors the long-shot/long-take—a means of contextualizing her characters within the broader social environment.

The film ends in a daring way that again highlights women's experience. As Angela gives birth we hear her scream and focus on her contorted face. We then see documentary footage of a newborn infant whose umbilical cord is being cut. The final shot of the film is a freeze frame of that baby (Figure 3.3).

Here, an exchange spoken earlier between obstetricians reverberates in our ears. They decry how grown men are tied to women by an umbilical cord which strangles their independence. Similarly, Petra's former lover says at one point, "You women scare us. Sooner or later we must hurt you."

As we stare at the image of the child, we wonder what kind of future it will face and whether it will be constrained by the same limitations of gender and convention that have haunted the world of *Loving Couples*. Clearly, Mai Zetterling hopes that it will not.

In sum, *Loving Couples* is a text that invokes all senses of the term "women's cinema." It is made by a female artist after an apprenticeship in other facets of the film industry. Furthermore, its narrative is based on the work of another female creator, writer Agnes von Krusenstjerna. Moreover, the drama confronts issues central to women's lives and appeals to a female audience: questions of marriage, pregnancy, motherhood, and the constraints of bourgeois convention. Finally, as a skilled craftswoman, Zetterling utilizes the varied

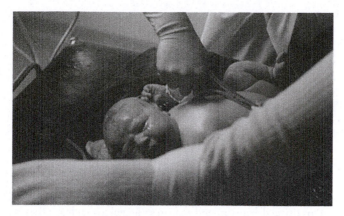

Figure 3.3   The final shot in *Loving Couples.*

Source: *Loving Couples,* Mai Zetterling, 1964.

discourses of cinema (the camera "gaze," editing, shot composition, etc.) to present a female perspective on the story told.

Related topics

Patrice Petro, "Classical feminist film theory: then and (mostly) now"
Maureen Turim, "Experimental women filmmakers"
Erica Levin, "Class/Ornament: cinema, new media, labor-power, and performativity"

Notes

1 "Mai Zetterling: Actor, Director, Feminist." http://edinburghfilmguild.org.uk/wordpress/
   ?page_id=1134 (accessed June 15, 2015). My emphasis.
2 Swedish Film Database. www.sfi.se/en-gb/Swedish-film-database/Item/?type=PERSON&itemid=
   173874&iv=BIOGRAPHY (accessed June 15, 2015).

References

Canby, V 1966, "Mai Zetterling Comments About Directorial Role," *New York Times,* September 15.
    Available from: www.nytimes.com (March 9, 2016).
Collins, G 1994, "Mai Zetterling, 68, Film Actress with a Second Career in Directing," *New York Times,* March 19. Available from: www.nytimes.com (March 9, 2016).
de Lauretis, T 1984, *Alice Doesn't: Feminism, Semiotics, Cinema.* Indiana University Press, Bloomington.
Doane, MA 1987, *The Desire to Desire: The Woman's Film of the 1940s.* Indiana University Press, Bloomington.
Haskell, M 1973, *From Reverence to Rape: The Treatment of Women in the Movies.* Penguin Books, New York, pp. 153–4.
Johnston, C 1999, "Women's Cinema as Counter-Cinema" in *Feminist Film Theory. A Reader,* ed. S. Thornham. Edinburgh University Press, Edinburgh, pp. 31–40.
Kaplan, AE 1990, "The Avant-garde Theory Film: Three Case Studies from Britain and the USA: *Sigmund Freud's Dora (1979),* Thriller *(1979),* Mulvey/Wollen's Amy *(1980)*" in *Women and Film: Both Sides of the Camera,* ed. AE Kaplan. Routledge, New York, pp. 142–70.
Kaplan, AE 2000, "Is the Gaze Male?" in *Feminism and Film,* ed. AE Kaplan. Oxford University Press, New York and Oxford, pp. 119–38.

Mulvey, L 2009, *Visual and Other Pleasures*, 2nd edn. Palgrave/Macmillan, Basingstoke, United Kingdom.

Pate, H 2014, *Tyrone Power 180 Success Facts–Everything You Need to Know About Tyrone Power*. Emereo Publishing, Aspley.

Thornburg, L 1974, "Mai Zetterling: The Creation of a New Mythology," *Journal of the University Film Association*, Vol. 26, No. 1/2, pp. 13–15.

Waldman, D 1981, *Horror and Domesticity: The Modern Gothic Romance Film of the 1940s*. University of Wisconsin–Madison, Madison.

Zetterling, M 1985, *All Those Tomorrows*. Grove Press, New York.

Further reading

Alison Butler. *Women's Cinema: the Contested Screen*. London: Wallflower Press, 2003.

An introduction to critical debates around women's filmmaking and how they relate to cinematic practice. Building on theoretical work by Claire Johnston and others, Butler argues that women's cinema exists inside other cinemas, reformulating the codes and systems of the major cinematic traditions from within.

Lucy Fischer. *Shot Countershot: Film Tradition and Women's Cinema*. Princeton, NJ: Princeton University Press, 1989.

This book relates the idea of a counter-cinema to theories of intertextuality and locates it in the broad context of recent feminist film, literary, and art criticism. Fischer employs an original critical model of the dialogue between women's cinema and film tradition in the very organization of the book. Each chapter discusses a theme or genre (such as the musical, the "double," the myth of womanhood, and the figure of the actress), counterposing two or more works—from the feminist and from the dominant cinema.

E. Ann Kaplan. *Women and Film: Both Sides of the Camera*. New York: Methuen, 1983.

Through her analysis of four films depicting different cinematic periods, Kaplan discusses how the male gaze (as the camera eye), through its position of power, has defined and limited woman as spectacle. She also describes women filmmakers' attempts to overturn the dichotomy and speak on film as subjects. Furthermore, Kaplan suggests that the Mother, who has been mostly overlooked in male representations of women, is a good place to look to locate a female voice outside patriarchal definitions.

Mariah Larrson, Anders Marklund, eds. *Swedish Film; An Introduction and a Reader*. Lund: Nordic Academic Press, 1990.

A collection of essays, organized in thematic sections, concerning the history of Swedish cinema. Some chapters focus on women in the film industry (e.g. one on writer Selma Lagerlöf and another on director Mai Zetterling's film *The Girls*).

Linda Thornburg. "Mai Zetterling: The Creation of a New Mythology." *Journal of the University Film Association*, Vol. 26, No. 1/2, *Women in Film* (1974), 13–15.

A discussion of several films by Mai Zetterling (including *Loving Couples*, *Dr. Glas*, and *The Girls*), arguing that her cinema fights conventional myths of womanhood and opens up new possibilities for female filmmakers.

Mai Zetterling. *All Those Tomorrows*. New York: Grove Press, 1985.

Mai Zetterling's autobiography recounting her personal life as well as her work as an actress (in both Sweden, England, and the US) and her career in documentary and fiction filmmaking.

4

SOUND AND GENDER

Kathleen M. Vernon

To the extent that sound has been treated as secondary, subordinate, and supplementary to the visual dimension of cinema, critical consideration of its nature and function has often been rendered in terms of gender. Viewed within the frame of the "ideology of the visible" (Doane 1985a: 55) that has dominated Western epistemology, sound stands opposed to vision in an implicitly gendered hierarchy that associates rational knowledge and the mastery afforded by the distance between viewer and object of vision with the sense of sight, and sound in its elusive yet enveloping presentness with "the emotional and the intuitive" (ibid.). In privileging the role of the visible over the audible and seeing over hearing, mainstream film theory and criticism have left these categories largely intact.

Indeed, the first serious academic studies of film sound published in the 1980s can be seen to reinforce the then dominant psychoanalytic paradigm in its understanding of cinema as a primarily visual medium structured by a controlling male gaze. Yet as the work of Laura Mulvey and other feminist theorists was read to exclude a role for women as anything but the projection of male desire, subsequent critics began to look to cinema sound in its different components, including music and voice, as a way to rescue a place for the female subject and feminine agency both within and beyond the film text. Pursuing such a notion, in *La voix au cinéma* French composer and sound theorist Michel Chion points to the promise of sound and rhythms as a potential "territory of freedom" for feminists, a fluid and musical domain rich in meanings and pleasures (1982: 8–10).

To provide a critical overview of the study of film sound and gender is to trace an arc from those initial and still influential approaches that consider the soundtrack as constrained by the same structural and cultural binaries and biases that regulate the gendered visual regime of cinema—and that largely concentrate their focus on the canon of classic Hollywood cinema—to other, recent studies informed by a plural and experiential model of spectatorship that also venture beyond the Anglo-European film canon. Increasingly attentive to cultural, sexual, and racial/ethnic differences, this work also incorporates a new set of conceptual and methodological models and reading strategies, including empirical and phenomenological approaches and queer studies. In seeking to present the key arguments that have shaped the debates over film sound and gender, I have organized the discussion that follows in two primary blocks, the first devoted to the analysis of film music and the second to discussions of the voice that lead to a general consideration of the materiality of sound in the context of a body-centered, haptic cinema.

Film music

By many accounts, music figures as the most highly gendered and specifically "feminine" of the different components of cinema sound. Such an understanding harkens back to long-standing Western suspicions of music that conflate its supposed abstract and non-referential nature and lack of fixed meanings with fears of (feminine) disorder, and emotional and sexual excess. Both Plato and Aristotle warned of music's moral ambiguity, while classical Greek literature thematized the ambivalent power of music vested in the female voice, on the one hand celebrating its beauty and capacity to immortalize heroics deeds, and on the other, warning of its seductive charms and magical power to lure men to their destruction, as manifest in the songs of the Sirens and Circe in the *Odyssey* (Brett 1994: 11; Segal 1994:17–18). In English Renaissance writings, the linkage between women and music served to upbraid both for their "essentially changeable nature, unpredictable and some-times irrational ... behavior" (Dunn 1994: 57). Music's sensuous sounds were said to give it the capacity to "penetrate the ear and so 'ravish' the mind" (ibid.).

Writing from the context of psychoanalysis, the work of Guy Rosolato offers another angle on the identification of sound and music with the feminine and the corporeal. Rosolato argues for the acoustic origin of the subject's emergence into selfhood, beginning before birth with the sounds perceived in the "sonorous envelope," of the mother's womb. For Rosolato, the infant's sustained contact with the soothing and "nutritive" voice of the mother provides "the first model of auditory pleasure" and the basis for all subsequent musical experience (1974: 81–2). This positioning of music as feminine has allowed feminist thinkers such as Julia Kristeva and Hélène Cixous to embrace the supposed irrationalism and emotionality of music as a source of subversive power. For Kristeva, music resides outside standard signifying practices and is intrinsic to her notion of "poetic language," a polysemic mode of expression that, in its anarchic force, "borders on the psychotic" (Kristeva, cited in Flinn 1986: 61). Cixous too stresses the privileged role of music within the female imaginary, as the expression of a sexuality that exceeds the codes and classifications of rational thought (1980: 246).

Despite the liberatory potential of the alignment of music and sound with the feminine in proposing an alternative to the image-centered theories of cinema narration dominated by the structuring male gaze, critics such as Mary Ann Doane and Caryl Flinn call attention to the dangers of consigning music, and woman, to the pre-rational and prelinguistic, to a space beyond signification. Notes Flinn: "The notion of music ... cast in terms of profoundly imaginary pleasures of disordered unsignifiability ... suggests that woman and music function beyond patriarchal inscription" (1986: 62). While accustomed to inhabiting the margins of patriarchy, she warns, woman should be wary of embracing the "utopian" temptations of self-exclusion. To do so is "to risk losing her[self] and music to imaginary obscurity, meaninglessness and social ineffectivity" (ibid.). For her part Doane warns of the dangers of an "erotics" of music and the voice, viewed here as a form of essentialism: "to mark the voice as a haven within patriarchy, or having an essential relation to women, is to invoke the specter of feminine specificity, always recuperable as another form of 'otherness'"(1985b: 174).

Nevertheless, such conceptions of music as antithetical or anterior to rational thought continue to shape the analysis of its role in film. In her pioneering 1987 book, *Unheard*

Melodies, Claudia Gorbman writes that music supplies "a necessary emotional, irrational, romantic, or intuitive dimension" to the other, "objective" elements of film (1987: 79). For the spectator/listener of the classical Hollywood film score, awash in a sonorous "bath or gel of affect," the primary goal of film music is clear: "to render the individual an untroublesome viewing subject: less critical, less 'awake'" (ibid. 5).

Subsequent analyses of Hollywood scoring practices by scholars such as Kathryn Kalinak, Anahid Kassabian, and Heather Laing show that film music can signify, but only within the limited parameters of the classical film score, rooted in nineteenth-century European orchestral styles and conventions that draw upon a repertory of shared social and cultural codings. Laing identifies a pattern of meanings and associations grounded in broader social and cultural constructions of gender dating back to the sixteenth century, with music coded as masculine "according to qualities such as clarity, system, understandability, strength, vigor, power, reason and manliness" while femininity was thought to be best expressed in "musical simplicity, tunefulness and modesty of scale," characteristics also prescribed for female musicians and listeners (2007: 13–14). Kalinak finds confirmation of the persistence of such musical typologies in the portrayal of the "good girl" in Max Steiner's score for John Ford's 1935 film *The Informer*. Emblematic in its characterization of feminine virtue, her theme is conveyed by violins and harp and marked by "simple triadic harmonies" (1992: 122). In contrast, when it comes to representations of women deemed disreputable, Hollywood scoring practices leave little doubt about the dangers of overt female sexuality, deploying the vernacular idioms of jazz, blues, or ragtime to signal their deviation from the norms of proper feminine behavior. Against the lush strings, tonal harmonies, and regular tempos of the standard symphonic repertory, the themes attached to the film's "fatal woman" feature saxophones and muted horns, chromaticism, dissonance, and syncopated rhythms (ibid. 120). Playing upon their association with urban black culture and its supposed uninhibited sexuality, notes Kalinak, "the classical score used jazz [and related forms] as a musical trope for otherness, whether sexual or racial" (ibid. 167).

Rather than providing a source of feminine self-expression, argues Laing, the consequences of this gendered musical inheritance result in a frustratingly restrictive position for women (2007: 10). The common practice of assigning leitmotifs or themes to characters can also be seen to bear this out, in the differential treatment of female and male protagonists. James Buhler argues that the frequent "doubling" of the love theme with the theme for the female lead suggests that she has no existence beyond her relationship with her male partner. This lack of symmetry, in which the heroine is denied an independent musical signature while the theme "for the hero establish[es] a musical identity for him that cannot be reduced in the same way," reinforces a male dominated point of view (2014: 367). Nevertheless, the persistent association of music with emotion and the irrational troubles its identification with male characters. Laing argues that since women are not expected to control their emotions, their close relation to music is taken for granted as a reflection of that fact. Normative masculine behavior, on the contrary, requires men to demonstrate their command over emotional expression so their distance from music represents a sign of that control. Thus Laing compares the profound implication with music experienced in *Letter from an Unknown Woman* (Max Ophüls, 1948) by the title character, Lisa, for whom it provides a source of intense emotion and pleasure, with the more distanced, professional relation to music evinced by the pianist and male protagonist Stefan (2007: 176–7). The playing that first attracts Lisa and comes to represent for her a kind of audio-fetish that stands in for his unattainable love also carries a counter meaning as evidence of his wasting of his artistic gifts and the love she would offer him, in favor of a series of sexual dalliances and the immediate but transitory gratification of fame.

Other studies, in several cases by these same critics, chafe against an overly monolithic view of the role of film music, identifying significant exceptions to these scoring patterns, even within the corpus of classical Hollywood films. Flinn proposes readings of the melodramas *Back Street* (John M. Stahl, 1932) and *Now, Voyager* (Irving Rapper, 1942) in which music "work[s] to make the female subject's special relationship to music active, pleasurable and meaningful" (1986: 69). In her analysis of David Raskin's score for *Laura* (Otto Preminger, 1944) Kalinak examines the ways the "positive" musical characterizations of the title character challenge the dominant conventions for representing female sexuality and highlight the tensions between the visual depiction (and opinions of the director and screenwriter) of Laura as a fallen woman and a more nuanced conception rooted in the novel by Vera Caspary on which the film is based (1992: 159–67).

More recent approaches seek to broaden the focus to account for significant changes in the nature and function of music in contemporary cinema within and beyond Hollywood. In *Hearing Film* Kassabian stresses the need to look beyond conventions based in nineteenth-century Romanticism, arguing that music "outside the classical Hollywood semiotic code" offers a wider range of possibilities for female characters (2001: 71). In contrast to the "unheard melodies" (Gorbman 1987) of the traditional composed score that tries "to maintain fairly rigid control over perceivers [the designation she prefers to the vision-centered term spectator]" (Kassabian 2001:2), she focuses on the increasing use of compiled scores, selections of pre-existing music and especially popular songs that invite audiences to bring to the film experience their individual associations and histories. The compiled score is thus held to favor not the passive assimilation of Gorbman's "untroublesome" spectator but an "affiliating identification" that "depend[s] on histories forged outside the film scene … and [that] allow for a fair bit of mobility within it" (Kassabian 2001:3). Kassabian finds an example of this opening to alternative identifications and subject positions in the music for the lesbian romance *Desert Hearts* (Donna Deitch, 1985) whose compiled score consists of some nineteen popular songs that stem from a range of idioms, although primarily country and western, and rock. In moving away from the "tight meaning system of classical Hollywood scoring practices" film listeners can draw on a range of associations that include the connotations of the music's respective genres but also more individual meanings produced by their relationship to specific songs. Kassabian argues that these musical choices are key to the film "escaping the trap of trying to represent lesbian sexualities in terms of Hollywood heterosexual feminine sexuality" (ibid. 73). By triggering spectator memories and emotions and bringing them into conscious awareness, she writes, the songs "both particularize [the two women's] relationship and provide particularizable paths of entry for identification" (ibid. 73).

In her 2007 article, "Auteur Music," Gorbman also attests to the scope of recent changes in film scoring practices, pointing to the shifts in industry economics (including the commercial potency of the soundtrack album, see Smith 1998), the influx of new musical idioms, the development of new digital recording and video editing technologies, and a "vastly more flexible range of ideas concerning the nature, placement and effects of music in movies." One major result, she announces, is that "[m]elodies are no longer unheard" (2007: 151). Her list of auteur *mélomanes*—i.e. directors for whom music functions as an "integral aspect" of directorial style—is long and varied and includes Agnès Varda, Quentin Tarantino, Jean-Luc Godard, Spike Lee, Sally Potter, Wim Wenders, Aki Kaurismäki, and Tsai Ming-Liang (ibid. 150–1). Gorbman highlights Tsai's *The Hole* (1998), a film that features a series of highly choreographed lip-sync performances by the female protagonist of pop songs by 1950s and '60s Taiwanese singer and actress Grace Chang that erupt in the otherwise drab and depressing setting of the film. This repurposing of earlier musical sources evokes, with significant differences, the work of another noted cinematic *mélomane*, Pedro Almodóvar. Over the course of his career the Spanish director has demonstrated his ability to mobilize the existing cultural associations of the Latin American bolero with its melodramatic declarations of romantic suffering rooted in exaggerated gender binaries in the service of individual expressions of transgressive desire. Inclusive rather than exclusive in their address, Almodóvar's musical choices give voice, for example, to the desperation of the gay lovers who converge for a last night of passion to the strains of Los Pancho's "Lo dudo" in *Law of Desire* (1987) while actively attending to the emotional needs of fellow characters and the film audience alike. In a strategy similar to the inclusion of songs by lesbian and gay icon Patsy Cline in *Desert Hearts* (Kassabian 2001: 73), Almodóvar has also recruited a roster of performers—Chavela Vargas, k.d. lang, Caetano Veloso, and Concha Buika—whose own mobile sexual (and national/racial) identities open pathways to multiple forms of engagement for spectator/listeners (Vernon 2005, 2013).

The voice in cinema

In cinema histories that treat the transition from silent film to sound, what is really at issue, as Rick Altman reminds us, is the ability to synchronize the sound of the human voice with the image of the actor viewed on screen (1980: 67–8). The work of Altman and Doane along with that of Michel Chion in France has been essential in setting out the terms of research and debate on the role of the voice in cinema. While Doane speaks of the "subordination" of the voice to the screen that "makes vision and hearing work together in manufacturing the hallucination of a fully sensory world" (1985b: 171), Altman reverses the equation, arguing for the priority of vocal sound over image. In its insistence on assigning the voice to a body—to the moving lips of a speaker—cinema engages in an act of ventriloquism: "pointing the camera at the speaker disguises the source of the words, dissembling the work of production and technology," and hiding the fact that it is words and language that stand at the origin of the world portrayed on screen (1980: 69). Although perhaps not the primary focus in these early writings, gender soon came to play a significant role in the attempts to unravel the relations not only between sound and image but also among voice, language, body, and technology.

In *Echo and Narcissus*, Amy Lawrence's study of women's voices in classical Hollywood cinema, she proposes a framework that is helpful in our analysis of significant work on the topic. In it she distinguishes three distinct but overlapping aspects of the female voice: the first relating to the reproduction of the voice by means of cinema/sound technology; the second regarding the woman's relationship to language and verbal discourse; and the third having to do with her access to self-expression and discursive authority (1991: 3). Lawrence's own study begins with an investigation of the pre-cinematic history of sound recording, the origins of an "ideology of the voice" that she argues has also shaped the treatment of the female voice in film (ibid. 9). She identifies a recurring concern in documents that chart the commercial development of sound technology in phonography, radio, and sound film with the "'problem' of recording, transmitting, or reproducing women's voices" (ibid. 29). Far from a "neutral" technology, she argues, sound recording was from the beginning grounded in the ability to record and reproduce the male voice, with women's voices viewed (or heard) as deficient, "naturally" less powerful, high pitched, and less pleasing to the ear (ibid. 29). Lawrence contrasts the negative responses to recordings of women's speaking voice with the generalized acceptance of the female singing voice. A speaking woman, in contrast to a woman singing, asserts her claim to a position of authority and is perceived as a threat to established gender norms and hierarchies (ibid. 18). Hence the subtext of the classic 1940s Hollywood films analyzed by Lawrence in their emphasis on women's voices as the primary "*source* of textual anxiety" (ibid. 5, emphasis in the original). In films such as *Blackmail* (Alfred Hitchcock, 1929), *Notorious* (Alfred Hitchcock, 1946) and *Sorry, Wrong Number* (Anatole Litvak, 1948), she argues, the material products and practices of sound and recording technology, "[t]elephones, phonographs, voice-overs and dubbing," are brought to the foreground as the means to "silence women and restore the primacy of patriarchy and the image" (ibid. 6).

If Lawrence focuses on the uses of sound technology in the attempt to deny female characters a voice, Kaja Silverman, in *The Acoustic Mirror*, takes the absence and impossibility of the female voice, in the sense of an independent or authorized point of view, as her point of departure. In classic Hollywood cinema, she writes,

> [w]omen's words are shown to be even less her own than are her "looks." They are scripted for her, extracted from her by an external agency, or uttered by her in a trancelike state. Her voice also reveals a remarkable facility for self-disparagement and self-incrimination. ... Even when she speaks without coercion, she is always spoken from the place of the sexual other.
>
> *(1988: 31)*

Silverman effectively assumes the subordinate role of sound, as manifest in the female voice, portrayed here not only in the service of the filmic illusion but as "a fetish within dominant cinema, filling in for and covering over what is unspeakable within male subjectivity" (ibid. 38). With an approach positioned squarely within the psychoanalytic paradigm (the subtitle underlines the predominance of the focus on "The Female Voice in Psychoanalysis and Cinema"), the book depicts the role of sound and voice as constrained to that of acting as an echo, or "acoustic mirror" of the structuring male gaze. Rather than offering an alternative to the vision-centered account of cinema production and reception, Silverman's study doubles down on the terms of the sound/image, proximity/distance, object/subject, passive/active, female/male binaries that define the model. Hence the male voice is said to aspire to the attributes of "invisibility and anonymity" that characterize the cinema apparatus while the female voice is identified with an objectified "spectacle and the body" (ibid. 39). Synchronized sound, the matching of voice with body in the Hollywood soundtrack, works to engender "a complex system of displacements which locate the male voice at the point of apparent textual origin, while establishing the diegetic containment of the female voice" (ibid. 45). The ultimate demonstration of this opposition of subject and object, power and powerlessness is found in the emphasis on the use of voice-over or voice-off, as a prerogative identified almost exclusively with the male:

> voice-over is privileged to the degree that *it transcends the body*. Conversely it loses power and authority with every corporeal encroachment. ... Pascal Bonitzer describes the embodiment of the voice in terms of aging and death, remarking that as soon as its source is revealed, it becomes "decrepit" and "mortal."
>
> *(ibid. 49, emphasis in the original)*

In her 2006 study, *Into the Vortex: Female Voice and Paradox in Film*, Brita Sjogren highlights the persistent visual bias in work such as Silverman's, finding that the latter goes farther than even Mulvey in her insistence on aligning subjectivity with a male-centered vision posited as "bodiless," "imaginary/visual," and "distanced" (2006: 27), a scenario she deems "unlikely to account for the experience of feminine subjectivity, or for the effect or the experience of the acoustic register of film" (ibid. 13). One approach shared by Sjogren and Lawrence that would better capture the experience of film sound, and the voice in particular, as sensory phenomena, targets the nature of vocal performance, both spoken and heard. Countering Silverman, Sjogren's reading of the female voice-over (she prefers the term voice-off) examines the final scenes of *Letter from an Unknown Woman*, in which Lisa's voice "speaks" the words of the letter read by Stefan. At that point in the film, for him, "Lisa's voice is unknown and anonymous, just as the title prepares us to find her. Magnified, lyrical and invisible. ... [t]he quality of her voice here is at least as remarkable as the words" (ibid. 66). Indeed, despite their different conclusions, Silverman, Lawrence, and Sjogren each acknowledge the inescapable duality of the voice, as the intersection between body and language, "meaning and materiality" (Silverman 1988: 44). Despite its passage through the process of mechanical reproduction, the recorded voice retains its corporeal traces (Lawrence 1991: 22–3)—what Roland Barthes has famously called "the grain of the voice"—a discernible texture that carries "the materiality of the body speaking its mother tongue" (Barthes 1977: 182). Where Silverman describes the particularizing traces of individual performance—"in the guise of accent, speech impediment, timbre or 'grain'"— as a "submersion" of the voice in the body, distant from the production of meaning (1988: 61), Lawrence reads these same distinctive markers as a source of authorial power in the case of the adult narrator Scout, voiced by Kim Stanley, in *To Kill a Mockingbird* (Robert Mulligan, 1962). Insisting that "it is the voice in sound that makes dialogue *matter*" (1991: 98, emphasis in the original), she affirms that Stanley's "specifically regional, feminine, *embodied*, voice on the sound track fills the emptiness of the words-as-language with a definite sensual pleasure. ... [A]ccent, enunciation, and vocal timbre ... call attention to the space *outside* of language and return us to the body—here, undeniably a *woman*'s body," (ibid. 184, emphasis in the original) thus enriching and asserting the authority of the woman's voice in the film.

This attention to what we might call the phenomenology of the voice in cinema has gained currency in the work of Martin Shingler and others who would move beyond psychoanalytic approaches, citing the calls by Altman, toward more historically grounded studies of film sound based on "close analyses of particular films rather than on ontological speculations that presume to cover all possible practices" (Altman 1992: 39). Shingler's 2006 article opens with an analysis of Bette Davis's distinctive vocal style in *All About Eve* (Joseph A. Mankiewicz, 1950) that details timbre ("firm and steady, deep throaty resonance, husky [not croaky]"), accent and inflection ("slight drawl, snide") and rhythm and intonation ("clipped pronunciation, staccato rhythm, punchy and percussive"), deeming it "totally unrealistic, totally theatrical, yet convincing." Davis's performance, he concludes, "might not be naturalism but it is credible, pleasurable and most certainly dramatic. ... and represents simultaneously one of the highpoints of the movie, of Bette Davis's film career and of classical Hollywood cinema" (2006:1).

Many critics (and audiences) have noted the importance of distinctive voices in the creation of bankable "picture personalities" and the establishment of star systems in Hollywood and elsewhere (deCordova 1990). It is telling that many of the most recognizable star voices notably depart from gendered vocal stereotypes. David Bromwich has called attention to the "signature touch" of Jimmy Stewart, in his use of a soft, higher pitched voice and stammer, often deployed in intimate scenes with women (cited in Shingler 2006: 2). Both Silverman and Lawrence point to the low and husky voices of female stars of the 1930s and 1940s like Mae West, Greta Garbo, Marlene Dietrich, and Lauren Bacall, although they draw opposite conclusions about their effects. While Silverman considers the vocal "excess" entailed by the alignment of a male sounding voice with a female body, as conferring "a privileged status vis-à-vis both language and sexuality" (1988: 61), Lawrence deems such voices "particularly apt for fetishizing and thus controlling" (1991: 88). Writing on the role of the voice in screwball comedy, Sarah Kozloff signals the importance of voices that elude gender conventions, noting that the most successful female stars of the genre such as Katharine Hepburn, Barbara Stanwyck, Carol Lombard, or Claudette Colbert exercise virtuosic control over voices that are "not conventionally pretty—that is, soft and melodious—they have edginess, perhaps raspiness" (2000: 194). For her part Erica Carter reminds us that the implication of voices and bodies in the cinema is not confined to the actors. Describing the effects of the rich contralto voices of stars like Dietrich and Sarah Leander on spectator/hearers, she evokes their androgynous quality, "transcendent and liquid," that "travel through the auditorium of a movie theater and resonate through the bodies of the audience" (cited in Shingler 2012: 80).

Such an understanding of the nature of sound, also articulated by Sjogren, as a "closer cousin to the 'senses of contact' than sight, as it penetrates the ear, activates the eardrum, inhabits the body" (2006: 31), brings us to an alternative model of the film experience proposed in theories of haptic cinema (Marks 2000) and embodied spectatorship (Sobchack 2004). (For more on phenomenological and haptic approaches to cinema see Chamarette, this volume.) In this conception, a film is received not simply by an eye (and ear), "not solely by an intellectual act but by the complex perception of the body as a whole" (Marks 2000: 145). Consistent with a larger critique of an ocularcentric ideology of the visible, the focus on sound and the body challenges the "myth" of the transcendent and distant spectator "centered" by the voyeuristic gaze. In its place stands a notion of cinema perception occurring across "multiple spatialities" within a continuum in which "the opposition between object and subject, inside and outside, here and there coincide in vigorous simultaneity" (Sjogren 2006: 34). Although Laura Marks acknowledges the lack of detailed attention to the soundtrack in her study of "intercultural cinema, embodiment, and the senses," *The Skin of Film*, she points to the haptic dimension of sound, noting the important role of "[m]usic, talk, ambient sound and silence" in such films, and for "the feeling of embodied experience they produce" (2000: xiv–xv). Marks reclaims the alignment of the body and the senses with women and feminism, not as some intrinsically feminine quality, but as a "strategy that can be used to describe alternative visual [and, I would suggest, acoustic] traditions" (ibid. 170). As a mode of creative practice and reception, embodied cinema proposes new forms of knowledge, shrinking the distance between perceiver and the object perceived; it "tends less to isolate and focus upon objects than simply to be co-present with them," as such corresponding to Trinh T. Minh-ha's notion of "speaking not about, but nearby" (ibid. 164) the objects and issues addressed in her films. The result is a significant reorientation in the role and position of the spectator whose attention and engagement, rather than being organized around identification with one or more specific figures, is "labile, able to move between identification and immersion" (ibid. 188).

Emerging from a cinematic context at some remove from both Marks's intercultural documentaries and the classic Hollywood cinema studied by Sjogren, the films of Argentine director Lucrecia Martel propose a sustained meditation on the immersive nature of film sound. In conjunction with a distinctive visual style marked by decentered and fragmented close-ups and a refusal to provide spectators a clear sense of spatial or temporal orientation, sound in Martel's films works to unsettle and subvert traditional perceptual and cinematic hierarchies. Set in the northwestern Argentine city of Salta, her three feature films, *La ciénaga/The Swamp* (2001), *La niña santa/The Holy Girl* (2004), and *La mujer sin cabeza/The Headless Woman* (2008), present as their setting and subject the claustrophobic domestic spaces of the provincial middle class dominated by women and children. In *La ciénaga*, the densely-layered soundtrack of rumbling thunder, buzzing insects, creaking bed springs, ringing telephones, and the drone of TV echoes the oppressive summer heat at the same time that it masks the lack of genuine communication among the family members who gather at a run-down country house. In a video-essay included with the Criterion collection DVD edition of the film, Martel proposes a lecture-demonstration on the properties of film sound. Presenting "La pileta invertida" (The Sideways Pool), the director displays a transparent tank of water tipped on its side, its rectangular shape and volume an analogue of the movie theater, the movement of the waves a visual representation of the effects of sound on the perceiver of cinema. Addressing the viewers she explains: "You see? Sound cinema has always been three dimensional" while the flat rectangle we see on screen "is an illusion … an optical illusion … called perspective." Sound is another matter, in that "[t]he space occupied by sound is real and material, the sound waves touch the spectator." While acknowledging the artifice involved in the creation of her cinematic universe, Martel stresses the continuities between the experience of film and our existence in the world, in the mutual implication of bodies and subjectivities submerged in a shared "ocean of air."

Martel is certainly not alone in her exploration of the heightened expressivity of the acoustic realm in recent cinema, made possible by the introduction of multitrack Dolby technology and its ability to (re)produce sounds with "their own materiality and density, presence and sensuality" (Chion 1994: 149). This attention to the expanded signifying capacity of the soundtrack coincides with the emergence of the interdisciplinary field of sound studies that has brought together scholars from the social sciences, humanities, and experimental sciences along with architects, artists, and composers. Investigating the ways soundscapes condition and express diverse experiences and identities within and across historical periods and cultures, these discussions provide a stimulating framework for ongoing studies of sound and gender.

Related topics

Patrice Petro, "Classical feminist film theory: then and (mostly) now"
Jenny Chamarette, "Embodying spectatorship: from phenomenology to sensation"

References

Altman, R. (1980) "Moving Lips: Cinema as Ventriloquism," *Yale French Studies*, 60, pp. 67–79.
———— (1992) "Introduction: Four and a Half Film Fallacies" in R. Altman (ed.) *Sound Theory, Sound Practice*, New York: Routledge, pp. 35–45.
Barthes, R. (1977) "The Grain of the Voice," in *Image, Music, Text* (Trans. S. Heath), New York: Hill and Wang, pp. 179–89.
Brett, P. (1994) "Musicality, Essentialism and the Closet," in P. Brett, E. Wood, and G. Thomas (eds.) *Queering the Pitch: The New Gay and Lesbian Musicology*, New York: Routledge, pp. 9–26.
Bromwich, D. (2002) "Between the Raindrops," *London Review of Books*, 24.4, p. 3.

Buhler, J. (2014) "Gender, Sexuality, and the Soundtrack," in D. Neumeyer (ed.) *The Oxford Handbook of Film Music Studies*, Oxford: Oxford University Press, pp. 367–82.

Carter, E. (2004) *Dietrich's Ghosts: The Sublime and the Beautiful in Third Reich Film*. London: BFI.

Cixous, H. (1980) "The Laugh of the Medusa" (Trans. K. and P. Cohen), in E. Marks and I. de Courtivron (eds.) *New French Feminisms*, Amherst: University of Massachusetts Press, pp. 245–64.

Chion, M. (1982) *La voix au cinéma*, Paris: Editions de l'étoile.

———— (1994) *Audio-Vision: Sound on Screen*, (Trans. C. Gorbman), New York: Columbia University Press.

deCordova, R. (1990) *Picture Personalities: The Emergence of the Star System in America*, Urbana; University of Illinois Press.

Doane, M.A. (1985a) "Ideology and the Practice of Sound Editing and Mixing" in E. Weis and J. Belton (eds.) *Film Sound. Theory and Practice*, New York: Columbia University Press, pp. 54–62.

———— (1985b) "The Voice in Cinema: The Articulation of Body and Space," in E. Weis and J. Belton (eds.) *Film Sound. Theory and Practice*, New York: Columbia University Press, pp. 162–76.

Dunn, L. C. (1994) "Ophelia's Songs in *Hamlet*: Music, Madness and the Feminine" in L. C. Dunn and N. A. Jones (eds.) *Embodied Voices: Representing Female Vocality in Western Culture*, Cambridge: Cambridge University Press, pp.50–64.

Flinn, C. (1986) "The 'Problem' of Femininity in Theories of Film Music," *Screen*, 27.6, pp. 56–72.

Gorbman, C. (1987) *Unheard Melodies*, Bloomington: Indiana University Press.

———— (2007) "Auteur Music" in D. Goldmark, L. Kramer, and R. Leppert (eds.) *Beyond the Soundtrack: Representing Music in Cinema*, Berkeley: University of California Press, pp. 149–62.

Kalinak, K. (1992) *Settling the Score*, Madison: University of Wisconsin Press.

Kassabian, A. (2001) *Hearing Film: Tracking Identifications in Contemporary Hollywood Music*, New York: Routledge.

Kozloff, S. (2000) *Overhearing Film Dialogue*, Berkeley: University of California Press.

Kristeva, J. (1980) *Desire in Language*, L. S. Roudiez (ed.) (Trans. T. Gora, A. Jardine, and L. Roudiez) New York: Columbia University Press.

Laing, H. (2007) *The Gendered Score: Music in 1940s Melodrama and the Woman's Film*, Aldershot, Hampshire: Ashgate.

Lawrence, A. (1991) *Echo and Narcissus: Women's Voices In Classical Hollywood Cinema*, Berkeley: University of California Press.

Marks, L. U. (2000) *The Skin of the Film: Intercultural Cinema, Embodiment, and the Senses*, Durham, NC: Duke University Press.

Rosolato, G. (1974) "La voix: entre corps et langage," *Revue Française de Psychanalyse*, 38.1, 75–94.

Segal, C. (1994) "The Gorgon and the Nightingale: The Voice of Female Lament and Pinder's Twelfth *Pthyian Ode*," in L. C. Dunn and N.A. Jones (eds.) *Embodied Voices: Representing Female Vocality in Western Culture*, Cambridge: Cambridge University Press, pp. 17–34.

Shingler, M. (2006) "Fasten Your Seatbelts and Prick Up Your Ears: The Dramatic Voice in Film. *Scope: An Online Journal of Film and Television Studies*, 5, pp. 1–14. www.scope.nottingham.ac.uk/article.php?issue=5&id=128. (Accessed February 5, 2016)

———— (2012) *Star Studies: A Critical Guide*, London: BFI/Palgrave Macmillan.

Silverman, K. (1988) *The Acoustic Mirror: The Female Voice in Psychoanalysis and Cinema*, Bloomington: Indiana University Press.

Sjogren, B. (2006) *Into the Vortex: Female Voice and Paradox in Film*, Urbana: University of Illinois Press.

Smith, J. (1998) *The Sounds of Commerce*, New York: Columbia University Press.

Sobchack, V. (2004) *Carnal Thoughts: Embodiment and Moving Image Culture*, Berkeley: University of California Press.

Vernon, K. M. (2005) "Las canciones de Almodóvar," in F. A. Zurián and C. Vázquez Varela (eds.) *Almodóvar: el cine como pasión*, Cuenca: Ediciones de la Universidad de Castilla-La Mancha, pp. 161–75.

———— (2013) "Almodóvar's Global Musical Marketplace," in M. D'Lugo and K. M. Vernon (eds.) *A Companion to Pedro Almodóvar*, Malden, MA: Wiley-Blackwell, pp. 387–411.

5

GENDER IN TRANSIT

Framing the cinema of migration

Sumita S. Chakravarty

Immigration is, arguably, the hot button issue of our time, rivaling in scope and complexity the role that "the national question" and "the Jewish question" played in previous eras. Not a day goes by without a news story of boats of migrants adrift at sea, of refugees who have drowned and asylum seekers who were turned away. A strong undertow of concern in host countries is the long-term effect of such migrations on local populations and cultures. From Australia to Indonesia and Malaysia to Lampedusa, in Italy and other European countries, migration is indeed a worldwide political, economic, and humanitarian problem. Not surprisingly, such ubiquity is reflected in the increasing body of work in cinema, both commercial and independent, documentary and fictional, male-centered, female-centered, and child-centered, in which filmmakers have tried to capture the experience of migrants and the impact of migration on host societies. There is also a growing critical literature on migration cinema that examines themes of exile and abjection (Naficy 2001; Marciniak 2006; Palmer 2011), home and belonging (Gedalof 2011; Kraenzle 2009; Yi 2015), borders and boundaries (Shepherd 2010 for Spanish film and literary texts; Capussotti 2003 and Luciano and Scarparo 2010 in relation to Italian migration; Levine 2008 for *beur* cinema in France), migrant subjectivity (Capussotti 2003; Podalsky 2010), institutional structures and cultural policy (Grassilli 2008), multiculturalism and transnationalism in metropolitan centers (Oliete 2010), history and memory (Mitchell 2013; Portuges in Sherzer 1996). New journals such as *Mobilities* and *Crossings: Journal of Migration and Culture*, started in 2006 and 2010 respectively, are devoted exclusively to the cultural dimensions of human migration. In short, migration has emerged as a key epistemology in the contemporary world.

Women filmmakers have not lagged behind in their own output. As Catherine Portuges writes of only one location (France),

> Disrupting and widening the horizons of contemporary visual culture, Claire Denis, Chantal Akerman, Josiane Balasko, Catherine Breillat, Aline Isserman, Diane Kurys, Tonie Marshall, Brigitte Roüan, Véra Belmont, Coline Serreau, and Agnès Varda all produced new work in the 1990s, exploring issues of national identity and ethnicity, sexuality and gender, and marginality and displacement.
>
> *(Portuges 2009)*

Others have cited films by immigrant women directors such as Gurinder Chadha and Deepa Mehta, who focus on diasporic issues or concerns from feminist perspectives; Marjane Satrapi and Samira Makhmalbaf, as transnational filmmakers from Iran; or Lucrecia Martel of Argentina as female auteur. The rubrics employed are as various as the works, for they range from transnational to national to postcolonial feminist traditions of scholarship.

Such multifarious work on migration cinema has yet to result in a synthesis, and one of the aims of the present essay is to attempt such a synthesis. This task calls for unorthodox methods, given that many of our familiar critical frameworks of nationality, class, gender, ethnicity, and race do not quite hold up under the pressures of ceaseless global migration and the forces it unleashes. The current European "migrant crisis" of 2015–2016 (called an exodus of near-Biblical proportions by some reporters), in which the divides of East/West, Christianity/Islam, home country/host country, and the like are being destabilized, may well give one pause. As Syrian or Iraqi refugees yearn to reach Germany or Sweden or Austria, white Christian societies all, older identity markers and ascriptions may well be under erasure. At the same time, the receiving countries, for their part, feel torn apart and fear grave political consequences as age-old cultures and traditions are perceived as threatened by the new migrants settling in their midst. This is the overall context for the present essay, and it leads me to take an empirical, inductive approach to the task of identifying the topoi of migration within Western societies. What does it mean to have people very different from oneself move in next door? How do films stage the conflicts that inevitably arise? What kinds of (grotesque or redemptive) transformations result from interactions with migrant characters? What forms does the "containment" of the migrant Other take? And how might one chart out the terrain of migration films that are, as they say, "all over the map?" In exploring such questions, I detect the presence of certain commonalities across a range of fictional films that allow me to point to the migration film as a putative *genre*, and to the strategies developed by this genre to connect to popular audiences. The question of gender becomes highly pertinent in this regard. I want to argue that, in this new "frontier," neither masculinity nor femininity follow predictable paths.

It might be helpful at the outset to describe some of the difficulties noted by scholars working in the area of migration cinema. Marciniak (2006: 66) warns against the "ghettoizing" that takes place in the discussions of "immigrant," "ethnic," and "minority" films. Moreover, many established feminist film scholars (McHugh and Sobchack 2004; Spigel 2004; Doane 2004; Jayamanne 2004) have critiqued the restrictiveness of theories of patriarchy, sexual difference, and the male gaze, and moved on to more "cinematic" (read "gender-neutral") elements for investigation, such as popular pleasure, cinema of attractions, or carnival. A movement away from "stereotypical representations of disempowered, voiceless minorities caught between cultures" (Kraenzle 2009: 92), a category to which female migrant characters are invariably relegated (cf. *The Border* (Tony Richardson, 1982); *Lilya 4-Ever* (Lukas Moodysson, 2002); *Sin Nombre* (Cary Joji Fukunaga, 2009)) may also be necessary.

Definitions and critical frameworks

Migration is, quite simply, the movement of a person or group from one country to another, or internally, from one region to another. It has, more recently, also come to mean movement itself, as people move (or are driven) across territories in search of economic opportunity or political refuge without necessarily reaching their desired destination. In the critical literature, the term "migration" often subsumes a host of related terms such as immigrant, exile, diaspora, émigré, transnational, and global. Migration, in turn, is sub-sumed within transnational feminist (and more general) media studies, and the two terms crisscross throughout the literature. Three rubrics have underpinned this research: post-colonial critique, exilic cinema, and transnational/global/world cinemas. Women's issues and contributions made specifically by female directors are addressed in books such as *Transnational Feminism in Film and Media* (Marciniak et al. 2007) and *Women's Cinema, World Cinema* (White 2015). The first discusses films from twelve different countries that "have been marginalized by the mechanisms of commercial distribution and have barely registered within canonical film studies" (Marciniak et al. 2007: 3). Bringing together critical transnational thinking with feminist theory and criticism of film and media culture, the essays in the collection explore "the ugly underbelly of 'the global village': racism, illegal border crossing, forced economic migration, xenophobia, and the traffic in women and children" (ibid.). Patricia White's book follows a similar structure, combining transnational and feminist frameworks to cast light on films made by female directors such as Jane Campion and Lucrecia Martel, Samira Makhmalbaf and Deepa Mehta, Nia Dinata and Zero Chou—as they explore social, economic, and sexual conditions in local/global con-texts. Much valuable work has also been done in drawing attention to the lives of migrant women in domestic labor (*Maid in America* (Anayansi Prado, 2005)) or to their experiences of struggle and marginalization. However, the "transnational" as an umbrella term can sometimes be a bringing together of different national traditions, rather than developed as a paradigm with its own modes of becoming.

In an interesting essay on Europe's struggle with migrants, Thomas Elsaesser (2006) advances the concept of "double occupancy" as a way to engage with the more metaphorical aspects of exile, foreignness, and dealing with a female, sexualized Other. He suggests that we pay attention to more allegorical attempts at depicting the problems of "foreignness" in contemporary Europe. Narratives of *double occupancy*, he notes, are at once tragic, comic, and utopian; they are about finding new symbolic spaces of co-existence. Elsaesser shows how a film like *Dogville* (Lars von Trier, 2003), although not about migration per se, stages the presence of a stranger within a stable community, thereby unraveling its veneer of self-regulation and harmony when faced with diversity and difference.

However, Elsaesser does not foreground the gendered dimensions of the narrative. It is worth recalling that Grace (played by Nicole Kidman) is not only stunningly beautiful and hence desirable to several of the male characters, but is also kind, thoughtful, and as her name suggests, gracious to a fault. The plot unfolds through a double irony: Grace's body is at once the cause of dissension within the community she has entered, even as the film critiques the narrow-minded and exploitative nature of those who have given her shelter. Women, it seems, cannot be seen as divorced from their bodies. In her analysis of *Maria Full of Grace* (Joshua Marston, 2004), Emily Davis (2006) raises similar questions about female characters and their redemptive status as child-like or child-bearing and child-rearing entities. She writes:

> I have to admit that there was initially something disturbing to me about the fact that the only two women who seem positioned by the film to create new lives for themselves are pregnant: Maria and Lucy's sister Carla. ... The use of the female body for production, as a mule, of "unnatural" commodities was rejected, while the body as vessel for "natural" reproduction remained unchallenged, obscuring the slipperiness of that very boundary.
>
> (ibid. 63)

Indeed, the female body as sexually and economically vulnerable is very much a part of the transnational genre, as Davis shows in her essay. Here her concern is with visual texts that depict the bodies of immigrants and refugees that are trafficked in the global marketplace. She notes, "Sexuality here in particular is a terrain of commodification, power struggle, and exchange" (ibid. 34). Using as her examples *The X-Files* (Chris Carter, 1993–2002), *Dirty Pretty Things* (Stephen Frears, 2002), and *Maria Full of Grace*, Davis links their representations of gender, race, sexuality, and class to more general anxieties about immigration, biotechnology, and labor. Nevertheless, I maintain that thinking of the body alone as adequate to discussions of women's representation fails to account for the new paradigms of (cross-)gender roles signaled by migration films.

My notion of "gender in transit" is meant to capture the instabilities of representation and analysis in migration cinema. The phrase entails a multiple process of mobility as it unfolds on *both* literal/thematic and metaphorical/symbolic levels. On the literal level, of course, migration entails precarious journeys to often unknown destinations, and, for female characters, sexual vulnerability along the way. Marciniak notes that "such 'exilic journeying' refers to physical movement across space, but also to identity shifts, linguistic traversing, bodily transformations, symbolic reconfigurations of one's 'I'" (Marciniak, 2006: 34). In transit also is the generic status of several films and literary texts that foreground women's role in border-crossings of all sorts. For example, Kate Mitchell discusses Australian Anna Funder's book *Stasiland* (2002) as of uncertain genre, poised as it is at the intersections of history, journalism, travelogue, memoir, and the historical novel. "Funder writes herself into the text as one of its characters, forming a bridge between now and then, here and there, outsider and insider" (Mitchell 2013: 92). The same might be said of the generic uncertainty of commercially released films such as *Chocolat* (Claire Denis, 1988), *Head On* (Ana Kokkinos, 1998), *Dirty Pretty Things*, and *Frozen River* (Courtney Hunt, 2008) in which social realism, action drama, suspense, and melodrama all co-exist. Finally, gender in transit suggests unexpected alliances that female characters make across racial, class, and gender lines. Significantly, such transformations affect white and male characters as often as they do figures more immediately recognizable as migrants in the context of Western societies. Does migration, then, signal a shift in the representational practices of gender relations long critiqued by feminist scholars? In her analysis of Hungarian filmmaker Ibolya Fekete's male protagonist film *Chico* (2001), Marguerite Fuller writes:

> Much of the film's power and its highly original feminism ... lie in its making visible and usable the transformative, interactive borderlands that it makes accessible everywhere, to everyone, whether the focus is macrohistorical or the smallest scrap of visual language. The film works to create space for cross-gender, trans-positional, and most conspicuously, transnational dialogues that marks the film both as feminist and as challenging some of Western feminism's most deeply held axioms.
>
> *(Fuller in Marciniak et al. 2007: 228)*

The concept of gender in transit, then, seeks to explore the transitional and transitory nature of alliances in a migratory, transnational age.

This essay proceeds in three parts: the first reviewed the major trends in the feminist study of migration cinema; the second presents a typology of general characteristics and tendencies of migration films; and the third analyzes *Frozen River*, a film in which gender intersects with complex legal and ethical issues as presented through the interactions of two female characters.

Migration cinema: a typology

How can one devise a methodology that cuts across the categories of nation, ethnicity, and culture to evoke the transnational in general and migration in particular? What does it mean to be literally and symbolically "in transit"? In what follows, I sketch out one modality through which I tap into the general sensibility that might be said to inform the genre of migration film. The examples I cite—*Gran Torino, Caché, District 9, The Border, Frozen River*—come from different production contexts (art house, independent, or commercial), are set in different locales, and involve different storytelling traditions (action drama, psychological thriller, suspense, science fiction), yet they seem to follow similar thematic trajectories in order to grapple with the phenomenon of migration. Centered on dominant social actors rather than the migrant characters, they reflect dominant attitudes towards migrants while at the same time questioning them. Issues of gender become interesting in this context, as these definitions are themselves at stake in situations where reversals are the norm.

Gran Torino (Clint Eastwood, 2008) is an action drama in which the white lead character finds himself next door to an immigrant family and slowly comes to terms with it; *Caché* (Michael Haneke, 2005) is an art film loosely structured as a psychological thriller in which a white French couple's comfortable bourgeois existence is disrupted when they start receiving videotapes ostensibly sent (although never revealed in the film) by an Algerian adoptee; *District 9* (Neill Blomkamp, 2009) is a science-fiction film about aliens, ostensibly serving up to its audiences a political critique of a refugee crisis. Set in contemporary South Africa, the film portrays the fortunes of a zealous official who seeks to get rid of an army of aliens. *The Border* is an early attempt to probe the narrative and ideological tensions resulting from the encounter of dominant American culture and illegal immigrants from South America. *Frozen River* is gritty social realism filmed almost in the style of cinema verité. It is the story of a trailer mom who is so alone and desperate that she agrees to participate in the illegal immigration trade at the Canadian–American border.

The films examine the *consequences* of migration—on the migrants themselves, on the host society and its representatives, on subjectivity. One key dynamic is the conflict between (female) ethics and the law (of the male-identified state). Following the law is no longer the ethical thing to do; rather, these protagonists are often confronted with stark choices that pit the human and ethical dimensions of a situation against legality, safety, and normative behavior. Audiences are invited to peer into these dark and shady spaces of ethical dilemmas in return for the thrills of suspense, action-packed chases, grotesque crime, and random violence. Unlike most accounts of migration films, I have chosen here to foreground migration as a factor within host society politics and white protagonist identities-under-reconstruction. I have avoided the familiar critique of patriarchal, bourgeois society in favor of pointing to the cracks envisaged in that society and a description of the 'big picture' of migration film.

Given space limitations, I will only elaborate on the "displacement" film type and unpack some of the commonalities across these very different narratives.

The critique of overdevelopment

In the examples considered here, the protagonist is a member of the dominant white community, but his or her life betrays a fundamental dissonance resulting in rage, loneliness, emotional tension, and unease. Dominant society is held up to ridicule or critique through characters who are shallow, grasping, unthinking, or highly materialistic. The opening

61

Table 5.1 Charting migration in cinema

Theme	Films	Story	Genre mixing
Survival narratives	El Norte; In This World; Dirty Pretty Things; Maria Full of Grace; Una Noche	Stories often follow the journeys and experiences of undocumented migrants	Action drama; melodrama; road movie
Settlement narratives	East is East; My Beautiful Laundrette; Head On; La Haine; Mississippi Masala; The Namesake; Joy Luck Club; Beautiful People; Bend it Like Beckham; Last Resort	Stories of first or second generation immigrants in Western countries and their problems with the host society, and the clash between parents and children	Social satire; city symphony; ethnic drama
Translation narratives	Lost in Translation; Chocolat; La Florida; Babel; Crash	Stories in which Westerners are caught in "a clash of cultures" and languages	Psychological drama; language
Exile narratives	The Tenant; Happy Together; 2046; Last Life in the Universe	Stories that focus on feelings of internal or external exile of protagonists; homelessness	Science fiction; political thriller; film noir
Globalization narratives	Sleep Dealer; Maid in America; The World; I Don't Want to Sleep Alone	Stories which explore the impact of the globalized economy on characters' lives	Human-technology interfaces; cultural contact
Conflict/ border narratives	Before the Rain; No Man's Land; Blackboards; Chico; The Crying Game	Stories set in war situations and border regions, showing the impact of war on all concerned	War film; episodic film
Displacement narratives	Gran Torino; District 9; The Border; Caché; Frozen River	Migration as a factor within host society politics and white protagonist identities-under-reconstruction	Action drama; social realism; suspense; melodrama; science fiction

sequence of *Gran Torino* shows the Eastwood character's family gathered in church for his wife's funeral. The sons joke about their father, the granddaughter is shown wearing clothes inappropriate for a funeral service, her pierced navel exposed, and the two grandsons mouth obscenities as they slip into a pew. Soon after, they rummage through grandpa's things to look for valuables to take away. Throughout the film, viewers are invited to identify with Walt Kowalski's contempt for, and distance from, his family.

In *Caché*, the well-to-do French couple, Georges and Anne, has a marriage that seems cold and sterile, lacking warmth, closeness, and mutual trust. In *Frozen River*, in upstate New York near the Canadian border, Ray Eddy has been abandoned by her husband, leaving her to care for their two sons with almost no money to even pay for food. Neither her employer nor her creditors have any sympathy for her condition. In *District 9*, protagonist Wikus van der Merwe is betrayed and ruthlessly pursued by his own father-in-law. In *The Border*, the protagonist (played by Jack Nicholson) is psychologically distanced from his wife, whose only activity seems to be to surround herself with creature comforts. The world of dominant culture is a bankrupt one in these films, driving the protagonists to feelings of fear, guilt, or impotence.

Proximities of difference, proximate differences

The narratives of these films are propelled by the sheer physical proximity of the Other, thus forcing a recognition from which there is no escape. Migration films highlight the contingency of life in a globalized world, resulting in unwanted intimacies of encounters with the Other. The ethnic neighbor next door, the ex-colonized servant, the Mexican border-crosser, the alien invader, the Asian gang member—these are the faces dotting the social landscape of the white protagonists. In *Gran Torino*, plot and character development are propelled by the moving-in of a large Asian family into the house next door to Kowalski. The family's older generation does not speak English, their habits and rituals are strange to the native-born American, and they encroach upon the protagonist's space both literally and figuratively. The French couple in *Caché* finds the proximity of an unknown surveiller strange and frightening as their movements are captured on videotapes and mailed to them. *The Border* and *Frozen River* intertwine the protagonists' fortunes with illegal Mexican and Asian migrants respectively. A reluctant bond develops between Ray and Lila Littlewolf, the Mohawk woman with whom she smuggles illegal immigrants across the border from Canada. And in *District 9*, the concept of "alien" is visually given monstrous form as well as shown as an invasion that throws the society into panic.

Redemptive schemas for white protagonists

The motif of redemption marks these migration films, and it is the redemption of the dominant character brought about through his or her interactions with the minority characters. This is quite overt in the case of Kowalski in *Gran Torino*, whose final act of self-sacrifice in order to 'save' his young protégé, Thao, is presented as a Christ-like gesture. Walt's character evolves from a bigoted and cantankerous old man, one who reaches for his gun at the slightest provocation, to one who eschews violence and helps to put a vicious group of gang members behind bars. The protagonist of *The Border* risks his life to track down the baby of a young Mexican woman, stolen by a human trafficker in order to be sold into adoption in the United States. Leaving the orbit of his own kind, he bonds morally with the lowly migrant whose kind he was assigned to pursue and bring to justice. Georges Laurent in *Caché* does not quite reach the transcendence of his own narrow socio-cultural mentality, but he is able to confront his repressed sense of guilt for having betrayed his Algerian playmate. He and his wife carve out a tentative peace by focusing on the well-being of their teenage son, Pierrot, and the last shot is of his school entrance where he is shown talking to Majid's son. And *Frozen River* ends with a dual redemption of the protagonist: her acceptance of her imprisonment for having broken the law, and her sense of identification with the Mohawk woman to whom she entrusts the care of her boys in her absence.

The specter of connections

The worlds of the immigrants and the Anglo characters are at once polarized and intersecting, and the films present spectral scenarios of connection or recognition. The cultural habitus of these strangers is initially presented in all its ethnographic distinctiveness. In *Gran Torino*, a party scene among the Hmong emphasizes this: Walt encounters a shaman who is staring at him. But the shaman can read into the misery and isolation that haunts the protagonist and thus a tacit understanding is established. In *Caché*, the spectral nature of the immigrant/native relationship is perhaps most forcefully emphasized. Majid lives in a ghetto-like area, he unceremoniously slits his own throat in Georges' presence, and we never learn who filmed this act in addition to all of the other videotaping. If the connection made is most tenuous in this case, Georges has at least finally confronted his past. *District 9* ends with the protagonist having turned into an alien himself. Isolated and ostracized by his own kind, Wikus retreats to the refugee enclave, District 9, in order to hide from his pursuers.

Humanism in a post-humanist age?

The concept of "humanism" has been in decline since the critical onslaughts of post-structuralism and postcolonialism. So what can one make of the recourse to a kind of humanist appeal made in these films? In the complicated debates around this idea(l), which I cannot go into here, there has recently been a revival of faith in human-ism, articulated in terms of universal human rights, a respect for the bodily integrity of all human beings, and, following scholars like Edward Said, a call for a worldly or secular and critical humanism. Can the cinema of migration be said to contribute to this project? The films, for all their bleakness, conclude with a message of hope that individual actors can connect with strangers, cultural outsiders, and ethnic others on the basis of their common humanity. The crossing of borders is affirmed in the way these films end, suggesting a striving for community, co-existence, and understanding. At the conclusion of *The Border*, the protagonist has shown his awareness of the humanity of a Mexican migrant who has lost her baby, and whose relief in getting him back brings the only smile we see on the officer's face throughout the film. *Frozen River* also suggests that community can be found in unlikely places, as Ray and Lila affirm each other's humanity through the shared feelings of motherhood. The closing shot in *Caché* suggests at least conversation between George and Anne's son Pierrot and Majid's son, crossing the cultural and historical distance between their fathers. *Gran Torino*'s protagonist walks a tightrope between revulsion for his neighbors and his implicit and evolving understanding of them as fellow human beings. And *District 9* goes so far as to merge human and alien forms.

Frozen River

Above, I have noted some of the ways in which *Frozen River* shares features of the migration narrative. Here I will go into some more detail about the gender dimensions of the film. According to Patricia White, the concept of women's cinema is characterized by women's access to the means of production, the commitment to telling women's stories, and an address to viewers' diverse gendered experience within a dynamic public sphere. (White 2009: 155). In Courtney Hunt's case, she raised the money herself and also wrote and directed the film. Drawing on her own experience of life "at the border," she notes her awareness of a smuggling culture and her interest in portraying a white woman and a Mohawk woman who are thrown together but do not like each other. In an interview she states,

> It's a story with some suspense, which grows out of the true motivations of the characters. I tell it in a really suspenseful way because that was the one commercial aspect of the movie that I could deliver to pay back my investors. And suspense makes you stay in your seat until the last frame because they need to see what happens to this woman.

She says, "I did love this idea of a white woman and Mohawk woman stuck in a car together and just seeing what happens."[1] Inspired by John Wayne films and the Bonnie-and-Clyde type narratives, Hunt infuses a grim story of the smuggling of human beings with the drama of desperation that ultimately ends in an unlikely female alliance and friendship.

Hunt's film brings together many of the tropes of the migration film: crime and punishment, legality and illegality, spatial and psychic borderlands, "primitive" economic arrangements of barter and exchange, and frontier mythologies of strength and ruggedness.

Frozen River does not have much to tell us about the "illegals" being smuggled across the border: they remain shadowy, exotic figures with a fleeting presence on-screen. There is only a brief moment of connection with one couple whose baby is hidden in a carry-on bag that Ray and Lila drop in a remote spot on the frozen river. When they learn of their mistake, they drive back to retrieve the bag and are able to revive the near-frozen baby. The real drama of settlement involves, not the new migrants, but the old ones, giving a historical dimension to this story of two down-and-out women. Competing narratives of national belonging, spatial and domicile rights, and the visual contiguity of native reservation and white-occupied land—these are occasions for verbal sparring between Ray and Lila. The following exchanges underscore these anomalies:

> Ray: This is a crime [smuggling migrants across the US–Canada border]
> Lila: There's no border here. This is free trade between nations.
> Ray (scornfully): This isn't a nation.

And again:

> Ray: I'm not crossing that. It's Canada.
> Lila: That's Mohawk land. The rez is on both sides of the river.
> Ray: How about the border patrol?
> Lila: There's no border.

A short while later, the film changes register as the two women not only occupy the same space (the front of Ray's car) but Lila taunts Ray about her marriage:

> Lila: Why did your husband leave you? Maybe he wanted a younger woman. That's what usually happens. I never have to worry about that. My husband's dead. He went down the river on a run. They never found him. Probably tangled in the river weeds somewhere.

By a process of constant reversals of power and vulnerability, Hunt's film is able to create a kind of parity between the two women, although Ray enjoys racial superiority where the white police officers are concerned: she will not be stopped by them, as Lila would be. Yet it is Lila who has "friends" in this area (her smuggler-contacts) while Ray has no one to whom she can turn for companionship or financial support. When she has to go to prison, it is Lila who steps in for her to look after her two boys.

The film dispenses entirely with the tropes of sexual vulnerability and the costs these extract. Instead, the harshness of the characters' demeanor matches the harshness of the landscape that they negotiate on a daily basis. The opening sequence of the film presents Ray's face in extreme close-up, showing an abundance of lines and a generally worn appearance. A brief shot of her quickly undressing and changing shows Hunt to be comfortable with showing a slightly aging female body. Similarly, Lila is short and plump, and hardly a standard object of beauty. Rather, in a world where men have either absconded or died (as their husbands have), women rewrite the rules of what constitutes family/life. Rather than sexual vulnerability, it is motherhood that defines these women, and the film turns into a maternal melodrama in its final sequences. Crime is punished, and because the US police cannot arrest a Mohawk on their own territory, Ray is the smuggler that gets arrested along with the two migrants they were transporting. Tearfully, the two women exchange places of mothering as Ray asks Lila to move in with her sons while she is in prison. Lila gets the emotional strength to take back her own baby from her mother-in-law and walk out of the latter's home with courage and dignity.

Frozen River's generic "instability" becomes the modality whereby the complicated and contradictory political, legal, moral, and existential ramifications of migration are explored. Making no prior assumptions of female solidarity, it nevertheless provides an opening for a gendered understanding of differences of race, ethnicity, and historical struggles. True, the migrants are marginal figures here, but perhaps their very commodification brings home this point. The real drama is reserved for the white protagonist whose subjective position the audience is invited to share, rather than Lila's; Lila is always mediated through Ray's evolving consciousness, even though she gets almost equal screen time to Ray. Nevertheless, at the film's end a new kind of "transnational" family has emerged, and the starkness, isolation, and penury of the landscape has made room for a carousel that offers joy (and hope) to this human assemblage.

In this essay I have tried to suggest a perspective that navigates between gender, genre, and geographies to mark the conceptual space of migration cinema. I have included films that are not generally regarded in this context in order to incorporate popular ("dominant") culture as a valid staging ground for discourses of migration. Only by opening up the parameters of critical inquiry can one avoid the ghettoization that Marciniak warns us about.

Related topics

Katarzyna Marciniak, "Revolting aesthetics: feminist transnational cinema in the US"
Sandra Ponzanesi, "Postcolonial and transnational approaches to film and feminism"

Note

1 www.huffingtonpost.com/melissa-silverstein/interview-with-courtney-h_b_116411.html (last accessed July 2016).

Bibliography

Capussotti, Enrica. (2003) "Exile and Asylum: Women Seeking Refuge in 'Fortress Europe.'" *Feminist Review*, 73: 148–52.
Davis, Emily. (2006) "The Intimacies of Globalization: Bodies and Borders On-Screen." *Camera Obscura* 62, 21(2): 33–73.
Doane, Mary Ann. (2004) "Aesthetics and Politics." *Signs: Journal of Women in Culture and Society*, 30(1): 1229–35.
Elsaesser, Thomas. (2006) "Double Occupancy: Space, Place and Identity in European Cinema of the 1990s." *Third Text*, 20(6): 647–58.
Gedalof, Irene. (2011) "Finding Home in *Bend it Like Beckham* and *Last Resort*." *Camera Obscura* 76, 26(1): 131–57.

Grassilli, Mariagiulia. (2008) "Migrant Cinema: Transnational and Guerrilla Practices of Film Production and Representation." *Journal of Ethnic and Migration Studies*, 34(8): 1237–55.

Jayamanne, Laleen. (2004) "Pursuing Micromovements in Room 202." *Signs: Journal of Women in Culture and Society*. 30(1): 1248–56.

Kraenzle, Christina. (2009) "At Home in the New Germany? Local Stories and Global Concerns in Yuksel Yavuz's *Aprilkinder* and *Kleine Freiheit*." *The German Quarterly*, 82(1): 90–108.

Levine, Alison J. Murray. (2008) "Mapping Beur Cinema in the New Millennium." *Journal of Film and Video*, 60(3–4): 42–59.

Luciano, Bernadette and Susanna Scarparo. (2010) "Gendering Mobility and Migration in Contemporary Italian Cinema." *The Italianist*, 30: 165–82.

McHugh, Kathleen and Vivian Sobchack. (2004) "Recent Approaches to Film Feminisms." *Signs: Journal of Women in Culture and Society*, 30(1): 1205–7.

Marciniak, Katarzyna. (2006). *Alienhood: Citizenship, Exile, and the Logic of Difference*. Minneapolis: University of Minnesota Press.

Marciniak, Katarzyna, Anikó Imre, and Áine O'Healy. Eds. (2007) *Transnational Feminism in Film and Media*. NY: Palgrave Macmillan.

Mitchell, Kate. (2013) "The Migratory Imagination: Anna Funder's *Stasiland* as Prosthetic Memory." *Crossings: Journal of Migration and Culture*, 4(1): 91–110.

Naficy, Hamid. (2001) *An Accented Cinema: Exilic and Diasporic Filmmaking*. Princeton University Press.

Oliete, Elena. (2010) "Brides Against Prejudices: New Representations of Race and Gender Relationships in Gurinder Chadha's Transnational Film *Bride and Prejudice* (2004)." *The International Journal of Interdisciplinary Social Sciences*, 5(5): 136–41.

Palmer, Lindsay. (2011) "Neither Here nor There: The Reproductive Sphere in Transnational Feminist Cinema." *Feminist Review*, 99 (Media Transformations): 113–30.

Podalsky, Laura. (2010) "Migrant Feelings: Melodrama, *Babel* and Affective Communities." *Studies in Hispanic Cinemas*, 7(1): 47–58.

Portuges, Catherine. (2009) "French Women Directors Negotiating Transnational Identities." *Yale French Studies*, 115 (New Spaces for French and Francophone Cinema): 47–63.

——— (1996) "*Le Colonial Féminin*: Women Directors Interrogate French Cinema." *Cinema, Colonialism, Postcolonialism: Perspectives from the French and Francophone World*. Ed. Dina Sherzer. Austin: University of Texas Press: 80–102.

Prime, Rebecca. Ed. (2015) *Cinematic Homecomings: Exile and Return in Transnational Cinema*. NY, London: Bloomsbury.

Shepherd, Neica Michelle. (2010). *Crossing Borders, Crossing Margins: Immigrant Women and Transnational Narrative in Contemporary Spain*. Ph.D. dissertation.

Spigel, Lynn. (2004) "Theorizing the Bachelorette: 'Waves' of Feminist Media Studies." *Signs: Journal of Women in Culture and Society*, 30(1): 1209–20.

White, Patricia. (2015) *Women's Cinema, World Cinema*. Durham and London: Duke University Press.

——— (2009) "Watching Women's Films." *Camera Obscura* 72, 24(3): 155.

Yi, We Yung. (2015). "Between Longing and Belonging: Diasporic Return in Contemporary South Korean Cinema." *Cinematic Homecomings: Exile and Return in Transnational Cinema*. Ed. Rebecca Prime. New York: Bloomsbury Publishing.

6

"NO PLACE FOR SISSIES"

Gender, age, and disability in Hollywood

Sally Chivers

In *Quartet* (2012, Dustin Hoffman), central character and former opera diva Cissy speculates about who first said, "Old age ain't no place for sissies." She remembers the phrase despite experiencing early symptoms of dementia because it contains a homonym of her name. This coincidence makes the phrase into a joke both about the creakiness of old bodies on screen and about her forgetfulness as an even further sign of the stereotyped deficits of old age. Cissy attributes the phrase to renowned Hollywood actress Bette Davis. Though the phrase's exact origins are difficult to trace, most sources do credit Davis. When and whether Davis ever did utter the famous words, associating the phrase with her makes sense. In her famed career as an actress, Davis faced the difficult choice, once she no longer looked like the part of the ingénue, of either going back on Broadway or taking on horror roles. In the end, she did a bit of both, but had to transform her star persona to remain working in Hollywood.

Davis's phrase picks up on a broader social sexism that makes a woman staying on camera past a certain age an act of bravery. Roles for women in mainstream cinema are limited enough, with the stock characters of ingénue and vamp still reigning. But when women grow older than about 25, they no longer easily qualify as ingénue, and past 30 their vampishness comes across as camp to an ageist audience. Aging in Hollywood, then, happens more rapidly than one might think. And old age presents a set of challenges that intensify the pressures already placed on women who work in the public eye. Since working into old age requires courage, "sissies," tainted with cowardice, would not be able to hack it. What is more, the term "sissy" is derived from sister but connotes emasculation, so the phrase hints at how gender shifts with age. In a world where femininity is tied to a youthful appearance, women cease to be considered feminine as they age. Contradictorily, as men age, they are considered less masculine and even feminized in a belittling fashion, similar to a "sissy" in the sense of girlish man. While there is exciting room to queer this shift and break down a number of cis-gendered binary oppositions, to date Hollywood has resisted doing so.

Hollywood is blamed and praised for its role in promoting the images that give the anti-aging industry its strength (Chivers 2011: xv). And, whoever said it first, the "old age ain't no place for sissies" phrase has been picked up by contemporary anti-aging movements that expect people to either overcome the physical challenges of growing older, or pay to have someone else help them do so. The supposedly encouraging phrase appears as the title for self-help books and humor tomes that joke about creaky bodies (Cook 2010; Linkletter 1988; Kaufman 2002), it provides the slogan for myriad products from mouse pads through mugs to t-shirts, it offers a label for collections of photography of older athletes (Clark 1986; Clark 1995), it offers a point from which numerous blogs can riff on the adversities of old age (Bennett 2009; Mrs. B. 2009), and it is the header for numerous Pinterest boards with diverse images of older adults being impressively active. Its logic insists that to match the ideal, an older person should accurately mimic a younger person. As that becomes increasingly difficult to do through appearance, excessive activity should make up for the difference. "Sissies," by extension, are the old people who, in opposition to the ideal, are perceived to lack the physical, emotional, and moral strength to look or at least act young. Ironically, appearing old—embracing aging even—especially to the extent of noticeable infirmity, spells failure to the point of cowardice by the logic of the influential phrase. Thus, the phrase, "old age ain't no place for sissies," articulates a relationship between negative interpretations of older bodies in terms of age and gender. It links an ideal old age not only to courage—as mental fortitude—in a decidedly gendered way, but also to physical ability. This chapter focuses on the thorny relationships among gender, old age, and disability, how the cinema contributes to those relationships, and how feminist theory might help us think about old age and disability conjunctively in a more productive way.

The age of film

Film has long been the domain of youth, with workers both behind and in front of the camera tending to be younger. Its early years were infused with a sense of newness, in terms of workers and in terms of the art form. But, just as the oldest Baby Boomers have refused to step aside in other careers, they have insisted on keeping their place within cinema, so that longer careers are becoming more normal as the boomers age. As a result of this transformation in the workforce, along with an increasing number of boomer audience members growing older with their stars, central roles for older adults have increased since the 1990s, resulting in a different set of mainstream films that feature older actors front and center, a phenomenon I call the Silvering Screen.

Even with an increase of significant roles, the plots associated with older characters remain limited: they tend to be about care, propelling late-life fantasies, or self-mocking, all carefully linked to the fear of inevitable physical decline. A survey of recent movies about aging insists that we must strive for a resilient independence in order to age well, more or less refusing to age—in compliance with the anti-aging industry's demands. Like Paul Newman in *Nobody's Fool* (1994, Robert Benton), Jack Nicholson in *Something's Gotta Give* (2003, Nancy Meyers), *About Schmidt* (2002, Alexander Payne), Jack Nicholson and Morgan Freeman in *The Bucket List* (2007, Rob Reiner), and Clint Eastwood in *Unforgiven* (1992, Clint Eastwood) and *Gran Torino* (2008, Clint Eastwood), men ought to still be able to stand up for vigilante justice while pursuing their final dreams, however gritty and limited they may become. While the older characters may not be able to achieve that independence entirely on their own, movies lead us to believe that being part of a longstanding monogamous couple will offer the freedom from institutional care that movies tell us we should all desire. People should try to arrange care support at home, as portrayed in *Amour* (2012, Michael Haneke), *Still Mine* (2012, Michael McGowan), *A Separation* (2011, Asghar Farhadi), and even *The Iron Lady* (2011, Phyllida Lloyd). Or a dogged spouse should save his/her partner from institutional care for as long as possible, such as in *Cloudburst*

(2011, Thom Fitzgerald), *Iris* (2001, Richard Eyre), and *A Song for Martin* (2001, Bille August). If people decide that institutional care is a good option, the movies tell them that they will find attentive care workers with labor conditions that allow them to notice residents' individualized needs and care for their physical, social and cultural selves in ways that allow for growth in all parties, including the loved ones they leave in the community, but only if they can afford it, as depicted in *Away from Her* (2006, Sarah Polley), *Quartet* (2012, Dustin Hoffman), and in even more subtle ways, *The Best Exotic Marigold Hotel* (2011, John Madden).

These are, of course, unrealistic portrayals. But fantasy in itself is not the worry. Film *should* introduce new possibilities and imagine alternate worlds. But the films' incessant reliance on problematic and damaging stereotypes that link age to disability, viewing disability only as negative, invites feminist scrutiny. Feminist film theory, given its focus on interlocking forms of oppression, has a distinctive role to play in drawing out the implications of understanding old age as always already related to disability, especially for women, and especially because of the gendered double standards that govern film representations of aging.

Hollywood's triple standard

To stay on screen as they age, both male and female actors have to assert their physical and mental fitness to compensate for popular fears that they necessarily become decrepit. The idea is that physical fitness and beauty are essential to mainstream cinema, while both are thought to fade over time. As with arguments about the male gaze, this process is also decidedly gendered, so that male and female stars have to assert their ongoing value in different terms, and women have to do so at much younger ages than men. As just one example, consider the contrast between the careers of Michael Douglas and his wife Catherine Zeta-Jones. In his late sixties, Douglas played Liberace in *Behind the Candelabra* (2013, Steven Soderbergh), and interviewers describe him as "whippy, bright-eyed, and only a little slack around the jawline," using somewhat condescending language that compares him to a young puppy, but still asserting his general youthfulness (Brooks 2013). He made public a detailed health report in order to assure fans that medical authorities had found him free of recently treated throat cancer. In explaining his illness and recovery, he quipped that his cancer had not been caused by fast living nor the frailties of growing older, but by the HPV virus passed on through oral sex. He then claimed that cunnilingus was also the cure, knavishly winking to his audience. He had to assert his ongoing physical health, and, in the process, was able to firmly assert himself as a virile sexual male capable of pleasing his much younger wife.

Meanwhile Zeta-Jones, 25 years Douglas's junior, receives fewer significant roles in her forties than previously. Even though she is not nearly as prominent in the public eye as she used to be, she faces ongoing public speculation about what interventions she relies upon to keep looking young, including whether she has resorted to cosmetic surgery. She demurs by expressing gratitude for the smaller roles that are "still coming [her] way," conceding at only 42-years-old that, "I'm not going to be the ingénue for the rest of my life" (quoted in McQuoid n.d.). The following year, at 43, she made sure to point out that she did her own stunts for *Red 2* (2013, Dean Parisot), including running in high heels, though she claims she would prefer skydiving. In doing so, she asserts herself to be excessively active, going beyond what would be expected for an actor in her twenties (Marcus 2013).

While both male and female actors make claims about their physical fitness, exaggerating it, in order to continue to work in the industry, female actors also dramatically change their physical appearance and the roles they agree to take on, or risk not being hired at all. This is an exaggerated form of what Susan Sontag (1972) calls the double standard of aging, in which women face double the stigma since they lose both youth and beauty. They also face the stigma at much younger ages than men, being considered too old to be matched in a heterosexual romantic role with someone their own age by the time they are 40, if not sooner. The example of Douglas and Jones points to a gendered *triple* standard of aging in Hollywood because it subtly illustrates how depictions of older people in cinema typically yoke together age and disability, even if only through claims of excessive ability. To better explain the insidiousness of this connection and suggest other ways forward, I will outline the contributions of disability studies and age studies to film studies.

Disability studies

Disability-studies scholars think of disability as akin to other forms of difference that invite critical scrutiny, such as queerness, racialization, and gender. They examine a shared history of oppression and expression that has largely been ignored. They consider disability not to be an individual physical or mental flaw but to be produced in relation to social structures and norms. For example, whereas millions of people rely on prosthetic devices such as contact lenses and glasses to see with 20/20 vision, those who still cannot achieve that level of vision with the aid of readily available devices are disabled by the lack of technology, not by their own eyes. A wheelchair enhances motion through a hallway until it meets a staircase that could have been a ramp. A child on the autism spectrum faces stigma at school because his classmates are socialized into mocking him. From the perspective of a social model of disability, physical and social barriers, such as stairs and stares, cause disablement.

Many humanities-based disability-studies scholars analyze patterns of representing disability. They have found that, rather than hidden, disability is ubiquitous in most narrative traditions. Often, a disabled character lurks in the background if only to propel the plot forward. Martin Norden (1994) surveys hundreds of Hollywood movies that feature characters with physical disabilities to reveal a pattern of isolation. He articulates the stereotypes of the sweet innocent, such as Tiny Tim, and the obsessive avenger, such as Quasimodo, that many later disability scholars rely upon to explain both disability's prevalence in film but also the danger these stereotypes create. Other disability film scholars explain how difficult disability is to define, since it is not always visible and since it is context dependent, demonstrating that disability images on screen often reflect a broader social context (Smit & Enns 2001; Chivers & Markotic 2010; Cheu 2013; Mogk 2013).

Rather than consider disability solely a site of oppression, disability-studies scholars and activists view disability as a fundamental way of being in the world with its own value that exceeds the social and physical limitations placed upon it. New forms of disability cinema such as *goodnight, liberation* (2003, Oriana Bolden) and *Berocca* (2005, Martin Taylor), as explained by Snyder and Mitchell (2008), offer a more radical way to conceive of disability that could transform the social world for the better because they declare that disability should be recognized as the center rather than the margin of cultural production.

Age studies

Similarly, humanities age-studies scholars think of old age as contingent, unfairly maligned, and valuable. Considering age as a cultural phenomenon, they explain how people are made old by their social and cultural surroundings (Gullette 2004). The arbitrariness of age identity offers one important avenue for analysis within age studies, as does the unfair treatment of women based on how old they appear. Age-studies scholars scrutinize the deep biases within the anti-aging industry that governs Hollywood, and they unpack the more subtle normative underpinnings of the edicts behind successful aging: the idea that an ideal older person ought to be relentlessly active.

Many age-studies scholars track patterns of representing old age, articulating the problems with how older characters are often portrayed. Too often, an older character appears as the butt of a joke, or as a way to make younger characters seem even stronger by comparison. E. Ann Kaplan (2001) has built on feminist film theory to reinterpret the patriarchal gaze as it affects older women on screen. Amir Cohen-Shalev (2011) has considered both the age of the filmmaker and the representation of older characters to demonstrate that though younger and older filmmakers may imagine late life differently, the topic is of intense interest and importance to people across the life span. Focusing on popular film, Pamela Gravagne (2013) shows how the cinema reveals dominant social views of growing old. Other scholars draw on examples to show how certain films that feature older characters offer new perspectives on both film and on aging (Swinnen 2012; Chivers 2011; Brooks 1999; Beugnet 2006; Saxton & Cole 2013; Dolan 2013).

Age-studies scholars draw on cultural production and analysis to transform popular thinking about old age as tied to deficit, as burdensome, and as frightening, to thinking about the rich potential that comes with an aging population. They highlight the deep creativity that arises from the changes that come with old age, and they emphasize the resistance to neoliberal models for valuing "productive" elders.

Feminist perspectives

Feminist theory, and especially its focus on inequality, ought to offer an antidote to intertwined ageism, ableism, and sexism. However, feminist scholars have been reluctant to pay attention to older women, particularly older women experiencing disabilities as the result of their aging. As Toni Calasanti and Kathleen Slevin (2006) point out, "an inadvertent but pernicious ageism" "stems from [feminist scholarship and activism] failing to study older people on their own terms and from failing to theorize age relations" (1). Feminist film theorists have drawn attention to the biases against representing women, including their sexualization, forced passivity, and limited roles, but they remain reluctant to consider older women. Even though the undoing of stereotypes typical of early feminist film theory invites straightforward challenges to the stunted depiction of older females on screen, feminist film theorists largely focus on the youthful fit female body and the gaze it is subjected to, without adequately considering how that gaze further oppresses older women.

Cinema offers an ideal environment to challenge the youthful focus of feminist theory because it is difficult to find films that do not rely on either age or disability, and often both together. Speaking of Bette Davis's role as "spinster" Charlotte Vale in *Now, Voyager* (1942, Irving Rapper), Tara Brabazon (2001) asks,

> What questions would the contemporary women's movement ask of Charlotte Vale? Re-evaluating texts such as this serve to inscribe, rewrite and interpret a feminist history. We need to return to Bette Davis, and her films. A new theory of femininity can emerge when we look at—and through—those eyes.

The way that cinema codes gender is similar to the ways in which it codes age as always already consisting of disability. Visual pleasure is complicated by the screen presence of figures that people are commonly taught to stare at or look away from out of fear or dread. Feminist counter-cinema could work harder to project compelling images of older women. Questions should be raised about how and why older audiences watch movies, especially how they are affected by digitalization and mobility. Aging sexuality, which has at least small appearances within the Silvering Screen such as in *Something's Gotta Give* (2003, Nancy Meyers), *Away from Her* (2006, Sarah Polley), and *Still Mine* (2012, Michael McGowan), raises new questions about female desire. Queer narratives complicate the usual care structure. For example, in Thom Fitzgerald's *Cloudburst* (2011) long-time lovers Stella (Olympia Dukakis) and Dot (Brenda Fricker) run away from Maine to try to reach Canada, where they can marry. This would give Stella legal status to make care decisions for Dot, whose granddaughter has tricked her into living in a nursing home. Along the way, they pick a young male hitchhiker Prentice (Ryan Doucette) and, as they come to realize that Stella is not capable of caring for Dot at home, they forge a new plan for Prentice to come back to Maine and help out. From one perspective, this reinforces the neediness of the older characters and the strength of the younger character. But from another perspective, it offers a vision of chosen family and interdependence, since Prentice gains a home he lacks and offers care work in return. However, as I argue elsewhere, Dot dies before this care plan comes to fruition, so the film stops short of its liberating vision (Chivers 2015b). There is, in short, ample room for consciousness raising and decentering within canonical and noncanonical film studies, focused on the topic of age and its depictions.

Though Davis's career trajectory met obstacles as she aged, Brabazon (2001) points out that there were more roles for older women in the 1940s, 50s, and 60s than in the late twentieth century, and she derides the related ridiculous older-male-much-younger-female screen couples that prevail. Despite an increase in films focused on old age, the hiring situation is still comparatively grim and older female characters are more likely to be killed off than to be the object of sexual desire. Notable older actors who have remained on screen, perhaps because it is in itself a courageous act, have recently begun to be extremely vocal about the limited opportunities and the sexist double standard that women face. When asked about the failure to cast 37-year-old Maggie Gyllenhaal (though vocal about the rejection, Gyllenhaal has not named the project) because she was considered too old to be the romantic interest of an actor 18 years her senior, Helen Mirren lashed out, saying "It's fucking outrageous ... It's ridiculous. And 'twas ever thus. We all watched James Bond as he got more and more geriatric, and his girlfriends got younger and younger. It's so annoying" (Quoted in Lee 2015). As *Vulture Magazine* aptly puts it, "Leading men age, but their love interests don't" (Buchanan 2013). Unfortunately, Russell Crowe made comments on the topic that perpetuate, without showing any understanding of, the double standard. He asserts,

> To be honest, I think you'll find that the woman who is saying that [the roles have dried up] is the woman who at 40, 45, 48, still wants to play the ingénue, and can't understand why she's not being cast as the 21 year old ... If you are willing to live in your own skin, you can work as an actor.
>
> *(Quoted in Anonymous 2014)*

Of his own changing career, he notes, "I can't be the Gladiator forever" (ibid.). Maybe not, but he can still be cast at 51 as the lead in a musical despite a demonstrable inability to sing, and it is far more acceptable for him to show wrinkles and gray hair while still being cast as his age than it is for women at least 10 years younger than him. The acceptance of a man's "own (aging) skin" is thus shown to be vastly different from that of a woman.

Conclusion

Disability and old age often share the category of social refuse, and perhaps because of that (i.e. because disabled people fear aging as much as the general population and older adults fear being treated the way disabled people are usually treated), disability studies tends to resist thinking about late life, and age studies has been slow to consider the implications of disability-centered scholarship for its development. Disability and old age are misinterpreted in broader popular culture as being about the body in solely negative ways, so it makes sense and yet feels dangerous to connect them. Indeed, the cinematic record I outline above, that conflates old age with either loss of ability or the need to assert ongoing ability, justifies those fears. While Hollywood cinema is the worst and most obvious offender, even alternative and international films (such as *Amour* [2012, Michael Haneke, France], *A Separation* [2011, Asghar Farhadi, Iran], *A Song for Martin* [2001, Bille August, Sweden], *Son of the Bride* [2001, Juan J. Campanella, Argentina], *Wrinkles* [2011, Ignacio Ferraras, Spain]) flirt with these connections. But the emancipatory tools of disability studies and the creative strength of age studies promise to be a formidable force if combined well. And film offers a rich tapestry to begin thinking about how the two fields could come together to change social thought and social action, as Leni Marshall (2014) explains is necessary when she creates the neologism "ageility" to describe a desired conjunction of disability- and age-based social movements.

In response to the Bechdel–Wallace test, the idea that a feminist would be most interested in a movie if it featured at least two female characters who talk to each other about something other than a man, the disability community has forged its own measure, aptly turned prescriptive by David Perry (2015): "cast disabled actors and tell better stories." While the conjunction of disability and old age may appear to complicate the goal, combining these tests with an age focus offers insight into how film could contribute to the transformation of damaging social ideas about aging. If films regularly featured two older female characters, talking to each other about something other than a man, playing their ages, embracing whatever physical and mental changes may have come as the result of time but not necessarily focusing the story on them, that could be immensely freeing and progressive. Certainly an increase in feminist film production that features aging in ways that challenge dominant assumptions about beauty and value would be a welcome addition to an already politically driven oeuvre. But along with that, a general critical awareness of aging in cinema will help transform social thought about growing older in the twenty-first century. An age-aware feminist perspective that situates disability as central to human experience would offer a new way to think about bodies, plots, and careers. With thinking about age prominent, rather than focusing on who qualifies to play the ingénue, a fairly dull stock character, filmmakers would be freer to draw out a range of roles that would offer new directions for women in cinema at all life stages, "sissies" and all.

Related topics

Patrice Petro, "Classical feminist film theory: then and (mostly) now"
E. Ann Kaplan, "Visualizing climate trauma: the cultural work of films anticipating the future"

Bibliography

Anonymous. (2014). "Russell Crowe: 'Hollywood Actresses Need to Act their Age.'" *Australian Women's Weekly.* (Online) December 15. Available from: www.aww.com.au/latest-news/news-stories/lucy-turnbull-the-power-behind-malcolm-22225. (Accessed September 15, 2015).

Bennett, R. (2009). "Old Age Is Not For Sissies." *Time Goes By.* Blog. September 11, 2015.

Beugnet, M. (2006). "Screening the Old: Femininity as Old Age in Contemporary French Cinema." *Studies in the Literary Imagination.* 39 (2): 1–20.

Brabazon, T. (2001). "The Spectre of the Spinster: Bette Davis and the Epistemology of the Shelf." *Senses of Cinema.* (Online) 13: not paginated. Available from: http://sensesofcinema.com/2001/feature-articles/spinster/. (Accessed October 14, 2015).

Brooks, J. (1999). "Performing Aging/Performing Crisis (for Norma Desmond, Baby Jane, Margo Channing, Sister George, and Myrtle)." In K. Woodward (ed.) *Figuring Age: Women, Bodies, Generations.* Bloomington: Indiana University Press. 232–47.

Brooks, X. (2013). "Michael Douglas on Liberace, Cannes, Cancer and Cunnilingus." *The Guardian.* (Online) June 2. Available from: www.theguardian.com/film/2013/jun/02/michael-douglas-liberace-cancer-cunnilingus. (Accessed September 14, 2015).

Buchanan, K. (2013). "Leading Men Age, But Their Love Interests Don't." *Vulture Magazine.* (Online) April 13. Available from: www.vulture.com/2013/04/leading-men-age-but-their-love-interests-dont.html. (Accessed October 15, 2015).

Calasanti, T. M. and K. F. Slevin. (2006). *Age Matters: Realigning Feminist Thinking.* New York: Routledge.

Cheu, J. (ed.) (2013). *Diversity in Disney Films: Critical Essays on Race, Ethnicity, Gender, Sexuality, and Disability.* Jefferson, NC: McFarland & Company.

Chivers, S. (2011). *The Silvering Screen: Old Age and Disability in Cinema.* Toronto: University of Toronto Press.

———— (2015a). "'Blind people don't run': Escaping the 'Nursing Home Specter' in *Children of Nature* and *Cloudburst.*" *Journal of Aging Studies.* (Online) 34: 134–41. Available from: www.sciencedirect.com/science/article/pii/S0890406515000602. (Accessed October 16, 2015).

———— (2015b). "Empty Husks: Age, Disability, Care, Death, and *Amour.*" In Claudia Wassman (ed.) *Therapy and Emotions in Film and Television.* London: Palgrave Macmillan UK. 72–88.

Chivers, S. and N. Markotic. (eds.) (2010). *The Problem Body: Projecting Disability on Film.* Columbus, OH: Ohio State University Press.

Clark, E. (1986). *Growing Old is Not for Sissies: Portraits of Senior Athletes.* Petaluma, CA: Pomegranate Calendars and Books.

———— (1995). *Growing Old is Not for Sissies 2: Portraits of Senior Athletes.* Petaluma, CA: Pomegranate Communications, Incorporated.

Cohen-Shalev, A. (2011). *Visions of Aging: Images of the Elderly in Film.* Eastbourne: Sussex Academic Press.

Cook, Dr. M. L. (2010). *Growing Old Isn't for Sissies.* Victoria, BC, Canada: Trafford Publishing.

Dolan, J. (2013). "Smoothing the Wrinkles: Hollywood, 'Successful Aging,' and the New Visibility of Older Female Stars." In C. Carter, L. Steiner, and L. McClaughlin (eds.) *The Routledge Companion to Media and Gender.* London and New York: Routledge. 342–51.

Gravagne, P. (2013). *The Becoming of Age: Cinematic Visions of Mind, Body and Identity in Later Life.* Jefferson, NC: McFarland & Company.

Gullette, M. M. (2004). *Aged by Culture.* Chicago: University of Chicago Press.

Kaplan, E. A. (2001) "Trauma, Aging, and Melodrama (With Reference to Tracey Moffatt's *Night Cries*)." In M. Dekoven (ed.) *Feminist Locations: Global and Local, Theory and Practice.* New Brunswick, NJ: Rutgers University Press. 304–28.

Kaufman, L. (2002). *Old Age is Not for Sissies: A Witty Look at Aging.* Charming Petites. White Plains, NY: Peter Pauper Press.

Lee, B. (2015). "Helen Mirren: Ageism in Hollywood is 'Outrageous.'" *The Guardian*. (Online) June 17. Available from: www.theguardian.com/film/2015/jun/17/helen-mirren-ageism-hollywood-women. (Accessed September 15, 2015).

Linkletter, A. (1988). *Old Age is Not for Sissies: Choices for Senior Americans*. New York: Viking.

McQuoid, D. (n.d.) "Just Call me Cath." *Stylist Live*. (Online) n.d. Available from: www.stylist.co.uk/people/interviews-and-profiles/just-call-me-cath. (Accessed September 14, 2015).

Marcus, B. (2013) "Catherine Zeta-Jones Would Rather Skydive than Run in Heels." *Vanity Fair*. (Online) July. Available from: www.vanityfair.com/style/2013/07/red-2-premiere-catherine-zeta-jones. (Accessed September 14, 2015).

Marshall, Leni. (2014). "Ageility Studies." In U. Kriebernegg, R. Maierhofer, and B. Ratzenböck (eds.) *Alive and Kicking at All Ages: Cultural Constructions of Health and Life Course Identity*. Aging Studies V. Bielefeld: transcript Verlag. 21–39.

Mogk, M. (ed.). (2013). *Different Bodies: Essays on Disability in Film*. Jefferson, NC: McFarland & Company.

Mrs. B. (2009). "Old Age Ain't No Place For Sissies." *Mrs. B.'s Brilliant Blog*. Blog. September 11, 2015.

Norden, M. (1994). *The Cinema of Isolation: A History of Physical Disability in the Movies*. New Brunswick, NJ: Rutgers University Press.

Perry, D. (2015). "The Disability Community's Bechdel Test." *Al Jazeera America*. (Online). August 30. Available from: http://america.aljazeera.com/opinions/2015/8/the-disability-communitys-bechdel-test.html. (Accessed September 15, 2015).

Saxton, B. and T. R. Cole. (2013). "No Country for Old Men: A Search for Masculinity in Later Life." *International Journal of Ageing and Later Life*. 7 (2): 97–116.

Smit, C. and A. Enns. (eds.) (2001). *Screening Disability: Essays on Cinema and Disability*. Lanham, MD: University Press of America.

Snyder, S. L. and D. T. Mitchell. (2008). "'How Do We Get All these Disabilities in Here?': Disability Film Festivals and the Politics of Atypicality." *Canadian Journal of Film Studies*. 17 (1): 11–29.

Sontag, S. (1972). *The Double Standard of Aging*. Toronto: Women's Kit.

Swinnen, A. (2012). "Dementia in Documentary Film: *Mum* by Adelheid Roosen." *The Gerontologist*. 53 (1): 113–22.

Further reading

McRuer, R. (2006). *Crip Theory: Cultural Signs of Queerness and Disability*. New York: NYU Press.

Swinnen, A. (2015). "Ageing in Film." In J. Twigg and W. Martin (eds.), *Routledge Handbook of Cultural Gerontology*. New York: Routledge. 69–76.

7

CHINESE SOCIALIST WOMEN'S CINEMA

An alternative feminist practice

Lingzhen Wang

In the late 1960s and early 1970s, women's cinema emerged as a new concept in Anglophone feminist film theory (cine-feminism), and soon developed into a political counter-cinema challenging mainstream commercialism and patriarchal language. By that historical moment, Chinese women directors had already been practicing institutionalized, socialist cinema for nearly two decades, endorsing the mainstream promotion of gender equality, socialist production, and revolutionary ethics. In the 1980s, however, when China underwent economic reform and its "open-door policy," after a decade of the Great Proletarian Cultural Revolution (1966–76), the Chinese government and intellectuals turned to the West for a universal model of modernization and cultural discourses. Consequently, the study of Chinese women's cinema, especially from the socialist period (1949–76), has situated its subject within the terms of debate set by Western feminist critics, centering its criticism on Chinese women directors' failure to produce counter, minor, or marginalized cinema. The problematic conclusion—that no feminist films were produced during the socialist period—requires a critical re-examination of the relationship between feminism and its specific political and economic contexts.

This essay reveals the lasting effects of Western cultural hegemony in the contemporary world; it also questions the discursive turn in the poststructuralist intervention that reconfigured feminism as a primarily cultural subversion, contributing to cine-feminist dismissals of the social, economic, and political dimensions of capitalism. Finally, and more importantly, this essay emphasizes Chinese socialist feminism as practiced in modern China, highlighting its alternative visions and conceptualizations of gender and cinema during the first seventeen years of the socialist period (1949–76).

Poststructuralist reconceptualization of women's cinema as counter-cinema

Western feminist film theory developed most significantly during the heyday of structuralist and poststructuralist theories of the 1970s and 1980s. Semiotics, which concentrates on the linguistic and cultural structures, systems, and conventions by which texts signify, helped feminist film theory to "shift its focus from the critique of the ideological content of films to the analysis of the mechanisms and devices for the production of meaning in films"

(Smelik 1998: 9). This shift transformed the perception of film as a reflection of reality to an active, systematic reproduction of dominant patriarchal cultural values, especially through its construction of subject positions for viewers' identification. Concerned with the gendered effects of the dominant mode of film production typified by Hollywood, feminist scholars also actively appropriated Lacanian psychoanalysis to account for the internal logic of sexual difference coded in dominant cinema. Structuralism, semiotics, and psychoanalysis indisputably helped feminist scholars break with the previous empirical and sociological study of films as realist texts. Furthermore, they led to the critical revelation of film as a coded, cinematic reproduction of a phallocentric system representing woman either as nonexistent and non-male (Johnston 1973/2000: 25) or as the object of male gaze and desire (Mulvey 1975) without desire of her own (Doane 1987). In the process of reconfiguring the disruptive and oppositional function of women's cinema, feminist scholars risked collapsing over-determined structures, or structuralist specificities, into a universal, ahistorical homogeneity (Caughie 1981: 126) that overlooked the contradictions and interplay among different structures and subjects, and inadvertently reinforced the coded condition of woman as a non-subject. This problem is evidenced in feminist scholars' original theorizations of Hollywood cinematic spectatorship as a relation involving one-way identification with the central male subject positions (Mulvey 1975). More critically, this ahistorical cultural homogeneity delinked itself from specific economic and social systems, and consequently not only universalized one particular feminist position, but also concealed its complicated and often complicit relationship to established economic and political institutions, inadvertently granting all women's cinema an independent, disruptive, and even oppositional status.

Women's cinema received criticism in the 1980s when Black and Third World feminism challenged Western feminism overall, especially its Western-centric, white, and middle-class orientations, but the counter-cinema concept remained unquestioned. In her 2002 book, Alison Butler redefines women's cinema as "minor" cinema (2002: 1), a term adapted from Gilles Deleuze and Félix Guattari's concept of minor literature—the literature of a marginalized group written in the major language. Butler argues that key features of minor literature—displacement, dispossession, and deterritorialization—characterize women's cinema. Butler's reformulation intends to expand Anglophone women's cinema to include the diversity of women's film practice around the world. However, by situating 1970s Anglophone feminist film theory and practice as the source of minor cinema, Butler suggests that minor cinema is but a natural growth of earlier women's cinema in contemporary, globalized expansion and production (ibid. 119). As a result, her concept of minor cinema risks legitimizing Western cine-feminist practice as the origin of all women's cinema practice worldwide. Furthermore, although minor cinema modifies the radical claims of counter-cinema as completely resisting the mainstream language, this notion still defines women's cinema as a marginalized practice, authored by an essentially marginal or deterritorialized group and thus automatically a politically subversive practice (ibid. 20–1).[1]

This persistent and influential conception of women's cinema as counter-cinema (or minor cinema), whether emerging from mainstream or avant-garde film, suggests a self-generating origin of feminist political practice, obscuring the relationship between feminist cultural practice and the socio-economic systems from which those practices emerge. A marginalized or displaced position, for example, does not necessarily correlate to a politically subversive or oppositional stance. Many marginalized practices are contained, and even supported, by the broader system. More importantly, marginalized practices often collaborate with central political and economic forces on other social issues or in different (geo)political realms. Although feminist experimental cinema remains marginalized in the Western capitalist system, this work is also endorsed within discourses of private property and the middle-class ideology of individualism. The elitist and male-centered status of avant-garde cinema has also been well institutionalized in dominant systems. While the terms used to define minor literature or cinema no longer appear oppositional to the major language, as Mulvey has claimed, this "minor" literature refers to the same elitist and male-centered avant-garde practice. Women's experimental cinema of the 1970s certainly became a critical force that revealed and challenged gender disparities in mainstream commercial cinema. But to envision women's experimental cinema as subversive of Hollywood, and thus challenging the capitalist patriarchy overall, belies a much more complicated relationship between Western feminist cultural practice and mainstream discourses.

My focus on the institutional nature of feminist practice is not to argue that feminisms may be simply reduced to, or totally determined by, existing or emerging institutions and paradigms without their own political and critical interventions. Nor am I suggesting that various feminist practices or cultures would take a unified form within the same institutional context. Rather, I posit that paying attention to the institutional background of feminist practices helps:

- reveal what makes feminist practice possible in different geopolitical locations and periods;
- understand the power dynamics between specific feminist practices and established as well as emerging systems, institutions, and discourses;
- more critically demystify the claim that feminisms are and could be independent from political, economic, and cultural authorities and institutions (whether imperialist, nationalist, or capitalist).

In other words, despite critical, political feminist interventions, feminist relationships with various institutional forces, some of which may be oppressive in other realms, are complicated. These interactions must be fully understood in order to assess both the strengths and limitations of particular feminist practices in history. Furthermore, this recognition also enables us to realize how certain limitations of feminist practice, within a specific context, are institutionally bound, and thus can only be addressed by transforming the broader economic and political system.

Despite the institutional component of all feminist practices, the extent of feminisms' integration into central political, economic, and cultural institutions differs across systems. Unlike first world feminist practices, which were mediated through either middle-class ideologies of individualism, property, and political rights or marginalized left-wing intellectual discourses, third world feminist practices were directly linked to central political movements of anti-imperialism, nation-building, and economic development. This significant difference compels us to re-examine the feminist component of third world nation-states, and how these nation-states advanced feminist practices in mainstream institutions and culture. Chinese socialist feminism warrants one such re-examination in particular.

Chinese socialist feminism: institutionalized and integrated practice

The global spread of Western feminisms, especially across China and other third world countries in the late-nineteenth and early-twentieth centuries, was a direct result of

Western imperialism, capitalist expansion, and colonial modernity. Although many versions of Western feminism traveled, not all feminist ideas and practices would take root and grow under local conditions. Socialist feminism, as a set of historical practices incorporated into the Chinese socialist revolution beginning in the early 1920s, differed markedly from feminism as a marginalized theory or intellectual discourse in the capitalist West. In China, socialist feminism represents an indigenization of theory that engaged itself with an anti-imperialist, anti-capitalist, and anti-traditionalist revolution in a particular geopolitical location. As a critical cultural discourse, Marxist feminism established itself early in the May Fourth Cultural Movement (Tong and Kang 2004: 66–7), articulating a central set of Marxist views on women's emancipation that included the abolition of private property ownership and capitalism, women's participation in social production and political governance, and the transition from a bourgeois women's rights movement to working women's class and gender liberation. With the establishment of the Chinese Communist Party (CCP) in July 1921, Chinese socialist feminism was more fully institutionalized.

At its Second Congress in 1922, the CCP passed a "Resolution on Women's Movement," formal guidelines for organized feminist activities that highlighted the Chinese women's movement as an integral part of broader proletarian liberation, as well as anti-imperialist and anti-feudal struggles (Li 2011: 159). Chinese socialist feminism continued to develop throughout the 1920s, directly engaging with the nationalist revolution and labor movements. In 1927, however, the Nationalists and the CCP split violently. The subsequent Nationalists' massacre of communist and women activists drove the CCP underground in all urban centers and led some of the most dedicated members to retry previous experiments at organizing Chinese communist forces among rural peasants.

In the late 1920s, the party undertook its most significant theoretical and practical transformations, including serious reflections on its feminist policy and affiliations. The CCP repositioned itself in relation to China's large rural populations of women rather than urban-based women workers alone. As part of the general sinification of Marxist theory, this reflexive change ultimately redefined Chinese socialist feminism. During this period, peasant women were depicted, for the first time in Chinese history, as those most oppressed in China's political, economic, religious, and social systems, and were tied explicitly to the Chinese communist revolutionary cause (Mao 1967: 44–6). Moreover, as the most subjugated group, Chinese peasant women, together with peasant men, were perceived as essential participants in the proletarian revolution that would bring structural changes to China. This recognition among CCP leaders helped to establish socialist feminism as a core component of future communist revolution.

By 1931, when the Chinese communist base Jiangxi–Fujian Soviet Republic was founded, the CCP Congress established concrete laws to enforce equality in status and participation, including constitutional guarantees and a new political ethic of egalitarianism. For the first time in modern Chinese history, women's social emancipation was promoted together with their economic and material emancipation. Implementation of these newly established laws was particularly emphasized (Croll 1980: 191) and special women's departments were established in all party organizations, along with local women's congresses to preside over women workers. Literacy classes and training courses were provided as well, to coach women activists in leadership techniques as well as to break down traditional gendered divisions of labor. In short, the CCP's 1931 policies and practices set the course for the institutionalization and development of the peasant women's movement in the soviet areas (Walker 1978: 60).

Public/official space and feminist cultural practice in the first seventeen years of socialist China (1949–66)

With the consolidation of the communist victory in China after 1949, socialist feminism gradually evolved into dominant, mainstream discourses and practices. In addition to guiding the promulgation and implementation of new marriage laws (1950–3) and championing gender equality and women's special interests, socialist feminism was also integrated into other major state movements, such as land reform and collectivization (1950–3), the Korean War (1950–3), early industrialization (1950–5), and literacy campaigns (1950–6). Indeed, socialist feminism constituted a central force in advancing all aspects of the newly established socialist system. This interdependence between feminism and other socialist practices resulted in the emergence of a politically constructed public/official space that was essentially, and simultaneously, feminist and socialist.

The subsequent development of socialist feminist mass culture was crucial in combating patriarchal values, advocating for women's interests, and promoting the new, proletarian, socialist woman subject in 1950s China and beyond. The new socialist-party-state sponsored and institutionalized feminist cultural production in ways that explicitly targeted patriarchy. Whereas socialist women's emancipation stressed the development of productive forces and economic emancipation, socialist feminist cultural practice launched unprecedented, unmatched mass campaigns against patriarchal customs in everyday lives.

Chinese socialist feminist practice was naturally a complex process, constantly interacting with national and international economic, social, and cultural conditions and developments, and not all initiatives succeeded. The severe economic and technological sanctions launched against China by the United States and other Western countries during the Cold War, for example, significantly constrained China's economic development, directly or indirectly contributing to uneven economic development in rural and urban areas and the persistence of gendered divisions of labor (Lin 2006: 60–83; Moise 2008: 38–144). Regional economics and local customs also demanded careful reflection and adjustment during various policy implementations. The fact that certain gender and class issues persisted in socialist China did not preclude extensive efforts aimed at women's and proletarian liberation. On the contrary, achievements in gender and class equality in socialist China were unprecedented both historically and globally.

Contrary to the conventional wisdom that construes state-sponsored endeavors as dogmatic and totalitarian, socialist feminist culture grew from diverse international and domestic influences, changed over time, and produced various representations and aesthetics. Variations in Chinese socialist feminist culture, however, do not suggest a lack of a coherent, central agenda. The idea and practice of "proletarianization" (Chen 2003: 278) distinguished Chinese socialist feminism from earlier Chinese feminisms, as well as from socialist feminism practiced in other countries (see also Anikó Imre's essay in this volume, on socialism, gender, and cinema in the Eastern European context). Indeed, proletarian women, broadly defined to include both rural and urban working-class women, emerged as the new political, social, and economic subject in socialist China. In cultural production, they became both a targeted audience and central characters. Mass media representations of working-class women as exemplary socialist subjects constituted a most critical and significant dimension of socialist feminist culture, illustrating "the arrival of a socialist modernity contingent upon shattering the fetters of Confucian, feudal and capitalist worldviews and their attendant patriarchal forms" (Chen 2003: 282).

Socialist feminist culture, including film production, therefore belonged to the political mainstream in China. Reflecting the multidimensionality of socialist feminist agency, Chinese socialist feminist culture did not represent gender as an isolated and independent category but rather situated gender in relation to other political and social agendas. Chinese socialist feminism, like other third world feminisms, displayed a pronounced nationalist character. Whether in content or artistic form, nationalism was an important component of socialist feminist cinematic practice. These central features of Chinese socialist feminist culture directly challenge prevailing assumptions that feminist cinema is a marginalized practice that necessarily resists, disrupts, and/or subverts mainstream ideology.

Wang Ping: the first Chinese socialist women director and the embedded cinematic authorship

Men had dominated Chinese cinema since 1905; women were not institutionally and socially supported to produce films, nor had any women directors produced more than one film in mainland China. In the new social system, however, a small group of women such as Wang Ping (1916–90), Wang Shaoyan (1923–), Yan Bili (1928–86), and Dong Kena (1930–), who had neither training nor experience in filmmaking prior to the founding of the People's Republic of China in 1949, was sought after by different film studios and entrusted to direct films. The new socialist belief that women could succeed in filmmaking accounted for the active recruitment of women directors in the 1950s and 1960s. Equally important, the establishment of public daycare and boarding schools in early socialist China provided key structural, material supports for socialist career women. The emergence of the first generation of Chinese women film directors, and their subsequent success, remains directly tied to the transformation of gender roles in socialist society, the national institutionalization of socialist feminism, and the formation of feminist public/official space in early socialist China.

In early socialist cinematic practice, the entire film industry was in the process of transforming itself from a profit-driven commercial enterprise to a proletarian, mass-oriented pedagogical apparatus working to construct new social and national subjects in line with proletarian revolution, public ownership, and socialist nation-building. National forms and styles became central for film theory and practice. The nationalist character of the communist revolution and the Cold War, especially the Korean War (1950–3), compelled 1950s socialist China to develop a new system of representation, emphasizing distinctly Chinese cultural and artistic characteristics, including folk art and popular culture. Workers, peasants, and soldiers became the main characters as well as the target audience for Chinese socialist films.

These cultural and social transformations did not entail a smooth teleological development in Chinese cinema and gender representation. Instead, they generated a dynamic process of negotiation that was continuously affected by an unstable political climate (both international and domestic), persistent influences of the past, and the varying backgrounds of individual authors and artists. In response to a radically new political-economic-social system, the first seventeen years of Chinese socialist cinema were highly experimental. If mainstream socialist cinema refers to all films produced in the state-planned economic system and state-owned film studios, it does not rule out changes, differences, or even contentions in the filmmaking process. As a matter of fact, Chinese socialist filmmaking entailed a process of dynamic political and artistic experiment, which simultaneously defined and contested the boundaries of a new national cinema.

It was within these historical and cinematic transformations that the first generation of Chinese women directors rose to prominence and continued to make socialist films through different experimental methods. Critical attention to the often overlooked dynamics between socialist cinema and gender illuminates the interdependent relationship between women and the socialist system, and the intimate interactions among gender and other political, social, and cultural institutions. Whereas poststructuralist feminism renders women's (cinematic) authorship into a textual signification that is barred from the historically constituted author in a given society, and from concrete social, political, and economic systems where meanings are produced and negotiated, Chinese socialist feminism highlights the interdependence of women's authorship and the socio-economic structure, emphasizing the critical role social and political institutions play in transforming gender roles in society and promoting women's historical agency in social and cultural productions. Women's cultural (cinematic) agency, as a result, is a highly embedded concept in socialist China, contingent upon dynamic interactions among different political, social, cultural, and individual forces.[2]

In the first seventeen years of socialist China, due to the multidimensional character of Chinese socialist feminism and the experimental nature of the early socialist cinema, Chinese women directors played multiple and different roles through filmmaking, producing diverse meanings, aesthetic styles, and critical voices in their films.[3] The remainder of this paper will illustrate Chinese socialist women's cinema by focusing on Wang Ping and her film, *The Story of Liubao Village*.

Wang Ping was the first woman film director in mainland Chinese history. Several of her films are credited with charting previously unexplored thematic and artistic territories. Among her best-known films are *The Story of Liubao Village* (1957), *The Everlasting Radio Signals* (*Yongbuxiaoshi de dianbo*, 1958), *Locust Tree Village* (*Huaishuzhuang*, 1961), and *Sentinels under the Neon Lights* (*Nihongdengxia de shaobing*, 1964). Her musical epic *East is Red* (*Dongfanghong*, 1965) remains an unprecedented achievement in and of itself. In 1962, Wang won the Hundred Flower Film Festival award for best director for *Locust Tree Village*.

Wang's extraordinary accomplishments evidence the significance of the socialist system. As socialist feminism emphasized multidimensional agency, and as Chinese women increasingly forged public and professional identities in the socialist era, women began to occupy multiple positions in history. For example, when directing *The Story of Liubao Village* (1957)—a love story between a communist soldier and a peasant girl during the Sino-Japanese war and the civil war (1945–49)—Wang Ping was simultaneously a socialist and revolutionary filmmaker in the August First Studio, a well-educated intellectual strongly affiliated with 1930s and 1940s left-wing drama and film, and one of the first Chinese career women in history to rely on socialist childcare and the public school system, especially after the loss of her husband. These positions did not always coalesce into a harmonious whole and negotiations and adjustments were constant. As central a concern as gender was for Wang, it remained a deeply embedded and complex factor in her life and work and thus demands examination at the intersections of multiple historical forces in modern China.

Socialist filmmaking proved to be highly collaborative; critical interventions could take place at many levels. Around the mid-1950s, the socialist public discourse on romantic love became marginalized, especially in cinema, because of romance's alleged ties to Western individualism and bourgeois sensibilities. Wang Ping, however, endorsed the original story by Hu Shiyan and screenplay by Huang Zongjiang, working closely with them in the process of revisions. The success of this film was certainly a result of Wang, Huang, and Hu's collaboration. Their shared left-wing intellectual backgrounds and communist revolutionary credentials compelled them to emphasize both the importance of individual *qinggan* (emotions or feelings) and the proletarian class revolution. Rather than viewing love and revolution as incompatible or conflicting, they strove to represent individual love and class revolution as interconnected goals, and as such questioned the official dismissal of individual emotions.

As a socialist film director, Wang Ping also succeeded in creating a new national cinematic form, marked by its distinctive poetic style and folk sentiment. The film's "feminine" style originates in Hu's story, which concentrates on an intellectual revolutionary's subjective views on emotional bonds, love, and revolution. Wang generally followed the structure of the story, but actively and creatively intervened when it came to cinematic style and expression. In her "Director's Notes," (Wang 1959) she describes her stylistic intentions as "a beautiful poem" (ibid. 151). This decision to create a poetic film reveals Wang's endorsement of the sentimental structure of the original story. More significantly, Wang's poetic and feminine aesthetic ventures beyond the story's original intellectual sentiment. She creatively expanded the poetic scale to include visual compositions of the Jiangnan rural scenery, folk music and culture, and the voices and facial expressions of proletarian figures. Many scenes, especially repeated scenery shots that appear in the first several images of the film, accentuate the poetic quality of the Jiangnan–Jiangbei area: white clouds, clear rivers, weeping willows, wooden bridges, small boats, scattered cottages, and windmills in the water-filled rice fields. The cinematic configuration of this landscape pronounces a visual, "feminine" style reminiscent of classical Chinese painting and poetry. Music plays an equal, if not more important, role in articulating the poetic sentiment of the film. Many have argued that this film's great popularity results partially from its folk love song, "Sunny Days of September." This song is repeated four times throughout the film, dividing the film narrative into stanzas and punctuating the development of the relationship between the hero Li Jin and heroine Ermeizi. As they sing, Li Jin and Ermeizi also express their personal feelings and become important emotive anchors for the narrative. Indeed, the film's aesthetic demonstrates Wang's unusual talent, as a devoted revolutionary artist, for exploring national forms that could reach a mass audience. She was unique in creating a Chinese cinematic style that combined classic poetic imagery with folk music and lyrics, integrating intellectual, individual sentiments with the emotions of the (soldier and peasant) masses.

Wang Ping's personal experiences and life trajectory also played a critical role in her adaptation of the film. Throughout her life, Wang actively participated in major cultural and political movements, from the left-wing drama and film movement of the 1930s to the communist revolution of the 1940s, to socialist construction in the 1950s. Wang's sense of independence and commitment enabled her to articulate her ideas in ways that ultimately diversified socialist mainstream cinema and contributed to the multi-level significance of her films.

One of the most significant revisions made by Wang Ping in her adaptation of *The Story of Liubao* centers on transforming the heroine of the original story, Ermeizi, from a distanced love object to a self-sufficient, down to earth, and brave peasant girl. Wang's own gendered experience as a young woman from the same region, and her self-consciousness as a woman intellectual and director, mattered significantly in the revision process. In her "Director's Notes," (Wang 1959) Wang Ping elaborates on Ermeizi's emotional and psychological state, distinguishing it from the romantic love the hero, Li Jin, feels for her. During their first encounter, whereas Li Jin is overwhelmed by his love for Ermeizi, Ermeizi, according to Wang Ping, is "hugely burdened by her own problems and has no intention of even considering love. Her thoughts completely center on how to save herself" (ibid. 154) from a local military bully who collaborates with the Japanese. Ermeizi's concern, "how to save herself," becomes her primary psychological motivation, and the central theme of her story, in Wang's film. Of the eighteen acts Wang discusses in her director's notes, five center on Ermeizi, highlighting her personal agency and her determination to seek help from Li Jin and the army. Whereas Li Jin distances himself from Ermeizi while he struggles to prioritize the revolutionary cause and army discipline over personal emotions, Ermeizi bravely steps out of an ordinary young peasant girl's role to initiate meetings with Li Jin. Wang's analysis of Ermeizi's character underscores how Ermeizi understands the revolutionary army to be the only hope for herself and her family, and therefore feels compelled to explain her situation to Li Jin in person. Until obtaining her personal freedom, Ermeizi does not reveal her feelings toward Li Jin (ibid. 160).

Wang Ping's revisions significantly strengthened the female character's agency, diversifying the representation of proletarian women in socialist cinema. In other canonical socialist films directed by men, such as *The White Haired Girl* (白毛女, 1950), set in a Shaanxi village, and *The Red Detachment of Women* (Hongse niangzijun, 1961), set in Hainan Island, peasant women's pre-revolutionary selfhood is defined largely by their victimization and their agency in the traditional discourse of family revenge (报仇). In *The Story of Liubao Village*, Wang articulates a different female peasant figure in pre-liberation Jiangnan, whose self-saving initiatives play an equal, if not more important, role in transforming her fate and future.

In conclusion, this brief re-examination of Wang's role in the filmmaking process for *The Story of Liubao Village* reveals several critical insights concerning socialist feminism, feminist culture, and socialist cinematic authorship in the first seventeen years of socialist China. First, mainstream and systematic institutionalization of socialist feminism, and the subsequent formation of a socialist public/official space that is essentially feminist, not only ushered in the first generation of Chinese women directors in mainland China but also gave rise to a popular and diverse socialist feminist culture that battled patriarchal traditions and ideas both directly and indirectly, and constructed new socialist female subjects. Proletarian women figures dominated the silver screen, but their routes to revolution, their psychological and emotional underpinnings, and their senses of agency were represented differently from one another.

Second, socialist cinematic authorship is a collaborative and contingent concept. Personal experience and subjective positions matter significantly in the processes of collaboration and negotiation. The political and pedagogical demands of socialist cinema required team efforts, while the experimental nature of 1950s film production also propelled writers and filmmakers to explore different and individual visions and versions of revolution, emotions, class, and gender. The final version of *The Story of Liubao Village* bears its three filmmakers' strongly individual and shared negotiations; the film's authorship is clearly contingent upon, as well as embedded in, their dynamic and experimental collaboration.

Finally, and more pertinent to any critical reflection on feminist cinema at the transnational scale, this study of socialist women's China challenges the widely held assumption that feminist cinema only occupies a counter, minor, marginalized, or independent position, regardless of its specific geopolitical and socio-political contexts. Chinese socialist mainstream cinema contained a distinctive feminist structure, dedicating itself to gender equality and socialist feminist causes even as certain historical limitations and individual artists' blind spots remain evident in some films. To dismiss socialist women directors' contributions to the production of feminist culture because they conformed to mainstream political and artistic ideologies betrays a dogmatic ignorance about different political and economic systems, as well as a hypocritical naiveté that willfully denies the intrinsic linkage between all feminist practices and their particular political and economic systems.

Zooming in on Chinese socialist women filmmakers, we find that their gendered negotiations articulate another layer of embeddedness. Women in socialist China did not form a monolithic or autonomous identity, nor did they experience historical transformations exclusively through a unified, "standard" woman's perspective. On the contrary, socialist feminism emphasized multidimensional agency, female authorship, and feminist articulations. *The Story of Liubao Village*, as a result, must be understood through Wang's contingent negotiations among multiple yet related sets of practices, namely: her active response to the socialist state's call for a new revolutionary cinema with a Chinese aesthetic that would reach the masses; her endorsement and further enrichment of an intellectual discourse on emotion, love, and intersubjective bonding; and her individual, revisionist articulation of a proletarian, female self.

Related topics

Anikó Imre, "Gender, socialism, and European film cultures"
Sandra Ponzanesi, "Postcolonial and transnational approaches to film and feminism"
Priya Jaikumar, "Feminist and non-Western interrogations of film authorship"

Notes

1 For an elaborate study of the cine-feminist concept of women's cinema and its implications for female authorship, see Wang, L. (2011) "Introduction: Transnational Feminist Reconfiguration of Film Discourse and Women's Cinema," in her *Chinese Women's Cinema: Transnational Contexts*, New York: Columbia University Press, pp. 1–44.
2 For a full-length study of Wang Ping and her films, see Wang, L. (2015) "Wang Ping and Women's Cinema in Socialist China: Institutional Practice, Feminist Cultures, and Embedded Authorship," *Signs: Journal of Women in Culture and Society*, 40(3), pp. 589–622.
3 For a detailed study of critical voices conveyed in socialist women's cinema, see Wang, L. (2011) "Socialist Cinema and Female Authorship: Overdetermination and Subjective Revisions in Dong Kena's Small Grass Grows on the Kunlun Mountain (1962)," in her *Chinese Women's Cinema: Transnational Contexts*, New York: Columbia University Press, pp. 47–65.

References

Butler, A. (2002) *Women's Cinema: The Contested Screen*, London: Wallflower.
Caughie, J. (ed.) (1981) *Theories of Authorship: A Reader*, London: Routledge & Kegan Paul.
Chen, T. M. (2003) "Female Icons, Feminist Iconography? Socialist Rhetoric and Women's Agency in 1950s China," *Gender and History* 15(2), pp. 268–95.
Croll, E. (1980) *Feminism and Socialism in China*, New York: Schocken.
Doane, M. A. (1987) *The Desire to Desire: The Woman's Film of the 1940s*, Bloomington: Indiana University Press; London: Macmillan Press.
Johnston, C. (1973/2000) "Women's Cinema as Counter-Cinema," in E. A. Kaplan (ed.) *Feminism and Film*, Oxford: Oxford University Press, pp. 22–33.
Li Jingzhi (李静之) (2011) *Essays on Chinese Women's Movements* (中国妇女运动研究文集), Beijing: Shehui kexue wenxian Press.
Lin, C. (2006) *The Transformation of Chinese Socialism*, Durham: Duke University Press.
Mao Zedong (1967) "Report on an Investigation of the Peasant Movement in Hunan," in Mao Zedong *Selected Works of Mao Tse-tung*, vol. 1, Peking: Foreign Languages Press, pp. 23–62.

Moise, E. E. (2008) *Modern China: A History*, 3rd edn., New York: Longman.

Mulvey, L. (1975) "Visual Pleasure and Narrative Cinema," *Screen* 16(3), pp. 6–18.

Smelik, A. (1998) *And the Mirror Cracked: Feminist Cinema and Film Theory*, New York: St. Martin's Press.

Tong Hua and Kang Peizhu (仝华 康沛竹) (eds.) (2004) *Historical Development of Marxist Feminist Theory* (马克思主义妇女理论发展史), Beijing: Beijing daxue Press.

Walker, K. L. (1978) "The Party and Peasant Women," in P. Huang, L. S. Bel, and K. L. Walker (eds.), *Chinese Communists and Rural Society, 1927–1937*, Berkeley: University of California Press, pp. 57–82.

Wang, L. (2015) "Wang Ping and Women's Cinema in Socialist China: Institutional Practice, Feminist Cultures, and Embedded Authorship," *Signs: Journal of Women in Culture and Society* 40(3), pp. 589–622.

Wang Ping (王苹) (1959) "Director's Notes on *The Story of Liubao Village*" (柳堡的故事导演阐述), in Zuo Lin (佐临) (ed.), *Collections of Film Directors' Notes* (电影导演阐述集), Beijing: China Film Press, pp. 150–63.

8

GENDER, SOCIALISM, AND EUROPEAN FILM CULTURES

Anikó Imre

I propose to reassess the influence of socialist ideas on the history and theory of gender-conscious filmmaking—a term I use loosely here to reference media practices that consciously reflect on the politics of gender. Of course, such a constellation involves much of the history of feminist cinema, which, in the West at least, reached its theoretical-political peak in 1970s avant-garde feminist filmmaking. The efforts of those filmmakers to resist the viewing comforts of classical Hollywood's realism were themselves inspired by the European formalist waves of the 1950s and 60s, which were, in turn, informed by socialist politics (Kaplan 2004). But while feminism as a political movement has been closely allied with socialist ideas from the beginning (Mulvey 2004), feminist histories and theories of film have rarely and barely taken into account the gendered film and media practices of actual socialist systems.

It is true that thinking about the intersection between actual socialism and feminist filmmaking brings to mind the names of select female filmmakers active during Soviet socialism: Věra Chytilová, Márta Mészáros, or Agnieszka Holland. But the very fact that the reference to feminist cinemas during state socialism only calls up a handful of auteurs who were not men indicates the limits of this approach. Compared to figures like Maya Deren, Yvonne Rainer, Sally Potter, Claire Denis, or Jane Campion, who conjure up deeply saturated histories of women's cinema, thoroughly elaborated and actively taught in Western curricula on film, gender, and feminism, the few isolated Eastern European and Soviet women directors present a problem to, rather than a transnational extension of, a gendered inquiry.

They are a problem since, for the most part, these women directors themselves denied any truck with feminism; and their films had to be forced into a gendered box specially fabricated for "East European" or "national" auteurs. More broadly, the limitations of an essentialist approach focused on female auteurs lead us to the two major stumbling blocks faced by socialist film: socialism itself, which was collapsed into state socialist authoritarianism and therefore considered in the West something that all filmmakers and intellectuals had to oppose; and the equally complex work of nationalism, which provided a matrix of automatic and primary self-identification for intellectuals and artists behind the Iron Curtain, reinforced by a Western matrix of reception towards socialist cultural products. These two powerful ideological blocks have acted as filters that reduced gender politics to the anti-Soviet politics of the national auteur, who might occasionally and incidentally be a woman (for women's cinema in the context of Chinese socialism, see Lingzhen Wang, this volume).

I propose that this spotlight on the Eastern European socialist national auteur has obscured and oversimplified some of the ways in which the entire Cold War competition was underscored by gender. Feminists from the postsocialist region of Central, Eastern and Southern Europe, and the Soviet successor states have recently begun to explore the implications of such a radically expanded understanding of gender politics (Bonfiglioli 2014; Regulska & Smith 2012; Reid 2002; de Haan 2010; Oates-Indruchová 2012; Havelková & Oates-Indruchová 2014; Ghodsee 2012). Their historical revision bypasses the monolithic geopolitical constructions of the Soviet Union and the United States and questions the two superpowers' determining ideological impact on their respective empires. It also blurs the temporal divide between socialism and its aftermath. As the editors of a recent collection of writing on "Gendering the Cold War" explain,

> Much recent revisionist work focuses on the history of women, gender, and everyday life. Along similar lines, we hope to explore here whether "gendering the Cold War" is a useful lens to examine the history and agency of ordinary women and men, and the role of gender in politics, systems of governance, and culture in CESEE—as influenced by or part of the Cold War competition between "the West" and "the East."
>
> *(Fidelis, et al. 2014: 163)*

Indeed, once we bracket the "superpower approach" that continues to dominate scholarship on socialism, we discover multileveled interactions among a variety of institutions and individuals involved in constant East–West technological, scientific, economic, and cultural exchanges (Autio-Sarasmo & Miklóssy 2011: 1–2). As a number of recent publications have demonstrated, such a view also opens up windows into the everyday life of socialism, inherently defying Cold War stereotypes of a repressive, isolated, joyless bloc (Bren & Neuburger 2012; Crowley & Reid 2010; Gumbert 2014; Gal & Kligman 2000; Penn & Massino 2009). As a part of this large-scale rethinking of the Cold War, feminist historians from or working on the former socialist region have also suspended the binary Cold War paradigm to show that state socialism, and its arm of state feminism, did not have an all-encompassing impact on women's (or men's) lives and ideological outlooks. Continuities with socialist feminist movements active in the region before World War II, which were also plugged into international feminist discourses and activism, could not be suppressed altogether during the socialist period. Besides, state feminism itself was an ambivalent force. While it generally associated feminism with a demonized capitalist West beholden to consumerism, it also afforded generous social provisions to women and adapted to shifts in socialist ideology with remarkable flexibility.

Such an understanding of the gender politics of the Cold War should revise entrenched perspectives on socialism and its film cultures as well. Singling out female directors as automatic carriers of filmic feminism or gender concerns is not likely to be the most productive approach. In fact, as I explain in the next section, art film as a form of expression might be a bit of a dead end in this exploration, since it is inextricable from the dominant "national cinema" approach and has been thoroughly instrumentalized as a currency in Cold War cultural exchanges between East and West. This process was part of a larger international pattern of Cold War cultural exchanges whereby, as Priya

Jaikumar writes in her account of non-Western authorship and gender in this collection, European festivals such as Cannes and Berlin valorized "humanism" as an "international film ideology," which allowed Asian and African filmmakers to be included in a male auteurist canon, "whose acclaim rested on criteria of artistry assumed to transcend gender and national politics through their universal humanism" (Jaikumar, this volume). In a version of this international humanism that was more specific to the East–West division within European socialism, art films served to validate local cultural nationalisms and their agents, East European artists, within a cosmopolitan circulation that formed and fixed ideas about socialism in the West. Because these ideas were so profoundly inscribed in a Cold War script of male universalist nationalism, I suggest we look elsewhere to understand the ways in which women and ideologies of gender have made a more transformative impact: towards the less scrutinized and more popular mass medium of television.

I want to harness the energy around feminist efforts to revise the history of gender politics under socialism in order to redirect attention to everyday gendered practices and identifications around television. As I also note, while these feminist approaches have been effective at demystifying the influence of state socialism on gender relations and the bipolar history of the Cold War, they have been less successful at, or perhaps less interested in, tackling the other monolith: nationalism.

Socialist film culture's gender politics

Scholarship on European socialist film with an explicit interest in gender has followed two main avenues so far: an older concern with female auteurs and a more recent concern with themes of gender and sexuality. These avenues often cross and combine. Both are legitimate and fruitful approaches, but both tend to be circumscribed by the historical and nationalistic scripts of the Cold War and a dialectic of assimilation and resistance to Western feminist paradigms. Examples of the female auteur approach include Catherine Portuges's (1993) excellent work on the cinema of Hungarian director Márta Mészáros, whose films exhibit a marked concern with realism, the family, female characters, and intimacy. The oeuvre of Věra Chytilová, particularly her 1966 film *Daisies*, has invited some feminist curiosity about the gendered havoc wrought by the film's two irreverent protagonists, Marie I and Marie II (Hanáková 2005; Lim 2001; Seiter 1985). However, gender is just one possible emphasis in the film's abundant readings, and not even the most preferred one, particularly in the postsocialist region. *Daisies* has also been amply discussed, and is regularly taught as a masterpiece of Czech or Czechoslovak cinema, a historical variant of Dadaism, or as an example of surrealist cinema—without regard for its gendered content, which is something hard to imagine for the work of most Western female directors (see Eagle 1991; Owen 2011; Žalman 1967–8; Parvulescu 2006).

My own earlier contribution to this kind of text- and auteur-centered recuperative work compared textual strategies and pleasures in Sally Potter's *Orlando* (1992) and Hungarian director Ildikó Enyedi's *My Twentieth Century* (1989) (Imre 2003), a film that takes a whimsical, personal look at historical events that occurred at the birth of the twentieth century through the eyes and adventures of twin girls separated at birth. Similar to other attempts at generating a cross-cultural feminist conversation, my reading came up against the problem that Enyedi's film had been incorporated into a national modernist canon in both its native Hungarian and its cosmopolitan European cinephilic circuits of interpretation. The only way to wrench *My Twentieth Century* away from? this mercilessly nationalizing and universalizing historical context was to push it into, or into the proximity of, a different kind of canon by insisting that it systematically produces a "female address" (a term borrowed from Teresa de Lauretis [1987]) that is comparable to that of *Orlando*. In a way, while such female-centered Eastern European films are fascinating in their subtle subversions of a masculine national canon, they also remain suspended within that canon. The best we can say is that directors like Enyedi adopted a masquerade that traded downplaying gendered readings for getting recognition within the male canon.

Within the international operation of socialist media, "socialism" entailed an East–West division, rather than commonality, particularly within Europe. Whereas in Western Europe and elsewhere in the "developed" world of capitalism, socialist ideas were distributed among and absorbed by a variety of subnational and cross-national groups, including those that represented feminist and LGBT interests, in the socialist East, these subnational interests were subordinated to, if not suppressed by, the primary force of nationalism. Even though socialist regimes successfully consolidated their long-term rule by mobilizing popular nationalism, the job of representing "the people" was assigned to a traditional, patriarchal, cultural-nationalist elite. This cultural elite's opposition to the socialist state and its pre-scribed aesthetic of realism borrowed from modernist and avant-garde practices but immediately "nationalized" the oppositional potential of these practices, leaving little room for subnational identifications.

This intellectual and creative elite also played a key role in international cultural diplomacy, particularly through the work of European festivals and awards. Films that displayed international, "humanistic" sensibilities, made by cosmopolitan artists who already belonged to a transnational auteur canon, were designated to be representatives of the national cinemas that together made up Eastern European cinema. Their auteurs—Andrzej Wajda, Krzysztof Zanussi, Miklós Jancsó, István Szabó, Jiří Menzel, Dušan Makavejev, Želimir Žilnik, among others—were key to a (pan-)European circulation that affected every level of film culture, from ideology through aesthetics to economics. Paradoxically, identifying Eastern European film cultures with a few highly visible auteurs imposed a national framework on the socialist bloc that was belied by the reality of a fairly integrated media production and distribution economy within Europe, secured, to a great extent, by the very international visibility and mobility of the same auteurs who were supposed to confer nationalistic authenticity on "their" own native cultures.

In other words, the art films selected for international circulation served a symbolic function that supported both the Cold War monolith of a radical divide between East and West and the monolith of nationalism. What dropped out in this symbolic construction around "national" art films was the national spectator, who remained a fictional or imagined character for the most part. The films that constitute national canons were produced and distributed strategically by institutions of socialist nation-states. At the same time, the films in question were viewed and legitimized mostly by Western-facing intellectual elites—the most educated and cosmopolitan population group in each country. While "national cinema" traveled within the narrow circuit of cultural institutions, national intellectuals, Western critics, and movie buffs, the actual national spectator avoided national cinemas and quietly migrated to television and popular films. Of course, as Andrew Higson (1989) writes, national cinema, at least in Europe, is always an idealistic, top-down, and para-doxical construction in that it foregrounds the most diverse and progressive elements within a national culture. In Eastern Europe, this contradiction—and the gap between national cinema and national spectator—was further deepened by the ideological pressure of Soviet occupation, with the exception of non-occupied Yugoslavia, which curtailed national independence and confirmed the historical leadership role assigned to national intellectuals (see Imre 2014).

Most recently, the legacy of auteurist, nation-based, interpretative, evaluative focus has been supplemented by a trickling of industry studies and a renewed attention to female auteurs. Most such new work has zoomed in on "figures" and "representations." This work has followed an approach drawn from cultural studies, essentially moored in textual readings that extrapolate to socio-political meanings. In this way, for instance, Krzysztof Zanussi's films have been retroactively queered in a way that defines "Polish national culture" (Jagielski 2013); 1960s Yugoslavian cinema has been reclaimed from oblivion by "fore-grounding some [of its] gendered motifs" and opening its "celluloid closet" (Jovanović 2012); and women have been highlighted in the science fiction genre (Mazierska & Näripea 2014). While this effort to detect textual subversion is novel in work on (post)socialist cinemas, it carries the belated whiff of an early "images of" criticism. Its revisionism remains local, not thorough enough to dislodge the ideological primacy of the Cold War or to break out of the coercive spotlight created around great directors occupying the canonical center of national cinemas.

A more effective intervention would have to borrow from the findings and methods of archival and ethnographic work on socialism and gender currently pursued in gender studies, and merge textual readings with work on labor, and on industrial and consumer practices. It would have to reckon with an ideological context where the modernist style originally developed to oppose the bourgeois indulgences of capitalist Hollywood cinema was taken up and appropriated by a male vanguard in order to oppose state socialism's early mandate of simplistic realism. In this context, if women wanted to get different, gendered ideas and voices across, they had limited choices: perform an assimilationist masquerade by taking up the modernist-nationalist mantle and twisting its subversive tools to serve more explicitly gendered structures; or re-embrace the aesthetic of state-approved realism along with women's social mission to serve as the conscience and nurturing mother of the nation, often in documentary or pseudo-documentary forms. A third choice was to leave film altogether for the less charged domain of television, which left more room for women's concerns and favored a more accessible aesthetic.

Television and gender during the Cold War

Television gives better access to the political, economic, and cultural life of socialism, and to the underlying gender politics of the Cold War, than film. In the most obvious sense, television was an institution that lived in the intersection of the public and domestic spheres, between top-down attempts at influencing viewers and bottom-up demands for entertainment. Whereas much of art and literature informs us of the relationship between the party leadership and the intellectual elite, TV gives us a sense of the real complexity of the relationship between the party leadership and the public. And because scholarly attention to socialist TV is relatively recent, the medium's cross-border production, circulation, and consumption have not yet been circumscribed by a nation-state-based approach.

In a less obvious way, television also grants us access to subtle but all the more significant divisions within the "public" that both socialist ideology itself and Cold War discourses about socialism envisioned as homogeneous. Instead of confirming the blanket oppression of the people by authoritarian or dictatorial leaders, the history of television highlights the more fluid workings of micro-oppressions and exclusions: of women, of non-normative sexualities, of foreigners, and of the Roma and other non white populations. This can be traced, first of all, in the way television, unlike film, targeted women as an audience. Not as a primary audience, as did 1950s TV in the United States, where the female consumer in the household was identified early on as a target of advertising. In socialist cultures, the default TV viewer remained the idealized socialist citizen, who was white, heterosexual, and male. In fact, men actually watched more TV than women because of the disparity between women and men when it came to spare time. While women were encouraged to take an equal part in the workforce, they continued to shoulder the full range of household and family duties without help, since "work" was only understood as paid work in the public sphere (Bren and Neuburger 2012: 191). This effectively meant a double or often triple shift for women, which left little time to enjoy television after work.

Rather than following a commercial logic, socialist television's special address to women derived from the communist concern with the "woman question," as defined by Engels, Bebel, Lenin, Luxemburg, Stalin, and other major ideologues (see Fodor 2002). The socialist period interrupted the pre-war trajectory of academic and activist feminism and filtered most gender-related politics and research through the "woman question." In effect, this meant policies that segregated women into a homogenized social group identified with special needs and tasks (reproduction, family care, and emotional labor) and with inferior skills for political participation (preference for emotional identification, insufficient ability to reason) (ibid.; Zimmermann 2010). When it came to TV programming, this meant that women were treated as a distinct demographic who needed targeted political-educational programs, similar to factory workers, college students, or the elderly. This niche address invariably revolved around the family and the household and focused on issues of care-taking, lifestyle, emotions, and education.

In the Soviet Union, by the late 1950s and early 1960s—precisely during the ascendance of TV as a mass medium—Nikita Khrushchev shortened work hours and expanded leisure time for Soviet citizens. Competition with the West in industrial and agricultural production gave way to competition based on technological advances and consumer lifestyles, holding out the promise of daily comforts after decades of strife and hardship (Evans 2011: 622). Television was not just a conduit in this shift but literally the centerpiece of the domestic sphere, bringing the promise of rest and relaxation into the apartments of mass housing estates (ibid. 624).

This shift in competition with the West, from production to consumption and "lifestyle," moved the spotlight onto women as key agents of socialist citizenship. Éva Fodor writes that, in Hungary, the "woman question" had been considered "resolved" by the end of the 1960s but was reopened following a 1970 party decree that put women's role in society back on the agenda. In the decade that followed, a variety of state institutions produced 110 reports on women's roles in society (Fodor 2002: 251). The single party-controlled women's organization, the Women's Council, published about forty books that, for the most part, focused on lifestyle and consumption, such as skin care, self-help, child rearing, divorce, and cooking (ibid. 249).

Public affairs programs directed at women showcased the "feminization" of the socialist ideological agenda during the "thaw" or "normalization" period that followed anti-Soviet uprisings in 1956 (Hungary) and 1968 (Czechoslovakia). Women were discovered by the party leadership as a key demographic in the Cold War competition to demonstrate the superior lifestyle that socialism provided when compared to capitalism. As a result, a marked shift towards more explicit propaganda content occurred in Hungarian "women's programs" of the 1960s. The Hungarian Central Committee's Agitational and Propaganda

Department's evaluation of public interest magazine programs for women such as *Lányok, asszonyok* (Girls and women) read:

> [Such programs] help the educational work of the Youth Communist organization, schools and the family in diverse ways. It is commendable that Television offers specialized programs to address women. These kinds of programs were rather apolitical at first; today, however, they are more politicized and pay more attention to the issues of working women and girls.
>
> (*see Hungarian Socialist Workers' Party Central Committee*)

Even in Romania, under the extreme political oppression of Ceausescu's dictatorship, such programs developed an agenda to promote the ideal socialist woman, modeled by Elena Ceauşescu. Programs discussed agricultural work, the working woman, women leaders in different professions, the revolutionary woman, and the many virtues of Elena. For instance, the May 27, 1984 broadcast of *Almanahul familiei* (*Family Almanac*) included the following topics, according to the *TV Guide*: school for mothers; food for newborn babies; how to harvest bee venom in your own garden; how to raise silkworms; quitting work for pregnant women or stay-at-home mothers; the home pharmacy; culinary recipes; and healthy lifestyles (Mustata 2013).

In the Soviet Union, the long-running game/talent show *A nu-ka devushki!* (*Let's Go Girls!*, 1970–85) was developed specifically as a form of Soviet "niche outreach." It was supposed to expand the narrow participant range of earlier quiz shows to include demographics other than male intellectuals and to demonstrate the versatility of Soviet youth in terms of professions, talents, and gender. *Let's Go Girls!* featured young women from female-dominated professions, such as tram drivers, bakers, and telephone operators (Evans 2015). To reinforce the legitimacy of Soviet women's double burden, the first half of each program was a contest among participants from a single profession, often shot in a factory. This was followed by the same women competing in homemaking skills. The eight semifinalists who survived the first half then competed in housekeeping and consumer skills. The organizers tried to downplay physical characteristics of beauty and to emphasize professional qualities and brains as well as taste in clothing and personal care?. *Let's Go Girls* was supposed to showcase all the ingredients of the ideal modern 1970s Soviet woman, who is superior in every way to the Western beauty contestant (ibid.).

As I discuss in detail elsewhere (Imre 2016), dramatic programming became an even more powerful vehicle for shoring up "socialist lifestyle" during the period of late socialism (1970s–1980s). Socialist "soap operas" such as the Polish *Czterdziestolatek* (*The Forty-Year-Old*, 1974–8), the Hungarian *A 78-as körzet* (*District 78*, 1982), and particularly the Czechoslovak *Žena za pultem* (*Women Behind the Counter*, 1977) and *Hospital at the Edge of Town* (*Nemocnice na kraji města*, 1977), all modeled ideal socialist lifestyles in ensemble dramas that encompassed the workplace and the family. Unlike historical dramas, which removed the narrative into the past and revolved around heroic male figures in the public arena, these domestic serials took place in the present and featured central female characters who acted as problem-solvers, liaisons between the public and private worlds. This regional genre put women center stage to emphasize the shift from production to consumption and lifestyle in the competition with the West; and processed the feminization of late socialist cultures without allowing feminist politics to seep in. Much like Western soap operas, these serials introduced communities that were metaphors for modern society, offering fictional, "feminine" pleasures of identification (Ang & Stratton 1995). In other ways, however, the socialist soap was a peculiar hybrid specific to the conditions of late socialism. Rather than addressing women only as consumers, it addressed them first and foremost as citizens, whose biological features simply assigned them to unique roles within the socialist collective. It was also distinct in tone and aesthetic as it absorbed the influence of other socialist TV genres, most prominently the didacticism of public affairs programs and the satirical tone of comedy shows.

Television's lower, feminized cultural status also made it a more accommodating place for female professionals than was the film industry. Valentina Leont'eva was longtime hostess of the Soviet program *Ot vsei dushi* (*From the bottom of my heart*), launched in 1972. As Christine Evans argues, it was crucial to have a woman host a program charged with giving an emotional boost to the party's embrace of socialist lifestyle and nationalist mythology (2015). Leont'eva's legacy is similar to that of Irena Dziedzic, hostess of the first Polish cultural current affairs/cultural magazine *Tele-Echo* (1956–81). While both Dziedzic and Leont'eva were accused of political conformism, both were seen as outstanding TV personalities with long-lasting legacies because of their ability to stir up intense emotions (Pikulski 2002: 54).

Television compelled but also allowed women to assert themselves in the available forms of masquerade—genres whose formal conformity to the regime's ideological preferences was beyond scrutiny. In Hungary, documentary or docufictional forms that foregrounded a socialist realist aesthetic and social commitment saw a golden age beginning in the 1960s, thanks to the work of some outstanding professionals. Women in the forefront of television documentary production often came out with highly gendered topics and treatments. But instead of taking on politics directly, women tended to be more effective when they employed the politics of empathy, calling public attention to the plight of neglected groups that needed care, such as children, the elderly, ethnic minorities, isolated rural populations, and the sick. In Hungarian TV, these productions included *Bognár Anna világa* (*The world of Anna Bognár*) in 1963, directed by Márta Kende, a moving documentary film that had a decisive impact on the emerging genre of TV sociography. The film portrayed a fifty-two-year-old blind woman living on a farm, who gets her vision back due to a successful eye surgery ("Megnéztük," *Rádió és TV Újság* 10 [1963]). Margit Molnár's documentary *Leányanyák*, (*Teen mothers*, 1970) created a stir when it explored the plight of pregnant teenagers. In the same year, Molnár also hosted a public affairs program called *Nők fóruma* (*Women's Forum*). Unlike the previous socialist educational "niche" program, *Lányok, asszonyok* (*Women and Girls*, 1964), each episode of Molnár's show was dedicated to specific areas where public culture blatantly discriminated against women and families: how children of divorced parents coped, or the effects of inflexible work schedules on the lives of mothers.

As these examples of television's role as the mass medium of socialism and the Cold War, and particularly of women's engagement in socialist cultures as television professionals and publics illustrate, reducing our vision to the usual perspective of art cinema is simply not enough; it leads to a distorted and simplistic view, obscured by entrenched histories of a bipolar Cold War order that favors masculine or male figures representing their respective national populations to Western viewers in exchange for admission into a universal male canon. To get a better sense of the gendered significance of film's or visual media's engagement with socialist ideas, we need to follow the course that leads to the everyday life of socialism charted by anthropologists and feminist historians, and extend it to the mass medium of everyday life. A medium primarily for domestic consumption, television makes visible an otherwise invisible cultural and ideological matrix that rested on a carefully monitored gender politics and mobilized women as key agents of socialist citizenship and Cold War competition.

Related topics

Lingzhen Wang, "Chinese socialist women's cinema: an alternative feminist practice"
Sandra Ponzanesi, "Postcolonial and transnational approaches to film and feminism"
Priya Jaikumar, "Feminist and non-Western interrogations of film authorship"

References

Ang, I. and J. Stratton (1995). "The End of Civilization As We Knew It: *Chances* and the Postrealist Soap Opera." In *To Be Continued ... Soap Operas Around the World*, ed. Robert C. Allen. London and New York: Routledge: 122–44.

Autio-Sarasmo, S. and K. Miklóssy (2011). "Introduction: The Cold War from a New Perspective." In *Reassessing Cold War Europe*, eds. Sari Autio-Sarasmo and Katalin Miklóssy. New York: Routledge: 1–15.

Bonfiglioli, C. (2014). "Women's Political and Social Activism in the Early Cold War Era. The Case of Yugoslavia." *Aspasia* 8: 1–25.

Bren, P. and M. Neuburger, eds. (2012). *Communism Unwrapped: Consumption in Cold War Eastern Europe*. Oxford: Oxford University Press.

Crowley, D. and S. E. Reid, eds. (2010). *Pleasures in Socialism: Leisure and Luxury in the Eastern Bloc*. Evanston, IL: Northwestern University Press.

de Haan, F. (2010). "Continuing Cold War Paradigms in Western Historiography of Transnational Women's Organisations: The Case of the Women's International Democratic Federation (WIDF)." *Women's History Review* 19(4): 547–73.

de Lauretis, T. (1987). *Technologies of Gender: Essays on Theory, Film and Fiction*. Bloomington: Indiana University Press.

Eagle, H. (1991). "Dadaism and Structuralism in Věra Chytilová's *Daisies*." In *Cross Currents 10: A Yearbook of Central European Culture*, ed. Vladislav Matejka. New Haven: Yale University Press.

Evans, C. (2011). "Song of the Year and Soviet Mass Culture in the 1970s." *Kritika: Explorations in Russian and Eurasian History* 12(3): 617–45.

Evans, C. (2015). "The 'soviet way of life' as a way of feeling." *Cahiers du monde russe* 56(2): 543–70.

Fidelis, M. G., R. J. Kirin, J. Massino, and L. Oates-Indruchová (2014). "Gendering the Cold War in the Region." *Aspasia* 8: 162–90.

Fodor, E. (2002). "Smiling Women and Fighting Men: The Gender of the Communist Subject in State Socialist Hungary." *Gender and Society* 16(2): 240–63.

Gal, S. and G. Kligman (2000). *Reproducing Gender: Politics, Publics and Everyday Life after Socialism*. Princeton, NJ: Princeton University Press.

Ghodsee, K. (2012). "Rethinking State Socialist Mass Women's Organizations: The Committee of the Bulgarian Women's Movement and the United Nations Decade for Women, 1975–1985." *Journal of Women's History* 24(4): 49–73.

Gumbert, H. (2014). "Envisioning Socialism: Television and the Cold War in the German Democratic Republic." https://vtechworks.lib.vt.edu/handle/10919/51557 (accessed January 5, 2016).

Hanáková, P. (2005). "Voices from Another World: Feminine Space and Masculine Intrusion in *Sedmikrásky* and *Vražda ing. Čerta*." In *Eastern European Cinemas. AFI Film Readers*, ed. Anikó Imre. New York: AFI/Routledge: 63–80.

Havelková, H. and L. Oates-Indruchová, eds. (2014). *The Politics of Gender Culture under State Socialism: An Expropriated Voice*. New York: Routledge.

Higson, A. (1989). "The Concept of National Cinema." *Screen* 30(4): 36–47.

Hungarian Socialist Workers' Party Central Committee, MOL—288f22/19596.öe./23. MSZMP KP, Agitációs és Propaganda Osztály (Department of Agitation and Propaganda files), Hungarian National Document Archives.

Imre, A. (2003). "Twin Pleasures of Feminism: *Orlando* Meets *My Twentieth Century*." *Camera Obscura* 54(18): 177–211.

Imre, A. (2014). "Postcolonial Media Studies in Postsocialist Europe." *boundary 2* 41(1), 113–34.

Imre, A. (2016). *TV Socialism*. Durham: Duke University Press.

Jagielski, S. (2013). "'I Like Taboo': Queering the Cinema of Krzysztof Zanussi." *Studies in Eastern European Cinema* 4(2): 143–59.

Jovanović, N. (2012). "My Own Private Yugoslavia: František Čap and the Socialist Celluloid Closet." *Studies in Eastern European Cinema* 3(2): 211–29.

Kaplan, E. A. (2004). "Global Feminisms and the State of Feminist Film Theory." *Signs: Journal of Women in Culture and Society* 30(1): 1236–48.

Lim, B. C. (2001). "Dolls in Fragments: *Daisies* as Feminist Allegory." *Camera Obscura* 16(2): 37–77.

Mazierska, E. and E. Näripea (2014). "Gender Discourse in Eastern European SF Cinema." *Science Fiction Studies* 41(1): 163–80.

Megnéztük (1963). *Rádió és TV Újság* 10.

Mulvey, L. (2004). "Looking at the Past from the Present: Rethinking Feminist Film Theory of the 1970s." *Signs: Journal of Women in Culture and Society* 30(1): 1286–92.

Mustata, D. (2013). e-mail to Anikó Imre, September 13.

Oates-Indruchová, L. (2012). "The Beauty and the Loser: Cultural Representations of Gender in Late State Socialism." *Signs: Journal of Women in Culture and Society* 37(2): 357–83.

Owen, J. L. (2011). *Avant-garde To New Wave: Czechoslovak Cinema, Surrealism and the Sixties*. New York: Berghahn.

Parvulescu, A. (2006). "'So We Will Go Bad': Cheekiness, Laughter, Film." *Camera Obscura* 21(2): 144–67.

Penn, S. and J. Massino, eds. (2009). *Gender Politics and Everyday Life in State Socialist East and Central Europe*. New York: Palgrave Macmillan.

Pikulski, T. (2002). *Prywatna historia telewizji publicznej*. Warszawa: Muza SA.

Portuges, C. (1993). *Screen Memories: The Hungarian Cinema of Márta Mészáros*. Bloomington: Indiana University Press.

Regulska J. and B. G. Smith, eds. (2012). *Women and Gender in Postwar Europe: From Cold War to European Union*. London and New York: Routledge.

Reid, S. E. (2002). "Cold War in the Kitchen: Gender and the De-Stalinization of Consumer Taste in the Soviet Union under Khrushchev." *Slavic Review* 61(2): 211–52.

Seiter, E. (1985). "The Political is Personal: Margarethe von Trotta's *Marianne and Juliane*." *Journal of Film and Video* 37(2): 41–6.

Žalman, J. (1967–8). "Question Marks on the New Czechoslovak Cinema." *Film Quarterly* 21(2): 18–27.

Zimmermann, S. (2010). "Gender Regime and Gender Struggle in Hungarian State Socialism." *Aspasia* 4: 1–24.

9

QUEER OR LGBTQ+

On the question of inclusivity in queer cinema studies

Amy Borden

Writing about queer cinema in 2010, film scholar Bob Nowlan asked if it was retrograde to consider queer cinema as a radical, politically inflected cinematic mode in light of what he saw as film studies' conflation of queer and LGBT identities. Had queer become, he asked, less about disrupting and more about creating a blanket of inclusivity under which non-heteronormative practices found safety (2010: 10)? Five years later, queer cinema scholarship continues to practice an inclusivity that can make it productively maddening to characterize even when viewed as a unique subdiscipline that draws from, but does not mirror, queer studies or film studies. Jackie Stacey and Sarah Street locate queer cinema's ability to avoid the compartmentalization and "drive towards quotable synthesis" found in academia to the fact that it has always "belonged as much to film and video makers, festival programmers and political activists as to academics" (2007: 1). If it has coalesced around anything fundamental, queer cinema scholarship values Alexander Doty's invocation of a "definitional elusiveness" (2000: 6) found in queer theory's fundamental "indeterminacy" (Jagose 1997:1).

One of the issues at play in valuing indeterminacy and the inclusivity that it may foster, as Nowlan points out, is the potential to erode the radical politics that drove queer cinematic articulations of the recent past. As more collections about LGBTQ+ cinemas are published, Nowlan's question about the radical inflections of queerness helps frame how we might pull apart film studies' conflation of queer and LGBT identities by focusing on queer studies and queer cinema studies' intersection at a point of radical subjectivity that builds on women's and lesbian/gay studies' "refusal of any identity-based foundational category" (Hall and Jagose 2013: xv). Distinguishing what is queer in film studies focuses attention on the fissures and joints in how queerness is conceived in international and multiregional queer cinema. The plurality of experiences articulated in international LGBTQ+ cinemas coupled with the, at times, self-consciously political aim of queer studies marks queer cinema studies as a particular site in which destabilized identities and modes of filmmaking find a common cause. Defining queer is something I consciously avoid doing throughout this essay because I am focused on its indeterminacy and non-foundational status. I use the terms LGBT and LGBTQ+ to signify identity-based analysis and filmmaking, adopting the latter as a current, more inclusive description. When I refer to LGBT identities or studies I am drawing attention to moments in film studies or film history when LGBT studies dominated discourse about identity or when the authors I write about have used the LGBT description in their own work.

This essay, then, locates the shared appreciation of the "radical" in queer and queer cinema studies to prompt its review of contemporary, international invocations of queerness as a film practice rather than a genre. The practice of queer filmmaking and the cinematic modes by which it is expressed value deviance and an activist aesthetic as a counterpoint to an increasing proliferation of positive Western cinematic and televisual LGBTQ+ representations. What I hope to do by surveying the field of queer cinema studies is to argue that this form of queerness is a resurgent mode of analysis in LGBTQ+ cinema studies that both stages a version of the perceived historical differences between LGBT and queer studies and that demonstrates how valuing radical process and aesthetic forms, as queer studies does, contributes to the difficulty in characterizing queer cinema as a genre. In doing so, contemporary, international queer cinema studies uses queerness to signal how process takes precedence over identity by valuing hybridity and indeterminacy and reasserts a celebration of the radical as a fundamental aspect of LGBTQ+ politics. This turn evokes the ethos of British filmmaker Derek Jarman's "difficult" self-identity:

> I didn't discover my sexuality to sell *in* – I want change. … To call Pasolini, or myself for that matter, "gay artists" is foolish and limiting, one day maybe we will dispense with boundaries and categories. I was never gay, queer maybe, difficult certainly, with good reason.
>
> *(2011: 168–9)*

Ultimately, I argue that queer cinema studies addresses films that draw on avant-garde and art cinema conventions to highlight the importance of performativity in contemporary queer theory and to celebrate an aesthetic subjectivity as an alternative to foundational gender-driven identities.

As both queer and gay and lesbian studies have understood them, the differences between queer and LGBT cinemas are available to us if we work backward and forward from the 1990s New Queer Cinema (NQC). It was this unique "moment," as characterized by B. Ruby Rich (2013: 16), that reinvigorated art cinema's embrace of queer values and offered a film and video "renaissance … just when the passionate energy that had characterized AIDS activism was flagging" (ibid. xiv). In 1991 and 1992 Todd Haynes' *Poison*, Tom Kalin's *Swoon*, Gregg Araki's *The Living End*, and Derek Jarman's *Edward II* were among the films celebrated at Sundance, distributed on the art cinema circuit, and characterized in both mainstream and specialist publications as ushering in an "art-full manifestation" of intervention, cultural product, and political strategy informed by activist collectives such as ACT UP and Queer Nation (Aaron 2004: 6). The use of art cinema conventions and non-classical practices in these films highlighted queer as a counter-cultural formation whose cinematic history values deviance in both cinematic style and characterization.

The films listed above, as well as later NQC films—Cheryl Dunye's *The Watermelon Woman* (1996) and Guinevere Turner and Rose Troche's *Go Fish* (1994)—emphasize the perversity of seeking identification and historical presence in images that are created within inherently straight cinematic institutions such as those expressed in a classical mode defined in part by historically stable temporalities. Jarman disrupts this stability with anachronistic mise-en-scène in *Edward II* and his earlier film *Caravaggio* (1986), by forcing viewers into an out-of-timeness where typewriters and punk music diegetically co-exist in the Italian Renaissance and a hybrid Elizabethan and modern England. Kalin performs a similar temporal disruption in *Swoon*, his adaptation of the early-1920s Leopold and Loeb trial, when he re-stages the famous shot sequence from *Rear Window* (1954) via which the audience is first introduced to Grace Kelly's Lisa, whose shadow sweeps over James Stewart's sleeping form. In Kalin's iteration, Stewart's hobbled Jeff is replaced by a reclining Loeb receiving a kiss from Leopold as the pair deliver Kelly and Stewart's kiss-punctuated exchange: "How's your leg? Hurts a little. And your stomach? Empty as a football. And your love life? Not too active." Complete with the original's slowed image, *Swoon* creates a cinematic temporality that recreates a fiction that has yet to occur in the film's 1920s diegesis. More than an homage or moment of pastiche, Kalin perverts the audience-familiar moment by suggesting the murderous 1920s duo are its origin, switching genders and sexuality, and, by embodying Kelly and Stewart, perverting their original roles. Kalin layers a temporal indeterminacy with a perversion of normalized social behavior: one pair, murderous boyfriends, and the other, heterosexual "opposites" who seek to restore a law and order balance across the courtyard.

One of the many reasons NQC takes such a place of prominence in the history of LGBTQ+ cinemas is that it simultaneously disrupted the drive for positive cinematic representations of lesbian and gay lives and the continuation of negative and stereotypical cinematic representations—lesbians as vampires, gay men as "sissies," the presumption that LGBTQ+ individuals are doomed to unhappy deaths—chronicled by Vito Russo (1981). Defiance at mainstream culture and also "the 'tasteful and tolerated' gay culture that cohabits with it" binds NQC films to each other (Aaron 2004: 7). It also offers a template for now-contemporary queer film theory's reassertion of activism. Propelled onto then-mainstream platforms, the defiance NQC filmmakers practiced was elevated to a cinematic activism that reached art cinema audiences via the 1990s boom in independent film institutions (Pierson 2014).

Alternatively, LGBT cinema has historically been understood as a mode of representation within established and LGBT-specific genres, like coming-out and family acceptance stories, that consumers recognize and which provide marketing differences for distributors. Surveying LGBT cinema across a diverse set of exhibition and distribution platforms depends on an understanding of genre as a marketing tool as much as it is about classifying texts and their cultural work. Because genres suggest objective status and discursive boundaries, conceiving queer cinema as an international practice rather than as a genre retains indeterminacy as the key value of queer studies. Including LGBTQ+ representations within established genres can articulate cracks created by the addition of queerness to classical film styles and forms not unlike those found when scholars read a film queerly. Stacey and Street describe the "queer move" as "the possibility of combining post-structuralist theory with sexual politics" (2007: 9). Alexander Doty describes the same as occurring "in a queer zone" in which one is "no longer 'being' or positioning myself as gay or feminine, and also not 'being' or positioning myself fully in the remaining gender and sexuality labels, including 'straight'" (2000: 9).

Doty cautions scholars that queer film critiques might not take "a radical, progressive, or even liberal position on gender, sexuality, or other issues. ... [Because] in practice, queerness has been more ideologically inclusive" (2000: 7). However, in the early 2000s queer cinema scholarship increasingly understands inclusivity as a push to value radical nonnormativity, recuperating past practices and forms, to counter the universalizing discourses that exist alongside the minoritizing tendencies Eve Sedgwick points to as one of the paradoxes of queerness (1994). This form of inclusivity runs counter to the increased visibility and claims of normality presented in mainstream representations of queerness. From a marketing standpoint gay and lesbian cinema includes any film about or featuring LGBTQ+ characters. Producing films marketed to a broad LGBTQ+ community contains its own set of norms that are often specific to production/distribution outlets. Filmmaker Jon Garcia has made a two-film cycle beginning in 2012 (*The Falls* and *The Falls: Testament of Love*) that allegorically casts Mormonism alongside gayness. While making the second film, which was funded by the self-identified LGBT production house Breaking Glass Pictures, Garcia was encouraged to increase the amount of sex in the film and to pursue set and costume designs that would appeal to a wealthier audience demographic by including in-kind donations from Banana Republic (Garcia 2015).

This anecdotal example of a recognizable homonormative style dominated by conceptions of white gayness is not the exclusive realm of male-dominated, mainstream, or independent narratives. Films that value homonormativity also exist in trans- and lesbian-focused narratives in mainstream and independent cinema. Typical of these stories, the most successful of which is Lisa Cholodenko's *The Kids Are All Right* (2010), *Kiss Me* (2011), a Swedish film directed by Alexandra-Therese Keining, adapts the opposites-attract trope of classic romantic comedies within a multigenerational story that depicts the dramatic coming to terms of Mia's father with her choice to leave her male fiancée for her father's soon-to-be second wife's daughter, Frida, an artistic, assured lesbian. Like *The Falls*, the film trades on a desire for acceptance and so-called normality within a privileged and apparently socially democratic Swedish family whose father's reluctance to accept his daughter's desires is the only danger in the Nordic-designed on-screen world. By film's end, the emotionally anxious Mia returns to her role as part of a couple, soothed by Frida's self-confidence, so that the coupling between the two is portrayed as a betrayal, but one whose result is ultimately a recoupling and return to a sun-dappled normality. Keining's and Garcia's films help us to see how a market-driven, character-focused LGBT cinema may now stand apart from a conceptualization in which "queer/queerness [is] related to the word's ability to describe those complex circumstances in texts, spectators, and production that resist easy categorization, but that definitely escape or defy the heteronomarmative" (Doty 2000: 7).

This understanding of queerness in film studies has only sharpened as we move further into cinema's second century. In their call to "Let copulation thrive," Matthew Hays and Thomas Waugh celebrate queer cinema studies as a subdiscipline that must deploy methods and theories that reflect the non-axiomatic "volatility of our objects and corpuses, [to] remain as eclectic, incoherent, and promiscuous as they are" (2014: 132). Hays and Waugh advocate for methods of study that ultimately value hybridity and seek in queer cinema studies a critical mindset also found in recent work that expands on questions of race, ethnicity, and European identities in order to push against a perceived normativity located in gay and lesbian studies. Nick Rees-Robert expressively uses queer to title his *French Queer Cinema* to highlight an alternative to what he sees as "a celebratory (white, middle class) 'gay pride' rendition of French cinema' (2008: 5). Similarly, Chris Perriam differentiates between queer and LGBT cinema by arguing that films, filmmakers, and audience have built a new Spanish queer cinema that moves away from what he terms "'cine-gay' ... a form of cinema which—while appearing to give visibility and kudos—obscures and closes off the routes to commitment and alternative cultural development, and is in that sense, anti-queer" (2013: 5). The anti-queerness read in a cinema of "gay pride" or a "cine-gay" reflects a turn in film studies to distinguish between queer cinema's politically inflected performativity and a cinema driven by positive representations for LGBTQ+ and so-called mainstream communities. This difference is chronicled in both scholarship about Western

European cinemas, many of which have a long history of representing queer lives on screen, and in the work of the AsiaPacifiQueer Network and subsequent scholarship that aims to de-Westernize queer Asian cinema studies (Yue 2014: 146).

As part of neoliberalism's drive to economize all aspects of our existence (Brown 2015: 17), LGBTQ+ "pride" is increasingly connected to neoliberalism's fusion of capitalism with rights discourse in service of a politics of normalization that privileges market dynamics. For instance, for many queer activists the marriage equality debate marks an occasion to examine how LGBTQ+ rights discourse has shifted from championing a radical form of inclusion and hybridity to a politics of normalization (Duggan 2002: 175–94; Herz and Johansson 2015: 1009–20; Boellstorff 2007: 227–48). Queer cultural critic Michael Warner considers normalization an ethics of shame that believes that to "overcome stigma [is] to win acceptance by the dominant culture" (1999: 50). Even as we trace a history of cinematic institutions that serve marginalized audiences, the harnessing of LGBTQ+ rights with neoliberalism's push to create markets yields an increasing number of specialized LGBTQ+ film and video producers/distributors/exhibitors as well as the inclusion of LGBTQ+ as a common VoD "genre." For example, Wolfe Video specializes in "mainstreaming films with gay content" through theatrical/festival distribution, DVD sales, and an online VoD platform.

Queerness recognized in the counter cinema practices of art and avant-garde cinema helps differentiate between queer cinema and an LGBTQ+ cinema that mainstreams LGBTQ+ identities. LGBTQ+ cinema draws from classical Hollywood style—narrative closure, spatial and temporal coherence, and a cause and effect plot—to build mainstream and community-oriented films that work to normalize LGBTQ+ characters. This classical mode of filmmaking values cinematic texts as a site in which the individual is featured, drawn, and offered as iconic representations addressed to community members and their allies who desire to see versions of themselves on screen. Here we can think of how such mainstream and independent films as *Pariah* (Rees, 2010), *Transamerica* (Tucker, 2005), and *Making Love* (Hiller, 1982) share a similar impulse to normalize an individual's identity within a community that views her/his gender identity as an aberration. Although each of the films mentioned above display one or more of the queer film attributes Alexander Doty identifies (2000: 6), ahistorically identifying them as queer becomes more difficult as the concept of cinematic queerness (re-)explores its deviant aesthetic and political potential.

One argument to be made, then, is that film scholars now see LGBTQ+ cinema as that which has taken on the attributes of twenty-first century market-driven representations, while contemporary queer cinema and its scholarship recovers an activist history of radical politics and aesthetics. Recent work about R.W. Fassbinder by David Rhodes and Ronald Gregg signals how new questions and configurations emerge around canonical queer films when scholars recover this history with methods of analysis drawn from queer studies. Rhodes reads the style of Fassbinder's Sirkian period and his *Fox and His Friends* (1975) as an expression of queer on-set and cultural labor. Fassbinder, via Rhodes, draws our eyes to his films' mise-en-scène to activate the on-set labor effaced by classical style. He provides an equation for how style and its labor are endemic to queer culture: "labor produces style and style records forms of specific labor; queer laborers have often (and notoriously) worked to produce style, and in doing so, have made labor a mode of queer world-building" (2012: 195–6). Rhodes argues that although questions concerning labor are often Marxism's purview, in this case, queer labor is closeted, requiring a queer methodology for reading cultural signs.

German cinema's engagement with homosexuality and queerness is not a recent development but one with a unique lineage representing "unconventional sexualities as allegorical, ornate, and enigmatic" from the gender-ambiguous Weimar period to the present (Kuzniar 2000: 1). Considering the nomadic, animated dykes in the short films of Claudia Zoller and Stefanie Jordan among other queer representations, Alice Kuzniar suggests, "if sexuality is contingently determined via word or image, the role played by an art or experimental cinema is crucial for fantasizing and promoting alternative representations" (ibid. 5). And in *Queer Cinema in Europe* Robin Griffiths asserts the subversive potential of deviance to show that "political and representational agency dovetails with the radical innovations of European 'Avant-garde' and 'Art-house' filmmaking to synthesize a common cause" (2008: 16). It is perhaps not surprising that much of the cinema that Griffiths, Perriam, and Rees-Robert read as pushing back against "pride," is made within independent, underground, or counter cinema traditions or explicitly engages with the naturalness of deviance as Lucía Puenzo does in the Argentinian *XXY* (2007).

Alice Kuzniar's work also calls to mind Richard Dyer's argument that queerness and noir were made for one another's surreptitious, uncertain natures (Dyer 2002). She privileges the performance of a queer style in queer German cinema's

> baroque display and theatricality that paradoxically hides as much as it reveals ... remind[ing] its viewer that sexual difference is not always something one can see; by disrupting and scotomizing the optic register, it challenges the accepted notion that cinema discloses and makes visible empirical reality.
>
> *(Kuzniar 2000: 5)*

Because of its ability to build worlds that participate in unique temporal and spatial relationships, the cinema is a distinct site in which the hybridity of queerness' radical and/or artful aesthetic may be practiced and actualized for spectators. As such, Leo Bersani and Ulysses Dutoit's analysis of how cinema can make not just duality but indeterminacy visible on screen is an important touchstone for queer cinema scholarship. They propose a form of aesthetic subjecthood visible in contemporary art cinema that suggestively reflects Judith Butler's arguments about performativity and repetition. Aesthetic subjecthood is a "renewable retreat from the seriousness of stable identities and settled being" that activates performance-based gender at the expense of gender as an identity-based foundational category (Bersani and Dutoit 2004: 9).

Remarking on performance, however, we should keep in mind that Butler differentiates between performativity and expression to explain how performativity is a ritualized repetition, "often ... of oppressive and painful gender norms to force them to resignify. This is not freedom, but a question of how to work the trap that one is inevitably in" (1992: 83). Her argument is not that one performs gender via an external stylization of the self even if that is one way her ideas have been received within increasingly comfortable, gender-fluid publics. Understanding Butler this way allows for the expression of identity via style without addressing how alternative representations often reinforce a consumer cloaking of reproduced cultural norms that fail to disrupt practices and foundational categories of identity.

Bersani and Dutoit demonstrate how art cinema images and their formal analysis are evidence of new connections of time, space, and matter, allowing them to "propose the implausibility of individuality" (2004: 6). Writing about Godard's 1993 *Oh, Woe is Me*, for example, they isolate his ability to multiply a single character by using a basic in-camera edit that appears as a jump cut: "she doesn't move from one position to another, rather, she simultaneously disappears and reoccurs to the side of herself" (ibid. 4). In the films they write about, none of which overtly concern gender or sexuality,

> the multiplication of being depends on a lessening of psychic subject-hood. More exactly, our reappearances as (mere) appearances depend on a certain type of withdrawal from realised being, a withdrawal we will associate with an aesthetic (rather than a psychological) subject.
>
> *(ibid. 6)*

Their focus on film's aesthetic and stylistic abilities is especially important when considering how cinema may manifest the flexibility of queer theory because, as they point out, narrative cinema's use of film stars and its focus on the individual character more than any other art celebrates the "primordial importance of individuality" (ibid. 8). This, they argue, is ripe for destabilization via formal reminders of cinema's ability to demonstrate how "the multiplication of the individual's positionality in the universe is, necessarily, a lessening or even a loss of individuality. We are not as distinct subjectivities but rather as that which gives appearances to different modes or functions of being" (ibid. 5).

An aesthetic subject is one that retreats from stable identities and asks that time, space, and matter are perceived to be in performance rather than representational. Subjecthood perceived in this way values practice over signification. Here I borrow from Karen Barad's work on performativity in which she argues that matter must be considered as much as its representation in discursive conceptions of the world. For Barad, "a performative understanding of discursive practices challenges ... the belief in the ontological distinction between representations and that which they purport to represent; in particular, that which is represented is held to be independent of all practices of representing" (2003: 802, 804). The ontological gap Barad points to between things and their images are manifest in the way art cinema and avant-garde cinematic practices participate in and display the mechanisms by which their diegetic worlds are created.

Like Bersani and Dutoit, Nick Davis's theorization of a desiring-image is less about applying queer theory to cinema and more about locating queer's fundamental "open-ended variation" within images (2013: 8). Davis articulates a Deleuzian-centered understanding of desire as a late-twentieth-century image regime on par with the movement- and time-images, insofar as each is a "constitutive dimension of *all* cinematic images" (ibid.). To ease the strictures of gay and lesbian representational politics that have historically played out between the poles of positive and realistic portrayals, Davis describes how "desire generates itself in endless permutations, stressing how framing, editing, mixing, and other formal techniques perform the work of desiring-production" (ibid.17). The desiring-image does not assign or elicit desire from characters. Instead, like the movement- and time-images, the desiring-image "goads us to rethink perception, relation, and collectivity as aesthetic and also political precepts" on the basis of desire's ability to flow unheeded (ibid.7). Distinct from the previous two image regimes, the new relations that arise from spectatorial rethinking are not the products of rational thought, but instead arise from desire as a means by which to reimagine a spectatorial "filling-in" or conjoining of images grounded in a politics of difference that "interrogates its own terms, goals, and presumed constituents" (ibid. 18, 9). The non-linear flows and construction of fluid constituencies Davis locates in the desiring-image reflect his understanding of production as the basis of desire and of cinema (ibid. 15).

He concludes that although "desire obeys firmly sexed, gendered, and object-oriented structures in most films, this preponderance does not define desire or banish its queerer potentials from abiding even in films that superficially refuse them" (Davis 2013: 15). He thus encourages readings of queer texts as not necessarily those made by and for queer audiences. Unlike previous queerings that applied a camp sensibility or located queer cultural connotations, Davis queers by invoking Deleuze:

> desire does not take as its object persons or things, but the entire surroundings that it traverses, the vibrations and flows of every sort to which it is joined, introducing therein breaks and captures—an always nomadic and migrant desire.
>
> *(Deleuze 1972: 292 quoted in Davis 2013: 15)*

Instead of seeing queer cinema as part of an identity-based project, Davis argues that identity in any form is counterproductive to understanding how the very queerness of desire restructures cinema's ability to represent. Rather than a perceptual system determined by a perceiving agent, the desiring-image removes that agent and in doing so shifts a classical cinematic focus rooted in identity to that of an image regime that presents the possibility, as Bersani and Dutoit describe, for "a renewable retreat from the seriousness of stable identities and settled being" (2004: 9). Davis's desiring-image celebrates desire as a mode of being—where being is a process rather than a state—for the cinematic image. The queer desiring-image offers an alternative to the stable individual with its disparate field of desire.

Davis employs Deleuze and Guattari's concept of minor art to escape the cyclical arguments concerning the politics of identity and a gay and lesbian cinema "of iconic 'representation'" (2013: 9). Queer filmmaking is a minor art not only because it is produced by culturally marginalized members of a major culture. Similar to other minor artists, the queer filmmakers he names—David Cronenberg, Rodney Evans, and Claire Denis, among others:

> politicize sense and syntax from their usual frameworks; politicizing these renegotiated structures; and endowing them with a collective value, less on behalf of existing "minorities" than for new coalitions that they catalyze among the oppressed and invisible, along previously unrecognizable lines.
>
> *(ibid. 5)*

It is the creation of new coalitions and the preponderance of desire both as an act depicted on screen and as the mode of thinking via which spectators make sense of formal and narrative juxtapositions that differentiate queer cinema from LGBTQ+ cinemas.

The destabilization of the individual to question the singularity of identity is the primary motivation behind queer cinema studies' resurgent valuing of practice over representation. This recurrent force reflects the ebb and flow of radical politics and the fight for recognition for LGBTQ+ communities and effectively illustrates Sedgwick's conceptualization of the universalizing and minoritizing tendencies in queer theory (1990, 1994). Refracted through the concerns of cinema studies, this fight is now translated into the question of whether performativity and its accompanying destabilization of images offers a possibility for queer theory's indeterminacy to join with avant-garde and art cinema practices. In doing so, the stakes of stable identities are highlighted even when these identities are portrayed in films that provide marginalized communities with self-recognition. While the radical politics of the NQC generation may have faded, they have been transmuted into queer cinema studies' engagement with the perceptual affects available in questioning how emergent images and their objects relate to one another.

Related topics

Rachel A. Lewis "Lesbian cinema postfeminism: ageism, difference, and desire"
Eliza Steinbock, "Towards trans cinema"

Bibliography

Aaron, M. (2004) "New Queer Cinema: An Introduction." In M. Aaron (ed.) *New Queer Cinema: A Critical Reader*. New Brunswick, NJ: Rutgers University Press, pp. 3–14.

Barad, K. (2003) "Posthumanist Performativity: Toward an Understanding of How Matter Comes to Matter." *Signs: Journal of Women in Culture and Society*, 28(3), pp. 801–31.

Bersani, L. and Dutoit, U. (2004) *Forms of Being: Cinema, Aesthetics, Subjectivity*. London: BFI.

Boellstorff, T. (2007) "When Marriage Falls: Queer Coincidences in Straight Time." *GLQ: A Journal of Lesbian and Gay Studies*, 13(2), pp. 227–48.

Brown, W. (2015) *Undoing the Demos: Neoliberalism's Stealth Revolution*. Cambridge, MA: The MIT Press.

Butler, J. (1992) "The Body You Want: Liz Kotz interviews Judith Butler." *Artforum*, 31(3), pp. 82–189.

Davis, N. (2013) *The Desiring-Image: Gilles Deleuze and Contemporary Queer Cinema*. Oxford: Oxford University Press.

Doty, A. (2000) *Flaming Classics: Queering the Film Canon*. New York: Routledge.

Duggan, L. (2002) "The New Normatively: The Sexual Politics of Neoliberalism." In R. Castronovo and D. Nelson, eds. *Materializing Democracy: Toward A Revitalized Cultural Politics*. Durham, NC: Duke University Press, pp. 174–94.

Dyer, R. (2002) "Queer Noir." In R. Dyer *The Culture of Queers*. New York: Routledge, pp. 90–113.

Garcia, J. (2015) *Professions in Queer Cinema*. Lecture to FILM 370: Queer Cinema, Portland State University. May 11.

Gregg, R. (2012) "Fassbinder's *Fox and his Friends* and Gay Politics in the 1970s." In B. Puecker, ed. *A Companion to Rainer Werner Fassbinder*. London: Wiley-Blackwell, pp. 564–78.

Griffin, S. and Benshoff, H. M. eds. (2004) *Queer Cinema: The Film Reader*. New York: Routledge.

Griffiths, R. ed. (2008). *Queer Cinema in Europe*. Bristol, UK: Intellect Books.

Hall, D. E. and Jagose, A. (2013) Introduction. In D. E. Hall *et al.*, eds. *The Routledge Queer Studies Reader*. London: Routledge, pp. xiv–xxi.

Hays, M. and Waugh, T. (2014) "Six Crises." *Cinema Journal*, 53(2), 126–32.

Herz, M. and Johansson, T. (2015) "The Normativity of the Concept of Heteronormativity." *Journal of Homosexuality*, 62(8), pp. 1009–20.

Jagose, A. (1997) *Queer Theory: An Introduction*. New York, NY: New York University Press.

Jarman, D. (2011) *Smiling in Slow Motion*. Minneapolis: University of Minnesota Press.

Kuzniar, A. A. (2000) *The Queer German Cinema*. Stanford, CA: Stanford University Press.

Nowlan, B. (2010) "Queer Theory, Queer Cinema." In J. A. C. Juett and D. Jones, eds. *Coming Out To The Mainstream: New Queer Cinema In The 21st Century*. Newcastle upon Tyne: Cambridge Scholars, pp. 2–19.

Perriam, C. (2013) *Spanish Queer Cinema*. Edinburgh: Edinburgh University Press.

Pierson, J. (2014) *Spike, Mike, Slackers, and Dykes: A Guided Tour Across a Decade of American Independent Cinema*. Austin: University of Texas Press.

Rees-Roberts, N. (2008) *French Queer Cinema*. Edinburgh: Edinburgh University Press.

Rhodes, J. D. (2012) "Fassbinder's Work: Style, Sirk, and Queer Labor." In B. Puecker, ed. *A Companion to Rainer Werner Fassbinder*. London: Wiley-Blackwell, pp. 181–203.

Rich, B. R. (2013) *New Queer Cinema: The Director's Cut*. Durham, NC: Duke University Press.

Russo, V. (1981) *The Celluloid Closet: Homosexuality in the Movies*. New York: Harper Collins.

Sedgwick, E. (1990) *Epistemology of the Closet*. Berkeley, CA: University of California Press.

——— (1994) *Tendencies*. New York, NY: Routledge.

Stacey, J. and Street, S. (2007) "Introduction." In J. Stacey and S. Street, eds. *Queer Screen: A Screen Reader*. London: Routledge, pp. 1–18.

Warner, M. (1999). *The Trouble with Normal: Sex, Politics, and the Ethics of Queer Life*. Cambridge, MA: Harvard University Press.

Yue, A. (2014) "Queer Asian Cinema and Media Studies: From Hybridity to Critical Regionality." *Cinema Journal*, 53(2), pp. 145–51.

PART II

Genres, modes, stars

This section considers film form (genres and modes of cinematic expression), as well as the most visible figure of the cinematic screen—the movie star—in the context of critical approaches to gender. Yvonne Tasker examines masculinity and race as they undergird the action film, war film, and the Western. Along similar lines, Anthony Hayt turns to the examination of gender in the slasher remakes, particularly in the context of post-9/11 cultural shifts and representations of motherhood and the family unit. Hilary Radner discusses the trajectory of one of the most recognized genres of women's film—the chick flick—while Belinda Smaill highlights documentaries as one of the most productive sites of feminist filmmaking.

Constance Penley, Celine Parreñas Shimizu, Mireille Miller-Young, and Tristan Taormino's essay calls for the need to de-stigmatize porn, while offering an introduction to the field of feminist porn and porn studies (their essay is a slightly revised reprint of their introduction to the important volume *The Feminist Porn Book* [2013]). Margaret Hennefeld turns to the past and recuperates female slapstick comediennes from historical oblivion, while Julie Grossman turns her focus to one of the most recognizable iterations of women in film—the *femme fatale*—showing how the figure continues to do important cultural work in films such as *Clouds of Sils Maria*. Maureen Turim focuses on women's experimental film, and highlights the work of Jodie Mack, Shirin Neshat, and Eija-Liisa Ahtila. Finally, Russell Meeuf looks at the current trends in transnational stardom (as distinct from the earlier versions of international stardom) through the case studies of Jackie Chan and Jason Statham.

Together, these essays illustrate various prominent discussions in feminist film studies that pertain to genres, modes, and start texts. While many of the essays offer overviews of some key debates in their respective areas, their focus is on diagnosing the current state of the field when it comes to the ongoing shifts in the interplay between gender and genre, film form and politics, as well as between movie stardom and the globalized flows of media texts.

10

CONTESTED MASCULINITIES

The action film, the war film, and the Western

Yvonne Tasker

Action, war movies, and Westerns have all been characterized as generic sites that are in some fundamental way *about* masculinity and it is certainly the case that these three interlinked genres provide an extraordinarily fruitful site for exploring codes of masculinity in Hollywood cinema. War, Western, and action films typically center on male protagonists and male groups. Plentiful examples of these genres feature provocative or challenging female characters—from Ripley in the *Alien* (Ridley Scott, 1979) series to Vienna, Joan Crawford's gun-wielding saloon owner in *Johnny Guitar* (Nicholas Ray, 1954)—and these can be usefully framed in terms of either female masculinity or long standing formulations of tough, resilient femininity. However, the genres' characteristic scenes of action, endurance, and violence offer iconic images of male strength and resilience which elaborate an idealized masculinity. Male mobility is a central trope of all three genres, one which repeatedly couples physical movement or scenes of action with themes of independence. The hero desires the freedom to move, challenging individuals, groups, and circumstances that present obstacles to such freedom; in some ways it is this tension or conflict that generates the narrative. Moral and physical strength are conflated in multiple ways through—diversely—the soldier's sacrificial heroism, the command of nature associated with the Western hero and the action hero's heightened/fantastical physical abilities. Each operates in different yet related ways across frontiers, a motif which serves to mark the mobility of the masculine hero. In this chapter I explore some of the visual and narrative strategies which delineate masculinity in different ways across these generic spaces. In framing issues such as violence and freedom of movement, paternalism and duty, hierarchies and teamwork, I aim to acknowledge both continuities and differences between and across these genres.

In the broadest terms the Western deals with the formation of America, its articulation of masculine identity bound up with the establishment of white male authority over territory and peoples that seemingly require subjection. National discourses of masculinity are central to the war film too of course, even those which adopt a less than patriotic stance towards a particular conflict (one thinks of war films such as *Apocalypse Now!* [Francis Ford Coppola, 1979]). Both Westerns and war films are action genres, with prominence accorded to scenes of combat and pursuit. Yet they are also frequently elegiac in tone, with narratives that are marked by loss as much as celebrating victory. Action too, although it has progressively trimmed scenes of reflection in favor of the chase, retains something of this loss, a vulnerability often expressed via the body of the hero. Indeed although these genres have long been understood as culturally conservative, tending to support a racial and gendered hierarchy that privileges white masculinity, scholars have nonetheless found considerable complexity and ideological nuance at work across the Western, war and action film (Kitzes 2007; Basinger 2003; Tasker 1993).

Myths of white masculinity in the Western

In his 1954 essay "Movie Chronicle: The Westerner" Robert Warshow wrote that the values of the Western are expressed "in the image of a single man who wears a gun on his thigh" (Warshow 1964: 105). The compelling and evocative myth of the Western hero centers on the frontier (a battle for territory) and depends on violence; it involves a white American masculinity which is deemed necessary for the formation of a lawful community, and thus the definition of the nation, but which cannot be fully incorporated. It is the violence of the hero that fascinates and troubles the society of which he is part. Whether an outlaw (*Stagecoach*, John Ford, 1939), isolated (*High* Noon, Fred Zinnemann, 1952), or an outsider (*The Wild Bunch*, Sam Pekinpah, 1968), the potential for violence points to the uncertain position of the Western hero. Such conflict is expressed through a Western set piece such as the gunfight staged through the main street of a small town—violence visible in the heart of a new community.

Western and war films certainly celebrate white masculinity and the violence with which it is associated. Yet these genres also explore the complexity inherent in stories of violence. Warshow writes that "The Westerner at his best exhibits a moral ambiguity which darkens his image and saves him from absurdity; this ambiguity arises from the fact that, whatever his justifications, he is a killer of men" (1964: 95). The justification referred to here is most often that male violence is required by circumstance rather than being actively sought out. The male hero may be drawn into violence on behalf of others or his nation; he protects and sacrifices or is willing to sacrifice himself. To some extent paternalism figures as little more than a pretext for the hero's propensity to violence (as perhaps a film such as *Taken* [Pierre Morel, 2008] might be read) yet in films such as *The Searchers* (John Ford, 1956) (much discussed in film studies over the decades) critics have argued that there is more nuance at work than a simple scenario of racial hatred and revenge. While Warshow is not explicitly concerned with questions of masculinity, it is clear that his resonant image of the "single man who wears a gun on his thigh" expresses a particular idea of manhood. The masculinity of the Western hero is embodied, suggestive of violence and of a disconnection from society.

It is a tenet of scholarship on the Western that the hero's violence is necessary to the establishment of a community that cannot comfortably assimilate him. *The Man Who Shot Liberty Valence* (John Ford, 1962) elegantly explores this dichotomy. The film's action turns on lawyer hero Ransom Stoddard (James Stewart) who has the courage to stand up against violence (embodied in the brutal form of Liberty Valance), yet whose subsequent political career is underpinned by an act of violence incorrectly attributed to him. It is Tom Doniphon's (John Wayne) covert shot that both saves Stoddard's life and builds his reputation. While this is of course intensely ironic, a parable of masculine myth-making, Stoddard does indeed demonstrate bravery throughout the film; his defense of the law and willingness to sacrifice himself for its values underpins the community's perverse willingness to bestow authority on him as a reward for violence. The film's splitting of moral and physical authority over the two male leads underlines the genre's more usual conflation of the two. It also draws out the extent to which the Western hero played by Wayne is an outsider, a positioning that *The Searchers* encapsulates in its framing of Ethan Edwards (also played by Wayne) on his arrival at the homestead (Figure 10.1).

The Western is replete with "land and horses" writes Warshow (1964: 93), symbolism that evokes the possibility of movement within a natural space that conveys both freedom and isolation. Writers such as Jim Kitzes (2007) have understood the Western in terms of an organizing symbolic framework, drawing out an overarching opposition between the wilderness (nature) and civilization (the emerging communities of the western United States). The Western exploits nature as visual spectacle and as a setting for conflict, its subjection or loss, a theme expressed in terms of enclosure (arable/cattle), technology (horses/trains), and genocide (the subjection, even eradication, of indigenous peoples). Action genres of all varieties feature lone heroes, men unbounded by ties of family or community. This is the cliché of the westerner, the man apart, a figure who sits more harmoniously in the natural landscape than within the boundaries of an emergent community with its rules and confinement. Such outsider iconography pervades not just the Western; indeed it underpins the action cinema that emerged in the 1970s and 1980s, its heroic figures demonstrating physical strength or endurance while remaining very much at odds with structures of authority. *Dirty Harry* (Don Siegel, 1971) is clearly legible in this frame, Clint Eastwood's central character serving for Eric Lichtenfeld as "the action film's first true archetype" (2007: 23). The characterization of traumatized Vietnam veteran John Rambo, protagonist of a series of successful action films through the 1980s beginning with *First Blood*

Figure 10.1　*The Searchers* encapsulates in the framing of Ethan Edwards (John Wayne) the outsider status of the Western hero.

Source: The Searchers, John Ford, 1956.

(Ted Kotcheff, 1982) draws on both war and Western iconography. Here genre conventions such as the warrior unable to renounce war, and the hero who is more at home in the wild, frame a scenario of violent action brought home to America, and present a masculinity that is fundamentally unstable.

Masculinity, comradeship, war

The hero of the war film too is an ambivalent figure, his nurtured capacity for violence both vital to the survival of the unit (if not the hero himself) and yet ensuring a separation from the values and routine of peaceful society. This said, it is interesting that the American war film consolidates as a genre in relation to World War II, a conflict conducted overseas and conventionally coded in terms of ideological goals rather than national interest (the rhetoric of the "good war"). Given the extraordinary losses and societal upheaval of the civil war, say, or the war of independence, we might expect these conflicts to be staples of Hollywood cinema. That they are not is suggestive of the need for a certain distance to sustain evocative narratives of masculine action. Thus the Western presents the violence that formed America as myth, while the war film locates that violence at a geographical remove. The modern action film is rather more generalized, defined not so much by setting as mode, its violence a source of spectacle and narrative urgency.

The war film presents military masculinity as adherence to a shared set of values, produced through the collective effort of training (whether depicted or not), coordinated by and around inspiring male leaders (*Paths of Glory* [Stanley Kubrick, 1957], *Sands of Iwo Jima* [Allan Dwan, 1949], even *Platoon* [Oliver Stone, 1986]). Teamwork and comradeship define the military masculinity of the war film. In contrast to the symbolism of land and horses and the freedom of mobility of the Western hero, the military unit is subject to discipline and constraint. This contrast is further apparent in the stance of soldiers in combat, repeatedly portrayed in crouching posture, low in the landscape. In war movies men advance (or at times retreat) cautiously, working together to survive in threatening landscapes. Moreover the violence of battle is punctuated by periods of stasis and boredom allowing interludes for the development of characters. Narratives that trace the progress towards becoming a solider effectively articulate a gendered rite of passage, becoming a man. What constitutes that manhood? The key elements include an appreciation of necessary violence, the suppression, but not eradication of emotion, a willingness to sacrifice oneself for larger goals and, in effect, for the nation.

If male partnerships and male groups with their particular hierarchical dynamic operate as a familiar feature of all three genres considered here, it is the war film in particular that tends to frame masculinity in the context of the group. The conventions of the American war movie, and the particular character of World War II combat film, have been extensively explored within film studies. Jeanine Basinger (2003) outlines the development of the form, identifying its first definitive articulation in *Bataan* (Tay Garnett, 1943). Basinger suggests that the hero of the combat film typically has the responsibilities of leadership forced onto him in some way—his responsibilities are acquired rather than sought out. This convention is continued in the modern action hero who does not look for the violent and dangerous positions in which s/he finds her/himself, but is equipped to deal with them as though s/he is perpetually ready for action. In both war and subsequently action films the hero is precisely the individual whose masculinity makes him (or her) suited to respond to challenges when they arise and to bring a capacity for violence into use.

John Wayne's Sergeant Stryker in *Sands of Iwo Jima* speaks to the particular character of the war film's military masculinity. Stryker is an outstanding and experienced soldier who is shown to be an effective leader. He is also a loner, violent and alcoholic. His personal pain (estrangement from his wife and son) is the clear cost of the very qualities that make him a successful soldier. While the battles provide the action focus of the film, *Sands of Iwo Jima* centers on Stryker's efforts to train a squad of Marines. "I'm gonna' get the job done," snarls Stryker in his first address to the squad, signaling his toughness and determination. Generational tensions subsequently emerge between Stryker as trainer/father figure and his reluctant squad, with Private Pete Conway (John Agar) explicitly rejecting the model of masculine distance and discipline that Stryker represents for him. These differences are ultimately resolved through the rigors of combat; in battle both Conway and Al Thomas (Forrest Tucker), overcome their initial hostility and learn that Stryker's methods are designed to keep them alive. That formulations of white American masculinity require the suppression of emotion is underlined via the hostility Stryker faces from the men he trains and then leads. Indeed, the very moment in which the men show their respect and even love for their leader is the moment at which he is unexpectedly killed, his death ensuring that a capacity for violence is passed on to a younger man who leads the team forwards. The poignancy (and shock) of Stryker's death is linked to the transformation he has effected in his men, as well as the transformation of Stryker himself (in the moment before his death he seems more connected with others than at any other point, happy even). It is almost a cliché of action cinema that such personal connections make the hero vulnerable. In a related manner the hero's violence is seen in part to be driven by loss, whether of a comrade or a loved one, such that affection becomes associated with death in action genres.

The war film's articulation of a veteran damaged by conflict echoes the overarching themes of the consequences of violence via its displacement beyond the confines of war. In the post-war period a greater number of Hollywood films featured an increasing ambivalence towards authority, with the action hero a figure willing to break rules to achieve the required goal. The characterization of heroes who are both violent and psychologically troubled or damaged would also become a more prominent feature of action genres. Robert Eberwein positions *Sands of Iwo Jima* as one among a group of films of the late 1940s in which heroes are presented as "psychologically troubled men." For Eberwein such retrospective war films involved "complicated examinations of leadership and authority" (2010: 23). Thus while a critic such as Thomas Doherty describes *Sands of Iwo Jima* as exemplifying hollow patriotism in its "sanitized guts and glory" (1999: 272), the film nonetheless depends on what is in effect a generic trope by which authority is first questioned and then (partially) legitimized. Stryker's benevolent tyranny and his men's resistance to it pose the question of what it is to be a man.

None of this is to suggest that war films (or indeed action films more broadly) are in some coherent way resisting the idealization of tough masculinity that was exemplified by Wayne in many of his roles. Rather it is to echo Warshow's understanding, discussed above in relation to the Western, that a violent hero is perhaps inevitably ambiguous. Differing scenes of violence or conflict, whether generic locations or different periods of a genre's development, draw that ambiguity out to a greater or lesser degree. Thus we can trace patterns over time or across the different inflections of war stories and Western films (films around the Iraq war as opposed to World War II; Western narratives of new agriculture or the expansion of the railways as opposed to those concerned with the precarious character of frontier law). Despite this vast generic range however, and while much about what it is to be a white man in America is explored with nuance that belies the familiarity of convention, neither the necessity of violence nor its centrality to formulations of white masculinity comes into question. Considering Warshow's perception of ambiguity via more recent feminist scholarship on masculinity we can add that the melancholic emphasis on male loss which frames the Western and the war film operates both to expose and re-secure male authority.

In the war film it is the interaction between comrades rather more than combat with enemies that forms character, in large part since enemies are frequently presented in crude undifferentiated terms. The platoon is founded on teamwork and the platoon movie is an essay in forging that team, often in the process playing out a metaphor for the nation. As Richard Slotkin observes, the cliché of the war film's multi-racial roll-call "expresses a myth of American nationality that remains vital in our political and cultural life: the idealized self-image of a multi-ethnic, multiracial democracy, hospitable to difference but united by a common sense of national belonging" (2001: 469). At the same time the multi-racial unit presented in *Bataan*, at odds with the segregated practices of the day, is, as Slotkin makes clear, constituted through a virulent racism directed towards the Japanese enemy. Thus the rituals of inclusivity enacted in *Bataan* and still familiar to contemporary viewers are premised on a deep contradiction; seeking "to overthrow American racism by appealing to the most basic American racialist myth, the myth of 'savage war'" (ibid. 483).

The war film's rendition of American masculinity reveals the relative construction of idealized manhood, contrasting different members of a team. If the hero is a soldier who is skilled in combat, understanding of risk, and protective in a paternalistic manner of those about him/her, the war film is also a genre that acknowledges the costs of these talents. Learning to kill is a recurrent theme, hence the training format whereby a seasoned officer inducts inexperienced or less experienced soldiers into teamwork and death. The possibility that a soldier may be too fond of death emerges consistently in Hollywood films of the 1950s. The protagonist of *Hell is for Heroes* (Don Siegel, 1962), for instance, is numbed by the prospect of returning home; he is reinvigorated by the news that the troops are to head once more into battle. The graphic violence (remarked on by contemporary critics and the office of the Production Code Administration) by which the death of German soldiers is portrayed, as well as the general cynicism towards the competence of those in command, suggests a war film that at least acknowledges the negative aspects of the violent military masculinity idealized in many examples of the genre (see Tasker 2015).

Racial discourse and the contested masculinities of action cinema

The strength, bravery, resourcefulness, and resilience associated with the white male heroes of Westerns and war films feeds the later development of the Hollywood action film. Both the Westerns of the classical Hollywood years and the World War II film that emerged as a coherent set of conventions through the 1940s operate as genres that center on and effectively celebrate white masculinity. The trend towards group or multiple protagonist action movies, already evident in 1960s hits such as *The Magnificent Seven* (John Sturges, 1960), and *The Dirty Dozen* (Robert Aldrich, 1967), has allowed greater space for diversity, albeit typically in the form of a multi-racial or multi-ethnic group organized around a white guy.

Black masculinities have most often been elaborated in Hollywood cinema via supporting roles; despite my comments above, African-American and Latino characters are figures rather than leaders in multi-protagonist formats. The twenty-first century proliferation of superhero films, for example, draws on a comic book iconography that incorporates but marginalizes black heroism (War Machine in relation to Iron Man for instance, or Storm in contrast to Wolverine), a relationship that the film franchises replicate. Periodic speculation as to the possibility of displacing white men as the stars of other high profile action franchises, notably the James Bond films, underlines how fixed these associations remain. Thus Angelina Jolie's turn as Evelyn Salt in *Salt* (Phillip Noyce, 2010) was framed as her rendition of Bond (with much media comment to the effect that the role had initially been written with a male star in mind), while periodic arguments for a Black Bond have attracted little momentum to date.

As action emerged as a genre in its own right during the 1980s it has functioned as a space that has allowed African-American, Latino, and Asian performers to take center stage. To what extent has this begun to shift the genre's framing of male masculinity? Iconic white male stars of Western and war films such as John Wayne and, rather later, Clint Eastwood, suggest the ways in which these genres mythicized a terse and tough formulation of American masculinity; the action star personas of Will Smith, Vin Diesel and Dwayne Johnson demonstrate the range of African-American and multi-racial action bodies and masculinities on contemporary Hollywood screens.

What sort of action masculinity is at work here? What cultural myths are drawn on and replayed? If the white Western hero evokes a history of racial violence—the suppression of indigenous peoples confirmed by their marginalization in visual and narrative terms within the overall spectacle of Hollywood action cinema—then does the African-American action hero point to a history of violence and racism that his presence both acknowledges and to some extent overcomes? I want to propose just two elements here, although there are many more questions that could be explored: the ways in which racial discourses are played out around the African-American hero, and formulations of female masculinity in this context.

Slotkin observes the frontier myth that is foundational for the Western is one that "depicts America as a racial entity" defined against the peoples it seeks to subject and through constituting African-Americans as "internal aliens, as 'others' and potential enemies" (2001: 473). (The construction of Latino/a ethnicity within the Western is also pertinent in this context.) The pattern he identifies in *Bataan*, whereby a (fantasy of a) racially inclusive American military is juxtaposed with Japanese forces portrayed through dehumanizing racist discourse, is one that has been reframed and replayed in countless action films. The narrative devices of alien invasion (in science-fiction variants of action) and zombie apocalypse (in horror variants) have proven particularly effective in this regard. Consider action star Will Smith battling other/less than human enemies across diverse action-driven films: aliens in *Independence Day* (Roland Emmerich, 1996), ranked robots in *I, Robot* (Alex Proyas, 2004), and mutated human hoards in *I Am Legend* (Francis Lawrence, 2007). The outsider/maverick qualities of the hero are thus mitigated in contrast to the radical otherness of the extra-terrestrial enemy.

Lisa Purse's analysis of *I, Robot* takes note of the way in which the "film swiftly and overtly attempts to connect Spooner [Will Smith] to cultural signifiers of 'African-American-ness,'" although this evocation of difference from the norm of the white male hero is displaced by Spooner's hatred and suspicion of all robots (2011: 117). Scholars such as Purse note both the significance of what Mary Beltrán (2005) has termed the "multiculti action film" and the limited challenge this poses to Hollywood cinema's organization of masculinity in terms of whiteness. In a subsequent essay Beltrán suggests that the industry perceives the value of youthful and Latino audiences that it seeks to reach through its multi-racial action movies and its use of stars who are framed as racially indeterminate. Of the commercial success of *Fast & Furious* (Justin Lin, 2009) Beltrán observes "Just as important as the car-fuelled spectacle, however, is the underlying ethos of the *Fast* franchise, that of an urban, multicultural, and presumably postracial world in which the story's heroes perform cultural border crossing with ease" (2013: 76). It is then in part the ability to articulate masculinity as a position of authority less entrenched in whiteness, and, critically, more culturally mobile that is at stake here.

This postracial discourse acknowledges difference, while it erases cultural specificity and tends to entrench existing relations of power. Similar effects of displacing and subsequently reinstating white men as the locus of American masculinity take place when we consider the position of women in contemporary action genres. The multi-protagonist team of modern action cinema regularly includes a woman who effectively embodies female masculinity. This now recognizable (if not perhaps overly familiar) supporting figure is understood in terms of an embodied militarized masculinity that can be performed by both men and women. Writing in the 1990s I proposed the term "musculinity" to convey the mobility of masculine tropes across different types of bodies than those of white men, whether inscribed in terms of biological categories of sex and/or race (Tasker 1993). My focus was 1980s/90s film cycles such as the *Alien* and *Terminator* series that gave a central position to female characters who embodied masculinity in intriguing ways. Qualities such as physical strength and emotional resilience are culturally understood in terms of men and masculinity, yet cinema has long suggested the possibility of a more fluid conception of gender. As the 1997 war film *GI Jane* (Ridley Scott) suggests, however, locating military masculinity around the female body involves discourses of female exceptionalism and a narrative development whose goal is the woman's acceptance/approval by the white male leader whom she helps to save under fire (see Tasker 2011).

Moreover the masculine woman who appears in the military unit of Hollywood films is repeatedly described in racial and ethnic terms, as Beltrán (2004) has explored. Latina star Michelle Rodriguez has become associated with tough action roles in films such as *Resident Evil* (Paul W.S. Anderson, 2002), *Avatar* (James Cameron, 2009) and *Battle Los Angeles* (Jonathan Liebesman, 2011). Purse suggests that Rodriguez' function in several of these films, in keeping with a larger racial logic of Hollywood cinema, is to "have to die or make way to enable a white character's ascendency" (2011: 121). Her intermittent role as Letty Ortiz in *The Fast and the Furious* franchise emphasizes her toughness and (of course) driving abilities (her character dies in the first film but is subsequently revealed to have lived, reappearing in the sixth and seventh films in 2013 and 2015). Action star personas such as Rodriguez and Smith as well as the wider context of Hollywood's multi-racial action franchises suggests a pressure on the genre's longstanding formulations of white masculinity. In noting the commercial appeal of heroes who engage in "cultural border crossing" we might recall that, as I have outlined here, it is the freedom to move and to act which characterizes idealized masculinity across the Western, war, and action genres.

In different ways and with varying degrees of success, the three linked genres considered in this chapter engage with developing discourses of gender and race that are so important to Hollywood formulations of action, and so contested within contemporary culture. Although the Western and the war film are framed by the—albeit highly mythicized—historical contexts to which they refer, action functions as a generic space that in contrast to many other Hollywood genres, has increasingly departed from any simplistic assumption that heroism equates to white men performing white masculinity. In pointing this out I am not suggesting that films such as *San Andreas* (Brad Peyton, 2015), for instance, offer any particularly complex challenge to the values of protective masculinity played out in contemporary action. Indeed the film's scenario, in which Dwayne Johnson stars as a helicopter pilot seeking to reunite his family in the wake of a massive earthquake, is rather conventional. Yet the extent to which male (and to a lesser extent female) stars of color perform such conventional heroism is by no means insignificant.

Related topics

Anthony Hayt, "Moving past the trauma: feminist criticism and transformations of the slasher genre"
Hilary Radner, "The rise and fall of the girly film: from the woman's picture to the new woman's film, the chick flick, and the smart-chick film"

References

Basinger, J. (2003) *The World War II Combat Film: Anatomy of a Genre,* 2nd revised edition, Connecticut: Wesleyan University Press.

Beltrán, M. (2004) "Más Macha: The New Latina Action Heroine" in Tasker, Y. ed. *Action and Adventure Cinema,* London: Routledge.

Beltrán, M. (2005) "The New Hollywood Racelessness: Only the Fast, Furious, (and Multiracial) Will Survive," *Cinema Journal* 44.2, 50–67.

Beltrán, M. (2013) "Fast and Bilingual: *Fast & Furious* and the Latinization of Racelessness," *Cinema Journal* 53.1, 75–96.

Doherty, T. (1999) *Projections of War: Hollywood, American Culture, and World War II,* 2nd revised edition, New York: Columbia University Press.

Eberwein, R. (2010). *The Hollywood War Film,* Malden, MA: Wiley-Blackwell.

Kitzes, J. (2007) *Horizons West: The Western from John Ford to Clint Eastwood,* London: BFI.

Lichtenfeld, E. (2007) *Action Speaks Louder: Violence, Spectacle, and the American Action Movie,* 2nd edition, Connecticut: Wesleyan University Press.

Purse, L. (2011) *Contemporary Action Cinema,* Edinburgh: Edinburgh University Press.

Slotkin, R. (2001) "Unit Pride. Ethnic Platoons and Myths of American Nationality", *American Literary History,* 13.3, 469–98.

Tasker, Y. (1993) *Spectacular Bodies: Gender, Genre and the Action Cinema,* London: Routledge.

Tasker, Y. (2011) *Soldiers' Stories: Military Women in Cinema and Television since WWII,* Durham, NC: Duke University Press.

Tasker, Y. (2015) *The Hollywood Action and Adventure Film,* Malden, MA: Wiley-Blackwell.

Warshow, R. (1964) *The Immediate Experience: Movies, Comics, Theatre, and Other Aspects of Popular Culture,* New York: Anchor Books.

Further reading

Buscombe, E. and Roberta E. Pearson, eds. (1998) *Back in the Saddle Again: New Essays on the Western,* BFI. (Collection which reflects on the Western, past and present, cinematic and televisual, through historical perspectives).

Cameron, I. and Douglas Pye, eds. (1996) *The Movie Book of the Western,* New York: Studio Vista. (Collection of perspectives on the genre—several foregrounding gender issues).

Doherty, T. (1999) *Projections of War: Hollywood, American Culture and WWII,* Columbia University Press). (Considers the war film in the context of ideological perspectives on World War II).

Eberwein, R., ed. (2005) *The War Film,* Rutgers University Press. (With chapters from World War I to Iraq war films, a useful introduction to the genre).

Jeffords, S. (1994) *Hard Bodies: Hollywood Masculinity in the Reagan Era*, Rutgers University Press. (Influential volume which explores discourses of Hollywood masculinity in relation to the cultural values of the 1980s and early 1990s).

Tasker, Y. ed. (2004) *Action and Adventure Cinema*, Routledge. (Collection of essays on the genre, several of which feature a particular emphasis on issues of gender and race).

11

THE RISE AND FALL OF THE GIRLY FILM

From the woman's picture to the new woman's film, the chick flick, and the smart-chick film

Hilary Radner

Introduction

The "woman's picture" of classical Hollywood made way in the 1960s and 1970s for the "new woman's film" and its avatars, most notably the "chick flick."[1] The waning of the chick flick in the form of the "girly film," following upon the 2007–11 global financial crisis, highlights how the new woman's film, far from disappearing, has continued to develop in the independent sector, including re-workings of girly film formulas, producing what might be termed "smart-chick films." These shifts in nomenclature underline a parallel trans-formation in the preoccupations of these films, which have in common that they primarily address a female audience and are concerned with guiding a woman towards a path of self-fulfillment. In its early phase, the woman's picture upheld a fundamentally masochistic vision of feminine fulfillment (Doane 1987). It was succeeded by the "independent woman's film"—a variation on the new woman's film of the 1970s—which introduced uncertainties and experimentations that questioned this masochism. The independent woman's film, in turn, was replaced by a frenzied fantasy of self-gratification in the form of the girly film during the 1990s, during the height of the popularity of the so-called "chick flick" (Radner 2011). Finally, the new woman's film of the twenty-first century, including the smart-chick film, promoted an ironic vision of the woman's fate, while sharing with its progenitors of the 1970s a sense of uncertainty about the possibilities for fulfillment that contemporary society offers to women.

The woman's picture

During Hollywood's classical era (1925–48, give or take a few years), the studios that dominated film production during the period considered women to be the most influential film viewers (Stokes 1999). Since the disintegration of the studio system beginning in 1948, as classical Hollywood transformed itself into Conglomerate Hollywood (Schatz 2013), movie moguls rarely took the mature woman's views into account, resulting in a decline in films made specifically for that audience (Schaap 2011; Radner 2014). During this same

121

period, young male viewers achieved canonization as the primary cinematic tastemakers on a global scale (Krämer 1999). Notwithstanding these shifts, the rise of feminist film scholarship beginning in the 1970s has largely focused on popular films understood as directed at a female audience.

This interest in films for women has produced two bodies of scholarship. The first reassesses the films of the classical Hollywood era (grouped under the term the woman's picture or the woman's film), extending into the early 1950s, produced during the period in which female audiences and female stars were seen to dominate the cinematic landscape. The second focuses on the films, referred to as chick flicks by the industry and reviewers, released after 1990.

Initial feminist film scholarship emphasized the woman's picture, which genre specialist Rick Altman describes as "a notion" that "was originally assembled out of female-oriented cycles within a variety of genres" (Altman 1999: 76). According to Altman, the woman's picture as a generic category was primarily generated by feminist film scholars, rather than the industry itself, which tended to be much more informal in designations, using terms as varied as "hanky pics" and "femme fare." The woman's picture, as a recognized genre, emerges, in Raphaëlle Moine's terms, "*a posteriori*," as a consequence of the development and propagation of feminist criticism (Moine 2008: 145, 146). According to her, the woman's picture came to function as an "interpretive category … when generic readings" of a set of films revolving around a central heroine and her concerns "became established as a fact of reception," notably within academia (ibid. 143).

The debated status of the woman's film, or woman's picture, led some scholars to claim that the genre is not specific to classical Hollywood, and not properly a genre at all (Neale 2000: 188–96). Periodicity has proved to be a problem, with the genre in its existing definitions exhibiting an unevenness of development peppered with exceptions. One unresolved methodological problem revolves around definitions of gender itself, with Hollywood conventions predominating, in which notions of male and female (or the quadrants, males under 25, males over 25, females under 25, females over 25) function as coarse categories of analysis, leaving aside any potential challenges to their validity. Concomitantly, notions of feminine subjectivity, drawing upon psychoanalysis and its relations to the woman's film, which animated discussions of the genre in the 1980s (Doane 1987), have enjoyed less importance in subsequent decades.

From classical Hollywood to new Hollywood

In defining the woman's film as an interpretive category, the work of feminist critic Molly Haskell, originally published in 1973, proved formative and, indeed, she is largely credited with establishing the category "the woman's film," its attributes and its sub-genres, which would be taken up by feminist film scholars such as Mary Ann Doane, and Janine Basinger (Haskell 1975:153–88; Doane 1987; Basinger 1993). Haskell is responsible for introducing the view—which has been upheld by feminists such as *New York Times* reviewer Manohla Dargis in the twenty-first century—that, with the demise of the family melodrama at the end of the 1950s, film roles for women, beginning in the 1960s, took a turn for the worse. Haskell maintained: "With the substitution of violence and sexuality (a poor second) for romance, there was less need for exciting and interesting women; any bouncing nymphet whose curves looked good in catsup would do" (Haskell 1975: 323–4). Notwithstanding Haskell's call to arms, the films appearing between 1960 and 1990 have been unevenly explored by feminist film scholarship.

Karen Hollinger's study of what she calls the female friendship film constitutes one of the few sustained analyses of film from this period (Hollinger 1998), in which she identifies issues that predominate in what she calls the "new woman's film of the 1970s," which include "the independent woman" and "female friendship;" however, she maintains that "[f]ilms dealing with independent women actually began to die out in the 1980s, or they merged with preexisting film and television genres." In her estimation, "[f]rom among these various categories of new woman's films, the female friendship film found the widest audience and greatest mainstream popularity" (Hollinger 2012: 44).

This genre, or cycle, which included films such as *Turning Point* (Herbert Ross, 1977), *Beaches* (Garry Marshall, 1989), *Fried Green Tomatoes* (Jon Avnet, 1991), and *Thelma and Louise* (Ridley Scott, 1991), while initiated in the 1970s and prominent in the 1980s and 1990s, "ran out of energy in the late 1990s," perhaps in response to "the increasingly conservative climate in the late 1990s and into the 2000s" (Hollinger 2012: 46); simultaneously, many attributes of the female friendship film were incorporated into what became known as the chick flick, which, because of its emphasis on fashion and consumer culture more generally and consequent potential synergies, in terms of product placement, or the creation of ancillary products, for example, proved more popular with Hollywood producers than the films discussed by Hollinger (Radner 2011:131).

The chick flick/girly film cycle (see below), such as *Romy and Michele's High School Reunion* (David Mirkin, 1997), arguably re-worked the terms of female friendship in the context of a changing society. As a narrative form, these films signaled the continuing importance of female friendship in the lives of women with a view to both feminism (in some mode or another) and consumerism. Fashion, in particular, provided a significant inter-text; many of these later films, such as *The Devil Wears Prada* (David Frankel, 2006) were dubbed "fashion films" and "female event films." Fashion magazines, highlighting the designs featured in these films, for example, provided free publicity for the film, encouraging interest in its release while also inviting women to imitate the outfits of its stars (Radner 2011: 136, 153–70).

The rise of the chick flick

Hollinger posits that two strands, cycles, or genres (depending on a terminology that remains a topic of continued debated) emerged in the 1990s, overshadowing the female friendship film—adaptations of literary classics and the chick flick, or girly film. Embracing a wide range of material, from the British heritage film (Higson 2003) to the female biopic (Polaschek 2013), adaptations and costume dramas have occupied an important place among films that appeal to the female audience; however, they also probably deserve to be considered in their specificity as a distinct genre that exists alongside the woman's picture as defined by feminist film theorists. Other genres, such as the softcore thriller (associated with the 1990s), which feminist scholar Linda Ruth Williams specifies as "not just for the boys," or the female detective film as a post-Hollywood cycle that re-writes an essentially masculine genre, complicate definitions of the woman's film without for that matter extending its life (Williams 2005: 420; Martin 2007; Gates 2011). In contrast, the romantic drama, continuing into the twenty-first century with films that are often based on popular novels—such as *The Notebook* (Nick Cassavetes, 2004)—has long been a narrative form associated with a predominantly female audience; however, unlike the woman's film, the genre places a couple, rather than a single woman, at the apex of its story (Todd 2014).

In contrast, the chick flick—popular films successful with women—mirrored the woman's picture in many ways, in regard to its emphasis on a woman around whose concerns the narrative revolves, and its return to marriage and heterosexuality as offering the norms that govern all relationships (as opposed to friendship, for example). The term "chick flick" gained international currency in the 1990s following the success of *Pretty Woman* (Gary Marshall, 1990) (Ferriss and Young 2008: 2). Like the woman's film, the chick flick as a category is nebulous with regard to the scope and range of films included. The term was often used to designate any successful popular film that appealed to women, including romances and adaptations. The chick flick was preceded by a similarly ill-defined literary genre known as chick lit (Ferriss and Young 2006).

Helen Fielding's popular British novel *Bridget Jones's Diary* (1996) is often credited with drawing public attention to the chick lit genre, which includes a range of variations, such as "mummy lit," "black chick lit," as well as national iterations, with countries such as Australia and New Zealand boasting their own chick lit authors and novels replete with local detail and locutions (Ferriss and Young 2006). "Chick flicks" were more explicitly identified with Hollywood cinema and American culture. American chick flicks, at least as these have been defined by feminist film scholars, featured more successful and conventional heroines, such as Kate Hudson in *How to Lose a Guy in 10 Days* (Donald Petrie, 2003), whose antics and persona were typically less farcical in tone (though still comedic and prone to self-deprecation) than those attributed to the eponymous Bridget (Radner 2011:123). In general, late-twentieth-century chick flicks avoided the high melodrama that characterized many women's films of the classical period, as well as a significant number of female friendship films such as *Beaches*.

Chick flick handbooks (see for example Berry and Errigo 2004), of which there are many, define these films broadly with the intent of guiding women to movies that they might enjoy across the decades and across national cinemas, often including canonized feminist films such as Jane Campion's *The Piano* (1993). Feminist scholars have focused more narrowly on a variation centered around a heroine whom Charlotte Brunsdon dubbed "the postfeminist girly" in 1997, looking back at *Pretty Woman* and *Working Girl* (Mike Nichols, 1987)—films that she claims are variously "girls' films" or "shopping films" and "share an address to, and a representation of, a new kind of figure, the post-feminist girly." Films in this cycle are often characterized by an "obsession with clothes," and "an exaggerated performance of femininity" (Brunsdon 1997: 81, 4; Radner 2011: 2–4, 26–41). In particular, Brunsdon contrasts these films with what she calls "the independent woman film" of the 1970s (Brunsdon 1997: 83), which she sees as more clearly influenced by second wave feminism and standing in reaction to the woman's film of classical Hollywood. Subsequent feminist scholarship has tended to associate the girly films with post-feminism, emphasizing their relationship with romance (Hollinger 2012: 57). Scholars such as Diane Negra associate them with a trend that she calls "retreatism," in which women repudiate feminism and its gains within the workplace to return to some form of domesticity focused on the home (Negra 2009).

Feminism and post-feminism

Brunsdon herself advocates a more nuanced approach than that advanced by Negra and Hollinger in the twenty-first century. She expresses doubts about the a-historical implications of the term "post-feminism," in particular the way in which it "installs 1970s feminism as the site of 'true' feminism, from which lipstick wearers and shoppers are excluded" (Brunsdon 1997: 102). She also questions the more commonly shared view that post-feminism as a term implies that the work and time of feminism is over. Nonetheless, she finds the category useful in describing this new kind of "girly heroine ... as it marks the considerable distance we find here, in popular representation, from popular representations of 1970s feminism" (ibid.).

Brunsdon's uneasiness with the term post-feminist in 1997 highlights the difficulties feminist scholars such as Negra (cited above) have encountered in approaching feminine popular culture, which was frequently marked by a profound ambivalence towards the status quo, while instructing women to accept it to the degree possible in order to negotiate circumstances most favorable to their own individual fulfillment (Radner 1995). This focus on the individual has been variously highlighted by terms such as "commodity feminism" and "neo-feminism" as well as explicit references to neo-liberalism more generally (Radner 2011: 6).

The emphasis on self-gratification in the girly film, and the idea that a woman should and could "have it all," clearly distinguishes these films from the woman's picture. In *Dark Victory* (Edmund Goulding, 1939), for example, Judith (Bette Davis) suffers from a debilitating illness in silence until she dies, happy in the knowledge that, having given up her hedonistic ways, she has discovered love and marriage; in *Fried Green Tomatoes*, the "friends" literally get away with murder. Though the friends' happiness is short-lived (one dies of cancer), it is unalloyed and occurs in this life, not the next; however, the female friendship film's conclusion, frequently tragic (as in the case of *Thelma and Louise*), suggested that women had not as yet found their place in the world. *Pretty Woman* ends on a more triumphant note, with Vivian (Julia Roberts) anticipating love, marriage, wealth, and even children at the film's conclusion. Sexual relations are depicted openly and chastity is no longer a virtue, which was not the case with the woman's picture.

For many feminist scholars, the development of the woman's film in the form of the chick flick in the late twentieth century is best understood as the outgrowth of neo-liberalism more generally within feminine culture (Radner 2011; Kaklamanidou 2015; McHugh 2015). Sometimes termed neo-feminism, this position is associated initially with figures such as Helen Gurley Brown. Beginning in the 1960s with her bestseller *Sex and the Single Girl*, Brown advocated that women, even married women, maintain their economic independence by working outside the home, but also that they use sex to achieve what they wanted (or needed) from society (and men), exploiting consumerism to ensure their desirability while also pioneering a form of the sexual revolution that encouraged women to take their pleasure where they found it (Radner 2011: 6–25). Arguably, the girly film, as identified by Brunsdon, represented, almost thirty years later, the arrival of Brown's principles to the big screen.

Importantly, women like Helen Gurley Brown were reacting not to feminism, but to the same conditions of inequity that feminism sought to remedy. Neo-feminism, as associated with figures such as Brown, does not follow on from second wave feminism; rather, it coincides with, or perhaps even pre-dates, it. Neo-feminism, however, had a firmer grasp not only of women's needs, but also of their desires, often secretly shared by feminists themselves, as evidenced in the many confessions of guilty pleasure (such as those cited in Brunsdon 1997: 83) on the part of self-proclaimed feminists when consuming chick flicks. Indeed, much of the history of feminist criticism, particularly with regard to popular cinema directed at female audiences in the post-classical period, is formed by a division between feminists such as Negra, and what might be called the new independent woman, as initially portrayed in the 1970s. Not coincidentally, in the "older-bird film" (a variation on the girly film) *Something's Gotta Give* (Nancy Meyers, 2003), the film's heroine Erica (Diane

Keaton), as a twenty-first century independent woman, is contrasted with her sister Zoe (Frances McDormand), a feisty faculty member in Woman's Studies from Columbia University. Erica gets her man and her happy ending. Zoe, we assume, goes it alone; the film does not present her story worthy of the viewers' attention.

Films such as *Something's Gotta Give* posit ethics as a matter of individual choice deployed within the limited context of the individual's immediate social group, usually some form of the traditional family grounded in heterosexual norms. From the perspective of many feminist scholars, popular culture itself—including chick lit and chick flicks most pointedly—systematically distanced itself from second wave feminism (see Hollows 2000; Whelehan 2005), as illustrated by Zoe's marginalization as a feminist in *Something's Gotta Give* (notwithstanding the fact that the film's depiction of her is affectionate rather than hostile). Simultaneously, these narratives incorporated ideas that seemed also to suggest a debt to this same movement, its ideals and its reforms in the figure of Erica as a twenty-first century embodiment of the independent woman. A deep sense of irony at life's betrayals permeates what might otherwise appear to be a bitter condemnation of certain potentially feminist tendencies inherent in the chick flick, a trait shared by chick lit.

The girly film as the prototypical chick flick

The girly film offered a potent example of how popular culture played out these issues while attempting to offer a fantasy vision of the woman who had it all. While not a genre in the strict sense of the term, though many were romantic comedies or had a strong romantic theme, these films appear roughly from 1990 to 2010, beginning with the release and phenomenal success of *Pretty Woman* in 1990 and concluding with the failure of the television program "Sex and the City" (HBO, 1998–2004) to establish a successful movie franchise in 2010 with *Sex and the City 2* (Michael Patrick King), and with the declining success of films such as *Confessions of a Shopaholic* (P.J. Hogan, 2009) in comparison with earlier fashion films such as *The Devil Wears Prada* or *Sex and the City: The Movie* (Michael Patrick King, 2008) (Radner 2014).

The girly films distinguish themselves from earlier female-directed material such as the woman's picture of classical Hollywood, the independent women films of the 1970s, and the female friendship films of the 1980s and 1990s, through their ironic and self-conscious tone, their emphasis on consumer culture, and their affirmation of a sexually active feminine subject. Imelda Whelehan's comments about chick lit as addressing readers for whom "femininity" was "something essential to them under threat by feminism" hold equally true for the girly film (Whelehan 2005: 177).

The cycle's coherency derives from its focus on a heroine at the center of her universe, usually employed and often living in an urban environment, motivated by individual fulfillment expressed through some form of consumerism (often manifest in a shopping sequence and a make-over for the heroine) as its defining trait. Similarly, this loose formula is associated with a set of stars best deemed to incarnate the girly heroine, such as Julia Roberts, Reese Witherspoon, Anne Hathaway, and Jennifer Lopez, as well as a number of directors, such as Gary Marshall and Donald Petrie, including a few women, such as Nancy Meyers. Indeed, girly films comprise many further variations such as the older-bird film or middle-aged chick flick, as in *It's Complicated* (Nancy Meyers, 2009), and the black chick flick, as in *How Stella Got Her Groove Back* (Kevin Rodney Sullivan, 1998), or the mother–daughter chick flick such as *Mamma Mia* (Phillida Lloyd, 2008), suggesting the flexibility of its formula to the degree that the heroine expressed a certain youthful "girlishness" (irrespective of her actual age) externalized through her investment in consumer culture (she looks "good") and her sexual availability.

The decline of the girly film and the return of the woman's film: the smart-chick flick

With the onset of the 2008 recession, such films, with their emphasis on fashion and consumerism, became less common, with fewer and fewer films made for a female audience, in keeping with Conglomerate Hollywood's focus on the more profitable young male demographic and the family film, associated with Disney. The nature of their audience has also been an issue. Girly films tend to be single quadrant films—appealing to women over 25, with men reluctant to attend. As Hollywood felt itself under increasing pressure, particularly when falling DVD sales accompanied diminished theatrical attendance, it was less willing to take risks on a film that, even if successful, would lack broad appeal. Contributing to this trend is the fact that women are willing to go along to movies directed at other quadrants: to those constituted by their partners, daughters, and sons (Radner 2014).

Hollywood sought to recuperate possible losses through cycles seeking to appeal to broader audiences, including: the proliferation of hybrid romantic comedies, often with a *raunch* factor and featuring a high-profile male star, such as *Friends with Benefits* (Will Gluck, 2011) with Ashton Kutcher; the gross-out, usually bromantic, romantic comedies associated with Judd Apatow; and a short-lived cycle of what were known as the romaction film, such as *Knight and Day* (James Mangold, 2010), and *Killers* (Robert Luketic, 2010) (Radner 2014). A recent cycle of comedies generated by female stand-up comics, such as Kristin Wiig, Melissa McCarthy, and Amy Schumer (a cycle initiated by the tamer and more sentimental Nia Vardalos in *My Big Fat Greek Wedding*, Joel Zwick, 2002), who seek to shock with their transgressive, scatological, and sexually explicit humor, offer a variation on the narrative device that places a woman at the center of her universe with a relatively broad appeal.

The decline of the girly film coincided with the development of the Young Adult (YA) genre directed at women under twenty-five, including the tween/teen franchises adapted from previously successful book series, such as the Twilight series, the Mortal Instruments series, the Hunger Games trilogy, and the Divergent trilogy, as well as films based on a single best-selling YA novel, such as *The Book Thief* (Brian Percival, 2013), and *The Fault in Our Stars* (Josh Boone, 2014), which appeal to older women as well as young adults. The teen franchises performed well at the box office, though far from outstripping the action adventure franchises geared towards young males. These productions proved more reliable at the box office than the hybrid romantic comedies, including bromances, which nonetheless gained increasing purchase on the multiplex audience. The success of the franchises was due, at least in part, to the built-in pre-established awareness created by the successful novels, heightened in the case of a series. Indeed, several films from these franchises aimed at women under 25 ranked among the top ten releases for their year. For example, *The Hunger Games: Catching Fire* (Francis Lawrence, 2013) ranked number five in 2013 worldwide grosses (Radner 2014).

These films distinguish themselves from the chick flicks of the 1990s and first decade of the twenty-first century by offering heroines, who, with rare exceptions, are oblivious to the world of fashion and feminine culture broadly defined, at least within the fantasy universe of the films. The actresses and actors who play the central characters in these films, however, have very visible lives on the red carpet, in the tabloids and through various forms of social media, in which they both actively and passively support the fashion system, in keeping with the increasing influence of celebrity in all areas of consumerism, especially those pertaining to style, including homewares, cars, art, and architecture (Church Gibson 2012).

An exception to this trend is the continued output of what might be called smart-chick films by independent directors, a recent iteration of the new woman's film, such as *Rachel Getting Married* (Jonathan Demme, 2008), *The Bling Ring* (Sofia Coppola, 2013), *Blue Jasmine* (Woody Allen, 2013), and *Enough Said* (Nicole Holofcener, 2013) (Radner 2015, 2016). These films enjoy a modest success at the box office, depend upon an international as well as a domestic market, and are frequently viewed through small screen outlets (Radner 2014, 2015). Thus, despite the decline in theatrically released films directed at female audiences, bemoaned by critics such as Manohla Dargis, increasing numbers of female directors, such as Lisa Cholodenko, Kat Coiro, Nicole Holofcener, Courtney Hunt, Kelly Reichardt, and Lynn Shelton, have emerged in this sector in recent years, making films that in many ways continue the tradition (with important variations) of the woman's film of classical Hollywood, as a genre that addresses the mature female audience, and which, in American film scholar Jeanine Basinger's words, "accomplishes one important thing for its viewers: It puts the woman at the center of the universe" (Basinger 1993: 15). Importantly, these women directors are very often white and middle-class, addressing issues and milieux identified with that same class, with a very few exceptions, such as Gina Prince-Bythewood, and Jennifer Phang.

The twenty-first century variations of the new woman's film, including the smart-chick film, in terms of outlook and topic are more closely related to the woman's film of classical Hollywood and the independent woman film of the 1970s than the girly film, clearly meriting, in terms of structure, and address, to be considered a continuation of the new woman's film of the 1970s. Arguably, they continue to explore formulas established by the girly film—for example, the wedding film as in *Rachel Getting Married*, or the marriage plot as in Holofcener's *Friends with Money* (2006)—while borrowing some of their characters from the independent woman's film. This latest version of the new woman's film distinguishes itself from the woman's picture, however, through its reliance on irony and its sense of a woman's right to self-fulfillment (even if rarely achieved). Unlike the typical indie film, the irony of which derives largely from the viewer's pre-supposed knowledge of cinematic conventions, smart-chick irony tends to revolve around the feminine condition, women's culture, especially consumer culture, as well as the nature of male/female relations, family relations, and social relations, often affirming the characters' distance as well as sympathy for the perspectives of second wave feminism as a form of naïve, if sincere, idealism. In this sense, the new woman's film in the twenty-first century represents a return to the uncertainties of the 1970s, but tempered by a sentiment of resignation in the face of a fragmented contemporary culture.

If the new woman's film and the chick flick have in common their reliance on irony, both forms also depend heavily on an international audience (the chick flick to a lesser degree). Similarly, particularly with the advent of film festivals, dedicated movie channels, and VoD, films are produced internationally with a view to a female audience—films such as the Chilean *Gloria* (Sebastián Lelio, 2013), which details the dilemmas of a divorced woman, underlining her national specificity, while addressing a global female viewer, whose empathy is implicit in the film's rhetoric. In this sense, the new woman's film testifies to the continuing influence, if modified, of some version of what might be termed a transnational feminism, as does the idea that women function as an international audience, with gender extending beyond nationality to create a global female audience.

As moviegoers and feminist film scholars, we may bemoan the decline of theatrical releases for female audiences and mature audiences, but, for all that, we should not ignore the new possibilities that cinema and its various avatars afford us in the twenty-first century. The new woman's film has continued to transform itself in response to changing social mores and to broad economic and technological developments, testifying to the resiliency and will-to-life of its audiences. Whether on Netflix or at our local multiplex, whether we are transfixed by Gina Prince-Bythewood's *Beyond the Lights* (2014) or the Chinese-American director Wayne Wang's sensitive female friendship film *Snow Flower and the Secret Fan* (2011), we are still watching, and will continue to do so.

Related topics

Yvonne Tasker, "Contested masculinities: the action film, the war film, and the Western"
Veronica Pravadelli, "Classical Hollywood and modernity: gender, style, aesthetics"

Note

1 An earlier version of some of this material appeared in Radner (2014); all references to box office figures, receipts, and rankings taken from boxofficemojo.com, unless otherwise specified.

References

Altman, R. (1999) *Film/Genre*, London: BFI.

Basinger, J. (1993) *A Woman's View: How Hollywood Spoke to Women 1930–1960*, Hanover, NH and London: University Press of New England/Wesleyan University Press.

Berry, J. and Errigo, A. (2004) *Chick Flicks: Movies Women Love*, London: Orion Books.

Brunsdon, C. (1997) "Post-feminism and Shopping Films," in C. Brunsdon *Screen Tastes: Soap Opera to Satellite Dishes*, London/New York: Routledge, pp. 81–102.

Church Gibson, P. (2012) *Fashion and Celebrity Culture*, London: Berg Publishers.

Doane, M. (1987) *The Desire to Desire: The Woman's Film of the 1940s*, Bloomington and Indianapolis: Indiana University Press.

Ferriss, S. and Young, M. (2006) "Introduction," in S. Ferriss and M. Young (eds.) *Chick Lit: The New Woman's Fiction*, New York/Routledge: Routledge, pp. 1–25.

Ferriss, S. and Young, M. (2008) "Introduction," in S. Ferriss and M. Young (eds.) *Chick Flicks: Contemporary Women at the Movies*, New York/Routledge: Routledge, pp. 1–25.

Gates, P. (2011) *Detecting Women: Gender and the Hollywood Detective Film*, Albany, NY: State University of New York Press.

Haskell, M. (1975) *From Reverence to Rape: The Treatment of Women in the Movies*, New York/Baltimore: Penguin.

Higson, A. (2003) *English Heritage, English Cinema: Costume Drama Since 1980*, Oxford: Oxford University Press.

Hollinger, K. (1998) *In the Company of Women: Contemporary Female Friendship Films*, Minneapolis/London: University of Minneapolis Press.

Hollinger, K. (2012) *Feminist Film Studies*, New York/London: Routledge.

Hollows, J. (2000) *Feminism, Femininity and Popular Culture*, Manchester/New York: Manchester University Press.

Kaklamanidou, B. (2015) *Genre, Gender and the Effects of Neoliberalism: The New Millennium Hollywood Rom Com*, London/New York: Routledge.

Krämer, P. (1999) "A Powerful Cinema-going Force? Hollywood and Female Audiences since the 1960s," in M. Stokes and R. Maltby, eds., *Identifying Hollywood's Audiences: Cultural Identity and Movies*, London: BFI, pp. 93–108.

McHugh, K. (2015) "Giving Credit to Paratexts and Parafeminism in *Top of the Lake* and *Orange Is the New Black,*" *Film Quarterly* 68.3, www.filmquarterly.org/2015/03/giving-credit-to-paratexts-and-parafeminism-in-top-of-the-lake-and-orange-is-the-new-black/ (accessed September 25, 2015).

Martin, N. (2007) *Sexy Thrills: Undressing the Erotic Thriller,* Urbana: University of Illinois Press.

Moine, R. (2008) *Cinema Genre,* trans. A. Fox and H. Radner, Malden, MA: Wiley-Blackwell.

Neale, S. (2000) *Genre and Hollywood,* London/New York: Routledge.

Negra, D. (2009) "Structural Integrity, Historical Reversion, and the Post-9/11 Flick," *Feminist Media Studies* 8.1, pp. 51–68, DOI: 10.1080/14680770701824902.

Polaschek, B. (2013) *The Postfeminist Biopic: Narrating the Lives of Plath, Kahlo, Woolf and Austen,* Basingstoke, Hampshire: Palgrave Macmillan.

Radner, H. (1995) *Shopping Around: Feminine Culture and the Pursuit of Pleasure,* New York: Routledge.

Radner, H. (2011) *Neo-Feminist Cinema: Girly Films, Chick Flicks and Consumer Culture,* New York: Routledge.

Radner, H. (2014) "Creating Female Audiences: The Decline of the 'Girly' Heroine and the Return of the Formidable 'Femme,'" *Comunicazioni Sociali* 3, pp. 357–67.

Radner, H. (2015) "Personal Cinema and the Smart-Chick Film: *Rachel Getting Married,*" in C. Perkins and C. Verevis, eds., *US Independent Film after 1989: Possible Films,* Edinburgh: Edinburgh University Press, pp. 155–64.

Radner, H. (2016) *The New Woman's Film: From Chick Flicks to Movies for Smart "Femmes,"* New York/London: Routledge.

Schaap, R. (2011) "No Country for Old Women: Gendering Cinema in Conglomerate Hollywood," in H. Radner and R. Stringer, eds., *Feminism at the Movies: Understanding Gender in Contemporary Popular Culture,* London and New York: Routledge, pp. 151–62.

Schatz, T. (2013) "Conglomerate Hollywood and American Independent Film," in G. King, C. Molloy and Y. Tziomakis, eds., *American Independent Cinema: Indie, Indiewood and Beyond,* London/New York: Routledge, pp. 127–39.

Stokes, M. (1999) "Female Audiences of the 1920s and Early 1930s," in M. Stokes and R. Maltby, eds., *Identifying Hollywood's Audiences: Cultural Identity and Movies,* London: BFI, pp. 42–60.

Todd, E. (2014) *Passionate Love and Popular Cinema: Romance and Film Genre,* Basingstoke, Hampshire: Palgrave/Macmillan.

Whelehan, I. (2005) *The Feminist Bestseller,* Basingstoke, Hampshire/New York: Palgrave Macmillan.

Williams, L. R. (2005) *The Erotic Thriller in Contemporary Cinema,* Edinburgh: Edinburgh University Press.

12

MOVING PAST THE TRAUMA

Feminist criticism and transformations of the slasher genre

Anthony Hayt

Since 9/11, a common trend in horror film criticism has been to focus on the genre as a way of understanding and processing the trauma of the terrorist attacks that forever changed the cultural landscape of America, and of the world. This approach is warranted, as several shifts in horror production and consumption have been noticeable since 9/11. We have seen a simultaneous increase in the number of horror films with successful box office returns; the proliferation of new subgenres, such as "'torture porn,' 'post-millennial horror road movie,' 'military horror movie,' and 'post-torture porn retro-slasher'" (Wetmore 2012: 18); and the rebirth of various tropes that had lain nearly dormant for decades, including zombies and vampires (both of which have been co-opted away from horror and turned into teen melodrama in various ways). There has also been a staggering number of remakes of horror films, including seminal titles like *The Texas Chain Saw Massacre* (1974/2003) (the original film's spelling is "chain saw," while the remake is spelled "chainsaw"), *Halloween* (1978/2007), and *Dawn of the Dead* (1978/2004) and other lesser-known films, including *I Spit on Your Grave* (1978/2010) and *House of Wax* (1953/2005), among dozens of others.[1] It is clear, then, that producers are creating new genre templates and successfully reinterpreting past texts to act as the allegories of a post-9/11 world. The criticism that explores these changes in terms of cultural trauma is, therefore, necessary and wholly justified.

As a byproduct of this shift in cultural studies to a focus on trauma studies, and concurrent with the shift toward the problematic term "post-feminism,"[2] gender criticism in horror has largely fallen by the wayside in the past decade and a half. This is perhaps nowhere more strongly stated than in Kevin J. Wetmore's *Post-9/11 Horror in American Cinema* (2012) wherein he argues that because terrorism is indiscriminant in its victims (men, women, and children are all fair game), the horror films that variously recreate terror in the post-9/11 era should not be approached through gender-inflected criticism (which he lumps into the categories of psychology/psychoanalysis and sex/sexual politics) (14–16). His brief nod to acceptable gender criticism of the last decade and a half's horror films is Susan Faludi's *The Terror Dreams* (2007), which discusses, among many topics, the idea that we recreate the events of 9/11 through a gendered lens—men are heroes and women are victims, widows, or caretakers (ibid. 57; Wetmore 2012: 15). Wetmore's commentary reenacts the misogyny of American culture at large, and of the "post-feminist" era specifically, by making moves to discount the importance of upholding the vigilance of gender-based political struggle in favor of more "important" political causes. For Wetmore, the dismissal of feminism manifests itself in the utilization of the trends mentioned above; culturally, it manifests itself in many ways, one of which is a divergence of the political parties along the lines of both sexuality and gun rights, whereby conservatives champion both traditional gender roles and the use of weapons domestically and abroad as a two-pronged defense against the dangers of the post-9/11 era (women's rights/effeminate men, and terrorists). This approach to horror studies is unacceptable, and while Wetmore has many excellent observations in his book, this essay offers a response to many of the trauma-theory based examinations of the current horror landscape by reclaiming a position of primacy for feminism, including a brief look at the place of the mother in the domestic space of horror and a reexamination of the once-iconic Final Girl. I do so while considering genre conventions, aesthetic and narrative choices, and comparisons to past films.

As a way of demonstrating how feminist film studies can productively complicate the already dynamic landscape of post-9/11 horror studies, I have chosen to focus on a set of five recent films that are all remakes of classic 1970s slasher films, *The Texas Chain Saw Massacre* (1974/2003), *Halloween* (1978/2007), *Friday the 13th* (1980/2009), *Friday the 13th II* (1981/2009) and *Halloween II* (1981/2009). In terms of their historical moment, the original films typify the nihilism of the post-Vietnam, post-Watergate era in which the US was no longer assured of the inherent goodness of a foreign policy based on Manifest Destiny. Domestically, social roles based on gender and race had begun to shift in the continued ripples following the feminist and civil rights movements, changes that left traditional social codes and behaviors in flux. These films were also products of a post-studio production period, another traditional structural system that was crumbling during the era. These independently produced films captured the attention of surprising and unprecedented numbers of viewers. They continue as canonical classics of their time and genre, offer up plots that manipulate traditional social myths, and work to ignore the past or the future through three main narrative trends:

- ignoring traditionally feminine traits for heroines, such as complacency, inaction, or romanticized visions of courtly love;
- complicating, distorting, or dismissing the sex drives of male and female characters;
- presenting very non-traditional versions of motherhood so as to deny both birth (the past), and death (the future).

Through these three main facets, the films challenge the traditional American melodramatic mode by creating evil that is amorphous and hard to define, providing no romantic narrative around which to build easily-identifiable character types, and showing no interest in generational progress through the typical triumph of youth over old age, or heterosexual pairing. The original films also challenge the traditional models of American storytelling by highlighting young female characters in positions of resistance to misogynist violence, a short-lived trope that is a product of the 1970s feminist movement.[3]

The post 9/11 remakes of these films tell a very different story about our current cultural moment. With the attacks on the World Trade Center and the Pentagon, America was able to redefine its domestic image in terms of a foreign policy that became structured around an us/them dichotomy that had not been as justified since WWII, nor as tangible since the Cold War era. This realignment of patriotic values replaced the post-Vietnam era emotions that had carried through the 1990s (after a brief break in the 1980s yuppie explosion) with the disillusionment of Generation-X, and allowed America to once again be the "Good Guys" reeling from an unprovoked attack (or so the rhetoric of the time would suggest). This repositioning was felt across the board in American culture. While the original 1970s slasher films eschewed emotional melodrama (the traditional mode of American storytelling), the remakes are steeped in family melodrama that highlights recovery from trauma via the recuperation of the family unit. The narratives do so through foregrounding generational tension, appointing the mother to a prominent (if flawed and always-to-blame) position, undercutting the autonomy of the Final Girl (the female hero who fights back against the killer named by Carol Clover in *Men, Women, and Chainsaws* [1993]), basking in the glory of male heroes, and celebrating the figure of the psycho-killer. All of these changes to the original stories help to realign the films' narratives with more traditional storytelling modes, traditional gender norms, and traditional social myths than the originals, revolving around mothers and sons, sex and violence, and a sense of history or time. Despite Wetmore's claims that the new films are just as nihilistic as the originals, in fact his concept of "original" is flawed, as he considers mostly 1980s slashers as the original texts to use as his measuring stick. But those films are almost all sequels to '70s or very early '80s films (which retained much of the 1970s aesthetic), and were much more comedic and silly than the films that truly started the slasher genre in the 1970s. By comparing the post-9/11 films to the 1980s works, the former are certainly darker and more nihilistic. However, by looking back to the true originations of the slasher subgenre and applying consideration of feminist concern for the roles of women, we see that the films are not nihilistic, and instead all push toward a vision of America that can suffer from violent tragedy and move on to recovery, as long as faith in the ideological norms of our nuclear-family past can be recalled and relied upon.

Horror has long had a reputation as a genre that has cultural caché for being subversive, dangerous, and taboo. Nowhere was this more evident than in the 1970s. Indeed, the ways in which the use, manipulation, views, and transgressions of the body cross the lines of cultural standards can support all of the above adjectives. And the remakes transgress the boundaries of the body and of decorum with even more detail, realism, and precision than their 1970s predecessors could ever hope to do due to increased CGI and special effects technology. But for all this visual transgression of boundary and limits, the remakes have lost much of their subversive bite when it comes to their overall ideological messages. The non-traditional quality of the mothers in the originals is made more apparent when seen in contrast to the remakes, in which mothers abound to help unify the family and also provide a scapegoat on whom blame can be heaped for the killer's actions. Similarly, the masculine-coded women seen in the character of the Final Girl are no longer the heroes for whom we cheer.[4] But post-feminist social anxieties obsess over concerns that men have gone soft, and to help allay this fear, these remakes place men in the position of the hero, reasserting a tenuous hold on the ever-precarious dominance of white masculinity.

As much as a horror film is about scaring the viewer, often in our culture the most fearful thing in a movie is not blood and guts, things jumping out in the dark, or ghosts from the past. Instead, the mother/motherhood takes that position. *Psycho* (Hitchcock 1960) is a perfect example of a film mother whose domination creates the fear, while in a film like *Invasion of the Body Snatchers* (Philip Kaufman, 1978), the action of (re)generation actually removes the mother from the equation with giant uterus-like pods producing copies of citizens as the source of terror and mayhem. The slashers of the 1970s follow in the footsteps of other horror in that they confront motherhood, reproduction, and regeneration head on; however, they do so in two very disparate and complex ways that set them apart from the majority of mainstream films and pop culture.

The 1970s films discussed in this essay tend to follow two main trends—that of removing the mother completely, or turning her into a killer—to deal with the ambivalence created by the fear of the mother's ability to give life, and her constant reminder that life can be taken away. The two films that typify this trend of erasing motherhood are *Massacre* and *Halloween*. In *Massacre*, the only hint of a mother (or any female presence at all in the killers' house) is the desiccated corpse of "Gran'ma," still dressed, sitting in a rocking chair in an upstairs room. Furthermore, the three men in the group appear to be devoid of any sexual drive; they seem genuinely baffled and laugh hysterically at Sally's offer to "do anything" if they let her go. They are clearly uninterested in sex even when it is offered, and their dismissal is part of what makes their crimes so baffling to an audience preconditioned to see the woman's sexual body as *the* object. This absence is mirrored in *Halloween*, as moments after a 6-year-old Michael murders his sister, we see his mother for mere seconds, standing motionless and speechless. We never see her again. It is implied by this scene that the young child, left alone with an inattentive sister while his parents were gone, in effect has no mother. It would seem, then, that two movies with no mother characters are also two movies wherein the killers have no specific sexual aims; there is no sense of sexualized violence here, but only a sense of violence in place of sex. Michael's specific aim seems unclear; he is not motivated by sex, and the fact that the women (and men, a point often forgotten) he kills are sexually active seems unimportant to him. Michael himself is not a sexual creature, and instead is driven by violence and a sense of family (a point introduced in the original sequel when we find out that Laurie is his sister). This trend, and that of the men in *Massacre* eschewing sex for violence, follows Carol Clover's formulation of the subversion of sex into violence, as outlined in *Men, Women, and Chainsaws* (Clover 1993). Furthermore, there is no mother for these men to blame—their actions are their own, and there is no bad upbringing or bad mothering to be used as an out. Instead of the mother's absence being caused by the younger generation dismissing her for being in the way either physically, socially, or psycho-sexually, the male killers in *Halloween* and *Massacre* have no mother hanging over their heads and, in a rarely seen trait in film, a mother is not to blame for the sins of her son(s).

Mrs. Voorhees, the surprise killer in *Friday*, brings us to the second way in which mothers in the 1970s slashers are uncharacteristically treated: they become the killer. This follows more closely the trajectory of women that Barbara Creed outlines in *The Monstrous-Feminine* (1993), whereby women, or some aspect of their femininity, are figured as the terror. In *Friday the 13th*, Mrs. Voorhees takes on a fairly traditional role of the blamed mother, in some ways showing ties to *Psycho's* (Hitchcock 1960) Mrs. Bates in that her love for her son is so powerful that it develops into unrelenting violence when the mother–son relationship is threatened (in *Psycho* by another woman, in *Friday* by death). But unlike Mrs. Bates, whose story we only hear through the mouths of men, Mrs. Voorhees is unashamed of her killing spree, and takes great pride in telling her story. Thus, the common fate of motherhood, wherein a mother takes the blame for the sins of her family via *their* interpretation of *her* language, actions, or motivations, is turned on its head when we hear Mrs. Voorhees give testimony of her own.

The remakes of these films variously change these 1970s characteristics by creating mothers where there were none, or by giving those that did exist a much more traditional role. "Tradition," in some cases, means that they are presented as scapegoats for their killer sons; in other cases, they are placed within the domestic sphere and charged with reconciling the family. In the wake of 9/11, it is clear that a cultural need for a halcyon past in which Mrs. Cleaver was the poster-woman for safety (despite her name), has turned what were once raw and outlandish films into escapist entertainment in which murder is wrapped up not in a BBQ bag, but in a pretty bow of traditional motherhood.

Realigning with tradition does not, however, stop at motherhood. In fact, all forms of femininity are brought back in line with a more traditional standard in the new films. This also goes for the ever-important character of the Final Girl, a character type first identified by Carol Clover. The feminism of the 1970s did not *cause* the Final Girl per se; but, looking back through the lens of the recent remakes, it is clear that these strong female leads were influenced by a social world in which feminism was a prominent political movement. Similarly, I am not arguing that just because Laurie Strode fights back and escapes Michael Myers in *Halloween*, the film is a feminist text. Instead, the important fact to note is that the rather isolated trend of having women as that final fighter was a fleeting one, and that this trend, when seen collectively, highlights a character type that is indicative of a brief cultural moment that *could* imagine the hero as a woman. The remakes, on the other hand, are inspired by a neo-conservative, post-feminist social milieu in which powerful female leads are considered un-needed and/or unwanted. They are erased or paired with a male hero who ends up saving them; or, in the case of the new *Massacre*, the strongly written Final Girl is undercut by constant aesthetic choices that highlight her sexuality, as she is set against a mother created to help relieve the blame of Leatherface.

Though the 2000s are significantly different from the 1970s in many ways, there are similarities between the time periods that impact how we consider post-feminism's role in a post-9/11 America. Both time periods are characterized by a deep-seated distrust of government (linked to wars in Vietnam and Iraq/Afghanistan) and changes in gender dynamics (the women's movement and the LGBTQ and Third Wave movements, including the rise of "Girl Power" in the 1990s).[5] Both time periods generate stories like horror films (more than the 1960s or the 1990s) that allow us to map our social fears concerning gender, foreign policy, and domestic anxieties onto the bodies of individuals. However, instead of exposing dynamic and culturally transgressive mothers, highlighting the decline of the American family, revealing a disinterest in the past or the future through nihilistic ennui, and embracing a powerful female character who could point out the flaws in the white, middle class nuclear family like the 1970s films did, the post-9/11 remakes focus on ways in which men attempt to reclaim a sense of power and superiority over their situations while repositioning women (mothers or otherwise) into traditional, family-oriented roles. This male superiority and female traditionalism often brings with it a heterosexual pairing (in contrast to a lone woman standing in defiance to patriarchal heterosexuality) and/or a glorification of the male hero, left to revel in his own bodily pain and moral victory. It also celebrates or excuses the killers' actions, often heaping that blame on their mothers or their victims.

The Texas Chain Saw Massacre is perhaps the most notorious of the original films considered in this essay. It combines the sheer terror it produces through visual effects, sound design, and a narrative with no explanation for the horrors that we witness. It also acts as a stylistic guide to later slashers because it introduces a group of teens that are killed in a rural setting, a trope that would become a staple of the genre. The remake, however, opts for heavy-handed changes to the plot that influence the gender dynamics of characters and changes in the aesthetics that devalue the strength of the Final Girl. While she is still present in the 2003 version, her wardrobe is pared down to nothing but skin-tight jeans and a midriff-baring undershirt, while lighting is constantly used to highlight her stomach and breasts. These

Figure 12.1 Sexualized cinematography and mise-en-scène in *The Texas Chainsaw Massacre* (2003) —Erin's costuming and top highlighting.

Source: The Texas Chainsaw Massacre, Marcus Nispel, 2003.

Figure 12.2 Sexualized cinematography and mise-en-scène in *The Texas Chainsaw Massacre* (2003) —Erin's low-angle shot in the meat locker.

Source: The Texas Chainsaw Massacre, Marcus Nispel, 2003.

stylistic changes have the effect of sexualizing the violence done to her in a way that was specifically avoided in the original film. The men in the original actually make it clear that her imprisonment is not sexual, but instead is linked to their demented take on their socio-economic position as out-of-work slaughterhouse workers (Figures 12.1 and 12.2).

But the stylistic changes also contribute to important transformations in the plot of the remake. The remake indicates a level of sexual activity in the "bad family" that was never present in the original, mostly by actually including women who represent violent, neglectful, or perverted forms of motherhood. While the original focuses on a family of men who are connected in unclear ways, and have as the only acknowledged female in the family unit a dead and desiccated grandmother, the remake works harder to create distinct generational family units while implicating perverse forms of motherhood as a root of the family's violence—a change which does double duty to blame mothers and to recreate a focus on traditional family structures absent from the original. This plot change is coupled with the fact that the slaughterhouse is still functioning, and that the family seems to have little if anything to do with its operations. Thus, the socio-economic tension of the original, a tension played out on the body of the Final Girl who manages to overcome her captors in her escape, is erased into an irrational indictment of motherhood that forgives the male violence against the overly sexualized heroine. The plot also diminishes the killer's culpability because, like Michael Myers in the remake of *Halloween* and *Halloween II*, the main monster in *Massacre* is given a sympathetic backstory to help the audience understand, end even rationalize, his violence. Thus, despite his horrible actions and supposed place as the villain, his responsibility is diminished and instead placed on the mother as she is indicted for raising a flawed son.

The next set of films to consider is the *Friday the 13th* (1980) and its sequel, *Friday the 13th Part II* (Miner 1981), as well as the 2009 remake, which is actually a reimagining of first three films …' with only a brief nod to the original. While the remake of *Massacre* creates mothers where once there were none, the new *Friday the 13th* erases the mother who is at the heart of the first film: Mrs. Voorhees. In the 1980 film, audiences assume that the killer is male. Made just two years after Johns Carpenter's *Halloween*, *Friday*'s plot of a group of teens killed before/during/after having sex sets the audience up to equate the killer with *Halloween*'s because it follows the same formula. However, the killer in *Friday the 13th* turns out to be the mother of a boy (Jason) who supposedly drowned while camp counselors were having sex instead of watching as lifeguards. The remake erases Mrs. Voorhees from all but a few minutes of the beginning of the film, and makes the killer Jason Voorhees (Jason would be the killer star of the many sequels to the original *Friday the 13th* throughout the '80s and '90s, having been resurrected somehow each and every time). This erasure of Mrs. Voorhees effectively silences the voice of one of film history's few mothers who is a killer, is allowed to tell her story with no one else's interpretation, and has pride in her own strength and conviction. Her erasure is coupled with the creation of a new male lead character who is living in the shadow of his mother's death (like Jason) and searching for his sister who has been imprisoned by Jason because she looks like his dead mother. This pits two motherless sons against each other, and instead of the Final Girl beheading Mrs. Voorhees to save herself, like in the original, she is relegated to embodying the dead Mrs. Voorhees long enough for her brother to save her by killing Jason himself. The film's entire gender dynamic changes because of this, and the aesthetic becomes almost like the '80s action films that Yvonne Tasker (1993) details in terms of their ability to show the bodies of men taking a beating and coming back for more. The remake also centers on solidifying the fractured family unit in reuniting the brother and sister, a trend found nowhere in the original.

The last two pairs of films are *Halloween* and *Halloween II*, co-written in 1978 and 1981 respectively by John Carpenter (he directed the former, Rick Rosenthal the latter) and then remade (written and directed) in order by Rob Zombie in 2007 and 2009. I have chosen to tackle these two pairs together because, unlike many horror sequels, both pairs have the same writer/director and diegetically, both pairs work to create a fluid timeframe from one film to the next (the sequels literally pick up where the first left off to help make the sequel more like a true second act than a separate film). Through a major re-writing of the original film's plot, Zombie uses his fan's sympathy toward his own musician persona to help bolster the sympathy felt toward Michael Myers, the films psychopathic killer. This manipulation of star texts and problematic sympathies is mirrored within the diegetic world as Dr. Loomis (Myers' psychiatrist) becomes famous for writing a book that details the terrors that Michael endured as a child, and the terrors that Michael inflicts on the main character, Laurie. This move works in unison with that of the sympathetic backstory that Zombie gives Myers by simultaneously erasing the focus on Laurie as the Final Girl/hero by both Michael (the monster) and Loomis (a male hero figure), a move reminiscent of the 2009 *Friday the 13th*. It also mirrors the fact that Loomis uses the sexualized violence perpetrated against Laurie for his own profit, just as Zombie uses the violent sexuality of his musician persona to proffer sympathies for the Myers character, thus exploiting his star text to sell the movie to a new audience. Furthermore, the role of the mother, completely absent in Carpenter's films, is central to the melodramatic framing of Michael in the remakes. Myers mother, played by Zombie's real-life wife Sherri Moon Zombie, refocuses the horror of Michael's violence on the broken home from which he came, essentially giving his acts a scapegoat relating to his mother and the family unit, of which it is made clear that she is the leader. This scapegoating is a trend of the post-9/11 films seen in *Massacre* as well as, to a lesser extent, *Friday the 13th*.

Not every post-9/11 horror fits the thesis I have laid forth in this essay. But a focus on emotional resolve, family structure, and the healing process necessary for a post-9/11 audience is still markedly present. Thus, even while a few films eschew the cultural conservatism of a post-feminism that ignores the need for strong women, the over-arching cultural need for hope squarely sets the new films in line with the melodramatic mode and traditional values. This type of cultural studies work cannot be done without the help of strong, feminist inflected criticism. The consideration of gender roles, family structures, and melodramatic plotlines must be considered in terms of trauma studies as well as feminist theory, as only by illuminating these basic tenets of American social structures will we be able fully explicate the post-9/11 cultural landscape.

Related topics

Yvonne Tasker, "Contested masculinities: the action film, the war film, and the Western"

Notes

1 For more on post-9/11anxieties in horror and related genres, see James Aston and John Walliss's (eds.) *To See the Saw Movies: Essays on Torture Porn and Post-9/11 Horror* (2013); Todd A. Comer and Lloyd Isaac Vayo's (eds.) *Terror and the Cinematic Sublime: Essays on Violence and the Unpresentable in Post-9/11 Films* (2013); and Guy Westwell's *Parallel Lines: Post-9/11 American Cinema* (2014).

2 Angela McRobbie's 2004 essay "Post-feminism and Popular Culture" and Yvonne Tasker and Diane Negra's "In Focus: Postfeminism and Contemporary Media Studies" (2005) concisely and clearly explicate the pervasive nature, and negative cultural ramifications, of post-feminism as a social mechanism that continues to show women as part of a system that allows for freedom only within the traditional structures of patriarchy. See also Deborah L. Siegel (1997), Carolyn Sorisio (1997), and Ann Brooks (1997) for a comprehensive overview of the fracturing of feminism.

3 Perhaps the two most influential works of feminist film theory that deal with horror are Carol J. Cover's 1993 *Men, Women, and Chainsaws* and Barbara Creed's 1993 *The Monstrous-Feminine*. These books are heavily informed by Julia Kristeva's *Powers of Horror* (1982) and the foundational "Visual Pleasure and Narrative Cinema" (1975) by Laura Mulvey. Other works include Linda Williams's "Film Bodies: Gender, Genre, and Excess" (1991); Barry Keith Grant's (ed.) *The Dread of Difference* (1996); and David Greven's *Representations of Femininity in American Genre Cinema* (2011); and Cynthia A. Freeland's "Feminist Frameworks of Horror Films" (1996), which urges a move away from psychoanalysis, a call that I work to answer here.

4 Clover highlights the ways in which the Final Girl is coded as masculine and the killer as feminized throughout *Men, Women, and Chainsaws*, and especially in the first chapter "Her Body, Himself."

5 For a concise history of the "Girl Power" and Riot Girls movements, see Kathleen Rowe Karlyn's article, "*Scream*, Popular Culture, and Feminism's Third Wave: 'I'm Not My Mother.'"(2003).

Bibliography

Aston, James and John Walliss. Eds. *To See the Saw Movies: Essays on Torture Porn and Post-9/11 Horror*. Jefferson, North Carolina: McFarland and Company, Inc., 2013. Print.

Brooks, Ann. *Postfeminisms: Feminism, Cultural Theory, and Cultural Forms*. New York: Routledge, 1997. Print.

Clover, Carol J. *Men, Women, and Chainsaws: Gender in the Modern Horror Film*. Princeton, NJ: Princeton UP, 1993. Print.

Comer, Todd A. and Lloyd Isaac Vayo. Eds. *Terror and the Cinematic Sublime: Essays on Violence and the Unpresentable in Post-9/11 Films*. Jefferson, North Carolina: McFarland and Company, Inc., 2013. Print.

Creed, B. *The Monstrous-Feminine: Film, Feminism, Psychoanalysis*. London: Routledge, 1993.

Doane, Mary Ann. "The 'Woman's Film': Possession and Address." *Home Is Where the Heart Is*. Ed. Christine Gledhill. London: British Film Institute, 1987. 283–98. Print.

Faludi, Susan. *The Terror Dream: Myth and Misogyny in an Insecure America*. 2007. New York: Picador, 2008. Print.

Freeland, Cynthia A. "Feminist Frameworks for Horror Films." *Film Theory and Criticism: Introductory Readings*. 1996. 6th Edition. Eds. Leo Braudy and Marshall Cohen. New York: Oxford UP, 2004. 742–63. Print.

Friday the 13th (Killer Cut: Special Extended Version). Dir. Marcus Nispel. New Line Productions, 2009. Blu-Ray.

Friday the 13th (Uncut). Dir. Sean S. Cunningham. Georgetown Productions, Inc., 1980. Paramount, 2009. Blu-Ray.

Friday the 13th Part 2 (Deluxe Edition). Dir. Steve Miner. Georgetown Productions, Inc., 1981. Paramount Home Entertainment, 2009. DVD.

Gledhill, Christine. "The Melodramatic Field: An Investigation." *Home is Where the Heart Is: Studies in Melodrama and the Woman's Film*. London: BFI, 1987. Print.

Grant, Barry Keith. Ed. *The Dread of Difference: Gender and the Horror Film*, 1996. 2nd Edition. Austin: University of Texas Press, 2015. Print.

Greven, David. *Representations of Femininity in American Genre Cinema: The Women's Film, Film Noir, and Modern Horror*. New York: Palgrave Macmillan, 2011. Print.

Halloween. Dir. John Carpenter. Compass International Pictures, 1978. Starz Home Entertainment, 2007. Blu-Ray.

Halloween (Unrated Director's Cut). Dir. Rob Zombie. Dimension Films, 2007. Dimension Home Entertainment, 2007. Blu-Ray.

Halloween II. Dir. John Carpenter. Dino De Laurentiis Corporation, 1981. Universal, 2001. DVD.

Halloween II (Unrated Director's Cut). Dir. Rob Zombie. Dimension Films, 2009. Dimension Home Entertainment, 2009. Blu-Ray.

Heywood, Leslie and Jennifer Drake. "Introduction." *Third Wave Agenda*. Ed. Leslie Heywood and Jennifer Drake. Minneapolis, MN: University of Minnesota Press, 1997. 1–24. Print.

House of Wax. Dir. André De Toth. Bryan Foy Productions and Warner Brothers, 1953. Warner Home Video, 2013. DVD.

House of Wax. Dir. Jaume Collet-Serra. Warner Brothers, Village Roadshow, and Dark Castle Entertainment, 2005. Warner Home Video, 2006. Blu-Ray.

Imitation of Life. Dir. Douglas Sirk. Universal International Pictures, 1959. Universal Studios Home Entertainment, 2008. DVD.

I Spit on Your Grave a.k.a. Day of the Woman. Dir. Meir Zarchi. Cinemagic Pictures. 1978. Elite Entertainment, 2002. DVD.

I Spit on Your Grave (Unrated). Dir. Steven R. Monroe. Cinetel Films, 2010. Anchor Bay Entertainment, 2011. Blu-Ray.

Jeffords, Susan. *Hard Bodies: Hollywood Masculinity in the Regan Era*. New Brunswick: Rutgers, 1994. Print.

Karlyn, Kathleen Rowe. "*Scream*, Popular Culture, and Feminism's Third Wave: 'I'm Not My Mother.'" *Genders*. 38 (2003). Online. January 30, 2014. www.atria.nl/ezines/IAV_606661/ IAV_606661_2010_51/g38_rowe_karlyn.html (last accessed July 16, 2016).

Kristeva, Julia. *Powers of Horror: An Essay on Abjection*. Trans. Leon S. Roudiez. New York: Columbia UP, 1982. Print.

Landy, Marcia. "Introduction." *Imitations of Life: A Reader on Film Television Melodrama*. Ed. Marcia Landy. Detroit, Michigan: Wayne State UP, 1991. 13–30.

McRobbie, Angela. "Post-Feminism and Popular Culture." *Feminist Media Studies*. 4.3 (November 2004): 255–64. Print.

Mulvey, Laura. "Afterthoughts on Visual Pleasure and Narrative Cinema." 1975. *Visual and Other Pleasures*. Bloomington: Indiana UP, 1989. 29–38. Print.

——— "Notes on Sirk and Melodrama." *Home Is Where the Heart Is*. Ed. Christine Gledhill. London: British Film Institute, 1987. 75–82. Print.

——— "Visual Pleasure and Narrative Cinema." *Film Theory and Criticism: Introductory Readings*. 6th Edition. Eds. Leo Braudy and Marshall Cohen. New York: Oxford UP, 2004. 837–48. Print.

Psycho. Dir. Alfred Hitchcock. Shamely Productions, 1960. Universal, 2010. Blu-Ray.

Schatz, Thomas. "The Family Melodrama." *Imitations of Life: A Reader on Film & Television Melodrama*. Ed. Marcia Landy. Detroit: Wayne State UP, 1991. 148–67. Print.

Siegel, Deborah L. "Reading Between the Waves: Feminist Historiography in a 'Postfeminist' Moment." *Third Wave Agenda*. Ed. Leslie Heywood and Jennifer Drake. Minneapolis, MN: University of Minnesota Press, 1997. 55–82. Print.

Sorisio, Carolyn. "A Tale of Two Feminisms: Power and Victimization in Contemporary Feminist Debate." *Third Wave Agenda*. Ed. Leslie Heywood and Jennifer Drake. Minneapolis, MN: University of Minnesota Press. 1997. 134–54. Print.

Staiger, Janet. *Perverse Spectators: The Practices of Film Reception*. New York: NY UP, 2000. Print.

Tasker, Yvonne. *Spectacular Bodies: Gender, Genre, and the Action Cinema*. New York: Routledge, 1993. Print.

——— "In Focus: Postfeminism and Contemporary Media Studies." *Cinema Journal*, 44.2, 2005: 107–10. Print.

Tasker, Yvonne and Diane Negra. Eds. *Interrogating Postfeminism*. Durham: NC. Duke UP, 2007. Print.

The Texas Chainsaw Massacre. Marcus Nispel. New Line Cinema, 2003. Warner Home Video, 2009. Blu-Ray.

The Texas Chain Saw Massacre. Dir. Tobe Hooper. Vortex, Inc., 1974. Dark Sky Films, 2008. Blu-Ray.

Westwell, Guy. *Parallel Lines: Post-9/11 American Cinema*. New York: Columbia UP, 2014. Print.

Wetmore, Kevin J. *Post-9/11 Horror in American Cinema*. New York: Continuum Books, 2012. Print.

Williams, Linda. "Film Bodies: Gender, Genre, and Excess." 1991. *Film Theory and Criticism: Introductory Readings*. 6th Edition. Eds. Leo Braudy and Marshall Cohen. New York: Oxford UP, 2004. 727–41. Print.

——— "Melodrama Revised." *Refiguring American Film Genres*. Ed. Nick Browne. Berkeley: University of California Press, 1998. 43–88. Print.

——— "'Something Else Besides a Mother': *Stella Dallas* and the Maternal Melodrama." *Imitations of Life: A Reader on Film and Television Melodrama*. Ed. Marcia Landy. Detroit: Wayne State UP, 1991. 307–30. Print.

13

SLAPSTICK COMEDIENNES IN SILENT CINEMA

Women's laughter and the feminist politics of gender in motion

Margaret Hennefeld

Perhaps no image caused early film spectators greater discomfort in the 1890s than the public eruption of female laughter: the convulsive explosion of ribs heaving in their tight corsets, loud ripples of vocal mirth issuing from the oral cavities, and, worst of all, the implication that inappropriate innuendos were not lost on female viewers. While many of these tense and uncomfortable visions of female laughter have been long since forgotten, they pose crucial historiographic challenges for feminist film scholars today, and remain broadly resonant and provocative reminders of the very deep-seated social anxieties about women's relationship to laughter and comedy. As this chapter will explore, slapstick comediennes in early cinema both enacted and reflected heated cultural debates about the relationship between gender, comedic pleasure, and feminist social politics. From early 1900s trick films about exploding housemaids, to 19-teens knockabout comedies depicting domestic assault, to 1920s flapper films about commodity capitalism, silent movies featuring slapstick comediennes represent archival traces that reveal crucial formations of modern feminism and popular screen culture.

During the years while moving pictures were emerging as a mass medium and commercial institution, there was an explosion of discourse attempting to regulate and constrain female laughter in public. In 1898, the *New York Herald* advised women to adopt something called "The New Laugh": "It is a laugh, all but the sound, all but the opening of the mouth and the showing of the teeth. It is fun and amusement personified, but all silence." At the same time as the *Herald* coaxed women to pursue an ethereal experience of laughter that would efface the role of the body, the *Woman's Home Companion* leveled its censorship at "the funny woman" ad hominem: "We know you are very funny, but one's face aches with continual smiling, and an exclusively funny diet is about as sustaining as a ration of mere pepper and salt." Whether a site of inappropriate bodily excess or of gastronomical starvation, the female laugh was characterized as corrupt, immoral, and distinctly unfeminine.

Yet, early motion pictures tell a completely different story about women and laughter. It was completely conventional and uncontroversial for women to laugh uproariously onscreen, exemplified by films such as *Rube and Mandy at Coney Island* (Edwin S. Porter, 1903), *Laughing Gas* (Edwin S. Porter, 1907), *Betty and Jane Go to the Theatre* (Roméo

Bosetti, 1911), *Daisy Doodad's Dial* (Florence Turner, 1914), and *The House of Fifi* (Viggo Larsen, 1914). In *Laughing Gas*, an African-American woman, Mandy (Bertha Regustus), experiences uncontrollable laughter after being given nitrous oxide (laughing gas) by her dentist, and then proceeds to spread her laughter contagiously throughout the public sphere: to fellow streetcar passengers, gospel churchgoers, white police officers, and even to a justice of the peace. In *Daisy Doodad's Dial*, a bored housewife practices for an amateur face-making competition in public, eventually getting herself arrested and then having hysterical visions at night of her own disembodied laughter and spectral facial contortions (Figure 13.1). In numerous bourgeois "comedies of manners" throughout the 19-teens and 1920s, women's laughter often functioned as the glue that held the film's narrative together.

For example, in *House of Fifi*—a German comedy made shortly before the eruption of World War One—a female hat shop proprietor practically causes the downfall of the Prussian Military by enticing high-ranking officers to purchase increasingly expensive ladies' millinery. As the gift exchange and marital cuckoldry plots get messy, Fifi (Wanda Treumann), reorients the spectator by halting narrative time, stepping outside of her film character's own body to share an ironic laugh with the spectator. Similarly, in American comedies from this time, such as *Love and Gasoline* (Mabel Normand, 1914), *Are Waitresses Safe?* (Hampton Del Ruth, 1917) with Louise Fazenda, and *The Danger Girl* (Clarence G. Badger, 1916) with Gloria Swanson, women's extra-diegetic laughter—residing between the fictive world of the film and the living body of the film spectator—provided an image for stabilizing the comic slippage of misidentifications sustained by a film's plot. Female laughter covered over the missing links in comedic film narration.

Beyond the literal image of women laughing, ladies frequently performed outrageous and perverse bodily gestures in order to provoke the convulsive amusement of laughing film spectators. For example, in popular films of what I call the *exploding housemaid genre* (see Hennefeld 2014a)—such as *Mary Jane's Mishap* (G.A. Smith, 1903), *A Shocking Incident* (AM&B, 1903), and *How Bridget Made the Fire* (AM&B, 1900)—working-class women accidentally incinerate or electrocute themselves while attempting to perform traditional domestic chores with modern mechanical devices. Using jump cuts adapted from vanishing

Figure 13.1   Daisy Doodad's Dial.

Source: Daisy Doodad's Dial, Florence Turner, 1914.

lady films—"now you see her, now you don't!"—women disappear in puffs of smoke after heaping too much paraffin onto the hearth fire. The instantaneity of the film cut was thereby synchronized with the spontaneous eruption of laughter it provoked for the spectator. Women's calamitous, contortionist, and disappearing bodies somehow had the power to mediate the otherwise very charged relationship between startling screen effects and uproarious spectator embodiment: between onscreen explosions and nervous spectator convulsions.

While audiences delighted in the spectacle of moving pictures throughout the 1890s—at vaudeville variety theaters, traveling shows, garden parties, and community centers—the physical encounter with women's laughing bodies in the public sphere provoked considerable displeasure. Society columnists advised their female readers "to banish the giggles once and for all,"[1] while derisive journalists warned all readers against the hazards of female senses of humor: "The funny woman per se is a pestilence in the land. Carelessly and roguishly she seeks only to make the world laugh, sends her merry shot and shells here and there and takes no note of the wounded in the field."[2] Women's humor was here ideologically weaponized—equated with military violence—while female laughter was singled out for public censorship and repression.

Early motion pictures, with their mystifying and slippery relationship to the history and presence of the bodies that they capture, possessed the tremendous capacity to defuse pervasive social anxieties about the eruption of women's laughter in the public sphere. Moreover, the instance of onscreen female comedy provided a curiously potent image for mediating the spectator's own bodily experience of madcap cinematic movement. Like comedy, which hinges on surprise, reversal, and incongruity, filmmaking is all about the spectacle of paradoxes: animating past moments and still photograms as if they had come back to life and were really moving again before our eyes. In late-nineteenth- and early-twentieth-century American culture, filmmaking and comedic performance represented crucial interlocking sites for women to redefine the norms and constraints of femininity. Meanwhile, the charged image of female humor onscreen gave filmmakers an impetus to experiment with both the aesthetic and formal potentials, and the social and political limits of narrative filmmaking (see Hennefeld 2014b).

Slapstick comedy and feminist film theory

The intersections between gender and comedic performance have always occupied uncertain places in both feminist film theory (with its polemics of anti-pleasure) and in film histories of slapstick comedy. Traditionally, silent film experts have focused on the genius of the male clowns—Charlie Chaplin, Buster Keaton, Harold Lloyd, Stan Laurel, Oliver Hardy, Fatty Arbuckle, et al.—occasionally mentioning Mabel Normand, Marie Dressler, or Marion Davies as afterthoughts. The ever-evolving spate of "forgotten clowns," including Harry Langdon, Charley Chase, and Raymond Griffiths, builds on the patriarchal canon of comics established in Walter Kerr's *Silent Clowns* (1990), Kevin Brownlow's *The Parade's Gone By* (1976), and William K. Everson's *American Silent Film* (1998). Recently, archivists including Mariann Lewinsky, Bryony Dixon, and Elif Rongen-Kaynakçi, as well as feminist historians such as Jennifer Bean, Jane Gaines, Steve Massa, Kristen Anderson Wagner, Jacqueline Stewart, Vicki Callahan, and Joanna Rapf, have helped to unearth and establish the significant presence of slapstick comediennes in silent film historiography. More than a game of archival lost and found, rediscoveries of *forgotten comediennes*—including Cissy Fitzgerald, Valentina Frascaroli, Sarah Duhamel, Gale Henry, Alice Howell, Elfie Fey, and

Josie Sadler—open onto heated debates about the politics of gender and cultural memory, feminist polemics of pleasure and anti-pleasure, and theoretical discourses of gender and sexual performativity through comedy.

The polemical exclusion of comedy from feminist theory has a long history: from Laura Mulvey's famous call for *the radical destruction of visual pleasure* (1975), to Hélène Cixous' puzzling erasure of comedy from her passionate redemption of "The Laugh of the Medusa" (1976), to Linda Williams' pointed exclusion of comedy from her gendered theorization of sexually charged "body genres" (1991), to pervasive tendencies to equate the comedic with the non-serious in recent feminist scholarship and activism. Cultural critics remain as uncertain about the relation between gender politics and comedic laughter now as they have ever been. Rather than *rescue* obscure comediennes from their historical invisibility— itself a desire deriving from a misogynistic fantasy of feminine impotency—it is the gesture of this chapter to put these missing archival links back into circulation. Forgotten slapstick comedienne films raise crucial questions about gendered modernity, comedic ambiguity, and the fluidity of feminist and political identification that speak centrally to our own present day political challenges and cultural anxieties.

Early cinema: the public politics of gendered laughter

Early film comedies exploited every imaginable gendered scenario about how women might negotiate the shifting meanings and pervasive instabilities of femininity in modern culture. Films such as *Mary Jane's Mishap*, *Athletic American Girls* (Vitagraph, 1907), and *The Suffragette's Dream* (Pathé, 1909) draw on the unique temporal and spatial capacities of filmmaking to offer up images of outrageous gender and social transformation. Women in these films, as I have mentioned, do extraordinary violence to their own bodies in order to adapt to their shifting conditions of everyday living. They spontaneously combust while doing housework, dismember their own limbs to expedite their labor efficiency, hot wire automobiles to flee from lecherous masters, or completely overthrow the sexual division of labor in comical visions of gendered modernity. The situations in these films range from suffragette activism to shoe store foot fetishism, to female mob uprising, to the pornography of walking over a subway grate while wearing an ankle skirt, to licking stamps in a post office. From episodic antics to full-scale revolution, film comedy represented a space for negotiating ruptures and impasses in classical ideals of femininity, as well as projected futures for radical feminist politics.

As Kristen Anderson Wagner (2011) has put it,

> Comediennes in early twentieth-century entertainments such as vaudeville and silent film were performing at a time when debates about women and comedy were at their most heated and when the very concepts of 'woman' and "femininity" were undergoing massive transformation.

In film comedies such as *A Sticky Woman* (Alice Guy-Blaché, 1906), *The Consequences of Feminism* (Alice Guy-Blaché, 1906), *Petticoat Camp* (Thanhouser, 1912), *When Women Vote* (Lubin, 1907), and *The Suffragette Sheriff* (Kalem, 1912), the cinematic temporality of comedy provided a testing ground for cultural producers to represent alternative visions of gender identity, filmmaking form, and the politics of cultural pleasure.

For example, *The Consequences of Feminism* satirically exaggerates sexist woes that feminist liberation would be tantamount to rote gender role inversion: men dressing and acting like women, and women like men. *How They Got the Vote* (Edison, 1913) literally holds time itself hostage to feminist political progress: traffic halts, bodies freeze in place, and time stands still until women earn voting rights. *Petticoat Camp* humorously depicts a group of outdoorswomen who go on strike from their domestic chores during a co-ed camping trip, and then leave the men's camp in ruins: women use the sexual division of labor as cultural leverage to reveal the instabilities internal to the construction of the very ideal of masculinity.

These archival films flaunt their striking and experimental images of inappropriate reversal and female bodily fluidity: images that thematize the liquidity of gender identity and of feminine social norms. They thereby exhibit the crucial importance of filmmaking for redefining the place of women's bodies in mass culture, as well as the fundamental role of gendered comedy in formative histories of cinema.

In films from the 1890s and 1900s, gendered comedy hinges on the uncertain place of women in the public sphere: the spectator laughs off the shock of tremendous social and civic upheaval. Anca Parvulescu describes early cinema as "a laughing gas party" in her broadly suggestive book on laughter, gender, and critical theory, and Miriam Hansen links early cinema's *excess of comic appeals* to the potential for early film spectatorship to represent a feminist, alternative public sphere: "a space apart and a space in between ... a site for the imaginative negotiation of gaps" (1994: 118) in one's own lived identity and experience of urban modernity. As Virginia Woolf has put it in her incisive but rarely quoted[3] 1905 essay on gender and humor, "All the hideous excrescences that have overgrown our modern life, the pomps and conventions and dreary solemnities, dread nothing so much as the flash of laughter which, like lightning, shrivels them up and leaves the bones bare" (1986: 60). In other words, laughter hinges on spontaneity—the jolt of surprise erupting into an explosive bodily convulsion—and the temporality of laughter is shot through with gender and social connotations.

For example, in *What Happened in the Tunnel* (Edwin S. Porter, 1903), a white middle-class woman and her African-American maid ride the train unaccompanied by a male authority figure, which makes them vulnerable to assault by a lecherous fellow rider. When the train enters a tunnel and the screen goes dark, the spectator perhaps fears the worst. This tension about sexual vulnerability gets parlayed into uproarious comedy through cinema's capacity for abrupt transformation and extreme reversal. The physical location of the tunnel motivates a prolonged jump cut. When visibility returns, the harasser appears in a compromised position embracing not the white lady but her black maid: the effect of a prank by the two women. This comedy of racial and class reversal thereby addresses pervasive anxieties about rape and sexual assault with the racist fantasy of a black woman's sexual unviability (further obfuscating the frequent, traumatic event of black women's rape, abduction, and impregnation by white men, for whom they signified not unviability but free sexual access). The film does not offer a social solution, so much as a temporary resolution forged through laughter. In an incessant chain of displacements, the spectator learns to accept women's increasing presence in risky public spaces by means of the astonishing, spontaneous temporality coordinated through laughter, gender and racial (mis)identifications, and motion picture projection.

As Woolf writes,

> Laughter is the expression of the comic spirit within us, and the comic spirit concerns itself with oddities and eccentricities and deviations from the recognised pattern. It makes its comment in the sudden and spontaneous laugh which comes, we hardly know why, and we cannot tell when.
>
> *(1986: 59)*

Whereas most writers on the comic, such as Freud and Bergson, emphasize the dilution of humor risked by over-explanation—slowing down the joke to the point that it no longer becomes funny—Woolf pointedly asserts that "If we took time to think … we should find, doubtless, that what is superficially comic is fundamentally tragic, and while the smile was on our lips the water would stand in our eyes" (ibid.). Woolf formulated her views on laughter, gender, and the slippery line between tragedy and comedy in a cultural landscape increasingly influenced by the motion picture technologies. As Laura Mulvey notes in *Death 24x a Second*, "The technological drive towards photography and film had always been animated by the aspiration to preserve the fleeting instability of reality and the passing of time in a fixed image" (2006: 18). However, comedy turns this dynamic on its head. For example, with the trick cut, the jolt of spontaneous transformation stands in for an anxiety about contingency and impermanence. With comedy, to return to Woolf's argument, prolonging the image of rupture risks exposing the basis of comic joy in the burden of tears.

This is precisely the tension driving early gendered film comedies and their push and pull between laughter and pathos—between gleeful social transformation and the utter terror of sexual violence that these films compulsively rehearse. Alice Guy-Blaché's transvestite post office comedy, *A Sticky Woman* (1906), epitomizes the tension between rupture and fixity, between domestic tradition and gender modernity, and between mirthful pleasure and raging anxiety at the heart of this genre. This film depicts the plight of a young housemaid whose bourgeois employer forces her to lick a slew of postage stamps consecutively while standing in line at the post office. Evoking Henri Bergson's definition of the comic as "a growing callousness to social life" (1911: 66), the woman automatically flaps her tongue like a trained seal, or a salivating automaton. However, unable to desexualize her mechanically flapping orifice entirely, she unfortunately attracts the attention of a prurient male bystander. Undiscouraged by her oral rigidity, the man actually calculates the precise interval of her licks, and then rushes in and kisses her just at the very instant when her tongue will flap out of her mouth.

The man takes advantage not of her sexual promiscuity, but of her mechanical precision. Made by one of the most prolific female filmmakers, Alice Guy-Blaché (who directed over 700 films in France and the United States between 1896 and 1920),[4] *A Sticky Woman* ends by highlighting the abrupt violence of the film cut itself. When the sticky woman and her sketchy assaulter get their faces stuck together due to some postage glue residue accumulated on her lips, an office boy rushes in and snips them apart. What a *difference* a cut makes: half of the gentleman's mustache becomes firmly glued to the sticky woman's face. Again, *A Sticky Woman* performs the rampant fluidity of sexual norms and gender identity through the comic spontaneity necessary to provoke laughter. The temporality of pleasure and amusement becomes a radical site of political opportunity for redefining cultural norms and social traditions.

Although exemplary, *A Sticky Woman* was by no means exceptional. There was a powerful osmosis between women's bodies and emergent film technologies, and comedy presented an irresistible means for exploring the slippery line between these two entities. Other early film comedies make this dynamic more explicit: in *Mary Jane's Mishap*, a British maid explodes out of the chimney while attempting to light her employer's hearth fire with paraffin. A jump cut incinerates her, while a double exposure (the superimposition of multiple photographic exposures) later allows her to return as a specter who haunts mourners at her own gravestone. Women assumed a fantastic range of shapes and textures, places and positions, sexual and racial identities in early filmmaking: transmogrifying themselves into micrographic nicotine fairies (*Princess Nicotine*, 1908), cutting off their own limbs to finish their housework on time (*The Kitchen Maid's Dream*, 1907), razing the public sphere in protest to win voting rights (*Kansas City Saloon Smasher*, 1901), or having spontaneous, female to male sexual reassignment by ingesting magical African seeds (*A Florida Enchantment*, 1914). The collision between comedy and filmmaking represented a crucial horizon for blowing up staid notions of classical femininity, and for exploring and redefining the aesthetics and politics of gender, sexual, and racial identification.

Transitional comediennes: polite laughter versus comic anarchy

There were heated debates in the late-nineteenth and early-twentieth centuries about the social meaning or value of laughter and comedy. Typically, the argument goes that we laugh at someone as a form of cruelty in order to correct her/his behavior. Henri Bergson defines laughter as "a social gesture that singles out and represses a special kind of absent-mindedness in men and in events" (1911: 46). Thomas Hobbes (1969), Boris Sidis (1913), James Sully, George Vasey (1877), and many other philosophers and intellectuals all made a version of this argument: that laughter represents a social tool for keeping people in line. It is always premised on *distance*—emotional and psychological distance—between the laughing subject and the object of ridicule. As the poet Charles Baudelaire argues, "Laughter is Satanic": it is an expression of moral and psychological superiority, as Sully puts it, "to laugh away something in [society's] members which it sees to be unfitting" (1902: 411). However, the explanatory power of this *corrective hypothesis* falls short depending on the example at hand. The instance of a woman getting assaulted for licking postage stamps too suggestively, or a suffragette dreaming about freezing traffic and holding time itself hostage to the future of voting rights equality, contrasts sharply with an eccentric walking into a door or a police officer getting hit over the head with a frying pan. The corrective force of laughter is radically diluted by the uncertain and shifting power dynamics that these feminist scenarios provoke.

Indeed, the gender dynamic of slapstick ridicule was always a major point of tension for industry filmmakers working in the comedy genre. Mack Sennett, the director of Keystone Comedies, purportedly lamented that

> men don't want to laugh at pretty girls, not convulsively anyway, and so the actresses who specialize in all-out slapstick tend to be women like Marie Dressler, Phyllis Allen, Louise Fazenda, Polly Moran, Dot Farley, Charlotte Greenwood, Martha Raye, and Judy Canova, whom the ordinary male wouldn't think of romantically anyway.
>
> (Dale 2000: 105)

Many Keystone films such as *The Fatal Mallet* (1914), *Teddy at the Throttle* (1917), and *Tillie's Punctured Romance* (1914)—featuring Normand, Swanson, and Dressler respectively —were famous for their repetitive, violent knockabout gags and ingenious choreography of the clown's bodily disintegration.[5] Slapstick violence always teeters between episodic repetition and the risk of irreversible, permanent damage. However, this anxiety about the permanence of bodily abuse becomes especially charged when women's bodies take on the simultaneous hyper-vulnerability and physical invincibility of the slapstick clown.

Sennett's claim that men do not want to laugh convulsively at pretty women (presumably because they would rather be doing other convulsive things to women's bodies, but also because it transgresses classical ideals of femininity as uncorrupted and ethereal) precisely and productively misses the point of why it was so exciting to see women performing in the slapstick genre. Audiences were obsessed with witnessing every possible permutation of women's bodily violation and rescue, and slapstick knockabout was a crucial component of *this perverse, undying fixation with testing the limits of female durability*. (The term "slapstick" itself derives from the commedia dell'arte *bataccio*: literally a slap-stick that makes a loud sound effect using two wooden slats while delivering a disproportionately mild blow to the body.[6])

The gender dynamics of comic violence drive the plot of many Keystone Comedies. In *Love, Speed, and Thrills* (Walter Wright, 1915), Minta Durfee plays the wife of recurring series character Ambrose (Mack Swain), who has the misfortune of saving an evil villain from hanging himself. After pulling the man off of a cliff by his noose, Ambrose invites this evil villain, Mr. Walrus (Chester Conklin), into his home, where Walrus proceeds to seduce Mrs. Ambrose, spurring a multi-car, extended chase sequence to save Ambrose's wife from abduction and sexual violation. The bodies of everyone involved become completely fantastic and invulnerable to harm. This is the joke of the chase scene: Mrs. Ambrose falls off of a high-speed vehicle at least a dozen times without a scratch. By actualizing and exaggerating the violence that the chase pursuit is meant to defer, this Keystone film lampoons the film industry's Victorian hangovers: the obsession with safeguarding women's bodies from vulnerability and exposure in the public sphere, which had become the plot point in a disproportionate number of film melodramas—epitomized by rescue films such as D.W. Griffith's *The Lonely Villa* (1909) and Lois Weber's *Suspense* (1913), both films about women who telephone for help[7] on the brink of sexual assault by violent intruders.

Mabel's Strange Predicament (Mabel Normand, 1914) uses situational comedy instead of high-speed motoring to represent the comic tensions between gendered decorum and bodily anarchism. Like many of the comedies of manners popular in the 19-teens—meant to address an aspirational or bourgeois spectator as opposed to ethnic or working-class publics[8]—this film centers on the inappropriate place of a woman's body in a fancy hotel and the series of misunderstandings that it triggers. Mabel plays a hotel guest, who is being pursued by a drunken tramp (Chaplin, in his first film appearance as this character[9]). Desperate to evade the tramp after accidentally locking herself out of her hotel room, Mabel runs through the hallways in her pajamas, sneaks into a strange man's room and hides under his bed, and eventually acts out all of her worst nightmares regarding what might happen to a lone woman residing in a commercial boudoir. This was a key pretext for outrageous female-centric and often feminist comedy in the 19-teens, especially espoused by Keystone: women's excess of vulnerability to public risk and exposure paradoxically drives them into a series of impossibly precarious, comical situations and positions.

Beyond Keystone's all-out slapstick effects, women's physical comedy sprang from a recurring, underlying tension about the viability of its own continued existence, ideologically, physically, and commercially. What would it mean for women's bodies to become funny in relentlessly new, dynamic, and surprising ways against the bourgeois upward mobility and institutional standardization of the American film industry? For example, vaudeville dynamo Eva Tanguay formed her own production company during a brief foray into filmmaking to star in two films: *Energetic Eva* (1916) and *The Wild Girl* (1917)—both of which test the comedienne's explosive bodily excess against the narrative constraints of early Hollywood constructions of femininity. *The Wild Girl* opens with footage of Tanguay's vaudeville act, featuring the comedienne posing in a towering headdress, with her unkempt curly hair poofing out beneath, and sporting glittering jewelry and attire, as a preface to a film about a deprived woman ("Firefly") who is separated from her wealthy parents at birth and then raised among gypsies. Film narratives were often organized around the need to rationalize these contradictory images of femininity as *viscerally unbound, politely decorous,* and *commercially resplendent*—all at once!

The codification of film's storytelling grammar was intrinsically bound up with these fraught negotiations of modern femininity. Florence Turner ("The Vitagraph Girl") fled to the United Kingdom to form her own production company and direct herself in a film comedy about a woman who is haunted by the cinematic incongruities of femininity. *Daisy Doodad's Dial* depicts the plight of a homemaker who trains relentlessly to compete in an amateur face-making competition. The plot is especially meta-cinematic in that Daisy Doodad must condense all of the nervous bodily spasms of slapstick clowning into her face—it is really a film about a woman who is preparing for her close-up. After performing some truly horrific facial gestures on a streetcar, Daisy eventually gets herself arrested for public indecency. Mystically, she then transmits her facial gestures over the telephone to her husband in order to instruct him to bail her out of prison. With the emerging syntax of film narrative and character identification—which hinged especially on frequent close-ups of faces—the diffuse bodily anarchism of the clown was often localized to specific body parts and physical gestures.[10] If Daisy can transmit her facial gestures over the telephone, her uncanny ability derives from the broader contradictions internal to comedienne perform-ance: women's aesthetic containment by the emerging conventions of narrative filmmak-ing, against their persistent, forceful, and inventive means for asserting the anarchic necessity of bodily play fundamental to the slapstick genre.

Comediennes blow up the home front

On the cusp of the eruption of World War One in 1914, comediennes portended the traumas of trench warfare by reducing their homes to catastrophic spaces completely uninhabitable for traditional domestic life. European films especially flaunted images of their slapstick comediennes running wild in front of the camera. Film actresses in Britain (such as Alma Taylor and Chrissie White who star in the *Tilly the Tomboy* [1910] series), France (Sarah Duhamel, Mistinguett, and Musidora), Italy (Lea Giunchi, Valentina Frascaroli), and Germany (Wanda Treumann, Rosa Porten) continued to indulge in bawdy, demonstrative gags long after moral censorship delimited comedienne physicality in early Hollywood filmmaking. Leading up to and during the war, European comic sensibilities were much darker and more overtly sadistic in depicting the relationship between physical realities of comic violence and the fantastic bodily indestructability of the slapstick clown.

For example, in the French comedienne series, such as *Rosalie* (Pathé, starring Sarah Duhamel, 1911–12), *Léontine* (Pathé, starring unknown actress, 1910–11), *Pétronille* (Pathé, starring Sarah Duhamel, 1913–14), and *Cunégonde* (Lux, starring unknown actress, 1912–13), women's gags routinely hinged on turning their domestic spaces into shambles. The trenches on the Marne were probably better fortified against horrific destruction than Rosalie's new apartment in *Rosalie Moves In* (1911), or Cunégonde's employers' domicile in *Cunégonde Receives Visitors* (1912). The instance of a woman taking a bath or acquiring a toy boat (*Betty's Boat*, 1911) would almost guarantee the erosion of every ceiling or floorboard in her home.

There were slews of uproarious female clowns throughout the messy transitional years of the 19-teens, and their performances—in addition to meriting the usual heap of qualifiers such as "ingenious," "virtuosic," and "acrobatic"—are foremost interesting on an existential level: comedy springs from the very legitimacy of its own premise. The comedic tension and nervous anticipation that erupts in convulsive laughter derives from audience and industry discomfort with the fundamental premise of laughing at women's bodily exposure and potential violation. American comediennes including Normand, Turner, Dressler, Swanson, Tanguay, and Durfee, as well as Flora Finch, Alice Howell, Fay Tincher, Polly Moran, Patsy De Forest, Gale Henry, and, *really*, too many other funny ladies to enumerate, provoked every manner of narrative pretense, aesthetic contrivance, or commercial gimmick for motivating the incredible popularity of comedienne slapstick.

Rather than regard this 19-teens period as a linear history of comediennes' increasing physical suppression, closer readings of these transitional comedienne films themselves reveal a very different image of female comedy and physical embodiment. Comediennes wrestled with the contradictions between moral politeness and shocking display, between censorship and transgression—a dynamic tension that often provided the very basis for the comic scenarios that fueled narrative filmmaking as an institution. As Alenka Zupačič argues in *The Odd One In* (2008), comedy is

> profoundly materialistic ... not simply [in] that it reminds us of ... the mud, the dirt, dense and coarse reality as our ultimate horizon (which we need to accept) ... [but] because it gives voice and body to the impasses and contradictions of this materiality itself.

Comedy always arises from the gap between *being a body* and *having a body*: between gendered physical experience and its own meta-image.

This contradiction between bodily risk and physical censorship—between unhinged exposure and scrupulous awareness—emerges from the fundamental tensions of modern feminism and gender politics. The conflict or impasse between bodily action and social identification has been of central interest to feminist film theorists, cutting across psychoanalytic writings on language and sexual difference (Mary Ann Doane, Laura Mulvey, Kaja Silverman); black feminism and critical race theory (bell hooks, Nicole Fleetwood, Jayna Brown); queer theory and activism (Teresa de Lauretis, Jack Halberstam, B. Ruby Rich); and contemporary geopolitics of postcoloniality, nation, and world cinema (Patricia White, Kathleen McHugh, Ella Shohat). Yet, comedy lingers as a largely overlooked terrain and a critical blind spot among these feminist discourses. The great extent to which female slapstick comedy speaks centrally to the key concerns and vital debates of feminist film theory still remains largely unrecognized. Slapstick comediennes of the silent era tenaciously exploit the gaping chasm between *identification* and *existence*—between the language of sexual difference and the matter of simply existing, a central problematic for feminist media scholars. These eruptive comediennes reveal cinema's formative aesthetic and narrative role in shaping modern feminism. They represent vivid traces of the slippery and mutually constitutive relationship between *female bodily identity* and *visually mediated subjectivity* that feminism has long staked out as a central terrain for its social activism and theoretical analysis.

Comic afterimages of the home in ruins

Perhaps no other image provided a more absurd or symbolically potent rejoinder to pervasive social anxieties about suffragette feminism than the utter disaster of slapstick comediennes' household labor. For example, female domestics blow up their own bodies and take their employers' homes along with them in the early comedies (*Mary Jane's Mishap* and *How*

Bridget Made the Fire); they turn their homes into amusement parks in awkward negotiations between traditional domestic responsibilities and modern cravings for excitement and adventure (*Betty, Rosalie,* and *Cunégonde* series); and they frequently burlesque staid gender norms, causing a crisis of roles and boundaries even in polite comedies of manners such as *The Patsy* (King Vidor, 1928) and *Mighty Like a Moose* (Leo McCarey, 1926).

In a broadly resonant example, *One Week* (Edward F. Cline, 1920), a bride (Sybil Seely) and groom (Buster Keaton) receive a portable, prefab house as a wedding present. An imaginary resolution to contradictory modern cravings for domestic stability and unprecedented speed and mobility, the house quickly proves to be a completely impossible space to inhabit. In one scene, Seely attempts to take a relaxing bath, despite the constant mayhem and reconstruction erupting around her. Given the inadequate protection of the house, the filmmaker must intervene: she drops the soap and an enormous hand emerges to cover the frame while she lifts her body from the tub to pick it up (Figure 13.2). The absurdism of revealing the hand of the censor, indeed a self-reflexive gesture, in a comedy that is all about the hilarious deconstruction of everyday pretenses, raises a far more pointed question: what precisely is being concealed and covered up here, the woman's naked body or her physical status in a slapstick comedy about the very disintegration of traditional domesticity?

Neither radically transgressive nor conservatively pathological, women's laughter and women's comedy reinforced ambivalent structures of spectatorship. Pervasive cultural discomfort about the instance of female laughter made the image of comedienne slapstick a ripe format for working through a series of negotiations intrinsic to silent film spectatorship,

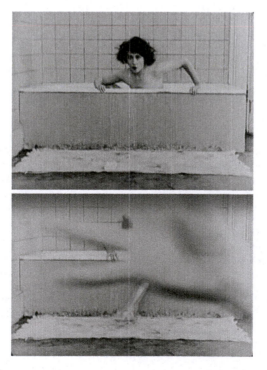

Figure 13.2 One Week.

Source: *One Week*, Edward F. Cline, 1920.

including the unstable limits between spectator and screen, the dubious social contexts of film exhibition, the collapse between gendered public and private spheres, as well as the uncertain ontological status of capturing and reanimating dead moments. Images of slapstick comediennes in silent cinema blowing up their homes, falling off motorcycles as if the road were a giant trampoline, or acquiring a mustache as a result of publicly licking postage stamps, remain as resonant now as ever, and continue to speak to our own present day feminist politics, media technologies, and gendered cultural fixations. Slapstick comediennes have haunted the very formations of feminism and modern media culture. It is long past time for their eruptive, unstable, and socially transformative bodies to reclaim their central positions in feminist film theory and women's media activism.

Related topics

Jane Gaines, "What was 'women's work' in the silent film era?"
Veronica Pravadelli, "Classical Hollywood and modernity: gender, style, aesthetics"

Notes

1 "Here's the New Laugh," *New York Herald* (1898).
2 "Without Tact the Humorous Woman Makes More Enemies Than Friends," *Woman's Home Companion* (1897).
3 Many thanks to Jeanne-Mathieu Lessard for finding this rare essay on laughter by Woolf (1986) and for generously sharing it with me.
4 See Alison McMahan's career profile of Alice Guy-Blaché on the Women Film Pioneers Project website: <https://wfpp.cdrs.columbia.edu/pioneer/ccp-alice-guy-blache/> (Accessed June 20, 2015)
5 For an excellent account of the gender politics of Keystone's slapstick film comedies, see: Robert King, "From 'Diving Venus' to 'Bathing Beauties': Reification and Feminine Spectacle, 1916–1917," in *The Fun Factory: The Keystone Film Company and the Emergence of Mass Culture* (2008).
6 For more on the displacement effects of the *bataccio*, see: Tom Gunning, "Mechanisms of Laughter: Devices of Slapstick." (2010)
7 For an excellent account of aural paranoia and the telephone motif in transitional silent cinema, see: Tom Gunning, "Heard over the Phone: *The Lonely Villa* and the de Lorde Tradition of the Terrors of Technology." (1991)
8 There has been a tremendous amount of scholarship detailing the cultural uplift, social gentrification, and institutional legitimacy of silent filmmaking during the nickelodeon era (1905–15). Key sources include Charlie Keil and Shelley Stamps (eds.), *American Cinema's Transitional Era: Audiences, Institutions, Practices* (2004); Allyson Nadia Field, *Uplift Cinema: The Emergence of African-American Film and the Possibility of Black Modernity* (2015); and Jennifer Bean, *Flickers of Desire: Movie Stars of the 1910s* (2011).
9 Although Chaplin appears as the tramp character in *Kid Auto Races in Venice* (February 7, 1914), which was released before *Mabel's Strange Predicament* (February 9, 1914), the latter was filmed first.
10 The 1920s flapper comedienne Colleen Moore exploits this tendency with the aid of trick photography, performing a series of cross-eyed facial tics in the silent Cinderella farce, *Ella Cinders* (Alfred E. Green, 1926), in a sequence best known as "The Eyes Have It." See Lori Landay's analysis of this film: "The Flapper Film: Comedy, Dance, and Jazz Age Kinaesthetics" (2002).

Bibliography

Baudelaire, Charles *The Essence of Laughter* (NY: Meridian Books, 1956).
Bean, Jennifer *Flickers of Desire: Movie Stars of the 1910s* (NJ: Rutgers University Press, 2011).

Bergson, Henri *Laughter: An Essay on the Meaning of the Comic* (New York: MacMillan, 1911).

Callahan, Vicki *Reclaiming the Archive: Feminism and Film History* (Detroit: Wayne State University Press, 2010).

Cixous, Hélène "The Laugh of the Medusa," in *Signs*, vol. I (Summer 1976), pp. 875–93.

Comic Actresses and Suffragettes: 1910–1914, curated by Mariann Lewinsky (Bologna: Ciniteca di Bologna, 2010), DVD.

Dale, Alan *Comedy Is a Man in Trouble: Slapstick in American Movies* (Minneapolis: University of Minnesota Press, 2002 [2000]).

Field, Allyson Nadia *Uplift Cinema: The Emergence of African-American Film and the Possibility of Black Modernity* (Durham, NC: Duke University Press, 2015).

Gunning, Tom "Heard over the Phone: *The Lonely Villa* and the de Lorde Tradition of the Terrors of Technology," in *Screen*, vol. 32, no. 2 (Spring 1991), pp. 184–96.

———— "Mechanisms of Laughter: Devices of Slapstick," in *Slapstick Comedy*, eds. Rob King and Tom Paulus (NY: Routledge, 2010), pp. 137–51.

Hansen, Miriam *Babel and Babylon*, (Cambridge, MA: Harvard University Press; Reprint edition, March 15, 1994).

Hennefeld, Maggie "Destructive Metamorphosis: The Comedy of Female Catastrophe and Feminist Film Historiography," in *Discourse: Journal for Theoretical Studies in Media and Culture*, vol. 36, no. 2, (Spring 2014a), pp. 176–206.

———— "Slapstick Comediennes in Transitional Cinema: Between Body and Medium," in *Camera Obscura*, vol. 29, no. 2 (2014b), pp. 84–117.

Hobbes, Thomas *Elements of Law, Natural and Politics* (London: Cass, 1969).

Horak, Laura *Girls Will Be Boys: Cross-Dressed Women, Lesbians, and American Cinema, 1908–1934* (NJ: Rutgers University Press, 2016).

Keil Charlie and Shelley Stamps, eds., *American Cinema's Transitional Era: Audiences, Institutions, Practices* (Berkeley, CA: UC Press, 2004).

King, Robert *The Fun Factory: The Keystone Film Company and the Emergence of Mass Culture* (CA: UC Press, 2008).

Landay, Lori "The Flapper Film: Comedy, Dance, and Jazz Age Kinaesthetics," in *A Feminist Reader in Early Cinema*, eds. Jennifer Bean and Diane Negra (Durham, NC: Duke University Press: 2002), pp. 221–48.

Massa, Steve *Lame Brains and Lunatics: The Good, the Bad, and the Forgotten of Silent Film Comedy* (GA: BearManor Media, 2013).

Mulvey, Laura "Visual Pleasure and Narrative Cinema," in *Screen*, vol. 16, no. 3 (Autumn 1975), pp. 6–18.

———— *Death 24x a Second: Stillness and the Moving Image* (London: Reaktion Books, 2006).

New York Herald "HERE's THE NEW LAUGH: Really Not So Much a Laugh as a Vocal Ripple of Merriment," reprinted in *Dallas Morning News*, September 11, 1898, p. 10.

Parvulescu, Anca *Laughter: Notes on a Passion* (Cambridge, MA: MIT Press, 2010).

Repplier, Agnes "A Plea for Humor," *The Atlantic Monthly*, Vol. 63, (February 1889), pp. 175–83.

Sidis, Boris *Psychology of Laugher* (NY: Appleton and Company, 1913).

Stamp, Shelley *Movie-Struck Girls Women and Motion Picture Culture After the Nickelodeon* (Princeton, NJ: Princeton University Press, 2000).

Stewart, Jacqueline *Migrating to the Movies: Cinema and Black Urban Modernity* (Berkeley, CA: University of CA Press, 2005).

Sully, James *An Essay on Laughter: Its Forms, Its Causes, Its Development, and Its Value* (London: Bombay, Longmans, Green, and Company, 1902).

The Woman's Home Companion "Without Tact the Humorous Woman Makes More Enemies Than Friends," republished in *The Cleveland Plain Dealer*, (October 10, 1897), p. 21.

Vasey, George *A Philosophy of Laughter and Smiling* (London: J. Burns, 1877).

Wagner, Kristen Anderson "'Have Women a Sense of Humor?': Comedy and Femininity in Early-Twentieth Century Film," *The Velvet Light Trap*, no. 68, (Fall 2011), pp. 35–46.

Williams, Linda "Film Bodies: Gender, Genre, and Excess," in *Film Quarterly*, vol. 44, no. 4, (Summer, 1991), pp. 2–13.

Woolf, Virginia "The Value of Laughter," in *The Essays of Virginia Woolf. Volume I. 1904–1912*. ed. Andrew McNeillie (London: The Hogarth Press, 1986), pp. 58–60.

Zupançic, Alenka *The Odd One In: On Comedy* (MIT Press, 2008).

14

FEMINIST PORN

The politics of producing pleasure

Constance Penley, Celine Parreñas Shimizu, Mireille Miller-Young, and Tristan Taormino[1]

What follows is a slightly edited introduction to *The Feminist Porn Book* (2013)—the first collection to bring together writings by feminist porn producers and feminist porn scholars to engage, challenge, and re-imagine pornography. As collaborating editors of this volume, we are three porn professors and one porn director who have had an energetic dialogue about feminist politics and pornography for years. In their criticism, feminist opponents of porn cast pornography as a monolithic medium and industry and make sweeping generalizations about its production, its workers, its consumers, and its effects on society. These antiporn feminists respond to feminist pornographers and feminist porn professors in several ways. They accuse us of deceiving others and ourselves about the nature of pornography; they claim we fail to look critically at any porn and hold up all porn as empowering. More typically, they simply dismiss out of hand our ability or authority to make it or study it. But *The Feminist Porn Book* offers arguments, facts, and histories that cannot be summarily rejected, by providing on-the-ground and well-researched accounts of the politics of producing pleasure. Our agenda is twofold: to explore the emergence and significance of a thriving feminist porn movement and to gather some of the best new feminist scholarship on pornography. By putting our voices into conversation, this book sparks new thinking about the richness and complexity of porn as a genre and industry in a way that helps us to appreciate the work that feminists in the porn industry are doing, both in the mainstream and on its countercultural edges.

So to begin, we offer a broad definition of feminist porn. As both an established and emerging genre of pornography, feminist porn uses sexually explicit imagery to contest and complicate dominant representations of gender, sexuality, race, ethnicity, class, ability, age, body type, and other identity markers. It explores concepts of desire, agency, power, beauty, and pleasure at their most confounding and difficult, including pleasure within and across inequality, in the face of injustice, and against the limits of gender hierarchy and both heteronormativity and homonormativity. It seeks to unsettle conventional definitions of sex, and expand the language of sex as an erotic activity, an expression of identity, a power exchange, a cultural commodity, and even a new politics.

Feminist porn creates alternative images and develops its aesthetics and iconography to expand established sexual norms and discourses. It evolved out of and incorporates elements from the genres of "porn for women," "couples porn," and lesbian porn as well as feminist

155

photography, performance art, and experimental filmmaking. It does not assume a singular female viewer but acknowledges multiple female (and other) viewers with many different orientations. Feminist porn makers emphasize the importance of their labor practices in production and their treatment of performers/sex workers; in contrast to norms in the mainstream sectors of the adult entertainment industry, they strive to create a fair, safe, ethical, consensual work environment and often create imagery through collaboration with their subjects. Ultimately, feminist porn considers sexual representation—and its production—a site for resistance, intervention, and change.

The concept of feminist porn is rooted in the 1980s—the height of the feminist porn wars in the United States. The porn wars (also known as the sex wars) emerged out of a debate among feminists about the role of sexualized representation in society and grew into a full-scale divide that has lasted over three decades. In the heyday of the women's movement in the United States, a broad-based, grassroots activist struggle over the proliferation of misogynistic and violent representations in corporate media was superseded by an effort focused specifically on legally banning the most explicit, and seemingly most sexist, media: pornography. Employing Robin Morgan's slogan, "Porn is the theory, rape is the practice," antipornography feminists argued that pornography amounted to the commodification of rape. As a group called Women Against Pornography (WAP) began to organize in earnest to ban obscenity across the nation, other feminists, such as Lisa Duggan, Nan D. Hunter, Kate Ellis, and Carol Vance became vocal critics of what they viewed as WAP's ill-conceived collusion with a sexually conservative Reagan administration and Christian Right, and their warping of feminist activism into a moral hygiene or public decency movement. Regarding antiporn feminism as a huge setback for the feminist struggle to empower women and sexual minorities, an energetic community of sex-worker and sex-radical activists joined anticensorship and sex-positive feminists to build the foundation for the feminist porn movement (Morgan 1980: 139).

The years that led up to the feminist porn wars are often referred to as the "golden age of porn," a period from the early 1970s to the early 1980s, marked by large budget, high-production-value feature films that were theatrically released. A group of female porn performers who worked during the golden age—including Annie Sprinkle, Veronica Vera, Candida Royalle, Gloria Leonard, and Veronica Hart—formed a support group (the first of its kind) called Club 90 in New York City. In 1984, the feminist arts collective Carnival Knowledge asked Club 90 to participate in a festival called The Second Coming, and explore the question, "Is there a feminist pornography?" (Sprinkle 1998: 149–51). It is one of the first documented times when feminists publicly posed and examined this critical query.

That same year, Club 90 member Candida Royalle founded Femme Productions to create a new genre: porn from a woman's point of view (Fuentes & Schrage 1987: 41–3). Her films focused on storylines, high production values, female pleasure, and romance. In San Francisco, publishers Myrna Elana and Deborah Sundahl, along with Nan Kinney and Susie Bright, co-founded *On Our Backs*, the first porn magazine by and for lesbians. A year later, Kinney and Sundahl started Fatale Video to produce and distribute lesbian porn movies that expanded the mission *On Our Backs* began.[2] In the mainstream adult industry, performer and registered nurse Nina Hartley began producing and starring in a line of sex education videos for Adam and Eve, with her first two titles released in 1984. A parallel movement began to emerge throughout Europe in the 1980s and 90s.[3]

By the 1990s, Royalle's and Hartley's success had made an impact on the mainstream adult industry. Major studios, including Vivid, VCA, and Wicked, began producing their lines of couples porn that reflected Royalle's vision and followed a formula of softer, gentler, more romantic porn with storylines and high production values. The growth of the "couples porn" genre signified a shift in the industry: female desire and viewership were finally acknowledged if narrowly defined. This expansion provided more selection for female viewers and more opportunities for women to direct mainstream heterosexual films, including Veronica Hart and Kelly Holland (a.k.a. Toni English). Independent, lesbian-produced lesbian porn grew at a slower pace, but Fatale Video (which continued to produce new films until the mid-1990s) finally had some company in its micro-genre with work by Annie Sprinkle, Maria Beatty, and Shar Rednour and Jackie Strano. Sprinkle also made the first porn film to feature a trans man, and Christopher Lee followed with a film starring an entire cast of trans men. There were also women working internationally during this period —Sachi Hamano was the first woman to direct "pink films" (Japanese softcore porn). Hamano directed more than three hundred in the 1980s and 90s to portray women's sexual power and agency, and challenge the representation of women as sex objects only present to fulfill men's fantasies (Selavy 2009).

In the early 2000s, feminist porn began to take hold in the United States with the emergence of filmmakers who identified themselves and their work as feminist including Buck Angel, Dana Dane, Shine Louise Houston, Courtney Trouble, Madison Young, and Tristan Taormino. Simultaneously, feminist filmmakers in Europe began to gain notoriety for their porn and sexually explicit independent films, including Erika Lust in Spain; Anna Span and Petra Joy in the UK; Émilie Jouvet, Virginie Despentes, and Taiwan-born Shu Lea Cheang in France; and Mia Engberg, who created a compilation of feminist porn shorts that was famously funded by the Swedish government.

The modern feminist porn movement gained tremendous ground in 2006 with the creation of The Feminist Porn Awards (FPAs). Chanelle Gallant and other staffers at sex-positive sex toyshop Good for Her in Toronto created the awards, which were open to films that met one or more of the following criteria:

> (1) A woman had a hand in the production, writing, direction, etc. of the work; (2) It depicts genuine female pleasure; and/or (3) It expands the boundaries of sexual representation on film and challenges stereotypes that are often found in mainstream porn. And of course, it has to be hot! Overall, Feminist Porn Award winners tend to show movies that consider a female viewer from start to finish. This means that you are more likely to see active desire and consent, real orgasms, and women taking control of their own fantasies (even when that fantasy is to hand over that control).[4]

These criteria simultaneously assumed and announced a viewership, an authorship, an industry, and a collective consciousness. Embedded in the description is a female viewer and what she likely wants to see—active desire, consent, real orgasms, power, and agency—and does not want to see: passivity, stereotypes, coercion, or fake orgasms. The language is broad enough so as not to be prescriptive, yet it places value on agency and authenticity, with a parenthetical nod to the possibility that not every woman's fantasy is to be "in control." While the guidelines notably focus on a woman's involvement in production, honored filmmakers run the gamut from self-identified feminist pornographers to independent female directors to mainstream porn producers; the broad criteria achieve a certain level of inclusiveness and acknowledge that a range of work can be read as feminist by audiences, critics, and academics. The FPA ceremony attracts and honors filmmakers from around the world, and each year since its inception, every aspect of the event has grown, from the number of films submitted to the number of attendees. The FPAs have raised awareness about feminist porn among a wider audience and helped coalesce a community of film-makers, performers, and fans; they highlight an industry within an industry, and, in the process, nurture this growing movement. In 2009, Dr. Laura Méritt (Berlin) created the PorYes campaign and the European Feminist Porn Award modeled on the FPAs. Because the movement has had the most momentum in Europe and North America, *The Feminist Porn Book* concentrates on the scholarship and films of Western nations. We acknowledge this limitation: for feminist porn to be a global project, more would need to be done to include non-Western scholars and pornographers in the conversation.

The work we do now, as scholars and producers, could not exist without early examinations of the history and context of pornography, including *Caught Looking: Feminism, Pornography and Censorship* by FACT, the Feminist Anti-Censorship Task Force (1986). Linda Williams's groundbreaking 1989 *Hard Core: Power, Pleasure, and the "Frenzy of the Visible"* opened the door for feminist scholars to productively examine pornography as film and popular culture, as a genre and industry, textually, historically, and sociologically. Laura Kipnis's 1996 *Bound and Gagged: Pornography and the Politics of Fantasy in America* made the strongest possible case that "the differences between pornography and other forms of culture are less meaningful than their similarities" (Kipnis 1996: viii). Jane Juffer's 1998 *At Home with Pornography: Women, Sex, and Everyday Life* urged us to pay close attention not just to the hardcore porn typically consumed by men but the uses of pornography in the daily lives of ordinary women. Since 1974 the film magazine *Jump Cut* has published more original scholarship on porn from a pro-sex, anticensorship perspective than any other media journal and by leading figures in the field, including Chuck Kleinhans, Linda Williams, Laura Kipnis, Richard Dyer, Thomas Waugh, Eithne Johnson, Eric Schaefer, Peter Lehman, Robert Eberwein, and Joanna Russ. More recently, Drucilla Cornell's *Feminism and Pornography* (2000), Linda Williams's *Porn Studies* (2004), and Pamela Church Gibson's *More Dirty Looks: Gender, Pornography and Power* (2004) cemented the value of porn scholarship. *The Feminist Porn Book* seeks to further that scholarship by adding a significant, valuable component: feminists creating pornography.

In the book, we identify a forty-year-long movement of thinkers, viewers, and makers, grounded in their desire to use pornography to explore new sexualities in representation. The work we have collected in the book defies other feminist conceptions of sexuality on screen as forever marked by a threat. That threat is the specter of violence against women, which is the primary way that pornography has come to be seen. Claiming that explicit sexual representations are nothing but gender oppression means that pornography's portrayal of explicit sex acts is a form of absolute discipline and subjugation for women. Within this frame, women who watch, study, or work in pornography bear the mark of false consciousness—as if they dabble in fire while ignoring the risk of burning.

The overwhelming popularity of women's erotic literature, illustrated by the recent worldwide bestseller, *Fifty Shades of Grey* by E.L. James (2011), and the flourishing women's fan fiction community from which it emerged, proves that there is a great demand among women for explicit sexual representations. Millions of female readers embraced the *Fifty Shades of Grey* trilogy—which follows a young woman who becomes the submissive sexual partner to a dominant man—not for its depiction of oppression, but for its exploration of erotic freedom. Women-authored erotica and pornography speak to fantasies women have, fantasies located in a world where women must negotiate power constantly, including in their imaginations and desires. As with the criteria for winning a Feminist Porn Award, these books and the feminist porn movement show that "women are taking control of their own fantasies (even when that fantasy is to hand over control)."

With the emergence of new technologies that allow more people than ever to both create and consume pornography, the moral panic-driven fears of porn are ratcheted up once again. Society's dread of women who own their desire, and use it in ways that confound expectations of proper female sexuality, persists. As Gayle Rubin shows, "Modern Western societies appraise sex acts according to a hierarchical system of sexual value" (1984: 279). Rubin maps this system as one where "the charmed circle" is perpetually threatened by the "outer limits" or those who fall out of the bounds of the acceptable. On the bottom of this hierarchy are sexual acts and identities outside heterosexuality, marriage, monogamy, and reproduction. She argues that this hierarchy exists so as to justify the privileging of normative and constricted sexualities and the denigration and punishment of the "sexual rabble" (ibid. 280). *The Feminist Porn Book* showcases precisely these punishable sex acts and identities that are outside of the charmed circle, and proudly sides with the sexual rabble. Spotlighting the numerous ways people confront the power of sexuality, this book paves the way for exploring the varieties of what were previously dismissed as perversities. At the same time, feminist porn can also expose what passes for "normal" sexuality at the center of that charmed circle.

One of the unfortunate results of the porn wars was the artificial fixing of a distinct antiporn camp versus a sex-positive/pro-porn camp. On one side, a capital P "Pornography" was a visual embodiment of the patriarchy and violence against women. On the other, Porn was defended as "speech," or as a form that should not be foreclosed because it might someday be transformed into a vehicle for women's erotic expression. The nuances and complexities of actual lowercase "pornographies" were often lost in the middle. For example, sex-positive thinking does not always accommodate the ways in which women are constrained by sexuality. But the problem with antipornography's assumption that sex is inherently oppressive to women—that women are debased when they have sex on camera—is that it ignores and represses the sexuality of women. For us, sex-positive feminist porn does not mean that sex is always a ribbon-tied box of happiness and joy. Instead, feminist porn captures the struggle to define, understand, and locate one's sexuality. It recognizes the importance of deferring judgment about the significance of sex in intimate and social relations, and of not presuming what sex means for specific people. Feminist porn explores sexual ideas and acts that may be fraught, confounding, and deeply disturbing to some, and liberating and empowering to others. What we see at work here are competing definitions of sexuality that expose the power of sexuality in all of its unruliness.

Because feminist porn acknowledges that identities are socially situated and that sexuality has the power to discipline, punish, and subjugate, that unruliness may involve producing images that seem oppressive, degrading, or violent. Feminist porn does not shy away from the darker shades of women's fantasies. It creates a space for realizing the contradictory ways in which our fantasies do not always line up with our politics or ideas of who we think we are. As Tom Waugh argues, participation in pornography, in his case as a spectator, can be a "process of social identity formation" (1992: 4). Indeed, social identities and ideas are formed in the act of viewing porn, but also in making and writing about it.

Strongly influenced by other social movements in the realm of sexuality, like the sex-positive, LGBT rights, and sex workers' rights movements, feminist porn aims to build community, to expand liberal views on gender and sexuality, and to educate and empower performers and audiences. It favors fair, ethical working conditions for sex workers and the inclusion of underrepresented identities and practices. Feminist porn vigorously challenges the hegemonic depictions of gender, sex roles, and the pleasure and power of mainstream porn. It also challenges the antiporn feminist interpretive framework for pornography as bankrupt of progressive sexual politics. As a budding movement, it promotes aesthetic and ethical practices that intervene in dominant sexual representation and mobilize a collective vision for change. This erotic activism, while in no way homogeneous or consistent, works within and against the marketplace to imagine new ways to envision gender and sexuality in our culture.

But feminist porn is not only an emergent social movement and an alternative cultural production: it is a genre of media made for profit. Part of a multibillion dollar business in adult entertainment media, feminist porn is an industry within an industry. Some feminist porn is produced independently, often created and marketed by and for underrepresented minorities like lesbians, transgender folks, and people of color. But feminist porn is also produced within the mainstream adult industry by feminists whose work is funded and distributed by large companies such as Vivid Entertainment, Adam and Eve, and Evil Angel Productions. As outliers or insiders (or both) to the mainstream industry, feminists have adopted different strategies for subverting dominant pornographic norms and tropes. Some reject nearly all elements of a typical adult film, from structure to aesthetics, while others tweak the standard formula (from "foreplay" to "cum shot") to reposition and prioritize female sexual agency. Although feminist porn makers define their work as distinct from mainstream porn, it is nonetheless viewed by a range of people, including people who identify as feminist and specifically seek it out, as well as other viewers who do not. Feminist porn is gaining momentum and visibility as a market and a movement. This movement is made up of performers turned directors, independent queer producers, politicized sex workers, porn geeks and bloggers, and radical sex educators.

In the first section of *The Feminist Porn Book*, "Making Porn, Debating Porn," feminist porn pioneers Betty Dodson, Candida Royalle, and Susie Bright give a grounded history of feminist porn as it emerged in the 1980s in response to the limiting sexual imagination of both mainstream porn and antiporn feminism. Providing a window into the generative and deeply contested period of the sex wars, these feminist pornographers highlight the stakes and energies surrounding the birth of feminist porn activism in the face of an antiporn feminism that ignored, misunderstood, or vilified them and their efforts. Bright's account of watching her first porn film, sitting among suspicious men in a dark adult theater, sets the stage for how the invention of the VHS player shifted women's consumption of porn and dramatically changed the marketplace.

In the last decade, a new war on porn has been resurrected and redefined by Gail Dines, Sheila Jeffreys, Karen Boyle, Pamela Paul, Robert Jensen, and others. Feona Attwood and Clarissa Smith (who would go on to launch the Routledge journal *Porn Studies* in 2014) show how this resurgent antiporn movement resists theory and evidence, and tendentiously reframes the production and consumption of porn as a mode of sex trafficking, a form of addiction, or a public health problem of epidemic proportions. In a sign of the increasing desperation of antiporn feminism in the face of the explosion of academic scholarship on porn and the expansion of access to porn on the Internet, Gail Dines, without explicitly naming names, held the editors of *The Feminist Porn Book* responsible for the massacre of six of our students in Isla Vista, California in May 2013. Even more dangerous than "porn culture" and its claimed murder-inducing effects on men, are the feminist apologists for porn who make their careers and please their boyfriends through studying it rather than joining with activists to denounce it.[5]

Attwood and Smith's work in *The Feminist Porn Book* powerfully exposes how feminist porn remains challenged and often censored in contemporary popular discourse. Lynn Comella focuses on the consequences of pornography going public. She examines one of the most significant elements of the emergence of feminist porn: the growth of sex-positive, women-owned-and-run sex shops and a grassroots sex education movement that create space for women to produce, find, and consume new kinds of pornography.

"Watching and Being Watched"—the second section of the book—examines how desire and agency inform pornographic performance, representation, and spectatorship. Sinnamon Love and Mireille Miller-Young explore the complex position of African American women as they watch, critique, and create representations of black women's sexuality. Dylan Ryan and Jane Ward take up the concept of authenticity in porn: what it means, how it is read, and why it is (or is not) crucial to feminist porn performance and spectatorship. Ingrid Ryberg looks at how public screenings of queer, feminist, and lesbian porn can create spaces for sexual empowerment. Tobi Hill-Meyer complicates Ryberg's analysis by documenting who, until very recently, was left out of these spaces: trans women. Keiko Lane echoes Ryberg's argument of the radical potential of queer and feminist porn and offers it as a tool for understanding and expressing desire among marginalized communities.

The intersection of feminist porn as pedagogy and feminist pedagogies of porn is highlighted in the penultimate section of *The Feminist Porn Book*, "Doing It in School." As porn scholars, Constance Penley and Ariane Cruz grapple with teaching and studying porn from two very different perspectives. For Penley, the challenge is how to teach porn as film and popular culture, as a genre and industry in an established film and media studies curriculum. Cruz describes her equivocal personal and political relation to porn as a black woman scholar negotiating both the politics of respectability and her contested space within the academy. Kevin Heffernan offers a history of sex instruction in film and contrasts it with work from Nina Hartley and Tristan Taormino in educational porn movies. Hartley discusses how she has used porn to teach throughout her twenty-five-plus years in the industry, and Taormino outlines her practice as a feminist pornographer offering organic, fair-trade porn that takes into account the labor of its workers. Performer Danny Wylde documents his personal experiences with power, consent, and exploitation against a backdrop of antiporn rhetoric. Lorelei Lee offers a powerful manifesto that demands we all become better students to achieve a more nuanced, discerning, and thoughtful discourse about porn and sex.

"Now Playing: Feminist Porn"—the book's final section—takes up questions of hyper corporeality, genderqueerness, transfemininity, feminized masculinity, transgressive racial performance, and disability. Jiz Lee discusses how they (Lee's favored gender-neutral pronoun) use their transgressive female body and genderqueer identity to defy categories. April Flores describes herself as "a fat Latina with pale skin, tattoos, and fire engine red hair," and gives her unique take on being (and not being) a Big Beautiful Woman (BBW) performer. Bobby Noble explores the role of trans men and the interrogation of masculinities in feminist porn while renowned trans male performer Buck Angel explodes sex/gender dichotomies by embodying his identity of a man with a vagina. Also concerned with the complex representation and performance of manhood in feminist pornography, Celine Parreñas Shimizu asks how race shapes the work of straight Asian male performer Keni Styles. Loree Erickson, a feminist pornographer and PhD candidate, represents not only a convergence of scholarship and sex work but one of the most overlooked subjects in pornography and one de-eroticized in society: "queer femmegimp." Emerging to speak from group identities previously missing or misnamed, the pieces in this section are by people who show the beauty of their desires, give shape to their realities, reject and reclaim attributions made by others, and describe how they create sexual worlds that denounce inequality.

As is evident from the contributions summarized above, *The Feminist Porn Book* explores the multiple definitions of feminist porn, but refuses to fix its boundaries. Feminist porn is a genre and political vision. And like other genres of film and media, feminist porn shares common themes, aesthetics, and goals even though its parameters are not clearly demarcated. Because it is born out of a feminism that is not one thing but a living, breathing, moving creation, it is necessarily contested—an argument, a polemic, and a debate. Because it is both genre and practice, we must engage it as both: by reading and analyzing its cultural texts and examining the ideals, intentions, and experiences of its producers. In doing so, we offer an alternative to unsubstantiated oversimplifications and patronizing rhetoric. We acknowledge the complexities of watching, creating, and analyzing pornographies. And we believe in the radical potential of feminist porn to transform sexual representation and the way we live our sexualities.

Related topics

Eliza Steinbock, "Towards trans cinema"
Jennifer Lynn Peterson, "*Green Porno* and the sex life of animals in the digital age"

Notes

1 Tristan Taormino, Celine Parreñas Shimizu, Constance Penley, and Mireille Miller-Young, eds., "Introduction: The Politics of Producing Pleasure" from *The Feminist Porn Book: The Politics of Producing Pleasure*. Copyright © 2013 by Tristan Taormino, Celine Parreñas Shimizu, Constance Penley, and Mireille Miller-Young. Reprinted with the permission of The Permissions Company, Inc., on behalf of The Feminist Press at the City University of New York, www.feministpress.org, accessed February 20, 2016.
2 See Susie Bright, *Big Sex, Little Death: A Memoir* (Berkeley: Seal Press, 2011) and Susie Bright, "A History Of *On Our Backs*: Entertainment for the Adventurous Lesbian, The Original: 1984–1990," http://rmc.library.cornell.edu/EAD/htmldocs/RMM07788.html, accessed July 16, 2016. See also, "About Fatale Media," accessed September 5, 2011, www.fatalemedia.com/about.html.
3 Feminists in Europe who used sexually explicit photography and film to explore themes like female pleasure, S/M, bondage, gender roles, and queer desire include Monika Treut (Germany), Cleo Uebelmann (Switzerland), Krista Beinstein (Germany and Austria), and Della Grace (England). In 1998, Danish film production company Zentropa wrote the Puzzy Power Manifesto that outlined its guidelines for a new line of porn for women, which echoed Royalle's vision: their films included plot-driven narratives that depicted foreplay and emotional connection, women's pleasure and desire, and male and female bodies beyond just their genitals. See Laura Merrit, "PorYes! The European Feminist Porn Movement;" (unpublished manuscript) and Zentropa, "The Manifesto;" accessed January 29, 2012, www.puzzypower.dk/UK/index.php/om-os/manifest, accessed on July 16, 2016.
4 Feminist Porn Awards, accessed September 5, 2011, http://goodforher.com/feminist_porn_awards.
5 "UCSB, Feminism, and Porn," Gail Dines, Huffington Post UK, accessed February 6, 2016, www.huffingtonpost.co.uk/gail-dines/porn-industry-and-misogyny_b_5427951.html.

Bibliography

Church Gibson, Pamela, ed. (2004). *More Dirty Looks: Gender, Pornography and Power* (London: British Film Institute).
Cornell, Drucilla, ed. (2000). *Feminism and Pornography* (New York: Oxford University Press).

Feminist Anti-Censorship Task Force ([1986] 1992). *Caught Looking: Feminism, Pornography and Censorship*, 3rd edn. (New Haven, CT: Long River Books).

Fuentes, Annette and Margaret Schrage (1987). "Deep Inside Porn Stars," *Jump Cut: A Review of Contemporary Media* 32, www.ejumpcut.org/archive/onlinessays/JC32folder/PornWomenInt.html (last accessed July 16, 2016).

James, E.L. (2011). *Fifty Shades of Grey* (New York: Vintage Books).

Juffer, Jane (1998) *At Home with Pornography: Women, Sex, and Everyday Life* (New York: NYU Press).

Jump Cut: A Review of Contemporary Media, eds. Julia Lesage, Chuck Kleinhans, John Hess, www. ejumpcut.org (last accessed July 16, 2016).

Kipnis, Laura (1996). *Bound and Gagged: Pornography and the Politics of Fantasy in America* (New York: Grove Press).

Morgan, Robin. (1980). "Theory and Practice: Pornography and Rape," in *Take Back the Night*, ed. Laura Lederer (New York: William Morrow: 134–40).

Nagle, Jill, ed. (1997). *Whores and Other Feminists*. New York and London: Routledge.

Rubin, Gayle (1984). "Thinking Sex: Notes for a Radical Theory of the Politics of Sexuality," in *Pleasure and Danger: Exploring Female Sexuality*, ed. Carole S. Vance (Boston and London: Routledge and Kegan Paul: 267–319).

Selavy, Virginie "Interview with Sachi Hamano," December 1, 2009, http://www.electricsheepmagazine. co.uk/features/2009/12/01/interview-with-sachi-hamano/ (last accessed July 16, 2016).

Sprinkle, Annie (1998). *Post-Porn Modernist: My 25 Years as a Multimedia Whore* (San Francisco: Cleis Press).

Waugh, Tom (1992). "Homoerotic Representation in the Stag Film 1920–1940: Imagining An Audience," *Wide Angle* 14, no. 2 (1992): 4–19.

Williams, Linda (1989). *Hard Core: Power, Pleasure, and the "Frenzy of the Visible"* (Berkeley: University of California Press).

Williams, Linda, ed. (2004) *Porn Studies* (Durham, NC: Duke University Press).

15

THE POSTMODERN STORY OF THE *FEMME FATALE*

Julie Grossman

Contemporary films that feature fatal women adopt various attitudes, although almost all of these works are deeply self-conscious about a legacy of stylistic traits and character types associated with classic film noir. Some of these more recent films exemplify a feminist affirmation of female power; others apply the *femme fatale*, as sexual badass, to a neo-liberal individualist agenda; still others offer a politicized critique of the construction of gender and power relations in the social world. This essay explores the abiding relevance of the figure of the *femme fatale*, not as a static object of vision, but as a dynamic critical tool for understanding the workings of gender in popular culture and society. Like other fictional icons—dominant televisual characters such as Walter White in *Breaking Bad* and Joan Holloway Harris and Peggy Olson in *Mad Men*—the figure of the *femme fatale* exemplifies the power of popular cultural representations to inform our notions of gender and social rules and, sometimes, to challenge them.

Erotic thrillers of the 1980s sought more to titillate, entertain, and resonate with classic film noir than, in most cases, to challenge gender roles. A spate of movies beginning with "B" for "blood," "body," "black"—such as *Blood Simple* (Joel and Ethan Coen, 1984), *Body Double* (De Palma, 1984), *Black Widow* (Rafelson, 1987) (also *Blue Steel* [Bigelow, 1989], *Blue Velvet* [Lynch, 1986], and *Blade Runner* [Scott, 1982]), their titles speaking the language of noir—adapted familiar narrative and character patterns to a new post-postwar era. Neo-noir films introduced a new strain of fatal female characters, beginning with Matty Walker in *Body Heat* (Kasdan, 1981). A pastiche of tropes most closely identified with *Double Indemnity* (Wilder, 1944), the film initiated a trend of exaggerating the noir male protagonist's dull-wittedness, presenting him as no match for the fatal woman who seduces then seeks to destroy him.

In classic film noir, the destruction of the male protagonist and the fatal woman constituted a critique of the American Dream—its failed promise of success and happiness seen through the perspective of marginalized figures. By virtue of their gender, women were always already such outsiders, an insight feminist readings of film noir brought to the table beginning with the publication of E. Ann Kaplan's *Women in Film Noir* in 1978. Amidst second-wave feminisms, and interestingly on the eve of the 1980s rebirth of the fatal woman in neo-noir, this landmark collection analyzed the so-called bad women in classic film noir as a symbolic expression of shifting power roles and a destabilized family in wartime and postwar America. The essays in the volume, such as Janey Place's "Women in Film Noir" (1978), opened up space for reading noir women in more positive terms, rather than simply as misogynist projections of male desire. The volume not only illuminated film noir's relevance to feminist discourse and theory, demonstrated in Christine Gledhill's book-end essays, but also found in psychoanalytic feminist theory a particularly resonant means of exploring different forms of agency, scopic regimes, and representation in film noir. Pam Cook's and Claire Johnston's essays, for example, paved the way for subsequent feminist psychoanalytic work on film noir, such as Mary Ann Doane's *Femmes Fatales: Feminism, Film Theory, Psychoanalysis* (1991)—which saw in the *femme fatale*'s masking and unknowability a powerful expression of male fears about female power—and also Joan Copjec's collection *Shades of Noir* (1993). Shifting critical attention from men's to women's stories, Elizabeth Cowie argued in her essay in *Shades of Noir* against a traditional reading of film noir's "mean streets" as a male "sphere," refocusing feminist film criticism on noir "women['s] roles which are active, adventurous and driven by sexual desire" (1993, 135). Elisabeth Bronfen's later essay (2004) lent the classic *femme fatale* a tragic dimension, boldly taking as her example Phyllis Dietrichson of *Double Indemnity* (1944), considered by many to be the quintessential opaque *femme fatale*. In their monographs, Helen Hanson (2007) and Philippa Gates (2011) "detected" and pursued the centrality of the female investigative role in film noir, Gates more recently averring that the "female detective brings with her an idealism" (2014, 33) that questions the centrality of cynicism in film noir. And Hanson and Catherine O'Rawe's 2010 collection explored the global, trans-historical, and feminist contexts that perennially shift the meaning of the *femme fatale*. As against this rich mining of the women's stories in noir, the excessive portrayal of the pathological fatal woman in neo-noir seems in many ways to flatten the critical terrain.

From its metaphorical side streets, classic film noir explored the dark underbelly of the American Dream. Neo-noir catapulted the deadly femme into the main streets and the mainstream of American culture in blockbuster thrillers such as *Fatal Attraction* (Lyne, 1987) and *Basic Instinct* (Verhoeven, 1992). However, a major change can be seen in that these films focus less on a flawed system (claustrophobic social settings for men and women, including domestic prisons and oppressive office life, and cops and war vets traumatized and corrupted by their proximity to violence) than on the weak men and powerful women who exploit their weaknesses.

Body Heat demonstrated that women should not be underestimated. As many have noted, Matty Walker "gets away with" her crimes, a major revision to the production-code-dominated films that saw women paying for their transgressions in classic film noir. More striking, however, is the film's cynical representation of women vying with men to cash in on their criminal endeavors for individual gain and pleasure, inaugurating the neo-liberal version of the *femme fatale* based on the assumption, as Samantha Lindop has argued about neo-noir, that "[I]ndividuals are constructed as entrepreneurial actors in every sphere of life, and are seen as rational, calculating, and self-regulating; with a life story that is the outcome of deliberate choices" (2015, 14).

Despite *Body Heat*'s focus on Reagan-era acquisitiveness, the film may offer a feminist through-line in Kathleen Turner's dynamic performance as Matty Walker—in moments, for example, when she mocks her husband's belittling of her, in much the way Gloria Grahame's dynamic Debby Marsh in *The Big Heat* (Lang, 1953) made fun of the men surrounding her, their domination eliciting her parody of them all as circus figures, "Now jump, Debby." In the restaurant scene in *Body Heat*, Matty says, "I'm too dumb. Woman, you know …," then, "I'll be right back. Then maybe we can talk about pantyhose or something interesting."

Following *Fatal Attraction*, in the 90s, movies such as *Basic Instinct*, *Body of Evidence* (Edel, 1993), and *The Temp* (Holland, 1993) featured men beleaguered by sexy pathological women. Yvonne Tasker aptly notes the following about Alex Forrest from *Fatal Attraction*: "Expressing the manifold contradictions of postfeminism, this attack on conventional femininity via the persona of the deranged noir woman is of a tangibly different quality than the examples featured in classic noir" (2013, 366). "[E]xhilarating and exasperating" for female spectators (Stables, 1998, 179), sexually alluring figures of horror in neo-noir (see Pidduck, 1995, 69) may be essentialized as opaque and pathological but they also enact a gender reversal that is, for many, pleasurable (see Cohan, 1998, 273). Because "the postmodern fatal woman is a creature of excess and spectacle" (Stables, 1998, 167), she has excited some viewers, while others may find these fatal women less interesting than the cultural debates—occasioned by these films' release—about the feminist, postfeminist, and/or reactionary portraits of gender, sexual orientation, work life, and the nuclear family reflected in society and the media generally (see Williams, 2009). I want to suggest that the most interesting postmodern story of film noir and the *femme fatale* will address questions beyond basic ones we associate with neo-noir and erotic thrillers that feature fatal women: Will the fatal femme kill (wield the iconic icepick beneath the bed)? Will she get away with her crimes and betrayals? These two questions may tantalize viewers, but they remain insular, plot-driven, and only really culturally resonant to the extent that they spike discussions in the media and academia about representations of bad, powerful, and/or sexualized women. For commercial gain, erotic thrillers exploit the spectacle of sex converging with murderousness; these films sell.

There is another sequence of films beginning in the 90s, however, that posits dangerous women as neither supernaturally violent nor pastiches of classic film noir *femmes fatales*. This includes Carl Frankin's neo-noir films *One False Move* (1992) and *Devil in a Blue Dress* (1995); Patty Jenkins's *Monster* (2003); David Slade's *Hard Candy* (2006); and David Fincher's *Girl with the Dragon Tattoo* (2011) and, to a lesser extent, *Gone Girl* (2014); and a number of David Lynch's films, notably *Blue Velvet*, *Lost Highway* (1997), and *Mulholland Drive* (2001): These films are critically oriented in exploring the *femme fatale* as a hierarchically gendered construction of men and women in an image-obsessed world: a media-created, media-driven *projection*.

Since the 1990s, these more critically minded films use these characters to question the source of the fatality they pose, analyzing the forms of cultural objectification that produce the *femme fatale* in the first place. This is a niche market of films, featuring so-called bad women lashing out against or struggling to survive within a culture that denies their subjectivity. These films often refer back to earlier noir films to suggest the continuities in gender representation, while employing a postmodern style or open-endedness to provoke thought and to suggest how unanswered many of the questions remain.

Carl Franklin's neo-noir films, for example, invoke generic features of film noir to see how their meaning changes when played out in the context of racial prejudice and complicated racial identities in America. In *Devil in a Blue Dress*, Daphne Monet's (Jennifer Beals) "untrustworthiness" has, in the end, to do with the fact that she is "passing" as a white woman to survive being of mixed race and in love with a prominent white man. Three years earlier, Franklin made the affecting *One False Move*, in which doubleness is similarly critique-oriented and about victimization based on racism. *Once False Move*'s dopey Sheriff Dale "Hurricane" Dixon (Bill Paxton) appears to be an ambitious Arkansas bumpkin, but it turns out that he sexually exploited the vulnerable Lila Walker (Cynda Williams) in the past, when she was seventeen and he was a married cop. In *One False Move*, the name Lila has adopted, "Fantasia," symbolizes her function as a screen onto which Dale projects his desires—and as a receptacle of men's fantasies in general. If Lila spirals toward crime and is separated from her son Byron, Dale represses his past into a psychologically jury-rigged fantasy of normalcy with a wife and daughter, Bonnie. In both of Franklin's neo-noir films, the so-called *femme fatale*'s duplicity is not part of a scheme to steal money or the expression of an opaque villain hell-bent on wielding power in any abstract sense. Her character is instead linked unambiguously to the particulars of racism. Unlike many of the women in neo-noir thrillers, these female characters do not fit neatly into categories. They exemplify the political legacy of film noir, carrying its critique into postmodernity.

Female vengeance has also played a central role in contemporary film noir representations of powerful women. The role of the avenging woman takes noir criminality beyond the representation of individual fictional characters to explore issues of exploitation and the victimization of women keyed to social realities. One of the most popular of these stories has been *Gone Girl*. As problematic as some elements of the book by Gillian Flynn and Fincher's film are—the film claims a feminist sensibility and yet exploits a fan base derived from wildly popular films like *Basic Instinct*, wanting it both ways—there are moments of clarity in the story regarding the nature of female rebellion against the oppressive roles women are led to play in order to succeed and sustain relationships. If classic film noir featured women defying sexist prescriptions for acceptable roles and behavior, *Gone Girl* explains a "new sexism" that leads "Amazing Amy" to feign the role of "Cool Girl." "Cool Girl" is "hot and understanding," illustrating the postfeminist expectation that women "[pretend] to be the woman a man wants them to be" (Flynn, 2012, 300). The critique of female role-playing in *Gone Girl* exemplifies Yvonne Tasker's insight into why discussions of film noir and the *femme fatale* remain important:

> The noir woman is snagged in what we might today term a sort of reputation management; her actions, illicit or otherwise, are explicitly framed by the need to *appear* a certain way. Thus, while noir is undoubtedly organized around male desires and male point of view, in its concern with appearance and perception, with the centrality of women's image for their being in the world, noir films articulate concerns that are hugely important for women and for feminism.
>
> *(2013, 360)*

Amy comments just before the "Cool Girl" passage that "Nick loved a girl who didn't exist" (Flynn, 2012, 299). Like the phantom *femme fatale*, the "Cool Girl" is a construct that is parallel to film noir's "space for the playing out of *various* gender fantasies" (Kaplan, 1998, 10).

A more bracing and less sensationalist film than *Gone Girl*, Patty Jenkins's *Monster* explores a process by which victims become criminal perpetrators. Charlize Theron plays Aileen Wuornos, a woman on the margins of society because of her class, gender, and sexual orientation. Dehumanized by her rape, Wuornos wreaks vengeance on the sexist society that has no viable role for her to play. She becomes a "monster." A searing film about the construction of fatal women in a world in which their only imagined agency is violent and revenge-oriented, *Monster* challenges the objectification of women, including in their Hollywood film roles, by casting the beautiful and usually glamorous Charlize Theron in the lead role.

In important ways, *Monster* echoes classic film noir's exposure of the objectification of women in film noir, women whose desires were punished by labeling and objectifying them as *femme fatales*. As Richard Dyer observed, "It is their sexuality that makes people remember Gilda and Laura as *femmes fatales* when they are nothing of the sort" (1998, 127). Such misreading of women as bad because their sexuality and their intelligence threaten patriarchal dominance is common not only in critical readings of film noir, but within the very stories themselves (as in Johnny Farrell's misreading of Gilda, Dave Bannion's misjudging of Debby Marsh in *The Big Heat*, and Jake Gittes's misapprehension of Evelyn Mulwray in *Chinatown* [Polanski, 1974]).

I have described two feminist strains of the postmodern story of the *femme fatale*—the politicization of her trials (exposing a corrupt society that proliferates her victimization) and the path of violent retribution she undertakes to find meaning in her own otherwise limited agency. A third strain I want to explore is the full-on postmodern stylization of the *femme fatale* figure in order to deconstruct her fabrication as gender ideation. These films, best exemplified by the work of David Lynch, play in narrative and cinematographic ways with the *femme fatale*, disrupting the ideological grounds on which she is often perceived. Hollywood's exploitation of female images serves as the backdrop for *Mulholland Drive* (2001), for instance, proliferating and double-exposing *femmes fatales* (and even foregrounding a poster of Rita Hayworth as Gilda, which inspires the amnesiac played by Laura Harring to call herself "Rita"). The process shows "how insubstantial—that is, fantastical— these images are" (Tasker, 2013, 367; see also Grossman, 2009, Chapter 5). Lynch's films are important revisions of film noir because their postmodern ambiguity destabilizes the objectification of the *femme fatale* (see Beckman 2012, 32).

Reaching beyond the genre of film noir further underscores the power and cultural significance of the *femme fatale*. In the last part of this essay, I would like to turn to a film that is not a noir movie, but mines the postmodern indeterminacy and volatility of this figure. Olivier Assayas's *Clouds of Sils Maria* (2014) invokes the idea of the *femme fatale* to undermine the objectification of women into types, the institutionalized reading of them as one thing or another. The film features not one *femme fatale* figure, but three versions of her (that are themselves based on and multiplied by other hovering fictional and non-present characters). The shifting position of the dangerous seducer defies an essentialized fatal woman and engages a more subtle investigation of female agency.

Clouds of Sils Maria turns on the idea that Maria Enders (Juliette Binoche) is asked to appear in a revival of the play *Maloja Snake*, which had, many years earlier, brought her to stardom when she portrayed the seductive temptress Sigrid. In the play, Helena is seduced by Sigrid, who becomes her assistant only to leave her in the end to pursue a life of travel and excitement. A distraught Helena wanders into the mountains, where, audiences assume, she commits suicide. Although actress Maria Enders powerfully identifies with the dynamic role that made her famous twenty years earlier— "I am Sigrid," she tells her assistant Valentine (Kristen Stewart)—she, Maria, agonistically returns to the play to portray the older woman.

In her first meeting with Diesterweg (Lars Eidinger), the director who wishes to cast Maria in the role of Helena, Maria extols the character of Sigrid, as "free, beyond everything." "[M]ost of all," Maria continues, "she is disruptive, unpredictable." Sigrid is, Maria's words suggest, a *femme fatale*, but also dynamic, like the vibrant cloud formation or "Maloja Snake" itself. The actress cast to play Sigrid, Jo-Ann Ellis (Chloë Grace Moretz), is, in the world of the film, a famous Hollywood bad-girl. When she meets Maria, however, she flatters the older woman's ego, appearing innocent and open. She orders chamomile tea, insisting to Maria, "I don't think you understand how much of an honor this is for me."

Jo-Ann claims that Maria is "Everything I ever wanted to be as an actress." "Because of you," she quietly intones, "I could pursue my vocation." Echoing Eve Harrington in *All About Eve* (Mankiewicz, 1950), Jo-Ann, however, is a master image-manipulator. She is Sigrid to Maria's Helena.

Sils Maria has a dizzying effect on viewers familiar with the careers of these actresses, particularly Juliette Binoche's and Kristen Stewart's. The film rejoins Binoche and Oliver Assayas, who wrote her breakout role in *Rendez-Vous* in 1985 and directed her in *Summer Hours* (2008). In *Sils Maria*, Jo-Ann Ellis's controversial excessiveness as a Hollywood star, including videos of drunken escapades and brawls that have gone viral, strongly echoes the celebrity profile of Kristen Stewart (whose character Valentine also mirrors Sigrid in the play within the film). Kristen Stewart's public controversies and romantic scandals remind us once again of Tasker's description of the challenge of the noir woman in her "reputation management."

Jo-Ann Ellis appears to be a *femme fatale* figure at the end of *Sils Maria*, when, just before the play begins, Maria approaches her to ask if she, as Sigrid, might accord her, as Helena, a meaningful look before the young woman leaves her: In this way, Helena might be given some dignity as worthy of at least a final gaze. Jo-Ann's response? "No one really gives a fuck about Helena at that point, do they?... This poor woman's all washed up. I mean your character, not you." "They want what comes next." Maria's justification for her request that Jo-Ann offer her a final gaze is that this is how *she* played Sigrid, twenty years earlier. Maria is challenged to accept that identities are a shifting process over time; roles in fiction and life are reshaped and migrate, blurring the boundaries that contain them.

One way in which this can be seen is in Maria's gradual change in dress. While she appeared at the beginning of the film as a conventionally glamorous woman, by the time Maria has her chilling exchange with Jo-Ann her garb is that of a man (Figure 15.1). With cropped hair and dressed in a man's business suit, Maria/Helena looks like the male protagonist in a film noir duped by the sexy *femme fatale* (Sigrid/Jo-Ann).

Sigrid is not only Maria's former "self" and Jo-Ann's role on and off the stage. She is also doubled in Valentine, Maria's assistant, for most of the story. As Maria struggles to inhabit the role of Helena, her young assistant runs lines with her in Sils Maria, a remote mountain region in Switzerland, where the women hike the landscape and anticipate the Maloja Snake, a stunning cloud formation whose fluid movement represents an alternative mode of existence to the forms objectified in the film's narrative (Hollywood celebrity, *femme fatale*).

As Helena and Valentine rehearse lines, the two act out the roles of ingénue turned vixen (Sigrid) and seduced older woman (Helena). But the way the scenes are performed, it is difficult to tell if we are watching Helena and Sigrid or Maria and Valentine, a

Figure 15.1 The doubling of woman's identity (*Clouds of Sils Maria*).

Source: *Clouds of Sils Maria*, Olivier Assayas, 2014.

blurring of fiction and life that blends the characters in the film with the characters in the play within the film. *Sils Maria* multiplies instances of role-playing to question the fixity of identities.

Maria desires Valentine, it seems, doubling the relationship between Helena and Sigrid. But the bond between Maria and Valentine is doomed, not because the latter consummates her role as *femme fatale*, although she leaves Maria, but because Maria does not value the younger woman's perspective, including her defense of Helena, whom Maria resists throughout the narrative. Maria finds Helena's treatment by Sigrid humiliating. She identifies with the female role she played when she was younger, especially with its restless dynamism: "The world moves, I want to feel that, I want to be a part of it. I want to travel," says Sigrid, in the play within the film. Valentine, however, rejects Maria's idealization of Sigrid: "I didn't read it like that. I see [Sigrid's] arrogance, her cruelty. And Helena's humanity. She's able to talk about her own pain. It's moving." Maria's inability to accept Helena is parallel to the problem posed by the figure of the *femme fatale*: Rather than viewing the *femme fatale* as a fixed unknowable object—the "simple" way chauvinist actor Henryk Wald [Hanns Zischler] sees Sigrid, for example, as a "a scheming girl that has [Helena] wrapped around her little finger"—she is dynamic, a *"femme vital"* (Osteen, 2013). Sigrid may shift to become Helena, as Maria has done, and *Sils Maria*'s postmodern play with fluid identities argues for embracing these changes.

Turning to perhaps the most notorious fatal woman in neo-noir, we see in Sharon Stone's portrayal of Catherine Tramell the knock-on effects of cultural obsessions with fixed character types. One of the most interesting elements of *Basic Instinct*'s cultural rever-beration is a discussion about Sharon Stone's age after the film's sequel was released in 2006. Arguing that the media will not allow the *femme fatale* to age, Rebecca Feasey attributes the failure of *Basic Instinct 2* at the box office at least in part to Stone's more advanced years (she was 48 when the film was released). Feasey's exploration of age and the *femme fatale* is important because it suggests that Stone's career was affected by a convergence of post-feminist emphasis on youth (see Tasker and Negra, 2007) and an objectification of the *femme fatale* figure. Audiences extend an objectification of female types within films to the life of the actress. They are fascinated by parallels between Gloria Swanson's life and Norma Desmond's, for example, which Billy Wilder exploited by including clips of a young Swanson from *Queen Kelly* (1929) in *Sunset Blvd* (1950). Aiding this conflation of "the girling of popular culture" (Lindop, 2015, 41) and the discourse of the *femme fatale* is the postfeminist sexism propelled by Paul Verhoeven in his comment about Stone that "Sharon is Catherine without the killing" (quoted in Feasey, 2012, 113) or by *Total Film* when it informs its readers that Stone "is one of our famous femme fatales … she'll always be the femme fatale from *Basic Instinct*" (qtd. in Feasey, 189). Apart from an obvious monetary incentive, the acquiescence to such typecasting may exemplify the postfeminist "Cool Girl" discourse, Stone here impersonating objects of male desire.

Clouds of Sils Maria takes up this objectification of women into types by suggesting the arbitrariness of such fixed positioning. Further, it destabilizes Hollywood conventions by focusing unusually on several vibrant female characters. *Sils Maria* challenges the idea that the fate of the fatal woman is to age within a society in thrall to fixed images of youthful female beauty. The postmodern story of the *femme fatale* opposes this trajectory by arguing for the necessity of change. *Clouds of Sils Maria* illustrates the beauty and fascination of such change in the charismatic performance of Juliette Binoche and the clouds of Sils Maria, encouraging us to consider gendered and social roles as dynamic and protean rather than static, provoking imaginative rethinking rather than passive acquiescence.

Toward the end of *Sils Maria*, Valentine and Maria climb the mountains looking for the Maloja Snake. As the camera records their hike beneath what we as viewers can see of the hills, only Maria reappears at one of its crests. Valentine's sudden disappearance is never explained in the narrative. Her sudden departure echoes Sigrid's abandonment of Helena, but also Helena herself, who was said in the original play to have wandered off into the mountains after Sigrid left, never to be seen again. Valentine's disappearance echoes David Lynch's treatment of the *femme fatale* figure in film noir, as Beckman understands it: "when the familiar character type of the femme fatale is removed from its interdependence on coherent narrative development and climax and emerges instead through different, overlapping, and incongruous layers of time, her function begins to shift" (2012, 43). Like Lynch's films, *Clouds of Sils Maria* can be said to "[open] up space for a revision of the role of the femme fatale" (ibid.).

The multiple roles for women in *Clouds of Sils Maria* allegorize the importance of the postmodern story of the *femme fatale*. She is a dynamic figure of female power who will not "stay still" (see Farrimond, 2012), but she is also a changeling figure that helps us to understand the gendered nature of power relations in society and culture. Such multiplicity is figured in the set design of *Maloja Snake*, the play within the film, with its mirrors and reflective walls: a sort of cubist rendering of a noir cubicled office space (Figure 15.2).

Figure 15.2   The multiplicity of set design (*Clouds of Sils Maria*).

Source: *Clouds of Sils Maria*, Olivier Assayas, 2014.

Figure 15.3   The women in *Mad Men*.

Source: *Mad Men*, Matthew Weiner, 2015.

The postmodern fiction of the *femme fatale* invites multiple chapters—perhaps one akin to the scruffy young writer's vision of a new "mutant" role for Maria Enders, a film he's writing in which she would play a "hybrid," "a creation of modern genetics but with a soul;" or a story from the fictionalized past, Joan Holloway Harris's or Peggy Olson's transgressions, to resonate with our own present (Figure 15.3).

One can even imagine a more fluid conception of the *femme fatale* generating a female Walter White (himself a noir adaptation of Walt Whitman). Such a portrait would not simply glorify murderousness, betrayal, or violence without context. This *femme* could be an Emily Dickinson or Elizabeth Barrett Browning, who, without being easily othered or turned into an object, might "break bad" against a claustrophobic environment to express her creative drive and agency.

Related topics

Patrice Petro, "Classical feminist film theory: then and (mostly) now"
Lucy Fischer, "Feminist forms of address: Mai Zetterling's *Loving Couples*"

Bibliography

Beckman, Frida. 2012. "From Irony to Narrative Crisis: Reconsidering the Femme Fatale in the Films of David Lynch." *Cinema Journal* 52: 25–44.

Bronfen, Elisabeth. 2004. "Femme Fatale—Negotiations of Tragic Desire." *New Literary History* 35.1 (Winter): 103–16.

Cohan, Steven. 1998. "Censorship and Narrative Indeterminacy in *Basic Instinct*." In *Contemporary Hollywood Cinema*, eds. Steve Neale and Murray Smith, 263–79. London and New York: Routledge.

Cook, Pam. 1978. "Duplicity in *Mildred Pierce*." In Kaplan, 68–82.

Copjec, Joan. 1993. *Shades of Noir: A Reader*. London; New York: Verso.

Cowie, Elizabeth. 1993. "*Film Noir* and Women." In Copjec, 121–66.

Doane, Mary Ann. 1991. *Femmes Fatales: Feminism, Film Theory, and Psychoanalysis*. New York: Routledge.

Dyer, Richard. 1998. "Postscript: Queers and Women in Film Noir." In Kaplan. Rev. edn., 123–29.

Farrimond, K. 2012. "'Stay Still So We Can See Who You Are': Anxiety and Bisexual Activity in the Contemporary *Femme Fatale* Film." *Journal of Bisexuality* 12.1: 138–54.

Feasey, R. 2012. "The Ageing Femme Fatale: Sex, Stardom, and Sharon Stone." In *Aging, Performance and Stardom: Doing Age on the Stage of Consumerist Culture*, eds. Aagje Swinnen and John A. Stotesbury, 109–30. Zurich: Lit Verlag.

Flynn, Gillian. 2012. *Gone Girl*. New York: Broadway Books.

Gates, Philippa. 2011. *Detecting Women: Gender and the Hollywood Detective Film*. Albany: State University of New York Press.

——— 2014. "Independence Unpunished: The Female Detective in Classic Film Noir." In *Kiss the Blood Off My Hands: On Classic Film Noir*, ed. Robert Miklitsch, 17–36. Urbana: University of Illinois Press.

Gledhill, Christine. 1978. "Klute 1: A Contemporary Film Noir and Feminist Criticism." In Kaplan, 6–21.

——— 1978. "Klute 2: Feminism and *Klute*." In Kaplan, 112–28.

Grossman, Julie. 2009. *Rethinking the Femme Fatale in Film Noir: Ready for Her Close-Up*. Basingstoke: Palgrave Macmillan.

Hanson, Helen. 2007. *Hollywood Heroines: Women in Film Noir and the Female Gothic Film*. London: I.B. Tauris.

Hanson, Helen, and Catherine O'Rawe. 2010. *The Femme Fatale: Images, Histories, Contexts*. Basingstoke: Palgrave Macmillan.

Johnston, Claire. 1978. *Double Indemnity*. In Kaplan, 100–11.

Kaplan, E. Ann. 1978, 1998. *Women in Film Noir*. London: British Film Institute.

Lindop, Samantha. 2015. *Postfeminism and the Fatale Figure in Neo-Noir Cinema*. Basingstoke: Palgrave Macmillan.

Osteen, Mark. 2013. *Nightmare Alley: Film Noir and the American Dream*. Baltimore: Johns Hopkins University Press.

Pidduck, Julianne. 1995. "The 1990s Hollywood Fatal Femme: (Dis)Figuring Feminism, Family, Irony, Violence." *Cineaction* 38 (September): 64–72.

Place, Janey. 1978. "Women in Film Noir." In Kaplan, 35–67.

Stables, Kate. 1998. "The Postmodern Always Rings Twice: Constructing the *Femme Fatale* in 90s Cinema." In Kaplan. Rev. edn., 164–82.

Tasker, Yvonne. 2013. "Women in Film Noir." In *A Companion to Film Noir*, eds. Andrew Spicer and Helen Hanson, 353–68. Chichester, West Sussex; Malden, MA: Wiley Blackwell.

Tasker, Yvonne, and Diane Negra. 2007. *Interrogating Postfeminism: Gender and the Politics of Popular Culture*. Durham: Duke University Press.

Williams, Linda Ruth. 2009. "A Woman Scorned: The Neo-Noir Erotic Thriller as Revenge Drama." In *Neo-Noir*, eds. Mark Bould, Kathrina Glitre, and Greg Tuck, 168–85. New York: Wallflower.

16

THE DOCUMENTARY

Female subjectivity and the problem of realism

Belinda Smaill

Few film genres are as significant for feminism as the documentary. It is overwhelmingly the genre to be taken up for advocacy purposes and as a tool within grassroots movements— the documentary genre is crucially tied to the politicization of women's experience. In comparison with fiction feature film, more women work as directors or in key roles in documentary production, making it critical to women's representation in the industry in many parts of the world. Despite this, documentary directors achieve a more modest public profile than their counterparts in fiction. Moreover, documentary has been under-theorized in scholarly approaches to media and cinema. In this chapter I take up the question of gender and documentary, exploring its relevance at the nexus of critical debates and filmmaking practice, both historical and contemporary.

Including documentary in a collection focused on *cinema* and gender might be seen as a point of contention: the opportunities for distributing documentary, and non-fiction formats more broadly, are extremely diverse and the genre has close associations with histories of television as much it does with those of cinema. Avenues for circulation are expanding, moreover, to include the proliferation of subscription television, the Internet, and streaming services. Nevertheless, while documentary may exist as a multiplatform media form, the *study* of the genre has been located in cinema studies accounts and approaches since the earliest days of the discipline—documentary has been understood and critiqued through the terms of film aesthetics, production practices, and audience address. This history of critique operates as a point of departure for this chapter. Specifically, I expand on the way gender has been addressed both by documentary filmmakers and scholars, focusing in particular on the problem of realism. I bring this historical discussion to an analysis of two recent examples: the first, *Stories We Tell* (2012) drawn from a North American context and the second, *First Australians* (2008), an Australian context.

Documentary past and present: the problem of realism

There are a number of pathways into the thicket of critical debates and field of film practice that has characterized the historical relation between feminist concerns and documentary. In the introduction to their landmark edited volume, *Feminism and Documentary*, Diane

Waldman and Janet Walker describe how, in the written accounts that emerged in the early days of documentary studies, women were absent:

> The relationship of '70s documentary studies to feminist concerns was primarily one of omission. Early '70s work on documentary neglected both the representation of women in the classics of the documentary tradition and the contributions of women to the documentary form.
>
> *(Waldman and Walker 1999: 4)*

Yet as these histories were being written, new women filmmakers were taking up the genre in unprecedented numbers as a way to represent the concerns of second wave feminism. In the late 1960s and early 1970s in the USA, the UK, and Canada, the genre was seen as a cogent way of raising awareness about social issues. The nascent institutions of documentary studies began to take notice of explicitly feminist work, even if films that were not explicitly feminist in nature "remained unaffected by feminist thinking" (Waldman and Walker 1999: 5). In the archive of feminist film debates, documentary as a category also received scant discussion, with pockets of analysis occurring most intensively in the 1970s and 1980s. I suggest that the perceived lack of attention to the conjunction of women and documentary owes much to the division that has developed between realist and non-realist forms of non-fiction filmmaking and the differing critical emphasis placed on the work that putatively falls on either side of this division.

I explore the permutations of this history, posing the different erasures, as well as the interventions of documentary feminism, as manifesting a problem of realism. This term, referring to the ways in which art or film (fiction or non-fiction) might resonate plausibly with viewers to offer a likeness of the world, is especially important for documentary. The genre encourages viewers to, in Elizabeth Cowie's characterization, "experience reality through recorded images and sounds of reality" (Cowie 2011: 1), fulfilling an expectation of and desire for "the fascinating pleasure of recorded reality as both spectacle and knowledge" (ibid. 3). Cowie's words leave the definition of documentary and its realism open, allowing for multiple styles and approaches to the representation of the real.

The problem of realism came to the fore in 1970s feminist film critique with Claire Johnston's essay "Women's Cinema as Counter-Cinema" (1975), and later, Laura Mulvey's "Visual Pleasure and Narrative Cinema" (1975). Both scholars argued that subjectivity and ideology were not simply tied to narrative and thematic concerns, but that the very formal structure (and apparatus) of cinema perpetuated the dominance of patriarchal perspectives:

> Any revolutionary must challenge the depiction of reality: it is not enough to discuss the oppression of women within the text of the film: the language of the cinema/depiction of reality [sic] must also be interrogated, so that a break between ideology and text is affected.
>
> *(Johnston 1975: 29)*

The depiction of reality referred to here is that seen primarily in commercial fiction film. Johnston's essay was inspired by new filmmaking of the time, and also influenced a diverse body of filmmakers who shared a desire to rethink the mediation or construction of the image —a new discursive system of cinematic conventions held the key to retraining consciousness in spectatorship. Much of this cinema employed non-realist strategies, a response to the critique of the ideological (patriarchal) underpinnings of realist codes. The films most associated with this moment include Mulvey's film with Peter Wollen, *Riddles of the Sphinx* (1977) and Sally Potter's *Thriller* (1979)—films that unravel narrative pleasure, particularly in response to Hollywood cinema. The urgency and allure of theorizing new conceptually sophisticated paradigms resulted in the canonization of largely North American works by filmmakers into the 1980s including Yvonne Rainer, Jill Godmilow, Michelle Citron, Su Friedrich, and Barbara Hammer in addition to British filmmakers Laura Mulvey and Sally Potter.

Much of this film work, especially in the 1970s, was posed in contestation with not only Hollywood cinema, but it also took issue with the established codes of realist documentary, such as observational camerawork, interviews, and voice over narration. Thus, the largely realist documentary produced by those working in activist and advocacy contexts in the feminist movement was debated on these terms, despite the fact that it emerged from a very different production context to that of Hollywood and had different aims. The interview format in particular was a key device for early feminist documentarians focused on giving voice to female subjectivity.

A number of scholars have questioned this simple division between realist and non-realist and its apportioning of value. Paige Schilt makes the point that "the uniformity of the critique has never been equal to the complexity of individual feminist documentaries" (Schilt 2006: 394), which often defy the imposition of either category. In part, this is due to the way "realist" has been equated with documentary proper (largely referring to classical modes of exposition including interviews and observational techniques), while "non-realist" has bracketed the non-fiction avant-garde, experimental and essayist forms and often been aligned more with art practice (see Scott MacDonald's *A Critical Cinema 2* (1992) for one example).

Predominantly realist documentary of this time is less attended to in scholarship and teaching contexts, seen more for its sociological content than its aesthetic innovations. It is easy to perceive these films as naïve or conceptually unsophisticated in their adherence to observational and expository styles, especially as these styles are more aligned with present-day television. Such a perception, however, glosses over the complexity of realism, realist style, and the documentary moving image, including histories of women working in male-dominated documentary production contexts. Prior to the 1970s, a number of women working as directors, editors and writers took on the conventions of the genre and pushed against the precepts of the time in nuanced ways, including Shirley Clarke, Esfir Shub, Catherine Duncan, and Helen Grayson. At the same time, it should be recognized that the different styles that are broadly bracketed by the problem of realism have not remained fixed—they have morphed into the present in ways that offer crucial insights into the current terrain of (feminist) documentary critique.

In 2006, B. Ruby Rich's editorial for a special "documentary studies" issue of *Cinema Journal* observed that the "landscape for documentary production, history, and theory is richer than it has been in the United States at any time since, perhaps, the last explosion: the direct cinema or cinema verité movement of the early 1960s" (Rich 2006: 109). Rich is observing a revival in documentary culture that expanded across the first decade of the twenty-first century. This was accompanied by a commercial "boom" as the market for feature length non-fiction film intensified, with the high point occurring between 2002 and 2006. Yet, as Thomas Austin observes, most of the financial high performers in the boom have been American and, moreover, it "was in part a discursive phenomenon, constructed in the output of film magazines, websites and newspaper" (Austin 2007: 14). Notably, documentaries exploring issues of gender, or even other axes of identity and subjectivity, are largely absent from this discourse and from the most visible and commercially successful products of this revival (for example, *Fahrenheit 9/11* (2004), *An Inconvenient Truth* (2006), *Supersize Me* (2004) or *Touching the Void* (2004)). The revival has also been characterized by the infamy (or controversy) surrounding a handful of (male) auteurs such as Werner Herzog, Errol Morris, and Michael Moore. Notably, Moore and Morris were key proponents in an earlier high point for the genre, one described by Linda Williams as a turn to a "postmodern" style of filmmaking (Williams 1998: 383).

While the highly visible and/or profitable products of the popular documentary landscape do not address feminist concerns, the numbers of filmmakers and artists interested in exploring the multidimensional issues, experiences, and institutions that expand around the socio-cultural formation of gender is steadily increasing. The field of documentary studies, if not cinema studies more broadly, has addressed clusters of this work (Smaill 2010; Renov 2004). Essayist and art cinema and video forms have attracted the most attention from documentary scholars in the 1980s and 1990s, the period prior to the one Rich describes. This includes the significant expansion of self-reflexive or autobiographical modes, areas of concentration for women filmmakers concerned with feminist questions (such as Pratibha Parmar, Ngozi Onwurah, or Trinh T. Minh-ha). Indeed, the mainstream revival of non-fiction filmmaking more broadly has been significantly influenced by the turn to first person address (Renov 2004; Lebow 2012). Less attention has been given to the development of predominantly observational and expository documentary over this time, with these examples more frequently associated with television and/or grassroots activist movements. Films in this tradition have continued to be a site of feminist enterprise. Perhaps the most visible forum for the independent distribution of this work is Women Make Movies, a New York based non-profit media arts organization that facilitates the production, distribution, and exhibition of independent films by and about women (see Debra Zimmerman's essay in this volume). In a different way television, especially public television, has played an important role in maintaining a significant role for socio-political realism amongst audiences and offering financial support (albeit increasingly meager) to documentary culture and filmmakers.

In documentary scholarship, explicitly feminist approaches have not been staked out as an identifiable sub-field, as is the case in some areas of film and screen studies. Instead, documentary scholars versed in feminist theory, such as Stella Bruzzi, Alexandra Juhasz, Janet Walker, and Patricia Zimmermann, work to confront a range of questions pertaining to women and female directors in a manner that binds them to the broader intellectual project of the discipline. Similarly, the contemporary output of documentarians concerned with gender includes not only those working under the banner of feminism but also many filmmakers who draw attention to women's human rights, gendered norms and female subjectivity in ways that are particular to their contexts but not necessarily in reference to stated feminist precepts. Recent examples of such films are as diverse as *India's Daughter* (2015), a film about the brutal rape of a Delhi student, its aftermath and widespread media coverage; *Dreamcatcher* (2015), an observational and personal examination of sex trafficking in Chicago; and *Finding Vivian Maier* (2013) which recounts, posthumously, the life and work of this previously unknown female photographer. Below I attend to further examples of this work, exploring different styles of realism and, by investigating how they open a space for feminist critique, viewing them through the lens of feminist documentary historiography.

Stories We Tell

While the documentary revival has focused on a group of high profile male auteurs, there has emerged a small but decisive stable of women directors, some new and some established.

These women have achieved critical, and sometimes popular, acclaim in recent years. The most recent success has been Laura Poitras' Oscar win for *Citizenfour* (2014). Poitras sits within a somewhat disparate group including Molly Dineen, Agnès Varda, Kim Longinotto, and, as I discuss in this section, Canadian actor and director Sarah Polley. *Stories We Tell* is Polley's first feature length documentary, and one that has gained considerable popular success in a commercial environment that is often less receptive to film focused on female relationships and female stories.

Polley takes a key role in the on-screen events of *Stories We Tell*, alongside family members, principally her siblings and her father, Michael Polley. It is a work of excavation: she digs into the events of family history, focusing specifically on her mother, Diane Polly, who died when Sarah was eleven. The film highlights her mother's vivacious personality, her intense love for her children and her wandering spirit. Most significantly, it explores the family myth that Polley's father was not Michael but rather a fellow actor Diane had been performing with at the time she became pregnant. The film follows a complex narrative structure, tracing events through multiple stories, showing that the storytelling structure is crucial to the interpretation. It does so by compiling a collage of super 8 footage and "faux" home movies (that include actors playing Diane and other characters), genuine archival photographs, interviews, and scenes in a sound studio recording Michael's voiceover.

The film can be compared with significant antecedents in the tradition of feminist documentary, most notably Michelle Citron's *Daughter Rite* (1979) and Su Fredrich's *The Ties that Bind* (1984). Both of these earlier examples feature the filmmakers reflecting on their own families and childhood with a particular focus on the relationship between the filmmaker and their mother. All use home movie footage, and furthermore, *Daughter Rite* uses actors to play the part of family members—a move imperceptible to many viewers. In all three, home movie footage is recast (slowed down in the case of *Daughter Rite*), filtered through the subjective lens of the filmmaker, blending its status as recorded reality with that of artifice. *Stories We Tell* shares much with earlier works such as *Daughter Rite*—by re-enacting past events, creating a new vision, it refuses a singular interpretation of the events it grasps. As Jane Feuer describes in relation to the earlier film, "a number of contradictory truths about women's lives with mother, 'truths' which deny the easy resolution provided by narrative closure" (Feuer 1980). It does so by employing a mix of devices (from realist and non-realist traditions) that are now common in documentary: multiple interviews, re-enactments, the on-screen presence of the filmmaker and archival footage.

Polley's film destabilizes documentary certainty in ways that also undo fixed notions of female identity, especially what it means to be a mother or a daughter. It does so through different spoken accounts and through the play of visual markers of identity. Diane appears in family photographs and home movies, but these faces of Polley's mother are not uniformly the same—the actor as doppelganger produces double-ness.

The film draws attention to the complexity of one woman's identity, prompting us to reflect on the typology of motherhood and posing it not as a trope but as a form of complex personhood. This is most striking in the sequence that refers to Diane's first marriage to George, the father of her first two children. Following the film's revelation that she had an affair with Harry (Sarah's biological father), Michael describes Diane: "Both Harry and I met a person who was bored with her life and wanted something more exciting." The frame is filled by a woman shot from behind, looking out a kitchen window and smoking a cigarette. The scene conveys both domesticity and discontent. The following sequence shows photographs of the real Diane with her first two children, both very young, and home movie footage of her wedding with George by her side. The voiceover of her eldest son describes how Diane felt "over controlled" and wanted to "get out from under." He goes on to note that when Diane left George she lost custody of the children, a situation unheard of in the 1960s. A younger son describes the anguish this must have caused their mother. Diane's life is governed by the expectations of marriage and motherhood and while the film shows how she works to meet these, it also conveys her as consistently troubled and restless.

While the viewer eventually learns the identity of Polley's biological father, the most compelling aspect of the film is not this revelation—it is instead the journey the viewers are asked to embark on. They are asked to indulge in the pleasure of the mystery as it unfolds, and to grapple with the figment of Diane (and her daughter) as it is multiply constructed in sound and image. This is perhaps where the film departs most significantly from earlier traditions. While it melds non-fiction and subjective retelling, confronting the problem of realism in explicit ways (thus keeping with a non-realist ethos), it also reserves a strong place for spectatorial pleasure. *Stories We Tell* harnesses the storytelling potential of narrative, of cause and effect and of the mystery of the (female) self. This mystery is not one that aims to mystify femininity—rather, it is an avenue to throw light on the lives of particular women and provoke questions about how to represent their specificity against the demands of gender norms. In Diane's case, the expectations of marriage and motherhood in the 1960s and 1970s. This crafting of the spectacle and knowledge of women's experience, to borrow Cowie's phrase, rethinks realism in a way that is implicitly feminist.

Stories We Tell sits alongside other notable examples that draw attention to femininity, and at times problematize the real of female subjectivity, such as Carol Morley's *The Alcohol Years* (2000) and *Dreams of a Life* (2011), and Anna Broinowski's *Forbidden Lie$* (2007). Indeed, Polley's film offers the most commercially successful example of such female-led documentaries, achieving significant theatrical release and multiple awards. It was also short-listed for an Academy Award in the category of best documentary. *Stories We Tell* is a singular example of how narrative pleasure, and female selfhood, can be harnessed on the path to confronting the problem of realism.

Rachel Perkins and the historical biographical documentary

I now move from discussing a single film to turn to the wider *oeuvre* of a filmmaker, one who also broadens the audience for the documentary representation of female subjectivity, but does so in a very different way, offering another strategy for documentary realism. Rachel Perkins is one of Australia's foremost film and television directors, and is of Australian Aboriginal heritage (*Arrernte/Kalkadoon* nation). Her work, although achieving significant international acclaim, is not valorized by the Euro-American system of box office figures and festivals that characterizes the documentary revival. Nevertheless, her approach to documentary and other screen genres is one that seeks to locate them at the center of mainstream national cinema and television. In particular, I am interested in how Perkins takes up the historical documentary, and the biographical mode within this, to bring into focus Aboriginal history and also to forge a place for women's voices and women's stories. Across her career Perkins has worked in multiple genres. Her first fiction feature, *Radiance* (1998), focused on three indigenous sisters and marked a turning point for indigenous women in Australian popular cinema. She has directed and produced musicals, television dramas, and multiple documentaries. Perkins is one of the most visible proponents of what has been termed Australia's new "Blak Wave" of indigenous filmmakers and artists.

This term encapsulates a body of film and television produced since 2000 that is both high profile and high budget, telling indigenous stories with indigenous film workers in key creative roles.

Perkins is co-founder, with Darren Dale, of the production company, Blackfella Films, which has collaborated with Screen Australia and public television to produce an important and sizable body of work. One of its most ambitious projects, *First Australians*, is a seven part documentary series that adopts the format of the large-scale historical-biographical documentary series. This format is often utilized to dramatize, in documentary form, epic events such as wars or the rise and fall of empires. Perkins, as producer and writer of the series, employs this mode of documentary realism in the service of reframing Australian narratives of nation for a mainstream audience. The series was made in collaboration with the national multicultural public broadcaster, the Special Broadcasting Service (SBS) as a multiplatform production, and all episodes can be viewed though the SBS web portal. Therese Davis offers a succinct description of Perkins' project:

> Over the years, Perkins has developed an international reputation by innovatively "Indigenizing" mainstream genres: melodrama, the musical and the biographical documentary. In *First Australians*, Perkins and her collaborators took on the enormous task of "Indigenizing" the international genre of the historical documentary, a project that would in the process become historical "event-television": a national media event.
>
> (Davis 2008: 104)

Specifically, the series takes up the work of prominent indigenous and non-indigenous historians (many of whom feature in the series) and crafts a series of seven semi-biographies, appropriating this approach to history to redraw notions of selfhood and nation.

I suggest that there is a feminist method in this redefinition of documentary, given its work in troubling dominant orthodoxies. More than this, the series is peopled with female experts, features a female narrator and brings to light a number of women's stories alongside those of men, with one of the episodes focused on the biography of a well known indigenous female figure of the nineteenth century, Truganini (*Nuenonne* nation). Titled "Her Will to Survive," this documentary episode (directed by Beck Cole), shares with the others a stylistic focus on interviews with historians, spoken quotes from individuals of the time, imagery from painting (landscape and portraiture), archival photographs and present-day images of historical locations. In Tasmania in the nineteenth century large numbers of indigenous people were killed by settlers or whalers, or died in missions due to disease. Truganini's biography is enmeshed with that of George Augustus Robinson, an untrained preacher who sought to establish a "friendly mission" for the last few hundred Aboriginal people living in the Tasmanian bush. Truganini, believing this was the only hope for her people, advocated for him.

The episode conveys the story of Truganini and her people largely through the different voices of historians. It creates a poly-vocal style, with meaning more firmly located in the narration than is the case with *Stories We Tell*. Early in the episode the viewer learns what was at stake for Truganini and others who decide to bargain with Robinson, becoming diplomats amongst their own people. Different commentators offer differing rationales. A voice recounts the words of Truganini as the camera zooms out from her portrait: "Our people were all being killed and it was no use fighting anymore and Mr. Robinson was our friend and would take us all to a good place." Describing why she might have worked to convince other Aboriginal people to join with Robinson, Professor Marcia Langton (*Yiman/ Bidjara* nation) addresses the interviewer:

> She perhaps thought she was offering them the chance of life as well … perhaps they would have been killed if they'd stayed where they were, by renegade settlers who were intent on murdering all Aboriginal people they found. There were after all, for a period of time, bounties on Aboriginal heads. They might have been murdered by sealers if they were living on the coast.

Later in the episode Langton describes the unique agency experienced by Aboriginal women who were able to move easily between white and indigenous worlds, seemingly posing less threat than Aboriginal men. Writer Bruce Pascoe (*Boonwurrung* heritage) recounts how whalers brutally killed Truganini's betrothed husband, abandoning him at and sea and cutting off his hands so he couldn't swim. As images of tumultuous waves against rocky cliffs cut to another painting of Truganini he states: "People wonder about Truganini's motivation for the things she did—she saw that." The documentary captures the complexity of Truganini's position, asking the viewer to perceive events from her point of view.

The series is remarkable not only for its attention to historical detail, but also for seeking out archival material to faithfully represent indigenous people, many of whom did not contribute to the written record or were seldom photographed. This particular episode interprets and produces Truganini's subjectivity as part of a national narrative. More than this, as Davis suggests, it engages an international dimension, adapting the long-form historical documentary genre. Ken Burns' monumental series, *The Civil War* (1990) was a key reference point for Perkins and others working on the series (Davis 2008: 106). Thus, the series consistently adheres to the conventions of realist documentary, while redrawing the map of Australian colonial history and interweaving it with female subjectivities—both historical figures and historians. With this subtle reframing the series adheres to a feminist approach, questioning both the patriarchal and British-settler representation of the past. This reflection on female-centric experience of the world might be seen as a mode of realism oriented towards feminist outlooks.

Perkins' filmmaking consistently contests the notion that indigenous femininity sits outside modernity and history. It does so through appropriating modes of documentary realism. Moreover, as an accomplished female director/producer, Perkins herself brings another notion of female indigeneity into view. She also highlights the importance, in the contemporary economy of documentary production, of the role of the producer as she negotiates institutions and genres in order to broaden the range of voices (and histories) that are elucidated in the Australian mainstream.

Conclusion

The question of women's film practice and the exploration, on-screen, of issues pertinent to feminism are not, it should be noted, identical. Yet, where documentary production is concerned, they frequently do converge, and this chapter has been primarily concerned with this intersection. Perkins and Polley's work does not fit the mold of "feminist documentary film" in straightforward ways. My reading has sought to bring them into dialogue with documentary histories, and its overlaps with feminist critique. These examples demonstrate how documentary that is grappling with the question of female subjectivity is doing so in different ways and for different audiences. They also show how women are working in a field of documentary production that is increasingly diverse. *Stories We Tell* and *First Australians* are, in their respective contexts, exceptional—one is a breakthrough autobiographical film and the other a high budget national series. Each in their own way, they show how female documentarians are gaining the status that is often the preserve of men, especially in the context of the documentary revival. This focus is not intended to reinscribe a paradigm that prioritizes exceptional women or to suggest that women film-makers and feminist concerns have been seamlessly integrated into the mainstream of documentary practice(s). Rather, these films reward a reading that seeks out connections between historical debates and new directions in documentary that both references and troubles the settled categories, such as realism, that constitute the documentary genre *and* gendered norms.

Related topics

Priya Jaikumar, "Feminist and non-Western interrogations of film authorship"
Debra Zimmerman, "Film as activism and transformative praxis: Women Make Movies"

References

Austin, T. (2007) *Watching the World*, Manchester: Manchester University Press.
Cowie, E. (2011) *Recording Reality, Desiring the Real*, Minneapolis: University of Minnesota Press.
Davis, T. (2008) "A Post-apology National History: *First Australians: The Untold Story of Australia*," *Metro*, 159, pp. 104–9.
Feuer, J. (1980) "Daughter Rite: Living with Our Pain, and Love," *Jump Cut*, 23, pp. 12–13.
Johnston, C. (1975) "Women's Cinema as Counter-Cinema," in C. Johnston (ed.) *Notes on Women's Cinema*, London: Society for Education in Film and Television, pp. 24–31.
Lebow, A. (ed.) (2012) *The Cinema of Me: The Self and Subjectivity in First Person Documentary*, London: Wallflower Press.
MacDonald, S. (1992) *A Critical Cinema 2: Interviews with Independent Filmmakers*, Berkeley: University of California Press.
Mulvey, L. (1975) "Visual Pleasure and Narrative Cinema," *Screen*, 16(3), pp. 6–18.
Renov, M. (2004) *The Subject of Documentary*, Minneapolis: University of Minnesota Press.
Rich, R. (2006) "Documentary Disciplines: An Introduction," *Cinema Journal* 46(1), pp. 108–15.
Schilt, P. (2006) "Feminism: Critical Overview," in I. Aitken (ed.) *Encyclopaedia of the Documentary Film*, New York: Routledge, pp. 392–8.
Smaill, B. (2010) *The Documentary: Politics, Emotion, Culture*, Basingstoke: Palgrave Macmillan.
Waldman, D. and J. Walker (1999) "Introduction," in D. Waldman and J. Walker (eds.) *Feminism and Documentary*, Minneapolis: University of Minnesota Press, pp. 1–35.
Williams, L. (1998) "Mirrors without Memories: Truth, History and *The Thin Blue Line*," in B. K. Grant and J. Sloniowski (eds.) *Documenting the Documentary: Close Readings of Documentary Film and Video*, Detroit: Wayne State University Press, pp. 379–96.

Further reading

Beattie, K. (2004). *Documentary Screens: Non-fiction Film and Television*, New York: Palgrave Macmillan. (An accessible and comprehensive account of recent and historical developments in documentary practice.)
Citron, M. (1999) *Home Movies and Other Necessary Fictions*, Minneapolis: University of Minnesota Press. (An award-winning depth study of feminist filmmaking practice from this key practitioner.)

Lesage, J. (1990) "The Political Aesthetics of the Feminist Documentary Film," in P. Erens (ed.) *Issues in Feminist Film Criticism*, Bloomington: Indiana University Press, pp. 222–37. (A re-print of a 1978 essay, one of the first to examine realist documentary from a feminist perspective.)

Trinh, T. M. (1993) "The Totalizing Quest of Meaning," in M. Renov (ed.) *Theorizing Documentary*, New York: Routledge, pp. 90–107. (A landmark essay that interrogates the construction of truth in documentary, employing a poetic style.)

Zimmermann, P. (1999). "Flaherty's Midwives," in D. Waldman and J. Walker (eds.) *Feminism and Documentary*, Minneapolis: University of Minnesota Press, pp. 64–83. (A feminist appraisal of the Flaherty Seminar, one of the key institutions for critiquing and promoting documentary in the United States.)

17

EXPERIMENTAL WOMEN FILMMAKERS

Maureen Turim

In 2005, an anthology entitled *Women and Experimental Filmmaking* edited by Jean Petrolle and Virginia Wright Wexman presented a corpus of filmmakers who had made significant contributions to the history of creative, alternative film praxis. Two years later, another anthology, entitled *Women's Experimental Cinema: Critical Frameworks*, edited by Robin Blaetz, presented a group of filmmakers that only overlapped with the previous anthology in the cases of Maya Deren, Abigail Child, Su Friedrich, and Joyce Wieland. In the introductions to each volume, the editors note that the constitution of the corpus could have included many filmmakers they did not finally include. All agreed on the importance of women experimental filmmakers at various periods in the history of avant-garde cinematic expression. Petrolle and Wexman included more filmmakers of color and those more directly addressing social issues in essayist form, while Blaetz concentrated on more formal experimentation with cinematic abstraction and personal poetics, including chapters devoted to Marie Menken, Gunvor Nelson, Carolee Schneemann, Barbara Rubin, Amy Greenfield, Barbara Hammer, Chick Strand, Marjorie Keller, Peggy Ahwesh, and Leslie Thornton. I begin this essay with citation of these two works not only because they represent fine scholarly attention to women working in experimental modes, but also as a prelude to my own remarks on the definition of experimental praxis: if viewed in its most expansive sense, it encompasses a celebration of women creatively innovating in filmic expression, yet this inclusiveness yields a corpus so diverse in expression that it becomes a collection of disparate examples. Ironically, such approaches often end up tied to biography, as they treat the body of work of individuals largely atomized.

Instead, my approach will be to highlight two filmmakers at present representing quite different polarities in experimental practice—Jodie Mack, on one hand, and Eija-Liisa Ahtila on the other—lacing the discussion of their work to others who preceded them or share common formal and conceptual ground with them at present. I will seek lines of connection, focusing on intertextuality across decades, to show how the collective project of women holds in common innovation in poetic filmic form, even while distinct variation in concerns abounds: some more narrative, some more essayist, and some more plastically abstract. My strategy of aligning these two film artists with others who preceded or are contemporaneous with them will provide an introduction to the field of women experimental filmmakers, though not one meant in any sense to be exhaustive, impossible in an essay of this length.

Jodie Mack works in visual abstraction, the mode in which pictorial reference and representation is minimal, while color, light, tempo, contrast, and rhythm are paramount—the type of film art explored by Cecile Starr and Robert Russett in their *Experimental Animation: Origins of a New Art* (1976). Her technique is often animation, in this case frame-by-frame capture by the camera of paper compositions. Mack redefines abstraction in relationship to a playful take on conceptual art and structural film; indeed humor and pleasure are as central to her "Let Your Light Shine" aphorism that names a series of her films, as is the exploration of glowing, flowing light and color.

Mack's work has a rich heritage of women who serve as precedents, for example, Lotte Reiniger, whose cut paper silhouettes create animated fairy tales and operas, an artistic innovation analyzed so well by Eric Walter White's *Walking Shadows: An Essay on Lotte Reiniger's Silhouette Films* (1931). In turn, Reiniger drew on a tradition of shadowplay in nineteenth-century paracinematic theatrical performance; while Reiniger's films are narrative, her sense of composition of the black cut paper against first white, and later, colored backgrounds may be seen in its abstract beauty. Mary Ellen Bute's *Synchromy No. 2* (1936) in black and white and *Synchromy No. 4: Escape* (1938) in the contrasting colors of orange triangular structures against a blue background lined in a black grid transform components into various configurations. In Bute's 1940 *Spook Sport*, made in collaboration with Norman McLaren, the abstract designs that chase each other across the screen suggest ghosts; and her *Tarantella* (1941) reworks some of these evocative shapes in a dance-like rhythm. Marie Menken, though working with representational rather than purely geometric images, develops a montage aesthetic that has been compared to abstract animation in such films as *Notebook* (1940–62), *Lights* (1964–66), and *Drips in Strips* (1963). Her *Eye Music in Red Major* (1961) abstracts the lights of New York, highlighting the color red, to create a play of color shining from the screen. Indeed, Shirley Clarke's *Bridges-Go-Round* (1958) rhythmically superimposes panning shots on New York City bridges and skylines in what ultimately becomes an abstracted play of architectural lines in movement and counter-movements. The color tints and the combined electronic and jazz score add to Clarke's exploration. Any still frame captured from this film is entrancing, yet viewing the film is rather an experience of motion itself, a transformation of fixed architectonics into a vision, fluid and always changing.

Thinking of these precedents, Mack's films can be seen as a revival of a tradition of abstraction in which women played an important part early on, though they were less well represented in the 1960s and 1970s expansion of this mode of filmmaking. Mack makes conscious reference to women's crafts such as quilting, and acquires materials for her films at dollar stores, and from the color samples of the paper industry, collecting and putting to new purpose materials in ways similar to female crafters who have layered their scrapbooks, collages, and quilts.

Her *New Fancy Foils* (2013) takes just such detritus, salesmen's sample books of fancy foils, as its found object to be subjected to artistic transformation. The film leaves traces of the origin of its shiny frames, by including marginal notes and markings indicating enterprises, addresses, and the notation of a contract exclusivity, "not to be used in candy trade 1965." The bold aesthetics of the 1960s, pop art alongside an ornate orientalism, turn this version of a flicker film, abstract patterning of colored frames, into a postmodern commentary on the precision and discernible organization of the structural film. Instead, we are left to wonder about order: why this series, why this return?

In Mack's *Undertone Overture* (2013), abstract color patches float by a black background, refracting prismatically rainbow-like light. Then triangles strung as mobile wind chimes reveal themselves. As the film softens focus, a more abstract incarnation and layered imagery presents whirling abstract zeros, geometric shapes, and oscillating all-over patterns.

It is important to note that as 16 mm film explorations, Mack's works remain rooted in the film gauge that experimental cinema most explored in its materiality. Mack remains committed to films mostly conceived, shot, and edited by the artist herself, the small-scale intimate production that allows one to take chances, to do the unexpected. Mack dares to be humorous and even quirky, charting a territory that experimental film occasionally explored, but is sometimes less recognized than its practitioners of high seriousness. Mack is also decorative in a manner that seems highly original, as her work is richly reflective on the life of shiny objects in culture, while it asserts the right of an artist to explore the pleasure of surfaces, designs, and reflections.

Mack's work in digital video, *Dusty Stacks of Mom: The Poster Project* (2013) is also the one that reveals the biographical aspects of her personal obsession with paper; it playfully documents her mother's now defunct mail-order business in selling printed posters as collector's items. The rolls of poster images create abstract sections offered as a salute to a family enterprise, even as it is folding. The visual play on the rolls and the unfolding of paper offers lively abstracted sections of the film.

In contrast, Ahtila tells stories in images and sounds that reconfigure narrative filmic experience. She works in film, but more often digital video, and though her work has a highly personal aesthetic, she works with a crew. Though some of her work is single screen projection, her experimentation is in highly narrative, highly cinematic multiscreen installations.

I wish to connect her work to film and video art installations by women such as Shirin Neshat, who like Ahtila, began her art career a photographer. Neshat's installation aesthetic draws on her work on portraiture incised with Farsi script. The installations juxtapose two or three screens, sometimes contrasting male and female roles, sometimes creating narratives. Like Ahtila, galleries and museums are her venue, and discussion on her work is likely to be found in art journals.

Shortly, I will look at the comparison between Ahtila's installations and the films of Maya Deren, Yvonne Rainer, Abigail Child, Marguerite Duras, and Chantal Akerman, in that all explore the spatiality of narrative while attuned to the secretive, inner dimension of the psyche. Though no one edits quite as rapidly and with such highly wrought vertical editing with the soundtrack as does Abigail Child in such films as *Mutiny* (1982–3) and *Mayhem* (1987), Child shares with these other women filmmakers what I have elsewhere called the exploration of the "Violence of Desire" (2005). So it is in respect to the enormous creativity that women filmmakers have shown for experimenting with the poetic form of narrative, with the inner thought forged from spectators' deep involvement with their complex imagery, that we can see the installations of Ahtila as the most entrancing current embodiment of experimental filmmaking.

Even Ahtila's shorter installations depend on narrative fragments, charged with characterization and performance expressed through a highly personal visual and auditory poetics. Her concern is desire and its loss. She also examines creativity and writing struggling with madness. She explores interiority, often of a female subject who is firmly situated in the architecture of a room, though permeated by the weight of various exterior forces. Inventive citations of surrealism and other modernist art forms, creative use of sequencing, intervals, and montage on both the image and soundtracks, as well as between them, challenge, delight, and disturb.

Where is Where? (2008) defies the category of installation due to its very length (45 minutes), and its insistence on being understood primarily through a chronological if multifaceted viewing taking in sequences on all of its four screens. It is distinctly spatial, a film designed for a multiscreen environment, and even for multiple viewings. As a temporal text, it asks to be absorbed as a discrete whole, even while it offers competing images at right angles to one another. Visitors unprepared to come to this installation with time to devote to it, who stroll through as they might other installation art, miss experiencing most of what it offers: in this it only underlines the demands of other Ahtila works. Hers is not an art for the passer-by. It grips, and demands sustained attention.

As preface to the main four-screen projection that comprises the bulk of *Where is Where?*, an animation in red and orange tones introduces motifs. Just before this ends, the spectators are beckoned beyond this antechamber by an illuminated enclosure of four screens, whose images define a wood in all directions, a bird on a branch in one image, and the voice of a woman who speaks of "thought cold as snow." A poet writing offers an ongoing motif of *Where is Where?* as her study becomes the stage of much of the action, portrayed again from a central viewing position in which each projected array of images can look out in all four directions. The scale of each view may vary, with interwoven closer shots that frame objects. An element of complex montage that animates this view of four walls of a room takes various forms, including sequential changes and the movement of figures from one image frame to the next. Invitations to the imaginary occur repeatedly, as the poet's arm stays behind, as if hung on a wall, or as words float off the page, and later, as she opens the door to a hooded death figure, only to have him opaquely demand words.

Interlaced black and white footage of Algerian streets under French colonial rule take over the screens, one by one, as prelude to the interweaving of another story, the report appended by Frantz Fanon to *Wretched of the Earth* (1961) that tells of two young Algerian boys who killed their French playmate, acting out their anger at French massacres of Algerian Arabs. The French soldiers who had been arresting Algerian men in black and white footage now appear in color to track their victims around the space of the poet's room. Then Ahtila restages the murder as shocking violence of young boys amid sand drifts. The interrogation afterwards by three adults, representing the clinical and legal assessment of the crime, moves the children's mental states back within the poet's walls. "How far must we enter into someone to understand him?" the poet asks after we return to her space via interludes outside and underwater. Indeed, Ahtila, in her tapestries of stories, spaces, and drifting temporalities repeatedly asks this question, addressing penetration and projection in various guises in all her installations.

Where is Where? ends with a coda, a single screen in yet another room, devoted to the images of shrouded corpses in Algeria, processed to appear perhaps as haunting memories. Wrestling with colonialism and female subjectivity, this work ties the war-torn disturbance of Algerian boys in the 1960s with the Finnish children of the poet. The peace of Finland suffers the uncanny invasion of despair via the poet's imagination, but the scenography includes a commercialized cereal, branded after the *Star Wars* franchise, as an indication of the interpenetration of war into personal sanctums.

This work iterates elements of so many of Ahtila's earlier works. A teacup spills over in slow motion in her film *Gray* (1993), much like the vase that shatters and recomposes in *Where is Where? The House* (2002) studies mental collapse within the confines of a room. *The Hour of Prayer* (2005) uses a four-screen folded scroll to mediate on death, and on a trip to Benin, connecting once again private life to lives on a global scale. A photographic diptych in the *Scenographer's Mind* (2002) juxtaposes an image of tall woods with a kitchen, as does *Where is Where?* Ahtila's works resonate with each other and with Charlotte Perkins Gilman's 1891 short story *The Yellow Wallpaper*, exemplifying the exploration of interiority characteristic in so many of the experimental narrative works whose comparative exam-ination reveals the shared principles of rendering narrative mysterious, open to dream structures, highly imagistic and associative.

Consider Shirin Neshat's installation trilogy composed of the works *Turbulent* (1998), *Rapture* (1999), and *Fervor* (2000). These three works are highly resonant as an ensemble, (as when they were shown together at the recent Hirshhorn retrospective [2015]). Each contrasts trajectories in contemporary Iran as experienced differently by men than by the women, each loaded symbolically to explore, in the words of Neshat, the "masculine and feminine in relation to the social structure of Iran" (Danto interview). In *Turbulent*, the trajectory is performing a song, but both performances are rendered conceptually, so that taken together they inscribe patriarchal domination, yet female rebellion. The man is framed centrally in the image, with a full, male audience behind him. He completes his performance to applause, then turns to bow to his audience, while in the opposing image a woman is seen from behind, in a chador, silent, with only empty seats behind her. Once his performance is complete, hers begins, as the camera, moving in a semi-circle, captures her singing frontally, but only for us, the viewers of this installation, and perhaps for the male singer in the image across the room, who once again has turned to face the camera. Her song is a contemporary vocalization, without lyrics, a direct expression of her emotions, the turbulence to which the title refers. Performed by its composer, Sussan Deyhim, a con-temporary Iranian singer living in New York, this work inscribes the exilic Iranian artist as voice of challenge. As Neshat says "An important aspect of *Turbulent* is that women in Iran are prohibited from singing in public, and there are no recordings by female musicians." Therefore, staging Deyhim, in exile, as if she had entered a theater in Iran to surreptitiously perform there, challenges a prohibition. Less often noticed in the installation is that the male singer, Shoja Azari, in performing a poem by the Sufi author Jalalad'din Rumi (1207–73 CE), does not simply represent the status quo of post-revolutionary Iran. While the poetic Sufi legacy had been claimed by the ruling powers, Sufi mysticism poses a threat to the ayatollahs' control of Shiite orthodoxy. The Iranian Ministry of Culture would try to remove Sufi poetry from Iranian songs in 2011. While *Turbulent* predates this crackdown, the choice of Sufi poetry offers, even in 1999, via the sensuality the poetry affords, an interpretation that the men encourage a future freeing of Iranian women, a subtlety missed by some who lack the references to Persian culture. Neshat understands contemporary Iranian culture as an ongoing artistic struggle against orthodoxy and control, and is cog-nizant that her status as émigré allows her to form works that perform a sensuous inter-vention that aims to recover both its poetic traditions and freedom.

Rapture takes this male/female organizational contrast to groups of 100 persons of each gender, whose movements become a choreography in differentiated spaces. The men's movement is within a citadel, the fortress Essaouira, in Morocco, built by Portuguese, and known to the film world as a site where Orson Welles shot *Othello* in 1951. The fortress, whose walls they climb, and along whose curved corners they amass, allows the male group to become shapes that complement the architecture itself. The women begin at the edges of this space, then undertake a journey across the desert to the sea, where, once having reached the shore, some women help launch others in a small boat. The imagery throughout ranges from group poses to group movement, always composed to create geometric and sculptural attributes to the image. Particularly striking are the images of the black-robed women scattered randomly across sand before the water. And as the women's boat launches, those aboard figure as refugees, setting off to explore an unknown future, an image whose reson-ance only grows in the years since the installation was made, as refugees from the Middle East become ever more numerous. It is worth noting that Iran is clearly not the sole referent here, nor in *Fervor*, which I discuss next; in staging the imagery in Morocco, and in replacing dialogue with gesture and the women's ululation, the specificity of one country opens to a resonant including of many.

Neshat's *Fervor*, explores the non-interactions of a hypothetical couple, a man and a woman who never meet, but in the opening shots pass each other. Both attend what appears to be the preaching of a sermon to a divided audience, though Neshat insists that, despite the religious citation of the Koranic Yosef and Zoleika narrative evoked to illustrate the dangers of sexual desire and sin, her mise-en-scène suggests a theatrical tradition of oration utilizing a painted backdrop. In the installation, two images are projected side by side, edited to create a mirroring effect between them. The angles on the preaching scene from behind the speaker offer a visual correlate of strict prohibitions on gender mixing and sexual exploration, as a curtain separates the men from the women wearing hijabs. The final image of the man and the woman departing, crossing each other in opposite directions in a narrow exterior corridor, suggests that the discourse sends them off in opposite directions, making it impossible for their bodies to meet, for the furtive fervor of their attraction to overcome the separate places they have been accorded in the discourse they assembled to hear.

Minimalist and precise, even when her subjects or her camera are in motion, there is a posed aspect to Neshat's imagery. Yet the sense in which she choreographs for the camera, as well as her connection to still photography, is reminiscent of the work of Maya Deren, so pioneering an experimental filmmaker that she can be said to have carved out innumerable exciting visual and audial paths that others have followed. Certainly Ahtila's installations resonate with Deren's, films as do those of Yvonne Rainer, Abigail Child, and Su Friedrich —three contemporary women filmmakers we will look at shortly. Deren's theoretical writing in *An Anagram of Ideas on Art, Form, and Film* (1946) sets the conceptual framework for her bold filmic expression, presenting the cinema as an instrument of discovery and invention. Ritual and children's games are both seen as inspirations for an experimental form in art-making.

Deren's dance background is most directly addressed in her *A Study in Choreography for the Camera* (1945), a collaboration with African-American dancer Talley Beatty aimed at presenting an entirely cinematic view of movement. The opening circular pan in a birch forest hauntingly shows Beatty dancing in slow motion in four different places within the camera movement, the last in close-up on his head as his arm rotates across the foreground, before cutting to a long-shot that continues his angular, then extended flowing movements by the water's edge. This exterior epiphany of the dancer's body introduces the gesture of an elongated step that will carry him across a cut to an interior space, where a series of rolling and gliding sensuous unfoldings of his body join in a match on action to his continued gliding in the opposite direction across a museum floor. In close-up, now in fast motion rotating his head and shoulders, his movement is compared to a multi-faced Buddhist sculpture behind him, which gives way to soaring leaps in the forest and lake setting—a montage that reaches a calm conclusion in a powerful image of the dancer attaining a stable and still widely-spread squatting pose, his back to the camera, his legs spread firmly and gracefully, his arms angular as he finally rests his hand on his thighs.

While many of Deren's films are female quest narratives, in which temporality is trans-formed through montage, slow motion, and stopped frames, this study of the male dancer adduces all that may be transgendered about poetically rendered modern dance, coalescing grace and refinement with power and intensity. *Meshes of the Afternoon* (1943), perhaps the best-known experimental film by a woman, strikingly explores the inner tensions of a woman struggling with her male partner while living in a bungalow in the Hollywood Hills, transforming this simple narrative situation into a series of hauntingly staged failed actions, entwining dream imagery with its unfolding disjuncture of time and space, its propelling of the woman's body up a staircase or across a room, in a finely tuned montage of rhythmic movements. *Ritual in Transfigured Time* (1946) again transforms everyday actions into rituals with unique rhythms, ending with a segment that elegantly turns to dancers, a male twirling two women off, a throw that ends in stop motion images of bodies frozen in motion, in a citation of the childhood game of statue-maker. *At Land* (1944) brings its female protagonist from the waves on the shore across many terrains, from inching her way over a table where others are dining, to a chess game, an associative spatial journey in which the textures of cinematography yield a continual play of the body connected to other materials and forms. Deren's work is open, suggestive, and intricate, an astounding shaping of paths that so many will follow in the years thereafter.

Deren's work is fascinating to compare to the cinematic expression of another dancer, Yvonne Rainer, whose exploration of everyday performative gestures is most prevalent in *Lives of Performers* (1972), though it remains an element of her mise-en-scène in virtually all her films. The simple act of walking on the streets of Berlin in *Journeys from Berlin, 1971* (1980) is an example, as is her bold frontal exposure of her chest, post-surgery, and the sensual encounters of lesbians in *MURDER and murder* (1996). Rainer's *Film about a Woman Who ...* (1974) has a notable section in which a woman named R is described as having come to understand murderous desires. The prelude to this development begins with a close-up of R's lover, D, looking at the camera as he says, "Because she has younger-looking breasts than you ... because she has younger-looking breasts than you." A medium long-shot follows, of R dressing in slow motion with D's voice-over: "I'll leave. I don't want you to go down there alone at this time of night." Then Y's voice: "Propelled by an avalanche of rage, her limbs catapulted her body into her clothing. She hardly knew what she was doing, and when her voice came out, it surprised her." R is seen in close-up as she says, "You're not moving fast enough." Y's voice continues her narration:

> He lost no further time and bolted out the door. Then she became aware of her heartbeat. When it had settled down she thought that she had never been that angry in her whole life. She thought she knew how someone could murder.

The post-breast cancer surgical scar imagery of *MURDER and murder* can then be seen intertextually as yet another commentary on the callousness of the fictive male lover. Across the films, the gestures have migrated, attained different political references and personal nuances, but remained consistent in their questioning of the context through which interpersonal interaction takes place, and the gestures of becoming a woman and becoming a wiser woman that her female figures adopt. A close-up on Rainer's face bearing written citations in *Film About a Woman Who ...* may be seen as a precursor to that layered textual inscription of photographic portraits of Neshat, though in Neshat's case the text is elegantly inscribed black Farsi lettering. Sound and image are orchestrated in Rainer's films to work in non-conjunction, allowing monologues and dialogues to be heard while other images unfold on screen.

In a quite different rhythm, Abigail Child, too, draws distinct tensions between her image and sound tracks. The overall rhythm is quicker, at times reaching a furious pace of fragments, percussive sounds, and punctuating silences. For example, her film *Mayhem* (1987) is divided into sections highlighting diverse elements of film history, restaged through scenes set in SoHo and the Lower East Side in New York, then cut as intervals roughly corresponding to narrative categories. The women chasing, telephoning, stretching out on a bed, or engaging in sex become, like the visual motifs of black and white dots and stripes, compositional elements that connect across the cuts, becoming a collaged representation of women's energetic movement across the history of film. The paradigmatic choice of elements disperses narrative events into restructured, virtual fragments corresponding to interrogations, chases, seductions, and dancing. One image of a telephoning woman, in which a woman places a phone between her spread legs to make a call, is reiterated with each repetition beginning and ending at slightly different points in the action from different angles on the action. A long section of the film includes a lesbian seduction in Japanese costume that seems to be drawn from a porn film, including jocular images of a cat burglar voyeur who eventually intrudes on the sexual activity of the women. Sound in Child's films may be as fragmented and montaged as the images, having a life both independent of the images, and yet seeking ironic conjuncture at key instances; in *Mayhem*, this is seen in a glorious play with sound effects as well as key, floating lines of dialogue that, rather than emanating from the scenes, operate in a unique relationship to them across a force field. What becomes apparent in repeated viewings is the highly structured and carefully composed poetry of image and soundtrack, a weaving together alongside an insistence on separate attention.

Equally carefully structured is Su Friedrich's magisterial film, *Sink or Swim* (1990). It divides into short segments, each given an abstract label: Zygote, YChromosome, XChromosome, Witness, Virginity, Utopia, Temptation, Seduction, Realism, Quicksand, Pedagogy, Oblivion, Nature, Memory, Loss, Kinship, Journalism, Insanity, Homework, Ghosts, Flesh, Envy, Discovery, Competition, Bigamy, and finally, a section titled after a mythological triumvirate: Athena, Atalanta, Aphrodite. Across this journey, a voice-over narration by a young girl recounts elements of Friedrich's biographical relationship to her father, set in the distanced third-person. The narration is nuanced, elegantly written, and the incidents compelling, accumulating the pain of his departure from the family, augmenting the distance already felt in his attempt to command her witnessing of the world through his perspective. Displacement is typical of the film's narrative structure, introducing fragments of imagery or concepts that reemerge later, unexpectedly. These displacements follow a dream logic, interweaving references to myths. The film's sexual undercurrents, its swiftly flowing sweep of desire and fear, is strengthened by images such as female body builders posing, a lion tamer subduing his cat with a whip, and words being struck onto a page on a mechanical typewriter. Images do not illustrate the stories but indirectly brush harshly against them, creating a friction. This is a film that has attained a wide audience, carried surely by the arch of the voice and the stories it tells, yet it remains rich and mysterious on repeated viewings, precisely because it is so indirect in its image and sound patterning, with the images themselves, formally short pieces of great beauty, subsequently revealing their *raison d'etre* as symbolic places from which to hear the film's voice.

All of these imagistic and audial innovations in narrative and poetic filmic expression might be interestingly compared to a threesome of Francophone filmmakers, Agnés Varda, Marguerite Duras, and Chantal Akerman. Of their works that were most experimental in form, there is still a relationship to feature production styles of the art cinema for Duras and Akerman, and to personal documentary for Varda. For our purposes here, it is Varda's shorts and late installation work that most fit into the discussion of experimental women's cinema, even while, as many have pointed out, there are shared threads to her corpus as a whole. Perhaps most powerfully, her *The Gleaners and I*, an autobiographical work (2000, 2002), gestures towards gathering images as it documents those who gather and use that which others reject. Her installation *Les Veuves de Noirmoutier* (2005), reedited in filmic form as *Quelques Veuves de Noirmoutier* (2006), recounts the moving stories of women of the island of Noirmoutier, who mourn their lost husbands. The installation presents each story as an element in an interactive image grid, with individualized sound posts watched by an audience who accesses each story from a chair reserved for just that segment. The cinematography is respectful of the women's faces, bodies, gestures, and their lives by the sea, so understated in its magnificent capturing of mourning as a continual bearing in the body of the memory of a lost relationship to another.

Voice and languid imagery, of course, also mark the work of Marguerite Duras, particularly in her dual "shadow" films *India Song* (1975) and *Son Nom de Venise dans Calcutta Désert* (1976), sharing their literary and strongly musical soundtrack, but offering in the former the staging of actions of observation and obsession, disinterest and self-containment, while the latter insists on shots exploring the ruins of the Indian mansion in which the earlier film took place, a space once filled with the suggestive movements of bodies, now depleted, a ghost space of what once moved there. Akerman's early film work, such as *Je Tu Il Elle* (1974), offering three distinct sections of performative narrative, exploring abjection and bisexuality, couples with her later installations such as *De l'est* (1993) to become one form that her experimentation takes. Her *Jeanne Dielman, 23, Quai de Commerce, 1080 Bruxelles* (1975) focuses understated minimalist attention on everyday gestures to a daringly emphatic degree, forging a temporal mode that stands as a marker for how to combine a subtle feminist sensibility with bold cinematic articulation.

Women's experimental filmmaking has become so vital that it is hard to remember that it emerged in a field of filmmaking especially dominated by men. Here I have not fully explored all the subcategories of experimental film, not separated out found footage work, for example, or explorations of sexuality and bodily exploration, or lesbian filmmaking from the broader concerns I have traced. For instance, found footage work is featured in Barbara Hammer, *Sanctus* (1990) which uses footage of 1950s motion x-rays, Michelle Citron's *Daughter Rite*, which combines her childhood home movie footage with a contemporary fictional frame, and Holly Fisher's *Bullets for Breakfast* (1992), that explores the western and its cultural reception. This exploration of intertextual resonance in the work by many experimental women filmmakers is meant only to trace some of the creative paths these artists have taken, to celebrate a shared exploration of womanhood in experimental aesthetic form.

Related topics

Patrice Petro, "Classical feminist film theory: then and (mostly) now"
Lucy Fischer, "Feminist forms of address: Mai Zetterling's *Loving Couples*"
Erica Levin, "Class/Ornament: cinema, new media, labor-power, and performativity"

Bibliography

Akerman, Chantal. 2004. *Chantal Akerman: Autoportrait en Cinéaste*. Paris: Cahiers du cinéma: Centre Pompidou.
Blaetz, Robin. 2008. *Women's Experimental Cinema: Critical Frameworks*. Durham: Duke University Press.
Clark, Vèvè A., Maya Deren, Millicent Hodson, Hollis Melton, and Catrina Neiman. 1984. *The Legend of Maya Deren: A Documentary Biography and Collected Works*. New York: Anthology Film Archives/Film Culture.

Danto, Arthur C. 2000. "Shirin Neshat." *Bomb 73* (Fall). http://bombmagazine.org/article/2332/shirin-neshat

Deren, Maya. An anagram of ideas on art, form, and film. 2001 [1946]. In Bill Nichols, ed. *Maya Deren and the American Avant-garde.* Berkeley: University of California Press.

Penley, Constance. 1989. *The Future of an Illusion: Film, Feminism, and Psychoanalysis.* Minneapolis: University of Minnesota Press.

Petrolle, Jean, and Virginia Wright Wexman, eds. 2005. *Women and Experimental Filmmaking.* Urbana: University of Illinois.

Rabinovitz, Lauren. 2003. *Points of Resistance: Women, Power & Politics in the New York Avant-garde Cinema, 1943–71.* 2nd edn., Urbana: University of Illinois Press.

Rainer, Yvonne. 1999. *A Woman Who … : Essays, Interviews, Scripts.* Baltimore: Johns Hopkins University Press.

Rice, Shelley and The Grey Art Gallery, 1999. *Inverted Odysseys: Claude Cahun, Maya Deren, and Cindy Sherman.* Cambridge: MIT Press.

Russett, Robert and Cecile Starr. 1976. *Experimental animation: Origins of a new art.* New York: Da Capo Press.

Sullivan, Moira, and Stockholms Universitet. 1997. *An Anagram of the Ideas of Filmmaker Maya Deren: Creative Work in Motion Pictures.* Stockholm: Stockholm University.

Turim, Maureen. 2005. "The violence of desire in avant-garde films." In: Jean Petrolle and Virginia Wright Wexman.*Women and experimental filmmaking.* Urbana: University of Illinois.

White, Eric Walter. 1931. *Walking Shadows: An Essay on Lotte Reiniger's Silhouette Films.* London: Hogarth Press.

18

TRANSNATIONAL STARDOM

Russell Meeuf

This essay explores the centrality of gender to the phenomenon of transnational stardom, arguing that what makes transnational stars "transnational" is their ability to navigate the gendered tensions of globalization. Recognizing that the historical process of globalization has created not just macro-level political and economic transformations but also transformations in everyday life and culture—including uneven transformations in the definitions of masculinity and femininity around the world—this essay explores how stars whose fame and labor cross national borders manage ideas about gender within global capitalism.

Definitions

Despite a spate of recent scholarship on transnational stardom (including my own recent books on the topic (Meeuf 2013; Meeuf & Raphael 2013)), the concept remains undertheorized in film and media studies, largely because the term itself lacks a coherent definition—or, at least, one that we can all agree upon. Scholars and critics have steadily examined case studies that epitomize transnational stardom—such as Jackie Chan, Maggie Cheung, Javier Bardem, Aishwarya Rai Bachchan, Chow Yun-Fat, Juliette Binoche, Zhang Ziyi, and many others—and yet the precise boundaries of the term remain elusive. What exactly does a star have to do to become "transnational?" Make movies beyond the borders of the country they were born in? Have fans in more than one country? Make movies in more than one language? Start in one national cinema and then make the move to Hollywood?

Sabrina Qiong Yu's (2012) excellent book *Jet Li: Chinese Masculinity and Transnational Film Stardom* tries to put this issue to rest by differentiating between "international stardom" and "transnational stardom." An international star is one that "achieves international recognition or fame, even if he or she never makes a film outside his or her own country," while a transnational star "physically transfer[s] from one film industry to another to make films" (Yu 2012: 2). This physical transfer, of course, most often means the transfer from one national film industry to Hollywood, thanks to the global power of the Hollywood film industry, but transnational star transfers are not necessarily limited to this common model (for example, it may include pan-European or pan-Asian stars or the work of Hollywood stars in other national industries). This definition is elegant and importantly foregrounds stars' labor to the definition of their stardom. Yu's detailed discussion of the evolution of Jet Li's transnational career offers an insightful exploration of race, gender, and national identity in relation to Li's mobile film career.

But this tidy distinction poses some problems, especially if the goal is to analyze how film stars *and* their mediated persona crisscross national borders, resonate with audiences, and contribute to definitions of modern identity. Yu's definition certainly helps explore how film performers move into different national production contexts and how that move impacts the construction of their persona, but how useful is it to separate the transnational circulation of the star and the transnational circulation of their fame? Yu's definition privileges production and labor over consumption and reception, suggesting that the cross-cultural exchanges of transnational stardom only occur when star *labor* crosses national borders. In turn, the dynamics of film and television *consumption* across national borders is categorized as "international" stardom. In both cases, moreover, these definitions assume a set of clear distinctions regarding national borders, national identities, and national cinemas that do not reflect the nebulous realities of globalization. Can the national identity of some films be clearly ascertained in a world of international co-productions? For that matter, can the national identity of some stars be easily understood? Are Hong Kong stars such as Jackie Chan "Chinese" after 1997? Is Neeru Bajwa, the Canadian-born actress who stars in both Bollywood and Punjabi films "Indian?"

The questions of so-called international stardom are not separate from issues of transnational stardom, as Yu defines it: for example, how stars from other countries are consumed in national or local contexts, how non-local stars might fit into local star systems, or how a range of stars from a variety of backgrounds form a constellation of meanings about identity and personhood. These questions are relevant to stars such as Jet Li who start in one national cinema and then make the move to Hollywood, but they are equally as important for understanding, say, the popularity of Hollywood stars like Will Smith beyond the borders of the US. Rather than separating these complexities into the categories of "international" versus "transnational," we should be putting these examples in dialogue with one another to better understand the projection of gender identities across national borders.

The circulation of stars and their performances across national borders, after all, has been at the core of modern stardom almost from its inception. Hideaki Fujiki's (2013) meticulous history of transnational film stardom in Japan's film industry from around 1910 through the early 1930s, for example, shows the power and popularity of US film stars in Japan, seeing Hollywood stars such as Mary Pickford, Douglas Fairbanks, Clara Bow, Rudolph Valentino, and others as key figures in the development of the Japanese star system. American stars, as Fujiki explains it, attracted passionate fans in Japan, acting as symbols of consumer modernity that sometimes affirmed and sometimes contradicted the dominant discourses of Japanese national identity. Moreover, American stars existed alongside popular Japanese stars, helping to shape the idea of stardom and public identity in Japan. American stars were not simply popular icons of Western consumer excesses against which Japanese stars were contrasted. Images of Hollywood stars often transformed the meanings and scope of Japanese stardom, prompting Japanese stardom to reflect the impact of Western consumer modernity in Japan, especially when it came to ideas of modern sexuality and personality.

For example, Fujiki situates the popularity of Clara Bow in Japan in the 1920s within the increasing cultural presence of the "modern girl" in Japan. While Japanese critics and authorities debated (and often bemoaned) the rise of the *moga*—a westernized, independent, consumer-driven version of the "modern girl" similar to the US idea of the "flapper"—images of Clara Bow offered a hugely popular spectacle of modern girlhood that helped define the concept in Japan. While some media discourses in Japan saw Bow and the rise of the modern girl as an affront to traditional Japanese femininity—seeing young women embracing Western dress and lifestyles as caricatures of vacuous consumer excess—other media discourses embraced the modern girl as a symbol of youthful liberation and modernity in a more culturally fluid Japan. Fujiki demonstrates how Bow's films and popular persona in Japan negotiated these cultural controversies and also helped shape the popularity of Japanese stars. Natsukawa Shizue, for example, emerged as both a counterpoint to and reflection of Bow's fame, offering the image of a more respectable modern girl who, unlike Bow, accommodated Japanese cultural attitudes about modern femininity while still embracing the modern girl image associated with Bow.

From this perspective, transnational stardom is not simply a matter of labor that crosses national borders. Rather, transnational stardom is one part of a larger transnational film culture—albeit one in which Hollywood continues to occupy the dominant role—where cinema provides a space of uneven cultural exchange. This space certainly includes transnational labor dynamics—not just the movement of acting labor across national borders, but also the transnational movement of all kinds of film personnel (for example, the steady stream of directors and cinematographers flowing into Hollywood productions ever since its inception). But equally important is the transnational circulation of visual media that creates moments of cross-cultural exchange, from the publicity images of Mary Pickford in Japan that helped make her a star there even before any of her films reached the country to the popularity of Indian actor Raj Kapoor in the 40s and 50s across Asia and Africa thanks to films like 1951's self-directed *Awaara* (in which Kapoor plays a character inspired by the international successes of English actor turned Hollywood star Charlie Chaplin), to the VHS-fueled cult fandom of Hong Kong action star Jackie Chan in the US in the 1990s, before Chan became a Hollywood star. Transnational labor flows and transnational consumption, in short, participate in a larger film culture that creates ephemeral moments of cross-cultural exchange, inspiration, and commonality.

In this way, cases of transnational stardom should be seen as examples of what Mary Louise Pratt (1991) calls "contact zones": spaces where different cultures and societies meet and grapple with one another within contexts of unequal social power such as colonialism or global capitalism. Kathleen Newman (2010) applies this concept to transnational film culture, proposing that transnational cinema operates by creating moments in which geographically diverse audiences forge momentary connections built around the shared experiences of global culture, even as that context seems to fade to the background behind intimate personal connections such as identification and emotional attachment. The contact zone, then, articulates the cross-cultural power of stardom:

> The powerful images and narratives surrounding media celebrities are a key example of such contact zones; the zones act as sites of transnational media circulation in which the constructs of nation or the inequalities of global capitalism, even when glaringly present, can be obscured or put aside in favor of the seemingly intimate and personal connections created by consuming transnational stars.
>
> (Meeuf & Raphael 2013: 3)

Understanding transnational stardom as a contact zone prioritizes the idea of exchange and intimate connections, seeing transnational stars not just as laboring bodies but as powerful images of identity and personhood in an increasingly globalized world.

A star becomes "transnational," then, not just because their labor or image circulates across national borders but also because they provide resonant narratives about the challenges of personal and national identity as the world has become more globally interconnected since the dawn of the twentieth century. Transnational stars are the performers through which audiences can imagine forms of borderless identity—especially borderless gender identities—capable of managing the tensions between the global and the local, between national identity and cosmopolitan culture. This definition certainly includes performers whose mobility between film industries is predicated on their ability to signify a sense of diversity or cosmopolitanism, whether framed as desirable (for example, the charming European-ness of Rossano Brazzi, or the sensual allure of Penelope Cruz in their respective Hollywood films), or else as a fascinating foreign threat (for example, Sessue Hayakawa's alluring villains as discussed by Miyao (2007)). It would also include stars born in one country who achieve most of their fame in another country, and whose "foreign" bodies are used to create narratives about identity in the modern world, encompassing, for example, the British and American films of Indian actor "Sabu" (see Jaikumar 2012), Mexican-born Dolores Del Rio in her Hollywood career, the Hollywood careers of Peter Lorre, Bela Lugosi, and Conrad Veidt discussed by Gergely (2012), as well as the career of Egyptian-born actor Omar Sharif, who played a range of cosmopolitan "foreigners" in US and British productions. Additionally, this definition includes stars whose work within a national industry crosses national borders and makes them a popular icon navigating identity in the modern world—for example, Hollywood stars who have garnered fans around the world, or Thai star Tony Jaa, whose continuation of the kinetic martial arts tradition of Bruce Lee and Jackie Chan has earned him an international cult following thanks to DVD and now streaming technologies. This definition is, admittedly, sprawling and nebulous, but it speaks to the expansive and diverse culture of stardom and transnational cinema.

By focusing on the cultural resonance of transnational stars rather than their mobile labor, this definition also provides a counterpoint to one of the most prevalent narratives concerning transnational stardom: that it involves an inevitable loss of cultural specificity. Much of the work tracing star migrations examines non-Hollywood stars seen as complex performers in a given national cinema, who then move into Hollywood productions where they are coopted into more stereotypical and commercial roles. Martin Shingler (2014), for example, argues that Bollywood mega-star Aishwarya Rai Bachchan becomes a vague signifier of international culture in her few Hollywood films. Likewise, Phillips' and Vincendeau's (2006) expansive project on European stars in Hollywood often focuses on the loss of national specificity in favor of stereotypical European-ness. While accurate, this perspective privileges the question of national identity over the issue of transnational appeal, and in the process, sees Hollywood as a vacuous, hyper-commercial bogeyman that strips performers of their "authentic" national identities.

However, rather than seeing the context within which stars attain work and fame across national borders as a consumerist morass that quashes national identity, some theories of transnational stardom point to the cultural transformations of modernity as necessitating powerful images of individuality. Much of this work is based around Richard Dyer's (1986) foundational work on stardom in *Heavenly Bodies*, which argues that stars provide not just models of different forms of modern identities, but models for the very idea of a discrete identity itself in a world marked by ideological contradiction and the fragmentation of personhood. Building off this idea, Stephen Hinerman (2001), for example, argues that global stars serve the cultural needs of individuals caught up in the transformations of globalization, functioning as a "blessing in the chaotic conditions of modern life" (196). For Hinerman, transnational stardom provides compelling models of identity that manage both national specificity and the global changes of modernity, providing "access points" through which globally disconnected individuals can envision their place in the systems of global modernity.

Gender is foundational to this theory of stardom, as the possibilities for identity amidst global modernity are deeply intertwined with definitions of gendered subjectivity. As R. W. Connell (2000) explains, the steady but uneven process of global modernization, first through colonization and today through global capitalism, are not macro-level, gender-neutral processes of political and economic change but rather inherently gendered systems that have radically transformed the global definitions of gender, both for those instituting an imperial agenda and for those brought into the fold of Western hegemony. Connell describes the emergence of a constantly-shifting "world gender order" in which Western conceptions of masculinity and femininity unevenly transform other gender systems around the world, while, simultaneously, processes of colonialism and global capitalism demand shifting forms of gendered behavior in the West.

In short, the tensions of gender within globalization—from the changes in family and social structures thanks to economic systems organized around industrial wage labor to the imposition of Western beauty norms onto non-Western cultures—are not incidental side effects of global modernity but the very heart of globalization itself. It should not be surprising, then, that as this process has unfolded historically, film stars have emerged as a key currency in a transnational world, acting as inspirational images of gender and personhood that can be shared and exchanged across national borders.

Transnational action masculinity

To illustrate how transnational stars dramatize these tensions and pressures of gender within global modernity, I want to focus attention on a set of gendered issues that has been particularly prominent in the history of stardom: the representation of violent men in contexts of capitalist labor. Global film culture has long obsessed over spectacles of men, muscles, and hyper-kinetic action. The action film genre (and before it the western) has long been one of the most profitable and popular global genres, not only for Hollywood but for a variety of international film industries seeking to capitalize on the spectacle of violent masculinity (for more on the action film genre, the western, and the war film, see Yvonne Tasker's essay in this volume). Such films have launched the careers of countless stars around the world, offering up images of male brutality, sculpted and otherwise "hard" bodies, and—importantly—masculine professionalism.

One of the most spectacular examples of this masculinity in the 80s and 90s was the global popularity of Austrian-born Hollywood star Arnold Schwarzenegger, whose string of popular action and adventure hits—from *Conan the Barbarian* (1982) to *True Lies* (1994)—made the former bodybuilder's sculpted physique one of the most recognized bodies in the world. For cultural studies scholar Simon During (1997), Schwarzenegger's fame illustrated the dynamics of what During calls the "global popular," the sets of films, television programs, stars, and other images that attain near-global pervasiveness. For During, the texts and images of the global popular did not necessarily demonstrate the triumph of an empty or superficial commercial culture on audiences around the world; rather, the fame of stars such as Schwarzenegger must be understood as a response to the very real cultural wants of diverse global audiences. As During puts it,

> the appeal of the audiovisual global popular is ... to be read in terms of the limited capacities of particular media to provide for individuals' needs and desires, especially male needs and desires, across the various territories that constitute the world image market.
>
> *(ibid. 815)*

Schwarzenegger, then, provides a deeply resonant set of images and narratives about men, male bodies, and the contexts of industrial labor. Schwarzenegger's films frequently place him in technological contexts, often seeing Schwarzenegger's taut muscles as an extension of the technological world, a physique created through machine-like maintenance (thus two of his most popular films—*Terminator* (1984) and *Terminator 2* (1991)—cast him as a cyborg, literally suggesting that his musculature is an impossible technological fantasy). His films indicate the importance of the human body as a key resource, although the power of that resource comes from its interactions with industrial technology, often the massive weaponry Schwarzenegger wields on screen. In this way, Schwarzenegger's fame should be understood in terms of its capacity to mirror the experiences of men's bodies within the global economy: the sensations of punishing physical labor and the symbiosis of men's work and machinery that defines the male labor market in much of the world. Of course, while mirroring the sensations of these experiences, Schwarzenegger also provides a utopian fantasy of strength and empowerment to overcome such sensations.

As During points out, Schwarzenegger is simply one in a long line of hard-bodied white men who dramatize the tensions of labor and identity in a changing world, from Schwarzenegger's direct cultural ancestors such as Eugen Sandow in the 1890s and early 1900s, or *Tarzan*-star Johnny Weismuller in the 30s and 40s, to other models of tough, violent, white men such as John Wayne. Wayne, in fact, was just as much of a global phenomenon in the 1950s through the 1970s as Schwarzenegger was in the 1980s and 1990s, with Wayne earning fans (and box office revenue) in coveted overseas markets. And like Schwarzenegger, the transnationally popular images of Wayne's large body deploying violence on screen dramatized many of the same issues concerning labor and professionalism. As I argue elsewhere (Meeuf 2013), Wayne's popular roles in the western genre emphasized not only his nomadic labor but also his ability to endure hardships and remain professional, providing a hyperbolic allegory of labor conditions in the developing world, where men's social and economic value was increasingly tied to demandingly monotonous wage labor and the necessities of labor migrations. (All the while, Wayne also provided a fantasy of embodied labor for white-collar men in the industrialized world). For both Wayne and Schwarzenegger, then, their stardom became transnational because they projected powerful images that managed the anxieties surrounding the male body and its labor in a particular historical moment.

Such tough, white men, of course, have been joined by a slew of Asian transnational action stars since the 1990s in articulating ideas about manhood and physicality. The popularity of Asian action stars in the 1990s de-centered the whiteness of the global action hero, using transnational stars to explore relations between Asia and the West as several Asian countries gained more global economic power. Several scholars have explored the global/local tensions at the heart of transnational stars from Asia—see, for example, Yu's aforementioned discussion of Jet Li's Hollywood career as he negotiates his national identity and existing Hollywood stereotypes of Asian men, or Anne Ciecko's (2001) analysis of contemporary Bollywood stars like Shah Rukh Khan, who blend traditional definitions of Indian gender roles with hyper-commercial Western personas. These tensions, however, are often managed through dynamic physical performances—especially for action stars— that envision the male body's ability to endure pain while executing super-human feats of strength and agility.

Examine, for example, the popularity of Hong Kong action star Jackie Chan, whose cult following grew in the US in the 1990s thanks to his reputation for accomplishing dangerous stunts and his humorous fight choreography (inspired in part by Hollywood comedian Buster Keaton). In addition to his films, Chan's fame centered on the outtake reels that show just how dangerous and real his stunt work is as he climbs, leaps, and fights his way through the bustling infrastructure of Hong Kong. Such images provide a different vision of action manhood than the "hard," white bodies of the 1980s, reveling in a model of agility, flexibility, and adaptability that mirrored the emerging world of cosmopolitan, corporate masculinity. At the same time, the pleasures of the visual spectacle of Chan at work still revolve around the sensations of physical labor, blending the very real dangers to the body of capitalist wage labor with a fantasy of dynamic movement and spatial mastery (see Gallagher 1997 for more on Chan). These pleasures are mirrored by other Asian stars inspired by Chan, notably Hong Kong star Donnie Yen (see Funnell 2013) and Thai star Tony Jaa, whose star persona equally revolves around the reality of his nearly impossible physical stunts (see Steimer 2013).

To illustrate these dynamics, examine the action antics of Jason Statham, who should be understood as a transnational star not just because of his work in different national film industries but because the spectacular images of his body engaged in violent antics also respond to contemporary anxieties surrounding manhood and labor in a global world. Statham, a former diver and model, found his way to movie stardom thanks to British director Guy Ritchie, who cast Statham in his fast-paced crime comedies *Lock, Stock, and Two Smoking Barrels* (1998) and *Snatch* (2000). After a few roles in Hollywood films, Statham earned his reputation as an action hero when he starred in the French action film *The Transporter* (2002), written and produced by Luc Besson and directed by Louis Leterrier and Hong Kong choreographer Corey Yuen. Statham often performs his own stunts, and his work in *The Transporter* films helped align his stardom with his martial arts prowess. Statham would star in two more *Transporter* films and a slew of British and Hollywood crime capers, including roles in the action franchise *The Expendables*, the quirky *Crank* series, and as the villain in the 2015 installment of the *Fast and the Furious* franchise. With perform- ances organized around his sharp-wit (delivered in his distinctive cockney accent) and dynamic martial arts stunt work, Statham has emerged as one of the most popular trans- national action stars of the new millennium.

His performance in *The Transporter* best illustrates how his star persona engages with issues of labor and manhood in a world of global capitalism. In the film, Statham plays Frank Martin, a former military officer who currently works as "the transporter," a driver for hire who will transport anything on time, no questions asked, with expert efficiency. But when he discovers that one of his "packages" is a beautiful young Chinese woman (Shu Qi) trying to stop a human trafficking organization, he must leave his cynical professional persona behind and single-handedly bring the traffickers to justice.

The film's narrative, in other words, revolves around the ethics of capitalism and labor in a world where one's work might have global repercussions. Statham's character tries to insulate himself from the morality of his labor by insisting on hard and fast rules: no names, no changes in the deal, and no opening the package. He tries to operate as a cynical entrepreneur who willfully ignores the larger contexts of his labor, focusing only on the immediate details that he can control. But when he learns that he is facilitating human trafficking, he has to confront the ethics of his work.

Of course, the narrative serves mostly as a backdrop to the action choreography, which provides a visual spectacle of men's bodies engaged in strenuous yet effortless labor. The real appeal of the film is found in the stylish, hyper-kinetic action sequences and the exciting performance of Statham's body as it flies through the air to kick down doors, or expertly fends off hordes of anonymous henchmen in the confined space of a bus. Statham's muscled body at work provides a variety of affective pleasures grounded in the sensations of labor: his body endures punishment and pain, exerts itself through intense physical feats, and yet seems to never really tire as he continues to execute his martial arts skills with expert precision, all the while engaging in violent acrobatics. His body, in short, offers up the sensations of physical labor while also insisting on a utopic fantasy of limitless skill and energy.

While the narrative of *The Transporter* establishes the context of men's labor within potentially unethical systems of global capitalism, the visual spectacle provides a fantasy in which men suffer from and yet transcend the constraints of their surroundings, literally turning the world of industrial capitalism into a playground as they dispense with the agents of the corporate world that try to reign them in. In one of the climactic fight sequences in the film, for example, Statham's character takes on a series of henchmen in a maze of shipping containers whose doors can open up and close off the passageways between the containers. Statham's character uses these doors to his advantage to constantly morph the space of action, in essence taking charge of the containers, which serve as a symbol of global trade (and the means through which human trafficking takes place in the film). Literally set against the infrastructure of global capitalism, the hero uses his physicality to make spaces of labor and exploitation his own.

In sum, Statham's transnational stardom hinges on his persona's sensational display of such gendered tensions, offering a kinetic spectacle of the male body that also reflects the anxieties of male identity and labor across national borders. It is not simply the fact that he has worked in different national cinemas that makes him a transnational star, but rather the ability of his persona to respond to the cultural needs and desires of (mostly male) audiences around the world that defines his transnational status. He is a transnational star because his persona and characters dramatize globalized circuits of labor and power, as exemplified by *The Transporter*. Clearly, the circulation of a star's labor and fame often overlap: the performers who get the opportunity to labor in different national contexts do so precisely because there is something resonant about their image and performances that speak to larger cultural concerns. Thus gender is not simply one intriguing aspect of transnational star performances but rather a foundational, defining characteristic of transnational stardom that weaves through issues of national identity, class, and opportunities for transnational star labor.

Related topics

Yvonne Tasker, "Contested masculinities: the action film, the war film, and the Western"
Sandra Ponzanesi: "Postcolonial and transnational approaches to film and feminism"
Tejaswini Ganti, "Fair and lovely: class, gender and colorism in Bollywood song sequences"

References

Ciecko, A. (2001) Superhit Hunk Heroes for Sale: Globalization and Bollywood's Gender Politics. *Asian Journal of Communication*, 11(2), pp. 121–43.

Connell, R. W. (2000) *The Men and the Boys*, Berkeley: University of California Press.

During, S. (1997) "Popular Culture on a Global Scale: A Challenge for Cultural Studies?" *Critical Inquiry*, 23(4), pp. 808–33.

Dyer, R. (1986) *Heavenly Bodies: Film Stars and Society*, London: Routledge.

Fujiki, H. (2013) *Making Personas: Transnational Film Stardom in Modern Japan*, Cambridge, University of Harvard Press.

Funnell, L. (2013) "Hong Kong's It/Ip Man: The Chinese Contexts of Donnie Yen's Transnational Stardom," in R. Meeuf and R. Raphael (eds.) *Transnational Stardom: International Celebrity in Film and Popular Culture*, New York: Palgrave Macmillan, pp. 117–38.

Gallagher, M. (1997) "Masculinity in Translation: Jackie Chan's Transcultural Star Text," *The Velvet Light Trap* 39, pp. 23–41.

Gergely, G. (2012) *Foreign Devils: Exile and Host Nation in Hollywood's Golden Age*, New York: Peter Lang.

Hinerman, S. (2001) "Star Culture," in J. Lull (ed.) *Culture in the Communication Age*, London: Routledge, pp. 193–211.

Jaikumar, P. (2012) "Sabu's Skins," *Wasafiri* 27(2), pp. 60–7.

Meeuf, R. (2013) *John Wayne's World: Transnational Masculinity in the Fifties*, Austin: University of Texas Press.

Meeuf, R. and R. Raphael (2013) *Transnational Stardom: International Celebrity in Film and Popular Culture*, New York: Palgrave Macmillan.

Miyao, D. (2007) *Sessue Hayakawa: Silent Cinema and Transnational Stardom*, Durham: Duke University Press.

Newman, K. E. (2010) "Notes on Transnational Film Theory: Decentered Subjectivity, Decentered Capitalism," in N. Durovicová and K. E. Newman (eds.) *World Cinemas, Transnational Perspectives*, New York: Routledge.

Phillips, A. and G. Vincendeau (2006) *Journeys of Desire: European Actors in Hollywood, A Critical Companion*, London: BFI.

Pratt, Mary Louise (1991) "Arts of the Contact Zone," *Profession*, pp. 33–40.

Shingler, M. (2014) "Aishwarya Rai Bachchan: From Miss World to World Star," *Transnational Cinemas* 5(2), pp. 98–110.

Steimer, L. (2013) "Tony Jaa: Hong Kong Action Cinema as Mode in Thai Action Stardom," in R. Meeuf and R. Raphael (eds.) *Transnational Stardom: International Celebrity in Film and Popular Culture*, New York: Palgrave Macmillan, pp. 139–62.

Yu, S. Q. (2012) *Jet Li: Chinese Masculinity and Transnational Film Stardom*, Edinburgh: Edinburgh University Press.

Further reading

During, S. (1997) "Popular Culture on a Global Scale: A Challenge for Cultural Studies?" *Critical Inquiry*, 23(4), pp. 808–33. An exploration of cultural studies work in an age of transnational culture.

Hinerman, S. (2001) "Star Culture," in J. Lull (ed.) *Culture in the Communication Age*, London: Routledge. Connects theories of stardom to theories of globalization and modernity.

Meeuf, R. and R. Raphael, (2013) *Transnational Stardom: International Celebrity in Film and Popular Culture*, New York: Palgrave Macmillan. Surveys a series of case studies in the history of transnational stardom.

Yu, S. Q. (2012) *Jet Li: Chinese Masculinity and Transnational Film Stardom*, Edinburgh: Edinburgh University Press. Offers a detailed exploration of transnational stardom, gender, and national identity through the case of Jet Li.

PART III

Making movies

"Making Movies" addresses various gendered aspects of the making and distribution of films. Priya Jaikumar and Patricia White both examine authorship in ways that challenge the centrality of the white male auteur. Jaikumar interrogates the notion of the auteur through feminist and non-Western frameworks, and White looks at the non-redemptive white female gaze in colonial/settler narratives in the work of Claire Denis and Kelly Reichardt. Eylem Atakav's essay critically addresses the representation of Muslim women in cinema. Atakav puts particular focus on the work of pioneering Muslim women filmmakers such as Haifaa Al-Mansour, in order to chart the encounter between women and Middle Eastern cinema. Anne Ciecko's piece considers the work of female directors in the African context, critiquing the discourse of pioneering filmmakers that has historically privileged male authors. Ciecko's essay discusses the intricacies of African film industries that sustain women filmmakers. Jaqueline Bobo's piece offers an overview of the contributions of Black women, primarily in the US context, to directing, but also to other aspects of filmmaking, such as editing. Tejaswini Ganti turns to the production of Bollywood's song and dance sequences, and locates, in the changing practices of casting backup dancers, the industry's shifting standards around privileging whiteness.

In her contribution, Jane Gaines interrogates the notion of women's work in the silent era, opening up the category of women to historical mutability and contingency—women as a "genre" in her words—in order to rethink the positions "women" have occupied in the history of the industry. J. E. Smyth looks specifically at female editors in the studio era, examining dominant film historiographical assumptions and highlighting female editors' own oral or written testimonies. Finally, Debra Zimmerman, the executive director of Women Make Movies, offers an overview of the institutional history of one of the few remaining organizations from the early days of feminist cinema that continues to distribute important international feminist documentary work.

19

FEMINIST AND NON-WESTERN INTERROGATIONS OF FILM AUTHORSHIP

Priya Jaikumar

Introduction

His scene has ended and he has been shot multiple times, but like Peter Sellers in the opening scene of *The Party* (Blake Edwards, 1968), the "author" in film theory refuses to die. Andrew Sarris, pioneer of auteur theory in the United States, noted with his tongue firmly in cheek that the predilections of auteurism as a mode of film analysis emerged most clearly in anti-auteurist criticism. By auteurists, Sarris was referring to theorists writing primarily from the 1950s through the 1970s, to trace signatures of a director's personal vision across a range of typically mainstream and studio films neglected by the canons of film criticism. In Sarris's words, critics of this mode of analysis (like Pauline Kael) found that auteurists

> were invariably male. ... They never bathed because it took time away from their viewing of old movies. They shared a preposterous passion for Jerry Lewis. They preferred trash to art. They encouraged the younger generation not to read books.
>
> (Sarris 2003: 22)

Behind Sarris's caricature of his opponent's position lay the truth that the directors most admired in auteur theory—including greats such as Alfred Hitchcock, Anthony Mann, Douglas Sirk, Max Ophüls, Nicholas Ray, Robert Bresson, Roberto Rossellini, Samuel Fuller, and Vincente Minnelli—were, without exception, white men working in European and American film industries. This fact was as much a product of the time and the film industries as it was a consequence of the category of analysis and prioritization of film theorists. But the combination of socially and theoretically exclusionary forms of erudition and obsession that characterized early auteurists, reminiscent of latter-day fanboy cultures, explains the defensive hermeneutics surrounding auteurism almost immediately following its originary moment.

In this essay, I map the conceptual distances between the proposal of auteurism and its revisions over the subsequent decades, in shifts that overlapped with the emergence of structuralist, poststructuralist, Marxist, anticolonial, and feminist theories that impacted film criticism. It should be understood that even those involved in a critical forensics of classical auteur theory found uses for reviving and revisiting it. Kaja Silverman sought to "return to the scene of the Barthesian crime, and to search there for both the murder weapon and the corpse of the deceased author" (Silverman 2003: 51; Barthes 1977). In this return, she found value in interpretive strategies "foregrounding" rather than "neutralizing" female authorship in classical Hollywood cinema, to prevent female authorial presence from "being occluded" by the masculinist biases of its industry, narrative, and visual machinery (Silverman 2003: 64). More recently, Patricia White has drawn attention to the significance of authorship to feminist film studies by noting that

> feminists have explored the work that has been made by women as an act of historical retrieval, a theoretical project of decoding biography and experience within film form and address, a site of identification and libidinal investment, and practical matter of equity.
>
> *(White 2015: 3)*

The feminist interrogation of authorship has to be considered in tandem with feminist investments in *female* authorship, just as non-Western interrogations of authorship must be considered in conjunction with their investment in *non-Western* authorship. Any critical examination of authorship must proceed from a grasp of why, despite feminist, deconstructive, black, Third World, and anticolonial criticisms of the concept since the 1960s, the idea of the author and the practice of auteurist criticism have endured in some guise.

Consequently, to understand the challenges posed by feminist and non-Western media and criticism to authorship, we must resist rigidifying them into positions of reductive antagonism to auteur theory, just as we must reject assumptions of *a priori* equivalence or solidarity between feminist and non-Western interrogations. To this end, what follows is a response to questions implicit in this essay's title:

- What are the relationships between "feminist" and "non-Western" interrogations? How and when were they allies? Alternatively, how and when have they designated distinct fields of analysis?
- If feminist and non-Western media and criticism are presumed to interrogate authorship, how do we account for the occasions when they embrace auteurism?
- If the oppositional and unspoken counterpart to "feminist" and "non-Western" is "patriarchal" and "Western" respectively, is it fair to assume that the latter terms are always invisible qualifiers of authorship? Should the feminist and the non-Western be understood primarily as the social and theoretical Other? Are they perennial outsiders who can at best look in interrogatively, disruptively, enviously, or anxiously?

Questions of gender and geopolitics in film authorship

The theorization of authorship in film typically follows a critical genealogy that includes Alexandre Astruc's essay "The Birth of a New Avant-Garde: The Camera-Pen" or *camérastylo* in 1948 (Astruc 1968), François Truffaut's "A Certain Tendency in the French Cinema" in 1954 (Truffaut 1976), Andrew Sarris's writings on Hollywood film directors collated in his book *The American Cinema* (Sarris 1968), and Roland Barthes's essay "The Death of the Author" (1977). Although not always part of this trajectory, Agnès Varda's notion of *cinécriture* or cinematic writing to define her body of work (Varda 1994), and Michel Foucault's essay, "What is an Author?," published in its English translation in 1979, have also been influential in thinking about film authorship. Each work created a constellation of concerns around the figure or idea of a film's author, and what is most compelling in these definitions is a foundational contradiction common to them all, which has been generative rather than debilitating to auteurist analysis.

Auteurism has always inhabited a contradictory space. The recognition of a film's director as its primary author is premised on the "romantic conception of the artist" as creative agent (Caughie 1981: 11), derived from bourgeois literary criticism, and from the notion that the author is a potentially profit-making individual, intellectually protected by a capitalist market. At the same time, theories of auteurism dismantle the author as human agent by seeking coherence not so much in the personality of the director but in the style of a range of cinematic texts. By seeking patterns across commercial and studio films dismissed by the artistic canon, auteurist criticism extended the range and focus of its film analysis. It went beyond discussions of a film's themes to such dispersed registers as cinematic style, mise-en-scène and editing patterns, thereby transforming the process of writing about films into a discovery and theoretical production rich with the specificities of film as a medium. As Sarris put it in assessing his own early writings, "if I had to do it all over again, I would reformulate the auteur theory with a greater emphasis on the tantalizing mystery of style than the romantic agony of the artist" (2003: 23). Auteurism elevated mainstream cinema to a cultural object no less worthy of study than the literary classics, while also signaling film criticism's disinvestment from the tools of literary analysis through a focus on cinematic language.

Nevertheless, the link between film and literary criticism persisted because the search for patterns in film language coincided with the dominance of structuralism and semiotics in Western literary theory, influenced by Ferdinand de Saussure's structural linguistics and Claude Lévi-Strauss's structural anthropology. The structuralist turn involved what Terry Eagleton (1983: 91–126) identifies as the demythification of language, society, and literature through a quasi-scientific methodology that sought to discern the rules governing linguistic and cultural systems. Radical to this approach was the notion that meaning was not pre-given or inviolable, but fluid and emergent through socially constructed and shared systems of signification.

Discerning stylistic coherence across variable film texts rather than assuming it to be unified by the author's personality did not resolve auteurism's foundational contradictions, but merely shifted them around. The demythification of art and cinema was accompanied by a mythification of the critical hermeneutics devoted to discovering latent textual meanings unavailable to the average spectator, creating what Caughie calls the "eureka syndrome" (1981: 128). Additionally, poststructural criticism's dispersal of the end-point of meaning beyond specific social structures to an infinite regression of signification systems exposed structuralism's tacit and unresolvable assumption of limits to its constructivism. For auteur theory, this appeared to auger the complete disappearance of the author, replaced by an intersection of discourses and institutions.

As film theorists noted, however, some level of structure or embodiment lingered even after the symbolic death of the author, embedded within assumptions of an enunciative perspective organizing the film, or in the expectation of a meaning-making and desiring subject watching it. Janet Staiger calls these the "dodges" to the authorship question (Staiger 2003: 28). Whereas the post-auteurist critique successfully dismantled capitalism's and humanism's ideological investment in the individual, the author's replacement with increasingly broader contexts for the emergence of a text evaded the question of productive determinants and avoided the "politically crucial question of causality in texts" (ibid. 29). Not only did the first wave of auteur theory treat the male director as a neutral and universalizable category for theorizing authorship but also "the attempted death of the author" arrived when such proclamations were particularly "non-advantageous for some individuals—feminists, gay and lesbian activists, and antiracists. Depriving us of our voices just as we are speaking more loudly seems like a plot" (ibid.). Authorship was a coveted and near-impossible goal for those who did not fit normative prescriptions of what authors should look like, and what they should make in order find institutional, critical, and popular acceptance. Recognizing that people were excluded from authorship because of their gender, race, or sexual preference was contingent on acknowledging that films had authors, with particular and privileged passages to authorship.

Equally significant, the deconstructed text was never *entirely* evacuated of the discourse of the individual and the "discourse of the body." Kaja Silverman uses Roland Barthes' essay "The Death of the Author" as a case in point. In the essay, Barthes analyzes Balzac's *Sarrasine* to find that the text is "made of multiple writings, drawn from many cultures and entering into mutual relations of dialogue, parody, contestation," but there is "one place where this multiplicity is focused and that place is the reader, not, as was hitherto said, the author" (Barthes 1977: 148). Silverman points out that Barthes' interpretation recuperates the reader as author, and divests authorship of its "paternal legacy" rather than erasing it completely (Silverman 2003: 54). By initiating his essay on the death of the author with a meditation on Balzac's narrative voice in *Sarrasine*, a novella in which the castrato Zambinella is a desirable woman, Barthes implicitly acknowledges that sexual difference is foundational to theories of authorship. Barthes' analysis of the codes functioning in this text is an interrogation into the interoperable networks of narrative and desire. To conduct such an analysis without reference to gender and sexual difference in society and culture would render the codes contentless and meaningless.

Poststructuralism's dispersal of the author into a textual system producing meaning and desire posed its own problems. Reading a film for "author effect" or "ideological effect" rather than for the author's personality meant that the analysis had to strain to be recognized as a study of authorship as such. This is one reason why feminist theories of cinema have been less readily identifiable as critiques of authorship. Though its impact on auteurism is an often-neglected aspect of the essay, Laura Mulvey's "Visual Pleasure in Narrative Cinema" (1975) shows the centrality of gender and sexual difference to the cinematic apparatus of Hollywood cinema, effectively replacing the focus on male authorship with a critique of larger (scopic and narrative) mechanisms of patriarchal pleasure and desire in film (Mulvey 1992). Sandy Flitterman recuperates Mulvey's reading of how "the unconscious of patriarchal society has structured film form" (ibid. 22) to write about its problematization of classical Hollywood cinema's regime of the authorial male gaze (Flitterman 1981). Introducing Flitterman's essay, Caughie notes that such feminist works serve "to problematize the look of the male director, to extend the dissolution of questions of authorship into questions of enunciation and subjectivity, and to give those questions a political priority" (Caughie 1981: 242). In the wake of feminist psychoanalytic criticism, auteurism had to articulate the agency of an author not only in relation to a film's enunciative apparatus but also in relation to its textual production of subjectivity, sexuality, and gender.

Flitterman's essay appears in the final section of Caughie's anthology because implicit in it are questions about the future directions for the study of authorship and feminist film theory. If the female is the object of desire and source of voyeuristic pleasure for cinema's heteronormative gaze, is feminist film theory's primary mandate the deconstruction of normativity? Must feminist filmmaking carry the burden of destroying cinema's pleasure? Before considering how Mulvey and Flitterman opened up feminism's critique of authorship rather than closing off its options, we have to recognize the frictions between feminist interrogations of authorship in the West and the West's valorization of non-Western male auteurs during the same period. One important instance of such friction was the articulation of humanism as an "international film ideology," embraced by European film festivals of the post-War era (Bordwell 2009). International film festivals like the Cannes (since 1946) and the Berlinale (since 1951) became an important locus for the inclusion of male Asian and African filmmakers into the Western auteurist canon. Although today these festivals can be a platform for female and feminist filmmakers operating transnationally—such as Mira Nair (an Indian American), Deepa Mehta (Indo-Canadian), Sofia Coppola (American), Jeong Jae-eun (Korean) and Samira Makhmalbaf (Iranian), among others—during the 1950s and 1960s they were largely an important site for the global recognition of *male* film directors from non-Western nations like India (Satyajit Ray) and Japan (Akira Kurosawa), whose acclaim rested on criteria of artistry assumed to transcend gender and national politics through their universal humanism.

Awards in US and European film festivals expanded awareness of non-Western cinemas within the Western canon, but they did not change authorship's definitional parameters. Non-Western directors were celebrated for their stylistic consistency and redemptive universalism in a manner that confirmed the humanistic vocabulary of Western auteurism, though the expanding geographical frame for auteurism had a corresponding and unac-knowledged gendered frame of repression. Not only did women from several non-Western nations have fewer opportunities to helm a film than their Western counterparts, but, as Andreas Huyssen argues about modernity, high art was also masculinized and mass culture feminized the world over, by excluding women as producers of art and by imagining them as objects of artistic representation, or as consumers of the emerging, expanding, and vilified popular media (Huyssen 1986: 44–62).

The entry of non-Western male directors into the West's auteurist canon points to the differing analytics and politics suggested by the terms "feminist" and "non-Western" in this essay's title. Whereas *feminism* manifests itself as a social movement, disciplinary practice and embodied life in different forms around the world, and offers insight into gender's asymmetrical hierarchies within socio-political, economic, and cultural realms globally, *non-Western* is defined by its negative ("non") status as a geographical designation outside the epistemic, social, and cultural paradigms of the West. Potentially, the two terms can speak to each other, but they can also speak across each other. If non-Western feminism abounds, so does Western Eurocentric feminism, non-Western misogyny, Western anti-colonial antiracist feminism, and so on. Of relevance to this discussion are the occasions when the politics of feminism and of a geographically multi-sited analysis have historically diverged in their priorities, and when they have intersected as modes of interrogation, particularly in the form of transnational feminism (Grewal and Kaplan 1994; Alexander and Mohanty 1997; Mohanty 2003; Marciniak et al. 2007).

One point of historical intersection was the Third Cinema movement. With its roots in the anticolonial struggles of Latin America, Africa, and South Asia, Third Cinema favored a collaborative rather than an individual mode of authorship. To quote from Solanas and Getino's manifesto:

> The man of the *third cinema*, be it *guerrilla cinema* or a *film act*, with the infinite categories they contain (film letter, film poem, film essay, film pamphlet, film report, etc.) above all counters the film industry of characters with one of themes, that of individuals with that of masses, that of the author with that of the operative

group, one of neocolonial misinformation with one of information, one of escape with one that recaptures the truth, that of passivity with that of aggression.

(1983: 27)

Third Cinema's call to rethink film authorship as the anticolonial work of a group or collective adhered to no idealized norms in aesthetics or genre, and attacked one of auteurism's fundamental assumptions. It shifted allegiance from the author as an individual or a diffuse presence immanent in a film's style to the principle of collective authorship that was dedicated to producing a revolutionary shift in consciousness, by any artistic means necessary. The move away from individual authorship to alternative modes of production, finance, and distribution was adopted as well by Jean-Luc Godard's Dziga Vertov group, and later film collectives like Dogme 95, reflecting a political dissatisfaction with capitalist film industries and infrastructures built on giving precedence to the individual, or the idea of an individual, who could sustain the industry's profit motive.

Arguably, the *"nuevo hombre"* or new man of Third Cinema (inspired by Che Guevara's personification of a revolutionary consciousness) has remained trapped in its masculine pronoun (as Sandra Ponzanesi similarly argues in her essay in this volume). Despite films like Humberto Solás's *Lucía* (1968, Cuba), which envisions political revolution as incomplete without sexual and gender revolution, the Third Cinema movement offered a more robust critique of race and class hierarchies than of gender and sex inequities. Nevertheless, Third Cinema's overall vision coincided with feminism's disordering of authorship in a few of ways. First, the emphasis on collaboration highlighted the problematic identification of authors with directors, which diminishes the contributions of craft and below-the-line workers who tend to be more diverse in terms of race, class, gender, and nationality (Caldwell 2013). Second, even without Third Cinema's anti-colonial manifestoes, global feminisms have produced a dispersed range of films with an intersectional politics and experimental aesthetics, which are no less revolutionary in intent or impact.

To offer a range of examples focused on female directors, women who were part of the LA Rebellion, such as Julie Dash, Zeinabu irene Davis, and Jacqueline Frazier, created works that were experimental in style and pertinent to questions of race and gender (Field et al. 2015). Dee Rees's work has been as much about film form as about queerness, race, and gender (Keeling et al. 2015). Black British cinema has included women like Pratibha Parmar and Ngozi Onwurah, whose films addressed nationhood, community, and diasporic identity in relation to style, gender, and narrative. The striking work of Australian filmmaker and artist Tracey Moffatt has been as acutely about indigenous lives as it is about gender and auteurism; and the Vietnamese filmmaker, theorist, and writer Trinh T. Minh-ha's collective of works similarly intervenes in discourses of art, postcoloniality, and auteurism. In striving for greater flexibility, freedom of content, and lower costs to produce work outside mainstream industries that could not accommodate them as directors, these filmmakers created work in a range of formats—from shorts, visual essays, and memoirs to documentaries and non-fiction. The few women critically recognized as auteurs, such as Marguerite Duras and Agnès Varda, cannot be easily situated in relation to their male contemporaries and affiliated film movements, indicating the limited imagination of authorship as an analytic category. Conventional definitions of feminism are also found wanting when confronted with filmmakers like Duras and Varda, or with mainstream directors like Katherine Bigelow and Farah Khan, whose gender critiques have been sly and ambiguous.

Auteurist criticism, which expanded the range of films considered worthy of study, is pushed to re-examine its own foundational paradigms and cast an ever-wider net to include such works. A focus on auteurism can easily bypass feminist films, because defining a film by its political content has often led to the erroneous minimization of its aesthetic and conceptual innovation. Such misunderstandings were replicated in feminist film theory, when Toril Moi disregarded "black or lesbian (or black-lesbian) feminist criticism" on the grounds that it did not deal with the "theoretical aspects of feminist criticism" (Moi 1985: 86; Mayne 2003: 78). The relationship of politics to aesthetics, of form to theory, and of the particular to the universal, returns us to Mulvey and Flitterman's interventions in the 1970s. Their readings of the cinematic gaze delimit neither the scope nor the focus of feminist film theory if we understand them to constitute a crucial but *localized* intervention, focused on the visual system of classical Hollywood cinema understood from a psychoanalytic rubric. Though translatable to different filmmaking contexts, their analysis cannot be presumptively universalized. It allows room for other possibilities, as shown by Mulvey's own turn to filmmaking in order to explore alternative contexts for film production. Fundamentally, anticolonial and transnational feminist interrogations of authorship have pressed a wider and global range of visual texts originating through multifarious modes of production, vision, and desire into consideration for auteurism. By so doing, they have shown that central to the theory of authorship is a geopolitical dialectic between dispersed but connected subjects and (affective, aesthetic, perceptual, psychoanalytic, politico-economic, and social) systems.

Examples from an institutionalized practice highlight the significance of the subject-system dialectic to theories of authorship. Recently, Hollywood has been confronted with controversies over how to credit co-directors for films awarded an Oscar in the best director category. Contract negotiations between the Directors Guild of America (DGA) and major film studios in 1978 led to the agreement that only one director could be assigned credit for directing a film (Elrick 2004). DGA was concerned that multiple directorial credits would erode a director's creative control, leading to the disproportionate influence of producers. The contract did allow for occasional waivers as exceptions (such as those granted to the Wachowski siblings and the Coen brothers). With transnational film productions on the rise, there have been more requests for waivers, but the DGA was prescient in anticipating and containing such exceptions, for while credit may be shared, the Academy Award for Best Director cannot be granted to a co-director. Those disregarded as co-directors at the Oscars recently have included Kátia Lund, co-director of *City of God* (Fernando Meirelles, 2002), Loveleen Tandan, co-director of *Slumdog Millionaire* (Danny Boyle, 2008,) and Christine Cynn, co-director of *The Act of Killing* (Joshua Oppenheimer, 2012), which were films that garnered the best director award for their first credited filmmaker.

In these instances (from Brazil, India, and Indonesia), the co-directors were all women. In the case of India and Brazil, the female co-directors were essential to the recruitment and directing of children from their country's urban slums. These women's labor as translators, possessors of local knowledge, and social facilitators pushed their creative control and input to secondary status. The social contract aspect of working on a film further complicated the question of their authorship, where to express dismay over the asymmetries of credit and publicity would have been to jeopardize future employment in a difficult industry. In these instances, bringing together non-Western and feminist interrogations of authorship reveals that the singular and normatively male director is central to the dominant paradigm of most film industries. It draws attention to the limitations and exclusions of the category of authorship in cinema, both as an industrial term and as a mode of analysis. It further emphasizes the need to think of auteurism not only in relation to film and media texts, but also in relation to the "power-geometries" (Massey 1991: 25) of gender, production, and finance globally.

Future directions

Feminist and non-Western perspectives on auteurism have greatly dispersed the field. If feminist criticism has tended to look at the production of desire within a discursive system of signification that excluded feminine and non-normative genders and sexualities, non-Western theories of film authorship have focused on the conditions of local, national, and transnational production, finance, and distribution that excluded the voices of entire races, nations, and classes. There have been two consequences of these interrogations. First, the analytical project of authorship has grown more ambitious as it attempts to discern several patterns of intersectionality defining a film. Second, with the dissipation of grand theories of auteurism, applying the lens of race, class, gender, or transnationalism to understand particular directors or specific films has sometimes seemed enough. The latter, though an important intervention, is a limited one. Cinema and media studies awaits the kind of gravity-shifting moment experienced in comparative studies (Gould 2011), where understanding that history and literature are geographically multi-sited provoked a radical revision of theory itself. In film studies, aesthetic analysis still defines a domain of allegiance that is distinct from cultural studies and political economy, disabling the possibility that these modes of analysis may reflect back on theory *collectively*, to review its terms. This is less a lament for the loss of grand theories of auteurism and more an optimistic agenda-setting for the coming together of aesthetic, historical, and political optics, to look at cinema and media's creative production from a decentered and poly-methodological perspective.

"I would venture to guess that Anon, who wrote so many poems without signing them, is often a woman," said Virginia Woolf (1957: 51). Woolf's Anon was not a creature of the past. She goes on and on (pun intended), and seeing her shadowy persistence dissipates the certitudes of authorship, while making visible those people who have remained anonymous in the recognition accorded to singular authors and auteurs. Inhabiting our contemporary world of multiplying platforms, feminist and non-Western interrogations of authorship can clarify the politics of visibility, paradigms of ownership, theories of subjectivity, and modes of recognition. With digital media's potential to disperse authorship, how we think of networked and collaborative work within contexts of ownership, policy, and political power increases in urgency. Such an interrogation of authorship calls not for an attack on classical theories of auteurism from a smug present of emancipation. It calls for a dialectical and historicized consciousness of the conditions defining authorship. It also asks us to question the authorship of our film industries, our policies, our states, our theories, our education, and our imaginations. The most significant interrogations of authorship will lie not only in the study of film form but also in revelations of how the norms and productive conditions of authorship have been working for and against creative and theoretical productions the world over, and in the active sustenance of venues for the screening, distribution, and viewing of feminist and anticolonial film and media. Increasing awareness of the visible and invisible authors behind every text and performance, and of the conditions that efface certain people and their labors, is a call to action that exceeds the remit of an interrogation.

212

Related topics

Patricia White, "Pink material: white womanhood and the colonial imaginary of world cinema authorship"

Sandra Ponzanesi, "Postcolonial and transnational approaches to film and feminism"

Anikó Imre, "Gender, socialism, and European film cultures"

Tejaswini Ganti, "Fair and lovely: class, gender, and colorism in Bollywood song sequences"

Bibliography

Alexander, M. and Mohanty, C. T. (1997) *Feminist Genealogies, Colonial Legacies, Democratic Futures*, New York: Routledge.

Astruc, A. (1968) "The Birth of a New Avant-Garde: La Caméra-Stylo," in P. Graham (ed.) *The New Wave*, London: Secker and Warburg, pp. 17–23 [1948].

Barthes, R. (1977) "The Death of the Author," in *Image-Music-Text* (translated by Stephen Heath), New York: The Noonday Press, pp. 142–8.

Bordwell D. (2009) "Observations on Cinema: Class of 1960," www.davidbordwell.net/blog/2009/08/02/class-of-1960/ (accessed December 12, 2015).

Caldwell, J. T. (2013) "Authorship Below-the-Line," in J. Gray and D. Johnson (eds.) *A Companion to Media Authorship*, Malden, MA: Wiley-Blackwell: 349–69.

Caughie, J. (1981) *Theories of Authorship*, London: RKP.

Eagleton, T. (1983) *Literary Theory: An Introduction*, Minneapolis: University of Minnesota Press.

Elrick, T. (May 2004) "Singularity of Vision: The Origin of the One Director to a Film Policy," *DGA Quarterly*. www.dga.org/Craft/DGAQ/All-Articles/0405-May-2004/Singularity-of-Vision.aspx (accessed December 15, 2015).

Field, A., J. Horak, and J. Stewart (eds.) (2015) *L.A. Rebellion: Creating a New Black Cinema*, Berkeley: University of California Press.

Flitterman, S. (1981) "Woman, Desire and the Look: Feminism and the Enunciative Apparatus in Cinema," in J. Caughie (ed.) *Theories of Authorship*, London: RKP, pp. 242–50 [1978].

Foucault, M. (1984) "What is an Author?," in P. Rabinow (ed.) *The Foucault Reader*, New York: Pantheon, pp. 101–20 [1979].

Gould, R. (2011) "The Geography of Comparative Literature," *Journal of Literary Theory* 5:2, pp. 167–86.

Grewal, I. and C. Kaplan (eds.) (1994) *Scattered Hegemonies: Postmodernity and Transnational Feminist Practices*, Minneapolis: University of Minnesota Press.

Huyssen, A. (1986) *After the Great Divide: Modernism, Mass Culture, Postmodernism*, Bloomington: Indiana University Press.

Keeling, K., J. DeClue, Y. Welbon, J. Stewart, and R. Rastegar (2015) "*Pariah* and Black Independent Cinema Today: A Roundtable Discussion," *GLQ: A Journal of Lesbian and Gay Studies*, 21(2), 423–39.

Marciniak, K., A. Imre, and A. O'Healy (2007) *Transnational Feminism in Film and Media*, New York: Palgrave Macmillan.

Massey, D. (June 1991) "A Global Sense of Place," *Marxism Today*, pp. 24–9.

Mayne, J. (2003) "A Parallax View of Lesbian Authorship," in V. Wexman, *Film and Authorship*, New Brunswick: Rutgers University Press, pp.76–86 [1991].

Mohanty, C. T. (2003) *Feminism without Borders*, Durham, NC: Duke University Press.

Moi, T. (1985) *Sexual/Textual Politics*, London: Metheun.

Mulvey, L. (1992) "Visual Pleasure and Narrative Cinema," in *The Sexual Subject: A Screen Reader in Sexuality*, London: Routledge, pp. 22–34 [1975].

Sarris, A. (1968) *The American Cinema: Directors and Directions, 1929–68*, New York: E. P. Dutton.

Sarris, A. (2003) "The Auteur Theory Revisited," in V. W. Wexman (ed.) *Film and Authorship*, New Brunswick: Rutgers University Press, pp. 21–9 [1977].

Silverman, K. (2003) "The Female Authorial Voice," in V. W. Wexman (ed.) *Film and Authorship*, New Brunswick: Rutgers University Press, pp. 50–75 [1988].

Solanas, F. and O. Getino (1983) "Towards a Third Cinema," in M. Chanan (ed.) *Twenty-Five Years of New Latin American Cinema*, London: BFI, pp. 17–27.

Staiger, J. (2003) "Authorship Approaches," in D. A. Gerstner and J. Staiger (eds.) *Authorship and Film*, New York: Routledge, pp. 27–54.

Truffaut, F. (1976) "Une certaine tendance du cinéma français," in B. Nichols (ed.) *Movies and Methods*, Berkeley: University of California Press, pp. 15–28 [1954].

Varda, A. (1994) *Varda par Agnès*, Paris: Cahiers du Cinema.

White, P. (2015) *Women's Cinema, World Cinema: Projecting Contemporary Feminisms*, Durham, NC: Duke University Press.

Woolf, V. (1957) *A Room of One's Own*. Harcourt, Brace, and World [1929].

20

PINK MATERIAL

White womanhood and the colonial imaginary of world cinema authorship

Patricia White

World cinema remains a key category in film studies and film culture, appropriately for the medium that helped define twentieth century global modernity. At the turn of the millennium, a renewed emphasis on defining and studying world cinema responded to new forms of economic and cultural globalization, as well as to the accelerated and dispersed adoption of media technologies that altered modes and flows of cinematic production, distribution, exhibition, and display. Within the context of these changes, cinema remains relevant as an object of study, distinct medium, and social technology due, on the one hand, to Hollywood's continued market expansion and, on the other, to its function within an economy of prestige linked to a vital global film festival network (English 2005). No longer dominated by European art cinema, but comprising work from Asia, Africa, Latin America, and the Middle East, as well as North American independent cinemas, sub-national and transnational formations, and so on, world cinema offers a cosmopolitan cultural antidote to still-prevalent global conflicts and uneven economic relations.

This investment of cultural capital in cinema's internationalism is not new: as Marijke de Valck shows in her study of film festival networks, the premiere European events in Cannes, Venice, and Berlin played an important geopolitical role in the post-World War II period (Valck 2007). In this context, festivals' elevation of the figure of the singular auteur reconciled ideologies of unique expression with those of national culture, and a canon of art cinema emerged that implicitly transcended political interests and colonial histories, hierarchies, and antagonisms. Discursively, the particular (the individual auteur's aesthetic vision) guaranteed the universal (film art as reparative).

By the end of the twentieth century, art cinema's Eurocentrism had been definitively challenged. In "Time Zones and Jetlag: The Flows and Phases of World Cinema," Dudley Andrew describes the impact on film culture of "a set of towering waves" initially set in motion by the worldwide events of 1968 and exemplified in his account by widespread acclaim at international festivals in the 1980s for the breakthrough films of China's Zhang Yimou and Taiwan's Hou Hsiao Hsien (2010: 76). Auteurism remained a distinctive dimension in this remapped world film culture, but its articulation with regional and national movements and waves had the potential to politicize the role of film art in the global cultural economy. In Andrew's timeline, economic and technological innovations since the 1990s quickly ushered in yet another phase of globalized film culture, one characterized less by world systems of circulation and more by instantaneity and saturation (ibid. 80–2). In the current phase, Hollywood's domination of world markets is answered with the cultivation of individual artists and aesthetic brands across the multiple nodes of global art cinema. Festivals, funding arrangements, and critical discourses challenge old distinctions between "center" and "periphery" as they vie to set terms of value.

Under these circumstances, young women directors have gained unprecedented access to the film festival circuit. Important prizes at the key European festivals have been awarded to such women as Samira Makhmalbaf, Sofia Coppola, and Claudia Llosa, and this recognition poses a challenge to the usual politics of authorship (White 2015: 40–1). Cinephilia has returned with a vengeance in the digital age, and this movie-love is notably global in scope. In the plethora of subscription services, online journals, websites, blogs, and aggregators that the cinephile can access, the coin of the realm remains the name of the author. But gender equity remains far from being achieved in this sector; a study of seven European countries finds that four in five films are directed by men, and films with male directors receive 84 percent of public funds (EWA 2016). Similarly, while the democratizing force of the internet accommodates fans of all genders and of all kinds of movies, gender hierarchies continue to mark the recognition of expertise and the judgment of value.

In *Women's Cinema, World Cinema* (2015), I look at how the increasing recognition of women directors from outside the US and Europe challenges visions of the world cinema auteur and how this challenge is managed discursively. Gender asymmetries are disguised either by emphasizing individual "genius" (privatizing) or by appropriating women directors' personae and work to stand in for concepts of "culture," in the sense of both "nation" and "taste" (domesticating). Rather than representing a country's cinema on neutral aesthetic terrain, these women directors are often over-identified with national trauma or a mythologized cultural heritage. It is my contention that gendered discourses of power remain operative all over the map of global art cinema, as do colonialist ones. The task is to untangle how they intersect: feminist methodologies are thus crucial to understanding the contours of contemporary world cinema.

The present discussion focuses on Claire Denis and Kelly Reichardt, two of the few women directors whose work and reputations have been decisively framed by understandings of authorship as expressive genius—as measured by festival invitations, award recognition, and critical reception. Such discourses of exceptionalism correspond to the two directors' privileged locations within the ecosystem of world cinema—France and the US independent sector. I will show how Denis and Reichardt refuse to abstract art from politics and instead position themselves reflexively by mapping discourses of exceptionalism onto gendered and racialized national and imperial narratives in their work.

Denis, the more established auteur, is the widely acclaimed director of a dozen features (plus documentaries and shorts) since her directorial debut with *Chocolat* in 1988—although, significantly, her path to feature film directing was more circuitous than that of her male peers (Mayne 2005: 14–15). Reichardt has completed six critically acclaimed features since 2006's *Old Joy*—although, again, her career shape is irregular, marked by a twelve-year gap between first and second features. Authorship—both as a critical construction and as a thematic and stylistic inscription in a filmmaker's oeuvre—"marks" these directors' location in relation to gender and nation. As white women recognized as "world class auteurs," Denis and Reichardt critique the concept of the transcendental author through their singular relationship to aesthetics and to privilege. Through story, style, and especially point of view, Denis and Reichardt show that gender cannot be thought outside "the world," and that a global optic ignores gender at its peril. Explicitly thematizing gender and colonial legitimacy, Denis's *White Material* (2009) and Reichardt's *Meek's Cutoff* (2011) point to an ethics of world cinema authorship (see Hole 2015).

Whites cut off

White Material is the story of a contemporary Frenchwoman desperate to bring in the harvest on her family's coffee plantation as the unnamed African country in which they have settled devolves into civil war. After a frightening, disorienting prologue that will be grasped only at the film's end, a cut to bright white outdoor light reveals the heroine Maria Vial (Isabelle Huppert), running through the brush in a pale pink dress, finally spotting an overloaded bus that has been pulled over by a soldier. At first the driver rebuffs her request to take her home, then gestures to the top of the bus. One of the Africans fleeing the area offers her a hand up, but she rides instead on the ladder, hanging on fiercely as the bus pulls out in a cloud of dust. We know nothing specific about setting or story—these bodies seem set in motion by the palpable dread that hangs over the landscape. Our bodies in turn respond viscerally to the evocation of heat, noise, and tensed muscle.

In Kelly Reichardt's *Meek's Cutoff* (2010), we follow a small group of 1840s pioneers on the Oregon Trail whose members have come to doubt their guide, Stephen Meeks. The film opens on the group taking on water before setting off across the baked earth. One of the men carves "lost" on a dead tree. The journey, based on an historical incident, is focalized through the perspective of one of the expedition's wives, Emily Tetherow (Michelle Williams). As the party trudges alongside the oxen, one wagon wheel obstinately squeaking, we hold steadily on a medium long shot of Emily in her pink dress, looking ahead with a fixed expression as she walks, her bonnet shading her face.

In both films, wordless long takes track women's bodies in arid landscapes; the protagonists' pale faces show resolve, if not desperation. The edges and depths of the frames hint at invisible threats as onscreen figures move without anchoring coordinates. Marked as the work of auteurs by theme and style, the films offer allegories of white female authorship inscribed within the colonial imaginary of global art cinema. The limited perspectives of these (post)colonial heroines pose questions of authorial accountability that register in both the unknown consequences of their actions and in the disquieting sensory experience of the viewer.

In her monograph on Denis, Martine Beugnet characterizes the French director's work in terms of "an aesthetics of the unsaid." "Her films shun well-defined characterizations and situations and favor transitory, mutating spaces," she argues (Beugnet 2007: 21). Coining the term "neo-neo realism," A. O. Scott notes a similar use of silence in Reichardt's work, calling her *Wendy and Lucy* (2008) a "modest, quiet ... study in loneliness and desperation" (Scott 2009: n.p.). Invoking space, place, and form rather than identity, these claims do not anchor authorship in gender. Indeed, each filmmaker prefers to be seen as "just a filmmaker" rather than as a "woman director" (Feinberg 2013: n.p.; Hornaday 2011: n.p.). Nevertheless, descriptions of their attention to the elliptical and the embodied capture the ways their work engages with feminist critiques of nationalist projects. Dramatizing the limits and costs of a circumscribed point of view in and through their fictions, Denis and Reichardt work to place cinema in service of a world of Others.

The films' distinctive style marks the point of view of the director's behind-the-camera gaze. At the same time, as I have argued in a comparison of *Wendy and Lucy* with Denis's *35 Shots of Rum* (2008), this gaze is spread over the surface or space of the film rather than delegated to a character (White 2009). Both the unsaid and the unblinking characterize the scenes described above: we hear the wind and grasp the high stakes of moving on in the right direction in the time that remains. In these austere and beautiful compositions, the skin of the white woman becomes visible as such. In this rendering visible, the "unmarked," what might otherwise be absent from consciousness, becomes marked *as* absence—of power and status in relation to certain men, and of consciousness of power in relation to place and to the other bodies and subjects that occupy it.

What does it mean to be implicated with the white women protagonists of these films? In both films, we are too close for comfort without access to interiority. We don't want to be Maria, yet the camera hovers over her shoulder. We don't know what Emily is thinking, yet the compositions that place her clustered with the other pioneer women (Zoe Kazan and Shirley Henderson), out of earshot of the men, make us stand with her as well. White skin thus structures spectatorial identification—both with and of these characters' particularity. Skin is itself portrayed as a structure, an "epidermal racial schema," to borrow Frantz Fanon's term (1967: 92). It is not (quite) that the white woman onscreen is fetishized, like Lillian Gish is through lighting, as Richard Dyer describes in his book *White* (1997: 86–7). Rather, her skin looks like it could burn up in the heat—turn red, freckle, autocombust. Its materiality rather than its ethereality is emphasized. She can no more escape her skin than we can shake the films' oppressive mood. Thus the formal precision of these auteurist films cannot be separated from the content; a white woman in an austere landscape triggers potent national myths of colonial entitlement. The heroines are enmeshed in history, but that history is rendered only obliquely; their partial perspectives acknowledge the costs of foreclosing on stories that remain unnarrated.

I argue that these heroines figure the women directors' own "exceptional" status within world cinema circuits and pose ethical questions about white female Euro-American authorship. In addition to their embrace of film aesthetics over action, both Denis and Reichardt look askance at hegemonic national narratives. Claire Denis may be an emblematic name in French cinema, but her body of work represents an ongoing exploration of the legacies of the French colonial presence in Africa. Her oeuvre is distinguished by a consistent displacement of her (gendered, racialized, national) position vis-à-vis the black male bodies who are her frequent subjects (Mayne 2005: 28). While Kelly Reichardt's films are distinctly American and unmistakably indie, they depict characters bypassed by dreams of American prosperity. Their regional settings make them not-quite national cinema, and they share the long-take, minimal dialogue, and global art-cinema aesthetic of "slow cinema" over the "quirk" of American independent features (Flanagan 2008; Newman 2011: 44). Circulating through global film festival networks, the films of both directors stand apart from, even as they stand for, national film practices.

But these filmmakers' work shows that it is not possible simply to "displace" oneself as a national subject—even exploiting as they do the predisposition to take female gender as "transcending" the political allegiance to nation. As Dyer points out in an analysis of colonial fictions, it is often in the white woman's name that the imperial project is undertaken. He traces, in the figure of the colonial mistress, a mix of traditional views of white women's civilizing mission and feminist ideals of independence (1997: 184–6). Both Maria and Emily are shown steadfastly "staying the course," even driving it. *White Material* and *Meek's Cutoff* take on the question of white female power and literal "direction," as their fierce heroines stand in the dust and make fateful choices about where to go from here.

White Material, set in contemporary Africa, is a film about the legacy of French colonialism, and *Meek's Cutoff* is an historical fiction about a foundational myth of US history;

yet both project an art-cinema aura of "timelessness"—with minimalist or elliptical narration and parable-like stories. This mode could be seen to favor an allegorical reading of the white characters' crises over an interpretation rooted in specific place and historical incident. Maria's spiritual bankruptcy is staged in an unnamed African country. In *Meek's Cutoff*, the dry, cracked earth of the plains makes a mockery of the settlers' land claims, and Emily's encounter with the party's Indian captive is staged to mirror her own difference from the white male norm.

But in the ways the films do conjure up "current events," they indicate that what is absent is not historical specificity, but historical consciousness on the part of the colonists. *White Material's* most haunting sequences are of child soldiers—doing drugs, sleeping among discarded toys, finally slaughtered by government forces. The rebel fighter known as the Boxer (Isaach de Bankolé) is loosely based on revolutionary leader Thomas Sankara, who became president of Burkina Faso in 1983, only to be assassinated four years later. Denis chose to film in Cameroon, where she had lived and made films before, in part because Burkina Faso was too unstable. The Boxer is wounded at the very beginning of the film, and the conflict is deliberately kept offscreen, while onscreen everyone ricochets from its impact.

Meek's Cutoff was written by Reichardt's frequent collaborator Jonathan Raymond, a Portland-based author from whose short stories Reichardt's earlier *Old Joy* and *Wendy and Lucy* were adapted. The quiet realism of those present-day tales of the US Northwest's lost and disenfranchised connects them to the historically themed *Meek's Cutoff*. Press materials liken the depiction of the disoriented wanderings of Americans on the Oregon Trail skeptical of their leadership to the twenty-first century occupations of Iraq and Afghanistan (*Meeks Cutoff's* press notes 3–4). Yet formally, the film's long takes emphasize phenomenological experience over the viewer's search for political commentary, and the arid expanses onscreen give no sign of territorial borders.

Moreover, even granted allegorical and geopolitical resonance, the films are far from epic in tone. Excepting a melodramatic turn in *White Material*, their narratives are quotidian, their settings domestic, their characters flawed, and their actions quite possibly pointless. They lack the reach of masculinist national and imperial myth, but nor do they dwell on the domestic concerns of classical women's pictures. The heroines are too opaque, the plots too slight. And the concept of "home" is taken apart at its very foundation. Child soldiers are murdered in Maria's bathtub; Emily throws her mother-in-law's rocking chair out the back of the covered wagon in order to lighten the load. Both films rework the iconic figure of the homesteading white woman common to fictions of empire and the US Old West alike. Historically and hegemonically, the colonial mistress is portrayed as the tamer of both Western masculinity and the childlike natives, imperial patriarchy's moral compass. "While white women conscientiously criticize and cause the downfall of [empire], they are also seen as impotent," Dyer observes (1997: 186). Similarly, critiquing patriarchy without dismantling colonial domination implicates Western feminism in imperial projects.

The iconography of the white woman in the western is just as mythic and contradictory. In her influential discussion of woman as sign in classical narrative cinema, Claire Johnston revisits Peter Wollen's assessment of John Ford as an auteur of the western. She comments:

> Ford's is a ... universe in which women play a pivotal role: it is around their presence that the tensions between ... the idea of the wilderness and the idea of the garden revolve. For Ford woman represents the home, and with it the possibility of

culture: she becomes a cipher onto which Ford projects his profoundly ambivalent attitude to the concepts of civilization and psychological "wholeness."

(1976: 213)

Martha, the mother whose image is revealed in the first shot of *The Searchers* (Ford, 1956), is the mythic example: all of the film's violence aims to recuperate its first opening moments when her gaze from the porch takes in the expansive western landscape. Reichardt refuses such mythic moments; she has remarked that if her film qualifies as a western, it is one told from the point of view of the woman who pours John Wayne's coffee.

Acknowledging the symbolic freight of white settler women, *White Material* and *Meek's Cutoff* implicate the colonial wives in imperial and expansionist projects. Maria is a stubborn hold out who ignores everything and bullies everyone around her to bring in the year's coffee harvest as the nation implodes with ethnic violence. Her lazy, selfish son (Nicolas Duvauchelle), who is eventually driven to monstrous violence and madness, hints at her own compromised moral character. Emily Tetherow is casually racist. Her response when she first sees the lone Indian (Rod Rondeaux) that the party will take captive is to load her gun. The film's poster image by artist Marlene McCarty shows Emily looking down the barrel of a shotgun, connoting both feminist empowerment and the vigilantism of settler colonialism, in its sand-and-yellow colors connecting her skin to the land she hopes to claim (Figure 20.1).

But Maria is also shown as a victim of patriarchal property rights; without consulting her, Maria's husband and father-in-law collude to sell the plantation to which she has no legal title. When the foreman of the temporary workers she hires after the others have walked off asks, "Are you the boss?" she answers: "I own nothing, but I run everything." Similarly, in *Meek's Cutoff*, Emily and the other pioneer women are pointedly excluded from decisions about their own fate. The men step away from camp to confer beyond earshot, handing the women the reins to the oxen but nothing else. The film takes up the women's aural perspective in these scenes, and the framing sets them apart. *White Material*, in turn, emphasizes the fatal partiality of Maria's perspective, often shooting her from behind or in profile. Both films derive a visceral intensity from the foregrounding of women's gazes and gestures, even when the protagonists lack insight, good judgment, or the ability to act.

The white women's alliances across race with men of color pointedly undermine white patriarchal power even as they lock white female privilege in place, leaving little room for women of color's perspectives. Unbeknownst to the men of her family, Maria shelters and tends the Boxer, dying leader of the rebel faction. Emily sews the moccasin of the nameless Cayuse captive. Yet their womanly ministrations are not recuperated as simply humane gestures. Maria's motives are ambiguous and suggest a forbidden eroticism; Emily explains her actions to another wife: "I want him to owe me something." Importantly, neither film depicts its protagonist's cross-race, cross-gender alliances as redemptive.

Meek's Cutoff offers a more explicitly feminist heroine—trusting their Indian guide, Emily symbolically takes over the "direction" of the trek from the men. When she raises the rifle a second time, it is to take aim at Meek just as he raises his weapon to shoot the Cayuse. But she has not decisively realigned her loyalties and disavowed her relationship to white colonial ambitions. Pointedly, she cannot understand the captive's message, and his words go untranslated for the viewer as well. The ending of *Meek's Cutoff* leaves us radically unsure about Emily and the settlers' fate. When the party reaches a lone, half-dead tree, they are faced with a decision about their route. In a shot from Emily's point-of-view, the Indian turns and walks into the vanishing point of the frame. The blighted tree stands as a

Figure 20.1 Marlene McCarty's poster design and drawing for *Meek's Cutoff*.

Source: Oscilloscope Laboratories

profoundly ambivalent sign: has the water it promises run dry? The film's cryptic last shot, of Emily's gaze, is deliberately obscured by its branches.

The limitation of—and to—the white women's point of view is the ethical challenge posed within the diegeses of *White Material* and *Meek's Cutoff*, and by the directors' authorial inscription in these films. Through a brief consideration of how each film brings to the fore concerns central to its respective director's body of work, I extend this challenge to a feminist critique of the very category of the auteur within world cinema circuits. First I link Denis's self-conscious exploration of French colonial history to an interrogation of French hegemony in the culture of art cinema, pointing to her intertextual racialization and displacement of Oedipal narratives. I then read Reichardt's location in relation to the auteurist style and aesthetic of world cinema as not only a displacement of Hollywood's cultural imperialism but also an ethical challenge to US independent cinema's understanding of its place in the world.

Claire Denis: African (anti-)Oedipus

In *White Material*, Denis revisits the question of white female colonial privilege explored in quasi-allegorical terms in her very first feature film. *Chocolat* (1988) depicts the waning empire from the position of the colonial female child (named, and standing in for, France). Denis spent her childhood in Africa as the daughter of a colonial administrator, and the legacy of empire remains a consistent theme in her work. *Beau Travail* (1999), perhaps her most widely acclaimed work, was filmed in Djioubti, and a number of her films are set in African diasporan communities in France. But she did not deploy a white female authorial avatar again until *White Material*. Instead, across her oeuvre, the white female director explores questions of desire, agency, and loss through black male bodies (Mayne 2005: 29). A reciprocity is constructed between white woman and black man within a forcefield of power relations that pushes both white male authority and black female experience to the margins, with ambiguous results. *White Material* takes up elements of *Chocolat* in an overt commentary on these themes and thus on Denis's own authorial position.

Adrian Martin speaks of a Denis film as a "diagram of bodies and desires" (2010); the colonial household of *Chocolat* is drawn along interracial, Oedipal lines. Although the film is not told from his point of view, Protée, the family's so-called "houseboy," is its most compelling figure (Cameroonian author Ferdinand Oyono's classic "Une vie de boy" is the film's literary source). France is allied with Protée and the other Africans who care for, converse, and play with her, against the white adults. But although the child may be innocent of exploitative intent, she is marked as forever an outsider, an intruder. Her mother, Aimée, seals the repression of her own attraction to the servant by firing him, in an arbitrary exercise of power. In what can be read as the primal scene of Denis's oeuvre, Protée rejects the daughter's attempt at rapprochement. France thus repeats her mother's story despite herself; the film shows that the privileging of female desire within the Oedipal narrative does not dismantle colonial exploitation.

The events of France's childhood are recounted in flashback. The visit to postcolonial Africa as an adult that frames the film is thus another repetition of thwarted desire, as is indeed the making of the film. *White Material*, produced twenty-five years later, is a rep-etition with a difference, one that explores the white colonial woman's complicity with the violence ravaging postcolonial Africa. Isaach de Bankolé, the "boy" of *Chocolat*, and a frequent actor in Denis's films, returns in *White Material* as the rebel leader, a comp-lementary fantasm of African masculinity. The actor's iconicity is highlighted by a diegetic mural depicting the Boxer with raised fists; the Boxer in the flesh is not an armed strong man but rather a mortally wounded and vulnerable one. His near wordlessness and the reverence in which he is held by the rebel soldiers shroud him in myth. While Protée opened up the familial dynamics of *Chocolat* to a broader historical canvas, suggesting a point of view and a future that Denis dared not narrate, *White Material* shows the nightmare implosion of the colonial household, where history obliterates the settlers' familial fictions. The Boxer moves into the room abandoned by Maria's son, who has become a crazed and cruel avatar of white colonial decadence. *White Material*'s shocking finale amps up the Oedipal drama when Maria, completing her frantic bus journey, returns to the plantation to find it in flames, and the Boxer, her ex-husband, and her son both dead. She finishes the job by brutally bludgeoning her father-in-law (Michel Subor). But this blow against patriarchy is drained of symbolic freight. If the white woman is revealed as the white man's heart of darkness in this final confrontation, it is a matter of indifference to the Africans.

Nor is the white woman's interiority of particular concern. Maria is simply referred to as *la blanche*; her skin is emblematic of her being. Huppert's casting contributes to a reading of what can be called Maria's *exteriority*. Denis tends to work with the same group of actors; her first collaboration with Huppert necessarily plays on the star's iconicity, from the seeming vulnerability of her pale, freckled skin to the fierce physicality of her performance style. She

Figure 20.2   Isabelle Huppert in *White Material*.

Source: White Material, Claire Denis, 2009. Courtesy IFC Films.

looks like a little girl in her pink dress, at once displaying and disavowing the power and privilege of white femininity (Figure 20.2). Indeed, her garments recall the pink and yellow dresses worn by both the child France and the mother Aimée in *Chocolat*. "A guy in Cameroon made them and they looked like dresses for white women in Africa," Denis comments. Wearing them, "I think [Isabelle] wanted somehow—I think she would not agree if she were here—but I think she did a kind of version of me or my mother" (Ratner 2010: 37–8). In collaboration with Huppert and French–Senegalese novelist Marie NDiaye (*Three Strong Women*, 2009), who co-wrote the film's screenplay, Denis interrogates white female colonial mimicry.

Kelly Reichardt: western visions

We have seen that the motif and materiality of the dress condenses *White Material's* gendered vision of settler colonialism. Female clothing is similarly emphasized in *Meek's Cutoff*. Pink material encodes "proper" femininity and contributes to the films' tactility. The film's costume designer Vicki Farrell describes her collaboration with Reichardt:

> In our initial discussions Kelly said she pictured Emily Tetherow in a rose pink dress. Everything spun out from there. ... Kelly was scouting and sending me these amazing pictures of the desert and I was sending her bleached-out swatches of calico.

Thus, in both films, what we might call a discourse of pink material exteriorizes the heroines' race and/as the delicacy and privilege attributed to their gender, determining their actions and point of view. Pictorially, the women in *Meek's Cutoff* are perfectly composed in their coordinated pastel garments, irradiated by the magic-hour cinematography (Figure 20.3). Yet there is no simple glorification of their pioneer "spirit." Instead of the housekeeping zeal of *Little House on the Prairie*, *Meek's Cutoff* shows women's work as repetitive, grinding routine.

As many reviews of the film note, the pioneer women's pink and yellow bonnets are not only a significant item of mise-en-scène, they are also a visual figure that marks women's limited perspective in the film and on history itself. The very-pregnant Mrs. White (Shirley Henderson) nearly loses hers in a moment of great tension—epitomizing both the tightly

Figure 20.3   Shirley Henderson, Zoe Kazan and Michelle Williams in *Meek's Cutoff*.

Source: Meek's Cutoff, Kelly Reichardt, 2010. Courtesy Oscilloscope Laboratories.

controlled aesthetic design of the film and the indexical force of its images. Trudging along at the rear of the party as it makes its habitual way from screen right to left when her bonnet blows away, she turns into the wind to retrieve it. She fights her way back, screen right, like Lillian Gish in Sjöström's *The Wind* (1928), finally snatching the scrap of material just before it disappears beyond the edge of the frame. The film's framing cuts a precarious foothold for the pioneers' action out of the unforgiving landscape.

The bonnets that literally restrict the pioneer women's range of vision are formally mirrored in Reichardt's decision to shoot the film in Academy screen ratio, a 1.37: 1 near-square rather than a rectangular format, which thus truncates the horizon. A tribute to the look of Anthony Mann's 1950s westerns, the choice of format is part of the film's oblique response to the legacy of the genre. Widescreen compositions would reveal too much, the director explains. Much of the film's drama is about what lies out of sight—will the party find water, will they be ambushed, will they discover they have walked in circles? We read the frame with the focused intensity the wives bring to their scrutiny of the paths before them.

The film's minimalism in plot, dialogue, and mise-en-scène deflate cinematic myths of the Old West: *Meek's Cutoff* is as much an indie auteur film as it is a western. Its parched landscape is distinctive to Oregon, where four of Reichardt's films to date are set and a territory whose connotations are far from settled in her oeuvre. In 1845, when the events of *Meek's Cutoff* took place, American identity was literally at stake in the border dispute between the US and Canada. A story of the Oregon Trail gone awry, *Meek's Cutoff* is, in a sense, the "back story" of the New West featured in Reichardt's earlier films. The characters played by Michelle Williams in both *Wendy and Lucy* and *Meek's Cutoff* displace white male heroes—driving the car, settling the west—with their ambivalent and precarious relationship to power in the foreground. Reichardt deterritorializes genre (the road movie and the western), to follow new itineraries, ranging over "western" spaces that are destined to be shared.

Her settlers walk. They also pitch camp, build fires, feed oxen, knit, and perform the myriad activities documented in the women pioneers' journals that Reichardt and Raymond read in preparation for the film. The press notes document *Meek's Cutoff*'s meticulous attention to material culture such as wagons, tackle, trunks, and bleached-out rose-colored material itself (2009). Rather than a static symbol of the homestead, Emily and the other women are always in motion, bodies synchronized with their gear: coffee grinder, cattle prod, and as we have seen, in key moments, rifle.

The white woman director

In *White Material*, Maria is similarly constantly operating machinery: minibike, truck, harvester, tractor, generator. We see this habitual work carved in her forearm as she hangs from the bus. The portrayal of female competence with equipment is a reminder of the woman behind the camera: I take the films' images of physical mastery, as much as their portrayal of the white woman's partial point of view and its consequences, as inscriptions of authorship. *White Material* and *Meek's Cutoff* both enact and critique the power white women have attained in the current remapping of world cinema. Neither film opens onto the many other stories these women and other Others could tell of these same times and places—indeed, both end with literal scorched earth. But their directors make the limits of their own perspectives, means, and competence part of their aesthetic and political projects, in films that both depict intersections of colonialism and gender and allegorize authorship as a dilemma of cultural authority.

Among the few women to be heralded as world cinema auteurs, Denis and Reichardt are also constructed as loners. This has posed a challenge to feminist readings of their work. Neither works in stereotypically women's genres, and many of their significant collaborators are male. Like Kathryn Bigelow, though in different ways, they are considered "tough." In an article in the *New York Times*, Dan Kios called watching *Meek's Cutoff* equivalent to "eating your cultural vegetables" (2011). In contrast to a "civilizing" mission, these directors offer "grit." Privileged as they might be, the French woman auteur and the US indie director refuse to stand in for "culture" in its benign sense, and instead hold themselves and their protagonists accountable to national narratives and their often-destructive paths through the world.

Related topics

Priya Jaikumar, "Feminist and non-Western interrogations of authorship"
Sandra Ponzanesi, "Postcolonial and transnational approaches to film and feminism"
Anikó Imre, "Gender, socialism, and European film cultures"

References

Andrew, Dudley (2010) "Time Zones and Jetlag: The Flows and Phases of World Cinema," in Nataša Ďurovičová and Kathleen Newman (eds.), *World Cinemas, Transnational Perspectives*. New York: Routledge, pp. 59–89.
Beugnet, Martine (2007) *Claire Denis*. Manchester: Manchester University Press.
Dyer, Richard (1997) *White*. London: Routledge.
English, James F. (2005) *The Economy of Prestige: Prizes, Awards, and the Circulation of Cultural Value*. Cambridge, MA: Harvard.
EWA. European Women's Audiovisual Research Network Report. February 2016. www.ewawomen.com/en/research-.html# (accessed March 3, 2016)
Fanon, Frantz (2008 [1967]) *Black Skin, White Mask*. New York: Grove.

Feinberg, Scott (2013) "Claire Denis, French Auteur, on Women Filmmakers, Attractive Actors and 'Bastards,'" *Hollywood Reporter* (October 18).

Flanagan, Matthew (2008) "Towards an Aesthetic of Slow in Contemporary Cinema," 16:9 29: 1.

Hole, Kristine Lené (2015) *Towards a Feminist Cinematic Ethics: Claire Denis, Emmanuel Levinas and Jean-Luc Nancy*. Edinburgh: Edinburgh University Press.

Hornaday, A. (2011) "Director Kelly Reichardt on 'Meek's Cutoff' and Making Movies Her Way," *The Washington Post* (May 19).

Johnston, Claire (1976) "Notes on Women's Cinema," in Bill Nichols (ed.) *Movies and Methods*. Berkeley: University of California Press.

Kios, Dan (2011) "Eating Your Cultural Vegetables," *New York Times Magazine* (April 29).

Martin, Adrian (2010) "In a Foreign Land," *Sight and Sound* 20.7: 50–1ff.

Mayne, Judith (2005) *Claire Denis*. Urbana: University of Illinois Press.

Meek's Cutoff press notes (2009) Oscilloscope Laboratories.

Newman, Michael Z. (2011) *Indie: An American Film Culture*. New York: Columbia University Press.

Ratner, Megan (2010) "Moving Toward the Unknown Other: An Interview with Claire Denis," *Cineaste* 36.1: 36–40.

Scott, A. O. (2009) "Neo-neorealism," *New York Times Magazine* (March 17).

Valck, Marijke de (2007) *Film Festivals: From European Geopolitics to Global Cinephilia*. Amsterdam: Amsterdam University Press.

White, Patricia (2009) "Watching Women's Films," *Camera Obscura* 72:152–62.

——— (2015) *Women's Cinema, World Cinema: Projecting Contemporary Feminisms*. Durham, NC: Duke University Press.

21

WOMEN, ISLAM, AND CINEMA

Gender politics and representation in Middle Eastern films and beyond

Eylem Atakav

Critical explorations of the relationship between Islam, cinema, and women contribute to academic debates around difference. This connection may be approached from different perspectives. One may think about the concept of representation in examining this topic: how are women represented in films produced in countries where Islam is the dominant religion? How do Islamic films represent women? Or, how do filmmakers who define themselves as Muslim represent issues around identity and cultural politics that inform discourses around womanhood? Furthermore, what kinds of themes and genres are chosen in films when the relationship between Islam and women is the focus of attention? How are Muslim women represented in cinemas of non-Muslim (predominantly Western) countries? One may approach these topics by examining questions around *women film-makers*: what kinds of films do women from Muslim countries produce? Are there common and/or recurring themes in their films? How are these films different, if at all, from those made elsewhere? Informed by issues around representation and modes of production, it is also possible for one to approach the topic from the perspective of *reception* studies: how are films about women and Islam received around the world? How are women's films from Islamic countries received within the country of their production and beyond? Do these films travel? In analyzing the relationship between cinema, Islam, and women, one may also choose to focus on *Middle Eastern film*. While this excludes areas outside Middle Eastern countries where Islam is the dominant religion, it enables a focus on comparable themes in the films of these socio-historical communities with shared geography and cultural and religious connections.

Feminist scholarship about Islam and cinema demonstrates that there are prevailing and longstanding discourses inherent in the ways women are represented in films (Akhavan 2015; Abu-Lughod 2002; Kahf 1999). As highlighted by recent research, Western media's approach to Islam and the Muslim world has historically been from the perspective of difference and opposition that has promoted misrepresentative and inaccurate knowledge about Muslim nations and cultures (Alsultany 2012). In Western media, women have, in numerable ways, been represented as veiled, oppressed, and urgently in need of rescue (Abu-Lughod 2002). Western ideas about womanhood in the Middle East are informed by religious stereotypes and the representations of Islam in the media in general, and films in particular. For instance, Hollywood films are inclined to show Islam as intrinsically oppressive towards women through the use of veiling and gender segregation to reinforce the so-called "backwardness" of Islamic societies. Indeed, Hollywood has endorsed a stereotyping of the "other" through the depiction of the "East" (Shohat and Stam 1994). The representation of Arab men, starting from the early days of Hollywood, and carrying through to the present, has varied from exotic men riding camels in the desert (for whom Arab women are only objects of desire), to terrorists and extravagantly oil-rich men (Donmez-Colin 2004). For instance, Iran has, for a very long time, mostly been (and, according to some, still is) known to the West for the astonishing *Not Without My Daughter*, a 1991 MGM film by Brian Gilbert, which tells the story of a suffering American woman who is attempting to escape from her barbaric and highly religious Iranian husband who becomes "traditional" when he returns back to Iran from America. In this, as its trailer puts it, "terrifying true story of a woman whose only fault is being American," Islam and Muslim women are depicted as backward, Iranian men as oppressive, and women in Iran as brutalized by a patriarchal culture. The oppressed woman narratives within films about Islamic countries are indeed numerous. However, it is important to question whether representations of Muslim women in Western films are any different from those produced within, for example, the Middle East—and if yes, how. For instance, the problem with *Not Without My Daughter* is in its monolithic portrait of Islam and Iranian women. To suggest this is not to position oneself as "defending" a particular religion over another, but to acknowledge the problematic nature of representing women and/in Islam in an ideologically reductive way. On the other side of the coin, for example, the *Sex and the City* franchise has long been seen as valorizing a narrow depiction of white, Western womanhood. This was arguably crystallized in *Sex and the City 2* (King, 2010). The film's representation of "Abu Dhabi" as a culturally and socially "backward" space, just like its representation of Muslim women as veiled, enigmatic, and oppressed, have received considerable scrutiny from film critics from around the world. The condescending tone of the film towards Muslim/Middle Eastern women was the most talked about part of the film in its reviews. Indeed, the film was deemed as "borderline racist" by *The Guardian* (Bradshaw 2010). A controversial sequence in which the four American women (Carrie, Samantha, Charlotte, Miranda) observe a woman wearing a burqa eating fries includes Samantha's comment that "it is like they [women] don't want to have a voice." Stephen Farber, from *The Hollywood Reporter* (2010), wrote about the film's "saucy political incorrectness." In addition, Wajahat Ali's *Salon.com* review observed that "nearly every single Middle Eastern female character in *SATC 2*'s imaginative rendition of "Abu Dhabi," is veiled, silent or subdued by aggressive men" (2010). Contrary to this, Govindini Murty argued, in *Libertas Film Magazine*, that [the film] satirize[d] Islam's treatment of women and points out that it is "the only big budget Hollywood film in recent years that dares to critique the repressive treatment of women in the Middle East." However, as outlined by the majority of its critical reception, the film uses normative representational strategies to paint a monolithic picture of Islam and its treatment of women as brutally violent and unjust. The key issue here has to do with the repetition of such stories through the circulation of films around the world. These films are as much about constructing a fantasy of the West as (by contrast) a place of freedom and progressive sexual politics as they are attempting to represent another culture.

One question that an ideologically problematic representation of women and Islam raises is: what alternative perspectives does this kind of popular narrative omit? Hollywood may have been the carrier of ideologies and images of the Islamic world, but with the increased number of films produced from within Middle Eastern or Muslim countries and by filmmakers of that origin, stereotypical images are progressively challenged and subverted, if less often seen by international audiences. This is not to suggest that Middle Eastern films do not conform to stereotypes. At times, they, indeed, do reinforce negative images of Islam in highlighting issues around women's oppression, yet these are typically used to critique the conditions that are consequences of cultural and religious values. Lina Khatib's work, for instance, compares Hollywood's and Arab cinema's engagement in filming the modern Middle East (2006). She suggests that *both* Hollywood *and* Arab films depict women's images/bodies as "authentic" symbols, while gender issues are emplotted as a tool of nationalism, although Arab cinema simultaneously attempts to subvert monolithic representations of the Middle East. While locating issues around the representations of Islam, women, and cinema, Khatib's research suggests that, in Palestinian cinema, for instance, the liberation of the country is linked with that of women (ibid. p. 12). As Khatib's examination of Algerian, Egyptian, and Palestinian films in relation and in contrast to Hollywood films suggests, women, femininity, and sexuality are used to symbolize the nation:

> [N]ation is symbolized by wholesome femininity. While sexually aloof women are used to symbolize the foreign enemy … Algerian and Egyptian films use gender as a mark of modernity, the latter symbolizing the oppression of Islamic fundamentalism through the representation of silent, veiled women while highlighting fundamentalism's immorality through depicting the hypocrisy of Islamic fundamentalist men in their relations with women in general.
>
> (*ibid.*)

In addition, representations in films from the Middle East can be full of nuances informed by cultural differences. The lack of access to the language of the culture in which the film originates may result in the reduction of a film's political significance and flatten its nuances. As Laura Mulvey (2006) rightly points out while writing about new Iranian cinema, discussions around and critiques of films from within the Middle East are invaluable contributions to the "texture" of understanding of these films that travel abroad. Indeed, it is through these debates that films can begin to "convey more explicit meanings and resonate beyond the appeal of the exotic" (ibid. p. 257). There are, indeed, many contemporary films, from countries where Islam is the dominant religion, that focus on women's experiences or offer more nuanced perspectives on Islamic cultures. These films predominantly circulate within international festivals, and are made by internationally renowned filmmakers, from Abbas Kiarostami (Iran), to Haifaa Al-Mansour (Saudi Arabia), Jafar Panahi (Iran), Asghar Farhadi (Iran), Nadine Labaki (Lebanon), and Nuri Bilge Ceylan (Turkey). Their films, and therefore the cultures of the Middle East, travel around the world and in film festival circles, and are primarily produced within a transnational context because of the funding they receive, and the filming locations and/or cast they use.

Representing women's empowerment

Within this framework, there are three prominent and recurring themes in films that address women in relation to Islam and cinema: women's status in Islam; the concept of violence against women that resonates across multiple layers of reference (physical, emotional, political, economic, sexual, military); and, rather contradictory to that, the use of powerful female characters. "Honor" killings, women's chastity, adultery, virginity, and forced marriage are topics which have a considerable impact upon women's lives and experiences in countries and communities where Islamic patriarchal regimes exist. Yet, this is not to suggest that these are issues of Islam. In fact, it is reductive and therefore problematic to imply that these issues affect Muslim women and Muslim societies only. Islam and tradition, in this sense, are frequently depicted as the reasons for women's oppression, as well as being presented as topics of criticism—particularly in films that have a feminist standpoint. Indeed, Middle Eastern films are critical sites for understanding the cultural politics of different national contexts. In these films, violence against women and women's empowerment coexist as powerful female characters subvert or critique that violence. For instance, Farhadi's *About Elly* (2009) and *A Separation* (2011), and Marjane Satrapi's *Persepolis* (2007) all have powerful female protagonists who defy religion and attempt to subvert the cultural positioning of women. Panahi's *Offside* (2006) is inspired by the day when the director's own daughter was refused entry to a football match in Iran. Iranian-American director Maryam Keshavarz's 2011 film *Circumstance* depicts the life of a teenage lesbian couple subverting cultural attitudes in Iran. *The Patience Stone* by Afghan writer and director Atiq Rahimi (2012) is a powerful drama that enters into the private lives of Arab women in a story about love, war, violence, sexuality, and marriage. In Nadine Labaki's latest film *Where Do We Go Now?* (2011), women are the source of power that brings back peace to a community living in an unnamed Middle Eastern village where Muslims and Christians live together. Another good example that reflects powerful Muslim women in films is Shirin Neshat's *Women without Men* (2009), which offers a view of Iran in 1953, when a British and American-backed coup removed the democratically elected government. Adapted from the novel by Iranian author, Shahrnush Parsipur, the film weaves together the stories of four women, whose experiences are shaped by their faith and the social structures of a patriarchal regime. Neshat explores the social, political, and psychological dimensions of her characters as they meet in a metaphorical garden, in which they critically reflect upon the religious forces that have shaped their lives.

Similarly, Eran Riklis' film *Lemon Tree* (2008) tells the story of a Palestinian widow who must defend her lemon tree field when a new Israeli defense minister moves next to her and threatens to have her lemon grove torn down. The vulnerability of a widow in a politicized, patriarchal context, and the land as embodied within the woman's body, are the focus of the film. Another film that is worth considering here is Syrian filmmaker Diana El-Jeiroudi's *Dolls* (2007). It was produced by Proaction Film, the only independent film production company in Syria that is in operation today. This documentary film explores the significance of the "Fulla Doll," the veiled version of the American Barbie doll, while at the same time asking questions about women's identity and their place in a society where Islam is the dominant religion. As Shohreh Jandaghian (2007) states, in *Dolls*, El-Jeiroudi attempts to reveal and critique a trend that commercially appropriates a female figure (that limits the mind, soul, and body of a young generation) into a female model informed by social and religious values. Another film that focuses on female agency in an Islamic culture is Labaki's *Caramel*, (2007). The film centers on the daily lives of five Lebanese women living in Beirut, and deals with the issue of virginity and sex before marriage. It conveys how women find ways to deal with the strict traditions and religious rules imposed upon them by a patriarchal society, through the story of one of the characters who has a surgery to become "re-virginized" before she gets married. All these examples present an array of stories on women and their experiences in Islamic cultures.

Violence against women and its critique in films

Although violence is a recurring motif in these films, it is typically heavily critiqued and condemned, rather than glamorized. Indeed, films about and by women from the Middle

East frequently offer a subversive response to the ways in which the female body is controlled in patriarchal regimes where religious discourses prevail. In thinking about strategies for alternative depictions of violence one may ask: how do women filmmakers represent violence against women while critiquing it?

One film that provides an answer to this question is Abeer Zeibak Haddad's *Duma* (2012), an extremely powerful documentary that focuses on the experiences of five Arab women. It is regarded as the first film that sheds light on violence against women and the sexual assault of women in the Arab world. What brings these five women together is not only the violence they endured in different ways, but also the silence imposed upon them by their families or society. The film creates a space for women to break the barrier of silence and fear, and speak overtly about their experiences of rape and abuse. In addition, there are a number of films that are produced by Palestinian filmmakers that focus on issues around gender in an attempt to visualize Palestinian resistance. These filmmakers generate new means of articulating and critiquing visions for Palestinian society. A case in point is Annemarie Jacir's *When I Saw You* (2013), which focuses on the story of a boy and his relationship with his father within the context of the Israeli–Palestinian conflict. The film is a reflection of the relationship between masculinity and violence. It marginalizes the male/masculine politics of the conflict, as opposed to marginalizing the story of the boy, whose refusal to accept artificial borders dominates the narrative. In addition, filmmaker Jacir's insistence on not wanting to be known for being the first Palestinian woman filmmaker, but rather for her films, is a thought-provoking position.

Another film that focuses on violence against women in communities where Islam is the dominant religion is Eylem Kaftan's bio-documentary *Vendetta Song* (2005). The film explores honor killings, gender inequalities, the traditional practice of arranged marriages, and the semi-feudal social structure in Eastern Turkey within the context of Islamic tradition. It problematizes the relations of the West to the East both within and outside Turkey, as the narrative is structured as a travelogue of a woman traveling from Canada to Istanbul, and then from Western to Eastern Turkey. The film questions whether there is a necessary or contingent connection between "honor" killings, patriarchy, and Islam. On one hand, it critiques traditional gender politics through its feminist discourse and, on the other, attempts to deconstruct the misperceived connection between Islam and violence against women; however, while doing so it also places emphasis on tradition rather than religion (Atakav 2015). The opening scene of the films immediately sets up a Western–Eastern distinction. The narrator types in English (suggesting a Western target audience) about her journey in and to the East. The use of photographic images is significant in highlighting the idea of difference. As she travels in Eastern Turkey, the director/narrator takes photos of the people she sees. The audience gets a sense here of the director acting like a tourist, which makes John Urry's phrase "the tourist gaze" relevant here (2002). Photographs—people frozen in an image—are suggestive of the idea that they will never change. Each time we hear the sound of the shutter, people are frozen and rendered inanimate, and this reinforces the distance between the filming subject and the filmed object. The tourist gaze offers signs which locate the particular tourist practices, not in terms of intrinsic characteristics, but through the contrasts implied with non-tourist social practices. So, by considering "the typical objects of the tourist gaze, one can make sense of elements of the wider society with which they are contrasted"—in this case Canada or the West (Urry, 2002, p. 2). *Vendetta Song* plays a significant role in revealing what is happening in Eastern Turkey in women's lives with strict customary practices, but one must also consider that people who are the objects of the gaze are aware of such gaze and this at times informs their (verbal, physical, or emotional) responses.

Saudi Arabian cinema, Islam, and women film pioneers

The first full-length feature film ever shot entirely inside the Kingdom of Saudi Arabia, *Wadjda* (2013), is directed by a woman, Haifaa Al-Mansour. The film focuses on the story of a 10-year-old girl (Wadjda) who wishes to buy a bicycle in a society that prohibits this act (due to religious views which suggest that riding a bicycle is tantamount to a girl losing her virginity). The story focuses on her bid to enter a Qur'an reading competition in order to secure the money necessary to purchase the forbidden item. But with regard to its own social and political context, the film itself was essentially forbidden: Al-Mansour had to film the story while hiding in a van and giving directorial orders through a walkie-talkie. There is a lot to be praised about *Wadjda*. Indeed, there are many powerful scenes in the film which delicately tell us about womanhood, girlhood, and women's place in a culture dominated by religious values and rules. The camera travels between a house, a school, a playground, a little street with a bicycle shop, and a rooftop. Wadjda, living within this limited and conservative space, is a witty, clever and, at the same time, powerful character whose imagination and ideas are limitless. It offers an interesting parallel with Al-Mansour, who had to film Wadjda's limitless world from within the very limited space of a van. The references to polygamy, significance attached to virginity, child brides, the implications of veiling, and religion's place in education make the film thought-provoking. One scene in particular is remarkable: Wadjda is secretly learning to cycle on the rooftop of her house, but she panics as her mother approaches, falls off the bicycle, and hurts her knee. As she cries out "I'm bleeding!" the mother covers her face with shame, mistakenly thinking her daughter is bleeding for having ridden the bike and losing her virginity. The scene is astutely narrated, skillfully performed, and brilliantly filmed. This scene, like many others in the film, offers a critique of gendered perceptions around girlhood in a religious context. What makes these scenes significant is their contribution to unpacking and thereby critiquing social values in a society where approaches to change in tradition and perceptions around gender are rather rigid. In an interview with the BBC (2013), Al-Mansour discusses the importance of introducing change in Saudi society while acknowledging that "[it] is a painful process." Change is embedded within the film through the image of a bicycle, which represents independence, mobility, freedom, and imagination.

Examining this pioneering film's critical reception raises crucial questions about the discourses that surround women, Islam, and cinema, particularly from the Arab world. The reviews of the film focus on the fact that the director was able to make the film within the limiting social and cultural context of Saudi Arabia. The marginalization of the accomplishments of the director as an artist are representative of the ways in which women filmmakers from countries dominated by Islamic cultures are talked and written about. Yet, this is also applicable to other women filmmakers from around the world. Writing about American cinema, for instance, Yvonne Tasker aptly argues that by virtue of their relative rarity, an interest in the work of women filmmakers and the language used to critique it "can often end up centering on the question of how they managed to get to the position they are in at all" (2010, p. 222). This is true for Wadjda's reception. The language used in the Western press to discuss issues around Islam and the Arab world further complicates this situation. It is perhaps for this reason that, in the case of *Wadjda*, Western reviews focus on the "backwardness" of Saudi Arabian culture in relation to its treatment of women (as also depicted by the film itself), rather than the cinematographic or cultural value of Al-Mansour's film. A case in point is Philip French's review (2013) of the film, in *The Guardian*: "One of the first features shot in Saudi Arabia, and certainly the first to be written and directed by a woman, this beguiling German–Saudi co-production turns upon an image that has been a cinematic metaphor for freedom, self-empowerment …" He further writes: "The story is an admirable necklace on which to string fact, anecdotes and insights that illuminate in a good-natured way the lives of women in an *unthinking, patriarchal, totalitarian society*" (italics my emphasis). Moreover, Hannah McGill (2013) writes about Wadjda as a "tomboy superheroine who gives pleasurable vent to the audience's frustration." She goes on to say, "For political reasons, it needs to show Wadjda as cowed and oppressed; yet for feel good reasons it wants to show her as indefatigable." These reviews that represent Western film critics' view on the film reflect and articulate larger intellectual and political questions about films from the countries and communities where Islam is the dominant religion. As outlined in the press kit of the film, critiques of the film from within Saudi Arabia are twofold: some say "The film is against our religion and values," "We shouldn't show our problems to the world," and there are also reviews that celebrate Al-Mansour's attempt to contribute to change in Saudi society. Some say "it isn't radical enough!" and some "it is only successful because it was made by a woman." One review states that the film will certainly be a great hit among Saudi women who will find pirate copies of the film to watch it. This raises a larger question about female authorship and about women's film history. If authorship is a discourse within which women filmmakers have been marginalized, and if Orientalism is the dominant discourse when critics write about films from the Arab world, then *Wadjda*'s reception and Al-Mansour's authorship are doubly marginalized. The reviews from different national contexts find different ways of negotiating female authorship and womanhood (as well as girlhood) in Saudi Arabia.

Documenting the veil: the case of Turkey

Turkey, as a country that straddles European and Middle Eastern cultural conceptions, identities, and values, has a unique position in the context of the relationship between women and Islam. Indeed, Islam and secularism have historically been a focal point of intense debate among groups with conflicting political and ideological interests in Turkey. Films, as products of cultural struggles in this historical, social, economic, and political context, offer a significant site for representing tensions and contradictions within a country that straddles the line between the modern and traditional, Western and Eastern, secular and religious. Turkish women have been the theme of several documentaries made for women, by women who live outside of Turkey, a number of which have been distributed by Women Make Movies over the last few years. These films tend to focus on the relationship between religion and women's place in Islam and in Turkey. Olga Nakkas' *Women of Turkey: Between Islam and Secularism* (2006), for instance, draws on interviews with women and examines the individual and political resonance of the headscarf and veiling. The film presents a positive image of Turkish women. Furthermore, Binnur Karaevli's *Voices Unveiled: Turkish Women Who Dare* (2009) provides a critique of the ban on wearing headscarves at the same time as touching upon issues including female officers in mosques, violence in the name of Islam, lack of education and economic dependence of women, women and Turkey's EU candidacy, and the tensions inherent between Muslim and Western cultures. Alba Sotorra's *Unveiled Views: Muslim Women Artists Speak Out* (2009), for instance, focuses on the life of five Muslim women, one of whom is a Turkish human rights lawyer.

Conclusion

All the films discussed above offer a fruitful area of further research to examine the relationship between women, Islam, and cinema. Indeed, women's cultural production and the very presence of women filmmakers from countries where Islam is the dominant religion make a difference, and contribute to the construction and redefinition of feminist cultural politics. The strategies of different women filmmakers of the Middle East offer distinctive motifs in cinematic style, as well as stunning examples of experimentation. Women's films are connected by similar processes of revising and reconceptualizing issues around gender, patriarchy, and religion. Feminist film studies has, for some time, recognized the plurality inherent in the concept of Woman as cut across by, for example, ethnicity, class, sexuality, and more recently age. It has also been the case that those popular and academic conceptions of feminism have privileged the white heterosexual woman. It is, therefore, significant to include discussions around women and Islam in the feminist studies of cinema which intervene into existing theories of film history, film genres, and film reception. New films and filmmakers emerging from different cultural and national backgrounds deserve scholarly attention as their mere existence calls for revisiting women's film histories, the history of Islam in/and cinema, as well as cinemas of the Arab world.

While this chapter cannot be exhaustive in its scope, it has aimed to address a number of issues related to the encounter between women and Middle Eastern cinema within the context of framing the significance of Islam. Hollywood representations of women in Islam are both subverted and to some extent legitimized by the films that emerge from the Middle East, exemplifying how the discursive hegemony of Hollywood is not easily relinquished. Nevertheless, the fact that women are also authoring these films and intervening in such debates is of significance in its own right, especially given the ways in which, at a representational level, women are perpetually required to embody and distill the political contours of the nation.

Related topics

Priya Jaikumar, "Feminist and non-Western interrogations of film authorship"
Anne Ciecko, "African 'first films': gendered authorship, identity, and discursive resistance"
Katarzyna Marciniak, "Revolting aesthetics: feminist transnational cinema in the US"
Maureen Turim, "Experimental women filmmakers"

Bibliography

Abu-Lughod, L. (2002) "Do Muslim Women Really Need Saving? Anthropological Reflections on Cultural Relativism and Its Others," *American Anthropologist*, Vol. 104, No. 3, pp. 783–90.

Akhavan, N. (2015) "Nonfiction Form and the 'Truth' about Muslim Women in Iranian Documentary," *Feminist Media Histories*, Vol. 1, No. 1, pp. 89–111.

Ali, W. (2010) "Sex and the City 2's Stunning Muslim Clich," Salon.com, www.salon.com/2010/05/26/sex_and_the_city_cultural_tone_deafness (Last accessed on August 12, 2015).

Al-Mansour, H. July 16, 2013, Interview, BBC HardTalk, www.bbc.co.uk/programmes/n3cstlf8 (Last accessed on May 8, 2015).

Alsultany, E. (2012) *Arabs and Muslims in the Media: Race and Representation after 9/11*, New York and London: New York University Press.

Atakav, E. (2013) *Women and Turkish Cinema: Gender Politics, Cultural Identity and Representation*, London: Routledge.

Atakav, E. (2015) "Honour is Everything for Muslims? *Vendetta Song*, Filmic Representations, Religious Identity and Gender Politics in Turkey," in *The Politics of Being A Woman: Feminism, Media and the 21st Century Popular Culture*, H. Savigny and H. Warner (eds.), London and New York: Palgrave, pp. 49–63.

Bradshaw, P. (2010) "Sex and the City 2," *The Guardian*, www.theguardian.com/film/2010/may/26/sex-and-the-city-2-review (Last accessed on August 12, 2015).

Donmez-Colin, G. (2004) *Women Islam and Cinema*, London: Reaktion Books.

Farber, S. (2010) "Sex and the City 2 Film Review," *Hollywood Reporter*, www.hollywoodreporter.com/movie/sex-city-2/review/29657 (Last accessed on August 12, 2015).

French, P. (2013) "Wadjda: Review," *The Guardian*, www.theguardian.com/film/2013/jul/21/wadjda-film-review (Last accessed on August 12, 2015).

Jandaghian, S. (2007) "Diana El-Jeiroudi talks about 'Veiled Barbie Dolls'" http://cinemawithout-borders.com/conversations/1327-diana-el-jeiroudi-talks-about-veiled-barbie-dolls.html (Last accessed on May 8, 2015).

Jankovic, C. and Awad, N. (2012) "Queer/Palestinian Cinema: A Critical Conversation on Palestinian Queer and Women's Filmmaking," *Camera Obscura*, Vol. 27, No. 2, 2012, pp. 135–43.

Kahf, M. (1999) *Western Representations of the Muslim Woman: From Termagant to Odalisque*, Austin: University of Texas Press.

Khatib, L. (2006) *Filming the Modern Middle East: Politics in the Cinemas of Hollywood and the Arab World*, London and New York: I.B. Tauris.

McGill, H. (2013) "Film of the Week: Wadjda," *Sight and Sound*, www.bfi.org.uk/news-opinion/sight-sound-magazine/reviews-recommendations/film-week-wadjda (Last accessed on August 12, 2015).

Mulvey, L. (2006) "Afterword," in Tapper, R. (ed.) *The New Iranian Cinema: Politics, Representation and Identity*, London and New York: I.B. Tauris, pp. 254–62.

Murty, G. (2010) "Sex and the City 2 Makes Fun of Islam!," *Libertas*, http://ronbosoldier.blogspot.co.uk/2010/05/sex-in-city-2-makes-fun-of-islam.html (Last accessed on August 12, 2015).

Shohat, E. and Stam, R. (1994) *Unthinking Eurocentrism: Multiculturalism and the Media*, Oxon and New York: Routledge.

Tasker, Y. (2010) "Vision and Visibility: Women Filmmakers, Contemporary Authorship and Feminist Film Studies," in *Reclaiming the Archive: Feminism and Film History*, V. Callahan (ed.), Detroit: Wayne State University Press, pp. 213–31.

Urry, J. (2002) *The Tourist Gaze*, London: Sage.

Wadjda Press Kit, http://razor-film.de/en/projects/wadjda, Razor Film (Last accessed on December 2, 2015).

Filmography

A Separation, Asghar Farhadi, 2011
A Wife for my Son, Ali Ghalem, 1982
About Elly, Asghar Farhadi, 2009
Caramel, Nadine Labaki, 2007
Circumstance, Maryam Keshavarz, 2011
Divine Intervention, Elia Suleiman, 2002
Dolls, Diana El-Jeiroudi, 2007
Duma, Abeer Zeibak Haddad, 2012
Lemon Tree, Eran Riklis, 2008
Midnight Express, Alan Parker, 1978
Not Without My Daughter, Brian Gilbert, 1991
Offside, Jafar Panahi, 2006
Persepolis, Marjane Satrapi, 2007
Sex and the City 2, Michael Patrick King, 2010
Silences of the Palace, Moufida Tlatli, 1994

The Patience Stone, Atiq Rahimi, 2012
Unveiled Views: Muslim Women Artists Speak Out, Alba Sotorra, 2009
Vendetta Song, Eylem Kaftan, 2005
Voices Unveiled: Turkish Women Who Dare, Binnur Karaevli, 2009
Wadjda, Haifaa Al-Mansour, 2013
Wedding in Galilee, Michel Khleifi, 1987
When I Saw You, Annemarie Jacir, 2013
Where Do We Go Now?, Nadine Labaki, 2011
Women of Turkey: Between Islam and Secularism, Olga Nakkas, 2006
Women without Men, Shirin Neshat, 2009

Further reading

Gole, N. (1996) *The Forbidden Modern: Civilization and Veiling*, University of Michigan Press.
   Examines the complex relationships among modernity, religion, and gender relations in the Middle East, including the concept of veiling, an insightful account of the Islam–West conflict, and the ways in which issues around gender, national identity, and Islam are portrayed by Western journalists.
Gross, R. M. (1996) *Feminism and Religion*, Boston: Beacon Press.
   Focuses on the historical role of women in all major world religions, including the impact of feminist scholarship on the study of religion and theology and examines feminist spirituality.
Laviosa, F. (ed.) (2010) *Visions of Struggle: Women's Filmmaking in the Mediterranean*, London and New York: Palgrave.
   Ten insightful essays focusing on identity, gender politics, political resistance, and violence in relation to both cinematic representation and the lives and status of women in Mediterranean culture (Israel, the Maghreb, Turkey, France, Greece, Italy, Spain, the Balkans, and Syria).

22

AFRICAN "FIRST FILMS"

Gendered authorship, identity, and discursive resistance

Anne Ciecko

In 2008, Focus Features, the arthouse division of NBC-Universal, launched a sponsorship program called Africa First, a competition to support the pre-production, production, or post-production of short films by filmmakers based within the African continent. The name Africa First has multiple connotations, including an overture of prioritizing African filmmaking, placing it at the forefront. The phrase might also suggest positionality, a hierarchical logic informed by hegemonic perceptions of developing economies and culture industries of what is variously considered the Global South or the "Third World." The declared mission of the Africa First financial support and mentorship initiative (which lasted from 2008–12) was to cultivate "auteurist" talent, as well as international profiles of African filmmakers (Sanogo 2015). Through this framing, such films may also potentially register as inaugural to particular audiences (e.g. first African films screened/viewed from particular nations, novel iterations of particular genres, etc.), as they circulate in the international image market. The African First project thus begs the question: What's at stake in being an African film "first?"

This essay questions numbered or ranked discourses and assertions of pioneer status, in an exploration of challenges in theorizing filmmaking from Sub-Saharan Africa. I approach the subject via the larger frames of national/transnational/world/global cinema studies and African cinema and media studies, with an emphasis on the role of gender. Always already problematic, "first film" labels (such as first African film, first black African film, first film from a given African nation made by a woman, etc.) and "Third World" or "Third Cinema" constructions are further complicated when viewed through a womanist, decolonialist, or feminist postcolonial prism. I survey here some key scholarly and mediated constructions of African filmmaking by women, recognizing the complexities of discourses of African gendered authorship, modes of production and reception, and the politics of representation. In particular, I examine cases of women filmmakers with work that collectively spans five decades, and demonstrates female agency and discursive resistance.

Issues of historicity and pioneer identities

In the introduction to his book *African Cinema: Post Colonial and Feminist Readings* (1999), Kenneth Harrow writes that, "It is important to recognize the inadequacy of regarding

African cinema as having one clear moment of departure—say the creation of the 'first' African film" (1999: x). African cinema's histories have long been linked with legacies of colonialism and neocolonialism that problematize modes of production, exhibition, and distribution in the continent. As Roy Armes has pointed out, "[o]ne characteristic feature both before and after independence was the dominance of western films on screens throughout Africa" (2006: 143). Indigenous stories and aesthetic strategies, as well as negotiations of tensions with the West, pervade African cinema. Variously observed taxonomies and tendencies of African cinema such as those identified by African filmmakers/critics Ferid Boughedir and Manthia Diawara (as recounted and extended by Françoise Pfaff 2004) demonstrate the heterogeneity of African cinema from the 1960s onward, even while narrative themes and subgenres became increasingly codified. With European art cinema providing an auteurist model of Second Cinema, African cinema came to represent "the cutting edge of a politically and artistically radical 'Third Cinema,' which explicitly rejected the capitalist world order of the West" (Murphy 2012: 104). However, these First/Second/Third categories do not function hermetically and without contradictions, with assertions of authorship and communal identities, cultural syncretism and authenticity, and the incorporation of didacticism and audiovisual attractions across postcolonial African filmmaking. With the rise of Nollywood as a global player, and the video-filmmaking boom and digital revolution that has radically altered the film/mediascape in Anglophone Africa especially, it can be argued that a commercially viable cinema is "manifested" as "what may be called a real 'first' cinema ... which competes with the so-called 'First Cinema' of the West" (Ukadike 2014: 230). Whereas Ousmane Sembène once exhorted that cinema is the night school of the masses (Ukadike 1994: 97), Nollywood is now being heralded as a model of successful homegrown film with popular appeal, although often fraught gender politics. (Nollywood audience is discussed in Ikechukwu Obiaya's essay in this volume.) For instance, one of Nollywood's preeminent film producers and woman filmmakers, the charismatic impresario Peace Anyiam-Fiberesima, CEO of the African Film Academy and founder of the African Movie Academy Awards, has highlighted the role of Nollywood in modeling accessible and entertaining stories about Africans for Africans.

Filmmaking by women in the African continent offers other layers to African film histories that frequently recognize and metaphorize the late Senegalese writer/director Ousmane Sembène as the "father of African cinema" (Ellerson 2004b: 185), a genealogicallyinflected and gendered claim that connotes influence, mastery, and enduring reputation. Similarly, his prominent status as filmmaker is reinforced by the invocation of the West African cultural figure of the "griot," tapping into timeless oral traditions, histories, stories, memories, and popular conscience and consciousness (Pfaff 1993: 13–14). Sembène's first feature film, *La Noire de…/Black Girl* (1966) is considered a landmark of African cinema on the global stage and "one of the first significant anti-colonial documents of Africa" (Cook 2004: 822). It also provides an indelible portrait of a woman who refuses cultural enslavement, and is a canonical exemplar of what Lindiwe Dovey has called African "male-authored feminist cinema" (2012: 18). Yet while Sembène has been heralded as a proponent of woman-centered narratives, a critic of patriarchy, and an advocate of women's rights, his cinematic legacy arguably remains the most dominant auteurist voice of male-dominated Sub-Saharan cinema.

Fellow Senegalese filmmaker Safi Faye was inspired by ethnographic filmmaker Jean Rouch, who she met in Dakar and who cast her in *Petit à Petit* (1969), his Niamey, Niger and Paris, France set ethno-fiction film about African immigrants. Faye subsequently trained as an ethnologist at the Sorbonne, where she wrote a doctoral dissertation on Serer ethnoreligious society in Senegal, a matrilineal culture that has survived colonialism and its aftermath (Ogundipe 2007). Notably, she was also the only African woman at the time studying filmmaking at the prestigious École Louis-Lumière in Paris. There she formally learned how to use film equipment and began to make her own short work including *La passante* (*The Passerby*, 1972), about her experiences as an African woman in Paris, and featuring her own performance as she walks the city streets with awareness of the male gaze and fantasies of exotic otherness. Her first feature film *Kaddu beykat* (*Letter from My Village*, 1975), celebrated at international festivals, blends documentary and fictional storytelling, and integrates collaboration as it is grounded in everyday life, community, and real-life practices and problems. *Kaddu beykat* has been described as "the first full-length film made by an African woman" (Barlet 2000: 9). However, others have contended that while Faye may be "the best known African woman filmmaker internationally … she is neither the first African woman filmmaker nor the only independent African woman filmmaker" (Schmidt 1997: 174). Faye herself has stated in interviews that she ambivalently accepts the role of being a "first" filmmaker (Ellerson 2004a: 194), although she is not comfortable with the seemingly submissive designation "woman filmmaker": "I think I am a human being like the others" (quoted by Reid 2006: 202).

Screen sisters and intersectionality

Such intertwined identities are also addressed in Beti Ellerson's 2002 pan-African documentary *Sisters of the Screen*, a pioneering project to gather and share information about women and African cinema. (This project also includes a book authored by Ellerson, *Sisters of the Screen: Women on Africa on Film, Video, and Television* [1999], and a transmediated afterlife as an interview compendium, database, and blog through the online repository she established, the Centre for the Study and Research of African Women in Cinema: www.africanwomenincinema.org/.) In the film, Safi Faye is one of numerous African and African diasporic film directors, producers, and actors interviewed (from Algeria, Burkina Faso, Chad, Comoros, Cote d'Ivoire, Democratic Republic of the Congo, Ethiopia, Ghana, Guadeloupe, Kenya, Madagascar, Niger, Nigeria/UK, Senegal, South Africa, Togo, the United States, Zambia, and Zimbabwe) at the Festival Panafricain du Cinéma et de la Télévision de Ouagadougou (FESPACO) in Burkina Faso, Vues d'Afrique Film Festival in Montreal, and other venues. While Safi Faye and Sarah Maldoror are recognized as two filmmaking pioneers, fissures in African film histories and identities are revealed as the documentary recounts events at the 1991 FESPACO where African diasporic women were asked to leave a discussion session focusing on challenges facing women in the African continent. Maldoror, one of the first women to direct a feature film in the African continent (the influential 1972 film *Sambizanga*, about the war for independence in Angola), was among those asked to leave because she was not born in Africa. In *Sisters of the Screen*, Maldoror expresses commitment to the representation of African history and culture through filmmaking, and chagrin at the lack of recognition of her Africanness (her enslaved ancestors were brought to the Antilles from the African continent). Integrating the filmmakers' struggles to express unity despite the differences of black identities within and outside the continent, and in various national/cultural and exilic/diasporic contexts, Ellerson's film provides a polyphony of voices and perspectives. It respects the specificity of experience, while also implicitly supporting a community-building and more inclusive black cinematic "womanist" perspective. Womanism as a concept and practice of black independent filmmaking by women, as described by Mark Reid, builds on the work of

African American writer Alice Walker, distinguishing it from white Anglo-American Western feminism (1993, 1991/2006). In addition to Womanism, Nigerian scholar Molaru Ogundipe-Leslie's term "Stiwanism," referring to "social transformation in Africa including women," offers another important reframing (1994). In *Sisters of the Screen*, the interviewed filmmakers, producers, and actors are asked to consider whether or not they exhibit female sensibility or gravitate toward certain types of African stories because of gender identity. Multiple subjects assert that they deliberately make or choose films with strong female characters.

The identity designations applied to and employed by women filmmakers with roots in the African continent display national, continental, racial, geocultural, ethnic, tribal, and hybrid affiliations and identity constructions. Likewise, they negotiate complex relationships with terms like "pioneer," which resonate with associations of colonialism, indigenous suppression, effacement, and exclusion. In their films and professional personae, these filmmakers may find political and artistic value in adopting strategic essentialism/native informancy and strategic intersectionality as means of inclusion, inversion, or reclamation (Ukadike 1994/1999). *Sisters of the Screen*'s testimonials reveal African continental divisions, such as Maghreb and Sub-Sahara, that also impact the rhetoric of collectivity and individual subject formations. For example, a Tunisian-born director interviewed in the documentary, Najwa Tlili, who has resided in Montreal since the 1990s, describes herself in terms of "multiple things at once," as an Arab woman who also embraces more collective or pan-African continental identity as "part of who I am" in terms of psychology and perceived emotional proximity. Burkinabe director Cilia Sawadogo refers to herself as half black and half white, "above all a citizen of earth." Born and raised in Madagascar, with a Malagasy mother and French father, documentary filmmaker Marie-Clémence Blanc-Paes mentions the challenges she has faced as person of mixed race: "I was born of a colonial orgasm." Chantal Bagilishya, Rwandan film producer based in France and displaced through the impact of genocide and exile, discusses the ways that working on African film projects, as someone who has lived mostly outside Africa, helps her to "connect" with the continent. Nigeria-born Ngozi Onwurah identifies politically and emotionally as black, and embraces the love of her white mother and grandmother, but sees herself as "removed from them culturally and politically." She compares her own films, *The Body Beautiful* (1991), an experimental autobiographical film about her own youthful racial identity and relationship with her mother, and *Monday's Girls* (1993), a BBC-funded documentary about coming of age rituals of Waikiriki women from the Niger delta, as different ways to access realities. Through it all, she says, "I definitely do have a female sensibility" that informs filmmaking.

Ellerson's efforts to represent the voices of African women filmmakers, producers, and actors address the fact that African film narratives so frequently focus on women, and that women have been instrumental to the development of African cinema and canonicity, although they have been largely written out of its history. For example, she attempts to revalue the contributions of Mbissine Thérèse Diop, the actress who played the iconic Diouana in Sembène's *La Noire de …* (as well as a small role in Sembène's *Emitai*, 1971); Diop experienced a harsh reception in Senegal after the release of *La Noire de …* , as some considered her to be Sembène's property, or morally compromised from having acted in the film (Ellerson 2010). In addition to contextualizing production and reception circumstances, Ellerson's documentary film includes audiovisual clips of screen performances by women in films directed by women, increasing exposure to films that need to be more widely seen. In the larger realm of African film history, as Lindiwe Dovey has pointed out, the relative absence of women filmmakers and the underrecognition of their contributions are exacerbated by the unavailability of their films, as well as the lack of investment in the distribution and preservation of their legacies (2012: 15–16).

Gendered desire and subversive auteurism

Focusing cinematic content and perspectives on women, Safi Faye's use of experimental documentary strategies, film scholar Gwendolyn Audrey Foster contends, "avoids the objectifying, colonialist tendencies of much documentary and ethnography" (2005: 179). With Faye's 1996 feature and latest film to date, *Mossane*, she has made over a dozen films; although, compared with acclaimed male auteurs from Senegal or the African continent more generally, her films are not widely available. Discursive embrace of Faye within a larger community of woman filmmakers helps raise exposure to this cinematic author/ agency. Of fifteen women, she is one of two African filmmakers included as an interview subject (along with Tunisian filmmaker Moufida Tlatli) in the feminist documentary *Filmer le désir: voyage à travers le cinéma des femmes* (Marie Mandy, 2004). The film provocatively asserts that women directors devoted to expressing feminist erotic aesthetics tend to treat the female body more holistically, and that the body is key to understanding the cinematic language of woman's filmmaking.

As a nod to Safi Faye's own filmmaking, such as her thirty-minute film *Selbé et tant d'autres* (1983)—a portrait of a woman with an absent husband who constantly labors to support her family while telling her story—*Filmer le désir* displays Faye as a speaking and acting subject, sewing by hand while talking about themes that inform her filmmaking and life as a woman. While her fingers work thread and needle through cloth, she discusses the roles of women friends and peers in informing each other about women's bodies and sexual pleasure: "We don't keep it inside if it's good." Her filmmaking extends this sharing of women's embodied knowledge and experience. *Mossane*, represented through an array of clips and Faye's words, deals with the erotic education of the titular young Serer woman in early adolescence (who has reached "marriageable" age) and the awakening of her own sense of desire and destiny, even in defiance of the plans and expectations of her family. Faye's words (spoken French and scripted Wolof) and the integrated visual images from *Mossane*, as well as her own face and body-at-work, convey a sense of intimacy and candor. A self-described departure from her earlier films that incorporate more overtly documentary explorations of rural Africa, *Mossane* is a personal "first" that extends the audiovisual and narrative vocabulary of her filmmaking, which previously combined documentary and improvisational performance with reenactments and fictionalized voiceovers, into more seemingly conventional narrative form. Faye calls *Mossane* "an ode to the beauty and purity of Senegalese women." Scenes from the film shown in *Filmer le désir* depict women touching bodies and being caressed by the camera in ways that reinforce subjectivity and haptic tactility/sensory experience: women bathing each other, two female friends talking about sexuality, and Mossane's confidante Dibor engaging in lovemaking in the context of a loving marital relationship that is charged with passion rather than passivity (Foster 2005). In the documentary, Faye suggests that she met and overcame some resistance in the shooting of the scene with the woman on top of the man; the woman controls her own pleasure and stops when she chooses, to make herself available to talk with her younger female friend. The filmmaker insists that these sorts of images and expressions are part of the "African" experience: "All of this belongs to my continent, Africa."

Performative acts such as Faye's participation in this documentary about desire and women's filmmaking, propose an expansion of African cinema histories and identities, and inclusion in a larger discourse of world cinema and gender. In addition to screenings and awards at major festivals like Cannes, Berlin, FESPACO, and elsewhere, Faye's film-making has been acknowledged on multiple occasions at forums devoted to the promotion of international women's filmmaking; for example, with tributes at Festival International de Films de Femmes de Créteil in 1998 and 2010 (Gemmeke 2012: 369).

Nervous conditions of production and reception

Funding for Safi Faye's filmmaking has included support from the French Ministry of Culture and from television stations and cultural organizations in France and Germany (Schmidt 1997: 175). Her aforementioned documentary *Selbé et tant d'autres* was funded by UNICEF, and her fiction feature *Mossane* was supported with televisual funding from France, Germany, the United Kingdom, and Senegal. *Kaddu beykat/Letter from My Village*, representing peasant labor struggles, was banned in Senegal due to its criticism of the government; and her films in general have been more widely screened in Europe than in the African continent.

For Zimbabwean writer and filmmaker Tsitsi Dangarembga, also interviewed in the *Sisters of the Screen* documentary, "the most important thing is to communicate," whether by novel, play, poem, or film script. Dangarembga, the author of what has been called a classic feminist postcolonial novel, the semi-autobiographical *Nervous Conditions* (1988), established a reputation as an important critic of race politics, cultural imperialism, and patriarchal oppression and gender inequalities in colonial Rhodesia and postcolonial Zimbabwe (Khader 2013: 61). "I wanted," the filmmaker has stated in a televised interview, "to see a girl like me in literature" (Dangarembga 2015). The success of Dangarembga's novel set the stage for her formal entrée into filmmaking, including film production training in Berlin. Dangarembga is associated with multiple contemporary Zimbabwean film landmarks. She wrote the story for *Neria*, a film about a widow's property rights (Godwin Mawuru, 1993), the highest grossing movie in Zimbabwean history. She also directed (and has a writing credit on) *Everyone's Child* (1996), a film about young orphan siblings struggling to survive after their parents die of AIDS; the latter was widely considered to be the first film ever directed by a black Zimbabwean woman.

While Dangarembga's contributions to Zimbabwean cultural life, African cinema and literature, and global women's authorship have been celebrated, the circumstances of foreign donor funding and social message-driven storytelling that surround her entry into the Zimbabwean film scene have been subject to critique. Recruited as a Zimbabwean authorial commodity, Dangarembga wrote *Neria* as a commission from Media for Development Trust, a European non-governmentally financed initiative. While her story was developed into a script by white American screenwriter Louise Riber, and directed by the late Zimbabwean filmmaker Godwin Mawuru, the film was frequently viewed and received as authored by Dangarembga, as arguably a way to assert its feminist perspective through a postcolonial African lens: "indigenousness, locality, authenticity, and being an insider in Zimbabwean cinematic discourse" (Thompson 2013: 74). Zimbabwean cinema itself has struggled to express its own sense of national identity while grappling with the larger regional "dominant and socio-historical environment of post-colonial Southern Africa" (Mhando 2010: 205). The wide popularity of films like *Neria* and *Everyone's Child*, and the use of Dangarembga's name to promote them, speaks to the building of a domestic audience, but also to what some consider neocolonial systems/perceptions of the functions of films.

Everyone's Child was also problematic in the ways that funding determined its subject matter and didactic developmental approach. Dangaremgba has been quoted as saying that yet another AIDS movie was not the film she wanted to make. While she has relaxed her judgment of the film over the years, she is still critical of its mode of production:

> [W]here a Non-Governmental Organization (NGO) has an issue and wants to give money to a production house to make a film about it. ... The fact that I made *Everyone's Child* was a result of the way the film industry has developed in Zimbabwe. ... I personally do not agree with that type of filmmaking. ... I think the role of creative narrative is to engage the individual, and that's how the message comes out, through that engagement, rather than as a message that engages the individual.
>
> (Rooney 2007: 60)

According to Dangarembga, Zimbabweans were initially receptive to "development films" as a way to see themselves onscreen, but they have grown weary of heavy-handed didacticism without a fully realized artistic vehicle. As a way to redress the compromise of voice and authorship in Zimbabwean cultural production, Dangarembga founded the Institute of Creative Arts for Progress in Africa (ICAPA) Trust in 2009. She has also worked with Women Filmmakers of Zimbabwe (WFOZ) and the International Images Film Festival for Women (IIFF), and established her own production house, Nyerai Films, that sees as its mission: "to make the unspeakable speakable ... by presenting difficult topics in the form of a compelling narrative, with all the visual and narrative spectacle that makes film engaging" (Ellerson 2011).

Beyond the (afro)future to unlabeled possibilities

Like Dangarembga, Kenyan-born and -based filmmaker Wanuri Kahiu has criticized the need to work for hire in African filmmaking, without creative freedom. She describes making documentaries for NGOs just to make ends meet, and is critical of the ways film and television projects have to be issue-based (AIDS, female genital mutilation, etc.) to receive funding (Kahiu 2010).

Kahiu was one of five filmmakers selected to participate in the inaugural Africa First program mentioned at the beginning of this essay. She was one of three women in the cohort that also included directors from South Africa, Senegal, and Rwanda. Her accomplished short film, *Pumzi* (2009), produced with financing from Focus Features, Goethe Institut, and Changamoto Arts Fund in Kenya (established to help Kenyan artists create new work and build new audiences), became instantly known as "Kenya's first science fiction film." A view of the post-apocalyptic near future, *Pumzi* (the Kiswahili word for air) is set in East Africa after wars and drought have made water a scarce and restricted resource, and humans have been forced to live underground. The film centers on a strong female figure, Asha, a museum curator who is inspired by an illicit dream and a box of soil in which she plants a seed that starts to grow. She escapes after she is denied an exit visa to explore the forbidden world outside, and to further investigate possibilities of sustaining life. She offers her own body as a sacrifice to nourish nature in jeopardy.

In addition to writing and directing *Pumzi*, Kahiu established her own production company, Dada Productions, and directed her first feature film, *From a Whisper* (2008), about the effects on survivors and their families in the aftermath of the 1998 bombings of

US Embassies in Nairobi and Dar es Salaam. *From a Whisper* won an array of prestigious African film awards. She also completed a documentary, *For Our Land* (2009), about the life of Wangari Maathai, Nobel Peace Prize laureate, environmental activist, and Kenyan woman, for the South African subscription television channel, M-Net and its "Great Africans" series (Focus Features 2008).

Inspired by Kenyan environmentalist Maathi's predictions, *Pumzi* has a transnational pedigree. In addition to its international fiscal formula, the short was filmed in South Africa, stars a South African actress and model, and was produced by South African producer and special effects artist Simon Hansen, who had previously produced the short *Alive in Joburg* that grew into the science fiction blockbuster *District 9* (Neill Blomkamp, 2009), as well as Hannah Slezacek and Amira Quinlan of Cape Town-based production company Inspired Minority Pictures. Screened at the 2010 Sundance Film Festival's New African Cinema Program, *Pumzi* was included in the DVD compilation volume, *Africa First: Volume One*. Kahiu was given authorial rights to the film; and in addition to festivals, it has been widely circulated through video-sharing platforms and social media.

In this last portion of this essay, I briefly address some of the ways in which media convergence (Jenkins 2004) has enabled the discursive reworking of identity designations of African women filmmakers. In particular, I discuss the ways Kahiu has used TEDx platforms (speaking to African and global audiences) to reread her own work, especially *Pumzi*, and her status as an author.

At TEDxNairobi (July 2012), Kahiu negotiates transnational discourses of Afrofuturism as an African-American diasporic invention by replanting it in the locus of continental Africa. She discusses Kikuyu myths, fables, and folk wisdom from her mother; Dogon cosmology from West Africa; Vusamazulu Credo Mutwa's Zulu folklore and stories of extraterrestriality; Kenyan funk group "Just a Band" (the subject of a documentary by Kahiu); the book *Who Fears Death* by a woman writer, Nigerian-American Nnedi Okorafor; as well as the blending of the spirit world and reality in the creative work of Nigerian male author Ben Okri, and in everyday African life. She insists that as Africans, "because we can't reclaim our history, we are now trying to project our future" (Kahiu 2012). She finds Afrofuturism a pan-artistic phenomenon that also uses technology from outside the continent in inventive ways, as exemplified by the Kenyan website AfriGadget ("solving everyday problems with African ingenuity"), as well as her own film, *Pumzi*. In the latter, Kahiu uses kinetic self-powered energy and layered technology as modes of communication (more "efficient" rather than emotive—something the filmmaker does not view as progress). She employs a dystopic narrative to address issues in contemporary African and global society.

In Kahiu's second TED talk at the African-focused TEDxEuston event in London in February 2014, she revises her position on Afrofuturism. She expresses the concern that science fiction in African cultural contexts is not a new phenomenon and is inherent in African storytelling; and that the label, when applied to her work, fixes it and segregates it from the larger human experience. To insist that *Pumzi* is the first science fiction film from Kenya downplays the presence of futurist discourses in the country, and the African continent more broadly. Kahiu discusses the strategic use of nationality to elude unwanted alliances based on ethnicity or tribe during times of national crisis and violence (as in post-election era Kenya in 2007–8). She argues for greater accountability to the future and to nature (the message of *Pumzi*), to "the kind of Africa I will leave behind." She perceives the role of a filmmaker as a creator of utopias, with the need to fill representational voids (as in the lack of love stories with healthy relationships in African cinema). She resists nomenclature that registers as exceptionalism, stating that she is not that unique:

> [M]y name is Wanuri Kahiu and I'm a filmmaker. And I say I'm a filmmaker and not an African or an East African filmmaker or a black female filmmaker or a Kenyan filmmaker, because I'm a filmmaker. That's what I am.
>
> *(Kahiu 2014)*

As discussed throughout this essay, filmmakers such as Safi Faye from Senegal, Tsitsi Dangaremgba from Zimbabwe, and Wanuri Kahiu from Kenya have grappled with restrictive labels throughout their careers. Histories of world cinema, and of African cinema more specifically, have tended to put primary focus on the contributions of male auteurs from the African continent, through tokenistic or re-hegemonizing primacy narratives. More dialogic and transmediated approaches may lead us to more inclusive appreciation of the complexities of gendered authorship and intersectional identities.

Related topics

Jacqueline Bobo, "Black women filmmakers: a brief history"
Ikechukwu Obiaya, "Nollywood, female audience, and the negotiating of pleasure"
Sandra Ponzanesi, "Postcolonial and transnational approaches to film and feminism"
Priya Jaikumar, "Feminist and non-Western interrogations of authorship"

Bibliography

Armes, R. (2006) "Early Cinematic Traditions in Africa," in L. Badley, R. B. Palmer, and S. J. Schneider (eds.) *Traditions in World Cinema*, New Brunswick: Rutgers University Press, pp. 143–59.

Barlet, O. (2000) *African Cinemas: Decolonizing the Gaze*, trans. by C. Turner, London: Zed Books.

Cook, D. A. (2004) *A History of Narrative Film*, 4th edn., New York: W. W. Norton & Co.

Dangarembga, T. (2015) interviewed by Makosi Mutambasi on the ZBCTV talkshow, "Makosi Today" www.youtube.com/watch?v=lVre1FUbrk4. (Accessed January 15, 2016).

Dovey, L. (2012) "New Looks: The Rise of African Women Filmmakers," *Feminist Africa* 16: 18–36; http://agi.ac.za/sites/agi.ac.za/files/3_feature_new_looks.pdf; www.africanfilmny.org/2014/new-looks-the-rise-of-african-women-filmmakers/. (Accessed January 15, 2016).

Ellerson, B. (1999) *Sisters of the Screen: Women of Africa on Film, Video, and Television*, Trenton, NJ: Africa World Press.

────── (2004a) "Safi Faye Interview," in F. Pfaff (ed.) *Focus on African Films*, Bloomington and Indianapolis: Indiana University Press, pp. 194–7.

────── (2004b) "Africa Through a Woman's Eyes: Safi Faye's Cinema" in F. Pfaff (ed.) *Focus on African Films*, Bloomington and Indianapolis: Indiana University Press. pp. 185–93.

────── (2010) "Thérèse M'Bissine Diop: A Pioneer in African Cinema" "African Women in Cinema" blog (April 28); http://africanwomenincinema.blogspot.com/2010/04/therese-mbissine-diop-pioneer-in.html. (Accessed January 15, 2016).

────── (2011) "Tsitsi Dangarembga: Filmmaker, Writer, Cultural Activist," (July 28); http://africanwomenincinema.blogspot.com/2011/07/tsitsi-dangarembga-filmmaker-writer.html. (Accessed January 15, 2016).

Filmer le désir: voyage à travers le cinéma des femmes (Filming Desire: A Journey Through Women's Cinema, 2000) (video) Belgium/France: Marie Mandy.

Focus Features, "Africa First" biography of Wanuri Kahiu (2008 recipient); www.focusfeatures.com/africafirst/recipients.php?year=2008. (Accessed January 15, 2016).

Foster, G. A. (2005) "Experiments in Ethnography" in J. Petrolle and V. W. Wexman (eds.), *Women and Experimental Filmmaking*, Champaign: University of Illinois Press, pp. 177–91.

Gemmeke, A. A. (2012) "Safi Faye," in H. L. Gates and E. Akyeampong (eds.), *Dictionary of African Biography*, Oxford University Press, pp. 367–69.

Harrow, K. (1999) *African Cinema: Postcolonial and Feminist Readings*, Lawrenceville, NJ: Africa World Press.

Jenkins, H. (2004) "The Cultural Logic of Media Convergence," *International Journal of Cultural Studies* Vol. 7.1: 33–43.

Kahiu, W. (2010) interview conducted at CinemAfrica Film Festival in Stockholm, Sweden; www.youtube.com/watch?v=uJ_vL2j8m1Q. (Accessed January 15, 2016).

——— (2012) TEDxNairobi talk; www.youtube.com/watch?v=PvxOLVaV2YY\. (Accessed January 15, 2016).

——— (2014) TEDxEuston talk; www.youtube.com/watch?v=4-BIlZE_78. (Accessed January 15, 2016).

Khader, J. (2013) "'None of the Women Are at Home': Culture, Unhomeliness, and the Politics of Expansion in Tsitsi Dangarembga's *Nervous Conditions*," in *Cartographies of Transnationism in Postcolonial Feminism*, Lantham, MD: Lexington Books, pp. 61–90.

Mhando, M. (2010) "The Geography of Cinema—Zimbabwe," in G. Harper and J. Rayner (eds.) *Cinema and Landscape*, Bristol, UK/Chicago: Intellect, pp. 203–18.

Murphy, M. (2012) "Art, Didacticism and the Popular in Francophone West African Cinema," in L. Khatib (ed.) *Storytelling in World Cinemas*, Volume I, New York: Columbia University Press, pp. 104–14.

Ogundipe, M. (1994) Ogundipe-Leslie, *Re-Creating Ourselves: African Women & Critical Transformations*, Lawrenceville, NJ: Africa World Press.

——— (2007) "The Sacred and the Feminine: An African Response to Clement and Kristeva," in G. Pollack and V. Turvey-Sauron (eds.) *The Sacred and the Feminine: Imagination and Sexual Difference*, London: I.B. Taurus, pp. 88–110.

Pfaff, F. (1993) "The Uniqueness of Ousmane Sembene's Cinema," *Contributions in Black Studies* 11: 13–19.

——— (2004), "Introduction," *Focus on African Films*, Bloomington: Indiana University Press, pp. 1–11.

Reid, M. (1991/2006) "Dialogic Modes of Representing Africa(s): Womanist Film," *Black American Literature Forum* 25, No. 2 (Summer): 375–88; reprinted in L. Phillips (ed.) *The Womanist Reader: The First Quarter Century of Womanist Thought*, New York: Routledge, pp. 193–206.

——— (1993) "Black Feminism and the Independent Film," in *Redefining Black Film*, California: University of California Press, pp. 109–24.

Rooney, C. (2007) "Interview with Tsitsi Dangarembga," *Wasafiri* Vol. 2, No. 2 (July): 57–62.

Sanogo, A. (2015) "Certain Tendencies in Contemporary Auteurist Film Practice in Africa," *Cinema Journal* 54 No. 2 (Winter): 140–9.

Schmidt, N. J. (1997) "Sub-Saharan African Women Filmmakers: Agendas for Research with a Filmography," in K. W. Harrow (ed.) *With Open Eyes: Women and African Cinema*, Amsterdam: Rodopi, pp. 163–90.

Sisters of the Screen: African Women in the Cinema (2002) (video) USA: Beti Ellerson.

Thompson, K. D. (2013) *Zimbabwe's Cinematic Arts: Language, Power, and Identity*, Bloomington: Indiana University Press.

Ukadike, N. F. (1994) *Black African Cinema*, Berkeley: University of California Press.

——— (1994/1999) "Reclaiming Images of Women in Films from Africa and the African Diaspora," *Frontiers: Journal of Women Studies*, Vol. 15, No. 1, Women Filmmakers and the Politics of Gender in Third Cinema, pp. 102–22; republished in D. M. Robin and I. Jaffe (eds.) *Redirecting the Gaze: Gender, Theory, and Cinema in the Third World*, Albany: SUNY Press.

——— (2014) "Video Book and the Manifestations of 'First' Cinema in Anglophone Africa" in N. F. Ukadike (ed.) *Critical Approaches to African Film Discourse*, Lantham, MD: Lexington Books, pp. 229–47.

23

BLACK WOMEN FILMMAKERS

A brief history

Jacqueline Bobo

In 2004, Julie Dash's *Daughters of the Dust* (1991) was selected for inclusion in the National Film Registry. A resurgence of widespread interest in films directed by Black women soon followed. This latter-day renaissance included films such as the young women's sports anthem *Love and Basketball* (2000), directed by Gina Prince-Bythewood, the coming-of-age Black lesbian exploration *Pariah* (2010), directed by Dee Rees, and *Selma* (2014), directed by Ava DuVernay. Foreshadowed in the contemporary period are landmark films from previous eras. Even though widespread knowledge of Black women's films is subject to intermittent cycles of intense mainstream interest, their body of work extends back to the beginning of the twentieth century. This essay traces Black women's film history—primarily African American women—giving particular attention to those films and filmmakers that have advanced the understanding of this wealth of creativity (See Ciecko, this volume, for a discussion of African women filmmakers).

Dash's *Daughters of the Dust* was the first US film directed by a Black woman to be placed in commercial theatrical release. Two earlier filmmakers, Jessie Maple and Kathleen Collins, were among the first Black women to create long-form dramatic narrative feature films: Maple directed *Will* (1981) and Collins directed *Losing Ground* (1982). First films produced by major Hollywood studios that were directed by Black women include: Euzhan Palcy's *A Dry White Season* (1989, MGM); Leslie Harris's *Just Another Girl on the I.R.T.* (1993, Miramax); and Darnell Martin's *I Like It Like That* (1994, Columbia). Martin would later go on to direct other noteworthy films and television programs, including the Oprah Winfrey produced made-for-television adaptation of Zora Neale Hurston's 1937 novel *Their Eyes Were Watching God* (2005, ABC). Martin joined Black women directors Gina Prince-Bythewood, with *Disappearing Acts* (2000, HBO), and Julie Dash, with *Funny Valentines* (1999, BET), as being the first Black women to helm media adaptations of Black women's literature.

Yet another significant benchmark for Black women filmmakers occurred when Camille Billops' co-direction of *Finding Christa* (1991) received the Grand Jury Prize for documentaries at the 1992 Sundance Film Festival. More recently, Ava DuVernay earned the Best Director Award at Sundance for her film *Middle of Nowhere* (2012). Moreover, Academy Award nominations in diverse categories are represented by DuVernay with *Selma* (2014) nominated for Best Picture and Best Song (winning in the latter category). An earlier

Academy Award nomination was garnered by director Dianne Houston for her film *Tuesday Morning Ride* (1995, Showtime).

Black women's films are corrective narratives, a form of "representational reparations" featuring aspects of Black women's lives, histories, and experiences different from those evident in mainstream films. Unheralded political activists such as Ella Baker, artists of the caliber of Sweet Honey in the Rock, and stylized documentaries looking at child adoption are a few examples.

Early work in the US context

Contemporary Black women filmmakers adhere to this hallowed tradition of cultural opposition, with evidence of similar intentions extending back to the earliest days of the twentieth century. Traveling evangelist Eloyce Gist created two known folk dramas, *Hell Bound Train* and *Verdict Not Guilty*, in the 1920s. During this same period Madam C. J. Walker created visual records of Black women's work history. Walker developed her retail business around manufacturing and distributing hair-care products and cosmetics for Black women, becoming one of the first Black millionaires. As part of her enterprise, Walker oversaw the production of training and promotional films about her cosmetics factory. She also owned the Walker Theater in Indianapolis, Indiana, which she opened after being charged a higher price at another local theater because of her race.

Novelist and folklorist Zora Neale Hurston produced ethnographic documentaries in the 1930s. Hurston was trained as an anthropologist, earning an MA in Cultural Anthropology from Columbia University, working with the noted ethnologist Franz Boas. Dr. Eslanda Goode Robeson, another anthropologist, also shot ethnographic films in the 1940s.

Among those early Black women filmmakers for whom documentation exists of their contributions, two others have received recognition: Madame E. Touissant, the personal photographer to Booker T. Washington, produced at least one film about Black soldiers who fought in World War I and Alice B. Russell, worked closely and productively on films produced by Oscar Micheaux, one of the earliest Black directors of feature films.

Work from the second half of the twentieth century

One of the first mid-twentieth century films directed by a Black woman was Madeline Anderson's *I Am Somebody* (1970), a groundbreaking documentary about Black female hospital workers who staged a successful 113 day strike in Charleston, South Carolina in 1968, and formed local 1199B of the national union of hospital workers (see Hole, this volume, who discusses the importance of this film in relation to the origins of feminist film and theory). Anderson was one of the first Black women to serve as executive producer of a nationally aired television series, "The Infinity Factory" for PBS in 1978, and was one of the founding members of the prestigious public affairs program "Black Journal," which began in 1965 and aired nationally on PBS. Yet another Madeline Anderson achievement was being one of the first Black women to teach cinema studies at a major university, Columbia Graduate School of the Arts, and was mentor to several of the earliest Black women filmmakers, notably, Monica Freeman.

Monica Freeman continued the practice of mentorship. Several of her film crews were made up entirely of Black women, many of whom are now established veterans. For Freeman's film, *A Sense of Pride* (1977), the female crew included Ayoka Chenzira, creator of a groundbreaking animated satire entitled *Hair-Piece: A Film for Nappy-Headed People*

(1984) and director of the ambitious feature-length narrative *Alma's Rainbow* (1993). Monica's crew also included Debra Robinson, who would go on to direct the innovative documentary about Black women comedians, *I Be Done Been Was Is* (1984), and the fictional feature story of a young Black girl's turmoil, *Kiss Grandmama Goodbye* (1992).

Filmmaker, cinematographer, and author Jessie Maple occupies a unique position in Black women's film history. Maple became the first Black female union cameraperson, earning entry into the International Photographers of Motion Picture and Television Union in 1974. Maple self-published a book of her fight to join the Union titled *How to Become a Union Camerawoman: Film-Videotape* (1977). In the midst of a flurry of productions by Black women in an array of formats, including shorts, documentaries, and experimental films, Maple directed two of the first feature-length narrative films by a Black woman: *Will* (1981) and *Twice as Nice* (1989), and in 1982 founded a venue for showcasing the films of independent Black filmmakers, 20 West: Home of Black Cinema in Harlem. Other Black women who later earned union camera operator status include Michelle Crenshaw, Jean Young, and C.A. Griffith.

Dramatic feature narratives extended the ability of filmmakers to connect with the familiar theater-going experiences of specific audiences. Kathleen Collins, with her two feature narratives, *The Cruz Brothers and Miss Malloy* (1980) and *Losing Ground* (1982), consciously designed her films for popular consumption. Collins understood that the effective use of cinema had the potential to evoke in the viewer a certain depth of response, similar to that experienced with other forms of art. In her films, Collins was concerned with utilizing the grammar of film to resolve the structural and formal questions unique to film as a medium. For independent filmmakers especially, tackling issues of structure was necessary if audiences were to gain an appreciation of cinema as more than a commercial vehicle.

Collins embraced the principle that cinema, like literature, has a language. In her films, a prime consideration was amplifying the potential of the medium. She was trained in France in the mid-1960s, and then earned an MA in film theory and production from the Middlebury Graduate School. Collins was greatly influenced by French director Eric Rohmer (*My Night at Maud's* 1969) and worked closely with unorthodox Black film actor/director Bill Gunn (*Ganja and Hess* 1973), actor Seret Scott, and her former student/later cinematographer Ronald Gray. Collins taught at the City College of New York and is considered by many filmmakers the finest editor of her era. She learned her craft by working with John Carter, one of the first Black union editors. Collins worked as an editor from 1967 to 1974 at WNET-NY.

A cluster of long-form dramatic narrative films directed by Black women followed Jessie Maple and Kathleen Collins in the 1990s and early 2000s. These films include: Leslie Harris's *Just Another Girl on the I.R.T.* (1992); Darnell Martin's *I Like It Like That* (1994); Cheryl Dunye's *Watermelon Woman* (1996); Zeinabu irene Davis's *Compensation* (2000); Neema Barnette's *Civil Brand* (2003); and Cauleen Smith's *Drylongso* (1999).

Drylongso is an especially provocative dramatic film that has a unique relevance for today. Premiering at the Sundance Film Festival, it aired on the Sundance channel and was named the Best Feature in the 1999 New York Urbanworld Film Festival. Smith also received the Movado Someone to Watch Award at the 2000 Independent Spirit Awards. *Drylongso* starts with the idea of the "endangered Black male," then evolves into a parallel look at the perils inherent in young Black girls' lives. *Drylongso* illustrates the risks facing Black youth in a touching, poignant look at the lives of "endangered Black youth." Cauleen Smith exhibited her training and skill with an earlier short experimental film, *Chronicles of a Lying Spirit (by Kelly Gabron)* (1992), that was one of the first films by a Black woman to be shown and celebrated at the famed Flaherty Documentary Film Festival.

Another documentarist, devout activist Jacqueline Shearer, director of the dramatic re-creation *A Minor Altercation* (1977), a story of the heated events in Boston in the 1970s surrounding the battles over busing—having Black children traveling to better schools in white neighborhoods—created a different form of filmmaking altogether. At the time of the film, Shearer was working with Boston Newsreel, a collective of activists committed to bringing about positive changes in the community. The attempt with the film *A Minor Altercation* was to depict both sides of the conflict, that of Black and White participants. In a later media project, the "Keys to the Kingdom" segment of *Eyes on the Prize II* in 1989, Shearer rectified what she considered the deflation of the busing conflict in *A Minor Altercation*, for she considered the busing issue to be one of racism against Black people. In the "Keys to the Kingdom," Shearer emphasized the courage of the Black mothers, illustrating their position in the frontlines of the busing issue, fearing for their children's safety against hostile white mobs, yet fighting for the rights of their children to have access to the best education available.

Shearer's two segments of *Eyes on the Prize II*—"Keys to the Kingdom," and "The Promised Land"—featured the artistry of noted film editor Lillian Benson, the first Black woman admitted to the American Cinema Editors, an internationally recognized honorary society of film editors. Benson received a television Emmy Award nomination in 1990 for her editing work with Shearer on "The Promised Land," a program that focused on the last year in the life of Martin Luther King, Jr.

Shearer and Benson also worked together on the path-breaking television documentary "The Massachusetts 54th Colored Infantry," a 1991 segment of the PBS series *American Experience*. Shearer's program was a sorely needed re-examination of the lives and histories of Black soldiers who fought in the Civil War. Although the story was dramatized in the Hollywood film *Glory* (1989), Shearer relied on Black historians, such as the well-respected Barbara Fields, to correct the misrepresentations in the earlier film. Black people—men, women, and entire families—lobbied and fought for the right of Black soldiers to enter the war and be treated with respect. The existence of an active Black abolitionist movement in Boston in the nineteenth century was also highlighted in Shearer's documentary, establishing that Black people were active agents in the fight for the abolishment of enslavement.

Jacqueline Shearer's media productions exemplified her principled stance that political activism and media production were integrally intertwined. To further the goals of media that were developed with honesty and integrity, Shearer testified before the United States Congress in her fight for funds for independent filmmakers. Shearer subsequently became the first board president of the funding agency Independent Television Service (ITVS) in 1992. Shearer's social activism is essential in understanding the responsibility thrust upon early Black women filmmakers. In her keynote address to a 1992 conference exploring distribution options for Black filmmakers, Shearer emphasized the intrinsic goals of the makers, that films are without merit "gathering dust on the shelf," and that "the production of a piece is not finished until and unless it plays to its audience."

Significantly, Julie Dash's *Daughters of the Dust* exemplified Shearer's sentiments. Through the efforts of an independent publicity campaign mounted by Black women, the film circumvented traditional venues to appear before audiences where the content reso-nated with their experiences. It is a work drastically different in subject matter and style from previous cinematic representations of Black women. Dash's film privileges Black women's history, emphasizing how women have survived and overcome historical oppressive circumstances through their personal and collective resources. The film

Figure 23.1   Julie Dash's *Daughters of the Dust* (1991).

Source: *Daughters of the Dust*, Julie Dash, 1991.

chronicles a multigenerational Black family at the turn of the twentieth century as they work through the legacies of forced removal from their African homeland and the tortuous regimens of enslavement. *Daughters of the Dust* is an exquisitely composed film dem-onstrating the skill and expertise of its director (Figure 23.1).

Julie Dash has an impressive body of work that includes the award-winning 16mm short *Illusions* (1983), a black and white film set in the war years of the 1940s about a fair-skinned Black woman who is an executive at a Hollywood studio. *Illusions* was declared the best film of the 1980s by the Black Filmmaker Foundation. Dash also directed *Funny Valentines* (1999), an adaptation of a short story by Black woman author J. California Cooper. Other recent Dash films include *Incognito* (1999), *Love Song* (2000), and the made-for-television *The Rosa Parks Story* (2002), starring Angela Bassett.

Similarly, Dianne Houston's film *Tuesday Morning Ride* (1995) offers an engaging look into lives not seen before in mainstream film. At thirty-five minutes in length, the film—starring legendary actors Ruby Dee, Bill Cobbs, and Vondie Curtis Hall, and based upon the 1933 short story "A Summer Tragedy," written by Arna Bontemps—is loaded with meaning and importance. Houston's portrait of a loving, elderly Black couple courageously facing debilitating illness is unique in cinema history. Two particularly memorable scenes—Dee as the blind character Jenny solo dancing to Nina Simone's "I Want a Little Sugar in My Bowl," and young Black people (actors Erica Gimpel, Cree Summer, and Curtis Hall) and their seemingly benign disregard of Black cultural traditions—demonstrate the sure-handed direction of someone well-versed in rendering Black cultural experiences.

Houston went on from there to become the Executive Story Editor and one of the directors for Steven Bochco's television series *City of Angels*, the only prime-time network television series in 1999–2000 to have a predominately Black cast and production per-sonnel. Previous to this, Houston was the Executive Story Editor for the 1990 television series *Brewster Place* (produced by and starring Oprah Winfrey), and had directed episodes of *The Education of Max Bickford* and *NYPD Blue*.

Actor and director Kasi Lemmons opens her first film, *Eve's Bayou* (1997), with the voice-over narration of the adolescent Eve Batiste (Jurnee Smollett) telling of the summer her Louisiana family began to disintegrate: "The summer I killed my father I was ten years old." The highest grossing independent film of 1997, *Eve's Bayou* is enveloped in spiritu-ality, Black folk practices, and the little understood religion of Voudou. The film gradually reveals its secrets in a beautifully photographed, evocative visualization of the spiritual mysticism and haunting story of a Black family in the South.

As an actor, Kasi Lemmons is known for her roles in films such as *Silence of the Lambs* (Jonathan Demme, 1991); *Hard Target* (John Woo, 1993); and *Fear of a Black Hat* (Rusty Cundieff, 1994). After *Eve's Bayou*, Lemmons directed *The Caveman's Valentine* (2001), with Samuel L. Jackson as a homeless schizophrenic; *Talk to Me* (2007), with Don Cheadle as an outspoken "shock jock;" and *Black Nativity* (2013), a musical loosely based on the 1961 play of the same name by playwright and poet Langston Hughes.

Terilyn A. Shropshire, the second Black woman to join the American Cinema Editors, edited three of Lemmons's films: *Eve's Bayou*, *Talk to Me*, and *Black Nativity*. Shropshire also worked with Gina Prince-Bythewood, editing *Love and Basketball* (2000), *The Secret Life of Bees* (2008), and *Beyond the Lights* (2014).

Prince-Bythewood's *Love and Basketball* is one of the most successful films directed by a Black woman. A confluence of circumstances surrounded the emergence of the film: the continuing impact of Title IX of the Educational Act of 1972; the media recognition of women's basketball and women's soccer directly after women's teams won gold medals at the 1996 Olympic Games; the inauguration of the WNBA in 1997; and the enormous media attention given to women's soccer with the US national women's team winning the World Cup at the Rose Bowl in 1999.

The critical and economic success of *Love and Basketball* led to Prince-Bythewood being selected to direct the critically acclaimed HBO adaptation of novelist Terry McMillan's *Disappearing Acts* in 2000. Prince-Bythewood later adapted and directed Sue Monk Kidd's 2002 novel *The Secret Life of Bees* into the 2008 film starring Queen Latifah, Jennifer Hudson, Alicia Keys, and Dakota Fanning. Prince-Bythewood gained screenwriting experience in network television with the series programs *A Different World*, *Felicity*, and *Sweet Justice*. She was nominated for an Emmy Award for her direction of a 1995 CBS Schoolbreak Special "What About Your Friends." Her recent film is *Beyond the Lights* (2014), a compelling story of a young Black singer's turmoil about the demands of being a celebrity performer. These names do not present an exhaustive list but give a brief overview of the range of film and television work undertaken by Black women working in media.

Focus on documentary: social movements, cultural movements

Early in the hospital workers' strike documented in Madeline Andersons's *I Am Somebody*, the hospital administrator declared to a national publication that he would never give in to people "who never had a grammar school education." In the face of armed state troopers, the South Carolina National Guard and retaliation by Charleston power brokers and community members, the Black female strikers held fast until hospital administrators compromised to end the strike. The battle was fierce and for outsiders it appeared the gains were small. One striker was questioned by a white reporter who appeared puzzled by the enormity of the battle waged for such a minimal change. It is a remarkable moment in the film when the striker offers her dignified response: "We won recognition as human beings, for one. We won recognition as human beings."

Recognition of the capacity of everyday human beings at the grassroots level to fight against debilitating oppression distinguishes civil rights legend Ella Baker, the subject of the documentary *Fundi: The Story of Ella Baker* (Joanne Grant, 1981). Grant's film illustrates the kinds of issues central to Black history and culture that Black women documentarians are highlighting in their work. Ella Baker (1903–86) had a profound influence on several generations of social justice activists. In the 1940s, she was field organizer for the National Association for the Advancement of Colored People (NAACP) and earlier had helped to found the radical organization In Friendship, which provided economic support to Black people in the South who faced financial hardships because of their political activism and attempts to register to vote. Through her organizing efforts, Baker honed her progressive ideas about social change, group-centered leadership, and that those involved in social movement organizations can be empowered to act on their own behalf if they participate in the decision-making process.

Baker's privileging of "participatory democracy" rather than authoritarian heads of organizations placed her in conflict with the leadership of the NAACP and later the Southern Christian Leadership Conference, the group that came into being through In Friendship's collaboration. The values of group-centered leadership and sustained organizing were the principles behind the organization for which Ella Baker was the guiding force—the Student Nonviolent Coordinating Committee, which became the inspiration for other activist groups in the 1960s, such as the Students for a Democratic Society. Young activists who followed Baker's lead were enabled to themselves leave deep footprints on movement activities. Bob Moses, currently still active, offered the designation of "Fundi" for Ella Baker. A word from Swahili that refers to someone in a community whose ideals are realized by passing on what they have learned to others, symbolizes Baker's lasting effect on embryonic leaders.

Both Bob Moses and yet another Ella Baker protégé, Bernice Johnson Reagon—the founding member of the a cappella group Sweet Honey in the Rock—were awarded the prestigious and coveted MacArthur Genius grants for their lifelong contributions to social justice movements. Reagon lauds Baker as her "political mother," for Baker's example of recognizing the potential for resistance in every individual, helping her to understand the power of music as a potent force in generating concentrated, large-scale opposition to varied manifestations of injustice. Reagon's goal in the formation of Sweet Honey in the Rock was to provide the inspiration that motivated people toward collective action for social change. Reagon herself is the subject of Michelle Parkerson's documentary *Gotta Make This Journey: Sweet Honey in the Rock* (1983). In this film, Reagon states that Baker's influence made her realize that songs can do more than make people feel good. Reagon's first singing group, the SNCC Freedom Singers, became a "singing newspaper," keeping people at the grassroots level informed of the actions in the small cities and towns where Black people were fighting for their constitutional rights.

The power of Bernice Johnson Reagon and Sweet Honey in the Rock to influence generations of activists is given life in *Fundi* and *Gotta Make This Journey*. In fact, the original song that Reagon composed for *Fundi*, "Ella's Song," accompanies other political documentaries, including *Yuri Kochiyama: Passion for Justice* (1994), directed by Pat Saunders and Rea Tajiri, and *Faith Even to the Fire: Nuns for Social Justice* (1992), directed by Sylvia Morales and Jean Victor. Again, these connections highlight the intersections between Black women's lives and activism in the work of Black women documentarians.

An influential author and activist who intersected three critical social movements—civil rights, feminism, and lesbian and gay rights—is intimately remembered in *A Litany for Survival: The Life and Work of Audre Lorde* (1995), directed by Ada Gay Griffin and Michelle Parkerson. Interviews with insightful artists and movement organizers, including longtime public mover and LGBT rights advocate Barbara Smith, Black Arts era essayist Sonia Sanchez, fiery Black lesbian poet Sapphire, and memorable Black gay writer Essex Hemphill, offer loving testimony to the life of a woman who demonstrated that political and cultural activism can be effectively translated through cultural forms.

In a similar vein of social and political relevance, scholar and prison reform advocate Angela Davis asserts that cultural practices have a primary role in the socialization process. In the documentary *A Place of Rage* (Pratibha Parmar, 1991), theory translates into reality in both form and substance. Parmar is a British resident of Indian heritage who was born in Nairobi, Kenya, and is a founding member of Black Women Talk, one of the first Black women's publishing houses in Britain. Her professed goal in the making of the documentary was to preserve the legacy of Black women's contributions in the far-reaching struggles and triumphs of civil rights movements. Parmar's stunning achievement interconnects historical resistance movements with political, social, and cultural activism through the lens of portraits of the public personae and political/cultural histories of June Jordan (1936–2002) and Angela Davis. At the time of her death, Jordan was Professor of African American Studies at the University of California, Berkeley, and the author/editor of twenty-eight books, essays, and novels for children. Rage, for Jordan, was a compelling force for organized resistance. Jordan made clear in her writings and actions that "rage has lost its respectability since the 1960s. The thing that you had in the civil rights revolution was an absolute, upfront embrace of rage and a working with that." An absence of rage against persistent evils in society, according to Jordan, leads to despair and the plague of drug abuse "taking out our young people in droves today."

Angela Davis, from an early age a fighter against systemic injustice, grew up in the segregated South in Birmingham, Alabama. Davis was thrust into the international spotlight in the late 1960s and early 1970s, when she was removed from her faculty position at the University of California, Los Angeles because of her membership in the Communist Party. Davis later became one of the first women on the FBI most-wanted list, when she was falsely charged with murder, kidnapping, and conspiracy when guns registered in her name were found in the possession of Jonathan Jackson, brother of prison reform activist George Jackson, who sought to free Black men on trial in Marin County in northern California. Angela Davis was eventually found not guilty of all charges, as she states, because of organized international efforts on her behalf.

At the beginning of *A Place of Rage*, June Jordan speaks emphatically of the revolutionary changes brought about through Black people's freedom struggles: "Things have changed absolutely in my lifetime. And they changed because we made them change." Clear evidence of the force of group actions reverberates when Davis recalls her imprisonment and the organized efforts of people on her behalf and against political repression:

> As I look back on that era, the historical significance of my case was that people took the organizing seriously; got together, built committees all over the country, all over the world; sent letters and telegrams and petitions to presidents and governors and judges. In the final analysis, there was nothing the government could do to counter that force. And that is why I was set free.

As can be inferred from the examples offered in this essay, whether in political documentaries, dramatic narratives, experimental works, or shorts, Black women's films are vital forces of historical re-construction. With their body of socially conscious work created in an industry that is not necessarily always welcoming, the filmmakers themselves form an integral component of a cultural movement, a configuration of activists that seeks to transform the status of Black women in the popular American imagination. Through faithful, complex, and varied representation of Black women's lives and histories, Black women's films are simultaneously historical exegesis, inspiration, and a call to action.

Related topics

Anne Ciecko, "Africa's 'first films': gender, authorship, identity, and discursive resistance"
Kristin Lené Hole, "Fantasy echoes and the future anterior of cinema and gender"

Bibliography

Alexander, George. (2003) "Kasi Lemmons." In *Why We Make Movies: Black Filmmakers Talk About the Magic of Cinema*. New York: Harlem Moon/Broadway Books, 253–71.

Anderson, Terry M. (1995) *The Movement and the Sixties: Protest in American From Greensboro to Wounded Knee*. New York: Oxford University Press.

Baker, Ella. (1973) "Developing Community Leadership." In *Black Women in White America*, ed. Gerda Lerner. New York: Vintage, 345–52.

Bobo, Jacqueline. Telephone interview with Jacqueline Shearer, October 13, 1992.

Browser, Pearl. (1995) "The Existence of Black Theatres." *Take Two Quarterly*. Columbus, Ohio: National Black Programming Consortium, 19–21.

Davis, Angela Y. (1990) "Black Women and Music." In *Wild Women in the Whirlwind: Afra-American Culture and the Contemporary Literary Renaissance*. ed. Joanne M. Braxton and Andree Nicola McLaughlin. New Brunswick, NJ: Rutgers University Press, 3–21.

Foner, Philip. (1980) *Women and the American Labor Movement*. New York: The Free Press.

Franklin, Oliver. (1981) "An Interview: Kathleen Collins." *Independent Black American Cinema*, (program pamphlet). New York: Third World Newsreel, 22–4.

Gibson-Hudson, Gloria J. (1995) "Recall and Recollect: Excavating the Life History of Eloyce King Patrick Gist." *Black Film Review* 8:2, 20–1.

MacDonald, Scott. (1998) "Cauleen Smith." In *A Critical Cinema: Interviews with Independent Filmmakers*. Berkeley, CA: University of California Press, 300–8.

Maple, Jessie. (1977) *How to Become a Union Camerawoman: Film-Videotoape*. New York: L. J. Film Productions, Inc.

Mask, Mia. (1998) "Eve's Bayou: Too Good to Be a 'Black Film?'" *Cineaste* 23:4, 26–7.

Miller, Darryl H. "Patience Rewarded in Sensitive, Unhurried 'Disappearing Acts.'" *Los Angeles Times*, December 9, 2000, F2.

Moon, Spencer. (1991) "Behind the Scenes: A Pioneer in Public TV." *Black Film Review* 6:4, 27–8.

Mueller, Carol. (1993) "Ella Baker and the Origins of 'Participatory Democracy.'" In *Women in the Civil Rights Movement: Trailblazers and Torchbearers 1941–1965*, eds. Vicki L. Crawford *et al.* Bloomington: Indiana University Press, 51–70.

n.a. (1976) "A Lady Behind the Lens: Jessie Maple Cracks Tough Cinematographers Union in New York." *Ebony* February, 44–52.

Nicholson, David. "A Commitment to Writing: A Conversation with Kathleen Collins Prettyman." *Black Film Review* 5:1 (Winter 1988/1989), 6–15.

Payne, Charles. "Ella Baker and the Models of Social Change." *Signs: Journal of Women in Culture and Society* 14 (1989), 885–99.

Shearer, Jacqueline. (1993) "Random Notes of a Homeless Filmmaker." In *Available Visions: Improving Distribution of African American Independent Film and Video Conference Proceedings*, ed. Jacqueline Bobo. San Francisco, CA: California Newsreel, n.p.

Shearer, Jacqueline. (1998) "How Deep, How Wide: Perspectives on the Making of *The Massachusetts 54th Colored Infantry*." In *Black Women Film and Video Artists*, ed. Jacqueline Bobo. New York: Routledge, 109–23.

Solomon-Godeau, Abigail. (1995) *Mistaken Identities*. Santa Barbara, CA: University Art Museum.

Wilgoren, Jodi. "Algebra Project: Bob Moses Empowers Students." *The New York Times*, January 7, 2001, 30–2.

Wilson, Melba. "All the Rage," *The Guardian*, October 3, 1991, 19.

24

FAIR AND LOVELY

Class, gender, and colorism in Bollywood song sequences

Tejaswini Ganti

What do the international pop or hip-hop stars Akon, Snoop Dogg, and Kylie Minogue have in common? They have all recently been featured on the soundtracks of prominent Hindi films, more commonly referred to as "Bollywood" films. The word "Bollywood," derived by combining Bombay with Hollywood, has become the dominant global term to refer to the prolific and box-office oriented Hindi language film industry located in Bombay (renamed Mumbai in 1995). The Hindi film industry is aesthetically and culturally distinct from Hollywood, but as prolific and ubiquitous in its production and circulation of narratives and images. Perhaps the most iconic and distinguishing feature of popular Hindi cinema, when compared to other filmmaking traditions in the world, is the presence of songs sung by characters in nearly every film. Regardless of genre—from gangster films to war films, from murder mysteries to period films, from vendetta films to love stories—popular Indian films contain sequences where characters burst into song (often accompanied by dance) for a variety of reasons having to do with narrative, characterization, spectacle, or viewing pleasure. The near ubiquity of elaborately choreographed and lavishly produced song sequences has become the marker of Bollywood's distinctiveness in the global media landscape, leading Gopal and Moorti to note in their introduction to *Global Bollywood*, "Frequently remarked upon by insiders and always remarkable to outsiders, song-dance occupies the constitutive limit of Bollywood cinema" (2008: 1).

Sound and music arrived in Indian cinema with the release of the Hindi film *Alam Ara* (*Beauty of the World*, Ardeshir Irani), on March 14, 1931, at the Majestic Theatre in Bombay. Advertised as an "all-talking, all-singing, all-dancing" film, this production, with its seven songs, established music, song, and dance as staples of Indian cinema. The centrality of music has its roots in older performance traditions which influenced cinema. Historians of Indian cinema trace the distinctive form of popular cinema to theatrical traditions such as classical Sanskrit drama, various forms of folk theater, and the nineteenth-century Parsi theater (Garga 1996; Rajadhyaksha & Willemen 1999). All of these traditions tightly integrated music, song, and dance, with each element being essential to the entire performance.

To those unfamiliar with popular Hindi cinema, song sequences seem to be ruptures in continuity and verisimilitude. However, rather than being an extraneous feature, music and song in popular cinema define and propel plot development. Many films would lose their narrative coherence if the songs were removed. Some scholars have described the popular film as operatic where the dramatic moments "are often those where all action stops and the song takes over, expressing every shade of emotional reverberation and doing it far more effectively than the spoken word or the studied gesture" (Prakash 1983: 115). Hindi film-makers spend a great deal of time and energy crafting the song sequences, which have a wide variety of functions within a film's narrative, as well as providing the main element of cinematic spectacle (Ganti 2013).

Hindi film songs also circulate in a rich, complex aural economy, where they take on a life of their own, disassociated from any particular film (Ganti 2000; Gopal and Moorti 2008). Until the early 1980s, film songs were the only form of popular music in India that was produced, distributed, and consumed on a mass scale, and even today film music accounts for the majority—nearly 70 percent—of music sales in India (Ganti 2013). While film music plays a significant role in the social and cultural life of urban Indians, the presence of songs in cinema had often been the object of ridicule and criticism by the press, state officials, and cultural elites, and film music did not warrant much serious scholarly attention until recently (Adamu 2008; Booth 2008a, 2008b; Gopal and Moorti 2008; Sarazzin 2008). For years, Hindi films were dismissed by most scholars and intellectuals as formulaic and escapist, with the song sequences cited as the primary evidence. Even filmmakers are critical or disparaging of these sequences and thus, rather than being an unquestioned feature of Hindi cinema, the production of song sequences are sites of tension, debate, and intense negotiation among members of the Hindi film industry (Ganti 2012b).

So how does one make sense of the enthusiasm and willingness with which some international recording artists have participated in the production of song sequences in a variety of registers—from rapping in a promotional music video for the 2008 film *Singh is Kinng* (Snoop Dogg), appearing onscreen in a song and dance sequence in the 2009 film *Blue* (Kylie Minogue), to singing the playback vocals for leading star Shah Rukh Khan in his 2011 film *Ra.One* (Akon)? I contend that it is only after the Hindi film industry is trans-formed into "Bollywood"—a globally recognized and circulating brand of filmmaking from India, often posited by the international media as the only serious contender to Hollywood in terms of global popularity and influence—that these collaborations become possible. One of the most notable changes since the onset of the millennium is the way Hindi cinema and the film industry more broadly have acquired greater cultural legitimacy from the perspective of the state, the English-language media, and English-educated/speaking elites in India.

This increased cultural legitimacy is a result of Hindi cinema and the film industry having undergone a process of "gentrification" in the late 1990s and early 2000s (Ganti 2012a). Just as urban gentrification is marked by a vocabulary of progress, renovation, and beautifi-cation, which is based upon the displacement of poor and working-class residents from urban centers, the gentrification of Hindi cinema was articulated through a discourse of quality, improvement, and innovation, based upon the displacement of the poor and working classes from the spaces of production and consumption. The results of this gen-trification were evident in the film industry, the films themselves, and the patterns of distribution and exhibition. Hindi films from the mid-1990s to the mid-2000s exhibited a growing concern with wealthy protagonists, resulting in a near-complete erasure of the working class, urban poor, and rural dwellers who were once prominent as protagonists/heroes in them. Additionally, more and more films were shot in North America, the UK, Australia, and Europe rather than in India, so that India itself was increasingly erased from the films. Secondly, the film industry had become progressively more insular and exclusionary, so it became very difficult for people without any family or social connections to break into the top tier of the industry. Finally, a new geography of distribution emerged which valued metropolitan and overseas markets and marginalized equally populous but provincial markets (ibid.).

This chapter will explain the consequence of this gentrification process in the best-known feature of Hindi cinema—its elaborate and spectacular song sequences. The discourse of improvement in the context of song and dance is marked heavily by the use of the terms "international" and "global" to denote value. I argue that in the case of song sequences, appearing "global" or "international" is predicated upon both the erasure and foregrounding of certain gendered, classed, and racialized bodies onscreen. Before delving into this point, it is necessary to understand the transformations that beset the Hindi film industry and its filmmaking practices after the advent of economic liberalization policies following IMF-mandated structural adjustment in 1991.

The changing political economy and media landscape of the Hindi film industry in the 1990s

After the IMF-mandated structural adjustment program initiated in 1991, the media landscape in India changed dramatically with the entry of satellite television in 1992, and the increased presence of Hollywood films in their dubbed and original English versions. These modes of electronically mediated entertainment posed new challenges for the Hindi film industry, and critically reshaped its filmmaking practices to deal with the competition for audiences posed by television and Hollywood. Although the film industry initially perceived the new channels as a threat, it settled into a symbiotic relationship with satellite television. These channels offered filmmakers new avenues to publicize, promote, and market their films and served as another source of revenue, since they were willing to pay large sums for the telecast rights of popular films. Many of the satellite channels continue to be hugely dependent on Hindi films, film music, film industry news, celebrity gossip, film awards shows, and stage shows featuring film stars for a steady diet of programming. Rather than diminishing the presence of films in popular culture, satellite television has reinforced the dominance of Hindi cinema and its stars in the Indian media landscape.

However, Hindi filmmakers acknowledged that they faced competition from television as a rival outlet for films, and with the increased popularity of certain prime-time reality shows and soap operas, as an alternative source of entertainment. Producers asserted that the pressures on the film industry were different since the advent of satellite television because audiences could not be taken for granted. Aesthetically, films in this period exhibited vastly improved production values that included digital sound, foreign locations, extravagant song sequences, and lavish sets. Much greater attention and emphasis began to be paid to the clothing, styling, and physique of stars, as well as the overall production design of films. In order to entice audiences into theaters, filmmakers spent a great deal of money and effort to project a cinematic experience and spectacle unavailable on television. The song sequences became the key site for cinematic spectacle, with producers spending inordinate amounts of money on the visualization of songs—between 30 and 50 percent of their total budgets. Many films, regardless of their theme and plot, had what was referred to as an "item number"—songs with lavish sets, spectacular costumes, hundreds of extras and dancers, and special effects, costing millions of rupees. An article in the English-language news magazine, *India Today*, explained that film scripts were increasingly demanding a "mega song," and that "song sequences today are autonomous entertainment attractions crafted with money, sweat, and care. With the financial stakes being higher, producers, directors, and choreographers labour to create that one hit number, to make the box office jingle" (Chopra 1997: 80).

The expectation that song sequences could be the key to box-office success was a result of songs having become the most significant form of a film's publicity, as Indian television was packed with film-based programming, mostly around film music, ever since the onset of cable and satellite television in 1992. Songs were recorded before a film commenced shooting, and a few of the song sequences were shot early on in the production phase so that they could be used to sell a film to distributors as well as be broadcast on television. Even before a film had completed production, sometimes months in advance, its song sequences started airing on the numerous film-based programs on television, or appeared as commercials in between other programs. Thus, it was during this moment in the mid-1990s that film music took on an increasingly important economic function within the Hindi film industry. In addition to songs' marketing function, the sale of music rights became another source of finance for filmmaking as audio companies vying for the top production companies in the industry were willing to pay sums that amounted to as much as 25 percent of a film's budget, since albums from successful Hindi films sold in the millions (Ganti 2013).

The changes precipitated by the liberalization of the Indian economy also facilitated the growing internationalization of the production and distribution of Hindi films. Filmmakers started to increasingly shoot a significant portion of their films in Africa, Australia, Europe, and North America. While Hindi films had been circulating internationally since the 1930s, and been popular among African, Eastern European, Arab, and Central Asian audiences for many decades, it was only in the late 1990s that Bombay filmmakers were able to reap revenues from the international circulation of their films. Hindi filmmakers began to consciously seek wider audiences outside India, by opening distribution offices in the UK and North America, creating websites to promote their films, and dubbing and subtitling their films in a variety of languages in order to expand their markets beyond the South Asian diaspora. Hindi films also became a visible part of the media landscape in the West, evident from the premieres of films in prestigious international film festivals like Cannes, Venice, and Toronto and the screenings of films in mainstream cinemas such as London's Leicester Square or New York's Times Square.

After the introduction of satellite TV, Films became markedly different from their predecessors in terms of themes and content as well. The most visible contrast was the nearly complete erasure of class difference and the tremendous focus on wealth. All signs of poverty, economic hardship, or struggle were completely eliminated from these films and the protagonists, rather than being working class or lower middle class as they were in earlier films, were typically incredibly rich—usually the sons and daughters of millionaires. Whereas wealthy businessmen were frequently the symbol of exploitation, injustice, and even criminality in Hindi films from the 1950s–80s, by the mid-1990s they were depicted frequently as benign, loving, and indulgent fathers. In earlier love stories, youthful rebellion was the norm; young lovers ran away together. However, during the 1990s, the theme of compliant lovers willing to sacrifice their love for the sake of family honor and harmony became the dominant norm (Ganti 2013).

Although the Hindi films from the mid-to-late 1990s, with their valorization of patriarchy, filial duty, feminine sexual modesty, and upper-class privilege, were much more conservative than films from earlier eras, their visual, narrative, and performance style made them appear more modern and "cool"—at least according to the film industry and the English-language press in India (Ganti 2012a). In addition to erasing the representations of the poor, rural, and working classes from the films, the changes in Hindi filmmaking—cited by industry members and observers as modernizing and becoming more sophisticated and fashionable—have also been responsible for erasing the actual presence of working class men and women in the profilmic space. The next section discusses how this erasure is most apparent in the world of background dancers.

Upmarket bodies

In the late 1990s, working class men and women who worked as dancers in the industry started losing jobs to more elite entrants referred to as "models" (by producers and other industry personnel—referring to the fact that these men and women either had worked as models in the fashion and advertising worlds or would be able to because of their appearance), as producers and directors preferred fairer skin and generally a more "upmarket" look for their films (Joseph 2000). While the men and women who worked as dancers in the industry did so to support themselves and their extended families, men and women who were "models" tended to be wealthy or upper-middle-class college students who were working for extra cash to spend on their consumption and leisure activities. *Outlook* magazine's article, "Bodies to Nobodies" described the plight of the dancers,

> Theirs are the bodies being pushed out of the frame—a human scenery that is rapidly fading out on the rearview mirror. Nobody wants them anymore. Not the voyeurs whose visual palates are shaped in the age of Diet Pepsi and the MTV song video. Not Bombay's dream manufacturers, who thrive on a mish-mash of Hollywood aesthetics and an updated racism. For these dancers, already occupying Bollywood's margins, annihilation is at hand.
>
> *(ibid.)*

The more elite men and women did not belong to the dancers union, Cine Dancers Association (CDA), but earned four to five times more. The article stated that while dancers earned 472 rupees for an eight-hour shift, the "models" could earn as much as 2,000 rupees for a shift. Although producers were not allowed to hire dancers who did not belong to the CDA, increasingly this rule was flouted, and members of the CDA periodically resorted to invading film sets to drive out the non-unionized dancers; however, given their relatively marginal position and lack of power in the industry, such tactics were not the norm.

Economics and imagined audiences were posited as the reason for these changes. The article asserted that, "With the overseas market becoming cardinal to commercial concerns, filmmakers like Yash Chopra and Subhash Ghai have begun to feel that traditional film dancers look too third-world for their tastes" (Joseph 2000). The article quotes many dancers' experiences of being told by choreographers, producers, and directors that they were not presentable because they were not suitably upper-class looking—such upper-class appearance most commonly signified by fair skin. One dancer recollected about a top actor, "We've heard he keeps telling his friends that he does not like the looks and the smell of poor dancers. He wants white-skinned college girls who smell good" (ibid.).

The article states that the woes of the CDA dancers started with the film *Dil to Pagal Hai* (*The Heart is Crazy*). This film, directed by Yash Chopra and released in 1997, was a production that I worked on briefly as an assistant during my fieldwork in 1996. The film was set against a backdrop of musical theater and most of the song sequences were elaborately choreographed set pieces with a number of dancers. The dancers were all students of Shiamak Davar—a dancer/choreographer who had started a dance school in Bombay in 1992, and who had gained fame and recognition as a modern/contemporary dancer who fused jazz dance with Indian movements. *Dil to Pagal Hai (DTPH)* was Davar's first foray into choreography for Hindi films and his dancers were young college-aged women drawn mainly from the elite social world of South Bombay. During the shoot, I was struck by the contrast between these women and dancers I had observed on other film sets. The dancers for *DTPH* arrived at the set usually in their own personal chauffeured cars, with their mothers accompanying them (rather than on their own in auto-rickshaws or buses); they spoke English among themselves (rather than Hindi or other Indian languages); they came wearing Western clothes such as jeans, t-shirts, and skirts rather than *salwar kameez*; and they were overall much fairer-skinned and in better physical shape than dancers I had seen on other film sets. At this moment in the late 1990s, what I was witnessing was a gentrification of the background dancer community where expectations about body type, skin color, and comportment disadvantaged dancers from lower-income and non-elite backgrounds.

The documentary, *Personality*, (Chowdhry, 2007) delves into the plight of such non-elite film dancers by focusing on one individual, Rajesh Rajput, an auto-rickshaw driver from Faridabad, Haryana, who travels to Bombay with the dream of becoming a dancer in Hindi films. He finds a choreographer who takes him under his wing, but since the choreographer himself is struggling to get established, Rajput has difficulty finding employment as a dancer. The film depicts the struggles of the CDA dancers and quotes the head of the union, "Producers want background dancers who look as good as the hero and heroines. They want girls who are 5′ 6 and fair-skinned. How can people as good-looking as stars be in the group dance?" (ibid.). The film also quotes some other dancers talking about the changes that have befallen the industry,

> Before what used to happen, anyone would get a chance as a dancer—whether you were dark or short. Nowadays, they really pick and choose. Today it is like this—"You're dark, we don't want you; we want someone who is fair and tall." The film line has changed: the songs have changed, directors have changed, producers have changed, cameramen have changed, the skin color has changed, the theaters have changed, everything has changed.
>
> *(ibid.)*

Rajput keeps losing out on assignments because he does not have the requisite "personality"— which the film defines as a Bollywood colloquialism referring to all aspects of male physical appearance such as height, weight, and skin color. Rajput states, "No one has a problem with my work, but sometimes they have a problem with my skin color, especially the last few years, choreographers have been getting pickier" (ibid.). Disillusioned, he finally gives up on his quest and goes back to his hometown, where he sets up a small business.

Another trend, which gained in prominence around the millennium, was to do away with Indian background dancers altogether, and use identifiably white Euro-American women as background dancers instead. The trend began with films that were shot in Europe and Australia, ostensibly because they were set there. However, by the mid-2000s, white women were showing up as background dancers in songs set in India as well, even in films whose narrative and style were completely local—for instance, *Lage Raho Munna Bhai* (*Keep It Up Munna Bhai*, Hirani, 2006), a film about a lovable gangster in Bombay who has visions of Mahatma Gandhi, and reforms the city's public culture through Gandhian techniques of nonviolence. The first song in the film has a sequence where *Munna Bhai* (the gangster protagonist) is dancing on a double decker bus winding its way through the streets of Bombay, accompanied by a dozen scantily clad white women dancers. An issue of the trade magazine *Film Information* in 2009 had an advertisement featured on its inside back cover of five white women wearing bikini tops, short, tight shorts, and high heels, announcing "For Film Shooting International Dancers & Models from Australia and UK available in India at Affordable Costs" (See Figure 24.1). One can notice the prominent emphasis of the terms "international" and "models" in the title of the advertisement.

Figure 24.1 Print ad for white Bollywood dancers.

Source: Film Information, Mumbai, 2009.

The popularity of foreign white dancers within the film industry is also based on ste-reotypes about white women's sexuality, specifically the sense that white women have different standards of modesty than Indian women. One of the subjects of the documentary *Beyond Bollywood* (Dow & Muchhala 2013), Pooja Kasekar, a young woman from Pune who moves to Mumbai to become a dancer within the film industry, explains the popularity of white women dancers in the industry in this manner: "Now there is such a demand for foreign girls because they agree to wear anything, any short clothes. Indian girls aren't as open and won't agree to wearing bikinis and panties on set" (ibid.)." Interestingly, at this point in the film, Pooja is on a film set shooting a song sequence while wearing the same short shorts and midriff baring top as the Eastern European lead dancer, Irena, whom she refers to as an "item girl," indicating her leading role in the elaborately choreographed, and frequently sexually charged spectacular song sequences termed as "item numbers" within film industry parlance. More than sartorial difference, what seems to be at play is skin color and varying perceptions of gender norms, as the choreographer asserts, "I had planned to cast Pooja as the lead for this song, but something happened and the director wanted some other look and that he got in Irena" (ibid.). From the film, the only difference visibly apparent between Pooja and Irena is their skin color, rather than their costumes or body types.

The intense colorism that plagues Indian society, where fair skin is extremely valorized as the ideal of beauty, manifests itself most blatantly in the Hindi film industry where, throughout much of its history, actresses have been disproportionately lighter skinned than the majority of the population. As the dominant glamor industry in India, Bollywood has prized actresses more for their appearance than their acting ability and currently, white women—usually models—from the UK, Europe, North America, South America, or Australia, or light-skinned women of mixed South Asian and Euro-American parentage, are able to garner roles as dancers and/or actresses despite their utter lack of film experience or knowledge of the Hindi language. Since 2003 onward, with the growing awareness of and interest in Bollywood, a slew of foreign women (Elli Avram, Nargis Fakhri, Jacqueline Fernandes, Yana Gupta, Amy Jackson, Katrina Kaif, Hazel Keech, Sunny Leone, Giselle Monteiro, and Evelyn Sharma, among others) have been showing up in India for modeling assignments and then inevitably making their way into the Hindi film industry, where some of them, like Kaif and Fernandes, have become very successful actresses.

The valorization of white female bodies becomes even more apparent when comparing the prominent participation of the three international recording stars—two African-American men and one white Australian woman—named at the beginning of this chapter. Of the three, only Kylie Minogue appears onscreen in a song sequence within the main narrative of *Blue*. While Snoop Dogg appears in a song that plays during the end credits of the film *Singh is Kinng* (Bazmee 2008), Akon is only heard and not seen in the film *Ra.One*, despite a great deal of favorable and laudatory press coverage about his presence in India, and his collaboration with the makers of the film. Whereas Minogue appears in a nightclub sequence, singing (and dancing) in English, Akon actually sings a song in Hindi, to which the lead actor, Shah Rukh Khan, subsequently lip-synchs.

White skin as a passport to Bollywood is extremely gendered, however. Foreign men, white or otherwise, are not able to gain inroads into the industry either as actors or as background dancers. The patriarchal nature of the film industry enables women without any kinship and social connections to the film world to gain entry because the success or failure of a film is not perceived to be dependent upon the lead actress. Like Hollywood, male stars wield a great deal more power in the Hindi film industry than their female counterparts.

Male stars are perceived as having greater box-office drawing power and thus are paid more and hired first. The prevailing attitude among distributors and producers is that actresses do not "open" a film, that is, they do not pull in the crowds and generate the sold-out shows that guarantee a successful first weekend at the box office. Thus, the narrative thrust of films and the financing structures of the industry are wholly oriented around the male star, and hence the industry is much less welcoming of actors who are unknown entities. For instance, by 2008, a little over 60 percent of the actors who appeared in leading roles hailed from film families; of the top ten male stars in the industry—those actors who generated the biggest box-office revenues and were the most sought after by producers—seven were either second or third generation members of the film industry.

Conclusion

While Bollywood is frequently celebrated outside of India for its colorful song sequences, and its aesthetic and narrative style is posited as a refreshing alternative to Hollywood, this chapter has delved into the internal hierarchies and prejudices of the Hindi film industry. It points out how international interest and acclaim is a symptom of processes of exclusion that I have characterized as gentrification whereby certain kinds of bodies are erased from the profilmic space. The growing international profile of Bollywood renders it as a site of tremendous opportunity and possibility—even for those who are unfamiliar with Hindi or the local context—but it is so for only a select few who conform to the longstanding beauty ideals in India that valorize fair skin.

Related topics

Sandra Ponzanesi, "Postcolonial and transnational approaches to film and feminism"
Erica Levin, "Class/Ornament: cinema, new media, labor-power, and performativity"

References

Adamu, A. (2008) "The Influence of Hindi Film Music on Hausa Videofilm Soundtrack Music," in M. Slobin (ed.), *Global Soundtracks: Worlds of Film Music*. Middletown, CT: Wesleyan, pp. 152–76.

Booth, G. (2008a) "The Bollywood Sound," in M. Slobin (ed.), *Global Soundtracks: Worlds of Film Music*. Middletown, CT: Wesleyan, pp. 85–113.

—— (2008b) *Behind the Curtain: Making Music in Mumbai's Film Studios*. New York: Oxford University Press.

Chopra, A. (1997) "A Musical Explosion," *India Today*, March 15: 80–5.

Chowdhry, V. (2007) *Personality*. United States: Dakoit Films, 85 min.

Dow, A. and R. Muchhala (2013) *Beyond Bollywood*. United States: Bollywood Project LLC, 58 min.

Ganti, T. (2000) "Casting Culture: The Social Life of Hindi Film Production in Contemporary India." New York: New York University; unpubl. PhD dissertation. Department of Anthropology.

—— (2012a) *Producing Bollywood: Inside the Contemporary Hindi Film Industry*. Durham, NC: Duke University Press.

—— (2012b) "No Longer a Frivolous Singing and Dancing Nation of Movie-Makers: The Hindi Film Industry and its Quest for Global Distinction." *Visual Anthropology* 25:4, 340–65.

—— (2013) *Bollywood: A Guidebook to Popular Hindi Cinema*, 2nd edn. London: Routledge.

Garga, B. D. (1996) *So Many Cinemas*. Mumbai: Eminence Designs.

Gopal, S. and S. Moorti (eds.) (2008) *Global Bollywood: Travels of Hindi Song and Dance*. Minneapolis: University of Minnesota Press.

Joseph, M. (2000) "Bodies to Nobodies," *Outlook Magazine*, January 4.

Prakash, S. (1983) "Music, Dance and the Popular Films: Indian Fantasies, Indian Repressions," in A. Vasudev and P. Lenglet (eds.), *Indian Cinema Superbazaar*. New Delhi: Vikas, pp.114–18.

Rajadhyaksha, A. and P. Willemen (eds.) (1999) *Encyclopaedia of Indian Cinema*. Revd. edn. London: British Film Institute.

Sarazzin, S. (2008) "Song from the Heart: Musical Coding, Emotional Sentiment, and Transnational Sonic Identity in India's Popular Film Music," in A. Kavoori and A. Punathambekar (eds.), *Global Bollywood*. New York: New York University Press, pp. 203–22.

25

WHAT WAS "WOMEN'S WORK" IN THE SILENT FILM ERA?

Jane Gaines

Not surprisingly, 1970s Second Wave feminism was immediately interested in the sociology of workplace gender typing. For the feminist film festivalgoer as well as the scholar at the time, the test of the crack in the "glass ceiling" became the silent era female director. She was epitomized in an early publication on women and film by the French Germaine Dulac (Figure 25.1) (Van Wert 1977), the American Lois Weber (Figure 25.2) (Kozarski 1977), and the French immigrant to the US Alice Guy Blaché (Figure 25.3) (Peary 1977). Although later the Italian director/producer Elvira Notari was brought to our attention (Bruno 1993), the American 1910s and 1920s came to stand as a kind of "golden era" of female directors, writers, and producers (Mahar, 2006). As early as the 1970s, silent film researcher Anthony Slide argued that "there were more women directors at work in the American film industry prior to 1920 than during any period of its history" (Slide 1977: 9). For another two decades, Slide's estimate haunted feminism and film. When in the 1990s another generation of scholars turned back to historical research after a twenty year lull, they found not only greater numbers of women in emerging international film industries but also examples of how these women wielded more influence than was first assumed (Williams 2014; Stamp 2015; Gaines and Vatsal 2013). While today we celebrate these women, we still cannot stop there because the numbers themselves tell us too little. First, the numbers only hint at the fluid work conditions at the emergence of cinema when, before labor became so strictly "gendered," almost anyone could do any job. Second, the enumeration of directors deflects attention from the number of women in other influential jobs such as writing and producing. Third, numbers eclipse the silent era indecision about the capacity of women to direct motion pictures. More women than men had this question put to them by journalists and they expressed differing opinions. Some claimed that women were "just as good" as men; others insisted that directing was "men's work" and that therefore women could not handle the job.

In the US and Europe, over the silent era, from 1896 until the coming of sound around 1926–7, the women's capability issue intensified. In the first decade, one finds arguments for the "natural" capacity or special "feeling" of women for making moving images, and antithetically arguments for the "unnaturalness" of women directing. A typical defense

Figure 25.1 Germaine Dulac, writer/director.

comes from American serial queen Kathlyn Williams, who in 1914 herself directed one motion picture film. Relying on the most popular of gendered values, she says that

> Women can direct just as well as men, and in the manner of much of the planning they often have a keener artistic sense and more of an eye for detail—and often it is just one tiny thing, five feet of film maybe, that spoils a picture, for it is always the little things that go wrong that one remembers.
>
> *(As quoted in Slide 1977: 102–3)*

As Antonia Lant describes it, by the 1920s the question as to whether women were constitutionally capable of directing motion pictures became subject to "debate" (Lant 2006: 562). One of the most negative positions was taken by British screenwriter Nerina Shute in 1929: "It is pathetically obvious that women can't produce films," she asserts, evidence of which she thinks are films made by British director Dina Shurey, which she judges to be "appalling." Women aren't "fitted for direction," she thinks, but

> A woman of ideas can be invaluable to a director, lending all sorts of feminine subtleties to his work, but *she cannot do the work herself.* You see, a really fine director is a mixture of artist and business magnate. He must have a commercial brain, and he must be able to handle men. Physically, he must endure all kinds of hardships and mentally he must be a creative genius.
>
> *(Shute 2006: 668)*

Figure 25.2   Lois Weber, actress/writer/director/producer.

A century later, the reasons men give for not hiring women indicate unchanged assumptions about women's fitness for a job still defined as too difficult for them. "Our actors are hard on women," one contemporary male director is reported to have said (Buckley 2015: C5).

Now let us stand back from this hundred-year-old "debate" about female directors to think about ways of approaching new research on women working in the first years of emerging national motion picture industries. Consider, for instance, how new research points to women at the advent of cinema stepping into all kinds of work. Imagine occupations. Then, imagine in the globalization that brought social upheaval to Europe as well as to Latin America, South Asia, and the Middle East, women, often with men, starting companies, stepping into the role of producer. Imagine further women, without men, writing, directing, and producing. This rich area still to-be-excavated is a testing ground for feminist theories of gender and these theories are themselves evolving. That is, these theories are in transition from an earlier *sociological* approach, including the gendering of work, to the more current *theory of feminist history* approach (Dall'Asta and Gaines 2015). One strand of this theory follows historian Joan W. Scott, who has argued that gender as a historical category remains an open "question" (Scott 2008). This theoretical approach to historical cases begins with the assumption that "women" has not always meant the same

Figure 25.3   Alice Guy Blaché, writer/director/producer.

thing historically. Or, to put it another way, "women" are not now what "women" once were. In these terms, the silent era "debates" about women's capabilities are the epitome of gender "questioned."

The *sociological* approach still supports the case feminists make against gender inequality in the workplace. That basic case, based on a grasp of race as well as gender hierarchies, is supported today by evidence, but in the 1910s, women had nothing more than a "hunch" that they were treated differently, if they had that at all. Today we look for evidence of discriminatory hiring as well as promotion; in the silent era, work experience led a few, like Kathlyn Williams quoted above, to argue that women were "just as good as" and hints that in a few respects women had the edge. But the case for "even better than" men was most strongly made by writers. For instance, US screenwriter Clara Beranger, referring to 1918 film releases, is quoted as saying that there were more "writers" who were women, implying that women were the *real* writers, that is, even better writers than men (Beranger 1918: 1128) (Figure 25.4). Thus an idea of female superiority and achievement was there in the silent era and available for another generation to claim again. Not surprisingly, Slide's argument that the ratio of female to male film directors was proportionately larger in the silent era than it has been in the century since has been recruited on behalf of the position that if women "had been" important directors, they yet "could be" in the future. Indeed, this historical comparison underwrote the 1970s US women's film festivals (Rich 1998: 29–39). Celebrating "forgotten" female directors advanced the idea that if women were as capable as men in the silent era, they still were, and that, therefore, they *should be* given a chance to

Figure 25.4   Clara Beranger, screenwriter.

take plum jobs as film and television industry directors. Finally, the 1970s *sociological* assumption added another rationale for more equal female as well as minority representation in numbers—the ideal of a more "representative" representation on the screen. Women, it was assumed, could be depended on to create popular screen dramas with female roles enlarged and transformed.

The *sociological* approach, however, has its limitations, especially as it encourages screen role models and their often unspoken rationale—the "positive image" ideal. Here, the "real image" of the marginalized could be held up to disbelieving exploiters of women and mirrored back as idealized selves. Putting to rest the expectation that changing popular representations can transform beliefs, Anthony K. Appiah, referencing the NAACP "image awards," argues that it is never certain that "a score of movies with good Negroes in them will change the mind of a single bigot" (Appiah 1993: 84). Corollary to the vain hope that popular images will change consciousness is the idea that only "real and true" representations can counter mainstream misrepresentations. But there is no popular representation without misrepresentation, by which we mean that popular images are by definition fantastically broad as well as sketchily drawn. Tribute to the importance of the earlier 1970s excavation moment but also testimony to the exhaustion of "positive images" sociology is the experimental film *The Watermelon Woman* (dir. Cheryl Dunye 1996). As a subtle critique of the search for "real" African American female historical counterparts, director Dunye invents a Black female actress. Dunye's invention, Fae Richards, discovered as a lost forerunner, even has an affair with a white female director who Ruby Rich thinks resembles lesbian film director Dorothy Arzner (Rich 2013: 67).

The film's narrative of archaeological discovery is replete with faux archival documents and distressed film footage. Thus *The Watermelon Woman* re-enacts while critiquing the genealogical search, or legacy based on a family tree analogy. Dunye's critique of the "positive image" ideal finally reminds us that the historical search for foremothers is always a strategic invention, even when used for progressive ends. Our archival search for empirical evidence is always a predetermined search, and what we discover are not "real" ancestors but idealized ones who may resemble the selves we most want to be today.

Then and now

A century later in the US, women are still not getting top directing jobs. The fact that only 4 percent of the industry's top-grossing motion picture films between 2003 and 2015 were directed by women dramatizes the persistence of gender inequity. Because today workplace discrimination on the basis of gender is illegal, the American Civil Liberties Union of Southern California in 2015 asked the US Justice Department to investigate Hollywood hiring practices that might violate the federal Equal Employment Opportunity statute (Buckley 2015: C1). But the argument that women *had been* directors in the first decades does not necessarily make the case that women *should be* directors today, just as producing more culture written, directed, and produced by women does not guarantee that we will "see ourselves as we wish to be seen" on the big screen. While the contrast between then and now dramatizes the intransigence of gender bias, there are more important reasons to return to the advent of cinema.

Joan W. Scott, updating her aforementioned formulation, elaborates:

> Gender is a useful category only if differences are the question, not the answer, only if we ask what "men" and "women" are taken to mean wherever and whenever we are looking at them, rather than assuming we already know who and what they are.
>
> *(2009: 48)*

We are thus cautioned to analyze ourselves in our moment as well as to take women's different selves in different times into consideration. Applying this approach to his study of female directors who worked at Universal Pictures in the 1910s, Mark Garrett Cooper cautions against feminist foregone conclusions, proposing instead that the historian consider the "puzzle" of sexism in the workplace, and asking us to think of some factors that might even override gender discrimination (avoiding feminist foregone conclusions is also discussed in this volume in J. E. Smyth's essay on female Hollywood studio editors). As he says of historical comparison: "Divisions of labor in the 1910s and in the 2010s might both be sexist and yet pose very different challenges for those seeking to transform or maintain them." This angle on historical research, he goes on, has contemporary implications, because, as he argues,

> to understand sexism as a puzzle is to deprive patriarchal culture of its sense of inevitability. It is to acknowledge that gender has a history and therefore a future, and it also reminds us of the contingency that dogs any historical explanation: no matter how pellucid the unfolding causes and consequences, events might have gone otherwise.
>
> *(Cooper 2010: xxii)*

Sex to gender

Now let us see what else a *theory of feminist history* can yield. Imagine then a time before feminist theory, when commentators groped for explanations as to why women could or could not command respect or operate the new technology—cameras and projectors. Consider the moment when "sex" was the only available term, before "gender" became the term preferred over "sex," decades before "gender" was introduced by means of Gayle Rubin's "sex/gender system" in 1975 (Rubin 2011: 34–5). Surprisingly, for a short time, we find an apparent obliviousness of what we now see as a gendered division of labor. Actress Olga Petrova, who in 1917 founded Petrova Pictures, is quoted as saying about directors that initially "the idea of their sex didn't occur to me" (Petrova 1986: 110). That is, "gender difference" as a way of explaining differential treatment was not yet available to women as a group. Strange as it may seem, many "women" in the 1910s would not have thought of themselves professionally as part of "women" as a group. As a working hypothesis, we might say that one of the ways that women writers learned that they were "women writers" was as they were recruited to write stories that would appeal to female audiences. As Shelley Stamp's research shows, the industry that later excluded women writers and directors originally sought out directors and writers like Lois Weber as a strategy for making moving pictures respectable. Women would help to draw in women (Stamp 2015). Perhaps it was also female fan magazine writers and early female film critics who encouraged women to see themselves as women. Italian critic Matilda Serao, aligning herself in 1916 with the female spectator, declares that she, too, is that spectator, and more precisely,

> it is a spectatrix (spettatrice) speaking to you, a spectatrix who now asks herself ... the reasons for her tears, her smile, her boredom ... a creature of the crowd, it is she whom you should move, whom you should please.
>
> *(Serao 2006: 99)*

Although some women were learning to think of themselves as a group, under some workplace circumstances, women (and sometimes men) could be oblivious of gender distinction and bias because of conditions that trumped the gender hierarchy—the pressure to get the job done. Or the very conditions of work in the fly-by-night industry postponed the gender typing of work that would later solidify. This postponement had an upside for women, especially in the first decade of the silent era. To grasp what this reprieve might have meant for women we could try to imagine the moment before gender typing, when everyone on the set did every manner of work (Mahar 2006: 38–9). DeMille screenwriter Beulah Marie Dix for instance, later recalled that

> One learned quite quickly what could and couldn't be done with a camera. ... Anybody on the set did anything he or she was called upon to do. I've walked on as an extra, I've tended lights—and anybody not doing anything else wrote down the director's notes on the script. I also spent a good deal of time in the cutting room
>
> *(As quoted in Brownlow 1968: 276)*

So it should be no surprise that women in the earliest years could end up on the top, directing, or on the bottom, typing. Let's not forget that in the first two decades there would have been all kinds of work on the set but no advertised "jobs." One testimony to the conditions of work fluctuation comes from Australian Alma Young, who started in

Figure 25.5   Gladys Rosson, accountant/executive secretary.

Los Angeles in 1921 as a translator from French into English. In her oral history she recalls that:

> In the old silent days you had an hour for lunch ... we'd go over to the drugstore, and I used to eat very fast and I would take only an half-hour, and then go and relieve the switchboard operator, because there was no one to do it. Between pictures, [I] met Jack Warner and had nothing to do and he told her to find something. So it didn't matter what they wanted to do, I was in on it. [me] answered fan mail. [I] read stories. I was in the property department. I was all over.

An area of further research might be the extent to which women, in contrast with men, held the widest variety of jobs on the set. At the entry level, they might have started doing secretarial work, but once with a "foot in the door," they could end up moving into slots in which someone, anyone, was needed. And since, especially in the 1910s, much "work" may have been undefined and therefore not gender-typed, for a time women might have done the kind of uncredited work that later came to be defined as that of "screenwriter" or "director" or "producer." The rules of the industry employment game were not as yet set.

Yet more women than men did work as clerks and stenographers typing scripts and memos in the fledgling US silent era motion picture ventures. At least one such woman, Gladys Rosson, however, became a powerful executive secretary with responsibility for viewing the daily rushes when her boss Cecil B. DeMille was too busy (Oleson 2013) (Figure 25.5). Or some like Bradley King at the Lubin Company and Virginia Van Upp at Metro Pictures started as typists and moved up to screenwriting and scenario editing (Gaines, forthcoming). At the typewriter, the secretary merged with the screenwriter. Who would immediately notice that she had moved up (Figure 25.6)? Some women established themselves as both film editor and scenario editor, the latter of which required more writing, as exemplified by Beta Breuil and Hettie Gray Baker, who emerged from the editing department to head up departments as scenario editors, Breuil at Vitagraph where Marguerite Bertsch later took over, and Baker at the Bosworth Company as well as at Fox (Gaines and Vatsal 2013).

Figure 25.6 Ethel Doherty, screenwriter.

Within this group of female writers, often women surrounded by women, one can find DeMille unit writers Jeanie MacPherson and Beulah Marie Dix as well as Clara Beranger, earlier quoted as saying that the *real* writers were women (Beranger 1918: 1128). Another such elite group of writers included the Academy award-winning Frances Marion, as well as Kate Corbalay at Metro-Goldwyn-Mayer. Fifteen of these accomplished women writers wrote or co-wrote screenwriting manuals (Gaines and Vatsal 2013). In her study of silent era film writers, Wendy Holliday has argued that in this job they exemplified "women rising to prominence and power, doing 'women's work'" (Holliday 1995: 134).

Gender exceptions and exceptionality

We may be dubious of the sociological approach and its corollary that minorities and women in positions of creative power will transform popular "representations," yet we celebrate the stubborn refusal of race as well as the gender straightjacket dictated by the times. We celebrate Chinese-American Marion E. Wong, who wrote, directed, and produced *The Curse of the Quon Gwon* (1916) (Lau 2013). Undoubtedly, questions about careers make the evidence that women worked in gender-atypical jobs fascinating and important. One thinks of the camerawomen like Margery Ordway, who wore pants like a male director (Gaines and Koerner 2013) (Figure 25.7). Here we could also single out Hungarian Frieda Klug, who worked in the motion picture import–export business (Dall'Asta 2010a: 311–13), Australian Señora Spencer, who ran the theater projector (Verhoeven 2013), and French Canadian Marie de Kerstrat, who with her son started the Historiograph Company in Montreal and, beginning in 1904, exhibited motion pictures on the North American East Coast (Lacasse and Duigou 1987). This is also not to forget that female vulnerability was parodied and its antithesis flaunted by the daringly defiant serial queen action heroines (Dahlquist 2013; Singer 2001).

To look at silent era gender exceptions as proof that women were "just as good as" men, however, only reconfirms that the standard of achievement is male-defined. So what if we turn the tables, following Clara Beranger, and ask whether male writers were "just as good as" the

THIS IS THE NEW FALL STYLE IN CAMERA "MEN"

Meaning, the style you could fall for. Nor is this a masquerade get-up. Margery Ordway, regular, professional, licensed, union crank-turner at Camp Morosco, has gone into camera work as nonchalantly as other girls take up stenography, nursing, husband-stalking.

Figure 25.7   Margery Ordway, camerawoman.

female, postulating gender reversal as well as other challenges to the going version of how men and women are "supposed to be?" And of course an upside down approach puts in check the tendency to look for historical figures who we take to be "just like us." To repeat: "Women" are not now what "women" were. To defer a second time to Joan W. Scott, her most radical reconceptualization of "gender" to date traces her own thought to a relinquishment of "gender" as a category. Her thinking, she says, moved from understanding "sex" as bodily and the default referent for gender to "sexual difference" as so elusive as to be "ultimately unknowable" to such difference as an "impossible referent" for gender. She concludes: "Gender is, in other words, not the assignment of roles to physically different bodies, but the attribution of meanings to something that always eludes definition" (Scott 2011: 6).

"Women" is a genre

Here then I take the new archival evidence of so many women from the first two decades of cinema as the source of theoretical ideas, circumventing what I call the kind of *gender intentionality* we seek to avoid. By this I mean the critical practice, analogous to authorial intentionality in literary studies, of seeking to trace all social situations to gender. So *gender intentionality* is a reliance on gender to explain the historic position of women. When we rely on a historically situated idea of gender without questioning "gender" we slip dangerously into gender intentional territory. My proposal is that we shift to the realm of fiction as a way around the empirical project of researching the lived experience of historical persons. If we take "woman" to be a "genre" or a "fiction," as Ann Snitow has suggested (1996: 517), we circumvent the old problem of "woman" as either biologically, sociologically, or culturally guaranteed. If, instead, we see "women" as like "genre," we are dealing with cultural connotation, narrative situation, and iconic figuration. We are even dealing with sets of conventions *into which men too can step*. This is why, if following Christine Gledhill, we see creative personnel as well as audiences, female or male, as able to "make and remake" popular genre films (2000); we see that over time they also "make and remake" "women," *that other genre*. While real historical women might have had significant creative input in the development of a craft, male directors, actors, and screenwriters, too, would have helped to develop narrative conventions, for example. Men may have stepped into the conventions of popular genre construction developed by women in the 1910s, conventions that only later became accepted practice for all screenwriters. Thus, if we take Wendy Holliday's insight to its logical conclusion, all writers, male and female, as well as all actors, can be seen as doing "women's work" (1995: 134).

Then why exclusively "women" at all? We have already seen how some silent era writers as well as directors claimed that women had the gender edge. Today, however, we may consider it a mistake to think that the sensibilities espoused in early moving picture narrative "belong" to women as opposed to men, and today we are on guard against lapsing into the idea that works of culture contain any inherent anything, remembering the important 1990s feminist critique of essentialism (Dall'Asta 2010b). Further, we cannot avoid an apparent inconsistency with which we come face to face here. As Snitow puts it, there is "the pressure to be a woman and the pressure not to be one" (1996: 517). Or, how does a woman succeed at being both a woman and not a woman? For although these historical women may have insisted that their gender advantage, prescribed as it had been, was "theirs alone," there is another way of viewing conventional "female" values, a way that is more in line with the theory that "women," like "genre," is conventionalized and subject to change (Gaines 2012). If we say that there is a better solution this does not, however, mean that Snitow's "to be or not to be a woman" is resolved. Another approach is to foreground the ridiculous arbitrariness of gender assignment. If we can find espoused values located in conventions rather than inscribed in persons gendered one way or another, the door is opened to seeing "feminine" values as historically *assigned* to women rather than to men, even attributed to men as they very well might have been in another ordering of world cultures. And I do mean that we are talking about gender *assignment*, subject to historical reassignment. Without a doubt, the male screenwriters who replaced women after the silent era were doing "women's work."

Related topics

J.E. Smyth, "Female editors in studio-era Hollywood: rethinking feminist 'frontiers' and the constraints of the archives"
Margaret Hennefeld, "Slapstick comediennes in silent cinema: women's laughter and the feminist politics of gender in motion"
Kristin Lené Hole, "Fantasy echoes and the future anterior of cinema and gender"

References

Appiah, A. K. (1993) "'No Bad Nigger': Blacks as the Ethical Principle in the Movies," in M. Garber, J. Matlock, and R. L. Walkowitz (eds.) *Media Spectacles*, New York and London: Routledge, pp. 77–90.

Beranger, C. (1918) "Are Women the Better Script Writers?," *Moving Picture World* 37. 7 (August 24), p. 1128.

Brownlow, K. (1968) *The Parade's Gone By*, New York: Knopf.

Bruno, G. (1993) *Streetwalking on a Ruined Map: Cultural Theory and the City Films of Elvira Notari*, Princeton, NJ: Princeton University Press.

Buckley, C. (2015) "A.C.L.U. Pushes for Inquiry into Bias Against Female Directors," *New York Times* (May 13), pp. C1, C5.

Cooper, M. (2010) *Universal Women: A Case of Institutional Change*, Urbana: University of Illinois Press.

Dahlquist, M. (ed.) (2013) *Exporting Perilous Pauline: Pearl White and the Serial Film Craze*, Champaign-Urbana: University of Illinois Press.

Dall'Asta, M. (2010a) "On Frieda Klug, Pearl White, and Other Traveling Women Film Pioneers," *Framework* 51.2 (Fall), pp. 310–23.

——— (2010b) "What It Means to Be a Woman: Theorizing Feminist Film History Beyond the Essentialism/Constructionism Divide," in A. Söderberg Widdig and S. Bull (eds.), *Not So Silent: Women in Cinema Before Sound*, Stockholm: Acta Universitatis Stockholmiensis, pp. 39–47.

Dall'Asta, M. and J. Gaines (2015) "Constellations: When Past and Present Collide in Feminist Film History," in C. Gledhill and J. Knight (eds.) *Doing Women's Film History: Reframing Cinema's Past and Future.*, University of Illinois Press, pp. 13–26.

Gaines, J. M. (2012) "The Ingenuity of Genre and the Genius of Women," in *Gender Meets Genre in Postwar Cinema*, C. Gledhill (ed.) Champaign, IL: University of Illinois Press, pp. 15–28.

——— (forthcoming) *Pink-Slipped: What Happened to Women in the Silent Motion Picture Industries?*, Champaign-Urbana: University of Illinois Press.

Gaines, J. M. and M. Koerner (2013) "Women as Camera Operators or 'Cranks,'" in J. M. Gaines, R. Vatsal, and M. Dall'Asta (eds.) *Women Film Pioneers Project*, New York: Center for Digital Research and Scholarship, Columbia University Libraries. https://wfpp.cdrs.columbia.edu accessed November 1, 2015.

Gaines, J. M. and R. Vatsal (2013) "How Women Worked in the Silent Film Industry," in J. M. Gaines, R. Vatsal, and M. Dall'Asta (eds.) *Women Film Pioneers Project*, New York: Center for Digital Research and Scholarship, Columbia University Libraries. https://wfpp.cdrs.columbia.edu/essay/how-women-worked-in-the-us-silent-film-industry/ accessed November 1, 2015.

Gledhill, C. (2000) "Rethinking Genre," in C. Gledhill and L. Williams (eds.) *Reinventing Film Studies*, London: Arnold, pp. 219–43.

Holliday, W. (1995) "Hollywood's Modern Women: Screenwriting, Work Culture, and Feminism, 1910–1940," Unpublished PhD diss., University of Southern California.

Kozarski, R. (1977) "The Years Have Not Been Kind to Lois Weber," in K. Kay and G. Peary (eds.) *Women and the Cinema: A Critical Anthology*, New York University: E. P. Dutton, pp. 146–52.

Lacasse, G. and S. Duigou (1987) *Marie de Kerstrat: l'aristocrate du cinématographe*, Quimper: Ressac.

Lant, A. (ed.) (2006) *The Velvet Seat: Women's Writings on The First Fifty Years of Cinema*, New York and London: Verso.

Lau, J. (2013) "Marion E. Wong," in J. M. Gaines, R. Vatsal, and M. Dall'Asta (eds.) *Women Film Pioneers Project*, New York: Center for Digital Research and Scholarship, Columbia University Libraries. https://wfpp.cdrs.columbia.edu accessed November 1, 2015.

Mahar, K. (2006) *Women Filmmakers in Early Hollywood*, Baltimore: Johns Hopkins University Press.

Oleson, Z. (2013) "Gladys Rossen," in J. M. Gaines, R. Vatsal, and M. Dall'Asta (eds.) *Women Film Pioneers Project*, New York: Center for Digital Research and Scholarship, Columbia University Libraries. https://wfpp.cdrs.columbia.edu accessed November 1, 2015.

Peary, G. (1977) "Alice Guy Blaché: Czarina of the Silent Screen," in K. Kay and G. Peary (eds.) *Women and the Cinema: A Critical Anthology*, New York: E. P. Dutton, pp. 139–45.

Petrova, O. (1986) "A Remembrance," in A. Slide (ed.) *The Memoirs of Alice Guy Blaché*, London and Lanham, MD: The Scarecrow Press, pp.107–10.

Rich, B. R. (1998) *Chick Flicks: Theories and Memories of the Feminist Film Movement*, Durham: Duke University Press.

——— (2013) *New Queer Cinema*, Durham: Duke University Press.

Rubin, G. (2011) *Deviations: A Gayle Rubin Reader*. Durham: Duke University Press.

Scott, J. W. (2008) "Unanswered Questions," in American Historical Review Forum: "Revisiting Gender: A Useful Category of Historical Analysis." *American Historical Review* 113. 5 (December), pp. 1422–30.

——— (2009) "Finding Critical History," in James Banner and John Gillis (eds.) *Becoming Historians*, Chicago: University of Chicago Press, pp. 26–53.

——— (2011) *The Fantasy of Feminist History*, Durham and London: Duke University Press.

Serao, M. (2006) "Parla una Spettatrice," *L'Arte Muta* 1. 1 (15 June, 1916), pp, 31–2,repr. as "A Specatrix is Speaking to You," in A. Lant (ed.) *The Red Velvet Seat: Women's Writings on The First Fifty Years of Cinema*, New York and London: Verso, pp. 97–9.

Shute, N. (2006) "Can Women Direct Films?," *Film Weekly* (10 June 1929), p. 12, repr. in A. Lant (ed.) *The Red Velvet Seat: Women's Writings on The First Fifty Years of Cinema*, New York and London: Verso, p. 668.

Singer, B. (2001) *Melodrama and Modernity: Early Sensational Cinema and Its Contexts*. New York: Columbia University Press.

Slide, A. (1977) *Early Women Directors*, South Brunswick and New York: A. S. Barnes & Co.

Snitow, A. (1996) "A Gender Diary," in Joan Wallach Scott (ed.) *Feminism and History*, New York and Oxford: Oxford University Press, pp. 505–44.

Stamp, S. (2015) *Lois Weber in Early Hollywood*, Berkeley: University of California Press.

Van Wert, B. (1977) "Germaine Dulac: First Feminist Filmmaker," in K. Kay and G. Peary (eds.) *Women and the Cinema: A Critical Anthology*, New York: E.P. Dutton, pp. 213–23.

Verhoeven, D. (2013) "Señora Spencer," in J. M. Gaines, R. Vatsal, and M. Dall'Asta (eds.) *Women Film Pioneers Project*, New York: Center for Digital Research and Scholarship, Columbia University Libraries. https://wfpp.cdrs.columbia.edu accessed November 1, 2015.

Young, A. Interview with Anthony Slide. Oral History collection. Margaret Herrick Library, Academy of Motion Picture Arts and Sciences, Beverly Hills, California. n.d.

Williams, T. (2014). *Germaine Dulac: A Cinema of Sensations*, Chicago and Urbana-Champaign: University of Illinois Press.

Further reading

C. Beauchamp (1997) *Without Lying Down: Frances Marion and the Powerful Women of Early Hollywood* (Berkeley and Los Angeles: University of California Press) takes an inside look at working conditions.

V. Callahan (ed.) (2010). *Reclaiming the Archive: Feminism and Film History*, (Detroit: Wayne State University Press) collects some of the best recent work in historiography.

C. Gledhill and J. Knight (eds.) (2015) *Doing Women's Film History* (Champaign-Urbana: University of Illinois Press) is the collection that challenges the field most provocatively.

H. Hallett (2013) *Go West, Young Women! The Rise of Early Hollywood* (Berkeley: University of California Press) makes the definitive case that Los Angeles attracted young job seekers.

A. McMahan (2002) *Alice Guy Blaché: Lost Visionary of the Cinema* (New York and London: Continuum) is the most comprehensive source on the earliest female director.

J. Mayne (1994) *Directed by Dorothy Arzner* (Bloomington and Indianapolis: Indiana University Press) remains the definitive study of the lesbian director.

J. Simon (ed.) (2009) *Alice Guy Blaché: Cinema Pioneer* (New Haven and London: Yale University Press) is a collection of writing about the early director.

T. Williams (2014). *Germaine Dulac: A Cinema of Sensations* (Chicago and Urbana-Champaign: University of Illinois Press) is the only comprehensive study of the French lesbian director in any language.

26

FEMALE EDITORS IN STUDIO-ERA HOLLYWOOD

Rethinking feminist "frontiers" and the constraints of the archives

J. E. Smyth

Film historians are gradually coming to terms with the substantial number of women involved in the Hollywood film industry during the twentieth century, yet recent research has largely focused on "pioneers" of the silent era, such as director Lois Weber, star and United Artists' co-founder Mary Pickford, serial star Pearl White, and screenwriter Frances Marion (Beauchamp 1998; Whitfield 2007; Gaines et al. 2013; Dahlquist 2013; Hallett 2013). Karen Ward Mahar (2008) and Mark Garrett Cooper (2010) have argued persuasively that masculine managerial business practices all but closed the directing profession to women by the mid-1920s, and this has led many to assume that women lost professional prominence in the industry. The scholarly consensus holds that by the end of the 1920s, the limitless frontiers of early Hollywood had closed, and many high-profile female filmmakers vanished from the industry. It certainly is tempting to use these mythical western metaphors to characterize the narrative of women's presence in Hollywood during the first few decades of the twentieth century—reading these women as female pioneers in a wide-open cinematic frontier town— but this discourse, as well as the assumption that women were utterly disempowered and lost creative control during the 1930s and throughout the studio era, is problematic.

While feminist historians of the silent era have turned to the archives and the industry trade papers to reconstruct women's widespread presence in the US film industry, I would argue that further study of the extant studio archival collections suggests continuity rather than change in women's work in Hollywood during the 1930s, 1940s, and 1950s. Although overall numbers of female directors declined (with Dorothy Arzner and Ida Lupino the great exceptions), women remained active in the industry as producers, writers, script readers, researchers, actors, costume and make-up designers, set dressers, secretaries, publicists, agents, and editors. This chapter will consider the historiographic issues raised by the robust number of prominent female editors working in Hollywood between 1920 and 1960, and will focus on four editors—Barbara "Bobbie" McLean, Margaret Booth, Anne Bauchens, and Jane Loring.

Although closely following the content of female editors' careers in the studio era, this chapter is also mindful of the discourse or form of early twenty-first-century women's film historiography. Recently, borrowing from journalist Louella Parsons' advertisement of

Hollywood as a new "West" for women, film historians have eagerly but rather naively appropriated the discourse of American frontier history, singling out great female film-makers as "pioneers" to promote early Hollywood as a "free" space for modern women (Hallett 2013: 99; Gaines et al. 2013). Is it adequate or even appropriate to construct a women's filmmaking canon using the same exclusionary language which erased women from active participation in earlier eras of US history? While some historians have argued that great women carved "pioneering" paths out of the wilderness, they tended to privilege the rare Annie Oakleys and ignore the scores of anonymous women of varied ethnic backgrounds who conceived of their experience through familial and community networks, kinships, and collaboration (Brown 1958; Riley 1988, 1993). In the same way, film his-torians schooled in conventional auteurism are committed to a hierarchy of work emphasizing directors as the definitive creative force in filmmaking (Sarris 1968; Robson and Kelly 2014). More recent feminist historians of the American West have offered a more complex framework for understanding women's history and their subjects' often ironic writings about the relative freedoms of the Wild West (Georgi Findlay 1996; Des Jardins 2003). Similarly, in their oral histories, memoirs, and professional writings, Hollywood's top female studio editors were ambivalent about their exceptional status and how Second Wave feminist aims interpreted their careers and attitudes toward Hollywood. Film historians, invested in auteurs, the golden West of silent-era Hollywood, and miso-gynist corporate empires, have edited their voices from popular histories of Hollywood.

* * *

Few realize how many of the "classic" films of Hollywood's studio era (1920–60) were edited by women: *The Merry Widow* (1925), *Chicago* (1927), *Mutiny on the Bounty* (1935), *Camille* (1937), *I Married a Witch* (1942), *The Bishop's Wife* (1947), *Twelve O'Clock High* (1949), *In a Lonely Place* (1950), *All About Eve* (1950), *Singin' in the Rain* (1952), and *The Ten Commandments* (1956), are only a fraction. The film industry did not deny these women public recognition either. Until recently, Barbara McLean was the most-nominated editor in the Academy of Motion Picture Arts and Sciences history, nominated seven times and winning for the Fox presidential biopic *Wilson* (1944); and in the industry publication, *We Make the Movies* (1937), edited by filmmaker Nancy Naumburg, Paramount's Anne Bauchens was asked to write about filmmaking from the editor's perspective. The only other woman contributing to the volume, Bette Davis, represented the actress' trade, while her Warner Bros. counterpart, Paul Muni, spoke for the men. The Academy nominated Bauchens four times beginning in 1934, when the editing award was created (for *Cleopatra*), in 1952 for *The Greatest Show on Earth*, and in 1956 for *The Ten Commandments*. She won for *Northwest Mounted Police* in 1941. One out of three editors nominated in 1934 was a woman, in 1935 two out of six nominees were women (Booth and McLean), one out of six in 1936 (McLean), one out of five in 1938 (McLean), and two out of five nominated films had female editors in 1939 (Spencer and McLean).

However, editors are all but ignored as creative artists in more recent scholarship on Hollywood. The exception is the still-active Walter Murch (*The Conversation*, 1974; *The English Patient*, 1996), whose perspective has been endorsed by prominent male directors and producers associated with modern auteur criticism, such as Martin Scorsese and Francis Ford Coppola. Some of their praise has given Murch an auteur glow despite the fact that directors have become more hands-on in the editing room since the studio era. As Anne Bauchens noted of directors in 1937, "While a few insist on cutting their own pictures …

they are very scarce" (Bauchens 1937: 199). It was far more common in the 1920s and 1930s for directors to simply leave the cutting to the editors and producer. But in her lively effort to bring attention to women writers in Hollywood, critic Lizzie Francke dismissed the "invisible" work of female editors from the studio era to the present: "[S]ewing up films in a dark room under the judicious eyes of the director obviously limited their participation in the story-telling process" (Francke 2000: 1). Francke's picture of editing during the studio era is ill-considered. Editors frequently put a rough cut together with little or no input from the director, and often the second editor's rough cut became, with a few minor changes, the final cut seen by audiences. Though editors were recognized by the industry during their careers, "professional" film history focused on the director as author, constructor, and enunciator of the cinematic language, all but unaware that for decades, Margaret Booth (MGM), Adrienne Fazan (MGM), Barbara McLean (Fox), Dorothy Spencer (Fox), Eda Warren (Paramount), Jane Loring (RKO/MGM), Blanche Sewell (MGM), Anne Bauchens (Paramount), Viola Lawrence (Columbia), Monica Collingwood (Goldwyn), Eve Newman (MGM), Irene Morra (Fox/Warner Bros.), Eleanor Morra (Fox), Alma Macrorie (Paramount), Frances Marsh (MGM), Mary Steward (Fox), Lela Simone (MGM), and Helene Turner (Paramount) were writing with celluloid and scissors.

There are obstacles in reconstructing the careers and influence of editors, male or female, for sadly, the extant production materials are not particularly helpful. The "archives," once avoided by critics and cultural historians ideologically suspicious of the studios but star-struck enough to interview directors John Ford, Orson Welles, and Alfred Hitchcock, have been key in adjusting historians' awareness of the limitations of traditional genre studies and director-based auteur frameworks. Yet for women in the industry and feminist film historians, this has been only a partial victory. While the Howard Gotlieb Center at Boston University was instrumental in acquiring the papers of actresses such as Bette Davis and Janet Gaynor, and more recently, the Academy of Motion Picture Arts and Sciences' (AMPAS) Margaret Herrick Library continues to add major collections for Katharine Hepburn, Eva Marie Saint, and other prominent female stars, the papers of non-acting female filmmakers are relatively scarce. Female editors simply did not save their papers after they retired; Booth's papers at AMPAS are scanty and focused on the last few years of her career with Ray Stark, and McLean destroyed hers. The major archives did not approach them for purchase or donation, and instead focused on acquiring the work of famous men: Cecil B. DeMille at Brigham Young University, Darryl Zanuck at the University of Southern California, and David O. Selznick at the University of Texas at Austin. Ironically, it is through DeMille's papers, memos, and story conferences (transcribed and edited by female secretaries and production assistants) that the prominent role of film editor Anne Bauchens emerges.

While Bauchens, McLean, and others exist in the production memos attached to major studio collections for Paramount, Fox, RKO, and MGM, editors' personal cutting notes do not often survive. Studio cutting continuities tell us nothing about how decisions were arrived at, and are merely brief, anonymous transcripts of shots. In some cases from the 1940s, directors such as Fred Zinnemann and George Stevens chose to preserve their own handwritten editing notes, but unlike John Ford, Henry King, Gregory LaCava, and Lewis Milestone, they represent director-editors who took charge of a rough cut beginning in the late 1940s when directors extended their control over the final cut. During the 1930s, it was far more common for producers and writers to develop a project, and once it was passed on to a director, an editor would do a rough cut and then take general direction from a producer and a supervising editor. This was the way McLean and other editors functioned at Fox, yet

McLean's cutting notes do not survive and only occasionally do story conferences reference Zanuck's discussions with McLean and plans to seek her advice.

Establishment histories of cinema and the Hollywood film industry abound, and the better-known writings of Terry Ramsaye (1926), Benjamin Hampton (1931), Leo Rosten (1941), and Arthur Knight (1957), published in the studio era, focus on a progressive historical model founded on technological, artistic, and commercial innovation dominated by a male cast of producers and directors. Though there are occasional references to Pickford, Jean Harlow, and Mae West, Pickford's work as a producer and West's skills as a screenwriter are glossed over. While Leo Rosten acknowledged the film industry as unique in its ability to empower professional women, he was concerned only with actresses such as Norma Shearer and Greta Garbo (1941: 362). Women were assumed to be on one side of the camera, while men were on both. But three other traces survive indicating the industry's more complex attitude toward female editors in the studio era: trade papers, syndicated press, and movie magazine articles on women active in the industry; the rarer collaborative history; and the star memoir.

Articles in the *Los Angeles Times* and *Vogue* revealed Barbara McLean's considerable power in creating Hollywood's most popular films, and her potential to make or break a star's career by cutting his or her footage (*Los Angeles Times* 1940; *Vogue* 1952). Nancy Naumburg's collaborative portrait of Hollywood film production, featuring essays by 16 key professionals, came about because, she argued, "The technique of the American film is the most highly developed and most widely imitated … [but] few people outside of the industry are familiar with it." Anne Bauchens began her career for DeMille as a teenager, and would be his chief editor for 40 years. A year before her essay on editing was published in Naumburg's book, *The Plainsman* (1936) had again earned her critical attention and was one of the biggest box-office draws of the year. At the time, Cecil B. DeMille was possibly the biggest auteur in the industry, a rare director-producer for Paramount from the 1910s. Yet Bauchens argued that, while "different directors and producers work differently with their editors," editors had influence on the set (1937: 199). Usually editors were hired a week or so before production and a second editor would actually assemble the rough cut (Margaret Booth worked in this capacity before moving up to supervising editor, but still managed the editing nuances of most of MGM's feature films each year). As Bauchens noted, editors were often on the set throughout production and often insisted on additional close-ups and intervened to ask directors to shoot "protection" shots so that material would be covered from several different angles.

But the strongest source of knowledge about female editors, or indeed any editors from the studio period, is the oral history. The links between oral history and women's history are extensive, and key women's historians of the 1970s focused on the recovery of women's presence in public and private life through oral histories. Many traditional historians responded with suspicion to oral history's problematic relationship with objectivity and concomitantly increased subjectivism, while forgetting how the content, preservation, and retention of textual documents focused on men in archives shapes current ideologies of historical worth and methodological canonicity. In 1971, film historian Tom Stempel, best known for his work on the importance of screenwriters at Twentieth Century-Fox, turned his attention to editor Barbara "Bobbie" McLean, Zanuck's right hand in the editing room and one of the only people who could persuade him that he was wrong. McLean's oral history with Stempel (1971, hereafter McLean) and Irene Kahn Atkins' 1976 interview with Booth represented further correctives to dominant director-auteur discourses on Hollywood, but the editors also proved resistant to contemporary efforts to see them as rare female "pioneers" in a male-dominated industry.

McLean began editing professionally in 1924, but she did not just assemble the cut. She was on the set as the cameras rolled, handling the sound, talking to the directors about the close-ups they needed to shoot, and looping. As she remembered, "[W]e did everything. Well, you can't do that today. I was very fortunate. I could get to every department and do everything, even to do a good deal of working on music." (McLean: 5). Her comments highlight a less-known aspect of film production in the late 1920s and 1930s: several key female editors not only hung around the sound and music departments, they also worked as writers and producers.

Margaret Booth, perhaps the most powerful editor during the studio period, wrote part of *Mutiny on the Bounty* (1935) but also, from 1936, worked as an assistant producer. The MGM *Studio News* is a lively source of monthly information about the studio's employees, ranging from secretary Ida Koverman (who many said ran both mogul Louis B. Mayer and MGM) to the legions of secretaries and script girls who formed softball teams and regularly played each other in competitive "league" matches. Booth, it noted, "one of our ace cutters, has recently been advanced to the position of assistant producer." It went on to describe her rise to power within familial terms: "Practically born with a pair of scissors in her hand, Margaret has been brought up with the picture business and will prove a valuable factor in her new job" (MGM *Studio Club News* 1936). When Booth gave her oral history interview with Rudy Behlmer in 1990, she did not mention this, only noting her promotion to supervising editor in 1936. But in her interview with another woman, fellow editor Irene Kahn Atkins, Booth was more revealing of the extent of her power: "I used to look at everything in the projection room, all the dailies from everybody's pictures at MGM. And Mr. Mayer told me that, if I didn't like anything, to tell him and he would have it retaken" (Kahn Atkins 1976: 53).

Booth owed her career to Irving Thalberg, who put her in charge of the studio's most prestigious films. But Thalberg also wanted her to turn director when she was working for George Cukor on *Camille* (1937), and pressured her to do this shortly before his death. Even with Thalberg's support, Booth declined, and later explained her decision: "I enjoyed what I was doing. And I said, 'I want to be the best, if I can, at that'" (Kahn Atkins 1976: 54). While it is tempting to read her rejection of directing in gendered terms, with Booth internalizing her subservience as an editor and accepting the gendered hierarchies of direction and creative control, the more logical and ironic motivation may have been her emulation of Irving Thalberg's approach to film authorship. The man most responsible for the look of MGM's releases from the late 1920s to his death in 1936 never liked putting his name on any picture's credits.

During the 1930s, producers and writers had far more impact on individual film productions than had previously been recognized (Smyth 2006). Many of Zanuck's archived comments on tightening aspects of scripts or planning a particular sequence were influenced by his conversations with Bobbie McLean, who was often looking at the script before the director was assigned. McLean always assembled the cut as shooting progressed; even Fox's John Ford did not cut his own films. Though Booth would later say that editors were "locked in" to what the director wanted, this wasn't strictly true (Kahn Atkins 1976: 53). In Booth's own words, Mayer would order retakes of any areas she did not like and while she was on the set, she frequently went down to the sound stage and said, "'I need a close-up. I can't cut that footage out unless I have a close-up to replace it'" (ibid.). But McLean also revealed that with many directors, and especially for her long collaboration with Henry King, she would be on the set even before shooting started, script in hand, discussing things with the director, but also disagreeing with him and often getting her own way. Zanuck always deferred to her judgment.

When asked to articulate what motivated their judgment, and how film editing translated as a language to the audience, McLean, Bauchens, and Booth had similar reactions: it was intuitive and based on their long experience of cutting a variety of work. Booth said that working with silent films enabled editing to function as an art form: "When you worked in the silent days, you learned about rhythm, and you learned to cut film like poetry" (Kahn Atkins 1976: 51). But different genres had their own styles. For a comedy like *Bombshell* (1933), Booth chose "such a fast tempo" that there wasn't "a sprocket hole in between each line of dialogue." That was the way she "loved" to cut (ibid. 55). Bauchens (1937) acknowledged that editors assembled scenes according to the script, but "each shot expresses a different phase of emotion or interest." Long shots were for information or spectacle, medium shots were to enhance clarity and the audience's relationship with the actors, and, while it was useful to focus on individual elements, "it is not always necessary to tell it in a close-up of a face" (Bauchens 1937: 204).

Who developed the grammar and style of Hollywood film language? While McLean learned her trade from working with Pickford and watching other (often male) editors, Booth gave credit to director John Stahl for teaching her, and giving Booth her first credits as a cutter. "He would tell me why he went into a close-up. He said, 'Always play it in the long shot unless you want to punctuate something'" (Kahn Atkins 1976: 52). Yet, Stahl also learned from Booth: it wasn't simply a case of male directors "schooling" female editors. When Stahl "couldn't get a sequence the way he wanted," he looked at a rough cut Booth had been practicing on with the outtakes and used that instead in the final cut (ibid.). Booth became so individual and skilled in her cutting that Thalberg assigned her to new directors to protect them from potential incompetence and help them to develop their style. She cut George Cukor's first picture and handled Lionel Barrymore's *The Rogue Song* (1930). Bauchens was even more explicit about the creative power of editors. She argued that the protection shots editors called for and sometimes directed were used "to give variety to the telling of the story" (Bauchens 1937: 200). She defended directors who shot multiple takes and versions, and disliked directors who camera cut, saying "You can never be sure exactly which of these will best tell your story until you have cut it one way and then, if it does not look right, tried it another" (ibid. 204). Yet Bauchens' preference for more film inevitably gave her and her editing colleagues more creative control over the final cut. Directors chose to camera cut to avoid producers and editors taking control over the final cut.

Unlike Bauchens, McLean was fortunate enough to work for a female studio head for several years—Mary Pickford. At Pickford's studio, collaboration worked on two levels: people worked for each other and with each other, often doing several jobs at once without complaint. As McLean recalled, "[I]f the script girls that worked on the set were sick, the assistant editor would run on the set and take notes" (McLean: 6). Artistic hierarchies did not exist on the set, even with someone of Pickford's status at the helm. According to McLean, Pickford also dressed the sets and made sure the editors had tea while they worked. However, McLean used the same collaborative, familial framework to describe her work with men at Fox. She was working for and with men—Hugh Bennett, Stuart Heisler, and Alan McNeil, but

> it was like family. It was like the whole family, so naturally you worked like mad because you loved every bit of it. You loved them, and you wanted the picture to be great, and you didn't mind how hard you worked. And that's the faculty that Zanuck had.
>
> (ibid. 8)

Zanuck never used her for "women's pictures" (she cut westerns, war pictures, and biopics predominantly), and she laughed that "naïve" Henry King and Joseph Mankiewicz understood "women's pictures" and romance more than she did. Zanuck, before he had met her, had assumed Bobbie was a man based on what he had seen of her work and the nickname her male colleagues used for her. After the strike in 1933, Alan McNeil went to Zanuck and asked that "Bobbie" be put back on the picture they had been working on in spite of the fact she had been on strike too. "They all called me 'Bobbie,' so Zanuck said, 'Get him back, get him back,' thinking I was a boy" (ibid. 10). She clearly enjoyed the fact that in addition to being "the only girl" who could change Zanuck's mind, she was just "one of the boys" to her editing colleagues. McLean resisted attempts to see the profession as feminine or subservient, but she also refused to highlight her gender as aberrant within the professional system of Hollywood. She replied bluntly to Stempel's question about why there had been so many top female editors: "Why? Because you have to be good or you wouldn't get there" (ibid. 120). She did not see herself as a pioneering feminist actively pushing barriers for women within a male-dominated system, but rather as a filmmaker who thrived within a collaborative environment that accepted and honored her work regardless of gender.

She moved up from assistant editor to editor when Zanuck discovered that his editing changes only occurred if "Bobbie" could hear his comments in the screening room. So from *Gallant Lady* (1933) onward, there she stayed (except when she directed the close-ups on *Affairs of Cellini*, 1934). But McLean did not simply transcribe Zanuck's desires. "When you got an idea, he would listen to you," she insisted (ibid. 43). Of her collaboration with Henry King, she would often get him to shoot a film her way:

> We used to have some little arguments. I'd spend a lot of time on the set and sometimes he would say, 'I'm going to do so-and-so-and-so-and-so.' I'd say, 'You are?' He'd say, 'Now what's the matter?' I'd say, 'Well, gee …' and I'd give my opinion on something.
>
> (*ibid*. 48)

It was take it or leave it with her, and most took it. When she had to do a picture with King, McLean grabbed the script and read it and discussed it with him. As for her autonomy as an editor: "I've always been pretty fortunate in being able to put the picture in the first cut as I saw fit … If you have it, and you can feel it, then you can get it on the screen" (ibid. 15). Her expertise was legendary at Fox, and McLean mused,

> Zanuck used to always put me on the pictures when nobody knew what to do technically … He knew I could handle it … I managed to sit in on the rerecording and everything. He trusted me to do that.
>
> (ibid. 66)

Bobbie McLean excelled in an environment where the majority of her co-workers were men, but she did not indicate there was any sexism. She eventually became head of the feature editorial department but, like Booth at MGM, disliked the added control of hiring, accounts, and administration.

McLean's oral history provides invaluable insight into editing practices during the studio era, and her influence on Fox's product on so many levels makes a strong case for McLean's "authorship" on key film texts such as *Song of Bernadette* (1943), *Wilson* (1944), *A Bell for*

Adano (1945), *Twelve O'Clock High* (1949), and *All About Eve* (1950). More traditional auteur critics who've noticed these patterns in Twentieth Century-Fox's continuity editing such as Jonathan Rosenbaum smugly dismiss it as Fox's "corporate signature." Yet, given McLean and other successful women filmmakers' comments on their attitudes toward working for the studios, McLean embraced the idea of studio collaboration. For Rosenbaum, a "corporate signature" was a slight on film styles determined by those other than directors (in Fox's case, a woman). According to this approach, artistry is reserved solely for directors (men) who receive all the creative credit in the film histories. But for McLean, working was a collaborative process where "family" tasks were shared and negotiated among members (her own father had taught her the editing trade in the mid-1920s), and from 1934, where individual artistry was honored at the Academy Awards. She, along with Booth and Bauchens, worked with one studio for many years, progressing to chief editor, but also multitasking and doing a variety of jobs within a given production.

Only two major studio-era Hollywood film editors' careers are covered through oral histories. How is the work of someone like Jane Loring reconstructed? Arguably Katharine Hepburn rescued her longtime friend's career from oblivion. In *Me*, Hepburn pointed out that some of Hollywood's best "cutters" were women (1996). Yet Loring, who first met Hepburn at RKO on the set of *Alice Adams* (1935), despite a brief mention in Anne Edwards' seminal biography of Hepburn (Edwards 1984: 138, 147), is still all but unknown to film history, despite working for decades with Pandro Berman as an editor, writer, and associate producer, first at RKO and later at MGM. In fact, Loring co-directed *Break of Hearts* (1935), worked on all of Hepburn's post-*Alice Adams* films at RKO, and went on to write *Dragon Seed* (1944) and write and co-produce *The Seventh Cross* (1944) with Spencer Tracy. Berman, always overshadowed by Selznick at RKO, was nonetheless an intelligent and capable producer, and he and Loring deserve considerable credit for the maverick Hepburn's early feminist works. The range and depth of Loring's work survives in the Turner/MGM script collections at the Academy library, but she appears as one of many collaborators on the scripts (and an uncredited editor) rather than as a named auteur (Howard Estabrook and John Huston's scripts are organized under their own collections). While Hepburn may have helped to promote Loring's career and acknowledged her late in life as a valued colleague, film historians should also be cautious about seeing Hepburn as a self-conscious feminist icon: ironically, she described herself as an old-fashioned, self-motivated "masculine" individualist. In her famous television interview with Dick Cavett in 1973, she denied being a modern feminist and claimed that she achieved her top status because she lived her life "like a man." Similarly, Booth and McLean highlighted their workaholic, studio-centered lives (neither had children) and displayed ambivalence about their "exceptional" status as *female* editors (Behlmer 1991: 16). Ironically, in embracing some traditionally masculine "pioneer" traits such as hard work and toughness, they aligned themselves with the mostly masculine collective of the studio rather than their collective political identity as women in the 1930s and 1940s, and its subsequent refraction in Second Wave feminist discourse. Yet, for many feminists working in the 1930s and 1940s, gender equality was truly achieved when women were able to do their work well, without the public drawing attention to their identities as women; in such cases, frontiers were not broached, but pointedly ignored. And, like Louis B. Mayer, these editors saw the studio as home, and the barriers between professional and private life collapsed into memories of a collaborative "family" workplace.

When she was interviewed at the height of Second Wave feminism, Booth shrugged off Kahn Atkins' efforts to see editing as exceptional women's work: "I really can't say why that was. It just seemed like girls took to that at that time" (Kahn Atkins 1976: 53). However, she quietly nurtured other young editors such as Dede Allen (*Bonnie and Clyde*, 1967) just as McLean promoted Mary Steward at Fox during the 1930s and 1940s. They may not have been conventional "pioneering" auteurs, but they were true organization women, viewing the studio system as a negotiable artistic hierarchy where women's perspectives shaped the language of Hollywood film. "Sewing," Ms. Francke? Hardly. McLean may wear white gloves in her famous 1952 portrait in *Vogue*, but only because she handled the negative. In most cases, she and her colleagues could cut it how they saw it, director or no director.

Related topics

Jane Gaines, "What was 'women's work' in the silent film era?"
Kristin Lené Hole, "Fantasy echoes and the future anterior of cinema and gender"

Bibliography

Bauchens, A. (1937) "Cutting the Film," in Nancy Naumburg (ed.), *We Make the Movies*, New York: W. W. Norton & Co., pp. 199–215.

Beauchamp, C. (1998) *Without Lying Down: Frances Marion and the Powerful Women of Early Hollywood*, Berkeley: University of California Press.

Behlmer, R. (1991). *Oral History With Margaret Booth*, Beverly Hills: Academy of Motion Picture Arts and Sciences.

Brown, D. (1958) *The Gentle Tamers: Women of the Old Wild West*, Lincoln: University of Nebraska Press.

Cooper, M. G. (2010) *Universal Women: Filmmaking and Institutional Change in Early Hollywood*, Urbana: University of Illinois Press.

Dahlquist, M. (ed.) (2013) *Exporting Perilous Pauline: Pearl White and the Serial Film Craze*, Urbana: University of Illinois Press.

Des Jardins, J. (2003) *Women and the Historical Profession in America*, Chapel Hill: University of North Carolina Press.

Edwards, A. (1984) *A Remarkable Woman: A Biography of Katharine Hepburn*, New York: Morrow.

Francke, L. (1996) "The Invisible Hand in the Cutting Room," *The Guardian*, March 28.

Francke, L. (2000) *Script Girls*, London: BFI.

Gaines, Jane et al. (ed.) (2013) *Women Film Pioneers Project*, Center for Digital Research and Scholarship, New York, NY: Columbia University Libraries.

Georgi Findlay, B. (1996) *The Frontiers of Women's Writing*, Phoenix: University of Arizona Press.

Gluck, S. B. (1977) "What's So Special About Women? Women's Oral History," *Frontiers: A Journal of Women's Studies* 2(2), pp. 3–17.

Hallett, H. (2013) *Go West, Young Women!*, Berkeley: University of California Press.

Hampton, B. (1970 [1931]) *A History of the American Film From Its Beginnings to 1931*, New York: Dover.

Hepburn, K. (1973) Interview With Dick Cavett, *The Dick Cavett Show*, September 14.

Hepburn, K. (1996) *Me*, New York: Ballantine Books.

Kahn Atkins, I. (1976) "Margaret Booth: Interview," *Focus on Film* 25, pp. 51–7.

Knight, A. (1957) *The Liveliest Art*, New York: Mentor Books.

Los Angeles Times (1940) "Women Behind the Screen," April 28: H10.

Mahar, K. W. (2008) *Women Filmmakers in Early Hollywood*, Baltimore: Johns Hopkins University Press.

MGM Studio Club News (1936) 12(1), December, Special Collections, University of Southern California.

Ramsaye, T. (1926) *A Million and One Nights*, New York: Simon & Schuster.

Riley, G. (1988) *The Female Frontier*, Lawrence: University of Kansas Press.

Riley, G. (1993) "Frederick Jackson Turner Overlooked the Ladies," *Journal of the Early Republic* 13(2), pp. 216–30.

Robson, C. and Kelly, G. (eds.) (2014) *The Celluloid Ceiling: Women Film Directors Breaking Through*, London: Supernova Books.

Rosenbaum, J. (1982) "The Cutting Edge," *The Movie*, www.jonathanrosenbaum.net/1982/07/the-cutting-edge/ (last accessed June 14, 2015).

Rosten, L. (1941) *Hollywood: A Modern Business Enterprise*, New York: Harcourt, Brace & Co.

Sarris, A. (1968) *The American Cinema: Directors and Directions, 1929–1968*, New York: Da Capo.

Smyth, J. E. (2006) *Reconstructing American Historical Cinema*, Lexington: University Press of Kentucky.

Stempel, T. (1971) *An Oral History with Barbara McLean*, Darryl F. Zanuck Research Project, American Film Institute.

Turner, F. J. (1893) "The Significance of the Frontier in American History," *Report of the American Historical Association*, pp. 199–227.

Vogue (1952) February.

Whitfield, E. (2007) *Pickford: The Woman Who Made Hollywood*, Lexington: University Press of Kentucky.

Further reading

Croughton, Amy H. (1937) "Film Editor's Role Growing in Importance: More Women Employed As Cutters." *Rochester Times Union*, 13 May.

Hastie, Amelie (2007) *Cupboards of Curiosity*, Durham: Duke University Press. Useful rethinking of women's film authorship by expanding the sources in the historical archive.

Murch, Walter (2001) *In the Blink of an Eye*, New York: Silman-James Press. Leading editor discusses the importance of editing and philosophies of continuity and discontinuity.

Schatz, Thomas (1988) *The Genius of the System*, New York: Pantheon. Still the most comprehensive understanding of the studio production process during the studio era.

Ware, Susan (1983) *Holding Their Own: Women in the '30s*, Boston: Twayne. A standby on feminism in the 1930s and the achievements of American women during the Depression. Contests the idea that "feminism" did not exist before the Second Wave.

27

FILM AS ACTIVISM AND TRANSFORMATIVE PRAXIS

Women Make Movies

Debra Zimmerman

Women Make Movies (WMM), the organization I have led since 1983, is one of the few feminist media organizations that remain active, of the many that were founded in the 1970s. It started as a neighborhood community project to train local women to make films and has grown into an internationally renowned distributor of films by and about women that has had a significant impact on the availability and study of global women's media. As B. Ruby Rich wrote in a *Camera Obscura* dossier marking the organization's fortieth anniversary,

> Internationally, what WMM has been able to accomplish, by recognizing crucial figures from Kim Longinotto to Pratihba Parmar, is a branding of the organization as a global crossroads for a transnational feminist media. As such, WMM has been able to influence university curricula deeply.
>
> *(Rich 2013:160)*

In this chapter I uncover the historical roots of the organization's transnationalism and explore how its commitment to diverse representation and its need for economic self suf-ficiency have contributed to its longevity and its influence on transformative feminist media praxis.

WMM was founded in 1969 by Ariel Dougherty and Sheila Page, who met at a women's liberation meeting and formed a film working group to document women's issues. They used the name Chelsea Picture Station from 1969 until incorporating as Women Make Movies in 1972. The original name intentionally did not include women: it referred to the group's location in the working class neighborhood of Chelsea and it was hoped that the name would be less intimidating to the women living there (Fallica 2013). Their intention was to be a community resource; they gave film production classes at the St. Columba Catholic church in the local housing project. A flyer from those days encouraged "Housewives, secretaries, mothers, *muchachas*" and others to "come and learn to make a movie" (Chelsea Picture Station Workshops n.d.). They also realized that cable was coming to NY and hoped to be granted the license to become the local public access station. The short films that were produced reflected the lives of the working class women who had never made films before, and included: *How to Cut up a Chicken* (Suzanne Armstrong, 1973), which was the first in a planned series on how to save money in cooking; *Fear* (Jean Shaw, 1974), a short drama of a woman successfully fending off a rapist; and *For Better or Worse* (Judith Shaw Acuna, 1973), how a woman's life changes after marriage.

These films regularly screened at community centers, senior citizen centers, the local library, public schools, a city park summer program, and on the Manhattan public access channel. It was the early 1970s and video was not yet widely used as a production format. One of the first grants that WMM received from the New York State Council on the Arts was to buy a 16mm Bolex camera which subsequently provided access to film production equipment when the organization evolved into a membership organization.

In 1976, *Healthcaring from Our End of the Speculum* (Denise Bostrum and Jane Warrenbrand) was finished; it was WMM' first hour-long documentary. It won a blue ribbon, the top prize in its category, at the American Film Festival, an important annual event organized by the Educational Film Library Association and screened at the original Toronto International Film Festival, then called the Festival of Festivals. The film was successfully distributed by WMM, both to alternative women's centers and women's health centers throughout the US, as well as to the traditional users of educational film: universities and public libraries. Although in 1975 WMM had hosted a Conference of Feminist Film and Video Organizations (CFFVO) that drew representatives from almost 70 women's media organizations from around the country, the organization's major activities had been, by design, local and focused on community outreach (White 2006: 147). The new distribution activities of the organization brought WMM out of the neighborhood to wider North American audiences. And with the success of *Healthcaring*, other women filmmakers started sending their films to WMM, looking for distribution.

During the years 1978–82, WMM continued its training program, produced two hour-long video documentaries, and held International Women's Film Festivals in 1980 and 1981. The work that WMM was doing in New York was mirrored by women's film organizations around the world, including women's film distributors. Along with Iris Films in California, which had organized the Feminist Eye, a similar conference to the one that WMM hosted in 1975, there was Cinema of Women (COW) and Circles in England, Cinemien in the Netherlands, Women in Focus Society in Vancouver, and Video Femmes in Québec. The film festivals put the WMM staff in touch with these organizations, as well as with women filmmakers working outside the US, and were WMM's first step into the international film scene.

In the 1970s and until video became a viable distribution format, putting a film into distribution cost thousands of dollars because of the price of 16mm prints. Most women filmmakers couldn't afford to make an internegative, which, although expensive, would have greatly reduced the cost of additional prints. Therefore, distribution prints were made from the original A and B rolls and, depending on the length of the film, cost between $500 and $2,000 (in 1970's dollars). WMM and three other women's film distributors started working together across borders to split the cost of internegatives. In addition, they found that they could better negotiate for rights to films by being able to offer a producer distribution in the US, Canada, England, and the Benelux countries. *Processo per Stupro* (*Trial for Rape*, 1978), which was made for the Italian television station RAI and won the Prix Italia, was one of the films that were distributed by all of the groups. Made by a Roman filmmakers' collective, which included Loredana Rotondo, Annabella Miscuglio, and Roni Daopoulo, it was the first documentary that recorded an actual rape trial and had enormous impact on the discussion of sexual violence in Italy (Bruno and Nadotti 1988).

In the early 1980s, WMM, like many other women's arts organizations, lost its funding from the newly installed Republican administration. In addition, New York State Council on the Arts, the organization's first government funder, declined funding citing the lack of permanent staff and leadership (Bender 1990). That, coupled with internal strife, almost caused the organization to close its doors. However, after a series of community meetings to discuss the future of the organization, a decision was made to refocus the organization's energies on its one earned income program: distribution. By this time, there were many women who had learned the skills of filmmaking; there were fewer opportunities for their work to gain distribution. By expanding the distribution component of the organization, WMM was able to provide critically needed services to both the users and makers of media and create an income stream that would serve as the basis of the organization's finances. Rather than solicit grants to subsidize activities, WMM would look to its constituents for support one rental or sale at a time. In retrospect, this decision was key in the growth of the organization. From a budget of $30,000 and one staff person in 1983, its budget grew to more than $300,000 in 1990. But perhaps even more important was the fact that 90 percent of its budget came from earned income, which gave the organization the ability to design its own future and the freedom to maintain a decidedly feminist and political mission.

Contrary to the commonly held perception that the Second Wave of the women's movement was predominantly white and middle class, WMM had long had the involvement of and commitment to women of color. From diverse representation in discussions and sessions at the first CFFVO and in terms of participants in the early workshops, to the films in the early distribution collection, WMM had a critique of mainstream media, which included the lack of representation by and about women of color (Fallica 2013).

In 1984, when I became the Director of WMM, the first project we undertook was Punto De Vista: Latina/ Point of View: Latina, the first touring exhibition of films by and about Latina women in the US. Not only did this reflect the Hispanic roots of WMM's Chelsea neighborhood, but by this time we had moved into the Taller Latinoamericano, a loft space which rented offices to Latino and cultural groups. The project was the idea of Rachel Field, a WMM board member who had recently made a documentary on midwives in Nicaragua called *Abuelitas de Ombligo* (1982). We acquired Syliva Morales' groundbreaking documentary, *Chicana* (1979) and Lourdes Portillo's first film, a short drama called *After the Earthquake* (1979). Originally intending to showcase the work of Latina women filmmakers from the US, we quickly realized we needed to look south of the border to Latin America for other films. There just were not enough films made by Latinas in the US to put together a touring program. I was the sole staff person at WMM at the time, so we put together an Advisory Committee which included Latina scholars, Catherine Benamou, then a graduate student, and a local filmmaker and activist, Bienvenida Matias. To our delight, we found that there were sister women's media organizations doing production and distribution of women's films in Latin and South America: Cine Mujer (Colombia), Cine Mujer (Mexico), and Grupo Miércoles (Venezuela). The Cine Mujer collective was founded in 1978 by two Colombian feminists, Eulalia Carrizosa and Sara Bright. Its mission was incredibly similar to WMM: "the production and distribution of films, documentaries and other educational materials and information on the situation and problems of women in Colombia and Latin America" (Cinematria Cineclub Feminista, 2011). From Cine Mujer we acquired *Carmen Carrascal* (Sara Bright, Eulalia Carrizoza, 1982) and *Y Su Mama que Hace?* (*And What Does Your Mother Do?*, Cine Mujer, 1981). From Grupo Chaski, a collective devoted to independent filmmaking in Peru, we found a film produced when the Miss Universe pageant was held in Lima: *Miss Universe in Peru* (*Senorita Universo en El Peru*, 1985). Other films directed by independent women filmmakers included: Monica Vasquez's documentary, *Tiempo De Mujeres* (*Time of Women*, Monica Vasquez, 1980) about women in Ecuador; Mexican filmmaker, Maria Novaro's first dramatic short, *Una Isla Rodeada de Agua* (*An Island Surrounded by Water*, 1985); and Valeria Sarmiento's *Un Hombre, Cuando Es Un Hombre* (*A Man When He is A Man*, 1982), an experimental documentary which looked at machismo culture in Costa Rica.

The Punto De Vista: Latina project was an excellent example of WMM's attempt to work both locally and globally. Once funding had been secured from the New York Council on Humanities, Beni Matias was hired to organize community screenings throughout the boroughs of NYC, showcasing work produced by filmmakers from all over Latin and South America. With this project, WMM's commitment to the distribution of international women's films was firmly established.

The project also reflected the growing use of video as a production and distribution format. In collaboration with Groupe Intervention Video (GIV) in Montreal, the project was broadened to include Brazil. GIV, which has been distributing women's video art since 1975, had made alliances with women's video collectives in Brazil and had subtitled some of their videos into English and French. Unlike the women's organizations in Colombia and Mexico who were able to secure funding from the government, in Brazil, women had to use a less expensive format and video was more prevalent (Marsh 2008). The Brazilian Lilith Video Collective was founded in 1983 by Jacira de Melo, Sylvana Afram, and Marcia Meireles and WMM acquired a number of their productions.

There were other initiatives that aided WMM in its development as a transnational organization. In 1984, the United Nations End of Decade Conference for Women's NGO Forum Planning Committee gave a mandate to the National Film Board of Canada (NFB) to organize a "comprehensive film forum to showcase the voice of women in film" (Harbourfront Corporation 1986). The NFB had founded Studio D in 1974 as "the first and only government funded film studio dedicated solely to producing feminist documentaries" (Vanstone 2007). As such, it was the likely choice for putting on the event. I was invited to become part of an International Steering Committee, which included 13 women involved in film production, distribution, and exhibition from the US, Australia, Brazil, the Philippines, Trinidad, Mexico, China, Czechoslovakia, India, Kenya, the Netherlands, and China. The committee was charged with finding women filmmakers, coordinating methods of film shipment, providing information necessary for the production of the festival catalog and recommending workshop topics and resource persons. FilmForum '85 had a budget of $330,000, an extraordinary amount of funding at that time, and the long-term goals and objectives laid out by the organizers matched the sum. These included "establishing international network channels for the distribution of women's films" to "facilitate the international showcasing of women's films" (Harbourfront Corporation 1986). The success of the FilmForum was thwarted by politics and other technical difficulties, but censorship almost undermined the event. Just days before the film festival was to begin in Nairobi, the Kenyan government insisted on its Censorship Board screening every film. But it was not just Kenya that used censorship to prevent films from showing. The American Consulate, which had assisted the event by shipping the US films through diplomatic pouch, refused to allow *Healthcaring* to screen, on the basis that African women would be offended by the explicit images of women's vaginas!

However, though not all of the short-term or long-term objectives of the FilmForum were reached, the difficulties of planning and implementing the event created strong bonds and an informal network of international women working in film. It was in Nairobi that the future transnational focus of WMM became firmly established. There, I had the opportunity to screen feminist films and meet filmmakers from all over the world. And, perhaps most importantly, lasting alliances were formed with the women's film distributors in England, Australia, and the Netherlands, who had collaborated long distance years before.

Over the next decade, WMM's distribution collection increased dramatically. From approximately 50 films in 1983, by 1995 there were 330 films in the collection and almost one-third of these were made by filmmakers from outside of the US and Canada. Another one-third were by women of color living in US and Canada. While the US was just beginning to explore the importance of multiculturalism in the art world—and one particular case in point was the outstanding conference, *Do The Right Thing*, organized by New York State Council of the Arts Film Program under the leadership of B. Ruby Rich— there was already a body of work produced by Black filmmakers in Great Britain. Britain's Channel 4 had a specific mandate to broadcast independently produced programs (Thomas 2012). Starting in 1982–3, it enfranchised production workshops to support and produce independent and diverse programming: the Black Audio Collective and the Sankofa Film Collective were two of the most successful. WMM acquired many films produced both in these workshops, as well as by filmmakers working alongside of them, including films by Gurinder Chadha and Ngozi Onwurah, including one of WMM's most successful films still in distribution, *The Body Beautiful* (Ngozi Onwurah, 1991).

During the late 1980s, as the collection expanded, WMM also collaborated on numerous exhibitions and events. The *Viewpoints: Women, Culture and Public Media* conference (1986), held at Hunter College, CUNY, was attended by more than 700 artists, practitioners, academic theorists, and community activists. Martina Attille, one of the members of Sankofa, was in attendance and screened *The Passion of Remembrance* (1986), which she made with Issac Julian and Maureen Blackwood. As Rich writes in *Chick Flicks*, "In its insistence on activism, embrace of multiculturalism and respect for theory, it [the conference] looks like a unique springboard from the seventies into the eighties" (1998: 342). She also cites the conference as the moment when Trinh T. Minh-ha was "recognized in a star-making capacity" (ibid. 341). WMM had been distributing *Reassemblage* (1982) for many years, and was in the process of releasing Trinh's second film, *Naked Spaces: Living is Round* (1985). *Reassemblage*, a film that "challenges the role of the colonialized 'other,' (Third World Women) as subjects of the filmmaker's gaze" (Foster 1995: 357), was one of the centerpieces of a collection of films WMM had released in 1986: New Directions: Feminist Films and Videos. The release of New Directions was a pivotal moment for WMM, as the collection explored the incorporation of feminist film theory into the practice of independent women's filmmaking. Along with *Reassemblage*, Sally Potter's seminal film *Thriller* (1979) and Michelle Citron's *Daughter Rite* (1980), the films in the collection brought important independent feminist work to the academy and theory to those interested in women's cinema. Although New Directions included films by Trinh and Valeria Sarmiento, most of the films in the collection were by and about white women. The acquisition of films by Black (which was used to mean women of color in the British vernacular of the times) women filmmakers from England, as well as films by emerging Asian women filmmakers in the US, video art by South American women artists, and films by Australian Aboriginal filmmaker Tracey Moffatt enabled Patty White, a WMM staff member, and I to curate a later exhibition at the Anthology Film Archives in NY entitled Changing the Subject: An International Exhibition of Films by Women of Color (c. 1990).

Women's film festivals played a major role in these acquisitions. Two festivals, in particular, were crucial to the continuing development of the WMM collection. Films des

Femmes, the women's film festival in France, founded in 1979 and held annually in a suburb outside of Paris, offered a wealth of films by international directors. Silence Elle Tournent!, the Montreal International Women's Film Festival which was founded in 1985 and ran until the early 1990s, was created in the image of its French sister festival. The work of Mona Hatoum, the Palestinian performance, visual, and video artist, as well as the early work of Pratibha Parmar, and many other films acquired by WMM, were screened at the festival. Though the Montreal event is defunct, the Créteil festival will have its thirty-eighth edition in 2016; these festivals were the predecessors of hundreds of other women's film events.

By the 1990s, WMM had grown into the largest distributor of films by and about women, and in 1997 celebrated its twenty-fifth anniversary with exhibits in Austin, Salt Lake City, Boston, Atlanta, and Washington, DC, as well as internationally in Brazil, Mexico, Korea, Taiwan, and Belarus. It also helped to organize Women and the Art of Multimedia, a conference at the Women's Museum in DC, one of the first to bring together women media artists and technologists. But not everyone was celebrating the work WMM was doing—namely, bringing films by the women who were most marginalized by the mainstream media to audiences around the country. For the second time in its history, WMM lost its funding from the National Endowment for the Arts (NEA) after being used as a right-wing scapegoat in an attempt to close the federal agency. Michigan State Representative Peter Hoekstra, head of the House Education and Workforce Committee's Subcommittee on Oversight and Investigations was quoted as calling WMM films "taxpayer-funded peep shows" in a *NY Daily News* article entitled "Pol Reels at Group's Racy Flicks" (Sisk 1997). WMM had sponsored grants from the NEA for *The Watermelon Woman* (Cheryl Dunye, 1996), as well as films by Yvonne Rainer and Su Friedrich. In addition, the organization received funding for its distribution collection and the production of an annual catalog. As C. Carr relates in a chronological accounting of the NEA Culture Wars, 14 WMM films were attacked because of their representation of female, mostly lesbian, sexuality (Carr 2008). The Congressional Record of July 27, 2001 noted that, "In 1997, the American Family Association distributed to most members of Congress clips of some of these and other pornographic films distributed by Women Make Movies" (Congressional Record 2001). However, because of the strength of its earned income and the continuing demand for its films, the loss of its NEA funding for 3 years barely created a ripple in the organization's activities.

The same was not true for women's distributors around the world. In 1979, the feminist film journal, *Camera Obscura*, sent out a questionnaire to six distribution companies specializing in films by women and five others that had collections of interest to women. In WMM' response it was noted that the organization was "in the process of becoming a professional film and video organization" and that "setting up a good video distribution network" was listed as a future goal (*Camera Obscura* Questionnaire on Alternative Film Distribution, 1979). By the late 1980s, of the six organizations focusing on feminist film, WMM was the only one continuing with the agenda of distributing only films by and about women. Femmefilms, a short lived nonprofit distribution collective, was no longer functioning; two other distributors, New Day Films and Cambridge Documentary Films, had broadened their collections to include independent films by men; and two others were no longer in business as distributors. As foreseen by WMM, in the 1980s video had become a viable distribution format. Although this seemed to be a positive development for WMM, as the cost of distribution was much lower, other distributors in the US feared that the ease of duplication and the ability for users to tape "off the air" signaled the end of independent film distribution. Two of the six feminist film distributors, Serious Business Company, run by

Freude Bartlett, and Iris Films, founded by five women including Frances Reid, closed their distribution programs. Fortunately for WMM, both groups assisted WMM's growth by assisting the organization in acquiring films from their collections. Two of those films—*Thriller* and *Daughter Rite*—had played a major role in the rebuilding of WMM, as two of the key films in the New Directions collection. They were written about extensively in a chapter in E. Ann Kaplan's influential book, *Women & Film: Both Sides of the Camera* (1983), and by 1985 had become a staple in the teaching of feminist film.

Outside the US, feminist distribution outlets were not faring much better, although the reasons had little to do with the advent of video. The Sydney Filmmakers Co-operative was founded in 1970 with a particular emphasis on film for, by, and about women. In 1986, it closed its doors when the Australian Film Commission decided to fund only one distribution entity—the Australian Film Institute. In the UK, where there were two feminist distributors, a similar scenario was taking place. COW was set up in 1979 and had a particular focus on theatrical release of contemporary feminist narrative film and feature length social issue documentaries. Circles, which was founded a year later was more interested in feminist experimental film and films by pioneering women filmmakers like Germaine Dulac and Maya Deren. In 1990, the British Film Institute, their major funder, informed both groups that their funding was being cut to an extent that only one organization would be funded. After attempts to merge failed, Circles relaunched as Cinenova in 1991 (Knight and Thomas 2008). For 10 years, Cinenova struggled with limited funding to build an effective organization and is now an unstaffed archive of their film collection. In Vancouver, the Women in Focus Society, founded in 1974, "to develop positive images of women and their life experiences through the promotion of female artists and producers by making their art more visible and easily accessible to the public," also had difficulties with funding and transferred its collection to the Satellite Video Exchange Society in 1993 (rbscarchives. library.ubc.ca 1974; vivomediaarts.com 2016).

In Julia Knight and Peter Thomas's case study on Cinenova (2008), they point to some of the factors that contributed to the demise of the organization: the lack of commercial viability, under-resourcing, a changing marketplace, and the relationship with funders. I believe there are additional reasons and other factors that undermined the ability of the distribution efforts in the UK. In the US, there is a huge educational market, unparalleled anywhere else in the world, and this market makes it possible for smaller independent distributors to exist. Additionally, in England, independent distribution was negatively affected by the wide availability of independent production on television channels, such as Channel 4. Coupled with the pay TV policy in Britain (a policy in which all television owners pay an annual license fee), taping off the air was a much more common practice in the UK. In addition, WMM also had a commitment to diversity that started with the early years of the organization. Both Circles and Vancouver Women in Focus Society suffered from their origins in an art world that was slow in responding to the need for diversity in structure, programming, and outreach. This changed somewhat in 1989, when the Women in Focus Society hosted an extremely successful event In Visible Colours: An International Film/Video Festival and Symposium for Third World Women and Women of Colour. Monika Gagnon rightly called the event "remarkable and groundbreaking" in *Conundrums: Race, Culture and Canadian Art* (Gagnon 2000: 55). After this, Women in Focus tried to diversify their collection but it was too costly.

The demise of so many other feminist distributors increased WMM's commitment to maintaining its focus on the distribution of films by and about women, but it also increased the pressure on the organization to continue to rely on earned income, rather than grants.

As a result, in the late 1990s, WMM solidified its focus on documentary and concentrated on acquiring important transnational films being produced by women filmmakers. Although the collection was narrowed in focus and the organization no longer acquired many short experimental and narrative films, the market for documentaries was growing. The staff began to launch major outreach campaigns for these social issue documentaries, a precursor to today's community engagement campaigns that have recently become the focus of documentary film funding. One of the first of these campaigns was for *Calling the Ghosts* (Mandy Jacobson, Karmen Jelinčić, 1996), about the war in Bosnia-Herzegovina—the first film that explored rape as a weapon of war. WMM released the film theatrically in NYC and then worked with Amnesty International to organize a tour to a dozen cities, with exhibitions at local art houses and media centers as well as screenings on local college campuses. Long after its broadcast on HBO's Cinemax, the film continues to be seen and used as an important resource in university and college sociology and women's studies classes as well as referenced in pedagogical articles on the teaching of violence in the classroom (Schulman 1999; Salibrici 2004).

In 2002, the organization released *Señorita Extraviada, Missing Young Women*, Lourdes Portillo's groundbreaking documentary on the hundreds of women being murdered on the border of Mexico and the US. This was followed in 2004 with the Academy-nominated short film *God Sleeps in Rwanda* (Kimberlee Aquaro, 2004), which depicted the courage of Rwandan women following that country's genocide. In 2007, *The Greatest Silence: Rape in the Congo* (Lisa F. Jackson, 2007) was released around the same time that the issue was covered on the front page of the *NY Times* (Gettleman 2007). When Jackson started making her film, it was a subject almost unknown to anyone without a serious interest in the region or in women's rights in Africa. After Zalmay Khalilzad, the US Ambassador to the UN, saw the film, he introduced Security Council Resolution 1820, which demanded the "immediate and complete cessation by all parties to armed conflict of all acts of sexual violence against civilians," and stated for the first time that "rape and other forms of sexual violence can constitute war crimes" (United Nations 2008). It is this type of feminist filmmaking practice that is at the cornerstone of WMM's transnational feminist activism.

For the last 15 years, WMM has continued its commitment to both the filmmakers whose films it distributes and to the organizations that use the films in their cultural, community, and educational work. This unique history, coupled with the continued dedication to feminism and diverse representations of women, has not only made WMM one of the few surviving feminist media organizations that were founded in the 1970s, but also a thriving advocate for quality films by women that advance a transnational feminist agenda.

Related topics

Anne Ciecko, "African 'first films': gendered authorship, identity, and discursive resistance"
Priya Jaikumar, "Femininst and non-Western interrogations of film authorship"
Katarzyna Marciniak, "Revolting aesthetics: feminist transnational cinema in the US"
Belinda Smaill, "The documentary: female subjectivity and the problem of realism"

Bibliography

Bender, P. (1990). *Women Make Movies, Inc: Portrait of a Grassroots Organization in the 1970s and 1980s*. Masters. New York University.
Bruno, G. and Nadotti, M. (1988). *Off Screen: Women and Film In Italy*. London: Routledge.

Camera Obscura Questionnaire on Alternative Film Distribution (1979). *Camera Obscura: Feminism, Culture, and Media Studies*, 1–2(3–1 3–4), pp. 157–75.

Carr, C. (2008). An NEA Timeline (Just the Lowlights). *On Edge: Performance at the End of the Twentieth Century*, C. Carr. 2nd edn. Hanover, NH: Wesleyan University Press, pp.237–44.

Chelsea Picture Station Workshops (n.d.). (flyer) New York: Women Make Movies archives.

Cinematria Cineclub Feminista (2011). *Homenaje a Cine Mujer Precursoras del Cine Feminista en Colombia*. (online) Available at: http://cinematria.blogspot.com/2011/05/homenaje-cine-mujer-precursoras-del.html (Accessed February 15, 2016).

Congressional Record (2001). Washington, DC: US Government, p. 12174.

Fallica, K. (2013). *Sustaining Feminist Film Cultures: An Institutional History of Women Make Movies*. PhD University of Pittsburgh.

Foster, G. (1995). *Women Film Directors*. Westport, Conn.: Greenwood Press.

Gagnon, M. (2000). *Other Conundrums: Race, Culture and Canadian Art*. Vancouver: Arsenal Pulp Press, pp. 54–6.

Gettleman, J. (2007). Rape Epidemic Raises Trauma of Congo Wa. *NY Times*. (online) p. 1. Available at: www.nytimes.com/2007/10/07/world/africa/07congo.html?_r=0 (Accessed February 15, 2016).

Harbourfront Corporation. (1986). *A Report on International Women's Filmforum/Nairobi 1985*. Toronto, Canada, p. 7.

Kaplan, E. Ann. (1983) *Women & Film: Both Sides of the Camera*. London: Routledge.

Knight, J. and Thomas, P. (2008). Distribution and the Question of Diversity: A Case Study of Cinenova. *Screen*, 49(3), pp.354–65.

Marsh, Leslie L. (2008) *Embodying Citizenship in Brazilian Women's Film, Video, and Literature, 1971 to 1988*. Dissertation. University of Michigan.

NY Times (2003). U.N. Says Congo Rebels Carried Out Cannibalism and Rapes. (online) Available at: www.nytimes.com/2003/01/16/world/un-says-congo-rebels-carried-out-cannibalism-and-rapes.html (Accessed February 15, 2016).

rbscarchives.library.ubc.ca (1974). *Vancouver Women in Focus Society fonds*. RBSC/OSC Archives. (online) Available at: http://rbscarchives.library.ubc.ca/index.php/vancouver-women-in-focus-society-fonds (Accessed February 15, 2016).

Rich, B. (1998). *Chick Flicks*. Durham: Duke University Press.

Rich, B. (2013). The Confidence Game. *Camera Obscura: Feminism, Culture, and Media Studies*, 28(1 82), pp. 157–65.

Salibrici, M. (2004). The Transitional Space of Hidden Writing: A Resource for Teaching Critical Insight and Concern. *Pedagogy: Critical Approaches to Teaching Literature, Language, Composition, and Culture*, 4(2), pp. 215–40.

Schulman, B. (1999). The Unsettling Subject of Violence in Women's Lives: Encouraging Notes from the Classroom Front. *Women's Studies Quarterly*, 27(1/2), pp. 167–84.

Sisk, R. (1997). Pol Reels at Group's Racy Flicks. *Daily News*. (online) Available at: www.nydailynews.com/archives/news/pol-reels-group-racy-flicks-article-1.759173 (Accessed February 15, 2016).

Thomas, P. (2012). The British Workshop Movement and Amber Film Collective. *Studies in European Cinema*, 8(3), p.202.

United Nations (2008). *Security Council Demands Immediate and Complete Halt to Acts of Sexual Violence Against Civilians in Conflict Zones, Unanimously Adopting Resolution 1820 (2008)*. (online) Available at: www.un.org/press/en/2008/sc9364.doc.htm (Accessed February 15, 2016).

Vanstone, G. (2007). *D is for Daring*. Toronto: Sumach Press.

vivomediaarts.com (2016). *Women in Focus Society; VIVO Media Arts Centre*. (online) Available at: www.vivomediaarts.com/archive-library/special-collections/women-in-focus-collection/ (Accessed February 15, 2016).

White, P. (2006). The Last Days of Women's Cinema. *Camera Obscura: Feminism, Culture, and Media Studies*, 21(3 63), pp.145–51.

PART IV

Spectatorship, reception, projecting identities

This section considers one of feminist film theory's earliest interests—the spectator—charting developments in thinking about audiences as they intersect with new media, reception-based approaches, and fandom. Claire Pajaczkowska's essay examines the emergence of psychoanalytic film theory and its application beyond the gaze to new media-based documentaries, such as *Amy* (2015). Jenny Chamarette offers an introduction to thinking about film through a phenomenological lens, centering the body and sensation over psyche-based models, while Felicity Colman looks at the appeal of Gilles Deleuze's thought for feminist film theory, alongside the debated issue of the Deleuzian spectator. Janet Staiger gives a thorough overview of the history of reception studies as it relates to feminist concerns, while Katie Morrissey extends thinking about social audiences to the ever-expanding field of fan studies. In his contribution, Ikechukwu Obiaya looks at female audience reception in the Nollywood context. Finally, both Veronica Pravadelli and Rachel Lewis look at the representation of women onscreen, or what possible identifications are projected in the 1930s Hollywood film and contemporary lesbian intergenerational romance narratives, respectively. Pravadelli focuses on a shift in the representation of the modern woman around 1934, while Lewis compares contemporary "post-feminist" representations of intergenerational desire with counter-representations in the work of Cheryl Dunye and Jan Dunn.

Taken together, these essays offer a range of feminist approaches to thinking about viewing, and the relationships between media texts and their audiences. They also speak to historically and geographically located modes of analyzing spectators and audiences.

28

PSYCHOANALYSIS BEYOND THE GAZE

From celluloid to new media

Claire Pajaczkowska

This chapter provides a brief history of the concept of the gaze as it has been developed in psychoanalytic and feminist film theory, and then discusses three further developments of the theory that have emerged in recent decades. It discusses the relationship between the gaze as structured by the "classic realist text" and the gaze and scanning in the context of recent digital technologies of filmmaking. The discussion of cultures of oculocentrism incorporates both a feminist approach to cinematic sound and new research on the primacy of tactile, haptic, and other sensorial registers as cultures of embodied knowledge. The chapter concludes with an analysis of the documentary film *Amy (The Girl Behind the Name)* (Asif Kapadia, 2015) exploring how psychoanalytic theory can be used to analyze films that derive from new media.

The first wave of writing on gender and cinema, such as the *New Yorker* film critic Pauline Kael's book *Kiss Kiss Bang Bang* (1968) and screenwriter/critic Marjorie Rosen's *Popcorn Venus: Women, Movies and the American Dream* (1973) initiated a critical discipline which informed many scholarly and cultural practices. It was possible for film criticism to explore many innovative conceptual tools, possibly because cinema did not, until recently, enter the canon of academic respectability. As a product of industry, commerce, and new mass-media technologies, film was a deeply ambiguous object for academic study, and as such was regarded with ambivalence. It was, arguably, this "liminal" (Turner 1969), or edgy, status that enabled us to deploy interesting new methods of analysis to answer questions about sexuality, gender, narrative structure, and iconography. Hierarchies of high and low culture, of difference and indifference, were inverted as the feminist critical paradigm engaged with cultures and methods beyond the academy. It is the discourse of film analysis, and especially the critical reflections on identity, sex, and gender, that have proven to be methodologically groundbreaking.

Why psychoanalysis?

The critical questioning of gender stereotypes within cinema soon led to a feeling that concepts of "objectification" and "the sex object," although accurate, were not quite complex and nuanced enough to explain the impact and influence of cinema, and a search for more apposite analytic methods was begun. Critics had noted the absence of significant female roles in cinema, and that, in the rare event of central roles for women, these film plots tended to feature the spectacular rise of female protagonists and their subsequent fall, or symbolic humiliation. Critics turned to narrative theory to deconstruct the patterns and conventions of cinematic storylines. The analysis of narrative revealed that stories were plotted using cinematography to articulate point of view. The same conventions of framing, lighting, and camera movement were used in cinematography to represent gender roles. Critics sought to understand, in greater depth, the structures governing the connection between point of view, photographic perspective, and subjectivity, and therefore existing theories of iconography became integrated with cinematographic analysis (Barthes 1955; Lesage 1986). Barthes, for instance, noted that the face of Greta Garbo was deployed as an icon that functioned as a mask to exceed the naturalism of film narrative.

In understanding the exact collusion between imagery, cinematic pleasure, and narrative structure, no theory was more powerful than the structuralist "apparatus theory," with its integration of theories of ideology, specific signifying systems, and unconscious phantasy. Psychoanalysis was understood as a method of deconstruction.

As a culture of the new, a culture of the mechanized, industrialized, and urbanized world, cinema, in the past century, has become iconic of modernity itself. From a sideshow attraction at the music hall, the pier, and the picture palace, to the live streaming of digital media, films are viewed on billions of devices everywhere, but not only is the structure of cinema ubiquitous—the pace and speed of technological innovation within cinema has accelerated as well. Films are now seen on emails, on social media, and in digital games, redefining the boundaries between public and private spaces, between factual and imaginary realities. New technologies mean that processes of production are increasingly democratized. The mechanisms of dissemination, too, are readily available to people without either specialist cinematographic training or the traditional power and social capital of the media barons and movie moguls.

How has this accelerated democratization of access to cinematic production affected the culture of the moving image? For much of the twentieth century, from discussions of Eisenstein's work to postmodern auteurism, film critics and theorists have argued that cinema is an "art" that is equal in cultural status to the canonical fields of opera, theater, painting, architecture, music, and literature. A different critical orthodoxy proposes that the value of film is its status as "the movies"—the popular, mass culture of a post-industrial crowd. In film theory it was usual to apply different forms of analysis to auteurist cinema and genre films. Not until the emergence of the gender question did the theory of apparatus, applicable to cinema as a whole, become fully articulated.

The unconscious structures of cinema

Apart from the interesting experiments of the Frankfurt School sociologists and critical theorists, it was not until the application of psychoanalysis to film that psychoanalysis was used as anything other than a specialist therapy or specialist sub-genre of literary and art theory. It was the structuralist turn which changed this. Anthropologists and sociologists of modernity noted that to study cinema is to study the most significant structures of culture and society itself. Just as religion became the object of analysis for the earliest sociologist, Émile Durkheim, so the structures of contemporary mass culture are cinematic. Similarly, Durkheim's follower Max Weber proposed that one of the most powerful forms of culture within the rational-legal matrices of capitalism is the irrational pull of "the charismatic." To analyze and decode cinema is to study the structures, thoughts, ideas, and fantasies of modernity. Cultural theorist Raymond Williams defined cultural thinking as a "structure of feeling" (Williams 1954). And nowhere are the material effects of irrational but charismatic feelings more evident than in cinema. Using both the structuralist and culturalist paradigms of analysis, inaugurated by Durkheim and Williams respectively, it is in the structures of cinema that the most fundamental patterns and myths of human thought and behavior can be found. Lévi-Strauss' concept of an "architectonic" system of the human mind, aptly interpreted by Barthes, became the methodological principle for deconstructing the hair-styles of televisual and cinematic Romans.

The structuralist paradigm of analysis, with its origins in the French human sciences, Soviet formalism, and Freudian psychoanalysis, generated a toolbox of concepts such as narrative structure, semiotic codes, specific signifying systems, and the power of iconography.

Psychoanalysis was integrated within structuralism as one possible method of deconstructing fundamental logics determining patterns of division and union of signifying elements. The presence of the dynamic unconscious was accepted by the human sciences as a provisional description of mind that could be used until neuroscience might provide a more materialist description. The patterns of unconscious thoughts and the logic of unconscious "reason" are best understood by psychoanalytic theory of the dynamic unconscious. A post-positivist theory of society includes the Freudian theory of mind, which is understood as only partly conscious of the forces by which it is governed.

Concepts such as the Oedipal (ambivalence) dynamic were used to analyze stories of conflict and quest, no different from narratives in Greek tragedy or literature. However, film analysts found that the stories in cinema are very different, in form if not in content, from the stories in mythology, religion, and literature. The uniqueness of cinematic language is in the relationship between story and plot. In film, the story is completely different because of the way in which it is "told"—a vital dualism described by Christian Metz as the tension between "story" and "discourse" (Metz 1975). Metz uses the linguistic theorist Émile Benveniste's distinction between "*histoire*" and "*discours*," two functions of language, to identify two different kinds of voyeurism within the signifying system of cinema.

Metz argues that this is a vital psychic mechanism of both cinema and video, and he distinguishes between *histoire* (the story or narration which is issued by an all-knowing but unseen intelligence) and *discours* (the act of telling, the material practice of making meaning). Two consequences of this analytic method followed. One was the insight that this kind of textual deconstruction offered to ideological analysis. The second was the development of textual analysis into apparatus theory. The apparatus theory of Jean-Louis Baudry, like Metz's concept of the "imaginary signifier," explored further the psychoanalysis of voyeurism, unconscious fantasy, and sexual identity (Baudry & Williams 1974).

It was, and is still, of ideological interest that in classic realist texts the imaginary transparency of *histoire* is valued as being superior to, or more truthful than, the subjective form of *discours*. Historians often note that realism and naturalism are the genres that found popularity within "bourgeois" culture, in societies in which middle-class values are considered the norm.

The apparatus of cinema as a realist or naturalist genre of storytelling tends to maintain the conventions that propose that "neutral" objectivity is superior to embodied "subjectivity." Feminist filmmakers have used textual innovations to foreground the point of view and the voice of the first-person narrator. Postmodern critics have challenged this idea of the distinction between objective and subjective, "*histoire*" and "*discours*," by suggesting that all enunciation issues from a subjective interest, and that it is only possible to make culture which recognizes "the end of history," or the end of the myth of a disinterested neutrality of authority. The critique of the classic realist text, as a structure of conventions, is of real interest to feminist analysts, as most of the conventions reiterate the distinction between a masculine objectivity, which is disembodied and transcendental, and therefore authoritative, and a feminine subjectivity which is embodied, and therefore suspect. The critique of the classic realist text was considered an essential strategy for new feminine and feminist filmmaking. Counter-cinema (Wollen 1982; Johnston 1973) was considered a vital experimental strategy for implementing cultural and ideological change. Audio and visual tracks were combined in ways that challenge the production values of conventional continuity editing. Intertextuality was a strategy that combined different genres and styles of film within a text (Johnston 1973).

This was first proposed by Jean-Louis Baudry (1974), who suggested that a psychic "apparatus," as defined by Freud and Lacan, fits with cinematic conventions of classic realist cinema through a process of denial of difference. Just as spectators in the auditorium sit with their backs to the projector, without occlusions to their gaze at the large and luminous cinema screen, watching photogenic actors in a sequence of carefully edited shots that create a fiction of disembodied omniscience (seeing all without being seen), so the unconscious instinct for voyeurism is gratified. The neural capacity for "persistence of vision" denies the intermittent images, and creates an illusion of continuity. Baudry further analyzes the structure of different kinds of identification within the spectator–screen mechanism, pointing out that the primary identification of scopophilia or voyeurism between self and screen is overlaid with a secondary ego identification of self and characters. As the secondary identification is more readily brought into consciousness and discussed, the pleasures of gratification of the primary "gazes" (of the camera at objects, the spectator at the screen) are repressed and remain unconscious.

It was French theorist Christian Metz, and British filmmakers and theorists Peter Wollen and Laura Mulvey, who further developed this analysis into a fully gendered articulation of the unconscious of the cinematic apparatus. In 1975, Mulvey's essay "Visual Pleasure and Narrative Cinema" was published in *Screen*, triggering five decades of debate, critical analysis, and creative practice in film, with many applications extending into literature, art history, critical theory, and qualitative methods in social science. Mulvey noted that the textual structures of realism, which tend to repress primary identification as a "controlling and curious gaze," (Mulvey 1975: 8) give spectators the illusion of omniscience and omnipotence, and are congruent with a phallocentric ideology. Applications of Mulvey's theory produced the observation that cinema is one instance of an ideology which entitles predatory fantasies of sexual control to become enacted or gratified without consciousness, or by a "splitting" of the ego. Mulvey's essay proposes techniques of counter-cinema as experimental methods for deconstructing the apparatus (see also Johnston 1973 and Wollen 1982). Wollen proposed several characteristics of counter-cinema, including narrative intransitivity or the interruption of sequential editing, to counter the illusion of narrative transitivity or the illusion of causality, which is observed in the conventions of traditional realist continuity editing. The "aperture," or open-ended text, is offered as an alternative to the imaginary closure which seals separate realities within the conventions of film genres. Intertextuality or multiple diegeses are offered as countering the realist conventions of a single or unitary diegesis. It was suggested that unpleasure, or radical and revolutionary beauty, might become an alternative sublime to challenge the traditional forms of satisfaction sought by traditional audiences. Mulvey and Wollen made a series of highly influential experimental films which deployed counter-cinema techniques to construct narrative differently (see, for example, *Riddles of the Sphinx* 1977). These films juxtaposed still and moving image using montage techniques and a variety of soundtrack experiments to generate different forms of representing sexual difference.

The impact of Mulvey's essay was very generative. Filmmakers experimented with cinematic techniques that would construct a "female gaze." An influential collection of essays, *The Female Gaze: Women as Viewers of Popular Culture* (Lorraine Gamman and Margaret Marshment 1988), and E. Ann Kaplan's 1983 text "Is the Gaze Male?," indicated the extent to which the concept had articulated the concerns of two generations of feminist filmmakers and theorists. In 1989, feminist film journal *Camera Obscura* published a special issue, entitled "The Spectatrix," which reviewed the many debates on female spectatorship that developed in response to Mulvey's apparatus theory. The concept of the gaze was adopted, by extension, to describe the point of view of such other subordinate symbolic categories, such as the "queer gaze" (Gamman & Evans 1995), the "postcolonial gaze" (Said 1978), the "oppositional gaze" (hooks 1992), and the "imperial gaze" (Kaplan 1997).

Several essays questioned the attribution of gender to ocular positions of dominance and subordination within a series of textual structures. The concept of the gaze was no longer limited to the original formulation of a specific apparatus of the classic realist Hollywood film text. Theorists, inspired by Mulvey, found other articulations of gender and power within Hollywood cinema. Filmmakers, both independent and mainstream, responded to the influence of feminism and experimented with a range of strategies for constructing new conventions of representing sexual difference. The discussion of psychoanalytic method in film analysis continued to generate a specific focus on interpretative methodology in film theory. Kaplan's major essays, including "Is the Gaze Male?" were published as *Psychoanalysis and Cinema* (1990).

The debates proliferated, and a decade after Mulvey's essay was published, Gaylyn Studlar proposed a further development of the apparatus theory. Whereas Mulvey focused on the unconscious Oedipal dynamic and its effect in predisposing the spectator to a hypersensitivity to optical meaning and to fantasies of castration and bodily damage, in her essay "Masochism and the Perverse Pleasures of the Cinema" Studlar explores the range of sensory and ideational experiences that are considered, in psychoanalysis, as specific to the pre-Oedipal stages of subjective development (1984). The realm of pre-Oedipal subjectivity is of significance to gender because this is the stage in infancy and childhood which is experienced in close proximity to the psyche and the body of the mother, thereby activating a whole matrix of sensory, affective, and symbolic structures. Mulvey correctly identifies scopophilic instincts as integrally connected to epistemophilia, the desire to know everything, and thus catering to ego instincts of control and sadism. She analyzes the primary identification of the spectator in classic realism as shoring up the narrative structures of controlling and punishing cinematic objects of desire and seduction. Moreover, Mulvey suggests that the seductive images of women are especially desirable and frustrating, and that these are therefore objects of ritual and symbolic humiliation and punishment, gratifying the sadistic element of unconscious instincts.

Studlar explores this predicament further in her book *In the Realm of Pleasure* (1993), questioning the division of identification between masculine and feminine spectators, in order to propose that there is something seductive and pleasurable for the spectator in their state of regressive helplessness, sustained and entertained by the apparatus. This she rightly identifies as "masochism," a sensory pleasure in the activity of passive receptivity. If this is configured as the passive accommodation of emotional brutalization, this is the spectatorial equivalent of an orgiastic climax of sensory excitation. Masochism may result as a response to the spectator's immobility in the space of the cinema, but it is a pleasure of control, as it consists in eliciting the active agency of another to act upon the unconscious wishes of the ego, whereas unpleasure would, in cinematic terms, be the capacity to experience the psychic work of tolerating frustration (the unpleasure of counter-cinema). Studlar, drawing on Gilles Deleuze's study of Sacher-Masoch's book *Venus in Furs* (1971), explores the cinematic pleasures of the spectator's unconscious narrative agency based on the ego pleasure of passivity, which is doubly controlling, as this requires the setting up of a scenario in which the perpetrator is compelled to act on the victim. The passive/masochistic aspect of the ego derives pleasure from the gratification of the unconscious ego, and this, notes Studlar, is the cinematic gratification of the apparatus of the classic realist text.

Psychoanalysis beyond the gaze

There are two directions in which the psychoanalytic study of film and gender has developed beyond the theory of the gaze. The first is through contestations of the primacy of the optical, by close readings of the significance of acoustic, haptic, and cross-modal forms of sensory processing activated by signifying systems such as films. The second is through analysis of the kind of attention that is generated by new digital media, as distinct from the apparatus of the classic realist text and its viewing in the cinema auditorium. Alongside the development of debates about the female spectator and the new codes of textuality that digital practices create, a number of other ways in which psychoanalysis is used to think about gender and cinema have developed.

Theorists Mary Anne Doane (1991) and Kaja Silverman (1988) developed a textual psychoanalysis of classic realist cinema, investigating sensory experience and the meaning of sound and the acoustic register. Doane's concept of the voice in cinema as a sensory and imaginary space of embodiment offers different registers of textual analysis. Doane is especially interested in the way that the phenomenon of infantile omnipotence is a fantasy that underlies cultural texts. She argues that vision and scopophilia/voyeurism are not necessarily hegemonic within this configuration of the body ego. Acoustic sensory experience can be a source of imaginary plenitude as richly significant as the visual, yet this activates a different series of meanings. She discusses the concept of the film text as a "body" in relation to the imaginary body of the infantile ego, and articulates cinema's regressive pleasures and gratifications of the senses. For Doane, there are more textual strategies available to feminism than the unpleasure of counter-cinema proposed by Mulvey.

Silverman's concept of sound as an "acoustic mirror" offers a different perspective on the pleasures of entertainment, where the audience is "held" in the acoustic environment of cinematic texts. Silverman builds on the Lacanian concept of the ego as a psychic mechanism that is structured through the mirror stage, advancing the concept of cinema as providing an acoustic mirror that offers a self-identity not necessarily specular in foundation.

Doane proposes that there are films which contain significant episodes where protagonists advance the story through auditory means rather than through an exchange of secondary gazes. In effect, Doane, like Studlar, questions the hegemonic status of the Oedipal complex and suggests that the maternal pre-Oedipal dynamic may be accountable for a substrate of meanings that persist beneath the traditional iconographies of sexual difference. Another challenge to the ideology of oculocentrism described by Baudry is the reconsideration of the significance of tactility and sensory processing as cross-modal.

Miriam Hansen (1995: 364) notes this "holding" quality of the immersive experience of the pleasures of popular cinema, suggesting that "entertainment" has etymological roots in *tenere* (Latin, "to hold"), offering thereby another set of origins for the satisfactions of the holding functions of primary identification within the gaze. Hansen does not deploy psychoanalysis to account for this holding function of the cinematic pleasure of mass audiences, but her observations as a historian suggest that the group phenomenon of cinema as popular culture operates as a manifestation of what British psychoanalyst D. W. Winnicott calls a "holding environment," (Winnicott 1953: 89–97) which can trigger powerful emotional experiences.

This specifically psychoanalytic theory—that the ego is built up of representations of cross-modal interchanges between visual, tactile, kinesthetic, and acoustic experiences that function to symbolize, and thus "contain," emotional experience—finds recognition in the exploration of theories of affect and the haptic. Following this direction, American cultural theorist Giuliana Bruno's *Atlas of Emotion: Journeys in Art, Architecture and Film* (2007) starts with the work of Siegfried Kracauer and Walter Benjamin to extend the reach of the paradigm that emerged through film theory into architecture and art. Developing a concept of the haptic as a sense that translates tactile sensory processing into optical registers, this extraordinary book offers new frontiers to explore (for more on haptic approaches to spectatorship see Chamarette, this volume).

The second development of psychoanalysis beyond the gaze emerges from the advance of new technologies of making, storing, and disseminating digital imagery. New digital technologies, in both hardware and software, have revolutionized the ways that cinema is experienced and understood. Scanning has replaced gazing as the principal form of attention paid to moving image data. Since television and broadcast media began to replace cinema in the mid-twentieth century, there has been a steady increase in the diversification of media through which moving image culture is encountered. It is no longer even possible to refer to these multiple forms, generically, as film or cinema. Visual data is now commonly streamed; most young people no longer watch television but access content, including feature-length films and entire television series, online, either on laptops, tablets, or smartphones. The diversification of platforms for storing and distributing film and visual time-based media has changed the terms of spectatorship. The scale of the screen image, in relation to other optical data, is no longer impressively large, nor exclusive. It is no longer experienced as a source of plenitude or luxury. The ubiquity of gaming as a medium of navigating narrative and digital space is transforming the relationship between visual pleasure and narrative cinema as described and analyzed by Baudry, Metz, Wollen, and Mulvey. Most transformative of all is the way that social media, combined with smartphone technology, has made the interface between maker and spectator into one of complete reciprocity. The vocabulary of spectatorship now includes the concept of the "selfie," and indeed the manufacture of "selfie sticks," has enabled spectators to become pro-filmic events, without the intermediary of a producer, scriptwriter, director, or cinematographer. Blogging and vlogging (video blogging) expands the range of voices finding broadcast form, and multiplies the concept of the ownership of the means of distribution. This instant democratization of the means of recording and transmitting filmic records, statements, and creations has been noted as having extraordinary agency in such political events as the series of political uprisings known as the Arab Spring, and continues to have dramatic agency in providing photographic evidence of, for example, police brutality against black victims in the US or South Africa.

The forms of attention which are generated by this technological transformation are tracked and studied by psychoanalysts, amongst others. Cultural theorists describe the effects of this digitization of communication as a rhizomatic, or "flattening," effect on focus:

the postmodernist concept of the absence of the center vis-à-vis the attraction of the margins, or the continuous folding of the margins into the center, indicates a new form of attention. Some of the anxieties leveled at this technological change are familiar, resonating with the anxieties expressed about the effects of modernity in the fin-de-siècle city. This has become absorbed as a form of intertextuality within film culture. Once noted by Peter Wollen as a characteristic of counter-cinema, the meta-textual or self-referential qualities of the means of production now take on a multiplicity of meanings.

A good example of this complexity is found in *Amy (The Girl Behind the Name)*, a 2015 British documentary directed by Asif Kapadia. Focusing on the life of singer-songwriter Amy Winehouse (1983–2011), from a 13-year-old singing with friends, to her death from alcohol poisoning at 27, the film is composed of extracts from home movies, television footage, archival documentary footage from concerts and clips from phone movies, YouTube and blog posts, and interviews.

The subject of the film, which was shown to critical acclaim at the Cannes Film Festival and Edinburgh International Film Festival, and won the Oscar for best documentary feature, is the subcultural capital (Thornton 1995) that is generated when media and celebrity reflect their fascination with each other, the laser-like intensification of intertextuality producing a recursive feedback resonance loop of attention and interest. That this is more than an abstract concept is evident in the fact that the film was immensely meaningful to popular audiences, becoming the highest-grossing documentary ever, and making over £3 million at the box office on the first weekend of its release. With a production budget of £3 million it earned over £23 million on general release. It is extraordinary that a documentary film made solely of fragments of found footage, interspersed with the recordings of voiceovers and live interviews (but without any talking heads), should achieve critical acclaim and general popularity simultaneously.

Baudry describes the attraction of the cinema screen as "bordered with black like a letter of condolence" (1974: 44), and this is explicitly evident in *Amy*. The film traces the compelling attraction of the jazz chanteuse icon to a young Jewish girl from Southgate, north London. Amy's fascination with the power of the traces of tragic experience in the voices of the singers she most admired becomes materialized in the fascination of the mechanisms of celebrity culture. Art and life imitate one another in a mirroring alienation that makes Douglas Sirk melodramas look like the *Friends* television series. In Sirk's *Imitation of Life* (1959), he demonstrates the power of an identification with stardom, which makes a girl deny her black mother and identify with the illusion of Hollywood celebrity. Sirk uses the power of the blues music at the final scene of the funeral to augment the poignancy of the experience. In *Amy*, we see the singer fascinated by the promise of fame, and in this film it is the voice of the blues that reveals her contradictions. *Amy* lays bare the devices of reality television culture, which measures its successes by the metrics of television ratings, and, therefore, will push at the boundaries of ethical concern in order to produce an ever more sensationalist spectacle of the ideological effects of the cinematic apparatus on "ordinary" people. Merely 120 years since its birth, cinema has evolved into a medium which devours the stars it creates.

It is interesting that the focus of *Amy* is the voice of the singer. Her appearance is spectacular, beautiful, and compelling, and the film follows the way that the adoration of her looks generates sadism. The comedians who are filmed making jokes about the self-destructiveness of the singer are presented as the mouthpieces of an audience, as much as examples of especially vindictive celebrity-seekers. The fragments of home movies and archival footage from concerts and auditions reveal the fragmentary narrative of a girl trying to construct a facilitating environment for herself from the illusory reflections of the gaze of others. The metaphor for addiction—as self-medication or a doomed attempt to generate a reliable environment to replace the one which has fragmented and left the ego vulnerable—is complete. The fragmented medium of the film's narrative is visible and visually palpable in the "haptic visuality" of a chaotic life, constantly on the move from one stage to the next. The denial of this fragmentation is what keeps Winehouse afloat, and is what helps the spectator maintain the thread. It is the voice of the singer which others recognize as having the texture of suffering: the growl in the throat, the tremor and instability of affect; the semiotic which constantly promises to overwhelm the symbolic, which keeps the spectator locked into a profound bond of empathy. The singer's voice is her pain, the cry of affect, and is simultaneously the expression which appeases the pain and contains the suffering in words. If the gaze of the media proves inadequate to sustain Winehouse's need for a facilitating environment, it is this insufficiency that precipitates a turn to the tangible materials of "substance," and to the control over the intermittent doses of the returned gaze. The words of the songs, traced through Amy's notebooks, diaries, and journals, like the words of the witnesses and friends or professionals around her, seem lucid but powerless in comparison with the strength of her voice. It is, as Barthes noted, "the grain of the voice" (1977) which carries, holds, and grips us. More compelling than the *tenere* of entertainment, the grain of the voice is the focal point, or "punctum," of the picture.

Beyond the gaze, the spectator is brought to the *per-sona:* the person articulated through sound. The film's subtitle, *The Girl Behind the Name*, suggests the person behind the mask (and *persona* is the word for the mask used in Greek tragedy), constructed to amplify the voice in order to reach the whole audience in the amphitheater. It was in this search for the experience of being loved, or trying to generate, by means of singing and by being reflected back in the admiring gazes of the media, a "good enough" holding environment, that we are shown the mechanism by which subjectivity itself is made and unmade. In *Amy* the spectator is addressed as a viewer and as a user of digital social media, as both emitter and receiver of messages, which are shown as multiple and heterogeneous, contradictory and contested. The viewer can, with sensory modality and with affective resonance, "feel," in the textures of differences between media, voices, and images, the way that the interplay of activity and passivity within gazes is experienced as a medium of "holding." The scopic regime of cinema is articulated, in the unconscious, with other sensory modalities, such as sound, movement, and haptic visuality, in ways that invite readers to create new applications of psychoanalytic and feminist textual analysis.

Related topics

Kathleen Vernon, "Sound and gender"
E. Ann Kaplan, "Visualizing climate trauma: the cultural work of films anticipating the future"
Jenny Chamarette, "Embodying spectatorship: from phenomenology to sensation"
Belinda Smaill, "The documentary: female subjectivity and the problem of realism"
Patrice Petro, "Classical feminist film theory: then and (mostly) now"

Bibliography

Barthes, R. (1955) "The Face of Greta Garbo," in *Mythologies* (1972), London: Cape, pp.56–7.
——— (1977) "The Grain of the Voice," in *Image, Music, Text*, selected and translated by S. Heath, London: Fontana, pp. 179–89.

Baudry, J. L., Williams, A. (1974) "Ideological Effects of the Basic Cinematographic Apparatus," *Film Quarterly*, 28.2, 39–47.

Bruno, G. (2007) *Atlas of Emotion: Journeys in Art, Architecture and Film*, New York: Verso.

Deleuze, G. (1993) *The Fold: Leibniz and the Baroque*, London: Athlone Press.

Deleuze, G. (1971) *Masochism: An Interpretation of Coldness and Cruelty*, New York: George Braziller.

Doane, M. A. (1991) *Femmes Fatales: Feminism, Film Theory, Psychoanalysis*, London: Routledge.

Gamman, L., and Marshment, M. (eds.) (1988) *The Female Gaze: Women as Viewers of Popular Culture*, London: Women's Press.

Gamman, L., and Evans, C. (1995) "Reviewing Queer Viewing: Gaze Theory Revisited," in C. Richardson and P. Burston (eds.), *A Queer Romance: Lesbians, Gay Men and Popular Culture*, Oxford: Routledge, pp. 13–56.

Hansen, M. (1995) "America, Paris, the Alps: Kracauer and Benjamin on Cinema and Modernity," in L. Charney and V. R. Schwartz (eds.) *Cinema and the Invention of Modern Life*, Berkeley, CA: University of California Press, pp. 262–402.

hooks, b. (1992). "The Oppositional Gaze," in *Black Looks: Race and Representation*, Boston: South End Press, pp. 115–31.

Johnston, C. (1973) "Women's Cinema as Counter-Cinema," in C. Johnston (ed.) *Notes on Women's Cinema*, London: London Society for Education in Film and Television.

Kael, P. (1968) *Kiss Kiss Bang Bang*, Boston: Little, Brown.

Kaplan, E. A. (1983) "Is the Gaze Male?," in *Psychoanalysis and Cinema* (1990), London: Routledge.

———— (1990) *Psychoanalysis and Cinema*, London: Routledge.

———— (1997) *Looking for the Other: Feminism, Film and the Imperial Gaze: Nation, Woman and Desire in Film*, London: Routledge.

Lesage, J. (1986) "D. W. Griffith's *Broken Blossoms*: Artful Racism, Artful Rape," in C. Gledhill (ed.) *Home is Where the Heart is*, London: British Film Institute.

Marks, L. U. (2000) *The Skin of the Film: Intercultural Cinema, Embodiment and the Senses*, Durham, NC: Duke University Press.

———— (2002) *Touch: Sensuous Theory and Multisensory Media*, Minneapolis: University of Minnesota Press.

Metz, C. (1975) "Story/Discourse: A Note on Two Kinds of Voyeurisms," in *The Imaginary Signifier: Psychoanalysis and the Cinema*, Bloomington, IN: Indiana University Press, pp. 91–8.

Mulvey, L. (1975) "Visual Pleasure and Narrative Cinema," *Screen*, 16.3, 6–18.

Rosen, M. (1973) *Popcorn Venus: Women, Movies and the American Dream*, New York: Coward, McCann and Geoghegan.

Said, E. (1978) *Orientalism*, London: Routledge & Kegan Paul.

Silverman, K. (1988) *The Acoustic Mirror: The Female Voice in Psychoanalysis and Cinema*, Bloomington, IN: Indiana University Press.

Studlar, G. (1984) "Masochism and the Perverse Pleasures of the Cinema," *Quarterly Review of Film Studies*, 9.4, 267–82.

———— (1993) *In the Realm of Pleasure*, New York: Columbia University Press.

Thornton, S. (1995) *Club Cultures: Music, Media and Subcultural Capital*, London: Polity.

Turner, V. (1969) *The Ritual Process*, Harmondsworth: Penguin.

Williams, R. (1954) *Preface to Film*, London: Film Drama.

Winnicott, D. W. (1953) "Transitional Objects and Transitional Phenomena," *International Journal of Psychoanalysis*, 34, 89–97.

Wollen, P. (1982) *Readings and Writings: Semiotic Counter Strategies*, London: Verso.

29

EMBODYING SPECTATORSHIP

From phenomenology to sensation

Jenny Chamarette

Film-phenomenology is written from the perspective of the now. What do you see when you sit in front of a film—in the cinema, on your laptop or tablet or mobile device, in a park with an open-air inflatable screen, on television, or in a dilapidated warehouse with performers enacting parts of the film in front of you? What do you experience? Do you remember that you have a body that is connected to and through your eyes? Or do you become so engrossed in the film that you wince if flesh is pierced or a fireball erupts from a car, as if you were inside the world of the film yourself? Do you shiver from the over-active air-conditioning in the cinema or classroom, or are there goosebumps on your skin from a particularly shocking film sequence? Do you feel invited by the film to consider something other than what you see—what you hear for instance, what you are enticed to reach out to touch, or even to smell? These questions are phenomenological: they are about interrogating, describing, and accounting for the conditions that give rise to, or emerge from, the experience of viewing film.

Let's say that a conventional approach to "reading" a film is a little like imagining that you are looking at a film text as a surgeon would do, scrutinizing her patient on the operating table, aiming to examine the inner organs, to excise unwanted material or patch up damaged tissue, or to establish a diagnosis. If we carry that analogy further, into a phenomenological approach, imagine that you are not the surgeon, nor the film a "patient" on the operating table, but you and the film are part of the whole room, the whole hospital, the time and the place of the town in which the hospital is based, the sound of the ticking clock and the buzzing of neon lights overhead and the movable lamps, the beep of the monitor and the rustle of cloth, the moment of breath and the beats of many hearts. Imagine that you are observing yourself observing, just as you are observing what is observed in the film. That means paying attention to the things that are unsaid, the objects that fall out of the frame, the off-screen, and the on-screen, and yourself. It also means understanding the ways in which you come to use the terms "I" or "we" when writing about film. Is the "I" position necessarily less useful because it acknowledges your own subjective positioning with relation to the film? Many academic writing courses discourage the use of "I" in undergraduate writing, and yet, film-phenomenology attempts to recuperate the validity of a subjective writing position, rather than trying to maintain the pretense of an omniscient or transcendental "I." Film-phenomenology also attempts to discuss the ways in which viewing

311

bodies—and the bodies in and on film—are situated in specific environmental and cultural contexts, which are not more or less important than the film, but which will necessarily permeate any account, description or analysis of it. Before I go further however, the term "phenomenology" itself warrants some explanation.

Phenomenology is the study of things as they appear in the world. While this concept seems simple enough, the ways in which phenomenology manifests itself, particularly in the study of gender and cinema, become more complex. Phenomenology is often identified as an alternative to philosophy—but this is confusing, because many of the individuals associated with the emergence of phenomenology were themselves European philosophers of the eighteenth, nineteenth, and early-twentieth centuries. As is so often the case, this list reads in the masculine: Georg Wilhelm Friedrich Hegel, Edmund Husserl, and Martin Heidegger are all associated with the emergence of phenomenology as a philosophical field (for introductory guides to these, see Stern 2013; Russell 2006; Gorner 2007). But perhaps it is not helpful to begin with the philosophical origins of phenomenology, particularly because phenomenology itself is not interested in origins or roots. It is interested in the now: what we see, how we perceive, and how those perceptions shape or become the world that is constitutive both of our environment and of us.

In this chapter, I am not just seeking to connect feminism with phenomenology, or phenomenology with film, but gender, film, *and* phenomenology. I am also interrogating terms of varying familiarity to Film Studies—spectatorship, embodiment, and sensation. This is no doubt a difficult task. But it is important to identify those aspects of thinking about film that destabilize film as a detached object of cool observation, an object that can be decoded or "read" as a text. If studies of spectatorship acknowledge that the screen is not the only site where meaning is made for a film, then studies of embodied spectatorship go one step further. They attempt to talk about the ways that film relates to and affects a film viewer's entire bodily experience: her breathing, her sensation, her memory, and her emotion.

Feminist perspectives on film-phenomenology question conventional hierarchies of the subject who looks (the cinematic spectator) and the object that is looked at (the film). They also question the dualisms that have pervaded western Enlightenment critical thought: mind over body, sight over all the other senses, language above bodily experience, sensibility over sensation, depth over surface, and articulation over inarticulacy. Like other kinds of questioning discourse—queer theory, critical race theory, postcolonial studies, critical disability studies—feminist film-phenomenology tries to uncover and make visible the dichotomies that are already present in any attempt to describe the world of film "as it is." Our perceptions are never excluded from the world that we are in and the world that makes us. As the French phenomenologist Maurice Merleau-Ponty discusses, we are always "beings-in-the-world" in the sense that Heidegger suggests, but that also means we are embodied beings, who perceive the world before we can philosophize about it (Merleau-Ponty 1962).

We cannot consider our perception of the world separately from the world itself—and because we cannot do this, we also cannot conceive of *ourselves* as separate from the world. This rather mystical statement is actually quite radical: it implies that we cannot talk about a subject and object with any kind of clear distinction. When we look at film, what film looks at, and the positions from which we look, these are part of a continuum, rather than distinct and separate concerns. Perhaps this is the most significant difference between psychoanalysis and phenomenology: where psychoanalysis is interested in uncovering the unconscious subject and object relations or power systems within a film, phenomenology is interested in the ways that film experience manifests itself, which may indeed flow between subjects, objects, and others that slip beyond the category of either "subject" or "object." Phenomenology is not interested in the subject so much as it is interested in subjectivity—the ebbs and flows of life that emerge in our experience of it, including in relation to film. This also means that time, and the flow of time, are important to phenomenological and sensory studies of film (Chamarette 2012; Mroz 2012). Film experience has the capacity to make time concertina-like: it is possible for an event in time to be both there (on the screen) and *then* (recorded at another time).

Though phenomenology emerges from a nineteenth century German school of thought, the most prominent phenomenological thinkers adopted by Film Studies are not German but French: Jean-Paul Sartre, Simone de Beauvoir, and particularly Merleau-Ponty (Sartre 1936, 1943; Beauvoir 1949; Merleau-Ponty 1964). Inspired by Husserl and Heidegger's transcendental phenomenology, and by new discoveries in gestalt psychology, Merleau-Ponty's writing on aesthetics, sexuality, non-linguistic communication, art, and indeed his short essay on cinema, all discuss ways of accounting for the world as it is perceived and lived existentially (Merleau-Ponty 1964, 1968; Johnson 1993). Although he died prematurely in 1961, Merleau-Ponty greatly influenced both Sartre and Beauvoir. Beauvoir's *The Second Sex*, often cited as the first example of feminist phenomenology, describes women's lived, situated experience in Western Europe in the 1950s (Beauvoir 1949; Heinämaa 1999). This kind of existential phenomenology has an enduring legacy in studies of embodiment, spectatorship, and sensation in film. Feminist phenomenology in particular demonstrates that the lived experience of being-in-the-world, and the nature of the world as it is experienced, are as related, as varied and as different, as every individual's life experience. Feminist phenomenology questions the unspoken assumptions of phenomenology, particularly in terms of the ways that bodies live, experience, and are situated in their environments. For instance, Judith Butler's critique of Merleau-Ponty's *Phenomenology of Perception* takes him to task for failing to adequately account for the gendered situation of his own body in relation to the body-subjects that he writes about (Merleau-Ponty 2002; Butler 1988).

It was not until the 1990s that Film Studies returned to the phenomenological questions previously asked by the French phenomenologists, as well as the Frankfurt School and by Siegfried Kracauer (Koch 1985, 2000: 11–25). Since the mid-1970s the dominant theoretical paradigm in Anglo-American studies of film had been psychoanalysis, which had also been a dominant mode of thinking, not just in film, but in cultural studies and critical theory more broadly. Consequently phenomenology took something of a backseat in the mid- to late-twentieth century. Nonetheless, feminist film scholars such as Annette Kuhn and Constance Penley, writing in the late 1980s and 1990s, point towards a revival in phenomenological thinking and film. Kuhn, writing in 1994, highlights both potential conflicts and productivity between phenomenology and feminist film theory:

> it remains as yet unclear whether a metapsychology of cinema grounded in phenomenology would be capable of meeting the demands that feminism would make upon it. Nevertheless, more than one feminist film theorist has suggested that an encounter between feminist film theory and phenomenology might well prove productive.
>
> *(206)*

This is more hopeful than Penley, who, writing five years earlier, doubts phenomenology's capacity to deal with the "unconscious" of the film, or to analyze and actively critique the implicitly political aspects of film (as a medium and form) and cinema (as a broader culture of viewing). She views the role of a "phenomenology of cinema" as overtly descriptive, and thereby lacking in critical engagement, "its mirroring exaltation of film gradually giving way to a desire to develop critical tools going beyond description to an analysis of the aesthetic, psychical and social functioning of cinema" (Penley 1989: 37).

In the early 1990s Alan Casebier advocated a Husserlian feminist phenomenology of film. He argues that feminist film theory's critiques, both of cinematic realism and phenomenology, had no ground because they failed to understand the originary Husserlian purposes of phenomenology (Casebier 1991: 119–36). Unlike the hybrid, "impure" phenomenologies that appear in Anthropology, Gestalt Psychology, or Film Studies, Casebier advocates a transcendental phenomenology, where the objective is to bracket off naïve assumptions of film experience in favor of a reduction to pure consciousness. This seems like an impossibly difficult endeavor, and is at a significant remove from existential and situated phenomenology which acknowledges, rather than brackets off, the gendered implications of everyday experience. Combined and hybrid phenomenologies, which acknowledge the situated environments in which any phenomenologist finds herself, seem better equipped to address the inevitable non-neutrality of any kind of description or relation of viewer and viewed, and therefore seem to have a greater level of affinity with feminist film theory (see also Penley 1989).

Before I go any further, I want to stop here for a moment. Again, this chapter is leaning into the past. It is a tempting habit to seek meanings, origins, and evolutions in the past of a discipline, particularly one as rich and fascinating as feminist film theory. This is an urge that comes from storytelling: finding a beginning, middle, and end to film-phenomenology, and the assorted topics of this chapter (embodiment, spectatorship, and sensation). In the very first line of this chapter, I wrote that film-phenomenology is written from the perspective of the now. My "now" is a moment of thinking: about how to invite you, the reader, to move from a fairly conventional history of ideas about film and phenomenology, to a phenomenological and embodied practice of film scholarship, theory, and perhaps even filmmaking, that makes it possible to discuss film with insight and acuity.

The bedrock, if you like, of film-phenomenology, is one shared with many other kinds of thinking about cinema. That bedrock is close, detailed observation and description. If the idea of description sounds neutral to the ears of a Film Studies or literary studies scholar, perhaps we need to take a few leaves out of Anthropology's book: a discipline that is always concerned with the relationship between the person describing or writing about the human interactions unfolding before her, and the people who are being described. The idea of phenomenological description is not solely owned by the discipline of philosophy: in 1973 the anthropologist Clifford Geertz used the term "thick description" to emphasize how detailed observation, not just of an event or phenomenon, but also of the complex contexts in which it arose, is both deeply revealing and profoundly analytical (Geertz 2000 [1973]). Penley, writing in 1989, critiques the literature that then existed on phenomenological approaches to film and to cinema; perhaps what she could not at that time predict was the emergence not of one singular, doctrinal type of phenomenology but of many plural film-phenomenologies. Gaylyn Studlar points towards this possibility in 1990, when she discusses the affinities between Merleau-Ponty's "enworlded" phenomenology, and its conjunction with sociology, psychology, and feminist theory. Studlar's most hopeful suggestion is that feminist phenomenology has the potential to produce "a reflective awareness of film and a more open, progressive, and precise orientation to the relationship between women's phenomenological experience of the world and of film" (72). Ultimately, she even suggests that this reflective awareness can serve as a conduit between film theory and scholarship on the one hand, and filmmaking on the other.

Studlar's comments seem somewhat prophetic in this light. Vivian Sobchack's *The Address of the Eye*, published two years later, theorizes a phenomenological account of film experience. In her opening to this well-known volume, Sobchack transposes Merleau-Ponty's terms into a different context, in order to describe film as "an expression of experience by experience" (Merleau-Ponty 1968: 155, cited in Sobchack 1992: 3). Behind a deceptively simple vehicle of "description" emerges a whole philosophical complex of issues about subjectivity, about language and the ways that we articulate thought, about emotion and the role of feelings and sensations in any form of expression. What that gives rise to is not just a first step towards critical engagement, as Penley described in 1989: description is already critical engagement, if those observations also take into account the contextual and unstable relationships of the observer and the observed.

A key example of this, as well as a beautiful and lyrical one, is Sobchack's well-known description of the opening shot of Jane Campion's *The Piano* (1993), where she recognizes her own inescapable bodily responses prior to any intellectual distinction between her own position as a viewing subject, and the film as a viewed object (Figure 29.1, 29.2). Following a succinct gloss of the film's opening shots, Sobchack proceeds to a phenomenological description of her viewing experience. It is worth quoting her writing at length here, not only for its cogent illustration of film-phenomenology at work, but also because of its clarity and rigor:

> As I watched *The Piano*'s opening moments—in that first shot, before I even knew there was an Ada and before I saw her from *my* side of *her* vision (that is, before I watched *her* rather than her *vision*)—something seemingly extraordinary happened. Despite my "almost blindness," the "unrecognizable blur," and resistance of the image to my eyes, *my fingers knew what I was looking at*—and this *before* the objective reverse shot that followed to put those fingers in their proper place (that is, to put them where they could be seen objectively rather than subjectively "looked through"). What I was seeing was, in fact, from the beginning, *not* an unrecognizable image, however blurred and indeterminate in my vision, however much my eyes could not "make it out." From the first (although I didn't consciously know it until the second shot), my fingers *comprehended* that image, *grasped* it with a nearly imperceptible tingle of attention and anticipation and, off-screen, "felt

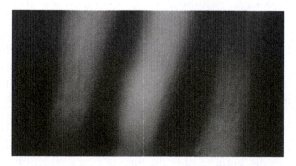

Figure 29.1   First Shot from *The Piano* (Jane Campion, 1993).

Source: The Piano, Jane Campion, 1993.

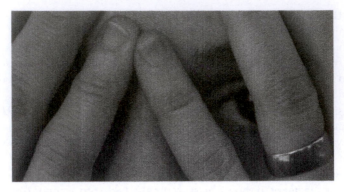

Figure 29.2   Second, reverse shot in *The Piano* (Jane Campion, 1993).

Source: The Piano, Jane Campion, 1993.

them-selves" as a potentiality in the subjective and fleshy situation figured on-screen. And this *before* I refigured my carnal comprehension into the conscious thought, "Ah, those are fingers I am looking at." Indeed, at first, prior to this conscious recognition, I did not understand those fingers as "those" fingers—that is, at a distance from my own fingers and objective in their "thereness." Rather, those fingers were first known sensually and sensibly as "these" fingers and were located ambiguously both off-screen and on—subjectively "here" as well as objectively "there," "mine" as well as the image's. Thus, although it should have been a surprising revelation given my "almost blindness" to the first shot, the second and objective reverse shot of a woman peering at the world through her outspread fingers really came as no surprise at all. Instead, it seemed a pleasurable culmination and confirmation of what my fingers—and I, reflexively if not yet reflectively—already knew

(Sobchack 2004a: 63)

Contemporary film-phenomenology, discussions of embodied spectatorship, and analyses of cinematic sensation have taken a somewhat different path from the earlier intellectual debates of Koch, Penley, and Kuhn. The contemporary approaches of scholars such as Sobchack, Laura U. Marks, and Martine Beugnet look beyond a feminist critique of psychoanalytic topoi of looking, fetishizing, and mystifying. Instead they take as their focus the film experience—both film and viewing. Sometimes the detailed descriptions of moving images, editing, sounds, and their bodily effects in film-phenomenological accounts can sound almost formalist in their scrutiny of detail. Yet the difference between a textual analysis of film form, and a phenomenological description of film, is that phenomenological description does not place a boundary between the film's aesthetic operations and the individuated bodily experience of the viewer—just as Sobchack's words above indicate her subjective experience of viewing as both "here" within her body, and "there" within the film. Film-phenomenological descriptions do not value category distinctions between viewer and viewed, seer and seen, nor do they imagine that the spectator is psychically or culturally "sutured" into the film, or that she identifies with the film and the film's protagonists. Rather, imagined or real bodily responses—sensory, physiological, pre-conscious, or proprioceptive—are privileged over and above the textual and linguistic signification or meaning of the film, or the ways in which spectators identify with or are called into the film.

Inevitably, this preoccupation with the body also leads to a concern with the senses, and sensations that are called upon, in the experience of film viewing and filmmaking. One of the most successful ways in which film scholars employing phenomenological frameworks have approached film is via an understanding of the ways that the senses and the body, and not just the brain (which we conventionally associate with the housing of the mind), produce knowledge and understanding. Among the most well known of these are Antonia Lant's discussion of the relationships between art histories of haptics and early cinema, Marks' essay on haptic images and video art, Sobchack's aforementioned essay on proprioceptive kinesthesia and *The Piano*, and Jennifer M. Barker's writing on the "musculature" of film—its capacity for sensory perception and expression (Lant 1995; Marks 2002; Sobchack 2004a; and Barker 2009: 63–119).

Theories of embodied spectatorship and sensation have another important function: they validate feeling as a means of thoughtfully articulating responses to film. Feeling, sensation and emotion: in short, affect, is a staple ground for many film-phenomenological accounts. Where other approaches from neuroscience, cognitivism, and Deleuze Studies overlap with some of the concerns of phenomenology, hybrid accounts of cinematic emotion and affect have flourished (see Rutherford 2009; Laine 2011; McKim 2011). While not all explicitly feminist, these interrogations of the emotional valence or agency of film nonetheless revise binaristic accounts of knowledge as deriving solely from reason and rational thought. They give space for the possibility of emotion, sensation, and affect as forms of thinking, knowledge, and agency emerging from an encounter with film. Phenomenological studies of affect and gender continue to flourish in scholarship on film, and while the scholars named above offer key examples of this work, it is reasonable to say that most of the scholars discussed in this chapter engage substantially with emotion and affect. After all, how could one separate emotion from lived experience, situated in an encounter with a moving image?

Mid-twentieth century feminist phenomenologies have also accelerated the development of feminist studies of film embodiment and sensation. This is where the writing of Simone de Beauvoir, and later, Iris Marion Young, becomes important. Young's essay about situated, lived body experience, "Throwing Like A Girl," is particularly significant for contemporary orientations of film-phenomenology that discuss the complex embodiment of women and girls (Young 1989). Katharina Lindner's work on the athletic body on film draws meaningfully from the frameworks of Young's philosophy and the queer phenomenology of Sara Ahmed, in order to question the dynamics of an active, strong, physically adapted body in relation to gender identity represented on-screen (Ahmed 2006; Lindner 2012). Kate Ince's writing on feminist phenomenology and the films of Sally Potter and Agnès Varda is perhaps the closest, and the most astute, in bringing the conceptual heritage of feminist phenomenology to bear on the work of contemporary female filmmakers (Ince 2012, 2013).

But it is not only theoretical and scholarly approaches to film that continue to explore the relationships between feminism, phenomenology, embodiment and sensation. In the past ten to fifteen years, a range of films from popular cinema, artist's moving image, and art cinema have emerged that lend themselves to the kinds of attentive description and analysis common in film-phenomenological accounts. These films are often not narrative-driven, though their impact is equally as effective through modes of sensory apprehension. These works demonstrate a different kind of duration, and attentiveness to the complexity of color and diegetic sound; techniques such as close-miking are a repeated motif, so that the breath, as well as the voice of protagonists, are recorded richly. These films lend themselves to close looking—they are not necessarily aesthetically "beautiful" in the sense of manicured artifice—but their formal, aesthetic, and technical details of color, costume, lighting, skin, and medium offer up an invitation to phenomenological description. For instance, the films of Andrea Arnold, Claire Denis, Lucile Hadžihalilović, Mia Hansen Løve, and Lynne Ramsay, have been praised for their close proximity to and with their protagonists' lives, observing the unfolding of action alongside, rather than always in front of them. The protagonists, too, run counter to cinematic narrative conventions. They are children, or young working class women, or young professional women: characters whose vulnerability and precarity is made manifest in the aesthetics and soundscapes of the films. Scholars Liz Watkins, Laura McMahon, Davina Quinlivan, Emma Wilson, and Lucy Bolton, have all explored, in different avenues, this sense of precarity and vulnerability in the work of the filmmakers named above, through color, texture, light, sound, contact at a distance, flesh, opacity, and skin (Watkins 2015; McMahon 2012; Quinlivan 2009; Wilson 2012; Bolton 2011).

It is not clear whether film-phenomenology or studies of film-sensation have influenced these types of filmmaking, but certainly critics and scholars within this field have identified contemporary forms of filmmaking that emphasize proximity, touch, blurriness, and explicit bodily acts of a sexual or violent nature. The particular forms of the blurry close-up and its elicitation of texture, touch, and eroticism have led feminist scholars such as Laura U. Marks and Martine Beugnet to relate this attention to a relationship of haptic visuality and cinematic intimacy between screen and viewer (Marks 2000; Beugnet 2007). The notion of haptic visuality comes via the nineteenth century art historian Aloïs Riegl, whose invocation of contact through a sense of vision, rather than a sense of touch, is taken up by Gilles Deleuze in his books on cinema: *Cinema 1: The Movement-Image*, and *Cinema 2: The Time-Image* (See Deleuze 2005a, 2005b; Marks 2002). While Marks talks about haptics as a kind of erotics, texture or mimesis, Beugnet discusses haptic visuality as a means of accessing subjective formlessness and visceral penetration, particularly in relation to the group of films and filmmakers attributed the collective term "The New French Extremity"— filmmakers such as the above named Denis, Olivier Assayas, Gaspar Noé, Vincent Dieutre, Catherine Breillat, François Ozon, Bruno Dumont, and Philippe Grandrieux among others. Beugnet takes up as a point of departure the derision of film critic James Quandt, who berated these films for their lack of content or moral integrity (Quandt 2004). In fact, the ethics of the New Extremity, in relation to the formal and conceptual issues raised by their phenomenological description is the subject of ongoing debate (see Kendall and Horeck 2011). Though the concern with film's surfaces, materiality and its "body" runs throughout much of this kind of scholarship, more recent work has expanded the address of touch to a philosophical refusal of contact (McMahon 2012) and investigations of texture (Widdis 2012; Fife Donaldson 2014).

There is no convenient mechanism by which feminist film theory neatly converges with feminist phenomenology, theories of embodied spectatorship, or explorations of film-sensation. It would be helpful if these studies did have an expedient teleology from a: feminism to b: phenomenology (or a: phenomenology to b: sensation, or a: spectatorship to b: embodiment). But the nature of formative interdisciplinary studies is that they approach their objects of enquiry from as many positions as possible. Film-phenomenology, as I have noted elsewhere, is not a single discourse or methodology (Chamarette 2014). There is no template model or method to "apply" to a film text, because doing so would go against the grain of phenomenological enquiry.

We could say instead that film-phenomenology is a collection of embodied approaches to film experience, which try to account for phenomena, but which resist interpretation through one framework. Film-phenomenologies try to discuss the shivers and the goose-bumps, the sudden emotional reactions and the resistance to the darkened room, but maybe they don't always succeed in doing so. There are many future directions for feminist film-phenomenology, and many of those intersect with the lived experience of others who have been historically and culturally marginalized. Film-phenomenologies or studies of film-sensation in relation to disability and complex embodiment, for example, may help question the body-normative assumptions implicit in feminist phenomenological inquiry (Sobchack 2004b; Chamarette 2013). For this reason too, queer and intersectional phenomenologies are important future directions, as Ahmed has already identified (Ahmed 2006; Lindner 2012), as are phenomenological interrogations of non-human worlds (see Pick 2013). But maybe there are also some things which cannot be said, but which are instead expressed—through film itself. In a way, film *is* phenomenology: a way of seeing the world, and us.

Related topics

Felicity Colman, "Deleuzian spectatorship"
Dijana Jelača, "Film feminism, post-cinema, and the affective turn"
Claire Pajaczkowska, "Psychoanalysis beyond the gaze: from celluloid to new media"
Kathleen Vernon, "Sound and gender"

References

Ahmed, Sara (2006) *Queer Phenomenology: Objects, Orientations, Others*. Durham, NC: Duke University Press.
Barker, Jennifer M. (2009) *The Tactile Eye: Touch and the Cinematic Experience*. Berkeley and LA; London: University of California Press.
Beauvoir, Simone de (1949) *Le Deuxième sexe*. Paris: Gallimard.
——— (2011) *The Second Sex*. Trans. Constance Borde and Sheila Malovany-Chevallier. New York: Vintage.
Beugnet, Martine (2012 [2007]) *Cinema and Sensation*. Edinburgh: Edinburgh University Press.
Bolton, Lucy (2011) *Film and Female Consciousness: Irigaray, Cinema and Thinking Women*. Basingstoke: Palgrave Macmillan.
Butler, Judith (1988) "Sexual Ideology and Phenomenological Description: A Feminist Critique of Merleau-Ponty's *Phenomenology of Perception*" in Jeffner Allen and Iris Marion Young (eds.) *The Thinking Muse: Feminist and Modern French Philosophy*. Bloomington and Indianapolis: Indiana University Press, 85–100.
Casebier, Allan (1991) *Film and Phenomenology: Towards a Realist Theory of Cinematic Representation*. Cambridge: Cambridge University Press.
Chamarette, Jenny (2012) *Phenomenology and the Future of Film: Rethinking Subjectivity Beyond French Cinema*. Basingstoke: Palgrave Macmillan.
——— (2013) "*Sur mes lèvres*, Deafness, Embodiment: Towards a Film Phenomenology of a Differently Ordered Sensorium" unpublished paper, available via podcast: http://backdoorbroadcasting. net/2013/03/jenny-chamarette-sur-mes-lèvres-deafness-embodiment-towards-a-film-phenomenology-of-a-differently-ordered-sensorium/ Accessed August 27, 2015.
——— (2014) "Embodied Worlds and Situated Bodies: Feminism, Phenomenology, Film Theory" *Signs* (Winter 2015) Vol. 40, No. 2, 289–95.
Deleuze, Gilles (2005a [1983]) *Cinema 1: The Movement-Image*. London: Continuum.
——— (2005b [1985]) *Cinema 2: The Time-Image*. London: Continuum.
Fife Donaldson, Lucy (2014) *Texture in Film*. Basingstoke: Palgrave Macmillan.

Geertz, Clifford (2000 [1973]) "Thick Description: Toward an Interpretative Theory of Culture" in Clifford Geertz, *The Interpretation of Cultures*. New York: Basic Books, 3–30.

Gorner, Paul (2007) *Heidegger's Being and Time: An Introduction*. Cambridge: Cambridge University Press.

Heinämaa Sara (1999) "Simone de Beauvoir's Phenomenology of Sexual Difference" *Hypatia*, Vol. 14, No. 4, (Autumn), 114–32.

Ince, Kate (2012) "Feminist Phenomenology and the Films of Sally Potter" in Jean-Pierre Boulé and Ursula Tidd (eds.) *Existentialism and Contemporary Cinema: A Beauvoirian Perspective*. New York; Oxford: Berghahn Books, 161–73.

––––––– (2013) "Feminist Phenomenology and the Film Worlds of Agnès Varda" *Hypatia*, Vol. 28, No. 3 (Summer), 602–17.

Johnson, Galen A. (ed.) (1993) *The Merleau-Ponty Aesthetics Reader: Philosophy and Painting*. Evanston, IL: Northwestern University Press.

Kendall, Tina and Tanya Horeck (eds.) (2011) *The New Extremism in Cinema: From France to Europe*. Edinburgh: Edinburgh University Press.

Koch, Gertrud (1985) "Ex-Changing the Gaze: Re-Visioning Feminist Film Theory" *New German Critique*, No. 34 (Winter), 139–53.

––––––– (2000) *Siegfried Kracauer: An Introduction*. Trans. Jeremy Gaines. Princeton: Princeton University Press.

Kuhn, Annette (1994) *Women's Pictures: Feminism and Cinema* (2nd edn.) New York and London: Verso.

Laine, Tarja (2011) *Feeling Cinema: Emotional Dynamics in Film Studies*. New York: Bloomsbury Publishing.

Lant, Antonia (1995) "Haptical Cinema" *October* Vol. 74 (Autumn): 45–73.

Lindner, Katharina (2012) "Situated Bodies, Cinematic Orientations: Film and (Queer) Phenomenology" in Saër Maty Bâ and Will Higbee (eds.) *De-westernizing Film Studies*. London; New York: Routledge, 152–65.

McKim, Kristi (2011) *Love in the Time of Cinema*. Basingstoke: Palgrave Macmillan.

McMahon, Laura (2012) *Cinema and Contact: The Withdrawal of Touch in Nancy, Bresson, Duras and Denis*. Oxford: Legenda.

Marks, Laura U. (2000) *The Skin of the Film: Intercultural Cinema, Embodiment, and the Senses*. Durham, NC: Duke University Press.

––––––– (2002) "Video Haptics and Erotics" in Laura U. Marks, *Touch: Sensuous Theory and Multisensory Media*. Minneapolis, MN: University of Minnesota Press, 1–20.

Merleau-Ponty, Maurice (2002 [1962]) *Phenomenology of Perception*. Trans. Colin Smith. London: Routledge.

––––––– (1964) *Sense and Non-Sense*. Trans. Hubert L. Dreyfus and Patrician Allen Dreyfus. Evanston, IL: Northwestern University Press.

––––––– (1968) *The Visible and the Invisible*. Claude Lefort (ed.) Trans. Alphonso Lingis. Evanston, IL: Northwestern University Press.

Mroz, Matilda (2012) *Temporality and Film Analysis*. Edinburgh: EUP.

Penley, Constance (1989) *The Future of an Illusion: Film, Feminism, and Psychoanalysis*. Minneapolis, MN: University of Minnesota Press.

Pick, Anat (2013) "Three Worlds: Dwelling and Worldhood On Screen" in Anat Pick and Guinevere Narraway (eds.) *Screening Nature: Cinema Beyond the Human*. New York: Berghahn, 21–36.

Quandt, James (2004) "Flesh and Blood: Sex and Violence in Recent French Cinema" *Artforum*, February, no pagination. Online article available at http://www.artforum.com/inprint/id=6199 Accessed August 9 2016.

Quinlivan, Davina (2009) "Material Hauntings: The Kinaesthesia of Sound in *Innocence* (Hadžihalilović, 2004)" *Studies in French Cinema*, Vol. 9, No. 3, 215–24.

Russell, Matheson (2006) *Husserl: A Guide for the Perplexed*. London: Continuum.

Rutherford, Anne (2009) *What Makes a Film Tick? Cinematic Affect, Materiality and Mimetic Inner-vation*. Oxford: Peter Lang.

Sartre, Jean-Paul (2004 [1936]) *The Transcendence of the Ego*. Trans. Andrew Brown. Abingdon: Routledge.

——— (2003 [1943]) *Being and Nothingness*. Trans. Hazel E Barnes. Abingdon: Routledge.

Sobchack, Vivian (1992) *The Address of the Eye: A Phenomenology of Film Experience*. Princeton, NJ: Princeton University Press.

——— (2004a) "What My Fingers Knew: The Cinesthetic Subject, or Vision in the Flesh" in Vivian Sobchack *Carnal Thoughts: Embodiment and Moving Image Culture*. Berkeley and LA; London: University of California Press, 53–84.

——— (2004b) *Carnal Thoughts*. Berkeley: University of California Press, 179–204.

Stern, Robert (2013) *The Routledge Guidebook to Hegel's Phenomenology of Spirit*. London: Routledge.

Studlar, Gaylyn (1990) "Reconciling Feminism and Phenomenology: Notes on Problems and Possibilities, Texts and Contexts" *Quarterly Review of Film and Video*, Vol. 12, No. 3, 69–78.

Watkins, Liz (2015) "Unsettling Perception: Screening Surveillance and the Body in *Red Road*" *Paragraph* Vol. 38, No. 1, 101–17.

Widdis, Emma (2012) "Socialist Senses: Film and the Creation of Soviet Subjectivity" *Slavic Review* (Fall) Vol. 71, No. 3, 590–618.

Wilson, Emma (2012) "Precarious Lives: On Girls in Mia Hansen-Løve and Others" *Studies in French Cinema*, Vol. 12, No. 3, 273–84.

Young, Iris Marion (1989) "Throwing Like A Girl: A Phenomenology of Feminine Body Comportment, Motility and Spatiality" in Jeffner Allen and Iris Marion Young (eds.), *The Thinking Muse: Feminism and Modern French Philosophy*. Bloomington: Indiana University Press, 51–70. Originally published in *Human Studies*, No. 3 (1980), 137–56.

30

DELEUZIAN SPECTATORSHIP

Felicity Colman

J'ai faim, J'ai froid

(Akerman 1984)

The philosopher Gilles Deleuze (b. Paris 1925–95) published two books devoted to the cinema—*Cinema 1: The Movement-Image* (1983) and *Cinema 2: The Time-Image* (1985). These contribute to his philosophical oeuvre, and have yielded specific methodologies for the discipline of the Philosophy of Film, in particular for the continental style of Film-Philosophy (cf. Bogue 2003; Colman 2009, 2011; Mullarkey 2009; Sinnerbrink 2011: 90–116), and for feminist film theories that think difference creatively (cf. Kennedy 2000; Butler 2002; MacCormack 2008). Deleuze's work on the system of images that the cinema produces arises from an historical era of the emergence of telematics in the late 1970s, where the convergence of information and computers enabled a networked environment that caused society to undertake a reappraisal of the perimeters of its aesthetic domains (Nora & Minc 1981: 4; Lyotard 1984; Deleuze 1986: 18–19). Through this, Deleuze's philosophy of film enables analysis through an attention to the units of experience that the cinema creates, and provides an open system of expressive language with which to articulate the dimensions of ideas, events, and information that the cinema opens up, registering changing conditions in the world.

Deleuze's philosophy of film, and his philosophical system in general, provide film scholars with a number of expressive tools, as well as a creative philosophical approach with which to describe their responses to cinema. In particular, an inspection of some of the divergent ways in which concepts labeled as "Deleuzian" are used in feminist film theories reveal a number of different theoretical positions, and often conflicting accounts of what Deleuze's philosophy of film actually contends in relation to the notion of spectatorship and cinema. Deleuze mentions "the spectator" several times in both of his *Cinema* books, a point that is often overlooked in discussions of Deleuzian approaches to spectatorship. This chapter begins by setting out Deleuze's position on the cinematic spectator, and then examines some of the differing applications of what might constitute a feminist oriented "Deleuzian spectator."

Deleuze's cinema spectator

Deleuze's methodological approach to the cinema arises from a number of central notions found throughout his philosophical oeuvre—on the topic of difference, and the creation of concepts. What the cinematic spectator is for Deleuze, and by extension, the Deleuzian approaches to analysis of the cinema, differ from those recognized as standard disciplinary approaches to film analysis and criticism in the twentieth century—for example, that of auteurist, cognitive, ideological, feminist, post-colonial, psychoanalytic, semiotic, and technological analyses, all of which influence the prevalent types of spectatorship theory (see Hayward 2000: 343, for a summary of film theory spectatorial positions until 1980, and for a critique of these, see Colman 2014: 73–5). Richard Rushton argues that Deleuze's work is "out of position in mainstream film studies," the reason being that: "Deleuze has no explicit conception of the *cinema spectator*" (Rushton 2009: 47, original emphasis). In fact, what Rushton highlights is that Deleuze's position does not comply with the "*Screen*" style spectator theory (named after the influential UK-based film theory journal of the same name, which dominated English language film spectatorship theories of the 1970s–80s; for more on this approach to spectatorship see Pajaczkowska, this volume). Rushton notes that *Screen's* theoretical approach tended to follow Louis Althusser's model (Rushton 2009: 49), where Althusser's theory of Ideological State Apparatuses is applied by various theories, to posit the cinematic apparatus and the film spectacle as either ideologically positioning or being directed by the spectator's position (Althusser 1971; Baudry 1974–5). *Screen* theory also tended to be dominated by attention to a range of psychoanalytical and or semiotic modes of theorization of the relationship between the film and spectator. As Rushton points out, *Screen's* language of "suture, gaze, ideological apparatus, reality effect, and so on" (2009: 47) is a film theory vocabulary that Deleuze does not use—and there are philosophical reasons why he does not do so, as I discuss below. Rushton argues that there is, however, an "implicit theory of spectatorship to be found in the *Cinema* books" (Ibid.), identifying in Deleuze's film theory a spectator that is created by the film, as a "consciousness [that is] formed by what happens in the film" (Ibid. 48). Rushton offers two models with which to describe this position: that of the notion of immersion, and that of a mode of absorption. Rushton applies these terms to describe Deleuze's model of spectatorship as a "challenge" for film viewing (Ibid. 53). Deleuze does not refer to immersion, and his sense of absorption differs to that of Rushton, and so the question remains: what exactly constitutes Deleuze's position on the spectator of film?

The expression of creative difference, as it is rendered in and by the creative arts, is one of the catalytic themes throughout the work of Deleuze. For Deleuze, *difference* refers to an immanent difference within an event or thing; a difference to itself (Deleuze 1994: 28–9, 294). To think with the concept of difference itself as an internal specificity, offers an alternative theoretical position to a sense of difference that is based on a predication—that is a judgment of something that it is not, or of opposition. Deleuze's philosophical non-binary position is useful for thinkers of identity, as the Deleuzian conception of difference challenges any representational hierarchical model that replicates and at the same time is productive of measurable resemblances described as same, or as "other." Instead of a philosophy based on negation, working with difference as a concept of creation is Deleuze's methodological approach for challenging the idea of the "nature of things," or the singular essence of something, and this critical approach is one adopted by Deleuzian film theorists such as Barbara M. Kennedy (2000), Anna Powell (2005), and Patricia MacCormack (2008). In his work Deleuze repeatedly examines questions concerning the creation of ideas, seeking to precisely define how those new concepts lend themselves to the creation of new forms, and multiple assemblages of things, which affect the ideas that created them in the first place (Deleuze 1994: 207). Deleuze's philosophy of the creation of concepts draws upon examples of creative intensity—what Deleuze and his co-author Felix Guattari describe as affects and percepts. They apply these concepts to examples from the theater, music, literature, poetry, film, fine arts, and from non-human entities; and the biological, geophysical, and animal worlds—all in relation to the question of how creative actions and forms produce thought (cf. Deleuze 1994; Deleuze and Guattari 1987a, 1987b). In addition to this work on how creative forms are productive of a breadth of innovative philosophical concepts and discourses, Deleuze's revisionist history of philosophy includes the work of Henri Bergson (b. Paris, 1859–1941), whose conception of space and time as a singular durational whole, leads Deleuze's methodology in his conception of the cinema to attend to the paradoxical position of time, as formed by the moving, time-based image that film generates. If taken together, Deleuze's notion of creative difference and the moving image's aggregation of differences are productive of a relational philosophy of the cinematic image, one that is concerned with the "practice" of the creation of concepts (Deleuze 1989: 280). This site of a creative practice, with its attendant methodological tools, is what makes Deleuze's philosophy of interest for media based theories, and a position that leads feminist thinkers to the formulation of original theses on cinematic experiences.

Deleuze is a *cinéphile*, and that he drew heavily upon the Parisian cinematic culture in which he lived is evidenced in the films that he takes as applied examples in his philosophy of film. Deleuze mentions a large number of male filmmakers in comparison to the work of just a few women directors in his *Cinema* books: Chantal Akerman (1950–2015), Shirley Clarke (1919–97), Germaine Dulac (1882–1942), Marguerite Duras (1914–96), Michèle Rosier (1930–), and Agnès Varda (1928–). Deleuze's approach to the cinema is as a conditional place where philosophical concepts can be formed through the informatics of the moving sound-image. Within this site, Deleuze's position towards the spectator is largely two-fold, as the spectator's role is to produce or "participate" (Truffaut, cited by Deleuze 1986: 241 n.7), as well as to be stimulated by the images. For example, attending to an aspect of what film theory calls the *mise-en-scène*, Deleuze describes color in relation to Varda's films as not a semiotic reference or index to a particular object, but in terms of its affective "power" that will "absorb" the situation on screen, including the characters and "spectator" (1986: 118). Through this approach, Deleuze's method of analysis begins as empirical observation—seeking to grasp things in themselves, which in turn is generative of specific meanings that, when developed through a combination of the sets of images that a given film produces, are generative of systems of images. This system, as he will argue, gives rise to a cinematic ethics of thought, in and to which the viewer contributes as an internal component, as an image among other images; and this marks his difference to the range of *Screen*-style theories of spectatorship concerned with the forms of external relation a spectator might have with film. It is with the process of how film contributes towards an image of thought that Deleuze concludes his *Cinema* books.

The *Cinema* books were written in the first half of the 1980s, at the start of the use of home recording devices that made possible repeated viewings. The films referred to by Deleuze are just prior to this technological facility of on-demand viewing; they are ones experienced by Deleuze in a cinema theater, which results in a very specific kind of spectatorial experience. In addition to these technological considerations for the kind of film-philosophy that Deleuze produces, there are a number of significant historical factors that contribute to the position on the cinematic viewer that his theory takes, marking it as different to that of mainstream film theory of the same era. First, although he is writing in a pre-internet era, we might note Deleuze's attention to the advent of the digital media, where changes in communication technologies result in a controlled set of data being made available to a spectator. This era of the late 1970s to early 1980s is at the very beginning of the realization of the huge social and political changes about to occur with the distribution of information (including images), and the effects upon the user/s of that information. In *Cinema 1*, this background consideration is evident as Deleuze argues that the ways in which the "information" of a film on screen communicates "data" to the "spectators" is contingent upon the values that are produced by the sets of images from the cinema, through the creation of the image, and through various forms of movement that modulate "the object" (Deleuze 1986: 2, 19; 1989: 27, 32). Engaging Bergson's proposition on the relations opened by the moving image in terms of its translation of things over time, Deleuze argues that "the movement-image is matter itself;" the data is "signaletic material" (1989: 33). In *Cinema 2*, Deleuze enlarges this conception of the movement-image, describing the ways in which the image changes through different forms of time, changing images (of all kinds: mental, relational, etc.), and creating different thought processes (Ibid. 23, 203). Secondly, Deleuze's interest in the spectator is given in the context of his philosophical investigation into regimes of representational logic, and the background of French critical theory's focus on structuralism and semiotics. In Deleuze's taxonomy of the cinema, the images and signs that films produce include the spectator, but only as an abstract component of the film system—as a sign, or as an image. While Deleuze constantly addresses the reader as spectator of the film in his *Cinema* books—through a complicit account of snippets of scenes, dialogue, or single phrase characterizations of films, and filmic themes, by the use of first person plural pronouns such as "our," "ours," "we," and "us," signaling the shared situation of the filmic image, and from attention to "the spectator's condition of vision" (Deleuze 1986: 91) to the collapse of a modernist perception for a different kind of expression of the image, such as in the films of Antonioni, where "the distinction between the spectator and the spectacle" is eradicated (Deleuze 1989: 5)—this spectator is just a part of the taxonomy. Through both *Cinema* books, Deleuze notes "the spectator" of films through specific instances, referring to what the "spectator's conditions of vision" do to the image (Deleuze 1986: 91; see also Deleuze 1986: 2, 24, 48, 74, 202; Deleuze 1989: 5). To construct his image taxonomy, Deleuze argues that the image is constructed either as an element of the mise-en-scène, *or in terms of a "mental image," and is produced through the filmic "chain of relations" (Deleuze 1986: 200–2). In reference to Akerman's films, Deleuze writes that*

> the chain of states of female body is not closed … in the same place or in space, a woman's body achieves a strange nomadism which makes it cross ages, situations and places (this was Virginia Woolf's secret in literature)
>
> *(Deleuze 1989: 196)*

Thus taking the situation of the body—as image—into a durational condition in which the "spectator" is "included" (as a taxonomic component), contributing to the "transformation" that images can bring, which Deleuze argues is a different form of image creation to one that is created through the relational chain of action, perception, and affections being produced by the film image (Deleuze 1986: 200–1; 1989: 202).

Deleuze takes these two key notions of the creation of the image, and its distribution as data sets, in his siting of the spectator. In Deleuze's philosophy of cinema, film is articulated in the recognizable terms of a system of images; the key forms of which are the movement-image and the time-image. In this system, Deleuze's focus on the spectator is considered through Godard's "pedagogy of the image," by which he means the ways in which the viewer is educated by the conditions of the image (Deleuze 1986: 13) to think and see things through different paradigms, as we see with the various arguments of Deleuzian film theorists (cf. Kennedy 2000; Powell 2005), in particular some which orient their analysis of screen images towards a feminist reading, as we will now discuss.

Becoming a feminist spectator, after and with Deleuze

First wave feminist film theory critiqued mainstream representations of women, aiming to develop theories for a "counter-cinema" (Johnston 1973), and a language with which to express the range of experiential (cognitive, sensorial, aesthetic, and political ideas) and referential (gendered, sexed, racialized) images that the cinema produces from a feminist position (see Humm 1997). Feminist film theories grew from a mix of the psychoanalytic theoretical models that argue there is a gendered positioning of the spectator (Mulvey 1975), and from semiotic and technological theories that offer a critique of the construction of a subject, via the apparatus of film itself (cf. Doane 1982; Silverman 1988). These largely Eurocentric theories are supplemented by analyses of representation, exposing the binarist negative position that the notion of a "gender" position establishes, critiquing class and race biases in feminist film theory (hooks 1996; Keeling 2007), and examining the problems in textual "readings" of the moving image (see Silverman 1988). While theories of spectatorship, and a single or multiple "spectator" vary, what they do have in common is a desire to express a response that is appropriate to the film viewing experience.

Deleuze's philosophical system manifests in multiple ways in feminist film scholarship, and the notion of a Deleuzian spectator is not an agreed upon, singular position. Different film theorists draw from various aspects of Deleuze's single-authored and co-authored work with Guattari, rather than just from his film-philosophy. Deleuzian and Guattarian concepts contribute the expressive tools for conceptualization of a philosophical system of critical analysis of various film forms. These include the terms of difference, creation and creativity; the notion of the subject and subjectivity as difference, the notion of a minor literature; of becoming; of the people-to-come; lines of flight; assemblages; the Body without Organs; nomadology; the terms of affect, perception, and action, as well as a Deleuzian cinematic glossary of neologisms (such as any-space-whatevers; hodological space; noosigns), with which to express the variations in images that the cinema produces. Deleuze's fascination in the *Cinema* books for the ways in which certain films offer a liberation from prescribed modes of being (such as we see with his address of Akerman), where the body is not limited by its gender coding, and other imaginings of worlds, times, and locales are able to be articulated for their complexities, all provide a currency for analysis of the moving image. It is thus no surprise that we see Deleuze's non-hierarchical semiotic system used for the interpretation and analysis of the moving image, as well as the complex coded expressive language of the image in the *Cinema* books, taken up by feminist film scholars who recognized the political potential of this system.

Prominent film scholars who have thus far developed specifically feminist methodological approaches for film analyses of spectatorship that draw from Deleuzian concepts for their logic include Gaylyn Studlar (1984, 1988), Barbara Kennedy (2000), Alison Butler (2002), Anna Powell (2005), and Patricia MacCormack (2008). These, and other scholars, have applied central notions of Deleuzian philosophy, either in conjunction with, or as deviating from feminist film theoretical models, in terms of what "spectatorship" might mean. Patricia Pisters (2011), for example, joins Deleuze's thinking about the mental images that film generates with neuroscientific theoretical models, in order to extend Deleuzian thinking to twenty-first-century technological platforms. Theoretical positions range from those focused on just one or two key philosophical concepts, to a more broadly applied "Deleuzian" position on the topic, which is, as we have seen, one where, within Deleuze's system of images, the spectator becomes just one of many components of an image. This theoretical position not only challenges the orthodoxy of one-way screen to subject relations but also allows theorization and speculation concerning the complexities that screen images offer within the continuum of images. As Deleuze notes, "men themselves are only mental functions, or 'neuronic messengers'" (1989: 121).[1]

Feminist film theories using Deleuzian approaches can also be divided between those that contend that Deleuze's work has an account of cinematic spectatorship (e.g. Gaylyn Studlar 1984, 1988), or those that argue that there is no theory of spectatorship in Deleuze (e.g. Teresa Rizzo 2012). On the side that refutes a Deleuzian theory of spectatorship, Rizzo approaches Deleuze and film in relation to what she describes as "a Feminist Introduction," arguing that "If feminist film theory has been slow to take up Deleuze's *Cinema* books, it is precisely because they lack any serious engagement with spectatorship, which is the very foundation of psychoanalytic feminist film theory" (Rizzo 2012: 3). Rizzo states that neither volume of the *Cinema* books "addresses spectatorship directly" (Ibid.). Rizzo's characterization of Deleuze's project in the *Cinema* books is misleading here, as Deleuze does explicitly address "the spectator" in both volumes, as described above. However, Rizzo's approach is decidedly Deleuzian, as she conducts her analysis of several films using terminology and broad concepts from Deleuze's work on difference, Deleuze and Guattari's work on assemblages, and their feminist interlocutors. Rizzo replaces the historical film indexical term of "spectator" with "film-viewer" (Ibid. 7). Aiming to "approach the film text and film-viewer relationship through a new framework or logic" (Ibid. 10) by exploring the "affective connections between the film and the viewer" (Ibid. 7), Rizzo takes what she argues is Deleuze's silence on the issue of the spectator, and describes instead his account of the "perception-image" in terms of her film viewer, as a model that is "a particularly provocative idea for feminist film theory as a cinematic consciousness that accommodates multiple perspectives at the same time challenges binary thinking" (Ibid. 29). In contrast to Rizzo, a reading that affirms a use of Deleuze's concepts in relation to spectatorship in the cinema is evident in Gaylyn Studlar's work on the pleasures found in looking (1984, 1988). Studlar's work signals a significant active position that enables a specifically Deleuzian spectatorial film theory, and as such, her work offers a distinctive thesis from those of Mulvey, Doane, and Rizzo. Mulvey argued that "the woman" was always constructed through what she sees as a masculinist bias and blindness of classical film theory, and of the film narratives' positioning of the spectator. For Mulvey, there is an inequitable balance of spectatorial power between a gendered male or female. In contrast, Studlar locates the spectatorial position not in terms of a binarist, culturally sexed subject, but following Deleuze, she concentrates on an account of the images within a film, and the signs that they produce, of which the spectator can be counted as one. Studlar develops a Deleuzian theory of the spectator's "masochistic desire" from Deleuze's 1967 book *Masochism: Coldness and Cruelty* (Studlar 1984, 1988). In *Masochism*, Deleuze distinguishes in the work of the nineteenth-century German novelist Leopold von Sacher-Masoch a particular set of symptomologies, concerning sexual prohibitions and associated states (Deleuze 1991: 58). Taking these symptomologies as signs, Studlar argues that, when they are manifested in certain film scenarios, they enable a conceptualization of the kinds of pleasures that the spectator is able to glean from films. Unlike Mulvey's position, Studlar argues with Deleuze that control does not have to be gendered either male or female when it comes to pleasure. Examining what she terms the "masochistic aesthetic" at work in the films of Joseph von Sternberg, Studlar argues that a spectator can decide to enter a (masochistic) fantasy, and assume a position where they are controlled "within" its "dynamics" (Studlar 1984: 270). The dynamism of an image, produced and configured by a certain type of film aesthetic, genre, or form, and its power to not only produce a "spectacle" (Deleuze 1989: 5) but also affect the spectators of the film, and even those within the film, as expressions of the conglomerated movement of images (as we see in Sternberg's films).

Spinoza's (b. Amsterdam, 1632–77) notion of affect is one that Deleuze develops throughout all of his work, and in the *Cinema* books it manifests to describe particular examples of where things change within a film, and how they affect not only the internal images of the film but also the external world of the viewer as well. Deleuze's work on affect, described in the *Cinema* books in terms of the affection-image, and as a part of the movement-image, is a concept that has greatly interested a number of Deleuzian thinkers of film and media forms (for examples see Angerer 2015: 1–24; Pisters 2011: 98–120). Focusing on the use of the concept of affect, Anu Koivunen (2015) maps out some of the contradictory practices among feminist film theorists who are interested in addressing notions of affect, and emotion, as it relates to film viewing experiences. Koivunen examines the theoretical attention to what she describes as a "new critical interest in experience, embodiment, affect, and emotion" (Koivunen: 97). This work, which Koivunen describes as "emotion trouble," articulates the ways in which "the sensory aspects" of viewing experience are repeatedly articulated by feminist film theories of the 1980s and 1990s, but as a "problem" that was "impossible" to address through the methodological tools of psychoanalytic and semiotic approaches to spectatorship (Ibid. 97–8). Koivunen looks to the work of theorists such as Laura U. Marks (2000), who draws from a Deleuzian vocabulary to develop a phenomenological position that relies on individuated spectatorial experiences of films in order to articulate different kinds of affective cognition of the filmic content. Marks insists on an account that involves discussion of the trans-hapticity of the affect of a film, a theoretical position contingent on the phenomenal experience of an undefined spectator. As Koivunen points out, this position makes Marks's concern with the image as a construction of a "political aesthetics" (among other things) count as Deleuzian, even as she paradoxically contends that Deleuze has no theory of spectatorship (Koivunen 2015: 105, 106). As Koivunen notes, while Marks argues that "we need a phenomenology of individual experience" (Marks 2000: 150; cited in Koivunen 2015: 106), in contradistinction, and following Deleuze's *Cinema* philosophy, Barbara Kennedy argues and demonstrates precisely the opposite; where, following Deleuze, we can logically follow that the individual spectatorial "body" is but a component of the overall film image (Kennedy 2000: 5; cited in Koivunen 2015: 106). Kennedy's proposal for a feminist film "aesthetics of sensation" is one that articulates the material body of film as an assemblage of desires and sensations, and is perhaps the closest to a categorically accurate Deleuzian spectatorial model. Although Koivunen runs through a number of different positions on feminist film theoretical "turns" to the use of "affect," including Deleuzian positions that address issues of affect and an interest in "embodiment," she contends that she can find no clear way through the "complexities of studying experience, affect and emotion" (2015: 110). However, a post-feminist film theory that develops a Deleuzian philosophy of the spectator can be located in scholars such as Kennedy, Pisters, and MacCormack, where the emphasis is not on a singular phenomenological account, but is one, as Kennedy argues, where "Deleuzian ideas also enable thinking of the ontological nature of film itself as a 'body' which moves in connection with other bodies" (Kennedy 2000: 79).

Like Barbara Kennedy, Patricia MacCormack is a philosopher who has taken the tools offered by Deleuze and Guattari's joint and solo works, to develop a new philosophy of film, which addresses the cinematic spectator in particular. In her book *Cinesexuality* (2008), MacCormack's focus is on the visceral viewing experiences that the cinema generates. Her position starts from inside the body, not external to it (as other feminist film theorists have tended to), aligning her conceptual position with the feminist philosopher Luce Irigaray. MacCormack's argument follows the non-hierarchical logic of the BwO (Body without Organs) (Deleuze and Guattari 1987a: 149–66), as well as Deleuze's *Cinema* books in their positioning of the spectator as a protean body—as the generator of the "hybrid fold of the image and spectatorial flesh" among other images, where the spectator is "becoming" the cinema itself (MacCormack 2008: 42, 46), and "[i]mages do not represent or describe entities but make their possibility in the world" (Ibid. 3). MacCormack's spectator can be said to be Deleuzian in her attention to the material affects of the visceral responsiveness that a spectator's body can have in her palpable experience with the cinema. MacCormack's work demonstrates one example of how what we can call a Deleuzian feminist spectator becomes, through a process of "absorption" into and within the image (Deleuze 1986: 118). This is articulated by MacCormack in terms of Deleuzo–Guattarian, rhizomatic processes, critiquing the traditional notion of a "spectator" of cinema (2008: 3), and instead allowing for multiple, non-hierarchical entry and exit points into the image, whereby she can argue that:

> Traditionally how we watch displays, to ourselves and others, our subjectivity and sexuality. How we see what we see is inextricable from how we "are seen to," systems of visual apprehension do not differentiate between the real and the represented because a relation of perception is always present. In this sense our spectatorial selves are already experienced before any image arrived – to be seen to be seeing in a certain way informs cinematic pleasure. Spectatorship is an event which cannot be witnessed. It is an event of unrevealable interiority. It repudiates the great system of visual signification in modern culture – that of "to be seen to."
>
> (Ibid. 2)

Future directions, spectatorial beliefs

To summarize, we can observe that adaptions of Deleuze's philosophy of creative difference for feminist film theory tend to use one or more of his philosophical concepts in order to thematically describe a particular type of film—such as Alison Butler's characterization of "women's cinema" not in terms of genres of melancholy or romance (for examples, see the essays in Gledhill 1987), but in terms of a "minor literature," following Deleuze and Guattari's work on Kafka (1987a); or Studlar's work on how a Deleuzian-inspired theory of masochistic desire might be developed to account for the viewer's interest in certain forms of cinema.

As Deleuze articulates it in the *Cinema* books, the "spectator" is always a part of the image, but not as a singular entity or individual subject. Rather, the viewer is an image among images. Because of the open system of image creation, different theorists are able to take aspects of Deleuze's taxonomy of cinema, and apply it to develop new conceptions of the film viewing experience (as Kennedy and Rizzo respectively show). For feminist theories of film spectatorship, Deleuze's political philosophy provides both the tools with which to think an expressive language for cinema viewing (as MacCormack demonstrates), and a complex conceptual ground upon which to develop ideas that are central to the feminist film theorist, critic, philosopher, and film practitioner, such as what the organizing logic of the medium, form, and spatial systems of film do to notions such as material reality, consciousness, subjectivity, and, implicitly, the spectator of film.

For feminist thinkers, Deleuze's work on the notion of difference, and what happens to the repetition and comparison of differences over time (Deleuze 1994: 41, 70–9), provides a powerful philosophical framework with which to approach film theory. Furthermore, detail of the constitution of spectatorship—as an active thing in itself—is addressed by attention to the material and intellectual elements and movements of the creation of images, over time. Deleuze concludes his *Cinema* books with a call for cinema to not film the world, but to film "belief in this world" (Deleuze 1989: 172), and it is this aspect of his work—thinking about what an ethics of the world might look like—that remains to be written by feminist film theorists.

Related topics

Jenny Chamarette, "Embodying spectatorship: from phenomenology to sensation"
Dijana Jelača, "Film feminism, post-cinema and the affective turn"
Jennifer Lynn Peterson, "*Green Porno* and the sex life of animals in the digital age"

Note

1 Deleuze cites Gaston Bounoure's description of Alain Resnais's work.

Bibliography

Althusser, L. (1971) "Ideology and Ideological State Apparatuses," in L. Althusser (ed.) *Lenin and Philosophy and other Essays*, New York: Monthly Review Press.

Angerer, M.-L. (2015 [2007]) *Desire After Affect*, N. Grindell (trans.), London and New York: Rowman & Littlefield.

Baudry, J.-L. (1974–5) "Ideological Effects of the Basic Cinematographic Apparatus," A. Williams (trans.), *Film Quarterly*, 28: 2, pp. 39–47, DOI: 10.2307/1211632.

Bogue, R. (2003) *Deleuze on Cinema*, New York and London: Routledge.

Butler, A. (2000) "Feminist Film Theory and Women's Film at the Turn of the Century," *Screen*, 41:1, pp. 73–9.

Butler, A. (2002) *Women's Cinema: The Contested Screen*, London: Wallflower.

Colman, F. (2009) "Introduction: What is Film-Philosophy?," in F. Colman (ed.) *Film, Theory and Philosophy*, Durham: Acumen, pp.1–15.

Colman, F. (2011) *Deleuze and Cinema: The Film Concepts*, Oxford and New York: Berg.

Colman, F. (2014) *Film Theory: Creating a Cinematic Grammar*, New York: Columbia University Press.

Deleuze, G. (1986 [1983]) *Cinema 1: The Movement-Image*, H. Tomlinson and B. Habberjam (trans.), London: Athlone.

Deleuze, G. (1989 [1985]) *Cinema 2: The Time-Image*, H. Tomlinson and R. Galeta (trans.), London: Athlone.

Deleuze, G. (1991 [1967]) *Masochism: Coldness and Cruelty*, J. McNeil (trans.), New York: Zone Books.

Deleuze, G. (1992) "Postscript on the Societies of Control," *October* 59, pp.3–7.

Deleuze, G. (1994 [1968]) *Difference and Repetition*, P. Patton (trans.), London and New York: Continuum.

Deleuze, G. and Guattari, F. (1983 [1972]) *Anti-Oedipus: Capitalism and Schizophenia*, R. Hurley, M. Seem, and H. R. Lane (trans.), New York: Viking.

Deleuze, G. and Guattari, F. (1987a [1978]) *Kafka: Toward a Minor Literature*, D. Polan (trans.), Minneapolis: University of Minnesota Press.

Deleuze, G. and Guattari, F. (1987b [1980]) *A Thousand Plateaus: Capitalism and Schizophenia*, B. Massumi (trans.), London: Continuum.

Doane, M. A. (1982) "Film and the Masquerade: Theorising the Female Spectator," *Screen*, 23 (September–October), pp. 74–87.

Gledhill, C. (ed.) (1987) *Home Is Where the Heart Is: Studies in Melodrama and the Woman's Film*, London: British Film Institute.

Hayward, S. (2000) *Cinema Studies: The Key Concepts*, (second edition), London and New York: Routledge.

hooks, b. (1996) "The Oppositional Gaze: Black Female Spectators," in b. hooks *Reel to Reel: Race, Sex, and Class at the Movies*, London and New York: Routledge, pp. 197–213.

Humm, M. (1997) *Feminism and Film*, Bloomington: Indiana University Press.

Johnston, C. (ed.) (1973) "Women's Cinema as Counter Cinema," in *Notes on Women's Cinema*, London: Society for Education in Film and Television, pp. 24–31.

Keeling, K. (2007) *The Witch's Flight: The Cinematic, the Black Femme, and the Image of Common Sense*, Durham and London: Duke University Press.

Kennedy, B. M. (2000) *Deleuze and Cinema: The Aesthetics of Sensation*, Edinburgh: Edinburgh University Press.

Koivunen, A. (2015) "The Promise of Touch: Turns to Affect in Feminist Film Theory," in L. Mulvey and L. Backman Rogers (eds.), *Feminisms: Diversity, Difference, and Multiplicity in Contemporary Film Cultures*, Amsterdam: Amsterdam University Press, pp. 97–110.

Lyotard, J.-F. (1984 [1979]) *The Postmodern Condition*, G. Bennington and B. Massumi (trans.), Manchester: University of Manchester.

MacCormack, P. (2008) *Cinesexuality*, Hampshire and Burlington: Ashgate.

Marks, L. U. (2000) *The Skin of Film. Intercultural Cinema, Embodiment, and the Senses*, Durham: Duke University Press.

Minc, A. and Nora, S. (1981). *The Computerization of Society*. Cambridge: MIT Press.

Mullarkey, J. (2009) "Gilles Deleuze," in F. Colman (ed.) *Film, Theory and Philosophy*, Durham: Acumen, pp. 179–89.

Mulvey, L. (1975) "Visual Pleasure and Narrative Cinema," *Screen*, 16:3, pp. 6–18.

Pisters, P. (2011), *The Neuro-image: A Deleuzian Filmphilosophy of Digital Screen Culture*, Redwood City: Stanford University Press.

Powell, A. (2005) *Deleuze and Horror Film*, Edinburgh: Edinburgh University Press.

Rizzo, T. (2012) *Deleuze and Film: A Feminist Introduction*, London and New York: Continuum.

Rushton, R. (2009) "Deleuzian Spectatorship," *Screen*, 50:1, pp. 45–53.

Silverman, K. (1988) *The Acoustic Mirror: The Female Voice in Psychoanalysis and Cinema*, Bloomington: Indiana University Press.

Sinnerbrink, R. (2011) *New Philosophies of Film: Thinking Images*, London and New York: Continuum.

Studlar, G. (1984) "Masochism and the Perverse Pleasures of the Cinema," *Quarterly Review of Film Studies*, 9:4, pp. 267–82, DOI: 10.1080/10509208409361219.

Studlar, G. (1988) *In the Realm of Pleasure: Von Sternberg, Dietrich and the Masochistic Aesthetic*, New York and Oxford: Columbia University Press.

31

FILM RECEPTION STUDIES AND FEMINISM

Janet Staiger

What is now understood as reception studies developed nearly alongside both second- and third-wave feminism, and within film studies each has contributed to the other's sophistication. This essay will approach this conjunction historically, tracing the emergence of each, chronicling three representative and influential debates in the 1980s that propelled the necessity for doing historical reception research, and concluding with a brief survey of several significant lines of reception research that begin in the late 1980s and continue through today.

The emergence of reception studies in relation to feminism

Like feminism, reception studies can be traced back many centuries. However, events such as World War II and the Cold War stimulated socio-cultural histories as scholars attempted to understand large-scale radical movements. Attention to how groups of people understood and could be mobilized by media became important. Also, considering taste cultures and emotional appeals in advertising as well as political life encouraged sociological, psychological, and, then, literary attention to individual and group interpretation and sway. By the 1960s theories of the "reader" were plentiful from scholars of the Constance School (Wolfgang Iser, Hans Robert Jauss), the revival of Bertolt Brecht's notions of distanciation and Georg Lukác's claims about the consequences of "realism," and the surge of negative hermeneutics (Jacques Derrida). However, from the generalized reader, people began to move to "ideal," "competent," and, occasionally, "real" readers. Stanley Fish's contribution of the notion of "interpretive communities" provided an explanation for the similarities among some reader activities (1976). By the mid-1970s, individualizing readers by some sort of identity became common: psychoanalytical theses from David Bleich and Norman Holland, semiotic dynamics from Umberto Eco and Jonathan Culler, and economic and cultural propositions especially from France (Louis Althusser) and from Britain's Birmingham School of Cultural Studies (Staiger 1992: 16–48; Staiger 2005).

The broader socio-cultural discourse also included conversations about women: women as author-producers, as images, and as readers. Kate Millett's *Sexual Politics* (1970) provided very unorthodox (and scathing) interpretations and evaluations of male authors. These and other feminist "non-normative" readings struck at the British heritage of Matthew Arnold's literary criticism and the US New Criticism's pantheon of great (male) authors. The presumption of a generalized, "correct" reading was harder to hold, at least for liberals and progressives; moreover, the social and political imperative was to historicize actual readings to help explain cultural trends. Feminist analyses of movies appear in the publications by Sharon Smith (1972), Marjorie Rosen (1973), and Molly Haskell (1974) and the initiation of the journal *Women and Film* (1972).

Although not an example of reception studies, Laura Mulvey's 1975 essay, "Visual Pleasure and Narrative Cinema," is a breakthrough piece for film reception studies because Mulvey stresses psychoanalytical reasons for *male* pleasure in the classical narrative film. This distinction between sexes in cinema-viewing breaks with the assumption that films operate the same way for everyone.[1] She argues that sexes split along the axis of the pleasure of looking—men are active viewers and women, passive (to be looked at). Promptly, the questions are, can women escape this dynamic? What are women's possible viewing pleasures, at least for the type of narrative films Mulvey is discussing?

Meanwhile, in feminist theory more generally, intellectuals such as Hélène Cixous and Luce Irigaray were promoting alternative psychoanalytical and social models of the woman based on bodily differences from men to understand female pleasures. For Cixous, "in the beginning are our differences" (1975: 893); for Irigaray, woman is "neither one nor two" (1977: 101). Working within this broad psychoanalytical conversation, by the early 1980s, Mary Ann Doane had raised matters of the female spectator's positioning for film analysis. In her "*Caught* and *Rebecca*: The Inscription of Femininity as Absence" (1981), Doane ponders the position of the female watching films supposedly directed at her: "women's films." Her conclusion is that the instability of seeing films in which she (the woman) is a commodified object results in a masochistic positioning. In "Film and the Masquerade: Theorising the Female Spectator," Doane extends the analysis to suggest that a female spectator might take on a masochistic positioning, or, also from Mulvey, she might assume a male viewing role, a "transvestitism" into a "'masculinization' of spectatorship" (1982: 80), but the female spectator might also flaunt her femininity as "masquerade," creating a gap between herself and the image and giving herself a sense of some agency. These propositions are fairly in line with Mulvey's calculations (1981) when she is asked to comment on the dreary outcome of her argument that women have few or no places for pleasure in watching narrative cinema. Meanwhile, Richard Dyer (1982) and Steve Neale (1983) raise questions about the dynamics involved with men viewing male bodies. This exploration of the implications of identities of sex, gender, and sexuality in watching movies continues through the 1980s by many important scholars, but the stage has been set for considering "readers/spectators" in terms of their positioned identities.

Characteristic feminist-reception debates of the 1980s

For feminist scholars, woman was a prime class of positioned identity. Three feminist debates during the 1980s illustrate that scholars could argue about the implications of representations; however, speculating without turning to some sort of material evidence would produce no resolution to the discussion. The three examples here circle around women as viewers of representations of women and illustrate the necessary break from speculating about hypothetical audiences to investigating socially contextualized ones (Staiger 1992: 45–8).

The first debate occurs primarily between E. Ann Kaplan and Linda Williams about *Stella Dallas* (King Vidor, 1937), specifically the ending in which working-class Stella Dallas looks from the street into the upscale home where her daughter is marrying an upper-class man. Kaplan (1983) argues that the film pulls the female spectator into patriarchy's place for women which, for the good mother, is self-sacrifice (giving up the child-as-phallus) and passive observation, and it suggests that Stella's choices are the right ones. Williams (1984) counters. She believes that female viewers would see the contradictions playing out between classes and the mother–daughter relationship, theorizing that women-as-spectators will identify with multiple contradictory subject positions (mother, wife, daughter) and experience viewing stances of masochism, transvestitism, and masquerade. Kaplan (1985a) responds that the film tries to argue that Stella's decisions were correct; moreover, Kaplan questions whether a 1930s spectator would be able to see the contradictions that Williams describes: the female spectator "experiences, perhaps, the conflicting demands made on woman, but accepts that woman is supposed to handle them" (ibid. 40). Kaplan stresses she is discussing the "hypothetical spectator constructed through the film's strategies" (ibid. 41) and emphasizes that a difference exists between a 1937 female viewer and the 1980s feminist although even the latter woman can be "'seduced' by the film's mechanisms" (ibid.). In follow-up dialogues, Patrice Petro and Carol Flinn (1985) observe that scholars will need to discriminate between "the construction of women both as [psychoanalytically positioned] spectators and as social audiences" (51). Kaplan (1985b) agrees with Petro and Flinn that scholars need to make a distinction between the subject position(s) a film offers and historical subjects.

Within the Kaplan–Williams discussion is also the beginnings of distinguishing between "women's films" and melodrama, which constitute another strand of feminist discussion in the 1980s about gendered preferences in genre and women's responses. The second debate is a couple of related conversations about the pleasures of two other types of "woman's" genres: the soap opera and the romance. In 1979, Tania Modleski sought to examine the pleasures of a non-Classical Hollywood narrative form which had large numbers of female viewers: the daily television soap opera. Modleski not only contrasts the soap with the romance but makes a social argument that the former fit well into the lives of women in the household. Soaps have on-going, daily rhythms of never-ending but interrupted narratives much like the experience of daily household toil. Soaps also thrive on stories that posit that not everyone can be happy all of the time. Additionally, the multiple story lines give viewers many characters with whom to identify, and the large ensembles create extended communities in which events are discussed among many characters with mini-climaxes simply complicating rather than resolving characters' lives. However, Modleski makes a couple of claims that made evident the need to test her hypotheses with real viewers. Modleski argues that the only person viewers do not like is the villainess whom they unconsciously envy, and she implies that viewers are sucked into these narratives, investing great attention while having little self-awareness about the stories.[2]

As this discussion developed, Annette Kuhn (1984) posited that understanding "women's genres," especially soaps which appeared on television rather than on the film screen, would require not only narrative analysis and discussion of the hypothetical "female" spectator but also theories of discourse to understand the social spectator in a very different sort of space than the one postulated by Mulvey's analysis (i.e., one with narrative disruptions, small screens, and conversation in the viewing area during the program, as opposed to the darkened movie theater). As well both of Modleski's latter propositions—hating the villainess and falling unselfcritically into the fantasy—were tested in an ethnography organized by Ellen Seiter, Hans Borchers, Gabriele Kreutzer, and Eva-Maria Warth (1989). These researchers studied how soap opera viewers (49 women and 15 men) fit watching soaps into their daily schedule and confirmed or clarified several of Modleski's theses. However, the results also indicated that the viewers resisted approving of many of the "ideal" mother's actions and were often fond of the villainess. Moreover, viewers were very savvy about the conventions of the genre and the medium, using their knowledge for fictional pleasure but also dismissing many of the unreal aspects of the text. Ien Ang's interviews (1982) with foreign watchers of the US television program *Dallas* (1978–91) also reveal a wide variety of strategies of negotiating with texts to make them pleasurable. Later work has pointed out that viewers are very cognizant about how the production of soaps affects the narratives: for example, stars going on hiatus for another project will suddenly end up in comas until they can return to the show; birth twins surprisingly appear some 30 years into main characters' lives. As the title of the essay summarizing the ethnography says, soap opera viewers ask that scholars "don't treat us like we're so stupid and naive" (Seiter et al. 1989: 223).

Simultaneously with conversations about soaps is the publication of another ethnography, Janice Radway's *Reading the Romance* (1984). Drawing from questionnaires and group interviews of a very close-knit community of female romance novel readers whom Radway calls the Smithton group, she unpacks their reading practices and their narrative preferences. She notes differences among these women, the sociological role of "Dot" who ran the bookstore the women used, and the sorts of narrative events which the women did not want in their stories. This book has been very influential in literary and film scholarship, both in its methodology and in its conclusions. The major criticism, however, is that as Radway tries to understand these women, she turns to psychoanalytical analysis of the actual Smithton readers, positing that because many of the women lived in patriarchal relationships with sometimes distant male partners, their preferred fantasies were a sort of compensation from and explanation for their everyday lives. The heroes in these fictional romances transform from cold, distant individuals to warm, feminized protectors (possibly substitute mothers for these readers), explaining why these women may prefer these sorts of stories. Radway (1991) has subsequently agreed that she stepped beyond the boundaries of her research in developing these assertions since her claims derived from an inadequate psychoanalytical study of real people. Despite the small missteps, in both the examples of soap operas and romances, by the late 1980s, scholars were rejecting (or at least labeling) "hypothetical" readers and viewers as such and were, instead, seeking material evidence of viewer/reader reception.

The Madonna discussions are the third debate. The commentary on how to interpret Madonna has been extensive. Should she be considered conservative or progressive? Modern or postmodern? For young women, a move backwards or emancipatory? From a feminist or postfeminist position? Her first albums and music videos began appearing in 1982. Discussion promptly ensued (Metz and Benson 1999). Within the scholarly community, John Fiske engages in an early analysis. In his *Television Culture* (1987), drawing from the concurrent British Cultural Studies tradition of investigating subcultures, he suggests that the use of gossip among Madonna fans allows them to see her as resisting patriarchal culture (1987: 125–6) and her admirers use her clothing styles in resistant ways no matter what the styles may mean in her performances, publicity photos, and videos (ibid. 233), giving the fans "a pleasure of control and empowerment" (ibid. 250). Much of Fiske's analysis is speculative, not specifically drawing from material evidence of those for whom he claims to speak (although he would do that soon for other case studies). However, Fiske does conjecture different audiences and postulates that Madonna means different things to them (1989: 124). These speculations continue with many scholars arguing these issues from numerous critical perspectives (for early essays, see Kaplan 1987; Bordo 1990; Curry 1990; Scott 1993; Andermahr 1994).

The work of Jane Brown, Laurie Schulze, and Anne Barton White moves the field into a full-fledged reception studies approach. In Brown and Schulze's 1990 study, they showed two Madonna videos to undergraduate students in a communications class. The students had a wide variety of interpretations. For example, for "Papa Don't Preach," almost all of the white women and all the black students thought the song was about pregnancy. However, in lines about keeping her baby, only 73 percent of the black women and 43 percent of the black men understood "baby" as referring to her child; the alternative interpretation was that "baby" was her boyfriend. Brown and Schulze also find that class mattered: the upper-class students were more hostile to the woman in the song. In Schulze, White, and Brown's 1993 essay, they consider why some people disliked Madonna and describe how these people could find ways to make Madonna a "low-other" (1993: 16). To substantiate the negative opinion, these people used four diatribes: she was commercial, not authentic; she was corrupting popular culture; she was a "bad" woman; and she was the "antitheses of feminism" (ibid. 17). Those who criticized Madonna as harming feminism often called themselves feminists, but Schulze, White, and Brown note that these people did not hold values often considered central to feminism, particularly the value of respecting people's choices in sexuality. As the scholars conclude, since what is feminism has no consensus, it would be difficult to locate Madonna as (or not as) feminist.

By the end of the 1980s, it was difficult to make propositions about what spectators do without noting which sorts of spectators were being discussed and without providing some evidence through study of discourse or directed research in interviews or ethnographies. This is not to suggest that feminist and gender analyses of textual representations were no longer valid. Rather, what could be claimed from these approaches needed to be restricted or clarified. Feminist scholarship was not the only arena in which this transition occurred; people working on other identities were simultaneously engaging in these conversations. However, in film studies, the strength of feminist scholarship was central in altering cinema and media studies, and reception studies became an important approach in trying to understand history and culture.

Significant lines of reception studies and feminist research from the mid-1980s

As the supplementation and testing of the generalized apparatus theory with historical and contextual research began to increase in the middle 1980s, many lines of research benefited that were central to feminism. And feminism/gender studies has and still does lead to the raising of many questions that reception studies attempts to answer.

An early line of research was about film audiences in the first years of US and other national cinemas. The questions were not only who they were (class, sex, race/ethnicity), but also whether there were lines of cohesion among them or if parts or all of them resisted the ideological implications of the films they were watching. Realizing that audiences were not naive viewers of film narratives meant that films which were sometimes opaque to 1980s scholars could be much more meaningful and coherent to early audiences (Staiger 1986b). Moreover, male and female audiences laughingly enjoyed villains, sexual innuendo, and male bodies (Mayne 1982; Staiger 1986a). Thus, an important strand of research developed examining how audiences of various identities hypothetically (Hansen 1986 and 1991, using German public sphere theory) and, in fact, responded to these films (Staiger 1995; Studlar 1996).

A second line of research developed out of the excitement about audiences at midnight and cult movies and, then, fans for many films and television programs. J. Hoberman and Jonathan Rosenbaum's *Midnight Movies* (1983) described the environment and crowd activities from the 1960s in theaters exhibiting experimental and underground films, with *The Rocky Horror Picture Show* (Jim Sharman, 1975) as the shining example (also Austin 1981). This research accelerated with attention to positioned identities. Of particular excitement to scholars were women using fictional characters to create their own narrative extensions from the "official" fiction, often with sexual story lines including homoerotic tales (Jenkins 1988; Penley, 1991; Jenkins 1992; Staiger 2005, 95–138). Criticizing the penchant to represent fans as irrational (Jensen 1992), scholars started thinking about whether fan activities indicated progressive or regressive tendencies (Fiske 1992). Certainly the experiences of female fans at fan conventions were evidence that female fans would encounter sexism while pursuing their interests (Bacon-Smith 1992).

Related to fan studies was the development of a reception studies approach to star and celebrity studies. Dyer's path-breaking work on stars (1986) included some analysis of historical discourses around stars, especially the figures of Judy Garland and Marilyn Monroe. Subsequently, two important ethnographic/interview studies of people's relation to stars appeared. Jackie Stacey reported in *Star Gazing* (1994) the various ways British women remembered responding to female stars during World War II. Joshua Gamson also examined audience identities and celebrity culture in *Claims to Fame* (1994).

As feminist scholars foregrounded LGBTQ and ethnicity/race identity intersections beyond sex and class by the early 1990s, reception research into those positioned identities and responses to media appeared as an important third line of scholarship. A mid-1980s essay by Elizabeth Ellsworth (1986) is a model of the use of theory, historical discourse evidence, and textual details to describe how lesbian viewers of *Personal Best* (Robert Towne, 1982) manipulated the narrative information into a storyline that would be pleasurable to them. Considering how lesbians might use stars and gossip to read films, Andrea Weiss (1992) provided historical information about lesbian lives in the early 1930s in her examination of potential ambiguities raised by the cross-dressing of actresses Marlene Dietrich, Katherine Hepburn, and Greta Garbo. Jane Feuer (1989) interpreted fan group audiences for *Dynasty* (1981–9), asking whether narrative or spectacle—especially the wonderful costumes worn by Joan Collins—was the prime pleasure for a subgroup of viewers enjoying camp reading strategies. By this point, however, scholars avoided assuming that sexual minorities will concur in their responses to films. This is obvious for *The Silence of the Lambs* (Jonathan Demme, 1991) in the arguments among gays and lesbians about the implications for potential misunderstanding of the cross-dressing villain, Jame Gumb, as homosexual (Staiger 1993/2000). Arguing for intentionally producing queer readings, Alexander Doty's *Making Things Perfectly Queer* (1993) has had a long-term impact in learning how to produce non-normative viewing practices for pleasure.

Although earlier social science research investigated how race and ethnicity affected the responses of television viewers (for example, Friedman 1978), in connection with interest in early film audiences, Mary Carbine (1990) and Greg Waller (1992) investigated black theaters and audiences, drawing attention to variety acts and musical performances that created opportunities for quite unexpected interpretations of mainstream film. Context—living in racist environments—produced bell hooks's account of the resisting black female spectator in her highly important essay, "The Oppositional Gaze" (1993).

A fourth line of reception research in these transitional years was affect and what has been labeled the "low genres." As Dyer describes these genres, they are ones based on "the effect that both producers and audiences know the film is supposed to have. … an effect that is registered in the spectator's body—s/he weeps, gets goose bumps, rolls about laughing, comes" (1985: 27). Important speculation and historical work occurred from feminist perspectives on audiences of "affect" genres, especially the genres of horror, sexual erotica, and "weepies." Watching slasher films in the theater, Carol Clover argued from the visible responses of adolescent males that they were identifying with the feminized, screaming females (1987)—a reading strategy that would allow them to avoid potential homoerotic identifications. Using historical exploration, Rhona Berenstein (1996) pointed out that a lot of the terrified behavior at horror films in 1930s theaters was part of dating rituals in which gendered conduct was not necessarily indicative of interior responses; it was a highly performative event. In terms of pornography, Dyer (1985) considered gay responses to gay porn, arguing that gay porn works differently than straight porn, and John Champagne cautioned that gay men browsing in porn film stores were not always particularly engaged with the films: so "stop reading films" (1997).[3] Although research into the "weepies" was long-standing, Sue Harper and Vincent Porter (1996) used a massive 1950s British population survey to determine which film scenes provoked emotional reactions of what sort for men and women. This creative access to traces of history has continued to help illuminate the historical reception of cinema.

The length of this essay precludes following through the important work of the last 20 years and also discussing many valuable items of research published before, during, and after the development of film reception studies. However, film reception studies and feminism have benefited each other, opening up lines of research and preventing generalized speculation, hopefully leading scholars to a better understanding of history. In particular, film reception studies requires that scholars avoid blithely making claims about textual effects and recognize the significance of positioned identities in experiencing media.

Related topics

Ikechukwu Obiaya, "Nollywood, female audience, and the negotiating of pleasure"
Katherine E. Morrissey, "Gender and fandom: from spectators to social audiences"

Notes

1 This is in terms of general critical practices. Hollywood filmmakers and polling experts had always recognized general viewing preferences for female, male, rural audiences, etc. (Staiger 2005: 33–44).
2 Also see Modleski's *Loving with a Vengeance* (1982) in which she includes her work on soap operas and also examines Harlequin romances and gothics.
3 Two important theorizations about the hypothetical spectator of sexual erotica are Dennis Giles (1977) and Linda Williams (1989).

References

Andermahr, S. (1994) "A Queer Love Affair: Madonna and Lesbian and Gay Culture," in D. Holmes and B. Budge (eds.) *The Good, the Bad, and the Gorgeous: Popular Culture's Romance with Lesbianism*, London: Pandora, pp. 28–40.
Ang, I. (1982/1985) *Watching Dallas: Soap Opera and the Melodramatic Imagination*, trans. D. Couling, London: Methuen.
Austin, B. A. (1981) "Portrait of a Cult Film Audience: *The Rocky Horror Picture Show*," *Journal of Communications*, 31, pp. 43–54.

Bacon-Smith, C. (1992) *Enterprising Women: Television Fandom and the Creation of Popular Myth*, Philadelphia: University of Pennsylvania Press.

Berenstein, R. J. (1996) *Attack of the Leading Ladies: Gender, Sexuality, and Spectatorship in Classic Horror Cinema*, New York: Columbia University Press.

Bordo, S. (1990). "Material Girl: The Effacements of Postmodern Culture," *Michigan Quarterly Review*, 29 (4), pp. 653–77.

Brown, J. and Schulze, L. (1990) "The Effects of Race, Gender and Fandom on Audience Interpretations of Madonna's Music Videos," *Journal of Communication*, 40 (2), pp. 88–102.

Carbine, M. (1990) "'The Finest Outside the Loop': Motion Picture Exhibition in Chicago's Black Metropolis, 1905–1928," *camera obscura*, 23, pp. 9–41.

Champagne, J. (1997) "'Stop Reading Films!' Film Studies, Close Analysis, and Gay Pornography," *Cinema Journal*, 36 (4), pp. 76–97.

Cixous, H. (1975/1976) "The Laugh of the Medusa," trans. by K. Cohen and P. Cohen, *Signs*, 1 (4), pp. 875–93.

Clover, C. J. (1987) *Men, Women, and Chain Saws: Gender in the Modern Horror Film*, Princeton: Princeton University Press.

Curry, R. (1990) "Madonna from Marilyn to Marlene—Pastiche and/or Parody?" *Journal of Film and Video*, 42 (2), pp. 15–30.

Doane, M. A. (1981) "*Caught* and *Rebecca*: The Inscription of Femininity as Absence," *Enclitic*, 5 (2), pp. 75–89.

—— (1982) "Film and the Masquerade: Theorising the Female Spectator," *Screen*, 23 (3–4), pp. 74–87.

Doty, A. (1993) *Making Things Perfectly Queer: Interpreting Mass Culture*, Minneapolis: University of Minnesota Press.

Dyer, R. (1982) "Don't Look Now: The Instability of the Male Pin-Up," *Screen*, 23 (3–4), pp. 61–73.

—— (1985) "Coming to Terms: Male Gay Porn," *Jump Cut*, 30, pp. 27–9.

—— (1986) *Heavenly Bodies: Film Stars and Society*, New York: St. Martin's Press.

Ellsworth, E. (1986) "Illicit Pleasures: Feminist Spectators and *Personal Best*," *Wide Angle*, 8 (2), pp. 45–56.

Feuer, J. (1989) "Reading *Dynasty*: Television and Reception Theory," *South Atlantic Quarterly*, 88 (2), pp. 443–60.

Fiske, J. (1987) *Television Culture*, London: Methuen.

—— (1989) *Understanding Popular Culture*, Boston: Unwin Hyman.

—— (1992) "The Cultural Economy of Fandom," in L. A. Lewis (ed.) *The Adoring Audience: Fan Culture and Popular Media*, New York: Routledge, pp. 30–49.

Fish, S. (1976) "Interpreting the *Variorum*," *Critical Inquiry*, 2 (Spring), pp. 465–85.

Friedman, N. (1978) "Responses of Blacks and Other Minorities to Television Shows of the 1970s about Their Groups," *Journal of Popular Film and Television*, 7 (1), pp. 85–102.

Gamson, J. (1994) *Claims to Fame: Celebrity in Contemporary America*, Berkeley: University of California Press.

Giles, D. (1977) "Pornographic Space: The Other Place," in B. Lawton and J. Staiger (eds.) *Film: Historical-Theoretical Speculations: The 1977 Film Studies Annual, Part II*, Pleasantville, New York: Redgrave, pp. 52–66.

Hansen, M. (1986) "Pleasure, Ambivalence, Identification: Valentino and Female Spectatorship," *Cinema Journal*, 25 (4), pp. 6–32.

—— (1991) *Babel and Babylon: Spectatorship in American Silent Film*, Cambridge, MA: Harvard University Press.

Harper, S. and Porter V. (1996) "Moved to Tears: Weeping in the Cinema in Postwar Britain," *Screen*, 37 (2), pp. 152–73.

Haskell, M. (1974) *From Reverence to Rape: The Treatment of Women in the Movies*, New York: Holt, Rinehart and Winston.

Hoberman, J. and Rosenbaum, J. (1983) *Midnight Movies*, New York: Harper & Row.

hooks, b. (1993) "The Oppositional Gaze: Black Female Spectators," in M. Diawara (ed.) *Black American Cinema*, New York: Routledge, pp. 288–302.

Irigaray, L. (1977/1981) "This Sex Which is Not One," trans. by C. Reeder in E. Marks and I. de Courtivron (eds.) *New French Feminisms*, New York: Schocken Books, pp. 99–106.

Jenkins, H. (1988) "*Star Trek* Rerun, Reread, Rewritten: Fan Writing as Textual Poaching," *Critical Studies in Mass Communication*, 5 (2), pp. 85–107.

—— (1992) *Textual Poachers: Television Fans and Participatory Culture*, New York: Routledge.

Jensen, J. (1992) "Fandom as Pathology: The Consequences of Characterization," in L. A. Lewis (ed.) *The Adoring Audience: Fan Culture and Popular Media*, New York: Routledge, pp. 9–29.

Kaplan, E. A. (1983) "The Case of the Missing Mother: Maternal Issues in Vidor's *Stella Dallas*," *Heresies*, 16, pp. 81–6.

—— (1985a) "Dialogue," *Cinema Journal*, 24 (2), pp. 40–3.

—— (1985b) "Dialogue," *Cinema Journal*, 25 (1), pp. 52–4.

—— (1987) *Rocking Around the Clock: Music Television, Postmodernism, and Consumer Culture*, New York: Routledge.

Kuhn, A. (1984) "Women's Genres: Melodrama, Soap Opera and Theory," *Screen*, 25 (1), pp. 18–28.

Mayne, J. (1982) "Immigrants and Spectators," *Wide Angle*, 5 (2), pp. 32–41.

Metz, A. and Benson, C. (eds.) (1999) *The Madonna Companion: Two Decades of Commentary*, New York: Schirmer Books.

Millett, K. (1970) *Sexual Politics*, Garden City, NY: Doubleday.

Modleski, T. (1979) "The Search for Tomorrow in Today's Soap Opera: Notes on a Feminine Narrative Form," *Film Quarterly*, 33 (1), pp. 12–21.

—— (1982) *Loving with a Vengeance: Mass-Produced Fantasies for Women*, Hamden, Conn.: Archon Books.

Mulvey, L. (1975) "Visual Pleasure and Narrative Cinema," *Screen*, 16 (3), pp. 6–18.

—— (1981) "Afterthoughts on 'Visual Pleasure and Narrative Cinema' Inspired by King Vidor's *Duel in the Sun* (1946)," *Framework*, 15–16–17 (Summer), pp. 12–15.

Neale, S. (1983) "Masculinity as Spectacle: Reflections on Men and Mainstream Cinema," *Screen*, 24 (6), pp. 2–16.

Penley, C. (1991) "Brownian Motion: Women, Tactics and Technology" in C. Penley and S. Willis (eds.) *Technoculture*, Minneapolis: University of Minnesota Press.

Petro, P. and Flinn, C. (1985) "Dialogue," *Cinema Journal*, 25 (1), pp. 50–2.

Radway, J. A. (1984) *Reading the Romance: Women, Patriarchy, and Popular Literature*, Chapel Hill: University of North Carolina Press.

—— (1991) "Introduction," in *Reading the Romance: Women, Patriarchy, and Popular Literature*, Chapel Hill: University of North Carolina Press.

Rosen, M. (1973) *Popcorn Venus: Women, Movies and the American Dream*, New York: Coward, McCann & Geoghegan.

Schulze, L., White, A. B., and Brown, J. D. (1993) "'A Sacred Monster in Her Prime': Audience Construction of Madonna as Low-Other," in C. Schwichtenberg (ed.) *The Madonna Connection: Representational Politics. Subcultural Identities, and Cultural Theory*, Boulder: Westview Press, pp. 15–37.

Scott, R. B. (1993) "Images of Race and Religion in Madonna's Video *Like a Prayer*: Prayer and Praise," in C. Schwichtenberg (ed.) *The Madonna Connection: Representational Politics, Subcultural Identities, and Cultural Theory*, Boulder: Westview Press, pp. 57–77.

Seiter, E., Borchers, H., Kreutzner, G., and Warth, E. (1989) "'Don't Treat Us Like We're So Stupid and Naive': Toward an Ethnography of Soap Opera Viewers," in E. Seiter, H. Borchers, G. Kreutzner, and E. Warth (eds.) *Remote Control: Television, Audiences, and Cultural Power*, London: Routledge, pp. 223–47.

Smith, S. (1972) "The Image of Women in Film: Some Suggestions for Future Research," *Women and Film*, 1, pp. 13–21.

Stacey, J. (1994) *Star Gazing: Hollywood Cinema and Female Spectatorship*, London: Routledge.

Staiger, J. (1986a) "'The Handmaiden of Villainy': *Foolish Wives*, Politics, Gender Orientation, and the Other," *Wide Angle* 8 (1), pp. 19–27, rev. and rpt., in J. Staiger, *Interpreting Films* (1992), pp. 124–38.

—— (1986b) "Rethinking 'Primitive' Cinema: Intertextuality, the Middle-Class Audience, and Reception Studies," *Society for Cinema Studies*, New Orleans, Louisiana, 3–6 April, rev. in J. Staiger, *Interpreting Films* (1992), pp. 101–23.

—— (1992) *Interpreting Films: Studies in the Historical Reception of American Cinema*, Princeton, New Jersey: Princeton University Press.

—— (1993/2000) "Taboos and Totems: Cultural Meanings of *The Silence of the Lambs*," rpt. in J. Staiger, *Perverse Spectators: The Practices of Film Reception*, New York: New York University Press, pp. 161–78.

—— (1995) *Bad Women: Regulating Sexuality in Early American Cinema*, Minneapolis: University of Minnesota Press.

—— (2005) *Media Reception Studies*, New York: New York University Press.

Studlar, G. (1996) *This Mad Masquerade: Stardom and Masculinity in the Jazz Age*, New York: Columbia University Press.

Waller, G. A. (1992) "Another Audience: Black Moviegoing, 1907–16," *Cinema Journal*, 31 (2), pp. 3–25.

Weiss, A. (1992) "'A Queer Feeling When I Look at You': Hollywood Stars and Lesbian Spectatorship in the 1930s," in A. Weiss, *Vampires and Violets: Lesbians in Film*, New York: Penguin Books, pp. 30–50.

Williams, L. (1984) "'Something Else Besides a Mother': Stella Dallas and the Maternal Melodrama," *Cinema Journal*, 24 (1), pp. 2–27.

—— (1989) *Hard Core: Power, Pleasure, and the "Frenzy" of the Visible*, Berkeley: University of California Press.

32

NOLLYWOOD, FEMALE AUDIENCE, AND THE NEGOTIATING OF PLEASURE

Ikechukwu Obiaya

The Nigerian film industry has witnessed tremendous growth, and its products have received a wide welcome across Africa and beyond (for example, see Cartelli 2007; Ugochukwu 2009; Kerr 2011; Waliaula 2014). (The industry is widely referred to as Nollywood. However, the term is used here with the understanding that it is restrictive in its scope of reference since, properly speaking, it only refers to that aspect of the Nigerian film production that has its main center in Lagos.) It is widely accepted that the Nigerian filmmakers have captured the popular imagination of peoples across Africa, thereby succeeding where so many others have failed (for a broader discussion of African cinema and the discourses around "pioneers" and "firsts," see Anne Ciecko's essay in this volume). The reasons for this welcome development can be traced largely to the fact that the audience involved feels identified with characters and narratives they encounter in the video films. Thanks to the "proximity of Nollywood to everyday stories" (Green-Simms 2012: 60), the consumers see the stories of the Nollywood-produced films as theirs. And this popularity has been an essential factor for the growth and success of the industry.

The great strength of the industry, according to Haynes (2007), lies precisely in this "proximity to popular imagination" (31). The filmmakers have often claimed that their films respond to the needs of their audience by showing the people what they want to see. Nevertheless, the films have often been criticized for their content, and the filmmakers have been accused of corrupting their audience by an undue focus on issues of witchcraft, fetishism, violence, greed, and sex. But this, according to the filmmakers, is what the audiences want to see, and they point to their booming sales as an indication that the viewers enjoy and accept their content (Abah 2008). Audience analyses such as those carried out by Adejunmobi (2002), Akpabio (2007), Okome (2007), and Esan (2008) support, to a large extent, the notion that there is proximity between the films and their audience.

Thus, the Nollywood film has been said to be

> a material production of the people in both senses of representing the existential realities of the populace as well as being itself a product of this reality [and] it reflects the people the way they are and the way they aspire to be.
>
> (Okoye 2007: 27)

But some have pointed out that the reality is not that simple. Rather than merely reflecting things the way they are, the films are used as a means of imposing a certain cultural outlook and ideology. As Dossoumon has noted, "the choices offered to the audience may at best be illusory because despite the appearance of choice, media texts often convey ideologies that reinforce the interests of those who control capital while suppressing and repressing other interests" (2013: 7).

One recurring concern in this regard has been the way women are presented in these films. Nollywood is said to frequently take on "the role of regulating gendered and sexual citizens" (Green-Simms 2012: 60), and women are "portrayed as wayward and of low morality, easily lured by material things, subservient to men, causes of family problems, fit for domestic rather than professional and career roles, lazy & dependent on men, etc." (Okunna 2002: 9). They are "either depicted as catalysts to misfortune or portrayed as victims of male folk" (Anyanwu 2003: 87). The films present a "limited range of restricted caricatures and stereotypes of women, usually set in opposition to each other, as either 'sirens' or 'ideal mothers' portrayed in the majority of the movies" (Harding 2007: 12). The ideal woman—a submissive wife and mother—is contrasted with the danger inherent in an economically, politically or socially independent woman (Abah 2008). However, Kerr notes that "most stereotypes have their equivalents in both genders, contrary to a perception that Nigerian videos scapegoat women" (2011: 72). But he is quick to add that,

> This apparent "equality," however, is deceptive. Some of the stereotypes are far more common for one gender than another (for example, far more female sex-workers than toy boys, far more wizards than witches, far more male than female tricksters). In addition, most of the stereotypes conform to gendered role expectations, for example that a man's infidelity is less culpable than a woman's, or that a violent gang of female armed robbers is more shocking than an equivalent male gang.
>
> (*ibid.*)

The Nollywood films have been criticized as being products "made by men for a female-dominated audience and defined by masculine heteronormative assumptions" (Bryce 2012: 79). As pointed out by Shaka and Uchendu, the "image of the Nigerian woman in video films is a fictional construct borne out of the repressed desires and imaginations of patriarchy" (2012: 7). The films supposedly "perpetuate the denigration of women's domestic life in Nigeria by espousing the values of the dominant ideology for women's domestic and social roles in society" (Abah 2008: 351). It has also been said that the films are being used as means of reinforcing the status quo and keeping the masses in check (Dossoumon 2013).

Such criticism leads to the questions of spectatorship that are at the heart of this study. The criticism ties in to the notions of patriarchal dominance as found in cine-psycho-analysis, but it fails to explain the great popularity that these films continue to enjoy among a good number of women. Are these women oblivious of the claimed patriarchal under-pinnings of the films, or is theirs a non-gendered, passive spectatorship? Does their con-tinued consumption of the product imply an alignment with the mode of portrayal of women in those films and an acceptance of what the films present as the social status quo?

In cine-psychoanalysis, the female spectator is a passive one created by the text in which the spectator is forced into an identification with the objectified role provided within the patriarchal narrative structure. To enjoy and make meaning of the text, the female spectator must assume the unified position of the male subject and suppress such differences as defined by gender, sex, class, race, and nationality. This notion of a feminine spectator constructed by the text is contrasted with "the female audience, constructed by the socio-historical categories of gender, class, race, and so on" (Gledhill 2006: 113). Such socio-historical categories make provision for the fact that, rather than being a passive absorbent sponge, the audience brings a measure of activism to bear on the text and could even manipulate it for its own purposes. The text could be said to be mediated by whatever the spectator brings along with her. Thus, the context of the consumption matters—that is, the spectators bring along their own background and socio-cultural/historical influences, and it is through this filter that the text is consumed.

Gledhill's proposal of the concept of negotiation seeks precisely to take these various factors into consideration. The concept, while avoiding an "overly deterministic view of cultural production," was intended to hold together "opposite sides in an ongoing process of give-and-take" (Gledhill 2006: 114). It is a process in which "meaning is neither imposed, nor passively imbibed, but arises out of a struggle of negotiation between competing frames of reference, motivation and experience" (ibid.).

The negotiation takes place at the three levels: institution, text, and audiences. At the institutional level, the producer must match ideological preferences and the desire for profit to the use-value of the product for the intended consumers. The textual level would call forth negotiations aimed at achieving credibility in the text while maintaining a balance of familiarity and innovation. Reception at the level of the audience is, according to Gledhill, "potentially the most radical moment of negotiation" (ibid. 116) given its variability and unpredictability. This is because each member of the audience will approach the text with her own socio-historical realities, and each person will carry out a different, even if similar, negotiation with the text.

> Texts must be studied in the context of their production and reception, and it must be recognized that they can be viewed differently based not only on the viewer's gender, but also on determinants such as class, race, and nationality.
>
> *(Hollinger 2012: 18)*

This approach thus leads to a greater attention being paid to the audience with methods such as interviews and surveys. The goal becomes that of examining how female audiences interact with various texts and what pleasures they derive from the texts. The method has, however, been criticized for not evaluating films in terms of their ability to "challenge or educate female audiences in a progressive feminist way" and for "validating texts that seem from a feminist perspective clearly bad for viewers" (Hollinger 2012: 19).

But such an evaluation cannot be carried out in isolation from the particular socio-historical contexts and experiences of the audience. Moreover, there is the danger of approaching a text with preconceived notions that one expects the text to fit into. The notion of "reading against the grain," for instance, begins with the assumption that the text contains a dominant patriarchal discourse, which should be undermined by seeking alternative readings. Bryce (2012), in this regard, argues that the presentations of the feminine in Nollywood films should be read as signs in Nollywood's modes of signification. According to her, "If many of the roles given to women appear to be 'negative,' we should not make the mistake of reading them literally" (2012: 84). She also suggests that, in the effort to understand the films, one should avoid "moral prescriptiveness and normativity" and instead take a "cue from an audience that understands femininity as an ambivalent sign for an era of transition" (ibid.).

Taking a cue from the audience

Although some of the Nollywood films are premiered in cinemas, the greater majority go straight to VCD and DVD, and are also broadcast on television as well as exhibited in video parlors. Other "sites of consumption" (Okome 2007) are waiting rooms and hair dressing salons. The films are thus seen all over the country. The films are largely "consumed in the context of the domestic sphere, which renders the appropriation of the videoed world as a familial engagement of the fiction of Nollywood" (ibid. 6). In the familial and other less formal contexts, such as the video parlor, the audience tends to be more actively engaged, making comments about the action on the screen. Okome (2007) notes the special role that this audience has in Nollywood but, at the same time, points out the paucity of studies to deal with issues surrounding the audience.

One of relatively few existing studies is that of Azeez (2013) who carried out a survey to find out how the audience understands femininity, as guided by socio-historic realities. The study was carried out to find out how Nigerian audiences, mainly women, perceived the representations of women in the Nollywood films, and whether they identified with such representations or not. The method used involved a series of focus group discussions with a cross section of people drawn from different socio-economic backgrounds and grouped in line with age, sex, ethnicity, and educational level. It was previously established that the participants were frequent consumers of the films.

While a majority of the educated women were of the opinion that the Nigerian films presented a distorted view of the reality of women, the general opinion of the "less-educated women" was that the representations were true to the reality. However, one of the conclusions reached in the article is that "the reality of women shown in Nigerian films is the reality, which African culture and discursive practice have created for women, or which the 'culture' wanted for women" (Azeez 2013: 160). The author nevertheless adds that for the better educated women that accepted this as being the reality, their response could be seen as a "conscious identification, with the possibility of resisting (or dis-identify[ing] with) the negative meanings of the representations" (ibid.).

This analysis, however, becomes rather problematic when the author tries to account for the acceptance by the less-educated women of the reality portrayed in the films. To put it simply, the acceptance of such reality by these women is attributed to their ignorance. Having had a forced meaning indoctrinated into the way they see and live their lives, these women are seen as unable to resist the meaning of the films because "they are not exposed to the cultures of resistance" (ibid. 163). This conclusion is a rather reductive one that fails to explain the interaction of the women in question with the text, and the pleasures that they derive from it. It is noteworthy that a few of the highly educated women held similar views to those of the lesser educated ones, which suggests that education was not the only variable that made the difference. Thus, rather than attribute this position to a lack of exposure, we need to investigate further the nature of the negotiation that female audiences may have with Nollywood films.

One could perhaps, in this context, better appreciate Bryce's admonition that moral prescriptiveness and normativity should be avoided in favor of seeking an understanding of the text from the perspective of the audience. It is true that the lack of certain competencies could lead to the audience being oblivious of the intended meaning, but this does not obviate the fact that the audience approaches the film with its own defined use-value that leads it to read its own meanings into the text. Furthermore, in trying to understand the way the Nollywood female audience consumes the industry's products, it is important not to overlook the reality of its being popular culture. According to Green-Simms (2012: 61), "Nollywood is unique among global film industries in that it is produced from below—which is to say that the class affiliations of the producers are often those of the mass consumers."

Study of a sample Nollywood audience

For the purpose of understanding better the way in which the feminine audience of Nollywood engages with the films, I carried out a survey. Among other things, the survey aimed to find out why the respondents watched Nollywood films in the first place; whether they had an affinity for the films; and what they thought of the way women were portrayed in the films. Thirteen women were interviewed for this survey. The interviews were semi structured, and the women were chosen by convenience sampling. Effort was made to ensure that the persons selected were representative of different educational levels and socio-economic status. Also, a key criterion that guided the selection of the respondents was that they needed to be regular consumers of the Nollywood films, and this was ascertained prior to inviting them to take part in the survey. However, there was a range in the extent of consumer practices within the group (two respondents watched Nollywood films considerably less than others). While the other women gave varying accounts of consumption that ranged from about twenty films a month to one film almost every day, the afore-mentioned respondents indicated that they watched the films "once in a while" and "once or twice a month." Nevertheless, their comments were still considered relevant to the study and retained.

In choosing the respondents, effort was also made to have a representation of different age groups and, as already indicated, of persons with different educational qualifications. Thus, the ages of the respondents ranged from eighteen to forty-six years. One participant was eighteen years old, four people were in their twenties, another four in their thirties, and four others were in their forties. As for the educational qualifications, two of the interviewees had secondary degree education; two were undergraduates; one had a college diploma; six were bachelor degree holders; and two of them held master's degrees. Their jobs ranged from cleaner, caterer, trader, and housewife to business woman, librarian, and banker, and these are indicated below at the first mention of the names. (The names that are used here are not their real names.)

One of the first questions posed in the interviews was aimed at establishing the use-value of the Nollywood films for the respondents. It was quite striking that for just about all the respondents the films had a practical use. The attraction of the films for Sandie (a caterer) lay in their portrayal of culture: "I watch them because they promote the Nigerian culture. They tell our story." This was a position shared by most of the respondents who also found in the films a means of learning about what was going on in the country. For example, Blessing (a shop keeper) said: "[From the films], I learn about our culture and traditions; I learn a bit of other languages due to the subtitles, and I get to see other countries because some of the films are made outside the country." For Nkiru (an undergraduate student), the films are "educative, interesting; they make you laugh; they also teach you things that are happening in society so you are not naïve."

It is safe to say that this use to which the respondents have put the films is not the primary one intended by the producers of the films. It exemplifies the notion that media texts could be put to unforeseen uses by the consumers. And, as Gledhill says, use "values vary according to particular groups of users and contexts of use" (2006: 114). Thus, for one of the non-frequent watchers, Ada (a business woman), the films were merely a means to "while away time" in moments of boredom, when there was nothing else on television, or a source of entertainment for her visitors. However, more striking is the comment of Lisa (a cleaner) who stated that:

> They also help with your relationship within your family. For example, when it comes to the issue of girls not being sent to school, they can learn a lot about being educated [from the films], and it could also expose their parents to the fact that girls are actually going to school. They also learn about another life, so I find it exposing.

This reading appears to contradict what has been identified as the supposedly dominant patriarchal discourse that seeks to subjugate the woman, especially a woman of lower socio-economic position. If one accepts the existence of this discourse, then one can identify this as an instance of reading against the grain.

A follow up question sought to find out from the women their preferences with regard to Hollywood and Nollywood films. The responses to the question indicated three different positions. One group expressed a clear preference for Hollywood films due to their technological superiority. This preference, nevertheless, did not prevent those in this group from watching the Nollywood films. Amaka (a banker), for instance, stated, "Truthfully, I prefer Hollywood [films]; they are very advanced; their films are well plotted." But she also admitted with regard to the Nollywood films: "I have seen so many, and I am still watching. Weekly, I see about three films."

A second position was expressed by those who, while acknowledging Hollywood's technological superiority, placed both industries on equal standing in terms of their liking. Angie (a librarian), for instance, stated: "Honestly I am indifferent, but Hollywood films present the suspense so well." However, some of those in this group expressed a tendency to watch more of the Nollywood films. As Nkiru noted, "I enjoy the both of them, but I watch Nollywood films more."

A third position was taken by those that clearly preferred the Nollywood films due largely to having a greater affinity towards them. As Amara (a house wife) put it, "I find that I can relate more to Nollywood movies because I am quite a traditional person; secondly, I am not so educated, so I really understand Nollywood, and I enjoy it more." This was similar to the statement made by Nkem (trader): "Ha, I don't know what they are saying in the foreign films; I can't understand their accents, and their films look unreal and complicated. I prefer films I can relate to my everyday life." But this preference, for some, was also hinged on a desire to identify with an industry that they saw as their own. Thus, in response to the question of whether she preferred Nollywood films, Blessing said:

> Definitely, this is my country, and I can relate to the stories being told. Also, we as Nigerians need to learn how to promote what is ours; Nigerians are too focused on what happens outside, in London and in America.

It is clear that the interaction with the Nollywood films by these women is the fruit of very deliberate choices. Statements such as those above, and the reality of the different expressed attitudes, underline the importance of recognizing the audience—in this case the female spectator—not as fixed abstract entities, but as human agents that interact with the text from within concrete socio-economic and historical contexts. There cannot be just a single position, and the recognition of different identities that the concept of negotiation provides for makes it possible to accommodate such differences of position.

The majority of the respondents were not happy with the way women are presented in the films, but their reasons for this varied. For some, the films fail to recognize the reality of today's world. Angie decried the failure of the films to adequately portray the abilities of women, an idea supported by Omofuma, who noted that there was a lack of "focus on a particular strength and character that women possess." According to Ola (a business woman):

> We are portrayed in a lot of ways, sometimes promiscuous, sometimes as helpless beings, and then those that portray us as independent frame it to look like it is bad to be successful—next thing, the lady can't find a husband. This one is career minded; her parents begin to insult her; she cries because her mates have children. It just seems like the Nigerian woman is under a lot of pressure.

One can read into such reactions a negation of the position that sees the female spectator as passive viewer that is made to identify with the objectified role that the patriarchal narrative structure provides. These respondents have clearly brought to bear on the text their own notions of what it means to be a woman. Their enjoyment of the text involves recognizing and setting aside aspects of it that do not agree with their own views.

Gledhill has indicated the improbability of consumers swallowing cultural experiences whole and in the exact way that they are presented by the producers of the text. Rather, the consumers can choose to identify or not identify with one or various of the positions that the text presents. This reality was made clear by the reactions of some of the respondents that expressed a concern about the way women tended to be dressed in the films. This was a reference to women dressed scantily in revealing clothes. Nkiru termed it "unrealistic." According to her, "The way women are portrayed is wrong especially when it comes to dressing. I mean, the way you dress in real life is not the same." Sandie saw it as a poor way of imitating other cultures: "I don't know what words to use to qualify it, but it is terrible, sad and negative. If we are trying to imitate Western movies, why must our women be naked?" However, persons like Blessing and Nkem held a different opinion. For them, the way women were represented in the films merely reflected the realities of society. According to Blessing:

> I don't see anything wrong with the way women are shown, for me this is the way we are. This is also the path the movie maker wants to follow; also these actresses are playing out a script, so I don't see anything wrong with it. They want to show exactly what is happening, and that is what they do.

Blessing's comment appears on the surface to be rather contradictory. On the one hand, she indicates that the mode of portraying women is merely a reflection of societal realities, but on the other hand, goes on to imply that there is something deliberate about the filmmaker's use of such representations. Bryce (2012) has indicated the need to seek cues from the audience as means of correctly interpreting the mode in which femininity is presented in the Nollywood films. This comment by Blessing is about the closest that any of the respondents came to expressing an awareness that the mode of representing women could be just a means of signifying other realities. Nevertheless, one must admit that there is not enough here for one to reach a definite conclusion that this audience reads the portrayal of the female body as a symbolic or discursive sign.

While affirming that the films merely reflect what happens in society, Nkem gives as an example the portrayal of the plight of widows in the films: "When a woman's husband dies, terrible things are done to her." It is worthwhile pointing out that Nkem is herself a widow. And, in response to a different question, she expresses her ability to identify with the stories or characters in the films: "I can relate to films about widows because I am a widow, and what they show is real, even traditional practices and festivals." This ability by the consumer to empathize with the narratives of the films was acknowledged by most of the respondents, even when it did not derive, as in Nkem's case, simply from the fact of having lived through similar experiences. It was an empathy heightened by the fact that the films were able to tap into and reflect the various social tensions with which the respondents were familiar, thus lending greater credibility to the films. The element of credibility was clearly a key factor in the negotiations that the respondents carried out in choosing to identify or not to identify with the filmic stories and characters, because many of them were quick to point out aspects that they judged as being either untrue or not completely in consonance with the "reality." This judgment was expressed more with respect to the question of whether the films were, to a greater or lesser degree, reflections of the Nigerian society. Most of the respondents, even those that disagreed with the way women were portrayed, agreed that the films were a faithful reflection of the society. According to Nike (a wholesaler):

> To a large extent, they show what is happening; they even serve as eye openers to those of us that are not really exposed to the truths in society. So, in that regard, they are doing an excellent job. I think they carry out their research very well.

Persons like Omofuma, however, did note that the films sometimes contained exaggerations. However, Lisa and Blessing chose to see the films as merely fictional representations and not to be taken seriously. Blessing spoke of the need to create a distance, while Lisa noted that some of the films "reflect what they have seen happen. But most of these films are fiction or exaggerated. I hear a lot of women get angry over this, but this is not something to really be bothered about." Thus, though these women had clearly expressed their enjoyment of the films, there was also a certain resistance on their part that undermines the notion of audience passivity.

About a third of the respondents were of the opinion that the way women were portrayed in the films was due to the stories being told from a male perspective. According to Ada, "Men make women out the way they want. Since it is a male dominated industry, it makes it easy for them to keep churning out rubbish." This was a view shared by Omofuma and Chidi. However, Ola, while acknowledging that in the past the films were narrated from "the man's perspective," notes that "now there is a bit of a balance. Women are beginning to tell their own story, in their own way."

The majority of the respondents, nevertheless, opined that the depiction of women reflected the perspectives of both men and women. According to Nkem, "To me, stories are told the way they are told; it has nothing to do with being a man or being a woman." On her part, Sandie thought that the stories were "told from the perspective of someone that deeply understands our culture; really it is a combination of both [sexes points of view]."

The variety of opinions expressed here make it easy to appreciate the point that reception is potentially the most radical moment of negotiation given its variability and unpredictability (Bobo 1995). There is awareness on the part of some of the respondents of a dominant approach, which they reject. However, the others do not recognize that such an approach exists. It is difficult to trace any of these positions to particular socio-economic circumstances because those that expressed them came from different backgrounds. But, taking a cue from Sandie's comment, one could posit that a negotiation has taken place in which the meaning of the text has been approached, and judged, from within the frame of reference of established culture, and sometimes as a way to challenge dominant assumptions.

Conclusion

Each woman in this survey approached the filmic text on the basis of her own socio-cultural/ historical realities, and her interpretation has been done through that prism. Although there are some commonalities in their interpretations, the differences that exist serve to buttress that meaning is not imposed or passively imbibed. Rather, negotiations do take place in which the socio-economic and cultural make-up of the audience have roles to play. The negotiations that take place involve the decisions of the respondents to accept or reject what they encountered in the films and the meanings that they chose to ascribe to them. The ideas or representations in the films were assessed using personal experience as a yardstick, and decisions were taken on the basis of their personal notions of how things are or should be. While the level of education played a role in the positions taken, it did not appear to be the main determining factor. The reading of the films appeared to be based more on whether the depictions accorded with the reality as observed in their social surroundings. This, for the most part, appeared to be a greater concern and was particularly reflected in the expressed use-values.

The women clearly made a conscious choice to watch the Nollywood films in preference to films from other industries. It is noteworthy that this preference cuts across educational boundaries, with each person, even the non-avid fans, having a use-value for the films. A strong determinant for reception was nationality. A good portion of the respondents embraced the films because they identified with them both in terms of their origin and in terms of the culture portrayed.

This identification, of course, did not blind them to the perceived flaws. Nevertheless, participation in the stories of the films, leading to their acceptance or rejection, was affected not so much by the flaws, but by whether there was an alignment with the stories experienced by the women in their own lives. It is perhaps here that most of the negotiation between the Nollywood filmmakers and their audience takes place, *the negotiation of ensuring credibility by clothing innovation with the familiar*. The filmmakers, in the negotiation at the institutional level, seek to increase their profit by providing for the use-value of their consumers, thus enhancing their pleasure. To do this, the filmmakers produce new films, with new stories, but make them familiar to the audience by grounding them in social realities that are known to the audience, including its female members.

While it is true that this grounding in known realities could facilitate the audience's acceptance of novel ideas, the negotiation approach helps to establish that this would not be a blind and unthinking acceptance. This is especially useful when examining the reception of the Nollywood films by women spectators. The criticism of the films as denigrators of women and vehicles for their subjugation raises questions about the popularity enjoyed by the films among a good number of women. Such criticism tends to treat the audience as monolithic and passive. However, audience analysis that uses the concept of negotiation gives a more accurate picture of the nature of this female audience. It makes it possible to affirm that this audience is constituted of fluid subjectivities and identities, and it is through such identities that meaning in the films is sought and completed. The concept is also valuable for affirming the nature of the female audience and identifying its pleasures.

Related topics

Janet Staiger, "Film reception studies and feminism"
Anne Ciecko, "African 'first films': gendered authorship, identity, and discursive resistance"

References

Abah, A. L., 2008. One Step Forward, Two Steps Backward: African Women in Nigerian Video-Film. *Communication, Culture and Critique*, Volume 1, p. 335–57.

Adejunmobi, M., 2002. English and the Audience of an African Popular Culture: The Case of Nigerian Video Film. *Cultural Critique*, Issue 50, pp. 74–103.

Akpabio, E., 2007. Attitude of Audience Members to Nollywood Films. *Nordic Journal of African Studies*, 16(1), pp. 90–100.

Anyanwu, C., 2003. Towards a New Image of Women in Nigerian Video Films. In: F. Ogunleye, ed. *African Video Film Today*. Swaziland: Academic Publishers, pp. 81–90.

Azeez, A. L., 2013. Audience Perception of the Reality in the Representations of Women in Nigerian Films. *Journal of African Cinemas*, 5(2), pp. 149–66.

Bobo, J., 1995. *Black Women as Cultural Readers*. New York: Columbia University Press.

Bryce, J., 2012. Signs of Femininity, Symptoms of Malaise: Contextualizing Figurations of "Woman" in Nollywood. *Research in African Literatures*, 43(4), pp. 71–87.

Cartelli, P., 2007. Nollywood Comes to the Caribbean. *Film International*, Issue 28, pp. 112–14.

Dossoumon, M., 2013. *Class and Gender Representation in Nollywood Movies*. s.l.: ProQuest.

Esan, O., 2008. *Appreciating Nollywood: Audiences and Nigerian "Films."* (Online) Available at: www.participations.org/Volume%205/Issue%201%20-%20special/5_01_esan.htm (Accessed June 9, 2009).

Gledhill, C., 2006. Pleasurable Negotiations. In: J. Storey, ed. *Cultural Theory and Popular Culture: A Reader*. Athens: University of Georgia Press, pp. 111–23.

Green-Simms, L., 2012. Hustlers, Home-wreckers and Homoeroticism: Nollywood's Beautiful Faces. *Journal of African Cinemas*, 4(1), pp. 59–79.

Harding, F., 2007. Appearing Fabu-lous: From Tender Romance to Horrifying Sex. *Film International*, Issue 28, pp. 10–19.

Haynes, J., 2007. Nnebue: the Anatomy of Power. *Film International*, pp. 30–40.

Hollinger, K., 2012. *Feminist Film Studies*. 1st edn. Oxon: Routledge.

Kerr, D., 2011. The Reception of Nigerian Video Drama in a Multicultural Female Community in Botswana. *Journal of African Cinema*, 3(1), pp. 65–79.

Okome, O., 2007. Nollywood: Spectatorship, Audience and the Sites of Consumption. *Postcolonial Text*. (Online) 3.9, August 2007 Available at: http://journals.sfu.ca/pocol/index.php/pct/article/view/763/425 (Accessed November 2007).

Okoye, C., 2007. Looking at Ourselves in our Mirror: Agency, Counter-Discourse, and the Nigerian Video Film. *Film International*, Issue 28, pp. 20–9.

Okunna, C. S., 2002. *Gender and Communication in Nigeria: Is this the Twenty First Century?* s.l.: Paper Delivered at the Department of Mass Communication, Nnamdi Azikiwe University, Awka, Nigeria.

Shaka, F. O. and Uchendu, O. N., 2012. Gender Representation in Nollywood Video Film Culture. *The Crab: Journal of Theatre and Media Arts*, Issue 7, pp. 1–30.

Ugochukwu, F., 2009. *The Reception and Impact of Nollywood in France: A Preliminary Survey*. (Online) Available at: http://oro.open.ac.uk/25340/2/Nollywood_in_France.pdf (Accessed July 14, 2016).

Waliaula, S., 2014. Active Audiences of Nollywood Video-films: an Experience with a Bukusu Audience Community in Chwele Market of Western Kenya. *Journal of African Cinemas*, 6(1), pp. 71–83.

33

GENDER AND FANDOM

From spectators to social audiences

Katherine E. Morrissey

Studies of fandom are part of a broader history of research on film spectators and the cinema (see Janet Staiger's piece on Reception Studies in this volume). At the same time, they represent a break from film studies traditions. "Fandom" is a term strongly linked with "fan studies," a line of research that emerged in the 1980s and 90s. Fan studies strategically moved away from the term "spectator" and many of the conceptions of spectatorship that were dominating film studies during this period. The research addressed in this chapter—feminist analyses of fandom—represents both a response to film theory prior to the 1980s, and a continuation of the work already being done by feminist film scholars of this period. Despite the complex relationship between spectatorship and fandom, the history of fan studies—and of feminist studies of fandom—is dependent on a legacy of feminist film studies scholarship.

In the 1960s and 70s, apparatus and psychoanalytic theory were popular theoretical frameworks in film studies. These approaches tended to see film spectators as a collection of individual psyches—minds that the film apparatus positions in a particular way. This view of cinema holds that film's technologies, formal and aesthetic codes, and systems of production/reception hold spectators within specific ideological perspectives and privilege certain views of the world. While informed by this framing of spectatorship, many feminist scholars also found it limiting. Analyzing film through a psychoanalytic lens helped reveal the ways in which classical Hollywood cinema privileges a white, heterosexual, and male gaze (Mulvey 1975). However, there were numerous spectators who were not white, male, or heterosexual. Jackie Stacey argues that: "an implicit textual determinism defines assumptions about spectatorship. ... the term spectator implies a unified viewing experience, and its usage carries with it a very passive model of how audiences watch films" (Stacey 2011: 646). Sharing these concerns, many feminist scholars began approaching spectatorship from additional angles (e.g. genre, target markets, television viewing habits) and blending textual analysis with more empirical research methods. Many film scholars also found themselves studying a broader range of media and production environments (e.g. film, television, and print).

Annette Kuhn's "Women's Genres" (1984) is a useful starting point for anyone who wants to understand this history. Kuhn outlines two ways of conceptualizing audiences: as spectators and as social audiences. Due to the different ways film and television technologies organize audiences and shape narratives, Kuhn argues that film and television scholars tend to study spectators differently. Kuhn organizes these approaches on a spectrum, with one end emphasizing text and the ways the text positions the viewer (spectatorship/film studies) and, at the other end, context and the social/industrial circumstances informing reception (social audiences/television studies).

For many feminist media scholars, the 1980s were marked by a move away from the study of spectatorship, or at least spectatorship as it had been understood prior to this period. Many scholars increased their focus on cultural contexts, systems of representation, and the structuring of identities and ideologies across media. There were also broader moves to research various production and reception contexts, incorporate trans-media analyses, and to study audiences using empirical research methods. In the process, one of the audience groups these scholars turned to was fans.

The interest in viewing contexts, the influence of television studies, and the focus on the social is evident in fan studies scholarship. Corresponding with Kuhn's binaries of spectatorship/film studies and social audience/TV studies, a great deal of the research on fandom has been connected to television texts and audiences rather than film. However, all forms of research come with their own limits and affordances. Wherever their work falls on the spectator/social audience spectrum, it is critical that feminist fan scholars consider how their approach to research will shape their questions, methods, and findings.

Conceptualizing fans

Being a "fan" implies an emotional connection between an individual and something, but there are many possible "somethings." For example, a fan may enjoy a particular film, sports team, or a type of food. With fandom, however, the suffix "–dom" is significant. It signals a broader and shared declaration of affection, a group status, and a space in which one fan's interests are shared with others. Fandoms are often identified with a particular text or media franchise (such as *Harry Potter* or *Breaking Bad*), or a media genre (for example, Japanese anime, Korean TV dramas, or science fiction). When researchers study fandom they often want to know how fans are engaging with media and making sense of popular culture. This means that analyses of fandom tend to center more on fans, fan communities, and fan practices than they do on the texts themselves. Additionally, contemporary fandoms are also highly digital. Fan interests are coded into user profiles on social media sites, and fan-marketing strategies have become a major part of selling any popular media product. Due to this, contemporary fan studies can be, simultaneously, a study of a fandom, of digital cultures and networks, and of an individual's social media use.

While fandoms commonly organize around media texts and franchises, fan studies research often starts with an Internet forum or a fan convention and may, eventually, circle back around to a television show or film. Alternatively, the research might focus on the materials fans produce (a work of fan fiction, a fan-made music video, a fan in costume, or a work of fan criticism) rather than the media texts they are engaged with. Contemporary studies of fandom cover everything from the Japanese fans of Hong Kong celebrities (Hitchcock Morimoto 2013) to female gamers and their use of social media (Gray 2015).

Today, research on fandom (feminist or otherwise) is much more likely to be tagged with key terms like fan, audience, user, consumer, and participatory culture than it is with the term spectator. It also tends to be associated more with fan studies than it is with film studies. However, fan studies is an interdisciplinary network of scholars with connected research interests. It draws upon a multitude of methods and conceptual approaches from other disciplines. Among the many concepts it draws upon, spectatorship and feminist analyses of female spectators continue to play a critical role in fan studies and its history.

Media Fandom, fan fiction, and slash

Historically, feminist analyses of fandom have tended to focus on three particular aspects of fandom: Media Fandom as a specific fan community, fans' creative practices (often within Media Fandom), and slash (male/male and female/female focused creative work and a genre closely associated with Media Fandom).[1] In part, Media Fandom became the focus of scholarly attention because it was, and continues to be, a predominantly female area of fan activity. It also constitutes a production network, as (mostly) female fans use it to connect with each other socially, engage in media criticism, and produce/circulate their own creative works.

Media Fandom emerged in the late-60s as an offshoot of Science Fiction Fandom, which has been in existence since the early twentieth century. While Science Fiction Fandom had been more exclusively focused on literary science fiction, *Star Trek's* popularity in the late-60s introduced many new people to the genre. Divisions formed between the older networks of *literary* science fiction fans and the newer *media* science fiction fans. While Science Fiction Fandom continued to publish fanzines, organize local interest groups, and put together large fan conventions, the growing body of media fans began developing their own traditions. By the late-60s, fan fiction began to appear regularly in *Star Trek* fanzines and many well-known genres of fan writing were developed in the late-60s and 1970s. There were also clear gender differences emerging between these two groups. While there were prominent female fans prior to this period, historically, the Science Fiction Fandom was predominantly male. In the wake of *Star Trek*, fandom demographics changed. Many of the media fans joining Science Fiction Fandom were now female (Bacon-Smith 1999; Coppa 2006; Jamison 2013; Lichtenberg et al. 1975; Verba 2003). While both male and female fans read fanzines, the fan fiction writers were nearly all women (Coppa 2006; Jamison 2013; Lichtenberg et al. 1975).

During this period, early slash fan works (homoerotic stories and fan art) began to circulate. "The premise" that two fictional characters like *Star Trek's* Kirk and Spock would be in a sexual relationship scandalized some and intrigued others. The Kirk/Spock premise quickly became a focal point for debate, fantasy, and for scholarly interest. While both adult content and slash were highly controversial, many female fans defended these practices and began to organize conventions and fanzines dedicated to these materials. Out of this, Media Fandom emerged as a space for (mostly) female fans, artists, and writers to share their enthusiasm for popular media, creative work, sexual fantasies, and media criticism. These three aspects of fandom—Media Fandom's high numbers of women, the creative and critical practices predominantly sustained and shared by women, and slash as an erotic and romantic storytelling genre developed by women—drew in many feminist scholars interested in gender, media, and spectatorship. In contemporary fan studies, the focus has broadened beyond Media Fandom, its practices, and slash, but this genesis continues to inform feminist fan scholarship today.

The beginning of fan studies

As a field of academic inquiry, fan studies traces its origins to a series of articles, books, and essay collections published in the 1980s and early-90s. In 1985, Joanna Russ published "Pornography by Women for Women, With Love." The following year, Patricia Frazier

Lamb and Diane L. Veith published "Romantic Myth, Transcendence and *Star Trek* Zines." Constance Penley's "Brownian Motion: Women Tactics and Technology" and Henry Jenkins' "Star Trek Reread, Rerun, Rewritten: Fan Writing as Textual Poaching" were published in a collection on film, feminism, and science fiction in 1991. In 1992, Camille Bacon-Smith published *Enterprising Women*, an ethnography of media fandom, and Henry Jenkins published *Textual Poachers: Television Fans and Participatory Culture*. Collectively, this research helped establish fan studies as a rich area of inquiry, and shaped the trajectory of fan studies for many years to come.

While these early studies of fandom are now an important part of the fan studies canon, at the time, most of them were more directly linked with feminist media criticism. Feminist media scholars were engaged in a broader effort to analyze women's culture, and advocated for academics to take feminized genres more seriously. Tania Modleski and Janice Radway published their work on romantic literature, film melodrama, and television soap operas during this time (Modleski 2007; Radway 1991). Arguing that these genres reveal deep contradictions about women's roles in society, feminist media scholars worked to validate women's culture and reclaim feminized genres like romance and serial television.

Media Fandom and its creative practices were also used to complicate the debate on women and pornography taking place across the feminist movement during this period. With Media Fandom primarily comprised of women, and with fan art/writing often sexually explicit, it was positioned as a female production space, and fan work as a female version of pornography. Explaining that, "the author doesn't live her life according to feminist theory, but draws her feminist theory from her life," Joanna Russ focused on her own relationship with pornography (Russ 1985a: 9). An academic, a well-known science fiction author, and a reader and writer of Kirk/Spock fan fiction, Russ theorized her own relationship with slash and argued that female fans "have—ingeniously, tenaciously, and very creatively— sexualized our female situation and training, and made out of the restrictions of the patriarchy our own sexual cues" (Russ 1985b: 86). In this way, Media Fandom and its creative practices were used to complicate feminist conversations on women and pornography and to challenge the idea that pornography is inherently misogynistic.

The excitement and optimism that these scholars feel when discussing slash fan fiction is clear across their writing. "[M]erely the premise" of these stories makes Russ' "automatic nervous system [do] the nip-ups" (Russ 1985b: 81). Similarly, Constance Penley describes herself as, "for the most part, completely ga-ga over this fandom" (Penley 1994: 319). The work done on fandom in the late-80s and 1990s has been criticized for its enthusiasm and described as exemplifying a problematic "fandom is beautiful" phase of fan studies scholarship (Gray et al. 2007). However, it is important to remember that most of these early scholars were not attempting to establish fan studies as a discipline or mark out its borders. Their research circled back and contributed to central questions for feminist media and film scholars then and now: What enables women's creative production? How do stories represent women's desires and life experiences? What can be learned from feminized genres? This work was done as part of a broader academic conversation on women's genres and the ways that female audiences negotiated between their particular life experiences and the ways that media texts imagined them.

Fandom goes digital

Fandom is a common feature of today's digitized culture. Contemporary media is typically designed with some degree of audience participation and interaction in mind. In particular, the remix practices now seen as commonplace in digital culture (fanvids and anime music videos, digital collage, machinima, etc.) have been strongly influenced by fans and their early adoption of digital technologies. Internet-based fandom and fan practices play a role in Henry Jenkins' theories of a contemporary convergence culture (Jenkins 2008), as well as Lawrence Lessig's arguments regarding the role of remix in digital culture and his recommendations for policy reform (Lessig 2008). However, digital fandom is not a new phenomenon. It has a surprisingly lengthy history, much of it shaped by fandom's quick adoption of digital tools and networks in the 1980s and 90s. For feminist scholars interested in the role of gender within emerging digital practices, Media Fandom continued to be a useful focal point for their analyses.

Soap opera fans were connecting on Usenet forums as early as 1984, making soap fandom one of the earliest to connect online (Baym 1998: 111). Talking about soaps in online forums provided these fans "with interpretive resources to which fans may not have access on their own" (ibid. 127). Nancy Baym argues that soap operas function as a pretext that fans use to connect with other people and discuss a range of topics "including emotion, relationships, and selves" (ibid.). This suggests that part of the appeal of fandoms and fan practices are the opportunities they offer for individuals to engage in particular topics of conversation, as well as discussing and deconstructing popular media.

As access to computers increased, the new technology and communication networks were often celebrated as more open and democratic means of communication. The reality, however, was more complicated. Digital fandom was not without its problems. Studies of computer-based discussion forums found they replicated preexisting social hierarchies and norms (MacDonald 1998: 133). The use of new technologies was limited to individuals with access to computers and the free time to use them. In the 1990s, computer users were a fairly elite and limited group (ibid. 150). Computers facilitated dialog between more people, but in 1998, Andrea MacDonald observed many female fans using private mailing lists to create hierarchies of exclusivity among themselves. MacDonald found that "old social practices merge with new[,] creating a different but not radically new discursive space" (ibid. 133). In practice, new communication technologies were being used to create exclusive discussion forums and email lists just as easily as they were being used to facilitate large forums for public discussion.

There are also important reasons why female fans might want to create their own smaller and more exclusive discussion lists. In 1994, at least 94 percent of Internet users were male (Bury 2005: 1). Female fans encountered a great deal of stigma when they tried to share their interests in the more generalized Usenet groups. For example, in the early-90s, female *Quantum Leap* fans reported feeling pressured to leave rec.arts.tv (MacDonald 1998). In response, they created one of the first private mailing lists for (mostly) female fans in 1991 (ibid. 146). Feeling harassed and dismissed in the public forums, "many female fans chose to stake out and colonize cyberspaces of their own" where they could engage in media criticism and share creative work on their own terms (Bury 2005: 2). Rather than retreating from the Internet entirely, female fans strategically withdrew, "refusing to accept the fan practices engaged in by male fans and gathering in spaces of their own" (ibid. 17).

These early mailing lists and Usenet forums blurred the line between public and private fan conversations. Pseudonyms were already a part of fandom prior to the Internet but, as the Internet's role in fandom grew, they became a standard practice. According to Sharon Cumberland, the paradox of cyberspace is that it offers "personal privacy in a public forum" (Cumberland 2011: 669). Female fans used this ambiguity "to explore feelings and ideas that were considered risky or inappropriate for women in the past" (ibid.). Pseudonymity enabled larger numbers of individuals to join different fan forums and websites. While fandom could carry with it some degree of stigma, now fans could participate without feeling that being "fannish" would be traced back to them in their daily lives. Overall, the gendered aspects of fan networks and practices that so intrigued earlier feminist media scholars continued on in fans' newer computer-based communication networks. The Internet also broadened fandom's scope and integrated existing fan practices with the digital technologies and new cultural trends emerging at this time.

Queering fan desires

By the late-90s, it was routine for research on fans to assert that Media Fandom was predominantly white, female, and straight. The problem with this assertion is that it carries with it a normative function. It continually reinforces the idea that there are fannish "norms" and, in the process, crowds out the experiences of non-white, non-female, non-straight, and non-cisgendered fans. Given that much of today's fan activity happens online, this image of the archetypal fan girl is more perceived than statistically verifiable. Rather than researchers questioning these assertions, asking how fandom reinforces them, or where the perception of a dominant type of fan is coming from, the claim has often been left unquestioned.

In contrast, many fans have begun to push back against the assertion that Media Fandom and slash are exclusive to heterosexual women. Polls and anecdotal evidence gathered by fans "suggest that the number of self-identified not-straight women is proportionally greater in [media] fandom than in the population at large" (Busse 2006: 208). While slash had traditionally been analyzed through a feminist frame, Rhiannon Bury argues that slash is less an undoing of masculinity and more a continual questioning of heterosexuality. In this context, slash can be "better understood as a queer practice" (Bury 2005: 31). Fans continually move back and forth between the familiar and unfamiliar, referencing societal norms, playing with their limits, and performing different identities. Within this interplay, Kristina Busse argues that fandom can become a performance of queerness and queer desires (Busse 2006). The performance may be a momentary experiment; however, its potentially transitory and temporary status continues to reaffirm it as a queer performance. For Busse, the destabilization of identity and fluidity of norms underlies many fandoms and fan practices and, again, reinforces its queerness.

Ongoing concerns and (seemingly) absent parties

As fandom has become more visible and fan practices more widespread, the broader image of "the fan" has changed from a persona that is socially stigmatized to one that is much more legitimated. Today, fandom is incorporated into media marketing strategies, monetized by Web 2.0 companies, and fan conventions like ComicCon have become major media events. And yet, as Kristina Busse reminds us, "if the mainstream embraces one form of geek, it risks excluding further or even negating the existence of whoever does not fit that new model" (Busse 2015: 111). This has become a growing area of concern for many feminist media scholars. If popular culture currently celebrates fans, it is typically the figure of the fan boy, and not the fan girl, that dominates popular imagination.

While feminist analyses of fans return again and again to Media Fandom, feminized fan practices and networks continue to be stigmatized, with female fans portrayed as hysterical, overly emotional, and unable to control and appropriately channel their desires. Mel Stanfill finds that the fans celebrated in media are typically those who learn to keep fannish excess under control (Stanfill 2010). The process of learning to be a "good" fan is one that also reaffirms white, heterosexual, and male privilege. While the overly enthusiastic or improperly desiring fan is able to learn self-control, this process affirms one model of fandom while stigmatizing another (ibid.).

Profit is also used as a means of sorting between valuable and unproductive fan practices. In popular culture today, there is now an entire industry built around professional fans covering popular entertainment, celebrities, and new media releases. These professional fans serve as arbitrators of taste and fan behavior. Suzanne Scott calls such an individual a "fantrepreneur," "one who openly leverages or strategically adopts a fannish identity for his or her own professional advancement" (Scott 2015: 148). Fantrepreneurs demonstrate that fandom can be a legitimate path towards professionalization and profit. However, a fantrepreneur is much more likely to be white and male. Women fantrepreneurs often face increased scrutiny and accusations that their fandom is faked or insufficiently proven (Scott 2015).

Popular media franchises like *Twilight* and *The Hunger Games* draw large audiences and have many female fans. However, when these media and their fans receive attention, they are often positioned as embarrassing invaders into "real" fan spaces (Busse 2015; Hills 2013). To do fandom improperly, embarrassingly, and excessively often aligns with being feminized or non-normative in a variety of ways. On the surface, gender norms shape how fandoms and fan practices are coded—either pathologized or valued as productive. However, there are many additional hierarchies—race, class, sexuality, age, etc.—which intersect with what, on the surface, is most easily visible as gender (Busse 2015).

Feminist analyses of contemporary fandom have broadened beyond Media Fandom and slash, but the emphasis on Media Fandom continues, sometimes problematically so. Although Media Fandom increasingly incorporates popular media from around the world, analyses of fandom continue to center on Western and English-language media. Research tends to center on Western and English-speaking fans who occasionally "dabble" in international media. This ignores the various international contexts for fan practices, the global circulation of contemporary media, and the many borders fandoms cross. Addressing these gaps requires more than the occasional study of non-Western fans. Bertha Chin and Lori Hitchcock Morimoto call for fan scholars to be more attentive to cultural flows and transnational contexts. They argue, "we need a more effective means of accounting for social and cultural differences in fan practices across borders both geographical and cultural" (Chin and Hitchcock Morimoto 2013: 105).

Feminist media scholars have paid a great deal of attention to the role of gender and sexuality within fandom. Much less attention has been paid to the experiences of fans of color and to the issues of race and ethnicity across fandoms. Despite this lack of scholarship, fans themselves are increasingly debating issues of race and ethnicity in fandom and across popular culture. In 2008, when the cast was announced for a film version of *Avatar: The Last Airbender*, many fans were outraged. Upset that movie producers were "changing the race of characters of color to white for reasons of marketability" fans organized an elaborate Internet-based protest campaign in response (Lopez 2014: 638). Lori Kido Lopez argues, "fan communities offer a potential space and set of tools for shifting conversations from fictional texts to the realities that they impact and rely upon" (ibid. 646). For feminist scholars interested in the relationship between personal and political, as well as the role of protest within today's digital culture, Lopez' observations underscore the need to study how and when fans connect their status as fans to broader social and political concerns.

More than thirty years have passed since Russ, Lamb and Veith, Penley and Jenkins first began to publish on and codify academia's understanding of Media Fandom. Despite this, analyses of fandom continue to circle around identity categories like gender and sexuality. Feminist analyses of fandom need to address the issues of class, race, and transnational media flows, and consider how they intersect with and shape fan experiences. In focusing primarily on gender and sexuality, whiteness is permitted to be an unspoken and seemingly neutral component of fandom. The reality, however, is that many members of Media Fandom are not white. Media Fandom's social networks extend globally, crossing beyond the borders of Western English-speaking countries. More importantly, despite the size and prominence of Media Fandom, it remains one node of fan activity. The ongoing lack of scholarship on transnational fandom, on the experiences of fans in non-English-speaking countries, and on the experiences of fans who are not white, middle class, and cisgendered is painfully apparent. This is a signal to fan scholars that our love of Media Fandom, and perhaps our conception of fandom as a whole, is problematically shaping the possibilities of our discourse.

Related topics

Janet Staiger, "Film reception studies and feminism"
Ikechukwu Obiaya, "Nollywood, female audience, and the negotiating of pleasure"

Notes

1 Specific fandoms will be capitalized in this essay in order to distinguish between specific fan networks and fandom as a general concept/activity.

References

Bacon-Smith, C. (1992) *Enterprising Women: Television Fandom and the Creation of Popular Myth.* Philadelphia: University of Pennsylvania Press.

Bacon-Smith, C. (1999) *Science Fiction Culture.* Philadelphia: University of Pennsylvania Press.

Baym, N.K. (1998) "Talking about Soaps: Communicative Practices in a Computer-Mediated Fan Culture," in: C. Harris and A. Alexander (eds.) *Theorizing Fandom: Fans, Subculture and Identity.* Cresskill: Hampton Press, pp. 111–29.

Bury, R. (2005) *Cyberspaces of Their Own: Female Fandoms Online.* New York: Peter Lang.

Busse, K. (2006) "My Life is a WIP on my LJ: Slashing the Slasher and the Reality of Celebrity and Internet Performances," in: K. Busse and K. Hellekson (eds.) *Fan Fiction and Fan Communities in the Age of the Internet.* Jefferson: McFarland & Company, Inc., pp. 207–24.

——— (2015) "Fan Labor and Feminism: Capitalizing on the Fannish Labor of Love," *Cinema Journal* 54, 110–15.

Chin, B., Hitchcock Morimoto, L. (2013) "Towards a Theory of Transcultural Fandom," *Participations,* 10, 92–108.

Coppa, F. (2006) "A Brief History of Media Fandom," in: K. Busse and K. Hellekson (eds.) *Fan Fiction and Fan Communities in the Age of the Internet.* Jefferson: McFarland & Company, Inc., pp. 41–60.

Cumberland, S. (2011) "Private Uses of Cyberspace: Women, Desire, and Fan Culture," in: M.C. Kearney (ed.) *The Gender and Media Reader.* New York: Routledge, pp. 667–79.

Gray, S.M. (2015) "Cultural Production and Digital Resilience: Examining Female Gamers' Use of Social Media to Participate in Video Game Culture" in A. Trier-Bieniek (ed.) *Fan Girls and the Media: Creating Characters, Consuming Culture.* Blue Ridge Summit: Rowman & Littlefield Publishers, pp. 85–99.

Gray, J., Sandvoss, C., Harrington, C.L. (2007) "Introduction: Why Study Fans?" in: J. Gray, C. Sandvoss, and C.L. Harrington (eds.) *Fandom: Identities and Communities in a Mediated World.* New York: NYU Press, pp. 1–16.

Hills, M. (2013) "'Twilight' Fans Represented in Commercial Paratexts and Inter-Fandoms: Resisting and Repurposing Negative Fan Stereotypes" in: A. Morey (ed.) *Genre, Reception, and Adaptation in the "Twilight" Series.* Burlington: Ashgate, pp. 113–29.

Hitchcock Morimoto, L. (2013) "Trans-cult-ural Fandom: Desire, Technology and the Transform-ation of Fan Subjectivities in the Japanese Female Fandom of Hong Kong Stars," *Transformative Works and Cultures,* 14 (Online).

Jamison, A. (2013) *Fic: Why Fanfiction Is Taking Over the World.* Dallas: Smart Pop.

Jenkins, H. (1988) "*Star Trek* Rerun, Reread, Rewritten: Fan Writing as Textual Poaching" *Critical Studies in Mass Communication,* June, pp. 85–107.

Jenkins, H. (1992) *Textual Poachers: Television Fans and Participatory Culture.* New York: Routledge.

Jenkins, H. (2008) *Convergence Culture: Where Old and New Media Collide.* New York: NYU Press.

Kuhn, A. (2000 [1984]) "Women's Genres," in E.A. Kaplan (ed.) *Feminism and Film.* New York: Oxford University Press, pp. 437–49.

Lamb, P.F., Veith, D.L. (1986) "Romantic Myth, Transcendence, and *Star Trek* Zines," in D. Palumbo (ed.) *Erotic Universe: Sexuality and Fantastic Literature.* New York: Greenwood Press, pp. 235–56.

Lessig, L. (2008) *Remix: Making Art and Commerce Thrive in the Hybrid Economy.* New York: Penguin.

Lichtenberg, J., Marshak, S., Winston, J. (1975) *Star Trek Lives!* New York: Bantam Books.

Lopez, L.K. (2014) "Fan Activists and the Politics of Race in *The Last Airbender*" in G. Dines and J.M. Humez *Gender, Race, and Class in Media: A Critical Reader.* Los Angeles: Sage Publications, Inc, pp. 637–47.

MacDonald, A. (1998) "Uncertain Utopia: Science Fiction Media Fandom and Computer Mediated Communication" in C. Harris and A. Alexander (eds.) *Theorizing Fandom: Fans, Subculture and Identity.* Cresskill: Hampton Press, pp. 131–52.

Modleski, T. (2007) *Loving with a Vengeance: Mass Produced Fantasies for Women,* 2nd edn. New York: Routledge.

Mulvey, L. (1975) "Visual Pleasure and Narrative Cinema," *Screen,* 16(3), 6–18.

Penley, C. (1991) "Brownian Motion: Women, Tactics, and Technology" in C. Penley and A. Ross (eds.) *Technoculture.* Minneapolis: University of Minnesota Press, pp. 135–61.

Penley, C. (1994) "Feminism, Psychoanalysis and the Study of Popular Culture" in N. Bryson, M.A. Holly, and K. Moxey (eds.), *Visual Culture: Images and Interpretations.* Middletown: Wesleyan University Press, pp. 302–24.

Radway, J.A. (1991) *Reading the Romance: Women, Patriarchy, and Popular Literature.* Chapel Hill: University of North Carolina Press.

Russ, J. (1985a) "Introduction" in *Magic Mommas, Trembling Sisters, Puritans and Perverts: Feminist Essays.* Trumansburg: Crossing Press, pp. 9–16.

Russ, J. (1985b) "Pornography by Women, for Women, with Love" in *Magic Mommas, Trembling Sisters, Puritans and Perverts: Feminist Essays.* Trumansburg: Crossing Press, pp. 79–99.

Scott, S. (2015) "'Cosplay is Serious Business': Gendering Material Fan Labor on Heroes of Cosplay" *Cinema Journal,* 54, pp. 146–54.

Stacey, J. (2011) "Feminine Fascinations: Forms of Identification in Star-Audience Relations" in M.C. Kearney (ed.) *The Gender and Media Reader.* New York: Routledge, pp. 641–54.

Stanfill, M. (2010) "Doing Fandom, (Mis)doing Whiteness: Heteronormativity, Racialization, and the Discursive Construction of Fandom," *Transformative Works and Cultures,* 8 (Online).

Verba, J.M. (2003) *Boldly Writing: A Trekker Fan and Zine History, 1967–1987.* Minnetonka: FTL Publications.

34

CLASSICAL HOLLYWOOD AND MODERNITY

Gender, style, aesthetics

Veronica Pravadelli

Classical Hollywood cinema and feminist film theory

Classical Hollywood cinema has contributed to the formation and development of Feminist Film Theory (FFT) more than any other filmic form or movement. In the 1970s and the 1980s, feminist scholars dissected the semiotic and psychoanalytic paradigms of Hollywood cinema in order to uncover the "patriarchal and capitalist ways of seeing" women, and to show "the reasons why women occupy the place they do in the world of the film" (Kaplan 1976: 7). In the process, they established FFT as an approach for studying filmic images and texts, as well as the relation between cinema and female spectators. If we wanted to encapsulate in a single concept the aims of FFT, perhaps we could say that its main aspiration was to study the mise-en-scène of female desire and how this in turn triggered for women in the audience a process of identification with the film's psychic scenarios. In other words, FFT devised a set of paradigms for studying how subjectivity is "constituted in the relation of narrative, meaning, and desire; so that the very work of narration is the engagement of the subject in certain positionalities of meaning and desire" (de Lauretis 1984: 106). But beyond this common scope, feminists engaged with classical cinema in different ways, offering competing interpretations of its representation of women and gender relations.

As is well known, in her seminal essay "Visual Pleasure and Narrative Cinema" (1975) Laura Mulvey argued that Hollywood cinema followed *à la lettre* patriarchal standards, and that female desire and sexuality could only be expressed in terms of passivity—what Freud had termed "normal femininity." But in those same years, Claire Johnston and Pam Cook offered a quite different perspective on American cinema. In their view, the classical text was more "open" than Mulvey would allow, since Hollywood was not totally complicit with patriarchy. Johnston and Cook investigated the possibility of a counter-cinema within Hollywood in relation to sexual/gender politics by refashioning the theory of the "progressive text" (Johnston 1979). While "Visual Pleasure and Narrative Cinema" has long been considered the founding episode of FFT, it is important to recall that in the 1970s and the 1980s the notion of progressive text was as important and influential as Mulvey's intervention. In fact, most feminist readings of Hollywood were, in one way or another, "progressive," as scholars tried to uncover the instances of female agency.

FFT reached its apogee at the end of the 1980s, when several book-length studies investigated the relation between female desire and film aesthetics by considering specific genres and/or authors. One may think to Mary Ann Doane's *The Desire to Desire* (1987), Gaylyn Studlar's *In the Realm of Pleasure* (1988), and Tania Modleski's *The Women Who Knew Too Much* (1988). Other important "feminist classics" including large sections on Hollywood cinema are E. Ann Kaplan's *Women and Cinema* (1983) and Kaja Silverman's *The Acoustic Mirror* (1988). At the time that such feminist classics were appearing, some started to question their semiotic-psychoanalytic model for its supposed ahistorical attitude, while others launched a renewed interest in historical forms of spectatorship. The paradigm shift from theory to history also brought a change with regard to the object of study. If classical Hollywood cinema had been the primary focus of FFT, for feminist historians, early and silent cinema became the key period to investigate. The turn to history did not necessarily mean that theoretical concerns were erased. But regardless of method, it is undeniable that, as feminists became more and more involved with early cinema, their interest in classical Hollywood declined. For this and other reasons—such as the influence of critical race theory and transnational paradigms—in the last 20 years or so Hollywood has been rather marginal in feminist film studies (and film studies as a whole), at least compared to its centrality in the previous two decades.

My take on Hollywood starts from the assumption that today one should study such a legendary era in movie history by engaging both theoretical assumptions and historical frameworks. The notion of the mode of representation is a key aspect for defining such changes. I define a mode of representation as the convergence of the cinematic imaginary (Bertetto 2003) and a film style. From the late 1920s to 1960, such a convergence changes repeatedly to the extent that even the very notion of classical cinema becomes untenable for this stretch of time (Pravadelli 2015). In looking at the cinematic imaginary, one can ask what the figures, the images, and the narrative trajectories that cinema repeatedly presents onscreen are? Moreover, what are the social and collective desires and how are they articulated differently for women and men? Undoubtedly, cinema was the period's most popular form of entertainment and thus simultaneously reflected and interpreted the contradictory cultural arenas of modernity, the New Deal, the war, and postwar period. But at any particular moment, the stakes were dramatically different for women and men. Feminist historian Joan W. Scott has argued that too often the theory of "sexual antagonism" between males and females "projects a certain timeless quality" (Scott 1999: 39). She invites scholars to overturn their perspective and investigate the "historical specificity and variability" of gender relations (ibid.). My work on Hollywood cinema hopes to make a contribution along this line by probing the changes in the representation of gender dynamics throughout the studio era.

Besides the cinematic imaginary, narrative technique and mise-en-scène also go through impressive transformations in the same period. Working on the convergence of cultural and formal paradigms, one can historicize Hollywood's modes of representation and better describe its participation in the production and dissemination of ideas, values, and desires in American culture.

In the short space of this essay, it is not possible to give an overview of the entire studio era. For a broader investigation both in relation to the issues addressed here and to larger historical scenarios, see my *Classic Hollywood: Lifestyles and Film Styles of American Cinema, 1930–1960* (2015). In this essay, I focus on the 1930s, as this period is traversed by two different phases or modes, which make clearly visible the necessity for a historical reorientation in the interpretation of Hollywood cinema. Another reason for choosing the 1930s is the fact that previous feminist work has more often chosen the 1940s and the 1950s—and genres like noir, melodrama, and the woman's film. Finally, in 1930s cinema the representation of gender is closely connected to class to the extent that "being a woman" depends on specific (i.e. historical) connotations of the relation between gender *and* class.

Gender, style, aesthetics in 1930s Hollywood

American cinema of the 1930s presents two modes of representation. The first arises with the advent of sound and ebbs around 1933–4. The second develops in the years immediately following and continues to the end of the decade. Such delineation marks the rise and fall of dominant trends, which almost certainly overlapped, but the differences are remarkable.

Robert Sklar has identified two Golden Ages within 1930s Hollywood. On the one hand, what he calls the "Age of Turbulence" during the Great Depression represents one of the more significant challenges to traditional values in the history of American media. On the other, the "Age of Order," a Rooseveltian countercurrent that emerged during the 1933–4 season, reemphasized traditional American values, patriotism, national unity, and family (Sklar 1994: 175–94). A stronger implementation of the Production Code is also responsible for such a change. As Richard Maltby has argued "the imposition of a 'new deal' in regulation, with its emphasis on the reestablishment of an explicitly patriarchal moral order, coincided with the start of Roosevelt's presidency" (Maltby 1995: 57).

The dominant configurations of desire and subjectivity are notably different in the two periods, particularly in relation to women. Feminist historians have shown that modernity changed women's lives much more than men's (Peiss 1986). This scenario also explains Hollywood's craze for stories of female emancipation and images of the New Woman. In fact, between the end of the 1920s and the early 1930s, American cinema continued to focus on the image of the young, self-assertive, and sexy woman, thus perpetuating the cult of New Womanhood that emerged in the early years of the century. This tendency would wane as the decade progressed. From about the mid-1930s, after the Production Code became more strictly enforced, the dominant narrative of female desire was tuned to the formation of the heteronormative couple and to marriage, while the figure of the emancipated woman became marginal. This shift in the representation of gender identity was matched by a concomitant transformation in film style. In the early 1930s, Hollywood cinema extended the use of visual techniques developed during the silent period that we may consider in light of the "cinema of attractions" (Gunning 1990). Around 1934, the classical mode of representation—namely, a rational and motivated mode of storytelling based on action, analytic editing, and dialogue—became dominant, while visual attractions and techniques tended to disappear.

In the transition years from silent film to sound, cinema was (still) the most effective form for representing modernity and urban life, as well as women's desire to emancipate. Surveys of the period and contemporary investigations in audience studies reveal that, in the 1920s and the early 1930s, women represented the majority of moviegoers (Stokes 1999). In those years, Hollywood produced a vast number of films centered on women, often written by women scriptwriters. Women, of course, loved to see images of the New Woman, exemplified by such divas as Gloria Swanson, Clara Bow, Louise Brooks, and Joan Crawford. As Mary Ryan has pointed out, "the new movie woman exuded above all a sense of physical freedom – unrestrained movement ... abounding energy – the antithesis of the controlled, quiet, tight-kneed poses of Griffith's heroines" and moved with "dashing spontaneity" into social, work, and higher education spheres (Ryan 1976: 369–70).

In the 1920s, the flapper represented the most important image of the modern woman, and consequently the flapper film became a production staple in all studios (Ross 2000). As this image waned, the figures of the working girl and of the performer (in her different guises as singer, chorus girl, comedian, etc.) became the most popular. If illicit sex was often a fundamental element of plot and character, women were defined, first and foremost by their position in the working sphere. What is also interesting was cinema's perspective in relation to social class. In many cases, rich women were represented as uninteresting partners, or worse, as boring. Aristocrats and rich men, engaged or married to women of their class, frequently were shown to fall in love with women of a lower class, who were livelier and funnier than their official partners. Coming from a poor background, these women embodied quite literally the modern impulse toward change and transformation. And their desire for a better economic condition led them away from home in search of a job. In a vast number of films, the heroine leaves her birthplace—a village or small town—and arrives in the big city to look for work, as in *An American Tragedy* (J. Von Sternberg, 1931), *Night Nurse* (W. Wellman, 1931) and *Baby Face* (A. E. Green, 1933) among many. The urban working-class girl is both independent and cheerful, sexually active, and fun. Therefore, upper-class men might find her more interesting than women of their own class, as the latter often tend to follow protocols and etiquettes and overall seem less alert in embracing the attractions of modernity.

The modern metropolis as the site of change and transformation is beautifully exemplified in those films in which young women tried to improve their status through work or sex—or both. The heroine's social rise did not simply involve a linear plot in the tradition of classical narratives based on cause and effect, however. Through formal devices drawn from the silent period, in the transition years to sound, American cinema expressed the New Woman's condition through visual spectacles that represented cinematically the ideas of movement and metamorphosis as well as the experience of excessive visual sensations typical of modernity.

Cinema's mode of representation relied on a convergence between classical style and visual attractions—that is, between plots of emancipation and spectacular imagery. Tom Gunning has suggested that when the narrative form won out, the cinema of attractions did not disappear but went "underground, both into certain avant-garde practices and as a component of narrative films, more evident in some genres (e.g. the musical) than in others" (Gunning 1990: 57). If we accept that the cinema of attractions represented an aesthetic solution to the condition of modernity, we must then historicize that concept and evaluate carefully the changing relation between attraction and narration. The cinema of the early 1930s is a fundamental episode in this trajectory, since it calls for a gendered reading of the aesthetic concept of attraction. In the woman-centered films of the period, visual attractions rely on the image of the female body, while narratives focus on stories of female emancipation. The convergence between form and content around the woman's body is a very peculiar solution that deserves consideration.

The relation between woman and modernity was expressed in particular by two types of visual attractions: the "urban dissolve" and the exhibitionist display of the female body. The urban dissolve is a specific code of silent cinema, a rhetorical strategy developed in particular by the city symphony documentary. It is an extended dissolve, a series of superimpositions of images of urban life which amplifies "cinematically" the city's dynamism. Shot in the most bustling areas of the metropolis, it shows masses of people walking or waiting, fast-moving lines of cars and trolleys, and other energized moments of everyday urban life. Our perceptual experience registers endless movement and change as the main condition of city life.

Figure 34.1   Blonde Venus (Josef von Sternberg, 1932).

Source: Blonde Venus, Josef von Sternberg, 1932.

Dissolves and visual polyphonies are often gendered—that is, related to the female body. Because they effectively exemplify the idea of metamorphosis, they are particularly fit for representing the modern woman's narrative of transformation. Urban dissolves can be brief interludes between scenes or extended segments usually placed at the beginning of the film. The first type is the most common and recurs frequently in films narrating a performer's rise to success. The apex of the protagonist's career is usually conveyed by dissolves fusing images of the artist's face or body with urban topoi and icons like neon lights and signs, skylines and buildings, etc. Notable examples include the depiction of Marlene Dietrich's success as singer Helen Faraday (a.k.a. Helen Jones) in *Blonde Venus* (J. Von Sternberg, 1932) (Figure 34.1), and Constance Bennett's rise to stardom as Hollywood actress Mary Evans in *What Price Hollywood?* (G. Cukor, 1932). Extended dissolves usually focus on the relation between women and the metropolis by linking and juxtaposing images of women and urban scenarios or scenes of urban life. When positioned at the beginning of the film, they may suggest a narrative texture as well as create a whole atmosphere directly relating woman to modernity. This second type is formally more complex and spectacular. It is also much less common than the first type. I would like to recall two rather stunning examples in *Glorifying the American Girl* (M. Webb, 1929) and *Three on a Match* (M. LeRoy, 1932).

Glorifying the American Girl starts with a prologue about four minutes long, made up of urban dissolves. It begins with a shot of a map of the United States, with long serpentines of women superimposed on top and moving across the map toward big cities. The image then transforms itself into a woman putting on a pantsuit, and then a woman dressed like a Ziegfeld girl. Images of women are then superimposed on shots of moving trains, automobiles, and congested areas of the city (Figures 34.2 and 34.3). The whole prologue thus develops the theme of "women and the metropolis" without narration. The rhetoric of dissolves visualizes the transformation of bodies and/in spaces, and is thus directly linked to the plot of social mobility recounted by the film. *Glorifying the American Girl* tells the story of a girl working in a New York department store, but dreaming of a career in the Follies. After working as a traveling performer, she will become an overnight success on Broadway. While the story of a young woman's rise to the heights of Broadway is not original, the use of the aesthetics of attraction is quite stunning and accounts for the film's anti-classical mode.

Besides the dazzling dissolves of the prologue, the sequences in Technicolor are essential to the spectacular component of the film.

Three on a Match also starts with a sensational prologue, thanks to the use of dissolves and parallel editing. The theme of female upward mobility has peculiar connotations since the plot concentrates on the trajectories of three young girls coming from different social backgrounds. Therefore, the relation between gender and class identity is essential to the film's message. As young girls Mary, Vivian, and Ruth attended the same public school in New York City. After losing track of one another, they meet again as adults. From this moment on their lives will be woven together. The film's strength resides in its rhetorical strategies, particularly in the opening episode. Here shots of the three girls are intertwined with superimpositions and dissolves of newspaper titles, city streets, sports events, and other

Figure 34.2   Glorifying the American Girl (Millard Webb, 1929).

Source: *Glorifying the American Girl*, (Millard Webb, 1929).

Figure 34.3   Glorifying the American Girl (Millard Webb, 1929).

Source: *Glorifying the American Girl* (Millard Webb, 1929).

episodes of urban modernity. The story of the three girls growing up in New York is framed within the context of modernity, from 1919 to 1930, through the use, once again, of the most modern filmic device, the urban dissolve.

A second strategy of attraction employed in the films of the period is the brazen exhibition of the female body. It is my contention that such a strategy is actively pursued by female characters, and that it is part of a process of transformation and emancipation. Contrary to FFT's argument that the spectacle of a woman ontologically objectifies her, I argue that one must interpret this topos historically. Compared to the Victorian ethos of purity, piousness, and subordination to the man, the exhibition of the female body and woman's free sexuality can be loci of empowerment. This scenario is often deployed in the context of live performance in front of a diegetic audience. Radical examples include Marlene Dietrich's numbers as a cabaret singer in *Blonde Venus* (and several of her other films), and Mae West's performance in *I'm No Angel* (W. Ruggles, 1933). In the "Hot Voodoo" sequence, Dietrich wears a monkey costume and sings to the sound of drums played by a band of "savages." As she reveals her identity, stripping out of her excessively sexual and racially coded costume, the audience is caught by surprise and shocked by her outrageous performance. It is Dietrich that elicits the audience's gaze. Such a strategy is repeated when she performs in Paris. Dietrich appears on stage dressed in a white tuxedo, like a mannish lesbian. The episode is structured around female agency, as her body and performance control both the audience's gaze and camerawork. In *I'm No Angel*, Mae West's performance is choreographed in a similar fashion. Tira is a sensational attraction as a lion tamer. When she concludes the dangerous number by putting her head inside the animal's mouth, the audience is both greatly entertained and excited. Like Dietrich, West controls the gaze and the reaction of the paying customers. In a curious reenactment of early cinema's strategy of attractions, the New York socialites who have watched the show thank her because she has given them "a thrill"—enabled them to experience a sensational emotion.

Notwithstanding their different personalities and acting styles, Marlene Dietrich and Mae West are among the most radical examples of female bodily display of the period. Patrice Petro has noted that Tom Gunning "says very little about the way in which the female body functions as a main 'attraction' in the cinema of attraction" (Petro 2002: 171). Indeed, like the cinema of attractions, Dietrich and West's bodies "directly solicit spectator attention, inciting visual curiosity, and supplying pleasure through an exciting spectacle" (Gunning 1990: 58). To conclude, the dynamic impulse of the (urban) dissolve and the exhibitionist display of the body are the most effective aesthetic and stylistic devices for narrating the transformation of the modern working woman.

Sometime around 1933—1934 the dominant mode of female representation veers toward the convergence of normative forms of desire and strong narrative structures dominated by action and dialogue. While visual attractions tend to disappear, linearity and causality further a rational mode of storytelling which, in turn, supports traditional forms of identity and lifestyle, especially for women. This new mode of representation dominates Hollywood until the end of the decade. This periodization is in tune with the transformations of censorship as 1934 is "a turning point in the administration of industry self-regulation" (Jacobs 1997: xi). In my mind, the notion of classical cinema only applies to this specific filmic form. While the figure of the New Woman was relegated to the margins, a renewed trust in masculinity emerges in the cinema of the period. Hollywood's ideological project in the "Age of Order" implies a reversal vis-à-vis the gender discourse of the previous years. Transgressive sexual attitudes were no longer supported and women's working careers were similarly thwarted. Women's experience was now mainly framed within marriage and the home. Emancipatory plots often had a negative outcome, and the formation of the heterosexual couple became the main target. In contrast to the earlier period, as well as to post–World War II cinema, classical cinema focused on plots of integration and comedy provided the main framework for narrating the integration of the heteronormative couple into the social order. While it is true that the screwball heroine usually enjoys sexual freedom, the narrative nevertheless develops within the precincts of marriage or remarriage. Moreover, the genre's progressive stance toward female sexuality is limited to upper-class women. The relation between gender and class is thus reversed in comparison to the previous years. While in the early 1930s women had dominated the industry at all levels, now the values of masculinity and family came back with a vengeance. For instance, an analysis of late 1930s box-office returns clearly shows a renewed interest in images of order, normalcy, and masculinity. Likewise, the public adored adventure films (a typically male genre) and costume dramas, while another male genre—the biopic—was highly praised by critics and a favorite at the Oscars. Such genres were not only adequate to address the classical thrust for linear structures, but they all focused on male agency and assigned women only marginal roles.

In this scenario, it is not surprising that, outside of the screwball comedy, female independence is typically frustrated. In 1930s cinema, strong women were often depicted as "bad," so that they could rightfully be punished. Bette Davis, for example, was the prototype of the "Hollywood Bitch." It is enough to think of *Of Human Bondage* (J. Cromwell, 1934), *Jezebel* (W. Wyler, 1938), *The Letter* (W. Wyler, 1940), and *The Little Foxes* (W. Wyler, 1941) (Fisher 2011). But perhaps the best example of the dynamics described here is *Dark Victory* (E. Goulding, 1939), in which a rich and pampered Davis concerns herself with anything but marriage. In the habit of passing her days at horse races and parties, she suddenly discovers that an incurable disease will cut her life short. After marrying her doctor, she leaves the city—a place of cultured entertainment and diversion—for the countryside in Vermont. There, she learns to be a good wife and lead a simple life. She will die alone in her bedroom while her husband is away. One can easily speculate that her early death is the effect of her modern lifestyle: had she spent less time in having fun and paid more attention to her symptoms, perhaps she could still be alive.

The shift in the representation of female desire and its connection to modernity is further evident if we look at Barbara Stanwyck's career throughout the decade. Alongside Joan Crawford, she embodied the role of a poor girl aspiring to glamour and riches better than anybody else. In the early 1930s, both actresses played key roles as young women attempting to raise their social status through hard work and/or sex. They played working-class women who moved to the big city in search of a job, as well as a variety of fallen and/or redeemed women. We can think to Stanwyck's roles in *Ladies of Leisure* (F. Capra, 1930), *Night Nurse*, *Forbidden* (F. Capra, 1932), *Shopworn* (N. Grinde, 1932), and the more famous *Baby Face*. In the intervening years, Stanwyck continued to play working-class characters struggling for upward mobility. But then her desire would be repeatedly unfulfilled as in *The Bride Walks Out* (L. Jason, 1936) and *Stella Dallas* (K. Vidor, 1937).

Frank Capra's *It Happened One Night* (1934) is a key text for testing the relationship between formal order and subjective normativity. The film shows that behind the freshness and independence of Claudette Colbert's flapper lurks a strong desire for marriage, and for the male protection/domination that goes along with it. Capra's film is a perfect example of classical style, since its core structure is founded on a correspondence between narrative and formal logic which relies "on notions of decorum, proportion, formal harmony, respect for tradition, mimesis, self-effacing craftsmanship, and cool control of the perceiver's response" (Bordwell 1985: 3–4). These strategies are essential components of a broader paradigm, since classical cinema represents the world as a system of oppositions. Formal and narrative dialectics are so central to classical style that any interpretation of its textual configuration cannot do without structural analysis (Bellour 2000). Informing the classical text at all levels, these differences systematically converge most effectively in the comedy's traditional male–female opposition. In *It Happened One Night*, such a mechanism is activated in the first two sequences or "movements," which introduce female and male protagonists, respectively. In tune with classical procedures, Ellie Andrews and Peter Warne are compared and juxtaposed at the same time. They are opposites of each other in social standards —Ellie a pampered heiress, Peter a penniless, but morally grounded, journalist—but also similar, since they are both introduced in the act of rebelling against a paternal authority figure. This analogy formally anticipates Ellie and Peter's eventual union.

The film's narrative trajectory focuses on the couple's evolving relationship, from their initial mutual disdain to their affection for one another. The quick rhythm of shots and precise connections between them ensure invisible style. There are also no moments of visual spectacle, which in turn draws attention only to the film's plot. The story can therefore unfold according to the principles of motivated action and causality. Thus, Ellie's desire to marry Westley also affords Peter the chance to regain his job, because of their coincidental meeting. Different from the sophisticated comedies of Hawks, Cukor, and McCarey, Capra's film maintains a traditional vision of sexuality and male–female relationships in line with a "return to order" rooted in the New Deal.

Historian Christina Simmons has argued that, in the 1920s and 1930s, the image of the flapper became the ideal positive female figure since she "both embodied the popular notion of the free woman and retained a softness that did not threaten men" (Simmons 1993: 31). As such, she was the ideal companion of the "healthy male," or an analogously positive image of the normative masculinity of the period. Sensitive and at the same time decisive, he assumed the function of a guide toward matrimony, as the flapper gladly ceded him command (ibid. 24–7). This description fits the couple in *It Happened One Night*. Despite her autonomy, Ellie needs Peter's help at every moment. Moreover, not only is the sanctity of marriage reestablished, but also that of family and parent–child relationships. Ellie's father allies with Peter in the literal implementation of the symbolic process described by Lévi-Strauss, in which men exchange their women to preserve social order.

Classical cinema's turn to masculinity is also evident in biopics and adventure dramas, as both genres are dominated by a male world (Pravadelli 2015: 56–68). In contrast to these genres, women had a leading role in screwball comedies. While from the mid-1930s the demise of the New Woman was undeniable, the genre of screwball comedy represented a partial exception. If comedy's main ideological project aims at integrating the couple within the existing social structure through marriage, several comedies of the period presented progressive forms of sexual interaction and female desire. While endorsing marriage, films such as *Sylvia Scarlett* (G. Cukor, 1935), *The Awful Truth* (L. McCarey, 1937), *Bringing Up Baby* (H. Hawks, 1938), *The Women* (G. Cukor, 1939), *My Favorite Wife* (G. Kanin, 1940), *His Girl Friday* (H. Hawks, 1940), and *The Philadelphia Story* (G. Cukor, 1940), represented the male–female relation as explicitly sexual.

In the screwball comedy, the dynamics between male and female protagonists subtends a clear equality of the sexes in line with the model of "companionate marriage" that emerged in urban areas in the 1920s, in which the sexual "satisfaction of both partners [are] principal measures of marital harmony" and social order (Cott 1987: 156–7). The comedies of the second half of the 1930s presented the most advanced model of gender relations of the period. However, the convergence of gender and class identity had strikingly changed in relation to the earlier years. In the classical era, only rich and aristocratic heroines could enjoy sexual freedom. While in 1940 the genre produced some of its best examples, that same year a film like *Kitty Foyle* (S. Wood, 1940) depicted the demise of the model of the New Woman for working girls. In that film, Kitty (Ginger Rogers) must choose between two men, and her choice is articulated along the lines of class difference (Doane 1987: 105). She will eventually choose a poor but idealistic doctor and refuse her aristocratic suitor. If, in the early 1930s, class difference could be overcome and women's upward mobility (and sexual freedom) was one of Hollywood's favorite topics, in the intervening years, working-class women were denied social mobility while spoiled aristocrats enjoyed romantic and sexual freedom. In the second half of the 1930s the change in the representation of female identity and desire vis-à-vis the earlier period is radical. While broad social, cultural, and industrial dynamics might explain Hollywood's transformation from the early sound period to the classical era, probing such changes in the iconography of woman is essential if we want to assess the gendered politics of modernity, as well as cinema's role in promoting values and desires of the modern woman.

Related topics

Margaret Hennefeld, "Slapstick comediennes in silent cinema: women's laughter and the feminist politics of gender in motion"
Erica Levin, "Class/Ornament: cinema, new media, labor-power, and performativity"
Hilary Radner, "The rise and fall of the girly film: from the woman's picture to the new woman's film, the chick flick, and the smart-chick film"
J. E. Smyth, "Female editors in studio-era Hollywood: rethinking feminist 'frontiers' and the constraints of the archives"

Bibliography

Bellour, R., C. Penley (eds.) (2000) *The Analysis of Film*. Bloomington: Indiana University Press.
Bertetto, P. (2003) "L'immaginario cinematografico: forme e meccanismi," in *Enciclopedia del cinema*, vol. 1, Rome: Istituto della Enciclopedia Italiana, pp. 62–78.
Bordwell, D. (1985) "The Classical Hollywood Style," in D. Bordwell, J. Staiger, and K. Thompson, *The Classical Hollywood Cinema. Film Style and Mode of Production to 1960*. New York: Columbia University Press, pp. 1–84.
Cott, N. (1987) *The Grounding of Modern Feminism*, New Haven: Yale University Press.
de Lauretis, T. (1984) *Alice Doesn't. Feminism, Semiotics, Cinema*, Bloomington: Indiana University Press.
Doane, M. A. (1987) *The Desire to Desire. The Woman's Film of the '40s*, Bloomington: Indiana University Press.
Fisher, L. (2011) "Bette Davis: Worker and Queen," in A. McLean (ed.) *Glamour in a Golden Age. Movie Stars of the 1930s*, New Brunswick: Rutgers University Press, pp. 84–107.
Gunning, T. (1990) "The Cinema of Attractions. Early Film, Its Spectator and the Avant-Garde," in T. Elsaesser (ed.) *Early Film. Space Frame Narrative*, London: British Film Institute, pp. 56–62.
Jacobs, L. (1997) *The Wages of Sin*, Berkeley, University of California Press.
Johnston, C. (1979) "Women's Cinema as Counter-Cinema," in P. Erens (ed.) *Sexual Stratagems*, New York: Horizon Press, pp. 133–43.
Kaplan, E. A. (1976) "Aspects of British Feminist Film Theory. A Critical Evaluation of Texts by Claire Johnston and Pam Cook," *Jump Cut*, 12–13, pp. 1–18.

Kaplan, E. A. (1983) *Women and Film. Both Sides of the Camera*, London: Routledge.

Kaplan, E. A. (1992) *Motherhood and Representation*, London: Routledge.

Maltby, R. (1995) "The Production Code and the Hays Office," in T. Balio, *Grand Design*, Berkeley, University of California Press, pp. 37–72.

Modleski, T. (1988) *The Women Who Knew Too Much. Hitchcock and Feminist Theory*, London: Routledge.

Mulvey, L. (1989 [1975]) "Visual Pleasure and Narrative Cinema," in L. Mulvey *Visual and Other Pleasures*, Bloomington: Indiana University Press, pp. 14–26.

Peiss, K. (1986) *Cheap Amusements. Working Women and Leisure in Turn-of-the-Century New York*, Philadelphia: Temple University Press.

Petro, P. (2002) "Film Feminism and Nostalgia for the Seventies," in P. Petro *Aftershocks of the New. Feminism and Film History*, New Brunswick: Rutgers University Press, pp. 157–73.

Pravadelli, V. (2015) *Classic Hollywood: Lifestyles and Film Styles of American Cinema, 1930–1960*, Urbana: University of Illinois Press.

Ross, S. (2000) "Banking the Flames of Youth: The Hollywood Flapper, 1920–1930," Diss.: University of Wisconsin–Madison.

Ryan, M. P. (1976) "The Projection of a New Womanhood: The Movie Moderns in the 1920s," in J. E. Friedman and W. G. Shade (eds.) *Our American Sisters. Women in American Life and Thought*, Boston: Allyn and Bacon, Inc., pp. 366–84.

Scott, J. W. (1999) "Gender: A Useful Category of Historical Analysis," in J. W. Scott *Gender and the Politics of History*, rev. edn., New York: Columbia University Press, pp. 28–50.

Silverman, K. (1988) *The Acoustic Mirror*, Bloomington: Indiana University Press.

Simmons, C. (1993) "Modern Sexuality and the Myth of Victorian Repression," in B. Melosh (ed.) *Gender and American History since 1890*, London: Routledge, pp. 17–42.

Sklar, R. (1994) *Movie-Made America. A Cultural History of American Movies*, rev. edn., New York: Vintage Books.

Steinberg, C. S. (1980) *Film Facts*, New York: Facts on File, Inc.

Stokes, M. (1999) "Female Audiences of the 1920s and Early 1930s," in M. Stokes and R. Maltby (ed.) *Identifying Hollywood Audiences*, London: British Film Institute, pp. 42–60.

Studlar, G. (1988) *In the Realm of Pleasure. Von Sternberg, Dietrich and the Masochistic Aesthetics*, New York: Columbia University Press.

35

LESBIAN CINEMA POST-FEMINISM

Ageism, difference, and desire

Rachel A. Lewis

In a *Buzzfeed* article published on December 12, 2015, entitled "What It's like to be a Lesbian Couple with a 20-Year-Plus Age Difference," LGBT Editor Shannon Keating discusses social media's reaction to the decision by actresses Holland Taylor (72) and Sarah Paulson (40) to make their lesbian relationship public (Keating 2015). While lesbian fans' response to the news of Taylor and Paulson's relationship has been overwhelmingly positive, many social media commentators have expressed discomfort with the idea of an intergenerational lesbian relationship. One of the "most-liked" comments on Facebook, for example, reads: "This is really gross. Not because they are gay, but because Sarah Paulson is dating the crypt keeper" (ibid.). While age differences in heterosexual relationships—especially those between older men and younger women—often go unquestioned within the mainstream media, heteronormative audiences are decidedly less comfortable with the possibility of intergenerational same-sex relationships between women. In the context of lesbian sexuality, intergenerational desire is frequently cast as a form of arrested psycho-social development, the product of repressed maternal and/or childlike longings that are inherently asexual. These heteronormative stereotypes have the effect of rendering lesbian desire invisible by discrediting the possibility of women's sexual agency outside the context of compulsory heterosexuality.

The subject of intergenerational desire has become a pervasive trope within representations of lesbian women in contemporary film and television. For example, three mainstream feature-length narrative films from 2015—Peter Sollett's *Freeheld*, Paul Weitz's *Grandma* and Todd Haynes' *Carol*—center on the challenges faced by queer women in intergenerational lesbian relationships. In Season 2 of the award-winning Amazon television show *Transparent* (Jill Soloway, 2014–15), an older lesbian-feminist poet and gender studies professor played by Cherry Jones (ironically, the ex-lover of Sarah Paulson) is depicted dating a series of much younger women. Despite the fact that all three mainstream lesbian films released during 2015 revolve around the subject of intergenerational desire, however, there have been very few studies to date that examine the relationship between age and sexuality in contemporary queer film and media (see, for example, Krainitzki 2015). Given the growing number of portrayals of intergenerational lesbian relationships, it is important to consider how age factors into the politics of lesbian representation in contemporary film and visual culture. Do current representations of intergenerational lesbian relationships merely constitute the reinscription of heteronormative stereotypes of lesbian monstrosity and/or asexuality in new guises, or do they offer up more complex, more subversive portrayals of female same-sex desire?

In the first part of this essay, I examine representations of intergenerational lesbian relationships in mainstream and independent narrative films produced during the past five years. Focusing particular attention on the recent films *Grandma* and *Carol*, I explore how intergenerational lesbian desire is incorporated into the current landscape of postfeminist media culture. By "postfeminism," I am referring to the kinds of media representations of feminism in which certain second wave feminist critiques of gender inequality are taken into account in order to be dismissed as no longer relevant or necessary (McRobbie 2008). As I argue, within the realm of postfeminist media culture, ageist configurations of female sexuality intersect with postfeminist articulations of lesbian identity as hypersexual and chic, divested of all feminist associations. In the second part, I consider representations of intergenerational lesbian relationships in independent, experimental queer films, such as Cheryl Dunye's mockumentary *The Owls* (2010) and Jan Dunn's Dogme 95 film *Gypo* (2005). Both of these films offer important critiques of postfeminism through the invocation of intersectional and transnational perspectives on female same-sex desire. In doing so, these films challenge normative postfeminist temporalities grounded in the idea of reproductive time in a way that allows for more diverse representations of age and sexuality in contemporary queer film and media.

Postfeminism, heteronormativity, and lesbian representation

> It is insane how pro-status quo some lesbian movies can be. The women who made this flimsy movie [Tru Love] have absolutely no backbone. Let's not break the age taboo, not that one. We must kill the "old lady" at the end to avoid dealing with the awkwardness of their future together and the unsightliness of their lovemaking. ... In a sense, [Tru Love is] interchangeable with another God awful lesbian movie: A Perfect Ending. The older woman is also killed at the end. ... Do these women [filmmakers] have any sense of history? Do they not know that lesbians have been traditionally killed off in movies and literature? Now they're killing the old lesbian. Reinforcing prejudice against old LGBT people. ... I hope the filmmakers are not lesbians, then we could simply say forgive them father, for they do not know what they say.
>
> *The Walden*

In the above critique, an anonymous reviewer on Amazon who goes by the name of "The Walden" calls attention to the problematic representation of intergenerational lesbian relationships on the part of contemporary queer women filmmakers. As The Walden points out, both Nicole Conn's *A Perfect Ending* (2012) and Kate Johnston and Shauna MacDonald's *Tru Love* (2014) conclude with the death of the older lesbian character. In *A Perfect Ending*, an older married woman, Rebecca Westridge, discovers that she is dying of cancer and seeks the services of a female sex worker (Paris) to provide her with a sense of sexual fulfillment that she never experienced with her husband. Rather predictably, the two women fall in love, before the film ends with Rebecca's tragic death. In *Tru Love*, meanwhile, a beautiful older woman, Alice, is introduced to the film's main character, Tru, in order to teach the latter about the virtues of lesbian monogamy and romantic love. The potentially radical implications of an intergenerational lesbian relationship are undermined by the film's rather ageist conclusion, however, when Alice mysteriously dies at the end of the film, leaving Tru free to resume a monogamous relationship with her younger ex-girlfriend, Claire. Peter Sollett's film *Freeheld* (2015), starring Julianne Moore and Ellen Page, similarly ends with the death of the older woman (Moore), who is fighting for domestic partner benefits for her younger lover (Page). While Paul Weitz's film *Grandma* (2015), starring Lily Tomlin, does not end with the death of the older woman, it nonetheless presents the intergenerational lesbian relationship as inconceivable. Only in Todd Haynes' film *Carol* (2015) do the lesbian lovers actually remain together.

In all of the aforementioned films (*Carol* excluded), intergenerational lesbian desire is rendered visible only to be made to disappear at the end of the film with the death or departure of the older woman from the relationship; in all of these films, the older lesbian pays a price, narratively speaking, for articulating her desire. It is perhaps in *Tru Love*, however, that the intergenerational lesbian relationship is policed most violently, in this case by Alice's daughter Suzanne who, it turns out, herself embarked on a casual sexual encounter with Tru some months earlier. As Suzanne rudely informs her mother, "You know she's [Tru's] a lesbian, a young lesbian. And you're neither." When it becomes increasingly clear that Tru and Alice have developed a close romantic bond, Suzanne tries her best to separate the two lovers. Her excuse for such behavior, she tells Alice, is that she was trying to "protect" her mother from Tru. As she comments, "You were sick. You were vulnerable. ... You're chasing her around. At your age, it's pathetic. ... You are my mother. Start acting like it." While Suzanne's jealousy is clearly designed to embody the narrative obstacle in the lovers' pursuit of happiness, the ending of the film nonetheless seeks to reinforce the ultimate impossibility of intergenerational lesbian relationships. At the end of the film, Alice is substituted with a much younger woman—both literally and metaphorically—as Tru is shown planning the same trip to Paris with Claire that she had been initially planning to take with Alice.

The policing of intergenerational desire in lesbian cinema in queer cinema is symptomatic of the regulation of female sexuality and aging within contemporary postfeminist media culture more generally. While postfeminist discourses celebrate female sexual empowerment, only certain women in postfeminist media culture—i.e. those who are young, upper middle class, able-bodied, white, and heterosexual—are granted the status of active, desiring sexual subjects (Gill 2007). As Sadie Wearing notes, within postfeminist media culture, the "rejuvenation" of the older woman is linked with her ability to remain youthful (Wearing 2007: 284). In this context, queer women who visibly defy the logic of heterosexual romance and consumption get cast as an aberration, leaving them open to ridicule for not acting their age, as we can see with Suzanne's comments to Alice in *Tru Love* that she should start "acting like" a mother. Of course, "acting like a mother" in postfeminist media culture means acting asexual. As Susan Liddy notes, within postfeminist media representations, motherhood is generally perceived to imply asexuality, while sexually empowered women are rarely portrayed as mothers (Liddy 2014). In *Tru Love*, sex occurs off screen, as the filmmakers deliberately choose to conceal the body of the sexually active, older queer woman. In *Grandma*, meanwhile, what is stressed throughout the film is less Elle's identity as a lesbian and more her status as an old widow, making age, rather than sexuality, the overdetermined signifier of representation. The desexualization of the aging lesbian body is also apparent in *Grandma* via Elle's own internalized ageism which prevents her from continuing her relationship with Olivia. As Elle comments to Olivia regarding the breakup of their relationship, "We always knew it was going to happen," and "You have a wonderful life ahead of you. I want you to have what I had."

The postfeminist narrative at work in *Grandma* becomes yet further evident in the context of the film's representation of feminism itself. When Olivia introduces Elle to her parents at the end of the film, Olivia's mother informs Elle that she was a women's studies major, to which Elle—herself a feminist poet and academic—sarcastically responds, "Congratulations." Moreover, when Elle finally parts with Olivia, she hands her ex-lover first edition copies of three feminist texts—Simone De Beauvoir's *The Second Sex* (1952), Betty Friedan's *The Feminine Mystique* (1963), and Germaine Greer's *The Female Eunuch* (1970)—in a gesture that is clearly designed to symbolize the idea of feminist generational divides. Not only does this scene conflate feminism and women's studies with second wave feminism, as indicated by the symbolic "hand over" of three classic texts from the second wave, but it also evokes the kinds of generational metaphors that are central to post-feminism. As Tasker and Negra comment, "the generational construction of girls and young women as enjoying the freedoms secured by the activism of their mothers and grandmothers is a repeated trope of postfeminist culture" (Tasker and Negra 2007: 18). In other words, not only do the postfeminist narratives at work in *Grandma* make use of the comic format to ridicule the idea of mature female sexuality, but they also extend this ridicule to feminism itself.[1] As Tasker and Negra observe,

> The ambivalence about aging that strongly characterizes such [postfeminist] fictions is also extended to feminism itself. As postfeminism has raised the premium on youthfulness, it has installed an image of feminism as "old" (and by extension moribund). ... It is the supposed difficulty of feminism, its rigidity and propensity to take things "too far," that a middle of the road, middle-class postfeminism rejects.
>
> (*ibid. 11, 19*)

The implied consequence of postfeminist representations of the aging female body and of feminist critical positions is a rejection of feminism itself. In this context, lesbian-feminist achievements of the second wave are acknowledged only to be disavowed as outdated, unfashionable, and decidedly un-chic. Such representations create a false dichotomy between, on the one hand, the political lesbian of the second wave as being anti-men and anti-sex and, on the other, the contemporary postfeminist lesbian who is depicted as both chic and apolitical. This binary construction of aging not only stimulates intergenerational conflict by placing groups of women in opposition to each other on the basis of chrono-logical age, but also limits the possibility of intergenerational lesbian relationships.

An alternative representation of an intergenerational lesbian relationship in contem-porary mainstream cinema is Todd Haynes' film *Carol*, which was nominated for five Golden Globe Awards and six Academy Awards. Haynes' film has received particular praise for its beautiful period details and cinematography, despite complaints by some lesbian fans on social media that the sex scene between the two female characters caters too much to the heterosexual male gaze. As Patricia White observes, *Carol* situates lesbian sexuality within a representational history characterized by tropes of the predatory lesbian and mother/daughter love (2015: 10–11). In *Carol*, Therese's defining characteristic is her youthfulness, as the age difference between the two female protagonists is central to the film's narrative conflict. As Carol's ex-lover, Abby, comments regarding Carol's new lover, Therese, "She's young. Tell me you know what you're doing." Carol similarly remarks on Therese's age when she temporarily leaves her to fight for custody of her daughter, Rindy, writing: "You seek resolutions and explanations because you're young, but you will understand this one day." By the end of the film, however, the age differences between the two female characters have been reconciled, as Therese does come to understand Carol's point of view and the merger of the two women's perspectives—which is foreshadowed throughout the film via the cinematography and constant mirroring—confirm their ultimate sameness. The film thus ends without conflict and we are left to assume that the two women are able to happily pursue a future together. Interestingly enough, this is not the case in Patricia Highsmith's novel *The Price of Salt* on which the film is based, where the economic inequalities between Carol and Therese, as well as the age differences between the two lovers, are repeatedly stressed throughout the narrative.

Despite the fact that *Carol* is set in 1950s New York, Haynes's film is nonetheless constructed from the perspective of the "postfeminist present" (White 2015: 11), which is perhaps why the two lovers are able to remain together. Within the world of postfeminist lesbian chic, only certain women—i.e. those who are slim, feminine, white, middle class, and able-bodied—can be sexual; only lesbian sexuality that has been divested of its feminist associations and that caters to the heterosexual male gaze, in other words, can be tolerated. Within this postfeminist media landscape, lesbian, bisexual, and heterosexual female characters become indistinguishable in terms of their traditional femininity and sense of fashion. In *Carol*, the ultimate fusion of the two lovers' perspectives is less an indication of equality and sameness and more the result of the erasure of differences within contemporary postfeminist media culture. In Haynes' film, age differences are effortlessly erased in favor of a depoliticized lesbian chic that can be assimilated into dominant and universal narratives of heterosexual romance and consumption. By contrast, older lesbian women in intergenerational relationships who do not conform to heteronormative models of beauty and desirability are made to disappear. In this way, we can see how ageist configurations of female sexuality combine with the dictates of postfeminist media culture to render intergenerational lesbian desire invisible.

Queer temporalities in lesbian independent filmmaking

Two lesbian-authored independent films that seek to disrupt postfeminist representations of female sexuality and aging through the queering of heteronormative narratives of chronological decorum and temporality are *The Owls* and *Gypo*. Dunye's film *The Owls* premiered the same year as another lesbian-authored film, *The Kids Are All Right* (2010) by Lisa Cholodenko. While Dunye and Cholodenko were both active participants in the New Queer Cinema movement of the 1990s—a movement renowned for its radical critiques of heteronormativity and gay liberalism (Rich 2000; Aaron 2004)—*The Kids Are All Right* met with predominantly negative reactions from queer cinema critics who rightly point to the film's conservatism (see, for example, Walters 2012). In *The Kids Are All Right*, the film's central characters, Nic and Jules, far from contesting dominant ideals of the heterosexual nuclear family unit, actually uphold and sustain them. As the director, Lisa Cholodenko, comments:

> Our intention wasn't overtly political. The subversion, as we saw it, was to be nonpolitical, and just to make this human story that was about a family that people could relate to, no matter what your identity or your sexual preferences were.
>
> (Walters 2012: 924)

Unlike *The Kids Are All Right*, however, *The Owls* tackles heteronormative representations of lesbian sexuality head on through strategies directly gleaned from the New Queer Cinema movement.

Dunye's film opens with scenes of homophobic protest in California regarding the passage of Proposition 8 against gay marriage. As a number of critics have pointed out, mainstream gay rights advocacy that emerged to prevent the passage of Proposition 8 was largely framed around liberal arguments about the need to allow "good gay citizens" the right to marry (Rohrer 2014). However, we soon learn that *The Owls*—far from offering an endorsement of gay liberalism, as in *The Kids Are All Right*—actually presents us with a stinging critique of homonormativity. In *The Owls*, Dunye stages her critique of gay normativity at the level of both form and content through the presence of negative queer characters and the inclusion of self-reflexive meta-commentaries by the actresses in the film. As Guinevere Turner, who plays the role of Iris comments, all of Dunye's characters are "hateable"—from the selfish and narcissistic Iris, to sex mad MJ, to self-indulgent Lily, and finally to sanctimonious Carol played by Dunye herself, who repeatedly subjects the other characters in the film to pedantic lectures about the importance of social activism and the work of Audre Lorde. Throughout the film, the two main lesbian couples—Iris and MJ, and Carol and Lily—are frequently shown exchanging insults. While Lily wants to return to London, Carol is trying to persuade her lover to have a baby. As Carol opines, in a queer parody of both hetero and homonormativity, "That's what saves a relationship, having a family."

A crucial subject within *The Owls* is the idea of aging and intergenerational divides between queer women. According to Dunye, the term "owl" stands for "older wiser lesbian." As Lisa Gornick, the actress who plays Lily remarks, "I think it's really important to cross-ageify." Through the inclusion of these meta-level commentaries by the actresses on age and queer identity, Dunye seeks to subvert the kinds of linear, chronological narratives that are central to postfeminist representations of gender and sexuality. Instead, *The Owls* critiques homonormative models of queer evolution culminating in marriage and depoliticized forms of gay liberalism by showing how lesbian identities are always contested and intersectional. What is crucial to Dunye's subversion of postfeminist discourses is her queering of normative temporalities. As discussed earlier, ideas of chronological decorum and the centrality of family time regulate postfeminist representations of lesbian sexuality. Within contemporary postfeminist media culture, the emphasis is on "temporally 'correct' bodies finding one another" (Wearing 2007: 298) and on rehabilitating characters in intergenerational lesbian relationships into a generationally acceptable sexuality. In *The Owls*, however, Dunye seeks to subvert traditional temporalities grounded in the concept of reproductive time through the film's non-linear narrative and lack of clear closure. As Cheryl comments at the end of *The Owls*, "a happy ending is something I don't look forward to." By queering heteronormative temporalities through the disruption of chronological time, *The Owls* offers us a critical opportunity to challenge the kinds of ageist binaries propelled by a linear understanding of time as moving inexorably towards a narrative of decline in old age. Unlike heteronormative and homonormative timelines, then, which are regulated by the idea of reproductive futurism, *The Owls* demonstrates how queer temporalities can open up a space for challenging hegemonic definitions of older women as asexual.

Another independent lesbian-authored film that offers a similarly queer perspective on intergenerational lesbian relationships is *Gypo*. Dunn's film—which is one of an increasing number of European, independent films produced during the last decade that focus on the subject of lesbian migration and border-crossing—revolves around an intergenerational lesbian relationship between Tasha, a young Roma refugee from the Czech Republic, and

Helen, an older married, white working-class Irish immigrant living in Britain. *Gypo* adopts many of the formal features I have identified elsewhere as characteristic of transnational lesbian cinema, including self-reflexivity; defamiliarizing structures that work to undermine traditional notions of cinematic realism; location shooting; the inscription of the filmmakers themselves within the film; the use of transnational spaces such as seaports, border zones and immigration controls; and, perhaps most importantly, the documentary realist approach to the presentation of subject matter and narrative (Lewis 2012). Located in the run-down seaside town of Margate, Kent, *Gypo* is set within the context of the alienated, post-industrial landscapes and desolate coastal towns that characterize British social realist cinema of the 1980s and 1990s. As the director has commented in interviews, *Gypo* recalls political events in Britain from the late 1990s, when a number of Roma refugees fleeing persecution in Slovakia and the Czech Republic were dispersed to the Kent coast as a result of government efforts to "spread the burden" regarding what they claimed represented a massive influx of refugees and asylum-seekers into the country (ibid.). Drawing on the kind of oceanic imagery characteristic of anti-miscegenation discourses, the mainstream tabloid media in Britain predictably labeled all Roma refugees "economic migrants" and denounced asylum-seekers in general for "flooding" the Kent area and "running down the welfare state" (ibid.).

In *Gypo*, Dunn relies upon social realism and a Dogme 95 aesthetic to deconstruct the popular xenophobic trope that links immigration control with welfare provision in order to call attention to new forms of economic racism emerging within twenty-first-century Britain (Lewis 2012). Dunn criticizes xenophobia and economic racism primarily by way of the intergenerational relationship between Tasha and Helen, using the women's lesbian relationship to stress the need for political coalitions between women across national borders.

The film's central character, Helen, constantly strives to make connections between her own experiences as an Irish immigrant living in Britain, and the kinds of anti-immigrant sentiments leveled at Tasha. Indeed, the intergenerational lesbian relationship between Helen and Tasha that constitutes the film's central narrative attempts to counteract neo-liberal economic ideologies, insofar as it seeks to rehabilitate discourses of welfare and social citizenship. In *Gypo*, the lesbian relationship between Helen and Tasha is articulated in language that attempts to reclaim the state of vulnerability (literally: the condition of being "susceptible to physical or emotional injury") as a necessary and pleasurable aspect of all human interactions. Although Helen is twenty-five-years older than Tasha and (as she puts it) "old enough to be [Tasha's] mother," their relationship is presented in terms that clearly contradict the notion of Tasha as the "more vulnerable" of the two women. Rather, it is Tasha who demonstrates the most sexual agency in the film, as it is she who takes an active role in seducing Helen. The latter is borne out by the fact that we are encouraged to view the sexual consummation of the relationship between the two women primarily from Tasha's perspective, rather than Helen's. In response to Helen's comment that, "you're so far from home and you're really vulnerable now," Tasha replies: "I don't feel vulnerable at all, but you seem to me the most vulnerable person I've ever met." By stressing Helen's role as a mother while also making her sexually desirable from Tasha's point of view, *Gypo* counters post-feminist representations of motherhood and intergenerational lesbian relationships as inherently asexual.

By framing lesbian desire in terms of discourses of mutual vulnerability and inter-dependency, *Gypo* suggests that it is the human activity of care that must form the basis of what it means to be a citizen in a welfare state. Through the film's unsympathetic treatment of Helen's husband Paul, Dunn seems to indicate that the problem with current conceptions of social citizenship lies not with the notion of human interdependency, but rather with masculinist constructions of independence and the corresponding negation of welfare that they imply.

Countering the kinds of xenophobic tropes that link national vulnerability to a crisis of borders, *Gypo* seeks to revalue the concept of human interdependency, not as a gendered condition of weakness demanding special protection but rather as a crucial aspect of social citizenship. As Judith Butler observes, the desiring body is, by definition, a vulnerable and precarious body. While vulnerability is the precondition for desire and eroticism, however, it is also the condition of injury and violence. For Butler, sexual rights discourses need to reflect the ways in which the body is both "bound" and "unbound" by desire, the body's proximity to pain and loss as well as pleasure. As she writes:

> We are always something more than, and other than, ourselves. ... Let us face it. We are undone by each other. If we are not, we are missing something. If this seems so clearly the case with grief, it is only because it was already the case with desire.
>
> *(2004: 51)*

For Butler, desire and mourning, which expose the contingency of sexual and bodily life, constitute the basis for imagining an alternative political community, one that is composed of, as she puts it, "those who are beside themselves" (ibid.).

By deconstructing postfeminist conflations of female aging with frailty and vulnerability, *Gypo* encourages us to rethink issues of welfare and social protection from a transnational standpoint. As the "welcoming" arm of the British nation, Helen represents a more politically accountable mode of hospitality from that invoked by xenophobic discourses that construct migrants as arriving in "waves" and "tides." Instead, Dunn uses the older lesbian character to present islands as spaces of interconnectedness and hospitality, rather than separation and insularity. By stressing the fluidity and permeability of national borders through the evocation of a specifically intergenerational form of lesbian erotic vulnerability, *Gypo* shows how the island can become a powerful reminder of our connection to others. In this context, the island can offer us a model of social citizenship that is inherently transnational in scope, one that recognizes both differences *and* connections between generations of women across national borders. This is a model of citizenship that asks us to grapple with the crucial question of whether, in an era of globalization, sexual rights and social provisioning can be limited to belonging at the level of the nation-state.

Conclusion

As this article demonstrates, the subject of intergenerational desire has become increasingly central to current representations of queer women's sexuality in mainstream film and television. For this reason, it is crucial that we interrogate the politics of contemporary lesbian representation in relation to discourses of gender and aging within postfeminist media culture. Through an analysis of the films discussed here, we can observe the heteronormative disciplinary forces through which female bodies are produced as gendered, classed, and aged within postfeminist media culture. In these postfeminist representations of lesbian sexuality, notions of asexual old age are used to shore up heteronormative ideals of feminine youthfulness and heterosexual romance in a way that renders intergenerational desire between women invisible. It is crucial that lesbian filmmakers begin to challenge such hegemonic definitions of older women as asexual and strive to create the kinds of representations of intergenerational lesbian relationships that validate the sexual pleasure and agency of older women—both queer and non-queer alike. As Joan Nestle eloquently reminds us,

> Issues like physical well-being, body size, menopause, emotional fragility are always there, waiting to be incorporated into daily moments of intimacy. ... As I have come to enjoy my own middle-aged sexual wisdom, I have also come to recognize it in other older women I see around me. Gray hair and textured hands are now erotic emblems I seek out.
>
> (Nestle 1991: 181–2)

With their queer form and content, independent lesbian-authored films such as *The Owls* and *Gypo* open up a space for more diverse representations of lesbian sexuality and aging than those typically offered up by postfeminist media culture. In doing so, they show how significant age differences between lesbians, rather than constituting a source of injury, can represent a crucial aspect of queerness itself.

Related topics

Sally Chivers, "'No place for sissies': gender, age, and disability in Hollywood"
Amy Borden, "Queer or LGBTQ+: on the question of inclusivity in queer cinema studies"

Note

1 The television show *Transparent* offers a similarly caricatured representation of feminism and, by extension, women's and gender studies.

Bibliography

Aaron, M. (2004) *New Queer Cinema: A Critical Reader*. New York and London: Routledge.
Butler, J. (2004) *Undoing Gender*. New York: Routledge.
Butler, J. (2006) *Precarious Life: The Powers of Mourning and Violence*. London: Verso.
Gill, R. (2007) *Gender and the Media*. London: Polity Press.
Keating, S. (2015) "What it's Like to be a Lesbian Couple with a 20-Year-Plus Age Difference," *BuzzFeed*. December 13. www.buzzfeed.com/shannonkeating/lesbian-age-differences#.yfJM4BWRd (Accessed March 1, 2016)
Krainitzki, E. (2015) "Ghosted Images: Old Lesbians on Screen," *Journal of Lesbian Studies*, 19(1), pp. 13–26.
Lewis, R. (2012) "Towards a Transnational Lesbian Cinema," *Journal of Lesbian Studies* 16(3), pp. 273–90.
Liddy, S. (2014) "Missing Persons? Representations of Mature Female Sexuality in British and Irish Film 1998–2011," *Postgraduate Journal of Women, Ageing, and Media* 1, pp. 38–66.
McRobbie, A. (2008) *The Aftermath of Feminism: Gender, Culture and Social Change*. London: Sage Publications.
Nestle, J. (1991) "Desire Perfected: Sex after Forty" in B. Sang, J. Warshow, and A.J. Smith (eds.) *Lesbians at Midlife: The Creative Transition*. Minneapolis: Spinsters Ink, pp. 180–3.
Rich, B. R. (2000) "Queer and Present Danger," *Sight and Sound* 10(3): 22–5.
Rohrer, J. (2014) *Queering the Biopolitics of Citizenship in the Age of Obama*. New York and London: Palgrave Macmillan.

Tasker, Y. and D. Negra (2007) "Introduction: Feminist Politics and Postfeminist Culture" in Y. Tasker and D. Negra (eds.) *Interrogating Postfeminism: Gender and the Politics of Popular Culture*. Durham: Duke University Press, pp. 1–25.

Walters, S. D. (2012) "The Kids Are All Right But the Lesbians Aren't: Queer Kinship in US Culture," *Sexualities* 15(8): 917–33.

Wearing, S. (2007) "Subjects of Rejuvenation: Aging in Postfeminist Culture" in Y. Tasker and D. Negra (eds.) *Interrogating Postfeminism: Gender and the Politics of Popular Culture*. Durham: Duke University Press, pp. 277–310.

White, P. (2015) "Sketchy Lesbians: *Carol* as History and Fantasy," *Film Quarterly* 69/2: 8–18.

PART V

Thinking cinema's future

This final section has been compiled with attention to the shifting landscape of media and technology. While digital technology has all but entirely replaced celluloid film stock, new media and streaming services have further challenged the primacy of the traditional movie-going experience. Some have called this a shift to post-cinema, as discussed in Dijana Jelača's essay, which looks at music video as an example of new media rewriting iconic cine-feminist scripts. Erica Levin examines allegories of production as they relate to new media, experimental film, and the body, focusing on Natalie Bookchin's *Mass Ornament* (2009) and its citation of Busby Berkeley's *Broadway Lullaby* dance sequence. Emerging directions in the field do not pertain to technology only—they also link to the environment more generally, as discussed by E. Ann Kaplan with respect to climate trauma films, as well as by Alexa Weik von Mossner, whose focus is on ecocinema and gender. Jennifer Lynn Peterson speaks nearby these concerns, with her discussion of cinema, animal studies, and the post-human, which takes Isabella Rossellini's viral *Green Porno* series as a case study. Katarzyna Marciniak highlights filmmakers who espouse transnational feminist sensibilities through the figure of the immigrant as an embodiment of revolting aesthetics, while Eliza Steinbock highlights the under-studied but rich domain of trans* topics in cinema. In the volume's final essay, Kristin Lené Hole returns to some of the field's overarching questions, drawing on tools from critical feminist historiography to examine the origin stories of feminist film and theory.

Together, this final group of essays vividly illustrates our claim in the volume's introduction—that the business of feminist film studies is unfinished, and, moreover, that it needs to be rethought in light of the ongoing shifts in technology, gender norms, social hierarchies, and transnational flows of power/knowledge. The future remains unwritten.

PART IV

Thinking critical about...

36

REVOLTING AESTHETICS

Feminist transnational cinema in the US

Katarzyna Marciniak

All political ideologies – but perhaps particularly those preoccupied with social hygiene, such as racism, xenophobia, eugenics, homophobia and misogyny – are mediated through revolting aesthetics.

Imogen Tyler, *Revolting Subjects* (2013)

Revolting suture

When I show my students Panama-born US-based Anayansi Prado's 2005 documentary *Maid in America*, which features three female Latina women working as *domésticas* in Los Angeles, one scene always provokes gasps from the audience. Guatemalan Judith gives birth to her son Everest, and we watch the moment of birthing in all its realistic details: in a tightly composed frame, with the camera placed at the level of Judith's head, we see the baby being pulled out of her, his tiny body covered in blood and other fluids, still attached to the mother by an umbilical cord. My students, bothered by the very idea of such proximity to the flesh, invariably always ask: "Why do we need to see *this*?" The *this*, involving "the taboo aesthetics of the birth scene" (Tyler, Baraitser 2013: 1), placed centrally in the frame, captures a delicate and precarious moment of intimacy that typically takes place off-screen. As viewers, they claim, we are not used to watching such scenes in full detail. We are not used to seeing such moments "so close." The birthing sequence stages what, following Jacques Rancière, we may call "the intolerable image"—intolerable because it is "too intolerably real" (Rancière 2009: 83).

For viewers, the problem with this birth scene has to do with one's forced proximity to liquid bodily substances and messiness. One confronts an overly close encounter with human "sliminess." The sensory power of the scene of birthing brings into play what Laura U. Marks calls "haptic visuality" (Marks 2000: xi), making viewers feel as well as see sliminess up close. However, I also want to suggest that what makes *Maid in America*'s birth scene particularly revolting is the relationship it poses between migrant disposability and birth. In the context of a larger discussion on "the stranger" and "the foreigner" in contemporary societies, following Jean Paul Sartre's claim that "to touch the slimy is to risk being dissolved in sliminess," Zygmunt Bauman uses the concept of sliminess as a metaphor for the foreigner's contingency and "viscosity" (Bauman 1995: 9). Watching Everest's birth prompts us to consider that, as humans, we all enter the world in this form. Through a kind of transference, though, this sliminess can become "attached" to certain foreign bodies, which are then vulnerable to ostracism, exclusion, xenophobia, and deportability.

The various meanings contained within the birth scene merit unraveling. Everest, named in the honor of the highest mountain, is a conflictual subject: by virtue of his birth in the US, he is a citizen but, as the son of an undocumented mother who, contrary to popular anti-immigrant sentiments, does not gain formal legitimacy through birthing, he is already in a tenuous position. He is legitimate but his parent is not, making him vulnerable to potential separation from his mother or exile from his native land. His undocumented mother is fully aware of her precarity and disposability, even as her work as a *doméstica* is valued by her employers.

The *feeling* of sliminess as provoked in the birthing scene produces shivers of disgust; it is as if we feel the sensation on the surface of our skin. And we shudder. Commenting on the politics of disgust, Imogen Tyler tells us that "disgust is an urgent, guttural aversive emotion, associated with sickening feelings of revulsion, loathing or nausea" (Tyler 2013: 21), which may translate itself into socially performed stigmatization. Tyler notes that there is a vigorous tradition of writing on disgust in the context of social critique (ibid. 22), but cinema presents a particularly potent site for exploring the politics and aesthetics of disgust.

Throughout her book, *Revolting Subjects: Social Abjection and Resistance in Neoliberal Britain*, Tyler plays with the dual meanings of "revolt" and "revolting subjects," messing up the boundary between the two seemingly distinct meanings of "revolting": an emotional register evokes an expression of disgust, while a political register refers to acts of protest and rebellion that trouble authority and defy forms of violence experienced by those deemed revolting. I see her notion of "revolting aesthetics" as a powerful critical lens through which to consider a compelling post-2000 archive of US independent feature films and documentaries associated with transnational liminality, precarity, and tenuous national belonging, which place female foreign protagonists at the heart of the diegesis (for more on the cinema of migration, see Sumita Chakravarty's essay in this volume). The originality of these films comes from the fact that, often with poise and nuance, they pull the abjected and marginalized characters out of the peripheries where they are typically placed and situate their subjectivities in the center of the frame. The narratives variously link female foreigners with the literal and conceptual images of waste, garbage, and places of exclusion that surround the bodily labor of immigrant women, while prompting the viewer to question axiomatic associations between female migrants and discourses of waste and disposability. These films are directed by a new generation of US-based women filmmakers, many of them first-time directors coming themselves from immigrant backgrounds: Iranian-American Ana Lily Amirpour, Spanish Almudena Carracedo, Arab-American Cherien Dabis, Panamanian Anayansi Prado, Colombians Paola Mendoza and Gloria La Morte, and Nancy Savoca, born in New York to Argentine and Sicilian immigrants and unique in this group as an already established filmmaker with a substantial, internationally acclaimed oeuvre.

The work of these women directors develops a distinctly feminist voice and feminist optic while drawing on migratory histories—their own or their families'—connecting them to territories in the Global South. These films urgently respond to such issues as migrant labor, economic exploitation, domestic servitude, xenophobia, and racism, collectively projecting, in Patricia White's words, "a transnational feminist social vision" (White 2015: 5). Echoing Stuart Hall, we might say that these films "welcome [us] to migranthood" (Hall 1996: 114). Specifically, though, they welcome us to female migranthood, calling into question the politics of invisibility, inaudibility, and marginality.

The body of work I bring into focus here forcefully signals the contemporary emergence of a feminist immigrant cinema that thwarts the mainstream representation of foreign femaleness, opposing what Trinh Minh-ha terms "the exotic and erotic feminine ethnic minority" (Trinh 1991: 115) and what I have called "palatable foreignness" (Marciniak 2007). I understand these films as working with a "revolting aesthetics" that ties spectators to the foreign female gaze and thus to a foreign subjectivity through various formal techniques. Revolting aesthetics refers to rupturing the hegemonic ways of perceiving social reality, making visible and audible "what had been excluded from a perceptual field" (Rancière 2003: 226). The birthing scene in *Maid in America* shows just such a revolting rupture. If my students feel a sense of revulsion, the film's political choice to show us the birth of a citizen from a "foreign" migrant body becomes that much more powerful as a challenge and a shock to spectatorial sensibilities.

I place this survey in the field of transnational feminist media studies, a newly forged area of interest that emerged with the publication of *Transnational Feminism in Film and Media* (2007), co-edited by myself, Anikó Imre, and Áine O'Healy. This field has built a conceptual bridge between transnational feminist discourses and transnational cinema and media, arguing that

> feminism … is not a decorative addition or an optional perspective that can be applied to studies of transnational media but an acknowledgment that transnational processes are inherently gendered, sexualized, and racialized. The borders they erase and erect affect different groups differently.
>
> *(Marciniak et al. 2007: 4)*

The films under discussion here show such borders—some formal, some physical, and some symbolic—while accentuating a close link between the usability and disposability of foreignness, particularly female, or feminized foreignness. What I call the "usability of the foreigner" underscores the process through which the foreigner's physical or emotional labor sustains the citizen, while she often falls into the category of disposability (Marciniak and Bennett 2016). I see the interrelated tropes of the "usability" and "disposability" of foreignness as symptomatic of the paradox of foreignness itself. In my earlier work, I talked about "quivering ontologies" to describe the ambivalent positioning of the figure of the foreigner—her destabilized subject position as it refers to both her nation of origin and her host nation (Marciniak 2006). All female protagonists in the films I discuss, although "quivering," nevertheless also perform the role of "revolting subjects," whether their revolt is performed through a lawsuit or through small, daily acts of resistance knowable only to themselves. They refuse to accept victimization or to give in to discourses of pity. When María in Almudena Carracedo's 2007 documentary, *Made in LA*, states, "we do … protest," she shifts our attention to immigrant audibility. In what follows, I focus on ways in which these transnational feminist films foreground the possibilities of protest or resistance for the abjected category of immigrant women.

Recyclability of marginalized lives

A scene similar to the birthing moment in *Maid in America*, showing not birth but a termination of pregnancy, occurs toward the end of *Entre Nos* (*Between Us*), the directorial debut of Colombians Paola Mendoza and Gloria La Morte. An immigrant drama released in 2009 at the Tribeca Film Festival, the film shows the protagonist, Colombian Mariana

(Paola Mendoza), in the communal shower during a self-induced abortion. As she bleeds, the camera remains in close-up on her face, registering her anguish and pain. Vision is restricted in the scene: we are allowed to see only her face, her feet, and the blood flowing into the drain. Even though the word "abortion" is not uttered, spectators understand that this is precisely the experience we are asked to observe "up close." We also understand that this is an agonizing decision for religious reasons. Shortly beforehand, Mariana attempts to enter the church but cannot bring herself to open the main door. She asks for forgiveness for the act she is about to commit by whispering to the church door. The poignancy of the shower scene is heightened by the fact that her daughter, sitting in the hallway on the floor, is simultaneously conducting a seemingly casual conversation with her mother about the New York summer heat and her dream of living on a big apple farm. Through the parallel cuts, we move back and forth between the daughter's face and Mariana's face, a strategy meant to underscore Mariana's devotion to her child whom she does not want to neglect even in such a distressing moment. While she expels the fetus she cannot afford to term to life, she tends to the child behind the shower curtain.

As the final credits reveal, the film is based on Paola Mendoza's own childhood and the story of her mother. The mother, Mariana, together with her two small children, joins her husband in Queens, New York. The husband, who only briefly appears onscreen, leaves the family and travels to Miami for a new job, making it clear that he is not coming back. As the narrative unfolds in a series of vignettes, we are sutured into the brutal details of Mariana's survival in the city where she and the children go from penniless to homeless. The formal organization of the narrative deliberately keeps spectators closely connected to Mariana and her children. We often see them in alleys as they search garbage bins looking for recyclables, which they later sell for cash. We see them struggling as they share a bit of food they can afford to buy. In one scene, the daughter eats a small bag of chips and licks the crumbs off her fingers while Mariana and the son watch silently. There are several scenes showing us how they spend their nights on park benches and on stairways, lying on pieces of cardboard. The precariousness of their situation and the progressive worsening of their circumstances are conveyed visually without much dialogue: Mariana's body becomes more and more emaciated; their clothes become dirty; Mariana has dark circles under her eyes. The pace of this episodic narrative is slow, allowing us to contemplate the metonymic correspondence between Mariana and her children, searching through the city's garbage, and their social status as disposable. Yet they are also potentially "recyclable," like the cans Mariana picks up because of her perseverance and revolt.

Despite these harsh circumstances, this is not a "rescue" narrative in which a well-meaning citizen might offer Mariana a way out. The three characters with whom Mariana forms some alliance are a presumably homeless black man who guards her recyclables, a Latina woman operating a taco truck who offers them food, and an Indian woman who supplies her with herbs for the termination of pregnancy. All of these alliances are with already socially marginalized characters who, we can assume, implicitly understand Mariana's endangered survival and the apparently inescapable sliminess of her social surroundings.

Usability and disposability: feeding off the foreign

While *Entres Nos* focalizes the undocumented immigrants' disposability and Mariana's battle against her unlivable life, Nancy Savoca's *Dirt* (2003) privileges the politics of encounter between the citizen and the foreigner, showing how such encounters are always political and rooted in hierarchical structures of domination. Like *Entre Nos*, *Dirt* symbolically privileges images of dirt and grime. An undocumented El Salvadoran, Dolores (Julieta Ortiz), cleans posh Park Avenue apartments in Manhattan and, while the film details Dolores's cleaning routines, it sutures its audience repeatedly into the rhetoric and imagery of garbage and dirt, and to racialized structures of oppression (Marciniak 2008). The opening scene literally and metonymically links Dolores to garbage. As she walks toward the building where she works, an inhabitant of the building, a white woman, stops her, saying: "Excuse me. You clean the apartment next to mine. You left two bags of garbage in the hall yesterday. Do you understand what I am saying? You understand garbage? GARBAGE! *Basura!* Basura? No *basura* in the hallway!"

The lives of undocumented women are always already precarious and their employment at best tenuous, but the relation between Dolores and the Ortegas is particularly striking in the film. The Ortegas are the family for whom she has worked for nine years until Mrs. Ortega decides to "run for office." Mr. Ortega explains to shocked Dolores:

> Claudia is taking a hard stand against the illegals in the city. Well, if the press finds out that we hired you, they're going to crucify her and she won't be able to run. … She goes on TV against illegals in the city.

The family's rejection of Dolores is particularly hurtful to her because she and the Ortegas share a Latino/a immigrant background. She is not dismissed by a "concerned" white American family but by her immigrant *compadres*, showing us that immigrants, too, can be susceptible to hypocrisy and xenophobic tendencies, especially when such attitudes suit their interests. The arrogance of the Ortegas in *Dirt* stems from the fact that they understand their formal and economic superiority, but also, crucially, from the perception that their domestic help is disposable.

This trope of "feeding off the foreign body" is also a central concern in Spanish-born Almudena Carracedo's 2007 Emmy-award-winning documentary, *Made in LA*. Here, too, we see a narrative preoccupation with undocumented Latina women who work in the garment industry in Los Angeles, sewing clothes for *Forever 21*, a chain store that sells cheap clothing for girls and young women. Privileging three women workers, Mexicans Lupe and María and Salvadoran Maura, the film reveals a profound irony about economic (in)justice: young women in the US can enjoy affordable garments because the garment workers, sewing into the late hours of the night, do not even receive a minimum wage while working in spaces infested with rats and roaches. As María says about her supervisor, "the woman made us work fast and didn't let us eat or go to the restroom. We worked locked in." Lupe, understanding that their undocumented status makes them easily exploitable and disposable, claims, "if you are undocumented … you basically don't exist."

Rather than accepting such blatant exploitation and succumbing to invisibility and silence, the women launch the lawsuit against *Forever 21*, which they eventually win after a long and uncertain three-year battle conducted with the help of legal counsel from the Garment Worker Center, a non-profit community center. The film documents their fight to win basic labor protections, while showing us how these women managed to organize their community to spearhead a national boycott against the company, which, until the very end, refused to acknowledge any responsibility for its actions. There are images of protest in this documentary, showing banners with slogans such as "Danger: Shopping Here Supports Exploitation;" there are also scenes of human exhaustion, doubt, fear, and a willingness to give up, all conveying a strong sense that revolting against injustice, while critical, is hard work.

Perhaps the most revelatory segment of the documentary is Lupe's trip to New York where she visits the Ellis Island Museum and The Lower East Side Tenement Museum, which has preserved a sweatshop from 1897 that housed Jewish workers from Poland. There, the mise-en-scène shows images stunningly similar to the scenes of the contemporary workplace in Los Angeles: sewing machines in dark, tight spaces, poor working conditions, lack of proper ventilation. At the museum, black-and-white images shot in close-up show women bent over the sewing machines. Learning about the immigrant history of the nation, Lupe says, "Like today. Everything remains the same." But she also looks closely at the images showing protest: "We Condemn Child Labor. Unity is Strength. Organize." Making another parallel between the past and the present, she looks at the camera and claims: "It says, 'organize.'" The revelation is thus about the historicity of immigrant revolt.

Difference: fascination and disgust

Many female protagonists from the films I have briefly discussed *feel* the weight of their difference acutely. This difference—embracing racial, ethnic, national, or economic and class positioning—is often a burden, exposing their foreignness and thus their vulnerability. This vulnerability is particularly heightened when the protagonists are undocumented and are thus concerned about the risks associated with their becoming visible and audible. Dolores in *Dirt* often walks with her head down, her body giving an impression of wanting to be shrunk. When walking into the Park Avenue apartment building where she works, she stays close to the walls, not wanting to draw attention to herself. She wants to be a shadow. The women boycotting *Forever 21* are constantly worried about how the visibility of the lawsuit might affect those among them who have a tenuous formal status and are thus potentially deportable.

Arab-American Cherien Dabis's 2009 feature debut *Amreeka*, based on autobiographical elements from her family's life in Ohio, makes foreign disposability and perceived "sliminess" poignant and often subtly comic (Figure 36.1). The film premiered at the Sundance Film Festival and has been praised as unique in that it privileges an Arab female protagonist whose representation resists any orientalizing of the Arab female body as alluring, docile, and exotic. Instead, the narrative offers the story of a single mother who sees herself as overweight and unattractive.

In contrast to the other female foreign figures I have discussed, Muna (Nisreen Faour) is a documented immigrant, but her experiences in Illinois, where she stays with her sister after her journey from the West Bank with her son, Fadi, are not necessarily easier. Coming from a Palestinian territory, she is always conscious of her difference and unbelonging: "If we don't belong here, we don't belong anywhere." Being subjected to surveillance at the daily checkpoints in the West Bank and constantly worried about the well-being of her son while living there, Muna knows well what it means to be targeted as suspect, but she does not expect the force of xenoracism that hits her and Fadi in Illinois. They are both targeted, but in different ways. Fadi is called "Osama," and his cousin's car is marked with the misspelled "Al-Kada," singling Fadi out as a potential terrorist. Muna, despite her training and experience in banking, cannot get a suitable job ("Don't blow this place up," says one of the men who interviews her for possible employment), and, determined not to be a burden to her sister's family, she ends up working as a server at White Castle, concealing this from the family as a potentially shameful situation. This is where she meets Matt, a white American young man and a high-school drop-out who works by her side serving burgers. Matt visually stands out, boldly embracing difference: his hair is blue; his lip is pierced; he

Oh..., don't blow the place up!

Figure 36.1　Muna during one of her interviews for a position in banking in Illinois.

Source: Amreeka, Cherien Dabis, 2009.

wears large earrings. We see Muna glancing at Matt many times, not necessarily with dis-approval but rather with curiosity. Knowing quite well that *difference* for her and Fadi is at best risky she has a hard time imagining that someone like Matt would willingly refashion his body this way:

MUNA:　Why you do like this?
MATT:　Why? You don't like it?
MUNA:　No, I like it.
MATT:　Ah, I don't know, I guess I think it's cool, makes me different.
MUNA:　You like to be different?
MATT:　Yeah, why would I want to be just like everybody else?

While for Muna difference signals discomfort and the pain of not belonging, for Matt being different is about playing with coolness and deliberate defiance. The difference between their subject positions is, of course, crucial. As a white man, he can afford to play with his body this way, while Muna and Fadi cannot. Fadi's American cousin, in fact, warns him that unless he reconfigures his body, he will be perceived in his new high school as an FOB (fresh off the boat), "training" him to wear a hoodie and to walk and move in an "American way." But, in an interesting twist, Matt also experiences ostracism for exposing his difference. At one point he is defending Muna in front of the bullies who target Fadi at school and hears the insult: "Shut the hell up, faggot." At this moment when disgust for difference is per-formed, an affinity between xenophobia and homophobia is exposed as the two quickly converge. Because of his visible difference and potentially ambivalent sexuality, Matt becomes a feminized other and is "put into a discourse of 'woman,'" to use Alice Jardine's phrase. Jardine elaborates, "The space 'outside of' the conscious subject has always connoted the feminine in the history of Western thought – and any movement into alterity is a movement into that female space" (Jardine 1982: 59–60).

Addressing the spectator as a foreign female: "badass" immigrant

In her well-known 1987 essay, "Rethinking Women's Cinema: Aesthetics and Feminist Theory," in which she discussed feminist filmmaking, Teresa de posited the notion of a "feminist *deaesthetic*." The prefix *de-* is crucial for her: it signals the need to interrogate and destructure the very act of representation. But precisely how can such a destructuring happen? Reading de Lauretis closely, one sees that she steers us away from the simplified rendition of feminist film as cinema that, on a thematic level, deals with "women's issues," or merely privileges female protagonists as narrative agents. Rather, the changes in the apparatus of representation she calls for embrace the levels of both content and form. They redefine aesthetic and formal knowledges and challenge the codes and conventions of commercial cinema. The purpose of such a redefinition, she proposes, is to desexualize violence, de-aestheticize the female body, and de-oedipalize narrative structure. In her analysis, she mentions Chantal Akerman's 1975 classic, *Jeanne Dielman, 23, Quai du Commerce, 1080 Bruxelles*, as a film that offers "a picture of female experience, of duration, perception, events, relationships, and silences" (1987: 131). Considering one of the central ideas of de Lauretis's theory—the notion that a film "addresses the spectator as female," (ibid. 137) regardless of the gender of the viewer—it is important to point out that de Lauretis does not simply advocate an easy, comfortable, and straightforward *identification* with the femaleness depicted onscreen. On the contrary, such modes of address, if effective, have the potential to defamiliarize and dislocate the spectatorial gaze.

We can observe such a defamiliarization of the spectatorial gaze in Ana Lily Amirpour's *A Girl Walks Home Alone at Night*. A British-born Iranian who grew up in the US, Amirpour introduced her directorial debut at the 2014 Sundance Film Festival. The film is a provocative example of an overt play with female foreignness. As the director acknowledged in interviews, her black-and-white film was inspired by the chador, the skateboard, and the vampire (Figure 36.2). Shot entirely in Persian and subtitled in English, the film is conscious of the politics of translation. This romantic thriller, hailed as the first Iranian vampire Western, is stylistically unusual as it mixes the Spaghetti Western, graphic novels, and the atmospheres of Jim Jarmusch's films, while also paying homage to expressionist aesthetics.

Rephrasing de Lauretis's notion, we might say that the film "addresses the spectator as a *foreign* female." At the heart of the narrative, against the background of an industrial wasteland, a mysterious Iranian female vampire skateboarder in a chador, known as the Girl (Sheila Vand), roams the streets of Bad City at night, attacking males who disrespect women. As a female predator and an avenger, she sucks the blood of "bad" men, leaving them lifeless. Her attacks are thus not random vampire acts, but actions motivated by a

Figure 36.2 The Girl roaming the streets.

Source: *A Girl Walks Home Alone at Night*, Ana Lily Amirpour, 2014.

Figure 36.3   The Girl and sliminess.

Source: A Girl Walks Home Alone at Night, Ana Lily Amirpour, 2014.

sense of social justice. The scenes featuring the Girl are powerfully rendered using long takes and close-ups, pauses and swift movement. There are many moments where the Girl stares directly at the camera, often motionless and speechless, challenging the viewer with her gaze and posture. In contrast to these moments, we also see the Girl skateboarding, gliding across the frame, her chador flowing like wings, conveying a sense of unrestricted mobility—a Muslim female *jouissance*, poking fun at the idea that chadors restrict women.

Although various reviewers presume that the film intends to portray a city in Iran, it was actually shot in Southern California, outside Bakersfield, the distinctive mise-en-scène featuring oil fields and smokestacks. Thus the film may also be read as portraying a US-Iranian community, suturing us into foreignness and immigrant culture. Traditionally, in cinematic history, the figure of the vampire connotes foreignness. F. W. Murnau's *Nosferatu* (1922) features a horrifying vampire who is a foreigner from the east, associated with plague and death that threaten not just individual characters but the entire community. While Nosferatu preys on women, The Girl, as a foreign female vampire who protects women, disrupts the binaries. She is associated with sliminess, but in a defiant way. A scene in which the Girl kills a drug dealer who abuses women unfolds slowly, visually emphasizing bodily fluids. She exposes her teeth and sucks the drug dealer's finger while he, being used to women servicing his erotic needs, does not even suspect her intentions. When she bites the finger off, she, again slowly, pulls the amputated digit out of her mouth, dripping blood and saliva. This is a spectacle of sliminess and symbolic castration—the revenge of the female foreigner against the sexual exploitation and subjugation of women (Figure 36.3).

Conclusion: "Justice is Always in Fashion"

Reflecting on cinema and feminist consciousness, Trinh Minh-ha writes:

> each film is a way of experiencing and experimenting with limits; it is a journey from which there is no turning back. In reversing, displacing, and creating anew the gaze, [a film by a female feminist director] will not be offering an object to look at but *an articulation of images to consider.*
>
> (Trinh 1991: 115, *my emphasis*)

By forging a filmic grammar of immigrant visibility and audibility, the new feminist immigrant cinema offers such "an articulation of images" for its viewers to consider. The power of this filmic grammar reveals itself in an accumulation of those images that call on us to "see" the bodies and "hear" the voices of those who typically only occupy the edges of the narrative.

The films under discussion were all produced in the post 9/11 era, a period that has witnessed the uneven diffusion of globalization, the feminization of migration, the fervor of anti-immigrant politics, the criminalization of racialized foreignness as well as the production of a fetishized rhetoric of "illegality." As I have suggested, these films play with the dual sense of revolting: by showing us aversive images of sliminess in various visual and audible forms (dirt, garbage, bodily fluids, hateful words), they demand that we ask how and why such aversions "stick" to the female foreign figures while simultaneously depicting these figures as revolting against their abject disposability (in one of the scenes in *Made in LA*, we see Lupe proudly wearing a red T-shirt that reads "Justice is Always in Fashion"). In this way, they themselves can be considered revolting aesthetic forms that disrupt what is allowable for us to see, to hear, and to imagine.

Related topics

Sumita Chakravarty, "Gender in transit: framing the cinema of migration"
Sandra Ponzanesi, "Postcolonial and transnational approaches to film and feminism"
Priya Jaikumar, "Feminist and non-Western interrogations of film authorship"

References

Bauman, Z. (1995) "Making and Unmaking of Strangers," *Thesis Eleven* 43, pp. 1–16.
de Lauretis, T. (1987) "Rethinking Women's Cinema: Aesthetics and Feminist Theory," in T. de Lauretis *Technologies of Gender: Essays on Theory, Film, and Fiction*, Bloomington: Indiana University Press, pp. 127–48.
Hall, S. (1996) "Minimal Selves," in H. Baker Jr, M. Diawara, and R. Lindeborg (eds.) *Black British Cultural Studies: A Reader*, Chicago: University of Chicago Press, pp. 114–19.
Jardine, A. (1982) "Gynesis," *Diacritics* 12, pp. 54–65.
Marciniak, K. (2006) *Alienhood: Citizenship, Exile, and the Logic of Difference*, Minneapolis: University of Minnesota Press.
Marciniak, K. (2007) "Palatable Foreignness," in K. Marciniak, A. Imre, and Á. O'Healy (eds.) *Transnational Feminism in Film and Media*, New York: Palgrave, pp. 187–205.
Marciniak, K. (2008) "Foreign Women and Toilets," *Feminist Media Studies* 8(4), pp. 337–56.
Marciniak, K. and Bennett, B. (2016) (eds.) "Introduction: Teaching Transnational Cinema: Politics and Pedagogy," in *Teaching Transnational Cinema: Politics and Pedagogy*, New York: Routledge.
Marciniak, K., Imre, A. and O'Healy, Á. (2007) (eds.) *Transnational Feminism in Film and Media*, New York: Palgrave.
Marks, L. U. (2000) *The Skin of the Film: Intercultural Cinema, Embodiment, and the Senses*, Durham and London: Duke University Press.
Rancière, J. (2003) *The Philosopher and His Poor*, trans. J. Drury, C. Oster, and A. Parker, Durham and London: Duke University Press.
Rancière, J. (2009) *The Emancipated Spectator*, trans. G. Elliott, London: Verso.
Trinh, T. M. (1991) *When the Moon Waxes Red: Representation, Gender and Cultural Politics*, New York: Routledge.
Tyler, I. (2013) *Revolting Subjects: Social Abjection and Resistance in Neoliberal Britain*, London: Zed Books.
Tyler, I. and Baraitser, L. (2013) "Private View, Public Birth: Making Feminist Sense of the New Visual Culture of Childbirth," *Studies in the Maternal* 5(2), pp. 1–27.
White, P. (2015) *Women's Cinema, World Cinema: Projecting Contemporary Feminisms*, Durham and London: Duke University Press.

37

TOWARDS TRANS CINEMA

Eliza Steinbock

This chapter takes up the designation of *trans cinema* as a provocation to think cinema's multiple components, including film texts, screen media, and spectators, from a *trans* perspective. Trans is a prefixial term for a range of non-binary and non-conforming gender identities, but it can also be affixed to man and woman (i.e. trans man) to signify the experience, past or present, of a transitional state of sexed being. Gender variance in cinema dates to the first films, and continues in popularity across screen media from television, to the Internet, to film industries, be they independent, Hollywood, or Bollywood. Since the late 1990s, a growing number of trans-specialized film festivals from Amsterdam to Beirut, Bologna, London, Los Angeles, Munich, Seattle, Sydney, Toronto, and Quito showcase national trans cinemas from around the world.

In fact, the history of trans cinema is so rich and varied it is remarkable how little sustained attention trans-focused moving images have garnered from feminist film theorists or genre specialists. To date, only one monograph has been published dedicated to *Transgender on Screen* (Phillips 2006), and this from within a mainly psychoanalytic and postmodern framework. Reviewed in *Screen* with the conclusion that it "offers such negative representations, a lack of complexity of thinking and a poor understanding of trans subjectivities," its singular presence makes the paucity of scholarly work that much more evident (Stewart 2008: 114).

In this chapter I find it imperative to begin by charting the possibilities for recovering films and cinematic concepts that speak of trans before it reached today's horizon of intelligibility, largely under the banner of transgender. Namely, in the silent era of film, "transformation" and "cross-dressing" on-screen emerged when sexological accounts were first debating the terminology and diagnostic criteria for transvestism and transsexualism. Laura Horak (2016) challenges us to rethink cross-dressing in transitional cinema through earlier respectable cultural forms in which cross-dressing did not carry the stigma of deviance it has today. I offer that Laura Mulvey's (1981) under-utilized concept of "trans-sex identification" for female spectatorship is an important (mis)recognition of transgender phenomena. Judith (Jack) Halberstam's (2005) development of "the transgender look" for films that challenge the binary ordering of gender and sexuality in order to affirm a trans identity and trans as desirable follows as a more recent intervention.

Thereafter the chapter will survey the field of research explicitly conducted on trans cinema in order to demonstrate the many in-roads that have been made into conceptualizing trans as different from, though overlapping with, queer and third cinemas. The "New Trans Cinema" and "Trans New Wave" all build on feminist, postcolonial, and queer film criticism to assert significant groupings of films, contemporary directors, and types of spectatorship. These explicitly canonizing gestures reclaim territory for trans cinema; they constructively move on from critiquing the inadequate stereotyping of trans characters largely written by, directed by, and played by cisgender (non-transgender) people.

Throughout, I signal the future of trans for cinema studies by highlighting how trans film has interacted with other kinds of cinemas. The analytical lens of trans offers complex understandings of gender that will enrich theorizing characters and narratives on-screen, as well as the aesthetic and affective experience of viewers. I am guided by Helen Hok-Sze Leung's short keyword entry on "Film" (2014) included in *TSQ: Transgender Studies Quarterly*'s first issue, which summarizes the important dimensions to consider when researching trans cinema. Does trans film feature self-identified trans characters, or ones that a viewer might recognize as trans; should it be made by or starring trans people regardless of content; must it be meant for a trans audience, have a trans aesthetic, or be open to trans interpretations (2014: 86)? She notes that "when and why a film is talked about as a 'trans film' tells us a lot about the current state of representational politics and community reception as well as trends and directions in film criticism" (ibid.). The presence of this chapter titled "Towards trans cinema" in a book dedicated to cinema and gender itself suggests within cinema studies a newfound inclusion of gender variance that is not subsumed under sexuality or deviance. As we move towards a greater understanding of all that the moniker trans cinema can teach us, let us begin by looking at its early incarnations.

Silent, but not unseen: trans cinema before the "talkies"

Cinema exploits our tried and true fascination with the human body's potential to transform. From the beginning of motion pictures, the cinematographic "fantastic views" of Méliès at the turn of the twentieth century feature the use of a stop-substitution trick shot to change a man into a woman. In early American silent film culture, Laura Horak (2016) details the evolution of cross-dressing women appearing in a range of genres, set in contrast to the low-brow comedic styling of cross-dressed men. At the heart of cinema's birth and experimental development of form are trans cinema aesthetics and preoccupations. Whether refurbishing the before and after photograph into an instantaneous substitution, or rendering theatrical cross-dressing acts into the pleasures of a sustained "illusion," the sensibility of trans-ness underpins the cinematic. Though these representations are more closely aligned with curiosity for the body's mutability than trans persons that we might recognize today, they do demonstrate the longitudinal resilience of gender nonconformity and its celebration on-screen.

Playing the impresario in most all of his films, Méliès swapped a magic wand for scissors. "Méliès was one of the first to think of the cinema in terms of cuts!" exclaims Gaudreault, who points to the often overlooked stigmata of the numerous cuts found through all of Méliès' films, hidden in the upper corner where the glue sutures together two distinct successive moments that comprise the trick effect (1987: 118). Even closer to the surgical slice and splice creative thinking, though, was how, along with developing his achievements in editing, Méliès developed a penchant for demonstrating an instant sex-change on film. Both the fast cut and gender transformation are birthed in the origin story of his "discovery" of the stop-camera technique. It occurred one day through a happy accident when he was filming at the Place de l'Opéra around October–November 1896, less than a half year after he began filmmaking. He claims that,

> the camera I used in the early days (a primitive thing in which the film tore or frequently caught and refused to advance) jammed and produced an unexpected result; a minute was needed to disengage the film and to make the camera work again. During this minute, the passers-by, a horse trolley and other vehicles had, of course, changed positions. In projecting the strip, rejoined [*ressoudée*: glued back together] at the point of the break, I suddenly saw a Madeleine-Bastille horse trolley change into a hearse and men become women.
>
> (*Méliès and Liebman 1984 [1929]: 30; additional translation from*
> *Gaudreault 2007: 171*)

While Gaudreault analyzes this excerpt to show Méliès rightly belongs to the history of editing, the quick change of men becoming women was perhaps more than just a lucky metamorphosis; it precipitated in cinematic aesthetics the avant-garde of surgical and hormonal science of sex transformation by at least a decade.

This first substitution or stop-camera trick, Méliès says, sent him into a frenzy of experimentation: "Two days later, I produced the first metamorphoses of men into women and the first sudden disappearances. ... one trick led to another" (1984: 30). Méliès was able to produce more than 500 films in the years 1896–1913. Wanda Strauven assesses that in his intact oeuvre of around 170 films at least a dozen focus on the transformation of a man into a woman, or a woman into a man, and sometimes with multiple changes (2014: 295). For example, in *L'Illusionniste fin de siècle* (*A Turn of the Century Illusionist*, 1899), Méliès jumps from a table and becomes his corseted assistant, who gets on the table and in turn transforms back into Méliès as she jumps to the floor.

Many more films employ examples of cross-gender dressing that flirt with the taboos instituted by then recent dress reform laws that prohibited one from appearing "in a dress not belonging to his or her sex" (Stryker 2008: 31–2). Audiences of *La Tentation de saint Antoine* (*The Temptation of Saint Anthony*, 1898), though, could safely witness the scandal of a crucified Christ transforming into a scantily clad woman or, in *Nouvelles luttes extravagantes* (*The Fat and the Lean Wrestling Match*, 1900), watch two women in fine dress suddenly become two burly boxers. Strauven contends that these *chirurgie filmique* (filmic surgery) scenes follow the logic of smoke and mirror transformation magic, but also science fiction (2014: 296). Indeed, Méliès appears often as the stock character of the mad scientist, most famously in *Le Voyage dans la Lune* (*A Trip to the Moon*, 1902), signifying the excitement and dis-ease many felt with scientific progress.

Laura Horak's study of early American moving pictures shows, through archival research, that since approximately 1908 cross-dressed women were a regular presence "in everything from 'temporary transvestite' comedies, to thrillers, melodramas, and sentimental children's stories" (2016: 1). Her monograph *Girls Will Be Boys: Cross-Dressed Women, Lesbians, and American Cinema, 1908–1934* counters the assumption that since dressing in the clothes of the opposite gender was illegal in many places in the US, female masculinity was stigmatized and taboo. While much on-screen male-to-female cross-dressing occurred in "low" comedy, the representation of women in suits, cowboy outfits, and the like were established modes of genteel cultural forms, such as theater, opera, and literature, and of cinema's cultural cousins of vaudeville and music hall. Hence, the cultural interaction between these media and institutions was more selective and strategic: positively valued cross-dressed female types, namely young, white, and attractive, were appropriated to "uplift" the film industry.

In addition to addressing audiences with familiar types, Horak contends that different generic tricks were developed to exploit "gender surprise" moments, incorporating reports of gender masqueraders and the mythologies of the American West in which physically fit white American women interact with rugged landscapes (2016: 2–4). The examples of "standard sex farce" between 1908 and 1919 predate the widespread sexological culture in which mannishness was read as lesbian, or even as transsexual. Therefore, once these ideas took hold around 1920, cross-dressing women in pictures was rarely a lighthearted "switch," such as that seen in *A Florida Enchantment* (Vitagraph, 1914), and instead came to demonstrate a serious attempt at European sophistication by referencing deviant sexual identities. The transition to cinema as a proper media institution that ushered in the "Golden Age" of Hollywood relied on silent screen stars like Edith Storey, Vivian Martin, and Betty Hart taking great pride and pleasure in cross-dressed acts, a pleasure which has now been silenced in cinema's cultural memory.

The seemingly trans affirmative roles, however, have little in common with today's largely normalized route of physical transition involving hormones and surgeries to alleviate the experience of gender dysphoria. Nevertheless, cinema and visual culture more broadly, seem to have paved the way for larger conceptual shifts with regard to interpreting sexual indeterminacy. The early cinematographic play with transformation and transvestism indicates that long before Christine Jorgenson attained her highly mediatized international celebrity for having a "sex-change" in the early 1950s, the visual field was peppered with sex-change type narratives as well as morphing imagery.

Trans-sex identification and the transgender look

Filmic editing enables actual body morphing and cross-dressing externally on-screen, but feminist spectatorship theory has also argued that psychic identification renders an internal transformation through visual and affective alignment (see also Silverman 1996). Written into the foundational texts of feminist film criticism addressing the Golden Age of American cinema is the problem of on-screen cross-identified characters as well as off-screen cross-sex identifications experienced by female-assigned spectators often framed as a scene of "masquerade" (see also Doane 1982). In a surprisingly direct way Laura Mulvey's essay "Afterthoughts on 'Visual Pleasure and Narrative Cinema' Inspired by King Vidor's *Duel in the Sun* (1946)" (1981), considers the female spectator as a psychically cross-dressing woman. She seems unaware, though, of borrowing one of the earliest descriptions of transgenderism from Magnus Hirschfeld's 1910 book *The Transvestites*, where he suggests the desire to live and be perceived as another sex is akin to psychic transvestism. Though her psychoanalysis is rooted in a fixed sex identity and misunderstands transvestism, it has the potential to offer a trans affirmative understanding of trans-sex identification in which sex is an unsettled marker. After examining the implications of this strain of feminist theorizing, I discuss how Halberstam's reading of "the transgender look" in the film *Boys Don't Cry* (1999) is key to dismantling the inevitability and dominance of the male/female and hetero/homo binary in narrative cinema theories.

In her groundbreaking "Visual Pleasure" essay, Mulvey starts from the fascination we all have with narrative moving pictures, and how our cinematic experience is reinforced by pre-existing patterns of fascination at work within the individual psyche and the social formations that have molded the masculine ideal subject. The mirror stage establishes a pleasurable looking mechanism, even if based on misrecognition, whereas the castration complex dredges up anxiety around sexual difference in the male. Mulvey concludes, "Hence the look, pleasurable in form, can be threatening in content" (1975: 19). The same type of voyeuristic pleasure in looking is very complicated for women, but her description of the "trans-sex identification" solution in the "Afterthoughts" essay (1981) is less uncommon, she claims, than one might think.

When watching a certain genre of Hollywood narrative films, the female spectator can either identify with the male gaze or, with the object of the gaze, namely the woman being looked at. Mulvey argues that women oscillate back and forth between identification with the man (active role) and identification with the woman as object (passive role). From a classical psychoanalytic point of view, a woman's "male identification" is a fact for young girls, which Freud terms a "regressive" phallic phase for the girl/woman who identifies with her father and makes her mother a love object. A woman's identification with masculinity is something temporary, something that the girl must get over on her way to fulfilling her "real" role as a heterosexual woman. Mulvey suggests that cinema is full of examples in which female characters may temporarily forgo becoming a wife and mother, enjoying instead a career, childlessness, and overt masculine or tomboy identifications. Usually these women, potentially coded as lesbian or even transgender men, have until the end of the movie to accept their normative role—often because they become overcome with true heterosexual love. This ending gives closure to the subject who is finally inserted into the symbolic order, giving the viewer the feeling that "order has been restored."

In discussing *Duel in the Sun*'s rebellious woman character, Pearl, Mulvey finds evidence of her ambivalence towards being a real woman: on the one hand she wants to adapt to the symbolic order through a heterosexual union, but on the other hand, she also feels attracted to enacting masculine behavior like riding and fighting. In turn, Pearl offers an ambivalent pleasure to female spectators: the fantasy of a "male life," which ultimately becomes "defused" into conventional gender roles. Mulvey describes films that revolve around the desire for masculine pleasures, action, and agency as a questionable viewing pleasure at best for women. Why? Apparently their split pleasures risk destabilizing sexual difference.

Of this pleasure in relating to the hero and his control over the diegetic world, Mulvey suggests the female spectator must secretly enjoy it; acknowledging this pleasure would interrupt its "spell of fascination" (1981: 29). The sense of being caught in the act amounts to a paralyzing shame felt on the occasion of gender non-conforming or male cross-identification. In her elaboration of Freudian theories of pre-oedipal active femininity for the spectator, Mulvey can only see a conflict ensuing from this "trans-sex identification," a restless shifting around in "borrowed transvestite clothes" (ibid. 33) that merely suspends the facticity of sexual difference. Mulvey's problematic assumption here is that the Imaginary is already overwritten by the Symbolic, foreclosing trans identification and queer desire experienced on-screen and off. Though the films themselves are highly restrictive in how one can access viewing pleasure, the presumption of a spectator's shame at adopting a queer or trans position in the film text can no longer hold. Why not make that masculinity your own, and properly account for female masculinity that is not a "failed" version of straight femininity?

Halberstam's analysis of slasher flicks in *Skin Shows: Gothic Horror and the Technology of Monsters* (1995), of reception and butch stereotyping in *Female Masculinity* (1998), and of various "transgender looks" in *In a Queer Time and Place* (2005), seeks to repair the assumption in much feminist film theory of a heterosexual, feminine and non-transgender female spectator. Following the groundbreaking work of Chris Straayer in *Deviant Eyes, Deviant Bodies* (1996) on how "temporary transvestite" films uphold normative sexual systems, Halberstam (2005) interrogates what happens in films when the trans narrative is not temporary. Often films typecast transgender characters but avoid the transgender gaze, that is, a way of looking within the film that sees a trans man or trans woman as they see themselves with enduring gender identities, even when a "reveal" (Seid 2014: 176) occurs that shows a differently sexed body. Halberstam directs us to examine how adjustments to the classic Hollywood technique of the shot/reverse shot—which establishes relations within the film and sutures spectators into position—becomes key to the dismantling of sex/gender stability within the cinematic grammar of a film (2005: 86).

Taking the Oscar winning feature *Boys Don't Cry* (1999) by Kimberley Pierce as an example of the "transgender look," Halberstam examines how it constructs a legitimate and durable gender by forcing spectators to adopt, if only provisionally, Brandon's gaze. Based on the true-life story of Brandon Teena, a young female-bodied person living in Nebraska as a man and dating Lana, the film's love scenes are crucial to maintaining Brandon's gender identity. During the film (and his life), Brandon is forcibly stripped, raped, and killed, cinematically comprising a series of increasingly horrific reveals. Halberstam analyzes how the sex scenes shot from Lana's point of view return during these other visual interrogations to override what the violators "see." Additionally, Brandon holds onto this alternate vision of his body/identity and appears as a clothed double, returning a confirming gaze to his stripped, split self. Halberstam concludes,

> Not only does *Boys Don't Cry* create a position for the transgender subject that is fortified from the traditional operations of the gaze and conventional modes of gendering but it also makes the transgender subject dependent on the recognition of a woman.
>
> (2005: 89)

This development within feminist film theory "opens the door to a nonfetishistic mode of seeing the transgender body—a mode that looks with, rather than at, the transgender body" (ibid. 92). Individual films nonetheless must take up the challenge of this new kind of portrayal.

Trans cinema: queer film's evil twin?

While feminist film theory raises the question of a trans character and viewing positions, queer film criticism historically has foregrounded the analysis of a transsexual person's portrayal in terms of sexual subversion. Leung (2014) explains the sibling rivalry between trans and queer cinema criticism resonates with Stryker's description of trans studies being the "evil twin" to queer theory (2004: 212). "Films that feature gender variance have always had a significant place in queer cinema," she writes, "but considerations of trans issues have tended to be subsumed under the focus on sexuality" (2014: 86). I submit that the nomination of a New Queer Cinema (NQC), by B. Ruby Rich (1992) and others, has worked to partially hide and partially build on the success of an independent trans cinema. Like queer cinema, which responded to the AIDS crisis and flourished with the advent of more accessible film production technologies, an increasing number of trans-created audio-visual works appeared in the mid-1980s and 1990s. First editions of transgender film festivals in Montreal (1997) and London (1999) sought to showcase the urgent and higher quality film and video works that developed out of this period. Though perhaps trans cinema gained wider attention later than films labeled queer, film scholars should be pressed to excavate trans films from under queer analysis. This involves de-subjugating trans forms of knowledge, and evaluating a film according to its place in the genealogy of trans cultural production.

Akkadia Ford (2015) has suggested the term "transliteracy" could be used to refer to literacy across media platforms, and to literacy of gender diverse lives represented in cinema. To produce new readings it is necessary that scholars invest in familiarizing themselves with transgender studies tenets such as, "considering the embodied experience of the [trans] speaking subject" to be an essential component to the political dynamics of the situation being analyzed (Stryker 2006: 12). By centering the trans speaking subject in films, we can ask about how they are given presence through voice and body (Heath 1981), what kind of agency they are allowed within the plot, and whether they have their own narrative arc. Trans cinema studies can also learn from the film criticism that developed around the NQC to assess the historical specificity of attitudes towards gender and sexuality expressed in filmic form.

B. Ruby Rich's assessment that "1992 has been a watershed year for independent gay and lesbian film and video" (2013 [1992]: 16) places the NQC into a moment of great momentum. NQC was hardly a coherent set of aesthetic strategies seen across films released in 1990–3; Rich described the films as "irreverent, energetic, alternately minimalist and excessive ... they're full of pleasure" (ibid. 18). Rather, Michele Aaron (2004) offers that it was defined by an attitude of *defiance* demonstrated towards history, death, formal conventions, and towards compulsory heterosexual culture or homonormativity.

This brings me to consider why in 1992 something *queer* was seen not just flickering on the horizon, but pulsating orange and hot. Why was it not also the year for popular yet radical *trans* film and video? For example, Judith Butler's *Gender Trouble* (1990) referred to Jenny Livingston's film *Paris is Burning* (1990), producing one of the first theorizations of transgender experience as *gender nonconformity*, rather than as a kind of sexual deviance. It set trans apart from lesbian, gay, and bisexual politics about sexual practices, and more into relation with butch–femme theories about practices of gender presentation and perception. Created during the AIDS crisis, *Paris* displays an artistic urgency to create, to document, and to cherish while also allowing for complex and cogent trans protagonists (of color!) to take up space on screen (even if framed by an exploitative white lesbian gaze, as accused, cf. bell hooks 1992).

Yet, *Paris* is not typically included in lists of the major NQC films; even the broadest overviews are clearly marked by gay and lesbian preoccupations. What would the story of NQC look like if instead of *Basic Instinct* (Paul Verhoeven), being an example of a key filmic text released in 1992, we looked at *The Crying Game's* (Neil Jordan) cultural trajectory, in which transgender figures are associated with dangerous illusion, and revolting abjection? Given Michele Aaron's claim in the introduction to the NQC reader that in the early 1990s "the queer figure *par excellence* was the transsexual" (2004: 6), one has to wonder whether the trans characters on screen were (mis)recognized as only queer. It did not help that behind the camera there was a persistent lack of (openly) trans directors representing their own perspectives.

Where the 1990s could have seen an under-siege and partially destroyed community coming together, instead we ended up with an LGB that added a fake T, to use a phrase from Dean Spade (2004: 53). The marginalization and evacuation of lived trans experience in the context of activism and cultural production was occurring no less in the film culture and festival circuit than in community spaces, as well as in the academy (see also Prosser 1998, Namaste 2000). Unsurprisingly, reductions of "trans" to liminality or betweenness is a renewable queer trope for subversion, returning in popular, and even so-called radical, films as a plot device. For example, implied trans women are represented as psychotic (*The Silence of the Lambs* [Jonathan Demme, 1991]), murdered (*Dressed to Kill* [Brian De Palma, 1980]), or prostitutes (*Dallas Buyers Club*, Jean-Marc Vallée, 2013), whereas transmen often appear as confused lesbians or as traumatized by their feminine bodies (e.g. *Salmonberries* [Percy Adlon, 1991]; Yitzhak in *Hedwig and the Angry Inch* [John Cameron Mitchell, 2001]).

Joelle Ruby Ryan's dissertation *Reel Gender: Examining the Politics of Trans Images in Film and Media* (2009) catalogs the most prevalent trans stereotypes in film and television, particularly from 1980–2005, during the heyday of queer filmmaking. She contends that the "transgender monster" is often depicted in B-movies and horror films as a dangerous perpetrator to cement fear of gender-transgressive others, who in reality are themselves frequently murdered in hate crimes. Though friendlier, the "transgender mammy" appears to exist in order to fix the problems of gender normative people, thus becoming reduced to an outwardly fabulous yet servile subjectivity. Most common in mainstream films and television, however, is the "transgender deceiver," who is not trans but someone who passes as another gender in order to (selfishly) obtain someone or something they want. All these stereotypes circulate within mass media across platforms and genres, from news reports of murders, to the reception of reality television like *I Am Cait* (2015–), to independent cinemas like *Ticked Off Trannies with Knives* (Israel Luna 2010) and the *Gendercator* (Catherine Crouch 2007), and mainstream films like *Predestination* (Michael and Peter Spierig 2014). In the following and final section therefore, I will discuss the revolutionary cinema that defies these stereotyping plotlines.

Contemporary sex, love, and alliances: Trans New Wave

Tristan Taormino's *Village Voice* article "The New Wave of Trans Cinema" (2008) refers to films by trans directors featuring trans-identified actors that are breaking boundaries in the pornographic genre. More broadly, Trans New Wave offers new visions of sex, love, and intimate alliances. Both Nicole Richter's coinage of "New Trans Cinema" (2013) and Ford's "Trans New Wave" (2015) stress the portrayal of fictional love relationships and non-fictional graphic sex in films that tell different kinds of stories. Operating outside the studio system, with a low budget and without recognition by major award-granting bodies, these films receive far less attention than titles such as *The Danish Girl* (Tom Hooper 2015), or the Amazon series *Transparent* (2014–). Ryan's research (2009) charts the emergence of a revolutionary figure, especially in a new wave of trans documentaries, such as *Toilet Training: Law and Order (In the Bathroom)* (Tara Mateik and the Sylvia Rivera Law Project, 2003) and *Screaming Queens: The Riot at Compton's Cafeteria* (Susan Stryker, Victor Silverman, 2005), whereas Wibke Straube's dissertation (2014) stresses the "utopian" potential of mainstream fictional trans films like *Breakfast on Pluto* (Neil Jordan, 2005) in that they offer "exit scapes" from normative culture for the trans character and spectator alike.

In terms of a new wave, four films released between 2011 and 2013 strike me as important diagnostic texts of our trans age in cinema. Jules Rosskam's *Thick Relations* (2012) and Negar Azarbayjani's *Aynehaye Rooberoo* (*Facing Mirrors*, 2011) both take the question of being in alliance with others as their starting point. Through narrative strategies, the characters are shown to activate a deep and moving affective identification across identities. In *Facing*

Mirrors, a young Iranian trans man fleeing home to avoid an arranged marriage ends up in the taxi of a young mother who is driving to pay off her husband's debt. They harbor each other's secrets, though companionship is far from simple given their difference in class, religious belief, and gender identity. Eventually, they come to see each other's hardship as equally unjust. The cast and director do not come out of queer or trans communities, but successfully set trans issues against the backdrop of tensions around Iranian social norms. We become privy to how compassionate alliances can be forged between what might appear to be incompatible identities.

Thick Relations is so much a creature of Chicago's thriving queer and trans scene that Rosskam classifies it as part documentary. The script was written during workshops with participating friends/actors, who were invited to create characters that were their ideal selves, however contradictory or difficult. The blending of these "real characters" into a narrative results in a vaguely coordinated plot of romantic tropes, daily life, and chosen family. The flow of the film takes place across a non-normative logic of kinship in which central characters express love to various relations, with all the ensuing beautiful confusion of who is together with whom and in what gender configurations. The thickness comes from having sex, certainly, but also from singing together, swimming, drinking, talking, eating— in short, from time spent sharing affection.

The other films also rethink the documentary form by employing a mixture of visual styles in order to track the self as it is creatively invented. Both *Like Rats Leaving a Sinking Ship* (Vika Kirchenbauer, 2012) and *Pojktanten* (*She Male Snails*, Ester Martin Bergsmark, 2012) are filmic texts that seek to do justice to one's own perception of being trans without employing the typical format of documentary confessing. *Like Rats* takes aim at the culture of transparency through garnering opacity, a concept Vika borrows from the postcolonial theorist Édouard Glissant, who writes against the colonialist's desire for intelligibility and purity. The film offers a contrary visual style to appearing transparent to the state, law, and psychiatry. *Like Rats* makes a plea for gender opacity by layering grainy super-8 images with imaginary family films. These images are overlaid with audio of Vika reading psychiatric assessments of her "incurably transsexual" condition and memories captured in possibly fictitious journal entries. Where Vika's transgender embodiment emerges at the intersections of social, familial, and psychic fantasy, *She Male Snails* posits imaginary conversations between two main characters silently sitting in a bathtub shaving and caressing each other. The other main images come from flashbacks of an unidentified youth and a snail's eye view of the woods held together by the implied filmmaker's voiceover narration. The documentation of transfeminine artist Eli Leven is associational; it departs from a clear narrative to try to do justice to Eli's dreamy inner world, and uncertain feeling of being in the outer world.

When taken together, these films translate traits from NQC into trans cinematic grammars. Firstly, they demonstrate an attitude of defiance towards formal conventions of genre, building on a long tradition of queer cinema that challenges the distinction between fiction and non-fiction, or the documentation of life from creative intervention into life itself. Given the importance of biographical narrative and life documentation to the regulation of trans life, however, these films seem less interested in subversive acts of defiance than in a restructuring of intimacy and political alliance.

In the coming years it will be exciting to see how filmmakers such as Silas Howard grow into larger creative roles, since he is the first openly trans man to direct a television series (*Transparent*, season 2, 2015, and season 3, 2016). Since transitioning and publicly declaring her identity as a trans woman, Lana Wachowski's enormous power as a Hollywood director, along with her along with her creative co-director and recently transitioned sister Lilly, is the focus of Cael Keegan's forthcoming book *The Wachowski's: Imaging Transgender* (expected 2017). Keegan aims to develop a theory of trans cinematic aesthetics tracing especially the advent of transgender politics through the evolution of digital cinema. Since Méliès' first edited sequences of substitution to CGI today, innovations in cinematic aesthetics converge with evolving gender concepts.

Stars in our eyes: trans by any other name

This chapter has sought to bring trans cinema into conversation with early film history, feminist film theory, queer film criticism, and American and transnational film cultures, and to point to the influential presence of trans auteurs. Far more research could be conducted on the many inflections of trans across cultures as well as the various fan communities and subcultures that cross-pollinate with gender diverse communities. For example, on the relation of punk culture to trans image-making, film and video artists such as Hans Scheirl (Steinbock 2013) and Vaginal Creme Davis have had an incredible influence on music, fine art, and performance. Even within more mainstream film cultures, historical scholarship might consider the singularity of early trans directors, like Ed Wood Jr., the self-identified transvestite who made the delirious "Glen or Glenda" (1953) in a period of post-war conservatism. Recently, Stryker has presented widely on her in-process experimental documentary *Christine in the Cutting Room* that re-defines Christine Jorgensen as a filmmaker in the atomic age, an "image-maker" professionally and personally. Finally, the writings of Leung (2006, 2009, 2014) acknowledge many hit films featuring trans protagonists out of Thailand (*Beautiful Boxer* [Ekachai Uekrongtham, 2004]), Japan (*Funeral Parade of Roses* [Toshio Matsumoto, 1969]), and Hong Kong (*Portland Street Blues* [Raymond Yip, 1998]), demonstrating that Asian cultural productions deserve more than a comparison with Western cinemas—instead, they should be considered as innovating their own traditions of transformative practices.

Much like queer was quick to become a captured radical impulse converted into a capitalistic niche market, trans focused film and television often finds itself shunted into a pretty package or a gory spectacle. The trans narrative of becoming yourself, of being true and authentic, is easily co-opted into neo-liberal fantasies of individualism and choice. The commercialization and whitewashing of trans stories erase trans struggles for justice. Self-determination only takes place in the face of, and despite medicalization, sexualization, and continued social stigma. In thinking towards a trans cinema, the best practices of film-making would offer alternatives to overproduced films like *Stonewall* (Roland Emmerich, 2015), which flopped and was critically dismissed for ignoring its historical trans of color protagonists. In comparison, there is a groundswell of excitement around *Happy Birthday, Marsha!* (forthcoming 2016) that foregrounds Marsha P. Johnson and her trans sisters of color in 1960s–70s New York as the true revolutionaries of the Stonewall rebellion. The dreamy, utopian, and fully political vision of Reina Gossett and Sasha Wortzel's film suggests that trans cinema has the potential to challenge more than gender in its form and content.

Related topics

Maureen Turim, "Experimental women filmmakers"
Belinda Smaill, "The documentary: female subjectivity and the problem of realism"
Amy Borden, "Queer or LGBTQ+: on the question of inclusivity in queer cinema studies"
Debra Zimmerman, "Film as activism and transformative praxis: Women Make Movies"

Bibliography

Aaron, M. Ed. 2004. *New Queer Cinema: A Critical Reader*. New Brunswick: Rutgers University Press.

Doane, M. 1982. "Film and the Masquerade," *Screen* 23.3–4: 74–87.

Ford, A. 2015. "Transliteracy and the New Wave of Gender-Diverse Cinema," *Fusion Journal* 5: n/p. Online at: www.fusion-journal.com/issue/005-fusion-changing-patterns-and-critical-dialogues-new-uses-of-literacy/transliteracy-and-the-new-wave-of-gender-diverse-cinema/ Accessed on December 16, 2015.

Gaudreault, A. 1987. "Theatricality, Narrativity, and Trickality: Reevaluating the Cinema of Georges Méliès," *Journal of Popular Film and Television* 15.3: 111–19.

——— 2007. "Méliès the Magician," *Early Popular Visual Culture* 5.2: 167–74.

Halberstam, J. 1995. *Skin Shows: Gothic Horror and the Technology of Monsters*. Durham, NC: Duke University Press.

——— 1998. *Female Masculinity*. Durham, NC: Duke University Press.

——— 2005. *In a Queer Time and Place: Transgender Bodies, Subcultural Lives*. New York: New York University Press.

Heath, S. 1981. *Questions of Cinema*. Bloomington: Indiana University Press.

Hirschfeld, M. 1910. *The Transvestites: The Erotic Drive to Cross Dress*. Trans. Michael A. Lombardi-Nash (1991). Amherst, NY: Prometheus Books.

hooks, b. 1992. *Black Looks: Race and Representation*. Brooklyn: South End Press.

Horak, L. 2016. *Girls Will Be Boys: Cross-Dressed Women, Lesbians, and American Cinema, 1908–1934*. New Brunswick: Rutgers University Press.

Keegan, C. forthcoming, expected 2017. *Andy and Lana Wachowski: Imaging Transgender*. Champaign: University of Illinois Press.

Leung, H. Hok-S. 2006. "Unsung Heroes: Reading Transgender Subjectivities in Hong Kong Action Cinema," *The Transgender Studies Reader*. pp. 685–97. Eds. Stephen Whittle and Susan Stryker. New York: Routledge.

——— 2009. *Undercurrents: Queer Culture and Postcolonial Hong Kong*. Vancouver: University of British Columbia Press.

——— 2014. "Film," *TSQ: Transgender Studies Quarterly* 1.1–2: 86–8.

Méliès, G. 1984 [1929]. "Cinematographic Views," Trans. Stuart Liebman. *October* 29 (Summer): 23–31.

Mulvey, L. 1975. "Visual Pleasure and Narrative Cinema," *Screen*, 16(3), 6–18.

——— 1990 [1981]. "Afterthoughts on 'Visual Pleasure and Narrative Cinema' inspired by King Vidor's *Duel in the Sun* (1946)," *Psychoanalysis and Cinema*. pp. 29–38. Ed. E. Ann Kaplan. New York: Routledge.

Namaste, V. 2000. *Invisible Lives: The Erasure of Transsexual and Transgendered People*. Chicago: University of Chicago Press.

Phillips, J. 2006. *Transgender on Screen*. Basingstoke and New York: Palgrave Macmillan.

Prosser, J. 1998. *Second Skins: The Body Narratives of Transsexuality*. New York: Columbia University Press.

Rich, B. R. 2013 [1992]. "The New Queer Cinema: Director's Cut," *New Queer Cinema: The Director's Cut*. pp. 16–32. B. Ruby Rich. Durham, NC: Duke University Press.

Richter, N. 2013. "Trans Love in New Trans Cinema," *Queer Love in Film and Television*. pp. 161–7. Eds. P. Demory and C. Pullen. New York: Palgrave Macmillan.

Ryan, J. R. 2009. *Reel Gender: Examining the Politics of Trans Images in Film and Media*. Unpublished dissertation. Bowling Green State University, Ohio.

Seid, D. M. 2014. "Reveal," *TSQ: Transgender Studies Quarterly* 1.1–2: 176–8.

Silverman, K. 1996. *The Threshold of the Visible World*. New York: Routledge.

Spade, D. 2004. "Fighting to Win," *That's Revolting! Queer Strategies for Resisting Assimilation*. Ed. Mattilda Bernstein Sycamore. Berkeley, CA: Soft Skull. 47–53

Steinbock, E. 2011. *Shimmering Images: On Transgender Embodiment and Cinematic Aesthetics*. Dissertation published by the University of Amsterdam.

────── 2013. "Groping Theory: Haptic Cinema and Trans-Curiosity in Hans Scheirl's *Dandy Dust*," *The Transgender Studies Reader 2*. pp. 101–18. Eds. S. Stryker and A. Aizura. New York: Routledge.

Stewart, J. 2008. "Review: *Transgender on Screen* by John Phillips," *Screen* 49.1 (Spring): 110–14.

Straayer, C. 1996. *Deviant Eyes, Deviant Bodies: Sexual Re-orientation in Film and Video*. New York: Columbia University Press.

Straube, W. 2014. *Trans Cinema and Its Exit Scapes: A Transfeminist Reading of Utopian Sensibility and Gender Dissidence in Contemporary Film*. Unpublished Dissertation. Linköping University.

Strauven, W. 2014. "Pour une lecture média-archéologique de l'œuvre de Georges Méliès," *Méliès, Carrefour des attractions*. pp. 1–10. Ed. André Gaudreault, Laurent Le Forestier and Stéphane Tralongo. Rennes, France: Presses universitaires de Rennes.

Stryker, S. 2004. "Transgender Theory: Queer Theory's Evil Twin," *GLQ: A Journal of Lesbian and Gay Studies*, 10: 212–15.

────── 2006. "(De)subjugated Knowledges: An Introduction to Transgender Studies," *The Transgender Studies Reader*. pp. 1–17. Eds. Stephen Whittle and Susan Stryker. New York: Routledge.

────── 2008. *Transgender History*. Berkeley, CA: Seal Press.

────── dir. *Christine in the Cutting Room*. (work-in-process).

Taormino, T. (2008) "The New Wave of Trans Cinema: The Latest Transporn Breaks Down Both Boundaries and Inhibitions," *Village Voice* : Posted April 8, 2008. Last Accessed January 5, 2016: www.villagevoice.com/news/the-new-wave-of-trans-cinema-6389366.

38

VISUALIZING CLIMATE TRAUMA

The cultural work of films anticipating the future

E. Ann Kaplan

This chapter addresses cinema's role in negotiating the catastrophe of climate change to come—a catastrophe we ignore at our peril. My essay focuses on climate dilemmas facing humans as a species as they are imaged on film. Central is attention to the psychological impact of pending climate disaster that is rarely dealt with; the cultural work such film fantasies perform with regard to gender and race will also be a main focus, along with the politics of climate change more generally.

While this research may be linked to the rapidly expanding field of ecocinema in media studies, what "ecocinema" really means is as yet unclear (see Alexa Weik von Mossner's essay in this volume for definitions). This may not be surprising, given that debates continue regarding literary ecocriticism research. If ecofeminists (such as Susan Griffin 1978 and Carolyn Merchant 1995) initiated much of the environmental interest in the 1970s, that work got little attention until male critics, like Lawrence Buell (1995, 2001) and Greg Garrard (2004), took up the cudgel. But Cheryll Glotfelty's co-edited 1996 anthology, *Ecocriticism Reader: Landmarks in Literary Ecology*, marked a moment when the disparate aspects of the field began to come together. This, in turn, spurred media scholars to think about ecology and cinema. Taking the environment as a new lens through which to look at cinema (very much as feminists used the lens of gender to open up new ways of seeing), an astounding array of books, many of them anthologies, has appeared in the last five years. Martin Lefebvre's 2006 volume, *Landscape and Film* was ahead of its time as a monograph, followed by Ursula Heise's *Sense of Place and Sense of Planet* (2008) but neither got much attention from film scholars at the time. It is interesting that more recent books are largely anthologies (not monographs) reflecting a wide range of disciplines and methodologies, as well as vastly differing theoretical frameworks (see, for example, edited collections by Tommy Gustafsson and Pietari Kääpä 2013, by Rust, Monani, and Cubitt 2013, Anil Narine 2014, and Alexa Weik von Mossner 2014). All lay claim to studying some version of ecological or environmental media research.

My work has a specific and narrower focus than much of the research in these anthologies. Whereas many scholars have focused on animals in film, or on wildlife films; studied the cultural history of cinema underwater; discussed environments in film including urban spaces; and many other topics, I am concerned with how cinema negotiates climate change as a special dire circumstance (implicitly) caused by humans. I develop the concept of pretrauma as a fearful futurist emotion. Inês Crespo and Ângela Pereira (2013) offer a rare article on Hollywood and climate change that at least deals with audience's fear in watching films. And Narine (2014) discusses "eco-trauma," and some aspects of his edited collection overlap with my concerns. However, the issue is not a consistent focus and pretrauma is not mentioned. My focus is on ways nature is being newly constructed as in a state of collapse— one backed up by science—and the pretraumatic impact of collapse on subjects (on both sides of the screen).

Fantasies of collapse proliferated in the wake of 9/11, which ushered in a new era of uncertainty across a range of concerns—from terrorism to immigration to climate change. Selected from a large inventory of futurist disaster cinema, the films in my project reveal the response of international artists to the dramatic ecological changes described by scientists and readily available in the various reports by the International Panel on Climate Change (IPCC), in international science journals, and all over the internet. The 2014 IPPC report was the most negative so far, showing the planet heating up faster than scientists had predicted earlier. While COP 21 (the 21st Conference of Parties to the United Nations Convention on Climate Change) held in Paris in 2015 offered a glimmer of hope, few believe the agreement is anywhere near what is needed. A new 2016 study predicts (a conservative estimate) a resulting sea-level rise of from 1.7 to 3.2 feet by mid-century (Gillis 2016). While we need to understand that such evidence itself relies on modeling from complex, often highly debated, data (as Kathryn Yusoff 2009, for example, has shown), inevitably one has to rely on science as evidence for what humans are facing. Clearly artists making dystopian fantasies, as well as documentaries, respond to predictions.

If Nicholas Mirzoeff, writing in 2014, was right—and I think he was—that issues regarding climate change and the Anthropocene (the era marking human impact on the planet as a geologic force [Paul Crutzen and Eugene Stoermer 2012]) should now be considered as important as gender, race, and class have hitherto been to humanities research, the question arises of how to situate the new category in relation to the other familiar ones. Most recently, in a reverse discourse, Mirzoeff has denounced Anthropocene research as failing to attend to race: much of the current suffering from climate change is a result of colonialism, and now post-colonialism (Mirzoeff 2015). The increasing flow of peoples into the North is caused as much by post-colonial environmental catastrophe (e.g. global US and European corporations polluting nations formerly colonized) as by war. As Dipesh Chakrabarty (2009) pointed out, the danger of conceptualizing humans, on the macro-level, as a species is that, like the term "man" used to signify all of humanity, this tends to occlude the poor, women, racialized peoples, and the invisible minorities who are already bearing the brunt of the first waves of environmental catastrophe. It is just such paradoxes that dystopian imaginaries proliferating since 2011 open up for study.

In these works, filmmakers and novelists create fictional worlds relating both to the end of "the mass utopian dream of a social world in alliance with personal happiness" (Buck-Morss 2002, ix), and to the destructive geological force that humans now constitute on planet Earth (Chakrabarty 2009), both arising from the development of a highly evolved global capitalism. Giorgio Agamben adds to Buck-Morss's analysis by showing how global capitalism has eaten away at the nation-state in ways that belie the optimism some held for a new world order in the decades following the two World Wars. Politics as usual (in the sense of viable debates between socialists and conservatives, especially in regard to climate change) is no longer possible in the current global situation driven by multinational financial markets (Agamben 1998, 2005). A cohort of younger scholars, in the wake of research by Bruno Latour (1993), Jane Bennett (2010), and others argue the need for completely new paradigms: see Timothy Morton (2013), Roy Scranton (2015), McKenzie Wark (2015). In addition, Naomi Klein (2014) has persistently argued that capitalism and catastrophic climate change have gone hand in hand for centuries. In a somewhat hopeful mode, rare in this discourse, she insists that creating a more equal society would serve the ends of saving the planet and justice. Yet in reality governments exploit anticipated dangers regardless of harm being done to many by their policies.

As a result, utopian discourses have given way to dystopian imaginaries on a scale rarely seen in earlier aesthetic periods. Apocalyptic imaginaries about the end of the world continue to emerge and to be given space in media reporting. *Interstellar* (Christopher Nolan, 2014) and *Snowpiercer* (Joon-ho Bong, 2014) are but the latest versions of a world transformed by a climate catastrophe. As Julia Kristeva puts it, "Films remain the supreme art of the apocalypse, no matter what the refinements, because the image has such an ability to 'have us walk into fear'" (1989). Fears and fantasies of climate disasters, in particular, haunt humanity. Evidence, from scientists as well as from our own increasing experiences of flashfloods, droughts, and sea-level rise, makes us anxious.

In trying to understand the complex psychological mechanisms that inhibit humans from coming together to save themselves and the planet, psychic processes not usually a central focus have to be understood. What affects hold people fixed to particular ideological structures, such as climate change denial? To what extent are such affects the result of unconscious fear of a traumatic catastrophe engulfing humanity? If we can understand the psychic processes involved, can we find ways to rupture the ideological structure through helping people understand how such structures entrap them?

I turned to dystopian screen narratives circulating widely in order to investigate these questions, theorizing that films offer a kind of pretraumatic experience for viewers (Kaplan 2015). I believed these scenarios would reveal underlying, perhaps repressed, fears and anxieties which could then be "read," as it were, and tell us something by their impact on viewers. For while scholars are still debating the degree to which trauma can be known or represented, most agree that individual and cultural trauma haunts victims and societies. It manifests itself in actions taken by politicians as well as by ordinary people, often without subjects understanding what is driving their actions. If in classic trauma, subjects "act out" instead of "working through" catastrophes from the past, in pretrauma subjects are haunted by what they fear is coming from the future. And dystopian fantasies offer precisely such visions.

The pretrauma climate genre needs to be addressed in Film Studies, since it deals with our potential future as humans as much as the nuclear disaster genre has in the past and present. Trauma resulting from the deployment of the atomic bomb in World War II (Hiroshima, Nagasaki) arguably produced the spate of powerful 1950s films anticipating nuclear catastrophe worldwide. The effects of radiation were evident in the ghastly suffering of innocent Japanese civilians, images of which circulated widely as time went on. The nuclear disaster sci-fi genre persisted through the 1960s, but as the Cold War has cooled, leaking nuclear power stations have come to haunt global imaginaries, supplanting fears of the bomb itself (see Schwab 2014). Furthermore, nuclear danger is now also linked to fears about improper storing of nuclear waste from power stations (see on this, for example, Michael Madsen's powerful docu-drama, *Into Eternity*, 2010). But while the nuclear genre comes close to what I want to address in this essay (i.e. futurist films about environmental collapse, a genre dealing with climate pretrauma), there is a temporal difference. An atom bomb or nuclear power station meltdown (such as happened in Chernobyl or Fukushima) produces a sudden, immediate devastating catastrophe. Climate trauma, on the contrary, is slow and gradual, as Ramachandra Guha (2000), Rob Nixon (2010), Sandra Steingraber (1997/2010), Elizabeth Kolbert (2014), and many others have amply shown. This temporal difference is significant: Because the violence of climate change is slow, the challenge in attracting public notice and concern is much harder than in the case of nuclear bombs or power station leaks (see Ken Ruthven 1993 for more on this).

The nearness of the new futurist climate disaster genre to the director's time justifies the term *pretrauma*, because the traumatic scenario is one already seemingly possible given scientific projections alluded to above. These films then are not allegories. They insist on the probability of the worlds shown or, to refer to Timothy Morton (2013), the possibility of humanity already experiencing the worlds shown in the films. The obsession with dates, numbers, time, and futurist elements in many titles emphasizes the probability of the trauma's occurrence—it already has a date! Such titles include *28 Days Later* (Danny Boyle, 2002), *2012* (Roland Emmerich, 2009), *The Day After Tomorrow* (Roland Emmerich, 2004), *12 Monkeys* (Terry Gilliam, 1995), and *District 9* (Neill Blomkamp, 2009). Often the date is noted early in the film, as in *Children of Men* (Alfonso Cuarón, 2006) when 2027 is prominently displayed or *Snowpiercer*, when again the date is showcased. Most of these films set in the future start with the world already destroyed, all welfare and political infrastructures gone.

A good example of a pretrauma film is M. Night Shyamalan's *The Happening* (2008). As in so many pretrauma films, the hero is a white male, and he saves not only the white woman and child, but others as well. *The Happening* unsettles viewers as regards the reliability of the environment. The film adopts the trope of a sudden event that changes the world, and starts with nature turning catastrophic. While the characters are traumatized as the event happens in the filmic present, viewers are in the position of witnessing an event that has not yet happened—experiencing, as virtual future humans, a kind of pretrauma or anticipatory anxiety. It is obviously a world to be avoided.

But the film that offers the clearest definition of the condition of pretrauma evident in the genre is Jeff Nichols' 2011 film, *Take Shelter*. *Take Shelter* is the only film whose white male *protagonist* is personally traumatized by something that has not yet happened, and offers this position to viewers. Curtis LaForche apparently suffers from classic symptoms of Post-Traumatic Stress Disorder (violent nightmares, terrifying hallucinations, disturbing flashbacks), but the trick is that the events that trouble him have not yet come about. While Post-Traumatic Stress Disorder is often marked by unheralded intrusions of *past* traumas into one's *present* experience, in pretrauma, something from *the future* interrupts the present. Events that have not yet happened cause trauma symptoms.

In *Take Shelter*, then, although to viewers Curtis may appear to suffer from nightmares or hallucinations caused by a form of paranoid schizophrenia, in fact, at the film's shocking conclusion, viewers realize his symptoms refer to the reality of a catastrophic climate disaster that ends the world (Figure 38.1). He has experienced a kind of "haunting from the future" (to adapt Schwab's concept).

The film opens with Curtis standing outside his garage. Alerted by something, he looks out at the sky and sees a strange, terrifying cloud, with unusual jagged shapes looming large. It apparently starts to rain, but when Curtis looks at his hand (which viewers see in close-up) instead of water he finds a brown oily substance. He looks up at the sky while the oil pours down on his head. At this point, the film cuts to Curtis in the shower, with *real* water pouring down. Audiences suddenly realize he is having a hallucination of disaster, namely a pretrauma experience. In depicting an example of the phenomenon of pretraumatic stress syndrome, the film offers spectators a representation of their own position as viewers of pretrauma films. That is, Curtis is in a similar position to that of the pretrauma film's

Figure 38.1 *Take Shelter* (Jeff Nicolls, 2011).

Source: *Take Shelter*, Jeff Nicolls, 2011.

viewers: his fantasies of catastrophic climate change are similar to the fantasies viewers experience in the genre which foresees or foretells future climate disaster.

However, there is a difference in positioning vis-à-vis the traumatic events: viewers watching film scenarios rarely suffer pretraumatic symptoms as directly or viscerally as Curtis, or to the same degree. They rather occupy the vicarious (or secondary) trauma position: By this, I mean the position of indirectly experiencing a traumatic event as a bystander or observer rather than being the one to whom the event happens. Following a screening, viewers may express only minor or no symptoms, depending on personal difference. Anticipatory anxiety perhaps best expresses what viewers endure in watching this genre of films. Whether such scenarios offer viewers a sense of mastery (some characters usually survive!) or are read as warnings and a spur to action most likely depends on who the viewer is and her prior experience. (The sociological essay by Crespo and Pereira [noted earlier] offers a start towards an interview research project that would be required to get a handle on audience response; and even then it is unreliable data).

But what about gender and race in these films? Moving to the micro-level, as a feminist, I am concerned with how gender is situated vis-à-vis global warming and how it emerges in the films that evoke climate trauma. Pretrauma disaster films, like *Take Shelter* or *The Happening*, unconsciously focus on *male* fantasies about a catastrophic future, as against those *females* might envision (Figure 38.2). It is not by chance that most of the narratives in the films, whether they are blockbuster Hollywood-style or films made beyond Hollywood, have a plot dealing with how white males survive the destruction while saving a woman or child (often from a minority culture), or die having brought a mother and child to safety (see for example *Children of Men*; *I Am Legend*; *Day After Tomorrow, 2012*; *The Book of Eli*, Hughes Brothers, 2010; *Snowpiercer*). When not being saved, women are largely absent from the narrative or play minor, sexist roles (see *Soylent Green*, Richard Fleischer, 1973; *The Happening*; *The Road*, John Hillcoat, 2009). While influential environmental critics and scholars address issues of environmental injustice and focus on women and minorities as the main victims, the full force of such gendered injustice appears to be bypassed in pretraumatic fictions, leaving serious class and gender issues to be taken up in documentaries and academic studies.

Race is also a problem: Most of the heroes in pretrauma climate films are white, although Denzel Washington and Will Smith play central roles in *The Book of Eli* and *I Am Legend*, respectively. However, their characters are not self-consciously portrayed as ethnic, and their race is not a central aspect of their characters. Black actors are given the parts but race is not interrogated as such. Sometimes, as in *The Road*, there are strange lapses of judgment

Figure 38.2   Pretrauma disaster films, like *Take Shelter*, unconsciously focus on *male* fantasies about a catastrophic future.

Source: Take Shelter, Jeff Nichols, 2011.

on the part of the director, as when John Hillcoat casts African American Michael Kenneth Williams in the role of The Thief who is stripped bare and humiliated by Man at the end of the film. Is Cuarón making a statement about US slavery? Or is he unconsciously reiterating a negative stereotype? It is hard to tell.

We might find one answer by turning to class privilege, economics, and still-lingering ideologies of white supremacy. If we think about the group that potentially has the most to lose from the complete collapse of the current world order, we would arrive at the white male. White men control much of the power and wealth in the world today, and while they may already be using some of that wealth to shore up refuge against climate catastrophe, ultimately life will become unsustainable for everyone on Earth. Todd Haynes, years ago, in his film *Safe* (1995) showed the extreme lengths to which an upper-class woman would go to avoid environmental pollution making her ill. Fantasies about what this group will face dominate prevailing scenarios. We know that there are so-called "survivalist" businesses (such as Red Shed or More Prepared) explicitly appealing to those with the luxury (and the wealth) to think about and prepare for catastrophe. Self-Reliance Expos are eagerly sought out by many males and "prepper" or survivalist TV shows, like *Doomsday Preppers*, proliferate. Meanwhile, white working class men are angry about the growing independence of women and the influx of immigrants, who are seen as a threat. Curtis LaForche in *Take Shelter* embodies the thinking of skilled white men as he builds an elaborate tornado shelter for his family in response to his pretraumatic hallucinations. One might say then that unconscious sexism and racism, together with white male anxiety, leads to the prevalence of narratives featuring white males struggling to survive in situations of societal collapse (for more on this, see Katherine Sugg 2015). The white male viewer is given a sense of mastery by identifying with the heroic behavior of the protagonists who offer their image back to them as compensation for their real-life impotence in the face of climate change.

But psychoanalysis moves us towards a deeper understanding of this masculinist bias of the genre, as Susannah Radstone has argued (2007). In general, on the macro-level, as I argue at length elsewhere (Kaplan 2015), the antidote to climate trauma is denial. I am tempted to read climate denial on this level as requiring the travel from melancholia to mourning that is familiar in trauma studies. Mourning, however, signals that the subject's loss is being worked through—the lost object is seen as separate as the subject grieves an irreparable loss while moving forward with her life. Few films show male loss being worked through. The films in general offer a dominant melancholic structure of feeling, and this powerful affective tone well represents the white male's sense of being stuck, fixed in a hopeless cycle of increasing loss. As Radstone notes, loss is "the foundation of both masculinity and patriarchy." She further claims that instead of recognizing loss and difference, male communities "project their losses onto the body of woman or … onto those relegated to the position of women and who come to stand for castration" (2007: 172).

Anne Anlin Cheng (2001) suggests something similar as she explicitly focuses on race. She notes that "The racists need to develop elaborate ideologies in order to accommodate their actions with official American ideals, while white liberals need to keep burying the racial others in order to memorialize them" (Cheng 2001, 11). I think Cheng means that guilt-ridden liberals wring their hands over what has been done to minorities going back to decimation of Native Americans and the horrors of slavery—gestures that do not necessarily benefit those same minorities. Meanwhile, racists strive to bring their twisted views into line with what the amended Constitution meant to enforce as regards racial tolerance and equity.

Female sci-fi heroines in the pretrauma genre are hard to find, and there are only two films in the pretrauma genre cohort that feature female protagonists. The Woman (she is never given a name) in *Blindness* (Fernando Meirelles, 2008) becomes a strong leader using her unique ability to see; and Offred (thanks to Margaret Atwood) in Volker Schlöndorff's adaptation of *The Handmaid's Tale* (1990) manages to survive entrapment largely via the inspiration of other strong women. Feminist literary science fiction is far ahead of cinema in the way gender and race are organized. It seems that Hollywood producers decided to focus their sci-fi on an appeal to a white male audience, perhaps unconsciously understanding that, indeed, this was the group with most to lose with the onset of climate catastrophe. By contrast, Ursula Le Guin and Octavia Butler (to name just two) imagine female protagonists and ways of dealing with the end of the world other than via the prevailing nostalgia and melancholy. Female authors engage readers with utopian fantasies of renewal or the development of new kinds of bodies in other worlds—bodies which replace the western male/female binary with new kinds of sexualities, and with worlds in which women are no longer always victims and helpless. It seems that while male fantasies dwell on nostalgia and melancholy, female authors seek ways to envision new worlds, new ways of being, or creative adaptation to climate change.

If a few pretrauma films have mitigating aspects (the Father in *The Road*, for example, is nurturing; Eli in *The Book of Eli* hands his powerful cudgel to the woman he saved to continue his mission; and the Woman in *Blindness* saves the day), that does not absolve the majority of unconscious male bias. If some of the films addressing young adults, like the *Hunger Games* franchise, focus on strong female teenagers, that genre raises a host of different issues (see Kelly Oliver 2016).

In movies made in the last few years, as one would expect, women figure far more prominently as brave scientists (Sandra Bullock in *Gravity*, Alfonso Cuarón, 2013; Anne Hathaway and Ellen Burstyn in *Interstellar*). Meanwhile, *Snowpiercer* offers a satirical image of the bluestocking stereotype (played with grimacing humor by Tilda Swinton), a Korean male hero who ends up helping destroy the white fascist leader, and the role Ed Harris plays as totalitarian leader is critiqued. But if gender and racial bias in these narratives is starting to change, the genre still remains startlingly white, with rare cases of an African American protagonist linked to the realities of race within the plot. Thus, such films, even when featuring African American protagonists, elide any deeper considerations about the links between race, gender, and climate trauma.

However, this discussion should not underplay the importance of viewers experiencing future collapsed worlds, along with the dire conditions that would prevail. Naomi Oreskes and Erik M. Conway (2014), constructing a report by a virtual future human amazed at the inability of twenty-first century humans to deal with global warming, hope to arouse readers to action. If the focus on deprived environments in films is never explicitly described as being a result of human action (most likely for political reasons), scenarios imply that human actions were involved. In any case, the climate conditions are traumatic, and viewers may even recognize environments that they have experienced. (Note that most of the films were shot on location.) If it is necessary to unpack the cultural bias across these genres on the micro-level, and generally speaking, it is correct to see the pretraumatic film addressing the white male cohort still so powerful and wealthy in the US, viewers no doubt are captivated by the macro-level of danger to humans as a species.

I want to end with thinking more broadly, from a psychological point of view, about what it means to live in the Anthropocene, taking the concept to include all the dangerous uses of resources and corporate exploitation of the planet and ethical issues involved. The recent cohort of scholars noted earlier would argue that the theories I have used above are no longer adequate to our dire situation. They insist that we are beyond the tipping point, and should start from that position. Given the entrenched politics, institutions, economic structures, and belief systems that exist, these scholars believe there are zero strategies available to provide any hope of containing the multiple levels of impact climate change has produced: The only hope is to develop new paradigms for surviving. But whether or not we need, as Wark says, "to process the feeling of living among the ruins" (2015, 4) an important question has been raised.

Sympathetic as I am to scholars' arguments, we need in any case to show empathy and caring while we can for those bearing the initial brunt of catastrophes from climate change. Morton believes that we are already inside global warming—that the end of the world has come. He argues that dystopian fantasies such as those I study inoculate us against the object that is already here; I argue that the narratives not only force us to face horror and fear, rather than relax, but may spur us to action. The texts I study tell us much about our present moment, which, whatever the future holds, we need to deal with as best we can.

Susanne Moser (2012), like me, is concerned about the ways in which extreme anxiety leads to depression and denial. The scenario as she outlines it includes our having done too little, too late, "resulting in our communities, economies and the ecosystems we depend on being overwhelmed by the pace and magnitude of climate change, and all attendant losses and disruptions" (Moser 2012, 903). She continues, noting that "we will experience a range of essential systems degrading over time, or collapsing outright, but in either case shifting into completely altered states" (ibid.). Moser believes that we need a cohort of leaders, "adept in a range of psychological, social and political skills, to navigate the inevitable human crises that will precede, trigger and follow environmental ones" (ibid. 904). They will need to guide people, she says, in "processing enormous losses, human distress, constant crises and the seemingly endless need to remain engaged in the task of maintaining, restoring and rebuilding ... a viable planet, and the only place the human species can call its home" (ibid. 905). Viewers able to take on board the losses shown in pretrauma films may find that Moser's words resonate. They may not only prepare themselves for "completely altered states" as systems degrade, but be ready to help others.

If female directors have been slow to direct films in the pretrauma genre, unlike their literary sisters, there is still time. Possibly, they may take on board some of Moser's ways of thinking. This genre is not going to go away any time soon. Indeed, in offering a section on the future of gender studies in film research, this Routledge companion volume encourages readers to think about where our field is headed and how changing historical realities, like that of climate change, have an impact on what we study. In using the lens of climate disaster as a way to study gender in a newly prevalent genre of dystopian cinema, feminist inquiry stays vital and in touch with dramatic socio-cultural change, such as that of global warming.

Related topics

Alexa Weik von Mossner, "Ecocinema and gender"
Claire Pajaczkowska, "Psychoanalysis beyond the gaze: from celluloid to new media"

Bibliography

Agamben, Giorgio. *Homo Sacer: Sovereign Power and Bare Life.* Trans. Daniel Heller-Roazen. Stanford: Stanford University Press, 1998. Print.

———. *The State of Exception.* Trans. Kevin Attell. Chicago: University of Chicago Press, 2005. Print.

Bennett, Jane. *Vibrant Matter: A Political Ecology of Things.* Durham, NC: Duke University Press, 2010.

Buck-Morss, Susan. *Dreamworld and Catastrophe: The Passing of Mass Utopia in East and West.* Cambridge, MA and London: MIT Press, 2002. Print.

Buell, Lawrence. *The Environmental Imagination: Thoreau, Nature Writing, and the Formation of American Culture.* Cambridge, MA: Belknap Press, 1995. Print.

Buell, Lawrence. *Writing for an Endangered World: Literature, Culture and Environment in the U.S. and Beyond.* Cambridge, MA: Belknap Press, 2001. Print.

Chakrabarty, Dipesh. "The Climate of History: Four Theses." *Critical Inquiry* 35.2 (Winter 2009): 197–222. Print.

Cheng, Anne Anlin. *The Melancholy of Race: Psychoanalysis, Assimilation and Hidden Grief.* Oxford: OUP, 2001. Print.

Crespo, Inês, and Ângela Pereira. "Envisaging Environmental Change: Foregrounding Place in Three Australian Ecomedia Initiatives." *Transnational Ecocinema: Film Culture in an Era of Ecological Transformation.* Eds., Tommy Gustafsson and Pietari Kääpä. Chicago: University of Chicago Press, 2013: 165–86. Print.

Crutzen, Paul, and Eugene F. Stoermer. "The Anthropocene." *The Global Warming Reader.* Ed. Bill McKibben. London: Penguin Books, 2012: 69–74.

Freud, Sigmund. "Mourning and Melancholia." 1917. *Strachey.* 14: 243–58. Print.

Garrard, Greg. *Ecocriticism.* London and New York: Routledge, 2004.

Gillis, Justin. "Seas are Rising at Fastest Rate in Last 28 Centuries." *New York Times,* February 23, 2016, A1, 10. Print.

Glotfelty, Cheryl and Fromm, Harold. (Eds.). *The Ecocriticism Reader: Landmarks in Literary Ecology.* Athens: U of Georgia Press, 1996.

Griffin, Susan. *Woman and Nature: The Roaring Inside Her.* New York: Harper and Row, 1978. Print.

Guha, Ramachandra. *Environmentalism: A Global History.* London: Pearson, 2000. Print.

Gustafsson, Tommy, and Pietari Kääpä. *Transnational Ecocinema: Film Culture in an Era of Ecological Transformation.* Chicago: University of Chicago Press, 2013. Print.

Heise, Ursula, *Sense of Place and Sense of Planet: The Environmental Imagination of the Global.* New York and Oxford: Oxford University Press, 2008. Print.

——— ed. "The Invention of Eco-Futures." *Ecozon@: European Journal of Literature, Culture and Environment* 3.2 (Autumn 2012): 1–10. Print.

Kaplan, E. Ann. *Trauma Culture: The Politics of Terror and Loss in Media and Literature.* New Brunswick: Rutgers University Press, 2005.

————. *Climate Trauma: Foreseeing the Future in Dystopian Film and Fiction*. New Brunswick: Rutgers University Press, 2015.

————. "Memory and Future Selves in Futurist Dystopian Cinema: *The Road* (2010) and *The Book of Eli* (2010)," *Routledge International Handbook of Memory Studies*. Eds., Trever Hagen and Anna Lisa Tota. New York and London: Routledge, 2016: 259–71.

Klein, Naomi. *This Changes Everything: Capitalism vs. the Climate*. New York: Allen Lane, 2014. Print.

Kolbert, Elizabeth. *The Sixth Extinction. An Unnatural History*. New York: Henry Holt & Co., 2014.

Kristeva, Julia. *The Black Sun*. Trans. Leon S. Roudiez. New York: Columbia University Press, 1989. Print.

Latour, Bruno. *We Have Never Been Modern*. Trans. Catherine Porter. Cambridge, MA: Harvard University Press, 1993.

Lefebvre, Martin, ed. (2006). *Landscape and Film*. New York: Routledge. Print.

Madsen, Michael. Interview with Helen Caldicott. "The Journey Our Nuclear Waste Must Take: Into Eternity." *If You Love this Planet*. July 15, 2011. Webcast. http://ifyoulovethisplanet.org/?page_id=254. (Accessed July 17, 2016)

Merchant, Caroline. *Earthcare: Women and the Environment*. New York: Routledge, 1995. Print.

Mirzoeff, Nicholas. "Visualizing the Anthropocene," *Public Culture* 26.2 (2015): 213–32.

————. "It's Not the Anthropocene, It's the White Supremacy-scene." Paper uploaded to Academia-edu. Not published.

Mitscherlich, Alexander, and Margarete Mitscherlich. *The Inability to Mourn*. New York: Grove Press, 1975.

Morton, Timothy. *Hyperobjects: Philosophy and Ecology after the End of the World*. London and Minneapolis: University of Minnesota Press, 2013. Print.

Moser, Susanne. "Getting Real About It: Meeting the Psychological and Social Demands of a World in Distress." *Environmental Leadership: A Reference Handbook*. Ed. Deborah Rigling Gallagher. Los Angeles and London: Sage, 2012: 900–8.

Narine, Anil, ed. *Eco-Trauma Cinema*. New York and London: Routledge, 2014.

Nixon, Robert. *Slow Violence and the Environmentalism of the Poor*. Cambridge, MA: Harvard University Press, 2010. Print.

Oliver, Kelly. *Hunting Girls: Sexual Violence from* The Hunger Games *to Campus Rape*. Columbia University Press, 2016. Print.

Oreskes, Naomi, and Erik M. Conway. *The Collapse of Western Civilization: A View from the Future*. New York and London: Columbia University Press, 2014. Print.

Radstone, Susannah. *The Sexual Politics of Time: Confession, Nostalgia, Memory*. London and New York: Routledge, 2007. Print.

Rust, Stephen, Salma Monani and Sean Cubitt. *Ecocinema Theory and Practice*. New York and London: Routledge, 2013. Print.

Ruthven, Ken. *Nuclear Criticism*. Melbourne, Australia: Melbourne University Press, 1993. Print.

Schwab, Gabriele. "Haunting from the Future: Psychic Life in the Wake of Nuclear Necropolitics." *The Undecidable Unconscious: A Journal of Deconstruction And Psychoanalysis*. 1 (1) 2014: 85–101. Print.

Scranton, Roy. *Learning to Die in the Anthropocene*. San Francisco: City Lights Books, 2015. Print.

Soper, Kate. *What is Nature? Culture, Politics and the Non-Human*. London and New York: Wiley-Blackwell, 1995. Print.

Steingraber, Sandra. *Living Downstream: An Ecologist's Personal Investigation of Cancer and the Environment*. New York: Da Capo Press, 1997/2010.

Sugg, Katherine. "The Walking Dead: Crisis, Late Liberalism, and Masculine Subjection in Apocalyptic Fictions." *Journal of American Studies* (2015): 1–19.

Thacker, Eugene. *Cosmic Pessimism*. Minneapolis, MN: Univocal Publishing, 2015. Print.

Wark, McKenzie. *Molecular Red*. New York and London: Verso, 2015.

Weik von Mossner, Alexa, ed. *Moving Environments: Affect, Emotion, Ecology and Film*. Waterloo: Wilfrid Laurier University Press, 2014.

Yusoff, Kathryn. "Excess, Catastrophe, and Climate Change." *Environment and Planning D: Society and Space*. 27 (2009): 1010–29. Print.

39

ECOCINEMA AND GENDER

Alexa Weik von Mossner

The medium of film is in multiple ways connected to its larger environment, an environment in which it is shot, edited, and screened, and that also produces the raw materials necessary for film production, distribution, and exhibition. Films are materially embedded in various environments and at the same time represent such environments on screen. Characters and their actions make stories, but these stories inevitably take place within some kind of setting, a cinematic environment. It may be natural landscape, like the Virunga Mountains in Michael Apted's *Gorillas in the Mist* (1988), or it may be urban and specifically built for the film, like the futuristic cityscape of Los Angeles in Ridley Scott's *Blade Runner* (1982). It may also be wholly artificial and virtual, such as Pandora's enticing forest in James Cameron's *Avatar* (2009). Regardless of the origin and degree of authenticity of a cinematic environment, characters stand in relation to that environment and to the nonhuman actors that populate it.

Studying film from an ecocritical perspective means paying attention to the ways in which such environments are represented, and how characters relate to them. It also means taking account of how race, class, ethnicity, sex, gender, and other social identity markers inflect and sometimes determine such relationships in the actual world and in its representation on film. There are multiple linkages between gender and a variety of environmental issues related to representation, access, sustainability, and justice. Susan Buckingham-Hatfield reminds us in *Gender and Environment* (2000) that in the developing world "women's work is often linked to the environment" and "much of that work is made harder through environmental degradation" (1). While many people in the West are increasingly more distant from the sources of their food, energy, and water supply, Buckingham-Hatfield suggests that women's biology and accepted social role as caregivers nevertheless makes them more vulnerable and more attentive to environmental hazards and to the environment in general, especially so if they belong to a minority group (ibid.). But it is not only women's relationship to the environment that deserves special attention from an ecocritical perspective. Recent research on queer ecology highlights important questions concerning the intersections of sexuality and environmental studies that broaden the scope of feminist inquiry. As ecocritic Greta Gaard has pointed out, "dominant Western culture's devaluation of the erotic parallels its devaluation of women and of nature" (2004: 22). In effect these multiple devaluations are mutually enforcing, which is why a chapter on ecocinema and gender must consider both feminist and queer studies approaches, which in many ways complement one another. The complex inter-linkages between gender, sexuality, and the environment are receiving increasingly more attention from scholars in the relatively young field of ecocinema studies, but to date there is no systematic ecocritical approach from a feminist, queer or gender studies perspective. What I will therefore attempt in this chapter is bringing together recent scholarship in ecocinema studies, ecofeminism, and queer ecology. In the final part of the chapter, I will also suggest some ways in which an integration of feminist film theory might further enlarge and enhance the analytical scope of the gender-related study of ecocinema.

Gender-related approaches to ecocinema: the state of affairs

Ecocinema studies scholars engage with a wide range of audiovisual texts and theoretical approaches. As Stephen Rust, Salma Monani, and Sean Cubitt explain in their introduc-tion to *Ecocinema Theory and Practice*,

> ecocinema studies is not simply limited to films with explicit messages of environmental consciousness, but investigates the breadth of cinema from Hollywood corporate productions and independent avant-garde films to the expanding media sites in which producers, consumers, and texts interact.
>
> *(2013: 2)*

While their influential anthology does not include a chapter with a specific focus on gender, the three editors acknowledge that "cinema that engages gender politics is ... an important consideration" for the field and suggest that existing work in ecofeminism and queer ecology "can easily be directed towards ecocinema" (ibid. 10). Although much of the work in ecofeminism and queer ecology does not engage directly with film or related media forms, it offers theoretical insights that help us think through the ways in which gender roles and relations are represented, interrogated, and reworked in ecocinema.

Ecofeminism is a broad and interdisciplinary area of research that links feminism with ecology. Writing in the mid-1980s, the philosopher Val Plumwood observed that the label was being used to denote "a body of literature whose theme is the link between the dom-ination of women and the domination of nature" (1986: 120). Plumwood went on to note the diversity of ecofeminist positions, but the field has nevertheless often been reduced to a singular position and then criticized for its essentialist claim that, because of their biology, women have a special and in certain ways privileged relationship to nature. Given the long tradition of portraying wilderness as feminine and in need of masculine taming that fem-inists such as Annette Kolodny (1984) detected in Western culture, such a claim was considered problematic. Over the past thirty years, however, ecofeminist scholarship has continued to grow and diversify, and it has generated a range of ideas that have sparked and inspired other ecocritical investigations. Gaard observes that "current developments in allegedly new fields such as animal studies and naturalized epistemology are 'discovering' theoretical perspectives on interspecies relations and standpoint theory that were devel-oped by feminists and ecofeminists decades ago" (2011: 26). Gaard's own work, and that of other prominent ecofeminists, among them Donna Haraway and Stacy Alaimo, continues to inspire ecocriticism and related fields in the environmental humanities. These influential scholars are also among the relatively few ecofeminists who have included film texts in their critiques of cultural and political practices.

Haraway's *Primate Visions* (1989) examines the history of primatology and the role of female researchers such as Jane Goodall and Dian Fossey in creating gendered "narratives of touch" (401) that were instrumental in generating public interest in gorillas, chimpanzees, and other primates. Haraway explores the ways in which many documentary formats of the time used the women as mediators to give their audiences a feeling of proximity to the great apes. "The politics of gender," she maintains, "are fundamental to the meaning of primate stories and to their role in political struggles in European and American culture over 'human nature'" (ibid.). Among the films she considers are wildlife documentary formats and Michael Apted's 1988 biopic *Gorillas in the Mist*, in which actress Sigourney Weaver "must seek the desired touch" (ibid. 145) with gorilla males in Rwanda, just like Fossey herself had been asked to display her physical proximity with the primates before she was murdered for her activism on their behalf. "In the late twentieth century," declares Haraway, "nature must be lucrative to endure," and in her view, Apted's film is part of "a dialectic of love and money" that turns the attention of Western viewers toward the spectacle of wild animals and the women living with them in seemingly benevolent forms of exploitation (ibid. 265). Barbara Crowther's 1994 essay "Toward a Feminist Critique of Television Natural History Programs" also engages with gender issues in wildlife film, noting a pervasive tendency on the part of filmmakers to cast the land as female and passive whereas wild animals are depicted as male and active. Female animals, she reports, are either not shown at all or limited to their role in procreation (Crowther 1994: 131). Although ecocinema studies had not yet constituted itself as a field, Haraway's and Crowther's considerations of the gender politics of human–wildlife relations on film belong among its earliest texts. In more recent years, a steadily increasing number of ecofeminists have included film in their analyses of culture, and although it has rarely been their central focus, they offer important insights about the role of gender and sexuality in the production and reception of ecocinema.

Noël Sturgeon's *Environmentalism in Popular Culture* (2009) includes a chapter on "Penguin Family Values" that juxtaposes its analysis of Luc Jacquet's wildlife documentary *The March of the Penguins* (2004) with its adoption by American right-wing Christians who saw in the film "an inspiring example of monogamy, Christian family values, and intelligent design" (120). Critiquing both the film and the public response to it from a "feminist environmental justice" standpoint, Sturgeon draws attention to pre-conceived notions of heteronormativity and asks pointedly whether it "matter[s] in terms of environmental consequences what kind of familial and sexual arrangements we make?" (ibid.). Her analysis suggests that it does, connecting such arrangements to environmental reproductive justice and stating that, like the wildlife films considered by Haraway and Crowther, *March of the Penguins* "follows a standard anthropomorphic script … in which animal mating and reproduction is consistently represented as a metaphor for human heterosexual romance and nuclear family" (ibid. 128; on this point see also Mitman 1999, Whitley 2014, and Wilson 1992). The irony involved in this particular choice of a metaphor is that penguins happen to be a species in which the bonding of same-sex pairs is so common that it has achieved iconic status as "a symbol for the naturalness of gay marriage" (Sturgeon 2009: 120). It is an irony that is not lost on Sturgeon, who concludes that "discourses of the natural are flexibly used in the culture wars around sexuality" (ibid. 128), often to the exclusion of other issues, such as the fact that the natural habitat of penguins is strongly affected by anthropogenic climate change.

Sturgeon's attention to gender and sexuality in the production and consumption of ecocinema is equally astute in another chapter in her book, which focuses on children's environmentalist culture. "Environmentalism," she argues, "has become the new moral framework for children's popular culture" (ibid. 103), a moral framework that raises concerns related to gender, sexual, racial, and environmental justice because of what is depicted as "natural." While her analysis focuses predominantly on the politics of representation behind popular American TV shows such as the TBS cartoon series *Captain Planet and the Planeteers* (1990–2), it could easily be extended to recent Hollywood blockbusters aimed at a global audience of children, such as Disney's animated feature *Happy Feet* (2006), and Pixar's *Wall-E* (2009). Both of these films raise important issues related to environmental sustainability and conservation but at the same time reaffirm dominant American norms of heteronormativity (even robots are clearly gendered and heterosexually inclined), interracial relations, and American exceptionalism (Whitley 2014; Weik von Mossner 2014b). Although they engage with ecological problems that affect humans and nonhumans around the world, the relationships between individuals and their environments are depicted as firmly circumscribed by dominant Western norms and values.

Stacy Alaimo's *Bodily Natures* (2010) interrogates such relationships from a materialist position, suggesting that the physical, material enmeshment of all human (and nonhuman) bodies in their wider environments has drastic consequences for the way we think about human–nature relationships. Like Haraway's "A Cyborg Manifesto" (1991), Alaimo's *Undomesticated Ground* (2000), argues that rather than trying to disentangle women from nature, as much traditional feminism has done, feminist theory should *transform* gendered dualisms, such as nature/culture, body/mind, or object/subject that have been used to oppress not only women but also nonhuman forms of life (4–14). In her more recent book, Alaimo aims at such transformation of limiting binaries through the concept of *transcorporeality*, which "emerges in environmental health, environmental justice, web-based subcultures, green consumerism, literature, photography, activist websites, and film" and entails the "recognition not just that everything is connected but that humans are the very stuff of the emergent, material world" (2010: 20). That this materially enmeshed state of the human matters in cinematic representation becomes clear in Alaimo's reading of Todd Haynes's *Safe* (1995), a film about multiple-chemical sensitivity, starring Julianne Moore. Multiple-chemical sensitivity is a condition that involves physical reactions to often very small amounts of chemical substances in one's immediate environment. Because such substances cannot be seen and are often not detected by other senses or even by most medical testing, the condition is very difficult to diagnose, which makes it hard for affected persons to communicate their ailment to other people in their lives. Haynes' film dramatizes this lack of communication through a distanced mode of cinematography that offers viewers an intriguing and somewhat oblique view at this complex medical condition and what it does to an upper middle-class housewife who is affected by it. Alaimo lauds Haynes for his invention of "ethical ways to represent invisible material agencies and 'deviant' human bodies" (2010: 24), yet unlike Roddey Reid's (1998) and Susan Potter's (2004) earlier explorations of the film, her analysis pays relatively little attention to *Safe*'s visual strategies. A focus on cinematic form is still rare in ecofeminist readings of film, perhaps because scholars working in the field tend to have a background in women's studies, literary criticism, or philosophy, rather than in film studies.

Nicole Seymour's take on Hayne's film from a queer studies perspective is much more rewarding in this regard. Taking the insights of queer studies seriously means to pay attention to non-conformity and deviation more generally, and to accept it as an alternative perspective on the (natural) world rather than dismissing or discarding it. With reference to both Reid and Potter, Seymour argues that *Safe*'s "queer visual techniques" draw attention to the film's marginal figures—to the movers, painters, gardeners, cosmetologists, and housemaids who surround the white female protagonist and who are subjected to much higher dosages of the toxins to which her body reacts so violently. Not only are "the service occupations depicted in the film … strictly gender-coded" (male movers and gardeners, and female housemaids, and cosmetologists), but Hayne's use of unaccustomed shot sizes, shot durations, and deep focus also draws viewers' attention to "this raced and gendered coding and its fallout," which is "rooted in socially unjust ideology, rather than natural facts" (2011: 45–6). Seymour's careful analysis of the film's "queer" narrative techniques reminds us that cinematic form is as important as content for ecocritical analysis and that a queer perspective entails more than just a focus on sexualities that deviate from social norms. As philosopher Catriona Sandilands puts it pointedly, "[i]t is not enough simply to add 'heterosexism' to the long list of dominations that shape our relations to nature, to pretend that we can just 'add queers and stir'" (1994: 21).

In their Introduction to *Queer Ecologies* (2010), Sandilands and Bruce Erickson take a closer look at Ang Lee's *Brokeback Mountain* (2005), suggesting that the film "displays quite dramatically three important junctures at which lgbtq (lesbian/gay/bisexual transgender/queer) and environmental politics (both defined broadly) intersect" (2010: 2). The first juncture is the film's "effective disarticulation of same-sex love and desire from gay identity" (ibid. 3). The two protagonists of the film are white, rugged, and extremely masculine cowboys who insist that they aren't "queer"—characteristics that make them more likely to generate sympathy in mainstream audiences because it plants them on the "right side" of an evolutionary binary that juxtaposes the fit and healthy with the perverse and degenerate. The second juncture concerns the film's evocation of a picturesque American wilderness as "a vast place of homoerotic possibility" (ibid. 3), thereby subverting dominant under-standings of wilderness as the place where heterosexual masculinity is tested and affirmed. The third juncture lies in *Brokeback Mountain*'s depiction of its protagonists as shepherds, which "locates the film in a long history of pastoral depictions of nature and, indeed, an equally long history of pastoral representations of male same-sex eroticism" (ibid. 4) that goes back to ancient Greece. In her book-length study *Strange Natures* (2013), Seymour offers her take on the film, which is sensitive to its visual strategies and narrative structure, and the way they thematize social surveillance and "the violence of public–private divisions that privilege reproductive heteronormativity and punish anything that falls outside of it" (106). The protagonists' public display of rugged masculinity, which runs counter to ste-reotypical notions of gayness, shields them from punishment as long as they manage to keep their sexual encounters in the private realm, which in this case, ironically, is out in the open wilderness of Brokeback Mountain. Lee's film is thus interesting not only for its represen-tation of non-heterosexual desire and affection, but also for its depiction of white mas-culinity, which at the same time affirms and subverts traditional masculinized roles and practices that we associate with the American western film and, by extension, with the American West.

Critiques of films that represent such roles and practices in a more traditional way can be found in David Ingram's *Green Screen* (2000) and Deborah Carmichael's edited collection *The Landscape of Hollywood Westerns* (2006). Sarah Mirk's recent review of George Miller's *Fury Road* (2015) suggests that even action blockbusters that ostentatiously celebrate dominant notions of masculinity can promote ecofeminist values. However, given that in many parts of the world and throughout much of cinema's history, heterosexual, white men and their beliefs and values hold central focus, it seems regrettable that to date, there is no comprehensive focus on masculinity narratives in cinema as they relate to the environ-ment. In fact, M. C. Allistor's *Eco-Man* (2004) remains the only book-length study dedicated to general ecocritical exploration of cultural representations of masculinity. It is an area that calls for further exploration, as does the intersection of gender and sexuality with other social markers of identity. Salma Monani's work on indigenous film cultures offers a good example of the issues that might be explored in an approach that combines an interest in gender not only with environmental justice concerns, but also with an attention to race and ethnicity, and to non-Western modes of thinking. Her essay on Navajo filmmaker Nanobah Becker's *The 6th World: An Origin Story* (2012) explores the science fiction short's "engagement with signature Navajo themes—the important status of women, corn, and land" (1) and the complex ways in which these themes are linked to Becker's thinking about climate change and the degradation of the planet (forthcoming 2016). Chia-ju Chang's treatment of the "Woman-Animal Meme" in contemporary Taiwanese ecocinema (2010) is another recent example of a gender-related approach to environmental film that considers the representation of non-white and non-Western identities.

Despite these various intersections between ecocritical film and gender studies, there is still relatively little in-depth engagement with the rich tradition of feminist film theory. An explicitly ecofeminist or queer ecological film theory has yet to develop, and one way to facilitate its emergence might be by bringing it into conversation with established feminist and queer theory approaches to film. I therefore want to dedicate the last section of the chapter to a brief exploration of potential points of transfer and connection.

Feminist film theory and ecocinema: potential concerns and directions

Like ecofeminism, feminist film theory is a vast field that is constituted by a host of different schools and national traditions. As Ann Kaplan notes in her introduction to *Feminism and Film* (2001), "the knowledge produced in feminist film study has varied with the goals, methods and interests of different feminist film scholars" (1). To date, Beth Berila's contribution to Paula Willoquet-Maricondi's edited volume *Framing the World* (2010) is one of few explorations of ecocinema that consciously draws on this varied body of knowledge. Laura Mulvey's seminal essay on "Visual Pleasure and Narrative Cinema" (1975) serves as a touchstone for Berila to discuss the affective appeal of Robert Redford's glamorous Hollywood productions *The Horse Whisperer* (1998) and *A River Runs Through It* (1992), which she juxtaposes with two activist environmental justice documentaries— Kate Raisz's *Toxic Racism* (1994) and Joseph Di Gangi and Amon Giebel's *Drumbeat for Mother Earth* (1999). Berila's essay suggests that gender-related film theory has much to offer when it comes to issues of visual pleasure in the reception of ecocinema. Feminist scholarship on documentary film (see, for example, Waldman and Walker 1999) might also be productive for an analysis of the issues it discusses with regard to the four films. Paula Rabinowitz reminds us that "gender is a central category within documentary rhetoric, though one often ignored, suppressed, or resisted, because it is not always clear who occupies what position when" (1994: 6). It has been suggested that the documentary filmmaker is in a position of power, not only because the filmmaking process imposes a recording "eye" on the life and world of the subject, but also because the filmmaker's stay in that world tends to be temporary, while the subject has no choice but to continue living in it. However, the documentaries that Berila considers remind us that the filmmakers themselves may be female and that they may be involved in the community they portray. Feminist approaches to documentary film have wrestled with such complex forms of representation and distributions of agency in nonfiction filmmaking. They might therefore be helpful for gender-related inquires of environmental justice and other "green" documentaries.

The interest in visual pleasure that is at the center of Berila's investigation is also present in many queer theory approaches to film. "The study of film," writes Ellis Hanson in his introduction to *Out Takes: Essays on Queer Theory and Film* (1999), "is especially important to questions of desire, identification, fantasy, representation, spectatorship, cultural appropriation, performativity, and mass consumption, all of which have become important issues in queer theory in recent years" (3). Hanson suggests that queer film theory should both build on and also question earlier approaches to gender, sexuality, and film, among them the field's heavy reliance on psychoanalysis for the exploration of cinematic affect, desire, and pleasure (ibid. 6). Feminist film scholars such as Janet Walker and Ann Kaplan have demonstrated that psychoanalytical approaches to film—and in particular trauma theory—*can* offer valuable analytical tools for speaking about experiences of environmental shock and loss (Walker 2014; Kaplan 2016, this volume). The contributions to Anil Narine's anthology *Eco-Trauma Cinema* (2014) offer additional examples of how trauma theory and related psychological approaches to film can be utilized for the analysis of the relationship between gender and environmental suffering in ecocinema. Queer theory approaches to film, with their attention to nonconforming modes of representation and performance, have the potential to enrich and extend these concerns.

Another potential avenue for future research concerns an issue that has already come up in the work of many scholars mentioned here: the role of affect in our responses to ecocinema and the way in which those responses are inflected and shaped by gender and sexuality. Haraway's investigation of the function of female researchers in cinematic "narratives of touch" about primates, Berila's concern with landscape shots that cue an emotional response in viewers, and Sandilands and Erickson's interest in *Brokeback Mountain*'s use of such landscape shots to frame its depiction of same-sex eroticism, all betray an interest in how films function on the affective level. Psychoanalytical film theory filtered through the lens of ecofeminism or queer studies offers one theoretical approach to these issues. Affect theory offers a second one. A third theoretical route leads through the camp of cognitive film theory, which also offers intriguing insights about cinematic affect and emotion, but so far has relatively little to say about gender, sexuality, or environmental concerns. All three of these theoretical routes can be viable for ecocritical work on film (on this point, see Weik von Mossner 2014c), and I have little doubt that they can also be traveled to speak about gender-related concerns.

My last suggestion for further research concerns a mode of cinematic narration that has long been a consideration for feminist film scholars, not least because it was (falsely) thought to be a genuinely "feminine" film genre: melodrama. Known for its ability to evoke strong emotions in viewers, the melodramatic mode was, for the longest time, connected to the family drama and other films targeted at female audiences. However, as Linda Williams has convincingly argued, traditionally "male" film genres such as the American western and the war movie also rely heavily on melodramatic storytelling (1998). In my own research, I have used feminist film theory to investigate how melodramatic storytelling conventions shape the form and content of a popular environmentalist Hollywood film such as Steven Soderbergh's *Erin Brockovich* (Weik von Mossner 2014a). The general assumption within ecocinema studies has often been that an "exaggerated" emotional investment necessarily prevents critical reflection on the part of the viewer, suggesting that melodramatic films cannot promote critical thinking and are thus cementing the status quo

(see, for example, Willoquet-Maricondi 2010). However, as the cognitive film scholar Carl Plantinga has pointed out, "there is nothing in the elicitation of strong sympathetic emotions that prima facie could be said to disable critical thought" (2009: 191). On the contrary, we have to consider the fact that "[t]he elicitation of emotion is not merely about feelings; it is also about ways of thinking and valuing that are encouraged by the text and precede and/or accompany emotional response" (ibid.). An ecofeminist approach that focuses on the narrative strategies of environmentalist melodrama might therefore help us better understand the emotional appeal of a global blockbuster such as James Cameron's *Avatar*, which owes its worldwide success to the fact that it was popular with male and female viewers alike across different cultures. The gender-related study of ecocinema in its various forms and modes might still be in its infancy, but it is a field with considerable potential.

Related topics

E. Ann Kaplan, "Visualizing climate trauma: the cultural work of films anticipating the future"
Jennifer Lynn Peterson, "*Green Porno* and the sex life of animals in the digital age"

References

Alaimo, S. (2000) *Undomesticated Ground: Recasting Nature as Feminist Space*. Ithaca, NY: Cornell University Press.
—— (2010) *Bodily Natures: Science, Environment, and the Material Self*. Bloomington, IN: Indiana University Press.
Allistor, M. C. (2004) *Eco-Man: New Perspectives on Masculinity and Nature*. Charlottesville, VA: University of Virginia Press.
Berila, B. (2010) "Engaging the Land/Positioning the Spectator: Environmental Justice Documentaries and Robert Redford's *The Horse Whisperer* and *A River Runs Through It*," in Paula Willoquet-Maricondi (ed.) *Framing the World: Explorations in Ecocriticism and Film*. Charlottesville: University of Virginia Press, pp. 116–33.
Buckingham-Hatfield, S. (2000) *Gender and Environment*. New York and London: Routledge.
Carmichael, Deborah, ed. (2006) *The Landscape of Hollywood Westerns: Ecocriticism in an American Film Genre*. Salt Lake City: University of Utah Press.
Chia-ju Chang (2010) "Putting Back the Animals: Woman-Animal Meme in Contemporary Taiwanese Ecofeminist Imagination," in H. Sheldon and Jiayan Mi (eds.) *Chinese Ecocinema: In the Age of Environmental Challenge*. Hong Kong: Hong Kong University Press, pp. 255–70.
Crowther, B. (1994) "Toward a Feminist Critique of Television Natural History Programs," in P. Florence and Dee Reynolds (eds.) *Feminist Subjects, Multimedia: Cultural Methodologies*. Manchester: Manchester University Press, pp. 183–90.
Gaard, G. (2004) "Toward a Queer Ecofeminism" in G. Gaard (ed.) *New Perspectives on Environmental Justice: Gender, Sexuality, and Activism*. New Brunswick: Rutgers University Press, pp. 21–43.
—— (2011) "Ecofeminism Revisited: Rejecting Essentialism and Re-Placing Species in a Material Feminist Environmentalism," *Feminist Formations* 23 (2) (Summer): 26–53.
Hanson, E., ed. (1999) *Out Takes: Essays on Queer Theory and Film*. Durham, NC: Duke University Press.
Haraway, D. (1989) *Primate Visions: Gender, Race, and Nature in the World of Modern Science*. New York: Routledge.
—— (1991) "A Cyborg Manifesto: Science, Technology, and Socialist-Feminism in the Late Twentieth Century," in Donna Haraway *Simians, Cyborgs and Women: The Reinvention of Nature*. New York: Routledge, pp. 149–81.

Ingram, D. (2000) *Green Screen: Environmentalism and Hollywood Cinema*. Exeter: University of Exeter Press.

Kaplan, E. A. (2001) *Feminism and Film*. New York and London: Oxford University Press.

————— (2016) "Memory and Future Selves in Futurist Dystopian Cinema: *The Road* (2010) and *The Book of Eli* (2010)," in Trever Hagen and Anna Lisa Tota (eds.) *Routledge International Handbook of Memory Studies*. New York and London: Routledge, pp. 259–71.

Kolodny, A. (1984) *The Lay of the Land: Metaphor and Experience in American Life and Letters*. Chapel Hill, NC: University of North Carolina Press.

Mirk, Sarah (2015) "The Ecofeminism of *Mad Max*." *BitchMedia*. May 22. https://bitchmedia.org/post/the-ecofeminism-of-mad-max. Accessed September 22, 2015.

Mitman, G. (1999) *Reel Nature: America's Romance with Wildlife on Film*. Cambridge, Mass.: Harvard University Press.

Monani, S. (forthcoming) "Science Fiction, Westerns, and the Vital Cosmo-ethics of *The 6th World*," in S. Monani and J. Adamson (eds.) *Ecocriticism and Indigenous Studies*.

Mulvey, L. (1975) "Visual Pleasure and Narrative Cinema," *Screen* 16 (3) (Fall): 6–18.

Narine, A., ed. (2014) *Eco-Trauma Cinema*. New York and London: Routledge.

Plantinga, C. (2009) *Moving Viewers: American Film and the Spectator Experience*. Berkeley: University of California Press.

Plumwood, V. (1986) "Ecofeminism: An Overview and Discussion of Positions," *Australian Journal of Philosophy*, 64: 120–38.

Potter, S. (2004) "Dangerous Spaces: *Safe*," *Camera Obscura* 19 (3): 125–55.

Rabinowitz, P. (1994) *They Must Be Represented: The Politics of Documentary*. London: Verso.

Reid, R. (1998) "UnSafe at Any Distance: Todd Haynes' Visual Culture of Health and Risk," *Film Quarterly* 51 (3) (Spring 1998): 32–44.

Rust, S., S. Monani, and S. Cubitt (eds.) (2013) *Ecocinema Theory and Practice*. New York: Routledge.

Sandilands, C. (1994) "Lavender's Green? Some Thoughts on Queer(y)ing Environmental Politics," *UnderCurrents* 6, pp. 20–4.

Sandilands, C. and B. Erickson. (2010) Introduction, in C. Sandilands and B. Erickson. *Queer Ecologies: Sex, Nature, Politics, Desire*. Bloomington: Indiana University Press, pp. 1–47.

Seymour, N. (2011) "'It's Just Not Turning Up': Cinematic Vision and Environmental Justice in Todd Haynes's *Safe*," *Cinema Journal* 50 (4): 26–47.

————— (2013) *Strange Natures: Futurity, Empathy, and the Queer Ecological Imagination*. Bloomington: Indiana University Press.

Sturgeon, N. (2009) *Environmentalism in Popular Culture: Gender, Race, Sexuality, and the Politics of the Natural*. Tucson: University of Arizona Press.

Waldman, D. and J. Walker (1999) *Feminism and Documentary*. Minneapolis: University of Minnesota Press.

Walker, J. (2014) "Eavesdropping in the Cove: Interspecies Ethics, Public and Private Space, and Trauma under Water," in Anil Narine (ed.) *Eco-Trauma Cinema*. New York and London: Routledge, pp. 180–206.

Weik von Mossner, A. (2014a) "Melodrama, Emotion, and Environmental Advocacy: A Cognitive Approach to *Erin Brockovich*," *Anglia: Journal of English Philology* 132 (2): 292–309.

————— (2014b) "Love in the Times of Ecocide: Eco-Trauma and Comic Relief in Andrew Stanton's *WALL-E*," in A. Narine (ed.) *The Cinematic Earth: Eco-Trauma Cinema*. London and New York: Routledge, pp. 164–79.

————— ed. (2014c) *Moving Environments: Affect, Emotion, Ecology and Film*. Waterloo, ON: Wilfrid Laurier University Press.

Whitley, D. (2014) "Animation, Realism, and the Genre of Nature," in A. Weik von Mossner (ed.) *Moving Environments: Affect, Emotion, Ecology, and Film*, Waterloo, ON: Wilfrid Laurier University Press, pp. 143–58.

Williams, L. (1998) "Melodrama Revisited," in N. Browne (ed.) *Refiguring American Film Genres: History and Theory*. Berkeley: University of California Press, pp. 42–88.

Willoquet-Maricondi, P. (2010) "Shifting Paradigms: From Environmentalist Films to Ecocinema," in Paula Willoquet-Maricondi (ed.) *Framing the World: Explorations in Ecocriticism and Film.* Charlottesville: University of Virginia Press, pp. 43–61.

Wilson, A. (1992) *The Culture of Nature: North American Landscape from Disney to the Exxon Valdez.* Cambridge, Mass.: Blackwell.

40

GREEN PORNO AND THE SEX LIFE OF ANIMALS IN THE DIGITAL AGE

Jennifer Peterson

The interdisciplinary field of animal studies shares much in common with feminist and queer theory. In the simplest terms possible, animal studies' foundational stance of questioning human dominance in every realm of existence (including critical theory) bears structural resemblance to feminism and queer theory's shared effort to interrogate the hegemony of patriarchy. As literary scholar Susan McHugh explains, "Nonhuman non-heteronormativity presents a profound challenge not just to identity forms but more importantly to disciplinary habits of thinking of human subjectivity as the default form of social agency" (McHugh 2009: 155). From a more materialist perspective, ecofeminist Carol J. Adams argues that there is an essential connection between patriarchal culture and meat eating; for Adams, the oppression of women and the oppression of animals "are culturally analogous and interdependent" (Adams 1990: 90).

We might locate another region of common concern in the domain of sexuality. The evidence is all around us, and the issue merits analysis more than ever in the digital era: animal images, like images of women, obsessively center on questions of sexual behavior. It is a commonplace to observe that the internet's *raison d'être* is porn ... and cats. Though these two categories (internet porn and animals on the internet) might seem unrelated, what happens if we consider their commonalities? (Indeed the porn-animal confluence has spawned many a meme and Tumblr site: visit the BarelyFeral Tumblr for starters.) Not just cats but animals in general thrive (as images) in digital culture. Animal reproductive habits function as one of the major motifs in nature documentaries, and YouTube is filled with animal mating videos. Although it is impossible to determine the amount of internet traffic devoted to it, pornography is now receiving sustained critical attention from feminist scholars working in the burgeoning field of porn studies (Grebowicz 2013; Williams 2014). While Constance Penley, Celine Parreñas Shimizu, Mireille Miller-Young, and Tristan Taormino are handling the topic of feminist porn elsewhere in this volume, this article aims to interrogate the convergence between animals, gender, and sexuality in contemporary digital culture. In order to find a point of focus on this large topic, I concentrate on a rather singular case study: the web series *Green Porno* (2008–9), directed by and starring Isabella Rossellini.

Green Porno crystallizes a set of concerns shared by feminism, media studies, and post-humanism, including sexuality, anthropomorphism, and the performative female body.

Each episode in the series takes the form of an educational film, presenting information about the mating habits of certain animals (insects and sea creatures, specifically). But *Green Porno*'s style of visualization is nothing like the staid presentation of facts one finds in the old-school classroom film. Instead, the series features Rossellini herself dressed as each animal—earthworm, firefly, barnacle, anglerfish—in colorful costumes made out of simple materials such as paper, foam, and lycra. There is no attempt at realism, and yet the series succeeds in educating viewers about animal reproduction while at the same time reveling in its polymorphously perverse blurring of human/animal and male/female boundaries. *Green Porno* is unique (and uniquely delightful), yet it is one of countless "novelty" videos to go viral in the hothouse environment of early social media in the late 2000s. As such a digital novelty, it is both exceptional and symptomatic. The fact that it is about sex, gender, and animals is what makes it of interest here.

Animal studies emerged as an interdisciplinary field in the humanities in the 1980s, the same era that fueled much feminist film theory. But until recently, animal studies has been much less influential than feminism; it has been gaining momentum in the last decade as related critical paradigms in posthumanism and the nonhuman have been gaining critical traction. Of course, there are many feminisms; likewise there are many perspectives within animal studies. Rather than trying to sketch an overview of animal studies' many forms, and rather than arguing for one or another version as the best approach, this article is motivated by the question: What do images of animals share in common with images of women in the digital era? I argue that *Green Porno* is an example of feminist performance that uses the figure of the animal to challenge normative concepts of sexuality.

John Berger's article "Why Look at Animals," first published in 1977, is arguably the foundational work of critical animal studies. In it, Berger makes the now-canonical argument that while animals have disappeared from everyday life in modernity, they have reappeared as signs of themselves in a set of specific practices: zoos, pets, children's toys. If he were to rewrite his essay now, Berger would most certainly address the proliferation of animals on the internet. Berger's essay was not explicitly feminist, nor did it engage with questions of gender, but it did establish the key point that when you look at animals (zoo animals in particular), "*you are looking at something that has been rendered absolutely marginal*" (Berger 1991: 24, italics in original). It is only a small step to recognize that the question of marginality or minoritarian status (whether actual, imposed, or strategic) has been one to which feminist film theorists have returned repeatedly over the years.

One of the key arguments of animal studies is that animals are rarely, if ever, represented as animals; rather they are constructed by and through their relationship to the human via anthropomorphism, allegory, or other anthropocentric constructs. Science might seem to come closest to the goal of objective representation, but even scientific images fail to represent animals as animals (see Daston and Galison 2007). Instead, scholars have argued, following Berger, that animals disseminate an *idea* of "nature" rather than nature itself. And "nature," as Raymond Williams famously wrote, "is perhaps the most complex word in the language" (Williams 1983: 219). We might start by pointing out that the word frequently exists as a category through which to define what or who counts as "human." Akira Lippit writes,

> As figures of nature that lack the capacity for speech and thus (self) reflection and (self) conception, animals are incapable of determining or regulating the discourse they put forth: they simply *transmit*. Animals are unable to withhold the outflow of signals and significations with which they are endowed.
>
> (*Lippit 2000: 21*)

In other words, animals take on a huge burden of signification in human culture that extends well beyond their material existence or biological function in the world. And as voiceless creatures who have a poignant ability to gaze back at us, animals have no power to determine or influence the tremendous load of signification with which they have been burdened.

Once this point is understood, it becomes necessary to identify the set of discourses animals signify. Individual animals have served allegorical purposes since antiquity (the lion signifying pride, the owl signifying intelligence, and so forth). But thinking more broadly across the meaning of animals as a general category, we can identify a much smaller set of key concepts associated with the animal in modernity, including categories such as reproduction, sentience, and death. In the case of animals on the internet, cuteness and sentimentality are clearly two dominant aesthetics. It would be reductive, however, to conclude that animals are allied with the feminine in contemporary culture, for horror and disgust also form major subcategories of animal imagery today. In this essay, I am concerned not only with the gendering of animals in visual culture but also with ways in which the image of the animal in the digital age connects to earlier visualizations of animals in film history. I argue that *Green Porno* demonstrates new media's remediation of formerly marginal topics and styles for mass audiences. In this case, *Green Porno*'s success demonstrates the popular appeal of a return-to-nature discourse that takes shape through the figure of the animal, a kind of vernacular rendition of the Deleuzian concept of "becoming animal" in the digital age.

Green Porno and animal drag

A series of very short videos depicting animal mating habits, the *Green Porno* series was created by Rossellini for the Sundance channel (episodes can be viewed online at the Sundance Channel website). The series debuted in May 2008 and quickly went viral. Produced, directed, written by, and starring Rossellini, *Green Porno* is a case of auteurism in which authorship is written on the body of the author herself. The success of the series hinges on Rossellini's ingenious remaking of her previous image as a movie star and model in favor of a series of whimsical performances in animal drag. Although much is made of her star persona and acting experience in the show's press coverage, Rossellini also returned to school while creating the series in order to study for a master's degree in animal behavior at Hunter College. In numerous interviews Rossellini has said that she chose to focus on animal sexual behavior because everyone is interested in sex, not science. In naming the series *Green Porno*, Rossellini acknowledges the internet's preponderance of porn, yet the particular iteration of sex in these short videos is anything but commonplace. Rather, these "sex scenes" are absurd, stylized, and frequently transgender, with Rossellini more often than not playing the male role. In other words, the series queers its two generic touchstones: the nature documentary and pornography. Two spinoff series followed (*Seduce Me* and *Mammas*), followed by a live stage version that continues to tour the United States at the time of this writing. Thanks to new media, along with her own performance and production talents, Rossellini has remade her career on her own terms in her late fifties and early sixties.

In combining the seemingly unlikely genres of the nature documentary and the sex video, *Green Porno* gleefully crosses the wires of each genre's cultural function, making documentary facts seem strange and short-circuiting the visual sexual gratification of pornography. This generic mash-up is made possible by a strategy of zoomorphism, in which a human dressed in artificial animal costumes pantomimes animal sexual behavior. We are all familiar with the seemingly inescapable gesture of anthropomorphism, familiar from children's stories, Disney films, and documentary films that project human characteristics onto animals, thus erasing animality and difference from the concept of the animal. *Green Porno*'s reverse anthropomorphism overturns this gesture, and instead presents a human who takes on animal characteristics. In dressing as an animal, Rossellini is not trying to pass as an animal. Rather, she reveals the anthropocentrism and artifice that fuels the human understanding of animals. We might best characterize this as a form of animal drag. Debra Ferreday has argued that forms of animal drag in popular culture (as practiced by "furries" and "cervine" fans of the online game *The Endless Forest*) function "as a kind of human-to-nonhuman cross-dressing that queers the boundaries of the human" (Ferreday 2011: 222). In her willingness to appear ridiculous, in her jubilant upending of every convention of feminine beauty, Rossellini manages to transcend the traditional role of feminine screen image to become something else: a human-animal-sexual hybrid. *Green Porno*'s zoomorphism blurs human–animal boundaries in the service of conveying information, but it also serves a purpose beyond simple education. *Green Porno* portrays nature itself as a queer domain and rewrites natural history as a queer science.

In each episode of *Green Porno*, as Rossellini appears dressed as an insect or a marine creature, she speaks in the first person while enacting the mating habits of each animal. "If I were a dragonfly … I would have compound eyes," begins the first episode, as a close-up of Rossellini's familiar visage dissolves into a close-up of her face in costume with bulging eyes and green bodysuit. The video continues, presenting a radically truncated dramatization of dragonfly sex accompanied by Rossellini's continuing first-person narration, which uses the future conditional tense. Here is the entire remaining text of the first episode:

> And I would see upwards, downwards, forwards, backwards. I would have a slim, slim body. I would have translucent, transparent wings. At the end of my slender body, I would have a pair of clasping organs. I would find a female, and I would grab her with them by the neck. She would twist her body to get to my genital pouch. But first, I will clean her vagina, to make sure she would only have my babies. Then, we would copulate. When finished, I don't let her go, but would drag her where I want her to lay our eggs. Then, release her.

The entire running time for this episode (minus credits) is only 48 seconds. Note the subtle shift between future unreal and real conditional tenses here: would/will. This slippage, which occurs throughout the series, helps blur the boundary between Rossellini as unreal animal and Rossellini as actual animal. This linguistic slippage is just one of several ways in which the series dissolves human–animal boundaries; here that dissolution is established on the level of discourse, but throughout the series that dissolution is also handled through characterization, costume, and performance.

The series' uncanny shift between human and nonhuman animality, played out through the presentation of Rossellini's voice and body, is echoed by the fluidity of sexed identities, as Rossellini adopts male, female, and hermaphrodite animal personas. Rossellini has said she chose to enact male animals more frequently than female ones in the series because: "Often the *males* are the ones that move. … It was already so absurd to play a worm or a barnacle that I didn't think it was a problem to play a male" (Hesse 2009). This statement disavows the unsettling effect of Rossellini's animal drag performances, however. In the episode "Whale," she appears dressed in a whale costume with a 6-foot erection (Figure 40.1).

Figure 40.1   Isabella Rossellini as a whale.

Source: "Whale" *Green Porno*, Isabella Rossellini, 2008.

As she stands, surrounded by other (paper) whales with giant erections, it is clear that this is a moment designed to render all penises strange. In fact, the entire series arguably works to undermine phallogocentrism, as penises are characterized as liabilities ("A penis has disadvantages in water, because it produces drag. And a dangling organ is in danger of being snagged") and sperm are described as "cheap." When, in the episode "Why Vagina?" Rossellini walks amid a comical forest of paper animal penises; she describes penis forms as secondary to the defining vagina. She explains that vaginas are different in different animal species, "so that I am not screwed by a bear. Penises. Species-specific. Each one unique to their respective vaginas."

In the episode "Praying Mantis" Rossellini mounts a (cardboard) female praying mantis and pantomimes the act of penetration, only to have her head bit off in mid-copulation a moment later while screaming, "Nothing stops me. I keep going! SEX!" In this episode and many others, Rossellini builds her animal drag performance to a frenzied climax of perverse pleasure that hinges on a unique blend of information and humor. Rossellini's human-animal-sexual hybrid embodiment retains some amount of uncanny disturbance even as it is rendered cute and inoffensive by the artificiality of the costuming and mise-en-scène.

Along with Rossellini herself, the highly artificial and stylized costumes and set design are a key part of the series' visual appeal. The show's co-producer and art director, Rick Gilbert, helped design the simple, low-budget, brightly colored sets. The costumes, designed by Andy Byers, are made out of everyday materials that might be found in a children's classroom. These important elements of mise-en-scène make it plain that the series is not aiming for a traditional documentary style approach to animal behavior. For all its artificiality, however, the series gets closer to portraying a concept of animality than many documentaries or, for that matter, a whole raft of Disney anthropomorphisms. Animality here is blatant yet unconscious, the paper costumes evoking subtle resonances in a way that live-action documentary footage does not.

Rossellini's animal performances are fluid, ever-changing, and somewhat monstrous, but at the same time delightful and funny. *Green Porno* focuses on animals not as sentimental or Oedipalized beings, but as creatures operating as micro-level agents with the power to destabilize established power structures. As such, it exemplifies the Deleuzian idea of "becoming animal," one of the more important concepts in animal and nonhuman studies today. For Gilles Deleuze and Félix Guattari, "becoming-animal" is not literally about humans becoming animals, but about a mode of relating to and envisioning animals, as an oppressed or minoritarian group (Deleuze and Guattari 1987). I am arguing that *Green Porno* is a kind of vernacular iteration of this idea, one that moves closer to a fantasy of becoming animal, but that really has to do with ideas of nature and the naturalization of sexual practices. While purporting to present facts about animal reproduction, these little episodes actually deconstruct the nature of sexual behavior itself, portraying the many surprising mating practices of animals as simply an existing multiplicity of (nonhuman) activities.

Digital novelties and sex as work

Green Porno must be understood within its production context at a particular moment in media history when social media was just emerging. The series became a set of early viral videos, rocketing across the internet in the early years of YouTube and Facebook, both of which had begun gaining momentum over the preceding two years, in 2006–7. *Green Porno* was specifically designed for multi-platform viewing, and it particularly targeted mobile phone viewers. The show got an early publicity boost when it was featured on *The Colbert Report* just one week after its debut. In that short piece, made for the transitional media form of cable TV (and subsequently reposted and shared on YouTube), Stephen Colbert got right to the heart of the show's uncanny sexuality: "Now, I happen to think Miss Rossellini is a very sexy woman, which makes this all the more disturbing. Isabella Rossellini is trying to get me to want to have sex with bugs!"[1] Although Colbert is of course making a parody of his sexual discomfort, other coverage in the popular press also highlighted the series' unusual tones of eroticism/uneroticism. One newspaper interview opens with the line,

> If you were one of those people who had Isabella Rossellini on your 'Five celebs I'm allowed to sleep with guilt-free' list, please just stop reading … and *certainly* never click to 'Green Porno' because that's where you will find the 'Blue Velvet' erotic goddess 1) dressed up in insect costumes … ; 2) simulating sex acts with giant fake bugs.
>
> (Hesse 2009)

As both of these responses make clear, Rossellini's star persona has been shaped to an inordinate degree by her role as Dorothy Vallens in *Blue Velvet* (David Lynch, 1986). Despite her long career as an actor, writer, model, and face of Lancôme cosmetics, *Blue Velvet* is Rossellini's most iconic role. *Blue Velvet* has been decried by some over the years for its spectacle of masochistic femininity: Vallens is sexually abused and seems to enjoy certain parts of it, although she is also portrayed as a victim. Regardless of one's interpretation of *Blue Velvet* (does it critique misogyny or reinscribe it?), the Vallens character reads as essentially sexual, reproductive, and inscrutable. These elements of seductive mystery became central to Rossellini's star persona—heightened by her European accent and foreign cinema royalty parentage (as the daughter of Ingrid Bergman and Roberto Rossellini). These characteristics are also cornerstones of the patriarchal image of women that feminist film scholars have been working to dismantle for decades. In her new role simulating sex in foam-and-paper insect and ocean mammal costumes, Rossellini picks up on the erotic dimension of her star persona and redirects it into the realm of the biological. Not only is Rossellini unconcerned with presenting herself within the traditional standards of feminine beauty, she self-consciously exploits the elements of her star persona associated with perverse or taboo sexuality. She also makes the most of her Italian accent at crucial moments

("My sexual drive is ze strongest!" she says while dressed as a male praying mantis) to play up the series' absurdist humor.

As short videos with content that stands out as unusual or eccentric against the backdrop of the mainstream mediascape, individual episodes of Green Porno function as "novelties." Like a novelty song or a novelty toy favor at a child's party, these episodes are minor, short, and markedly "different." The aesthetic or entertainment pleasure one takes in them is of a particular kind: quick, spectacular, short-lived. The internet is a paradise for this sort of novelty aesthetic; quick, spectacular, and short-lived is the viral video's stock-in-trade. "Novelty" is also a term for adult sex toys, and here the series' self-stated connection to pornography is worth interrogating. For these are not exactly "pornos." The Green Porno title functions as a kind of click-bait in the context of the digital mediascape, promising the viewer some kind of visualized sex, but then delivering nothing like one would have imagined. "Shrimp" and "Anchovy," for example, both turn into arguments for why it is either unethical or distasteful for humans to farm and eat these animals: "I lost my appetite," Rossellini concludes in both episodes.

Green Porno dramatizes sexual behaviors designed to produce offspring; at least in the series' first three seasons, sex is shown to be essentially reproductive. And yet along the way, there are many stories of domination, sacrifice, and death. The drone bee's penis breaks off after copulation, and he bleeds to death. The female limpet dies in the process of reproduction, although other attached males carry on, changing sex one by one as sequential hermaphrodites. Green Porno depicts animal reproduction as a kind of relentless work, work that we might argue falls into the contemporary aesthetic category of the "zany." Sianne Ngai (2012) argues that the zany is a potent aesthetic category in the digital age which, along with the cute and the interesting, constitutes a set of minor aesthetic styles that negotiate current exigencies. Ngai's analysis connects the zany to work; its particular affective mode is one of anxiety about production. She writes, "what is most essential to zaniness is its way of evoking a situation with the potential to cause harm or injury" (ibid. 10). The zany forms of work that Ngai describes (as particularly exemplified by Lucille Ball's character in *I Love Lucy*) create a "distinctive mix of displeasure and pleasure ... immediately confront[ing] us with our aversion to that [zany] character" (ibid. 11). Green Porno [ital] series exemplifies Ngai's point that through Web 2.0's proliferation of the zany, the cute, and the interesting, these aesthetic categories "do nothing less than reorganize the relation of subjects to postmodern geopolitical reality" (ibid. 14). Green Porno, I argue, uses the figure of the animal to reorganize its viewers' relationship to contemporary discourses of normative sexuality. In so doing, the series foregrounds the shared concerns of feminism and animal studies to undo the seemingly inviolable forces of "nature." By destabilizing some of the most deeply naturalized categories in culture, it is not only gender and sexuality that are rendered fluid; through this series of animal drag performances the territorializing line between the human and the nonhuman is also destabilized. This matters not only for animals, but also for those humans (people of color, queers, women) who have frequently been counted as "nonhuman."

Vaudeville, YouTube, and early cinema

Although Green Porno was presented and received as a novelty, it follows a preexisting tradition from vaudeville and early cinema, both of which featured numerous animal acts and performers wearing animal costumes. Indeed, the series' short-format comedic immediacy is a typical characteristic of what Henry Jenkins has called YouTube's "vaudeville aesthetic" (Jenkins 2006). Rossellini herself has drawn comparisons between her series and early cinema, saying in one interview, "I am not very technical, so my big inspiration is Georges Méliès, who made the first science-fiction films. Silent movies, to me, are a big inspiration" (Vitiello 2015). I want to conclude with a brief analysis of one particular early cinema short, *The Dancing Pig*, a 1907 film by the French company Pathé Frères which functions in the early twenty-first-century media ecosystem as a kind of cinematic prototype for *Green Porno*. Historically, *The Dancing Pig* exemplifies the common early cinema practice of filming established vaudeville acts. The vaudeville act shown in *The Dancing Pig* was filmed several times; the only known extant print displays a rather grotesque amorous pig. *The Dancing Pig* is a useful comparison because it was released on DVD by Flicker Alley in 2008, the year of *Green Porno*'s debut. *The Dancing Pig*, like *Green Porno*, is readily available on YouTube, which has the effect of rendering all media (from any time period, any country, and any mode of production) effectively equivalent.

The Dancing Pig runs at just under 4 minutes.[2] The film is a wondrous, nonsensical pastiche of interspecies romance, featuring dance performances, fluid gender identity (on the part of the pig), and two moments of pig disrobing. The film begins as a large pig (or rather, a person wearing a large pig costume) makes a series of failed romantic advances to a young dancing girl. She rebuffs him, and he is sad. We know this is a male pig because the large (and truly magnificent) pig costume he wears identifies him as such through jacket and bow tie. In retaliation for the pig's unwanted amorous gestures, the girl rips off his clothes to render him naked (though of course this is still a person in a pig costume, so there is no actual nudity). The pig, who is thoroughly anthropomorphized, cowers in shame, covering what would be its genital area with its hooves. But then the girl hands the pig a baton, and the two begin dancing joyously together, the pig forgetting its nudity. By the end of the dance, the girl has accepted the pig, and the two exit the stage hand in hand. The pair returns a moment later; this time the pig is wearing ladies' clothing (dress and hat). After a brief dance routine (during which the pig hams it up and sticks out its very long tongue), the two exit, only to have the pig return a moment later disrobed again, this time wearing only bloomers. The pig again hunches over in shame, but a moment later perks up, grinning broadly, and begins dancing again. The film concludes with a close-up tableau shot of the pig (in male clothing again) sticking out its tongue in a grotesque sexualized manner, baring its teeth.

As *The Dancing Pig* demonstrates, an uncanny play with animal sexual identities is not new to the digital era, but can be found in (admittedly marginal) visual traditions over a century old. YouTube is what links *The Dancing Pig* and *Green Porno*, both of which appear as novelty shorts in the chaotic easy-access world of digital media, which flattens historical differences. *Green Porno* revises the venerable tradition of animal vaudeville acts from early cinema such as that seen in *The Dancing Pig*. But while the two films share the practice of animal drag, it is only *Green Porno* that takes an anti-anthropocentric and feminist stance. Perhaps one front in the battle for the liberated future of moving images, then, can be found not in a technophilic fantasy of the new, but from within and out of the ruins of film history, through inspired practices of digital remediation and feminist performance like those found in *Green Porno*.

Related topics

Amy Borden, "Queer or LGBTQ+: on the question of inclusivity in queer cinema studies"
Felicity Colman, "Deleuzian spectatorship"
Alexa Weik von Mossner, "Ecocinema and gender"
Eliza Steinbock, "Towards trans cinema"

Notes

1 *The Colbert Report*, Season 4, Episode 52 (May 12, 2008). See clip at www.cc.com/video-clips/ k7k3ke/the-colbert-report-threatdown—cute-bears (accessed October 1, 2015).
2 There are many different versions of *The Dancing Pig* on YouTube. The historically correct one can be found at www.youtube.com/watch?v=IcCKPAnArsw (accessed July 15, 2016).

Bibliography

Adams, Carol J. (1990) *The Sexual Politics of Meat: A Feminist-Vegetarian Critical Theory*. New York: Continuum.

Berger, John (1991) "Why Look at Animals," in John Berger *About Looking*. New York: Vintage, pp. 3–28.

Cynthia, Chris (2015) "Subjunctive Desires: Becoming Animal in *Green Porno* and *Seduce Me*," in Michael, Lawrence and Laura, McMahon, eds., *Animal Life and the Moving Image*. London: British Film Institute, pp. 121–33.

Daston, Lorraine and Peter Galison (2007) *Objectivity*. Cambridge, MA: MIT Press.

Deleuze, Gilles and Félix Guattari (1987) "Becoming-Intense, Becoming-Animal, Becoming-Imperceptible … ," in *A Thousand Plateaus*. Trans. Brian Massumi. Minneapolis: University of Minnesota Press, pp. 232–309.

Ferreday, Debra (2011) "Becoming Deer: Nonhuman Drag and Online Utopias," *Feminist Theory* 12(2): 219–25.

Grebowicz, Margret (2013) *Why Internet Porn Matters*. Palo Alto, CA: Stanford University Press.

Hesse, Monica (2009) "Conversations: Isabella Rossellini Discusses Her *Green Porno* Project," *Washington Post*, March 29. See www.washingtonpost.com/wp-dyn/content/article/2009/03/26/ AR2009032604390.html (accessed October 7, 2015).

Jenkins, Henry (2006) "YouTube and the Vaudeville Aesthetic," on the "Confessions of an Aca-Fan" blog at http://henryjenkins.org/2006/11/youtube_and_the_vaudeville_aes.html (accessed October 30, 2015).

Lippit, Akira Mizuta (2000) *Electric Animal: Toward a Rhetoric of Wildlife*. Minneapolis: University of Minnesota Press.

McHugh, Susan (2009) "Queer and Animal Theories," *GLQ: A Journal of Lesbian and Gay Studies*, 15(1): 153–69.

Ngai, Sianne (2012) *Our Aesthetic Categories: Zany, Cute, Interesting*. Cambridge, MA: Harvard University Press.

Sinwell, Sarah E. S. (2010) "Sex, Bugs, and Isabella Rossellini: The Making and Marketing of *Green Porno*," *WSQ: Women's Studies Quarterly* 38(3, 4): 118–37.

Vitiello, Chris (2015) "Isabella Rossellini's *Green Porno* is Weird, Funny and Educational on the Science of Animal Sex," *Indyweek*, December 2. See www.indyweek.com/indyweek/isabella-rossellinis-green-porno-is-weird-funny-and-educational-on-the-science-of-animal-sex/Content? oid=4920924 (accessed December 30, 2015).

Williams, Linda (2014) "Pornography, Porn, Porno: Thoughts on a Weedy Field," *Porn Studies* 1(1–2): 24–40.

Williams, Raymond (1983) *Keywords*. New York: Oxford University Press.

Further reading

Adams, Carol J., and Josephine Donovan, eds. (1995) *Animals and Women: Feminist Theoretical Explorations*. Durham, NC: Duke University Press. (This anthology presents a series of analyses of animal representation and animal ethical issues from a feminist perspective.)

Cahill, James Leo (2015) "A YouTube Bestiary: Twenty-Six Theses on a Post-Cinema of Animal Attractions," in Katherine Groo and Paul Flaig, eds., *New Silent Cinema*. London, Routledge, pp. 263–93. (This article explores the explosion of animal imagery on the internet by analyzing 26 examples.)

Halberstam, Judith (2011) *The Queer Art of Failure*. Durham, NC: Duke University Press. (Halberstam argues that animated works such as The *Fantastic Mr. Fox* and the *Wallace and Gromit* series provide rich possibilities for rethinking collectivities, animality, and posthumanity.)

Haraway, Donna (1989) *Primate Visions: Gender, Race, and Nature in the World of Modern Science*. New York: Routledge. (Haraway's groundbreaking work analyzes the construction of nature in late-twentieth-century culture by focusing on the history of primatology.)

Haraway, Donna (1991) *Simians, Cyborgs, and Women: The Reinvention of Nature*. New York: Routledge. (This book contains Haraway's "Cyborg Manifesto," a seminal feminist theory essay and foundational text of posthumanism, which argues for the importance of the cyborg as a utopian figure that transcends traditional categories of embodiment such as biology and gender.)

41

CLASS/ORNAMENT

Cinema, new media, labor-power, and performativity

Erica Levin

The study of social class as it intersects with gender in film studies has tended to focus either on issues of representation or reception. In the first case, scholars have analyzed how the depiction of class and gender in specific genres, contexts, or periods operates as ideology. Scholars such as Biskind and Ehrenreich (1987) and Nystrom (2009) argue that shifts in the gendered representation of one class point to social and political uncertainties faced by another; arguing for example, that the depiction of working class masculinity in the 1970s indexes the anxieties of a shrinking middle class. Other scholars have drawn attention to the way shifting gender norms are inflected by class concerns. For example, Tasker (2002) analyzes how depictions of working women in New Hollywood cinema reflect shifts in the industry while betraying ambivalence about the broad cultural impact of feminist discourse. Focus on representational codes of class and gender in film studies is not without its critics. Concerns about the tendency to presume a neutral viewer whose own class perspective is either entirely determined by the text or otherwise deemed irrelevant have driven increased scholarly attention to the conditions of classed and gendered reception in specific viewing contexts. Often drawing upon ethnographic and archival sources, a reception approach takes up the question of how gender and class inflect new modes of mass spectatorship. The work of Hansen (1994) is exemplary in this regard. Her groundbreaking study, *Babel and Babylon*, looks at the film industry's promotion of a modern culture of mass consumption through appeals to viewers characterized by social and sexual difference, which in turn conditioned, she argues, the emergence of new contexts for intersubjective experience otherwise absent from the bourgeois public sphere.

This essay proposes an alternate model of analysis based on the allegorical strategies of reading that inform David James' revisionary survey of American avant-garde cinema (James 1989, 2005). It draws on insights generated by feminist film scholars' analyses of ideological codes of class and gender while keeping in view questions raised by film historians of mass spectacle and spectatorship. As a model focused on how films tell the story of their own production, James's allegorical mode of reading proves especially useful in the close analysis of experimental practices of appropriation, sampling, and montage that cite classical Hollywood cinema. The following essay models this mode of analysis by looking closely at *Mass Ornament*, a video installation by Natalie Bookchin made with found footage culled from YouTube that probes the conditions of performativity that shape the appearance of class and gender online today.

* * *

Webcam footage of an empty bedroom appears at the center of a dark screen. Unseen fingers tap at a keyboard, punctuating the ambient buzz of this otherwise mundane domestic atmosphere. Other casually empty interiors begin to appear and disappear alongside it on screen. Together they form a shifting, but always incomplete row of similar shots. The chatter of flickering televisions in these spaces contributes to a swell of white noise. A tinny recording of "Lullaby of Broadway" breaks through the din. The words "Mass Ornament" flash on screen. This sequence introduces a short video installation produced by the artist Natalie Bookchin in 2009. Bookchin is known for work that engages a wide range of new media formats. The *Databank of the Everyday* (1996), for example, uses a database to catalog digital photographs of banal gestures. In this and later work that involves interactive installation formats and video game platforms, she interrogates the biopolitical dimensions of information and surveillance culture. *Mass Ornament* calls attention to new cultural forms that have been fostered by the internet. The work pairs footage posted to YouTube of people dancing alone in their rooms with a soundtrack borrowed in part from the finale of *Gold Diggers of 1935* (1935), the first feature film directed entirely by the famed Hollywood choreographer, Busby Berkeley. Staged as a performance at the climax of Berkeley's depression era backstage drama, "Lullaby of Broadway" has been described by James as "one of the great film poems in the American cinema and one of its most succinct indictments of gender and class exploitation" (James 2005: 83). To begin then, this essay asks how gender, class, and the logic of exploitation appear in Bookchin's work, mediated through this reference to one of Berkeley's most noteworthy musical numbers.

Bookchin borrows the title *Mass Ornament* from Siegfried Kracauer, whose essay of the same name was first published in 1927. Kracauer takes as his titular subject the Tiller Girls, a troupe of dancers whose coordinated tap and kick routines prefigured the cinematic spectacles produced by Berkeley for the camera. Through the precise orchestration of highly abstracted and synchronized movement, dancers are transformed into what he calls, "indissoluble girl clusters" (Kracauer 1995: 76). No longer per-forming as self-possessed individuals; their limbs become abstract elements in elaborate visual designs and military-like formations. Kracauer reads the unfolding visual patterns made up of their fragmented movements as purely ornamental; "the star formations have no meaning beyond themselves" (ibid. 77). Though they serve no other purpose than the production of visual pleasure, Kracauer argues that they make manifest the "rational principles which the Taylor system merely pushes to their ultimate con-clusion" (ibid. 78). He observes, "The hands in the factory correspond to the legs of the Tiller Girl" (ibid. 79). The mass ornament is thus "the aesthetic reflex of the rationality to which the prevailing economic system aspires" (ibid. 79). But, he asserts, this rationality is ultimately false:

> The Ratio of the capitalist economic system is not reason itself but a murky reason. ...
> *It does not encompass man.* The operation of the production process is not regulated according to man's needs, and man does not serve as the foundation for the structure of the socioeconomic organization.
>
> (ibid. 81)

Though Kracauer is more concerned with the manifestation of the mass as an ornamental figure than with the social divisions its abstract configurations disavow, his account of the phenomenon suggests how capitalist ratio decouples precision choreography from the classed experience of factory labor it draws upon.

Taylorism—the theory of "scientific management" devised by the mechanical engineer Frederick Winslow Taylor—sought to increase the efficiency of capitalist production through the application of extensive time-and-motion-studies. Taylor's approach, outlined in his 1911 book, *The Principles of Scientific Management*, begins with the division of the design and management of production processes from their execution. "The most important object of both the workmen and the management," he writes, "should be the training and development of each individual in the establishment, so that he can do (at his fastest pace and with the maximum of efficiency) the highest class of work for which his natural abilities fit him" (Taylor 1911: 12). In practice, "scientific management" stripped knowledge and autonomy from workers and transferred increased control to their supervisors and managers. Under this system, time restraints and exacting guidelines for movement were set for specific tasks based on the rational principles of measurement and the study of energy expenditure. Taylor's scientific approach to the human body reduced it to a mechanistic device defined by its capacity for motor-like repetition, measured in increments of productive output. The segmentation of industrial production processes required by Taylor's methods yielded a new generalized conception of unskilled labor. The proletariat can be defined as the class with nothing to sell but its ability to work, what Karl Marx identifies as its "labor-power." Capitalism, Marx theorizes, exploits the difference between the cost of reproducing labor-power (through rest and nourishment) and the value of what that labor-power produces (goods manufactured, for example). Taylorization gave rise to an impossible fantasy of a non-fatigable worker engaged in the endless performance of simple, repeatable gestures, fueled by what Kracauer recognized as capitalism's "murky reason," reason that, in his view, failed to fully encompass human need.

The regimented training of the performative body under Taylorization corresponds to the emergence of the precision style dance popularized by the Tiller Girls. John Tiller, a bankrupt textile tycoon from Manchester, England, founded the dance company specializing in chorus line choreography in the early 1890s. The troupe offered young working class women a better-paid alternative to factory or mill work. Rehearsals were originally held in Tiller's defunct cotton processing plant, where he translated his experience with manufacturing into methods for training dancers to kick on cue. At auditions for the troupe, no one was asked to dance. Tiller took for granted that any woman in good health with the right measurements could be trained in his method, in effect treating dance as a form of unskilled labor. "The girls were 'Tiller-ized'" Kara Reilly observes, "in the same way Frederick Winslow Taylor's Scientific Management streamlined factory work through efficiency engineering" (Reilly 2013: 120).

In *Mass Ornament*, Bookchin also employs segmentation and abstraction to dissect movement into discrete units. She manufactures synchronization (or something approximating it) through deft editing. Her visual analysis of found YouTube footage recalls the methods of camera based motion-study that grew out of Taylor's theories, particularly through the work, who analyzed recorded movement to determine the most efficient or ergonomic way to complete a task. Bookchin, however, dissects movement that is purely ornamental, dancing which serves no purpose beyond the pleasure it generates. Her efforts highlight moments of visual correspondence between moves performed by distinct figures each isolated in their own video frame. If the choreography of

Tiller and Berkeley is synonymous with spectacular formations made up of many bodies moving in unison, then Bookchin's editing emphasizes the distance that separates individuals who nonetheless move in strikingly similar ways (Figure 41.1). Her work asks how the mass endures as a descriptive category in the age of pervasive computing and online social networks, and what new principles of production (and exploitation) might inhere in the ornamental forms to which these principles give rise.

Berkeley's "Lullaby of Broadway" opens on the small ghostly face of Wini Shaw surrounded by depthless black, a non-space, not unlike the blankness that frames the appropriated clips that appear and disappear throughout Bookchin's video. Shaw's face grows steadily larger as she sings the opening chorus of a song describing the nocturnal lives of "Broadway Babies"—"the daffodils who entertain" at downtown clubs and "don't sleep tight until the dawn," girls to whom "a daddy" says, "I'll buy you this and that." After the final lines of the lullaby intoning, "sleep tight baby," Shaw puffs on a cigarette while her upturned visage becomes a cutout in the darkness, a keyhole framing an aerial view of Broadway lined with lights. From there the film shifts into a dream-like reverie that takes the form of a city-symphony style montage. Much like Dziga Vertov's *Man with a Movie Camera* (1929), it depicts the collective rhythms of the work-a-day world.

The camera fixes on the gestures of young women in their bedrooms waking up and getting ready for work: an arm sweeps an alarm clock into a drawer, legs swing out of bed, a pair of feet glide into feather adorned satin slippers (Figure 41.2). These actions, depicted through a series of close-ups, offer glimpses of movement that evoke a collective body. Gestures refer to the social, which is to say, classed experience of participating in a world oriented around labor. These brief scenes highlight the means by which labor-power is restored through sleep and other forms of daily sustenance. The absolute, abstract non-space that opens the musical number throws into relief the appearance of gesture coded as social in and through this montage. As the sequence continues, people crowd the sidewalk and head *en masse* to the subway, where one by one they pass through a turnstile (for more on the urban dissolve sequencing in classic Hollywood cinema, see Pravadelli's essay in this volume).

Bookchin's pairing of appropriated YouTube videos with the strains of "Lullaby of Broadway" in *Mass Ornament* calls attention to the role that domestic space plays in Berkeley's musical number. But it also departs dramatically from its referent—in her work individuals never exit their private spaces to come together as a group. The video focuses on the non-narrative play between visual isolation and mimetic movement, while Berkeley's sequence, by contrast, shifts in register from city symphony to what David James describes as its "noir countermovement" facilitated by the introduction of a simple narrative structure.

Figure 41.1 Natalie Bookchin's *Mass Ornament* (2009).

Source: Mass Ornament, Natalie Bookchin, 2009.

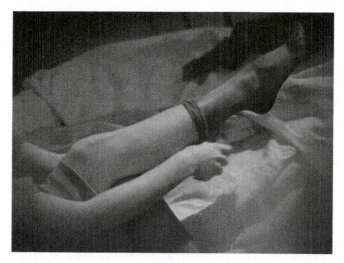

Figure 41.2   Glimpses of movement that evoke a collective body in *Gold Diggers of 1935*.

Source: Gold Diggers of 1935, Busby Berkeley, 1935.

The gender and class exploitation he highlights come to the fore with the appearance of a "Broadway Baby" who personifies the lyrics of the song.

As she steps out of a cab accompanied by a "daddy" in top hat and tails, her matronly neighbor airs some linens out the window above. When Baby bids farewell to her date and enters her apartment building, she is greeted familiarly by neighbors and the milkman on his rounds. Wearily ascending the stairs, she returns home to bed as everyone else moves in the opposite direction. Alone in her room, the camera fixes on her gestures in close-up. She gets undressed and swings her feet into bed, repeating in reverse the movements of the collective social body pictured earlier. James observes, this "montage of syntactically equivalent shots ... underscores its thematic contrasts between dusk and dawn and between the bed-times and working conditions of the different girls," and for that matter, the other older women and men she meets in passing (2005: 82).

The noirish turn that the sequence takes from this point forward pivots on Baby's threateningly liberated sexuality, much like the classic noir figure of the femme fatale theorized extensively by feminist film scholars (Kaplan 1978; for more on the femme fatale, see Grossman in this volume). At issue as well, I want to suggest, is the way her sexuality facilitates her capacity to apparently slip between classed identities. After morning fades to night, she wakes up and prepares to go out again. A shot of her sliding on a pair of elegant bedroom slippers calls back again to the earlier montage of women waking up collectively. A quick match cut of her feet in dancing shoes speeds the action along to a nightclub. There a dance performance takes place on a stage, mise-en-abyme within the larger musical performance. Baby and her male companion sit on a high platform by the edge of the stage, the only visible members of the audience. The emphasis on socially embedded gesture earlier in the sequence gives way here to formal abstraction in synchronized dance, leaving behind any trace of classed signification. Repetition generates ornamental uniformity rather than variegated social collectivity. Once the number begins, narrative momentum is suspended in favor of spectacular pleasure. Berkeley's choreography abstracts and monumentalizes the gestural movement that the camera earlier located in the work-a-day world.

The number begins with a couple dressed in white dramatically descending the stairs under a spotlight. Bookchin includes a brief clip of this scene in her video—also appropriated from YouTube—just after the title *Mass Ornament* flashes on screen. In the clip, we glimpse the first dancing figures to appear on screen, though only indirectly by way of their silhouettes. In Berkeley's musical number, the dramatic appearance of this dancing couple mirrors the visual isolation of Baby and her partner. Soon they are joined on stage by an army of figures wearing identical costumes in black, marching fascistically in lockstep. The women, encased in shiny black midriff-baring tops, appear as fetishistic totems of high Hollywood style (Figure 41.3).

Berkeley's mobilization of visual replication and the inversion of light for dark shift the image from the domain of shadows to that of ornament. The dancers twirl their partners and pound the stage with thunderous synchronized tap steps. At one point the camera hovers over a row of human torsos transformed through sequential movement into a series of machine-like gears turning automatically. Singing in unison, the dancers beckon Baby to join them on stage and she counters, "Why don't you come and get me?" Narrative momentum takes hold again as the mass ornament breaks down. Baby is drawn onto the stage and passed from one dancing partner to the next. The orderly mass disintegrates into an unruly crowd. Here the sequence lurches toward its dark climax. Baby flees the crowd, which now includes her male companion. They pursue her to a balcony where she seeks cover behind a pair of French doors. As she leans in to playfully kiss her lover through the glass, he flings the doors open with the full force of the crowd behind him, forcing Baby back and over the edge of the railing.

In the moment of her death, Baby's isolation from the mass takes a decidedly punishing turn. Her relationship to the dancers on stage remains ambiguously charged. Her movements mirror theirs, just as her evenings follow the daily rhythms of the working class women she lives among. Through her sexual association with a man of a different class however, she appears out of phase with these other figures. She slides into and out of her role as this man's "baby" as easily as she does a pair of satin bedroom slippers. Through her implied exchange of affection for such commodities, the film compares her to other working

Figure 41.3 "Lullaby of Broadway"—dancers in black.

Source: Gold Diggers of 1935, Busby Berkeley, 1935.

women who have nothing to sell but their own labor-power. She moves freely between their world and the world of her wealthy, bourgeois suitor. In the end, Baby is violently undone by her failure to assimilate perfectly to either domain. This failure precipitates the transformation of the orderly mass into the crowd. This crowd appears as the inverse image of the mass ornament, a fantasy formation of affectively charged, mimetic bodies reduced to an indissoluble cluster, no longer a dream image of rationality, but now its nightmarish opposite. The unity of the mass and its dark shadow, the crowd, figure a rationalist order that obscures the division between the working classes and their capitalist bosses.

James points out that Baby's brief, tragic story "inverts the saccharine resolution of the film's main plot" which involves a wealthy heiress and young hotel employee. It dramatizes what he calls "a social contradiction" in the form of "a surrealist nightmare of class consciousness," reflecting the "social realities" of the period, including the disproportionate exploitation experienced by working class women (James 2005: 83). It also suggests, I would add, how working women in this moment might come to find themselves out of synch with the gendered roles to which they would have been relegated in the past. The women who performed as the "Tiller Girls" were paid twice as much as their factory employed counterparts. They had the opportunity to travel extensively, though their experiences were often circumscribed by professional restrictions. Members of the troupe had to agree not to date while on tour and to give up their dancing careers once they were married. Doremy Vernon, a former Tiller Girl herself, draws upon interviews with other dancers in her historical study, *Tiller's Girls* to detail what it was like to transition back to working class surroundings after entering the public sphere as a performer on tour, often to exotic locations. Vernon highlights the difficulty of reassimilation faced by women who were forced into early retirement without much in the way of financial reserves. Finding their old living conditions shabby or dull after a brush with glamour, many described feeling lost or out of place. Family and friends would remind them how "they had stepped out of their class," implying they might have been better off had they never left (Vernon 1988).

"Lullaby of Broadway" is a reverie that unfolds along what Maya Deren describes as film's vertical axis, the domain of poetry which she contrasts to the horizontal axis of narrative (Deren 1970). James argues that Berkeley's film-poem anticipates the fascination in postwar avant-garde film with this poetic form, characteristic especially of Deren's "suicidal trance film," *Meshes of the Afternoon* (1943) (James 2005). He charts the development of a mode of filmmaking influenced by Deren, in which conflicts rooted in classed experience are decoupled from those bound up with gender and sexuality. Deren and many of her well-known queer acolytes, including Kenneth Anger and Curtis Harrington, focus on psychosexual conflicts staged in dream-like settings that seem cut off from the rest of the social world. Through the historical excavation of amateur and working class cinema, James calls attention to largely forgotten film histories that cut against this tendency. Elsewhere he discusses the evacuation of class from the study of film more broadly (James 1996). His revisionary survey of postwar filmmaking counters this tendency by focusing on the way films call attention to, or in his terms, "allegorize" the mode of their production (James 1989). Ranging across a wide span of filmmaking modes, including avant-garde, underground, independent, and experimental, he considers cinema's indeterminate and shifting imbrication in its political, cultural, and economic contexts. Following his lead, Bookchin's *Mass Ornament* calls to be read as a work that points to the process of its own production as it explores the contemporary conditions of mass spectacle.

Bookchin's cut-and-paste (or better, clip-and-repost) aesthetics are drawn directly from the digital online archives where she sources her material. She sidesteps narrative altogether in favor of audio layering and the simultaneous visual coordination of movement across discrete shots. Images of social collectivity in "Lullaby of Broadway" are generated through montage; working women wake up in their bedrooms and start the day. Scenes of synchronized choreography abstract gesture from this social context. The appearance of the mass (and the crowd as its dark shadow) screens out these lived experiences of working class life. Bookchin's *Mass Ornament* presents a negative image of these conditions of mass spectacle. The figures that pop up in separate frames in her video constitute neither a mass nor a crowd. The gestures they perform in their rooms are already mediated through mass spectacle; they do not add up to the kind of collective working class experience captured by Berkeley's Vertovian montage. As a result, signs of class in Bookchin's work are difficult to pin down. The accidental details of the interiors captured on screen may suggest traces of social meaning, but ultimately they resist signification. Does this particular bedspread or flickering television read as working class? Who can say for sure? What matters is that these banal spaces are private while at the same time imbricated in the emergence of a new kind of networked public sphere online, sustained by the proliferation of new media. Bookchin's work pictures the involution of the mass ornament in the age of YouTube. It asks how social bodies are mediated through online platforms. Classical cinema's embrace of the mass ornament set the stage for dramas in which social contradictions played out across bodies marked by class and gender difference. In "Lullaby of Broadway" the codes of class are conflated with gender in the figures of Baby and her bourgeois "Daddy." Scenes of working class life in Berkeley's film are largely represented through signifiers that are also gendered female and vice-versa. By contrast, most of the people that appear in Bookchin's video are female, but the inclusion of a few male figures engaged in similar dance moves suggests that gender does not function the same way in the work. The differences that structured the micro-drama of Baby's story in "Lullaby of Broadway" are no longer operative in Bookchin's *Mass Ornament*. Identity appears less fixed, more performative. Shifting registers from one mode of gendered or classed gesture to another is no longer threatening, if anything, performativity constitutes the normative condition of participation in this online public sphere.

The crowd in Berkeley's film betrays anxiety about the rise of mimetic politics—anxiety that erupts through the violence that underpins the sequence's fascist aesthetics. In Bookchin's work, we encounter the mediation of mimetic impulses through unseen networks of exchange. Bookchin describes her work as "trying to orchestrate a variety of quests to define and describe the self as a part of (and agent in) a larger social body" (Bookchin and Stimson 2011). Her work acknowledges that the risks of alienation and exploitation in undertaking this enterprise remain high. Throughout *Mass Ornament* view counts appear tagged to each appropriated video file. This subtle device points to new forms of abstraction and value extraction that have emerged with the rise of online media. At the same time, the work does much to call attention to the way the bodies on screen push against the constraints of isolation, conformity, and seamless digital exchange. Bookchin layers the soundtrack with noises produced by bodies bumping up against the surfaces of the spaces they occupy. Thuds, feet dragging, hands sliding down walls: these sounds bleed from one site to another, just as early in the work, the past bleeds into the present. Underscoring the connected distance between the bodies on screen, she asks what links the moment of the mass ornament's apogee in Berkeley's choreography to present conditions of sociability online. Looking at the way the work allegorizes the means of its own production through borrowed sound and strategies of montage brings this relationship into greater focus. Ultimately Bookchin's work is oriented toward the question of what might yet be possible, rather than what has already been. It visualizes a performative public sphere where mimetic desire does not signal the obliteration of class or gender difference so much as the powerful urge to make these differences matter in new ways.

Related topics

Maureen Turim, "Experimental women filmmakers"
Veronica Pravadelli, "Classical Hollywood and modernity: gender, style, aesthetics"

References

Biskind, P. and Ehrenreich, B. (1987) "Machismo and Hollywood's Working Class" in D. Bookchin, N. (2011) "Out in Public: Natalie Bookchin in Conversation with Blake Stimson" in G. Lovink and R. Miles (eds.) *Video Vortex Reader II: moving images beyond YouTube*. Institute of Network Cultures, Amsterdam. pp. 306–17.

Bookchin, N. and Stimson, B. (2011) "Out in Public: Natalie Bookchin in Conversation with Blake Stimson." *Rhizome Blog*, http://rhizome.org/editorial/2011/mar/9/out-public-natalie-bookchin-conversation-blake-sti/ Last Accessed July 15, 2016.

Deren, M. (1970) "Poetry and the Film: A Symposium" in P. Sitney (ed.) *Film Culture Reader*. New York: Praeger. pp. 171–86.

Hansen, M. (1994) *Babel and Babylon*. Cambridge, MA: Harvard University Press.

James, D. (1989) *Allegories of Cinema: American Film in the Sixties*. Princeton, NJ: Princeton University Press.

——— (ed.) (1996) *The Hidden Foundation: Cinema and the Question of Class*. Minneapolis, MN: Minnesota University Press.

——— (2005) *The Most Typical Avant-Garde: History and Geography of Minor Cinemas in Los Angeles*. Berkeley: University of California Press.

Kaplan, E. (ed.) (1978) *Women in Film Noir*. London: British Film Institute.

Kracauer, S. (1995) "The Mass Ornament" in T. Levin (ed.) *The Mass Ornament: Weimar Essays*. Cambridge, MA: Harvard University Press. pp. 75–88.

Nystrom, D. (2009) *Hard Hats, Rednecks, and Macho Men: Class in 1970s American Cinema*. Oxford: Oxford University Press.

Reilly, K. (2013) "The Tiller Girls: Mass Ornament and Modern Girl" in K. Reilly (ed.) *Theatre, Performance and Analogue Technology: Historical Interfaces and Intermedialities*. New York: Palgrave Macmillan. pp. 117–32.

Tasker, Y. (2002) *Working Girls: Gender and Sexuality in Popular Culture*. New York: Taylor & Francis.

Taylor, F. (1911) *The Principles of Scientific Management*. New York and London: Harper and Brothers Publishers.

Vernon, D. (1988) *Tiller's Girls*. Oxford: University Printing House.

42

FILM FEMINISM, POST-CINEMA, AND THE AFFECTIVE TURN

Dijana Jelača

This essay brings together the frameworks of post-cinema and the affective turn in order to examine how cultural echoes of film feminism reverberate from cinematic to post-cinematic platforms, as well as between different paradigms of subjectivity, and point to the continued vitality of feminist inquiry in understanding how shifts in screen technology influence the notion of womanhood as such. I first highlight relevant works in feminist film studies that have examined the links between cinema, spectatorship and the sensual (or the body), before turning to more recent studies of affect and the notion of the post-cinematic, in order to situate current shifts in both technology and scholarly inquiry. In the later parts of the essay, I analyze two music videos—as popular post-cinematic media forms—to illustrate how cinema and feminism are equally vital to the newer media, and function as sites of excess that challenge reductive conclusions about identity and subjectivity. With these case studies, I demonstrate how film and feminism continue to echo as important cultural touchstones in our post-cinematic present saturated with multiplying screens, viewing positions, and incommensurable subject formations.

Body of evidence: film, spectatorship, excess

The body, or the embodiment, of the subject is to be understood as neither a biological nor a sociological category but rather as a point of overlapping between the physical, the symbolic, and the sociological.

Rosi Braidotti (1994: 4)

In her influential essay "Film Bodies: Gender, Genre, and Excess," Linda Williams called attention to the ways in which certain movie genres trigger a sensational response, or "give our bodies an actual physical jolt" (1991: 2). In illuminating three "body" genres—melodrama, horror, and porn—(which, importantly, are carriers of low cultural status), Williams traced the ways in which our physical bodies, heretofore not frequently evoked in feminist film studies, represent a key site of spectatorial encounter, one that simultaneously conditions and reveals the ways in which gender, as well as class and taste dispositions, both inform, and are in turn informed by, our affective responses to viewing. Rather than being

446

merely gratuitous, Williams shows how excess functions as a system in itself, positioning body spectacle—orgasm, terror, or weeping—as central foci for gender (de)construction and its interaction with the concept of genre.

In the intervening years, a body of work has arisen that examines the physical body and its encounter with cinema more widely, through various modes of scholarly inquiry which could, in broad terms, be divided into two trajectories: cognitive approaches, (Bordwell 1985; Bordwell & Carroll 1996; Persson 2003; Smith 2003; Plantinga 2009), and phenomenological approaches (Sobchack 1992; Marks 2000; Kennedy 2000; see also Jenny Chamarette's chapter in this volume). Both trajectories sometimes turn to, and loosely rely on the findings of neuroscience, which has permeated emerging trends in film studies that have come to be dubbed psychocinematics (Shimamura 2013) and neurocinematics, or, the neuroscience of film (Hasson et al. 2008). While cognitive theory treats the spectator as an active information seeker, phenomenological approaches turn to affect, sensation and the body (which, in a Deleuzian model, is understood to be an assemblage with many parts) as central frameworks for understanding the film experience. In their summary of the two trajectories, Adriano D'Aloia & Ruggero Eugeni (2014) state that cognitive approaches focus on *viewer-as-mind* (or, spectatorship as a measurable, even quantifiable mental activity), while phenomenological approaches turn to *viewer-as-body* (or, spectatorship as embodied perception rooted in affect and the "logic of sensations" [5]). While this broad distinction rests on the premises of the mind/body split, it also illustrates how the two trajectories seem to be opposed to one another. Where they nevertheless align is in their critique of psychoanalytic film theory (including its feminist domain), and its seeming preoccupation with pleasure and desire, which, they contend, precludes other analytical approaches to spectatorship, film experience and its affective, or cognitive impact (Kennedy 2000; Smith 2003). However, cognitive film theory has not had much to offer in place of psychoanalytic understandings of sexual difference—a concept it frequently challenges, or elides altogether. For instance, Cynthia A. Freeland argues that: "psychoanalytic feminists construct genderized accounts of the tensions in horror between key features of spectacle and plot. But it is entirely possible to construct a theory of horror that emphasizes these same tensions without genderizing them" (1996: 201). In opposition to "psychodynamic feminist approaches," Freeland's proposed cognitive feminist theory of horror would "shift attention away from the psychodynamics of viewing movies, and onto the nature of films as artifacts that may be studied by examining both their construction and their role in culture" (ibid. 204). It is not clear, however, how and why such an approach needs to be premised on a dismissal of the insights of psychoanalytic feminist film theory, rather than placed in a meaningful conversation with it. In opposition to cognitive film theory, phenomenological approaches have been more attuned to the complexities of embodied difference and the hierarchies of power that (in)form experiences when it comes to subjectivity constituted through and around the work of cinema.

With this essay's focus on the future of feminist film theory, I am particularly interested in examining how some of the newer trajectories—most notably a turn to affect—can help us think about the feminist politics of "post-cinema." Post-cinema is here deployed as a term that does not designate the end of cinema, but rather situates cinema's current historical moment in the context of digital technologies which have overtaken the more traditional celluloid film form, if not rendered it entirely obsolete. Likewise, digital technologies have fundamentally changed the ways in which film is not only made, but also distributed and viewed. Nevertheless, echoes of cinema's celluloid past persist in the post-cinematic present, and frequently inform its envisioning of the future. If the proliferation of digital screen technology has ushered in a displacement of the centrality of a single dominant frame of representation, these multiplying digital screens frequently refer, in an intertextual manner, to cinema as an enactment of "feminist reverberations," where feminism is understood to function as "movements in space and time-history" (Scott 2002: 11). A similar movement, across time, space, and technological platforms, can be detected in film feminism and its reverberations that trigger intertextual references in the post-cinematic domain. Later in this essay, I discuss several prominent instances of film feminism functioning as a feminist reverberation in the post-cinematic domain, as a way to illustrate that a convergence of affect theory and post-cinematic technology carries significant scholarly potential for the future of feminist film theory.

Notes on affect, subjectivity, (post)cinema and (post)feminism

The affective turn developed in large part through the influence of the works of Gilles Deleuze on the one hand, and Silvan Tompkins on the other (for more on affect in the Deleuzian sense, see Felicity Colman's essay on Deleuzian spectatorship in this volume). Many theorists sought to engage their ideas about body, corporeality, sensation, and indeterminacy as a way to introduce into cultural studies what they saw as a blind spot: a consideration of the material body and its corporeal (in)consistencies. To that end, Steven Shaviro draws on the work of Brian Massumi to theorize what he calls "post-cinematic affect." "For Massumi," Shaviro notes,

> affect is primary, non-conscious, asubjective, or presubjective, asignifying, unqualified, and intensive; while emotion is derivative, conscious, qualified, and meaningful, a "content" that can be attributed to an already-constituted subject. Emotion is affect captured by a subject, or tamed and reduced to the extent that it becomes commensurate with that subject. Subjects are overwhelmed and traversed by affect, but they have or possess their own emotions.
>
> *(2010: 3)*

By extension, it may follow that what is uncontained cannot be entirely subsumed under a system of controlled meanings, or ideology. Yet when affect is attached to a subject and constitutes it at the same time, modes of recognizability depend on pre-existing structures of meaning, but also feeling. In the post-cinematic landscape where multiplying digital screens replace singular cinematic ones, cinema itself becomes an object of affective investment translated into nostalgia, melancholy, disavowal, or some combination of the three, but is never entirely subsumed under any of them, since, "behind every emotion, there is always a certain surplus of affect" (Shaviro 2010: 4). Shaviro summarizes the differences between the analog celluloid cinematic screen and its post-cinematic digital counterpart in the following way:

> Where analog cinema was about the duration of bodies and images, digital video is about the articulation and composition of forces. And where cinema was an art of individuated presences, digital video is an art of what Deleuze calls the dividual: a condition in which identities are continually being decomposed and recomposed, on multiple levels, through the modulation of numerous independent parameters (Deleuze 1995, 180, 182).
>
> *(ibid. 17)*

Yet this perpetual (de)composition may not be only post-cinematic: it echoes back to Williams' cinematic excess, or "a sense of over-involvement in sensation and emotion" (1991: 5) (which in many ways points to affect, even when she does not use the term itself). Williams describes in the body genres a spectatorial fascination with a body "beyond itself," or in "rapture" (ibid. 4)—in other words, a body so engrossed by sensation, or consumed by affect that it pushes beyond subjectivity, always existing in excess of any one subject position and of identity as such. This may be akin to Shaviro's post-cinematic affect—both processes are, in significant ways, gendered even when they push beyond static notions of gender. Williams notes that:

> Even when the pleasure of viewing has traditionally been constructed for masculine spectators, as is the case in most traditional heterosexual pornography, it is the female body in the grips of an out-of-control ecstasy that has offered the most sensational sight.
>
> *(ibid.)*

Shaviro, on the other hand, examines, in the post-cinematic figure of Grace Jones, how her persona crosses "the boundaries separating men from women" (2010: 20). Shaviro finds that Jones "embodies, and transmits, flows of affect that are so intense, and so impersonal and inhuman, that they cannot be contained within traditional forms of subjectivity" (ibid.).

Similarly, Williams focuses on how sensory reactions that float between the screen and the spectator in circular fashion may tap into normative notions about gendered bodies, yet her discussion of sensory overabundance nevertheless points to the ways in which subject positions constructed through body genres are not "as gender-linked and as gender-fixed as has often been supposed" (ibid: 8). In thinking about bodily, sensory responses to spectatorship, Williams uses Laplanche and Pontalis' 1968 theory of fantasy as a "place where 'desubjectified' subjectivities oscillate between self and other occupying no fixed place in the scenario" (ibid. 10). Extending the function of sensory excess and fantasy as a place of oscillation for "desubjectified subjectivities" may relate to affect theory's stipulation that affect is the excess that points to the edges of subjectivity rather than to its formation. I aim to explore affect as sensory excess that oscillates between the category of the subject or of identity, gendered or otherwise, and its perpetual dismantling. How does that oscillation between subject and beyond-subject operate in the context of post-cinema and its multiplying fields of not only vision, but sensory impact more generally? How can feminist film theory shift our understandings, as well as be shifted in its own right, in light of those transformations?

Existing scholarly approaches to cinema and affect frequently focus on films that portray or evoke heightened sensory, even sensationalist responses—for instance, a focus on cinematic violence, one of the "gross" factors in Williams' essay, has been examined in greater detail by authors like Carol Clover (1987), and more recently by Paul Gormley (2005) and Alison Young (2009). In *Deleuze and Cinema: The Aesthetics of Sensation*, Barbara Kennedy takes a wider approach, arguing that: "the look is never purely visual, but also tactile, sensory, material and embodied" (2000: 3). By extension, the sensory impact of cinema is important to consider not only when it amounts to excess, but rather as an all-encompassing and ever present process that needs to be accounted for if cinema's (shifting) influence on perception is to be fully understood. Drawing on Deleuze's philosophy, Kennedy proposes that feminist film studies move away from psychoanalytically informed notions of pleasure and desire, and moreover, away from the notion of subjectivity as such.

Through the Deleuzian framework, "subjectivity is subsumed through becoming, affect—and sensation" (Kennedy 2000: 6). While Kennedy's project is grounded in feminist politics, she adopts "post-feminism" as a paradigm that reflects "a desire to move outside a politics of difference or a politics of gendered subjectivities, to a micro-political pragmatics of becoming where subjectivity is subsumed to becoming-woman" (ibid. 21). Moreover, post-feminism is here linked with various other "posts" (postmodernist, post-theoretical, post-structuralist, post-semiotic, post-linguistic). However, even while she proposes it as a paradigm that would instigate a thinking beyond subjectivity (and essentialist notions of womanhood-as-identity), Kennedy concedes that post-feminism has been identified within larger cultural discourses as a term that suggests that feminism is no longer necessary or vital as a political project. While she resists such meanings, her use of the term cannot avoid association with such dominant implications about feminism-proper's obsolete status.

Instead of prefixing feminism with a word that denominates something beyond it, perhaps we can recast the meaning of feminism itself as a concept that should not be bound by one and one definition only, but rather seen as "becoming" in its own right. I therefore aim to retain the notion of feminism without the "post," even while simultaneously adopting the term post-cinema, since there exist important political implications that separate the two. While post-cinema has been deployed as a scholarly (and arguably apolitical) term that denotes digital technologies that have succeeded the analog film, post-feminism as a concept has frequently been deployed to the detriment of feminist projects as such, by way of implying their altogether obsolete status. As post-feminism has frequently been used as a means to depoliticize feminism, it remains a radical stance to insist on the latter term intact. I retain feminism as a concept that should not be prefixed with a "post," even when we talk about its transformation—via social change, theoretical shifts, technology, or shifting fields of perception—into something other than it had previously been.

And while Kennedy insists on a "beyond subjectivity" framework of Deleuzian becoming, some affect theorists have been careful to not dispel the notion of subjectivity altogether, recognizing its contingent relevance. For instance, Brian Massumi draws distinctions between affect and emotions, and argues that emotions are affect captured by a *subject*, or a "self-," where the hyphen denotes that "'self' is not substantive, but rather a relation" (2002: 14). And while there is always affect that exists in excess of subjectivity, there *is* nevertheless a subject being formed or made recognizable through his or her possession of different emotions. It is, then, precisely in the affective excess that "subjectless subjectivity" (Kennedy 2000: 46) is located, yet that excess never entirely does away with subjectivity altogether, but rather always already exists and is defined by its *simultaneous proximity and irreducibility* to subjectivity.

These notions of becoming, excess, and subjectless or desubjectified subjectivity can be returned to a feminist political project that sees "woman" as a figure who is always both becoming and becoming undone, yet is nevertheless important to retain, in all her conceptual instability. This figure is a site of political struggle over not only contested meanings, but also of continued material inequalities that persist even after the concept of "woman" is theoretically deconstructed as a phantasm (as Massumi notes, phantasms are real after all). And by strategically retaining the temporary stability of the notion of "woman" (while remaining mindful of the pitfalls of essentialism), we can recognize the continued vitality of feminism as a political project that challenges the status quo rather than descending into relativism. As structures of feelings that occasionally reverberate in the post-cinematic, feminisms could be seen as a paradigm that always already provides a nod to the incommensurable aspects of woman-as-subjectivity, by refusing to be entirely subsumed under the traditionally-defined frameworks of either womanhood or feminism (in other words, they are both in perpetual becoming). This is particularly the case in the context of the post-cinematic visual and aural landscape and its sensory impact. In what follows, I analyze two instances of post-cinema that converge affect, excess, (neo-)feminist frameworks, "beyond subjectivity," and womanhood at the same time, in order to illustrate a possible trajectory of film feminisms in the shifting technoscapes of our future.

Music video: feminist film reverberations

In his theorizing of post-cinematic affect across different media platforms, Shaviro places particular focus on music videos: "Films and music videos … are best regarded as affective maps, which do not just passively trace or represent, but actively construct and perform, the social relations, flows, and feelings that they are ostensibly 'about'" (2010: 6). The music video is a post-cinematic medium that frequently pays homage to the history of cinema and does so via intertextuality and quotation. In particular, there is a distinct tradition of female pop performers drawing overt links in their music videos to the female icons of the cinematic screen: Madonna's widely analyzed (and discussed in this *Companion* in Janet Staiger's essay on Reception Studies) references to classic Hollywood (in, for instance, "Material Girl," "Open Your Heart," or the David Fincher-directed "Express Yourself" and "Vogue") are a case in point. But beyond this classic example, there are the more recent, overt sci-fi film references in Ariana Grande's "Break Free" (Chris Marrs Piliero, 2014) and Taylor Swift's "Bad Blood" (Joseph Kahn, 2015). Music video has been deeply indebted to both cinema and film feminism, by way of recasting onscreen woman-to-woman solidarity from one medium to another, as well as by linking the cross-textual reverberations centered around female subjectivity through an appropriation that highlights women's agency (also known in the context of pop culture as "girl power"). These intertextual links between the cinematic and post-cinematic visual and aural landscape largely leave the notion of female subjectivity unchallenged, opting for a more traditional understanding of film feminist reverberations across time, space, and media platforms. However, several notable exceptions to this tendency exist, works that simultaneously uphold and undermine woman-as-subjectivity, in their casting of excess as a feminist structure of post-cinematic feelings.

Here I focus on two music videos that go beyond the "mere" homage of cross-media referencing, and stage moments of crisis through excess that points to the incommensurability of "woman" and "feminist" as stable subject positions. The first is Lady Gaga and Beyoncé's music video "Telephone" (Jonas Åkerlund, 2010). Structured as a film, it opens with shots of barbed wire and a prison exterior, coupled with exploitation film-style opening titles. That this is not "just" a music video designed to accompany a pop song is emphasized by the fact that the song itself does not start until well into the video, and thus the length of the video/film exceeds the audio limits of the song itself (something that is frequently done when the music video is positioned as a cinematic event—an approach popularized by Michael Jackson). "Telephone" also frequently nods to the post-cinematic proliferation of screens, as it switches between film camera and surveillance cameras. The song's sonic twitches are echoed in the interruptions of visual continuity, further reflecting a disintegration of the seamless cinematic framework to which "Telephone" is both indebted but also works at deconstructing.

Lady Gaga is ushered into the women's prison at the beginning of the video, presumably as a result of the murder she committed in her previous video, "Paparazzi" (also directed by Åkerlund, 2009). The video's first line of dialogue points to the threat of castration, a frequent fixture of psychoanalytic feminist film theory—upon undressing Lady Gaga, one guard tells another: "I told you she didn't have a dick." "Too bad," responds the other. A nod to feminist critiques of phallogocentrism, this exchange simultaneously represents a tongue-in-cheek response to the questions about Gaga's own subjectivity—in particular, questions about her sexual and gender identity. Indeed, this prison is a decidedly queer place whose occupants are ambiguous in many ways: a futuristic queer phantasm that houses unclassifiable figures, from their gender ambiguity to eccentric appearances that suggests a BDSM orientation of desire, and a preoccupation with the aesthetics and fetishism of style.

The video's film references are numerous and telling: from Wonder Woman—a multimedia fantasy of a supremely feminine superhero vixen (Figure 42.1)—to the 1974 women's prison exploitation flick *Caged Heat* (Jonathan Demme), to *Thelma and Louise* (Ridley Scott, 1991), to Quentin Tarantino's female vigilante saga *Kill Bill* (2003–4). These stages of film history referenced in "Telephone" are, more precisely, stages of the onscreen endurance of woman-as-subjectivity, whether her presence is feminist-leaning or exploitative (or somewhere between the two poles). "Telephone" draws these cinematic references together in order to recast female subjectivity through excess and incommensurability inside the post-cinematic domain.

When Beyoncé bails Gaga out of prison, she admonishes her nonchalantly ("You've been a bad girl. A very very bad bad girl, Gaga"), before stuffing a large bite of Honey Bun (a reference to *Pulp Fiction*) in her mouth and feeding a piece to Gaga, thus emphasizing the playful affect over serious reproach of female "badness." While Beyoncé sings her lines, Gaga takes Polaroid pictures of her: a woman gazing and imaging another woman, and an intertextual reference to two other cinematic feminist outlaws on the run—Thelma and Louise.

After Gaga helps Beyoncé poison her abusive boyfriend, Beyoncé addresses the camera with: "I knew you'd take all the honey, you selfish motherfucker." Gaga prepares the poisoned meal in scenes that are framed as edgy parodies of 1950s tropes of perfect housewives. The sweetness that is frequently called upon in the video—honey, Sweet Bee, maple syrup—and pin up, girly imagery are a reflection of feminine appeal which turns out to be lethal when Gaga poisons everyone with the sweet syrup.

Just as they are identified as feminist crusaders when they turn on Beyoncé's abusive boyfriend, the video turns to incommensurable excess: they kill everyone in the diner,

Figure 42.1   Wonder becoming-women: Lady Gaga and Beyoncé in "Telephone".

Source: "Telephone," Jonas Åkerlund, 2010.

Note: Music video.

including the dog. As they flee the scene (via the same Pussy Wagon driven by the murderous Bride in *Kill Bill*), Gaga says: "We did it, honey B. Now let's go far, far away from here." Echoing Thelma and Louise's promise to "keep going," Gaga and Beyoncé exchange the following words: "You promise we'll never come back?" "I promise." As a twenty-first-century, post-cinematic, cross-racial Thelma and Louise, Gaga and Beyoncé challenge the redemptive aspects of feminine woes, not placing their quest within firmly female-positive, or socially affirmative frames of reference. Rather, they are anti-heroes whose violent quest at times overlaps with, but is not entirely contained by, traditional feminist frameworks. And that is precisely what may make it decidedly feminist, if we position feminism as that which is always in the process of becoming, and which has not (yet) been domesticated when it comes to redemptive notions of subjectivity. Gaga and Beyoncé's acting in excess of the traditionally-defined feminist struggle—their violence extending beyond "mere" female empowerment and veering towards disruptive anti-social behavior altogether—all the while insistently referencing feminist cinematic milestones, envisions post-cinematic feminism beyond the subjectivity of womanhood altogether, one premised on excess more so than redemption, closure, and containment.

They cross hands as the car speeds ahead, in yet another reference to *Thelma and Louise*, albeit with an arguably more unnerving ending (Figure 42.2). Here excess is incommensurability: echoes of film feminism are mixed with the tongue-in-cheek excess of violence that posits the two women as both justified feminists *and* violent, anti-social outlaws. Whereas Thelma and Louise remained cast as victims of circumstances even when they became empowered crusaders for equality, Gaga and Beyoncé push beyond this moralistic recuperability and drive away into neo-feminist excess, beyond female subjectivity, as it were. In their departure into outlaw waters (or, in their going off "the grid," to use Massumi's terminology), they enact a kind of affective excess (where this phrase may be an oxymoron, because affect *is* excess) beyond traditionally feminist structures of feelings, and towards an uncharted territory that defies denomination and thus remains vital. Their becoming-feminist is, therefore, simultaneously coupled with their feminist undoing—a stance that performs an affective politics of partial (mis)alignment with traditional feminism all the while acknowledging its ongoing importance.

Figure 42.2   Post-cinematic echoes of film feminism: Gaga and Beyoncé as Thelma and Louise.

Source: "Telephone," Jonas Åkerlund, 2010.

Note: Music video.

The second video that circulates the affective excess of post-cinematic feminist feelings is Rihanna's "Bitch Better Have My Money" (Rihanna and Megaforce, 2015)—a radical, and radically political short film that sees Rihanna commit graphic violence against a rich white couple. Like "Telephone," the video's depiction of female outlaws echoes *Thelma and Louise*, but also another cinematic milestone that sees excess as a framework for depicting feminine woes: Brian de Palma's *Carrie* (1976). The end of "BBHMM" sees Rihanna walking in slow motion towards the camera, her face and body covered in blood, in a visual reference to *Carrie*'s monstrous feminine protagonist. And in another film reference—to *Faster Pussycat! Kill! Kill!* (Russ Meyer, 1965)— the female outlaws in the video are a cross-racial group of vigilantes whose leader is Rihanna herself, and who kidnap and torture a wealthy white woman. While throughout most of the video, it could be assumed that the "bitch" in the song's refrain is the kidnapped white woman, the final moments reveal that the "bitch" is, in fact, her accountant husband (played by Mads Mikkelsen, in a reference to TV's "Hannibal"), who embezzled Rihanna's money. This play on the gendered stereotypes of a culturally sensitive term calls attention to the repurposing of the term towards an unexpected meaning: calling out a man's capitalist power over the wronged woman, who enacts ultimate revenge by taking his life. The scene of excess is here staged through such a repurposing (and a critique of capitalist gluttony), but also through seemingly gratuitous drug use and excessive partying that occasionally interrupts the revenge plan, and sees the vigilantes not only "lose themselves" in drug-induced pleasure, but drug their prisoner as well. Moreover, the gang's excess is positioned as an exercise in "low class:" cheap motels, tacky clothes, junk food, all in juxtaposition to their prisoner's opulence and luxury. Later, excess is deployed as violence, at once studious and over the top (before slaughtering her accountant, Rihanna plays with the phallic tools frequently deployed as weapons of violence towards women in horror movies and TV shows like the aforementioned "Hannibal"—knife, hammer, the chainsaw). Sonically, the song dissolves while the video crosscuts between past and present, and sets up the scene of violence, which takes place off screen, as the spectator is privy only to its bloody aftermath.

In "BBHMM," Rihanna is a fighter for vigilante justice, but she is also a non-redemptive figure who cannot be merely coopted into an icon of female empowerment, since that would discipline her more threatening aspects. Indeed, Rihanna, as a pop cultural icon, is an unnerving figure who remains somewhat of an enigma—perhaps currently singular in her seeming lack of desire to appease the audience or cast an image of a friendly, girly, sexualized non-threat. In many ways, links can be drawn to Shaviro's analysis of the differences between Grace Jones and Madonna—two of Rihanna's most important predecessors— where Rihanna would act as a figure closer to Grace Jones, standing alone and apart from her audience because, as a black woman, she is "always already 'marked' as a body" (2010: 23). Taking into consideration the double bind that women of color find themselves in (simultaneously marked as both sexual and racial Others), Rihanna at the end of "BBHMM" is a figure difficult to identify with in appeasing feminist overtones—she both references and disowns her white cinematic predecessor, Carrie, while challenging the frameworks of gendered, racial, as well as classed prejudice premised on stable identity traits. She faces the camera in slow motion, simultaneously walking closer to us and into uncertainty, a black woman who is simultaneously familiar (in the echoes of Carrie), and an unidentifiable figure whose face does not reflect any recognizable emotion (Figure 42.3). She becomes a vigilante void which, in contradistinction to Lady Gaga and Beyoncé, does not drive away from us, but slowly moves closer towards us, embodying an inquisitive and threatening gaze that defies identification or classification, and that resides in affective excess itself.

Figure 42.3 Beyond subjectivity: Rihanna-as-Carrie returns the gaze.

Source: "Bitch Better Have my Money," Rihanna and Megaforce, 2015.

Note: Music video.

In lieu of conclusion: post-cinematic becoming-feminist

Both videos discussed in the previous section implicitly critique simple notions of female subjectivity and empowerment, and opt for an excessive restaging of becoming-feminine *and* becoming-feminist in the post-cinematic medium: the pop singer is both a feminist and a non-redemptive threat to the status quo, who cannot be entirely contained by female subjectivity or the feminist project. Perhaps that is where the figure of the post-cinematic feminist need always reside in order to remain a non-conforming, vital presence: placed within the familiar frameworks of feminist structures of feeling, as well as in perpetual excess of them.

If, as Brian Massumi argues, we need to draw a distinction between the conditions of emergence and re-conditionings of the emerged, where the former "are one with becoming" and the latter "define normative or regulatory operations that set the parameters of history" (2002: 10), we can also examine how these conditions and re-conditionings form a dialectic in the post-cinematic. For instance, both the conditions of emergence (or, in Deleuzian terms, becoming-woman) and re-conditionings of the emerged (or, regulatory operations that stabilize the subjectivity of "woman") coalesce in "Telephone" and "BBHMM" around a post-cinematic feminism that is necessary, vital, and radical, but also inadequate to fully account for the experience of bodies in movement. In affect, Massumi notes, "something remains unactualized, inseparable from but unassimilable to any *particular*, functionally anchored perspective" (ibid. 35). It is precisely where excess in the two videos—the inability to coopt the pop star into a singular feminist framework because she is cast in excess of it—speaks to the affective unassimilation, and where a functional perspective (or closure) is denied. Here I have suggested that reverberations of radical feminist politics may lie in the surplus of affect that circulates in the post-cinematic forms of popular music videos that position the traditions of both cinema and feminism as objects of reclamation and renewed radicalization of women's experiences in the twenty-first century. But these are reclamations that do not settle for fully assimilable modes of reflection. Rather than being seen as "mere" cooptation by popular culture, these music videos perform a more challenging role: they reflect the ongoing vitality and affective appeal of feminism not only across time and space, but also across shifts from one screen technology to another. They also reflect a shift towards becoming-feminist rather than embracing feminism as a stable notion of singular meaning. Feminism is a nomadic subject here, where "nomadic consciousness is a form of political resistance to hegemonic and exclusionary views of subjectivity" (Braidotti 1994: 23). Moreover, a challenge to stable categories of identity and subjectivity is a feminist methodology par excellence. In Joan W. Scott's words: "We need the feminist analysis of categories of identity not only to detect the differentials of power constructed by binary oppositions that are purported to be timeless, natural, and universal, but also to contextualize and historicize these categories" (2002: 11).

It may well be that feminism in the videos discussed here is at least partially utilized as a recognizable social script susceptible for commercial exploitation. However, such commercial exploitation is further complicated by the declaratively "post-feminist" climate in which these post-cinematic, yet film feminist reverberations arise, where identifying as feminist by way of challenging recognizable categories of identity still echoes as a radical act. Perhaps by extension, overtly referring back to the cinematic screen within a decidedly post-cinematic medium may be considered radical as well. Cinema and feminism thus become objects of radical nostalgia, a structure of feelings that renews the unfinished vitality of the two rather than merely delegating them to the finished business of the past.

Related topics

Jenny Chamarette, "Embodying spectatorship: from phenomenology to sensation"
Felicity Colman, "Deleuzian spectatorship"
Patrice Petro, "Classical feminist film theory: then and (mostly) now"
Janet Staiger, "Film reception studies and feminism"

References

Bordwell, D. (1985). *Narration in the Fiction Film*. London: Routledge.
Bordwell, D., and Carroll, N. (eds.) (1996). *Post-theory: Reconstructing Film Studies*. Madison: The University of Wisconsin Press.
Braidotti, R. (1994). *Nomadic Subjects: Embodiment and Sexual Difference in Contemporary Feminist Theory*. New York: Columbia University Press.
Clover, C. J. (1987). Her body, himself: Gender in the slasher film. *Representations* 20, 187–228.
D'Aloia, A. and Eugeni, R. (2014). Neurofilmology: An introduction. *Cinema and Cie*, special issue no. 22, 1–15.
Deleuze, G. (1995). *Negotiations 1972–1990*. Trans. Martin Joughin. New York: Columbia University Press.
Freeland, C. A. (1996). Feminist frameworks for horror films. In D. Bordwell and N. Carroll (eds.), *Post-theory: Reconstructing Films Studies*. Madison: The University of Wisconsin Press (195–218).
Gormley, P. (2005). *The New-brutality Film: Race and Affect in Contemporary Hollywood Cinema*. Bristol: Intellect Books.
Hasson, U., Landesman, O., Knappmeyer, B., Vallines, I., Rubin, N., and Heeger, D. J. (2008). Neurocinematics: The neuroscience of film. *Projections*, 2(1), 1–26.
Kennedy, B. (2000). *Deleuze and Cinema: The Aesthetics of Sensation*. Edinburgh: Edinburgh University Press.
Marks, L. U. (2000). *The Skin of the Film: Intercultural Cinema, Embodiment, and the Senses*. Durham: Duke University Press.
Massumi, B. (2002). *Parables for the Virtual: Movement, Affect, Sensation*. Durham, NC: Duke University Press.

Persson, P. (2003). *Understanding Cinema: A Psychological Theory of Moving Imagery*. Cambridge: Cambridge University Press.

Plantinga, C. (2009). *Moving Viewers: American Film and the Spectator's Experience*. Berkeley: University of California Press.

Scott, J. W. (2002). Feminist Reverberations. *Differences: A Journal of Feminist Cultural Studies* 13.3, 1–23.

Shaviro, S. (2010). *Post-cinematic Affect*. Park Lane: Zero-Books.

Shimamura, A. P. (ed.). (2013). *Psychocinematics: Exploring Cognition at the Movies*. Oxford: Oxford University Press.

Smith, G. M. (2003). *Film Structure and the Emotion System*. Cambridge: Cambridge University Press.

Sobchack, V. C. (1992). *The Address of the Eye: A Phenomenology of Film Experience*. Princeton, NJ: Princeton University Press.

Williams, L. (1991). Film bodies: Gender, genre, and excess. *Film Quarterly*, 44.4, 2–13.

Young, A. (2009). *The Scene of Violence: Cinema, Crime, Affect*. New York: Routledge.

43

FANTASY ECHOES AND THE FUTURE ANTERIOR OF CINEMA AND GENDER

Kristin Lené Hole

Forty years have passed since the publication of Laura Mulvey's "Visual Pleasure and Narrative Cinema" (1975), a text that is often made to do the work of representing a diverse and complex history of feminist theorizing. Put differently, Mulvey's essay has often stood in for the entirety of the feminist project as it related to cinema in the 1970s. This reduction of a complex moment of emergence—what I am calling the "event" of feminist film and theory —to a single text inevitably erases as much history as it makes visible. The occlusions this produces have detrimental effects for the ways in which we understand the field of feminist film studies in the present and how we articulate or imagine future directions. In her edited collection, *Reclaiming the Archive* (2010), Vicki Callahan writes that,

> the history that we present as feminists always implies a kind of reclaiming, rewriting, and recontextualization of materials. This self-critical turn is our central heritage from 1970s feminism, for it asks us what it means to write from a feminist perspective.
>
> *(5)*

In what follows, I am interested in this reclaiming, rewriting, and recontextualization specifically as it applies to narratives about the 1970s and the "event" of—or historical confluence of forces that has come to be known as—feminist film and film studies. Callahan's project evinces the kind of thinking that is crucial for feminist film and media scholars at this moment, as she is interested in "the continued influence of 1970s feminist film studies in relation to the current production of film history and feminist film theory," and in challenging our own "historical amnesia" about this intellectual inheritance (ibid. 4).

Indeed, many contemporary feminist film scholars are invested in giving back to the 1970s its historical complexity. Some more recent attempts to narrate particular histories of feminist film studies include B. Ruby Rich's *Chick Flicks: Theories and Memories of the Feminist Film Movement* (1998), Alexandra Juhasz's *Women of Vision: Histories in Feminist Film and Video* (2001), Vicky Callahan's aforementioned edited collection, Patricia Mellencamp's *Five Ages of Film Feminism* (1996), Patrice Petro's *Aftershocks of the New: Feminism and Film History* (2002), and the 2004 special issues of *Signs, Beyond the*

Gaze: Recent Approaches to Film Feminisms. While I can not address all of these texts in detail here, I view their impulse to revisit the beginnings of feminist film and film studies through the lens of critical feminist historiography. In dialogue with several historiographical concepts, the recent histories of feminist film/theory open up a discussion as to what cinema and gender as a field is, can become, or will have been, by inviting us to (re)consider our origin stories.

The troubling tendency to reduce the intellectual inheritance of 1970s to (a reductive account of) psychoanalytic theory and the concerns of white women persists. Not only does this tendency reproduce the very exclusions it aims to critique, it also serves as a shorthand dismissal for the contributions of feminist film theory to the field as whole, particularly in the work of scholars who do not situate their work in a feminist framework (see, for example, David Rodowick's history of film theory (2007) as discussed by Petro in her contribution to this volume; perhaps more disturbingly, Rich's memoir seems to participate in this reduction of "academic feminism" to some univocal psychoanalytic framework that belies its true diversity). Revisiting the 1970s to seek out what is lost when this historical moment is condensed to a particular theoretical paradigm or series of canonical films and texts is crucial to both how feminist film scholars situate themselves in this lineage and to maintaining the critical force that feminism in its many forms brings in the present.

What is at stake here is an understanding of feminist film theory *as feminist history*, and doing justice to those origins, so that the narratives about what feminist theory *was* shape how it is practiced today and, concurrently, shape an understanding of what needs to be done going forward. How feminist film scholars write about and historicize this intellectual history is a matter of political urgency—a politics of representation much like that which preoccupied feminist film activists and scholars in the 1970s. Petro is also concerned to point out in her essay (in this volume) that feminist film theory is increasingly being marginalized or written out of larger histories of the discipline, so it seems germane to pause and consider how feminist film scholars view their legacy and to insist on its ongoing political and intellectual force, in all of its current diversity. In what follows I turn to several methodologies from feminist historiography that are useful for thinking through our own origin stories and offer occasional "moments" or images that I find useful from filmmaking or theorizing for illustrating how I envision these concepts at work. I draw on the work of three feminist scholars —Joan Scott, Tani Barlow, and Victoria Hesford, to think about fantasy echoes, catachresis and the future anterior, and the "event" of 1970s feminist film studies, respectively. From Hesford's work I draw on the idea of the "eventfulness" of feminist film theory. That is to say, I am interested in how affect and emotion crystallize around particular figures or texts from the past, and how investigating those affects can open up this history and restore to it some of its density. This relates closely to Joan Scott's notion of the fantasy echo—a process of identification across time, for example, between "women." The echoes are fantasies in that they obscure real historically and culturally significant differences that color what "woman" means in any given moment. They are echoes because they are repetitions, identifications that recur over time, but are always and each time different. At the same time these figures of identification are themselves historical invocations that tell us something about the moment at which the identification occurs and how the past was understood at that moment of invocation (Figure 43.1). Fantasy echoes illuminate the process of forming a collective identity across time, however fractured that collective is in its historical reality. In the case discussed here, this collective identity is centered on feminist film activism and studies. Finally, Barlow's work on Chinese feminism mobilizes the concept of the catachresis—a term without a stable historical referent—to think about

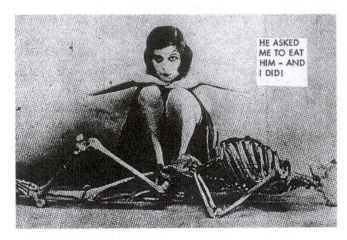

Figure 43.1   According to the journal *Women and Film* (1972), feminists were circulating images, such as this one of Theda Bara, captioned to reflect the current mood. Fantasy Echoes at work! (Author's construction).

the way that terms such as "women" are invoked at historical moments where the meaning lacks a secure content (one that is often only given retrospectively). For Barlow, the catachrestic term is deployed in the modality of the future anterior—it gestures as much to what *will have been* as to what is. These concepts are useful for reflexively engaging with the processes of identification that shape feminist film scholars' relationships to the past and for consciously constructing current histories that center what feminist film theory in the present *will have been* for future generations.

But before delving more into how these historiographical tools might work in practice, I want to make a few observations about the 1970s. These points are of course as much about the present moment as about a fidelity to the "truth" of the past. Inspired in part by Rich's account of the energy, collective action, and conviction of 1970s organizing, but also by earlier accounts such as Jan Rosenberg's *Women's Reflections: The Feminist Film Movement* (1983), I offer new ways of framing what the 1970s might mean for us today as we think further about the legacy we have inherited.

To begin, the then-nascent feminist film movement lacked discipline—in the sense of academic disciplinarity and in a more colloquial sense as well. It was connected to the world outside of the university and to feminist activism. It was committed to supporting women in making and exhibiting their work, and to organizing festivals and screenings to that effect. Since film studies were not yet institutionalized, they were also necessarily *inter*disciplinary. In fact the use of psychoanalysis itself can be read as an interdisciplinary thrust, akin to the use of sociological approaches to look at the representations of women in other works of the 1970s (such as Haskell's *From Reverence to Rape*, 1974). We can take from this period an incitement to working collectively, feeling accountable to constituencies both in and out of the university, and maintaining, in particular, a sense of feminist inter- and a-disciplinarity. Interdisciplinarity in our own time remains crucial in terms of developing film theory using feminist writing and theory from across disciplines and outside of the university. My attempt to enact such a practice is evident here in the desire to think about feminist film theory as an intellectual inheritance through the lens of feminist historiography.

Second, and related to the lack of respect for disciplinary boundaries, the 1970s were political. Johnston, Mulvey, and other canonical thinkers of the time were not writing solely for tenure or for solipsistic intellectual pleasure. Feminist theory emerged from a sense of commitment, of urgency, and of being relevant to real women. In her contribution to this volume, Petro references a recent interview with Laura Mulvey where she reflects on the origin of her seminal "Visual Pleasure" essay. In this 2015 interview, Mulvey emphasizes that the essay emerged out of what was essentially a form of consciousness-raising group— "a Women's Liberation study group, in which we read Freud and realized the usefulness of psychoanalytic theory for a feminist project." Its origin, then, was in women collectively speaking about and analyzing their experience as it intersected or was in tension with major intellectual currents of the time—a political sense of urgency and a need to diagnose women's situations in the present through the history of dominant images and ideas. Feminist visions, then, were filtered through dominant discourses, while their experiences modified and shaped these discourses to politically evaluate culture as they lived it. This is not to say that feminist film theory should not take theoretical and abstract forms. Rather, from the very beginning, there was a pervasive sense that feminist work matters—whether it is speculative, historical, or uses another framework. This commitment to political relevance has persisted over time and up until the present. Feminist film scholarship politicizes the field of representation and sees it as relevant to our lives, in large part by shaping and generating conceptions of the possible for marginalized groups.

Finally, feminist film (or we can add media here to update our object of study) was and continues to be feminist *theory* in its own right. Striking in this regard is Rich's account in *Chick Flicks* of the impact of Chantal Akerman's *Jeanne Dielman* (1975), so groundbreaking was the film in terms of its representation of female subjectivity. She writes,

> We felt we needed a new vocabulary to talk about the film, and set to work educating ourselves to deserve it. *In Chicago, we even had a study group on* Jeanne Dielman *for a while.* Our emotional investment in the film can't be overstated.
>
> (1998: 159; *italics mine*)

The affective and intellectual are not separable in Rich's avowal. The power of visual media to affect us, make us think, and offer us perspectives and knowledges at the limits of the articulable continues to inspire feminist film scholarship and filmmaking. This connection between affect and acting is a key component of thinking about feminist film theory as an "event."

In *Feeling Women's Liberation* (2013), Victoria Hesford interrogates the "eventfulness" of women's liberation in order to reopen what may seem to be a closed chapter in the history of women's second wave activism and theorizing. She does so in order to challenge dominant narratives about that history and the limiting occlusions of these accounts. Her archaeological method offers a useful template with which we can approach feminist film and theory's own disputed history. Both women's liberation and the origins of feminist film theory emerge in the same period—the contested "seventies"—and for good reason. Feminist film theory came out of real struggles—over representation, theoretical exclusion, unequal access to filmmaking resources, and women coming together to better understand their experiences in a patriarchal society.

Hesford argues for a more complex history of feminism rooted in challenging normative identities that continue to limit women in the present and to truncate the scope of how the political is defined. Methodologically, she unearths the intensities, affects, and emotions that have produced the artifacts composing our archive of memories of women's liberation. But rather than taking these objects and memories as evidence of identities, positions, and platforms, in her account they operate as points of access to a larger field of issues and problems, out of which the solutions offered by the "second wave" arose. This complex of problems persists in—even as it is largely obscured by—dominant narratives and feelings about the history of women's liberation.

To apply this method to feminist film theory's history then, would be to discern its canonical artifacts and to analyze the emotions that circulate around them, in order to reopen the past to its variegated reality and make available other points of identification. What now gets simplified and then typically dismissed via labels such as "cinefeminism," "cinepsychoanalysis," or "seventies feminist film theory" was a much more complicated event with multiple origins. These shorthand terms are also loaded with a variety of affects, from nostalgia to embarrassment to anger, and these affects are equally important for an analysis of contemporary feminist film theorists' relation to this intellectual and political inheritance. While this short essay form precludes any attempt to undertake the kind of detailed examination that Hesford does in her book-length study, I want to gesture here towards the need for a similar discursive and affective archaeology of the past to discover moments of repressed potential. This involves seeking out points where feminist film theory became entrenched as, for example, "psychoanalytic," and how those moments of solidification obscure a more diverse and unknowable revolutionary moment. As Hesford argues, in order to better understand the "something to be done" in the feminist present, we must relieve the past of its coherence and reopen the texts of our history that are often, even by feminist academics, deemed essentialist, simplistic, or no longer relevant to the struggles of women today.

To pay attention to feminist film theory's eventfulness involves interrogating the ways in which feelings about that period—and its later institutionalization in the 1980s—obscure its historical density. In this respect I gesture towards another commentary referenced in Petro's essay in this volume. This is Linda Williams's contribution to a 2004 *Signs* roundtable reflecting on the history of feminist film theory. Williams confesses that she "ha[s] more enthusiasm for Hugo Münsterberg than for Laura Mulvey ... I now feel weighed down by the burdens of what feels like orthodox feminist position taking." She also admits that the invitation to reflect on feminist film theory for the special issue as, "writing about a field that had once felt very exciting ... was, in the case of this essay 'assignment,' beginning to feel like an unwanted duty." Williams' honesty in these sentences provides us with an affective node that is useful for thinking through the event of feminist film theory and our relationship to this history in a way that I hope she herself would find useful. Her avowal illustrates the ways in which our feelings about the past—feelings which have solidified around precisely such objects as an essay—tend to prevent us from reexamining that past and rewriting or investigating our origin stories. The feelings expressed by Williams, in this framework, can provide us with a way *into* the event of "seventies film theory." Examining our emotions of shame or weariness towards certain texts, objects, and even image-memories as professors and scholars invites us to ask how the emotions that are produced between us and these objects have resulted in certain occlusions or foreclosures in the classroom. Indeed, Petro's own writing on "Film Feminism and Nostalgia for the Seventies" points out a "disturbing" tendency to nostalgia for the 1970s at the turn of the century. Within my framework here, this nostalgia becomes, like Williams' sense of burden, itself a way into the past as it shapes the present. To paraphrase Hesford, to approach feminist film theory "as an event is to approach it as both possibility and legacy" (2013: 14), to see it as both an eruption of the new and as operating in excess of its own moment and carrying over (consciously or otherwise) into contemporary ways of doing and thinking feminist film theory.

A return to texts of the past—films and essays—that are in danger of falling into oblivion because they are not canonized is a fruitful way to begin to reopen this moment of emergence and to find alternate figures or images around which to think through this timeframe. Joan Wallach Scott's notion of the fantasy echo is a way of thinking about collective identities— such as "feminist film scholar" here—as the result of identifications with figures across time. As Scott argues of the category "women," "the commonality among women does not preexist its invocation but rather ... it is secured by fantasies that enable them to transcend history and difference" (2001: 288). The echo is—like all repetitions—each time different. These identificatory "echoes" tend to minimize materially and historically significant differences that in fact divide women across time, while pointing to the important role of fantasy in constructing political identity. As Scott writes, "Identification (which produces identity) operates as a fantasy echo, then, replaying in time and over generations the process that forms individuals as social and political actors" (ibid. 292). Doubtless, many of the recent attempts at revisiting feminist film and theory of the 1970s, along with my own thinking here, engage processes of identification with the past of feminist film and theory. Mellencamp's book is a quixotic foray across films and texts that have created her somewhat diaristic narrative of feminist film history. Her schema of "five ages" of film feminism is imbued with affect, and turns to films and persons as diverse as *Gold Diggers of 1933* (LeRoy, 1933), Tracey Moffatt, Clara Bow, and *Something to Talk About* (Hallström, 1995). *A Fine Romance* is more a personal—and critical/intellectual—identification across time with texts and figures than it is a chronological historical overview of feminist film. Rich's book, by contrast, is a recounting of what to her were the key moments of an emerging movement—from a screening of Schneeman's *Fuses* to the work of Sara Gomez and Yvonne Rainer. By alternating between her past published writing and her current (late-1990s) reflections on what was happening in her life—personally and politically—at the time of their writing, her memoir foregrounds the role of identifications and affects in relating to and remembering the past. Juhasz's film, *Women of Vision* (1998), and the published collection of interview material that followed (2001), reveals that there are multiple origins at work in the history of feminist filmmaking and theorizing—but we reproduce the exclusion of these origins when and if we narrate the past as always already white/straight/middle-class/psychoanalytic. Juhasz's work uses oral history to reopen a lost time of collective organizing, thinking, and filmmaking. Her interviewees range from lesbian experimental filmmaker Barbara Hammer to Margaret Caples, an activist and arts administrator committed to social justice, who works for the Community Film Workshop and strives to make media production accessible to women of all races. Caples expresses ambivalence about early feminism's whiteness, an ambivalence shared by Frances Negrón-Muntaner, a Puerto Rican filmmaker and activist who places her work within feminist film history, but identifies more so as a queer and/or disaporic filmmaker. The book includes the voices of women of color whose media activism centers on AIDS activism (Juanita Mohammed), academics who focus on queer and Asian-American representation (Eve Oishi), and an artist, social justice activist and active sex worker (Carol Leigh). *Women of Vision* acknowledges diversity while simultaneously grouping the women included— racially, class-wise, and generationally— into a shared identity as feminist media "people." What her project makes visible is that the very occlusions and omissions that are located at the beginnings of feminist film theory are reproduced in the tendency to privilege those sites as the problematic, yet undisputed, origins of feminist film's intellectual inheritance. Juhasz's inclusion of voices from a variety of demographics that are involved at different levels of feminist cinema offers a much-needed corrective that opens up the past to new images and voices and celebrates this originary multiplicity.

This points to the necessity of—to the extent possible—understanding our own invocations as themselves historical. To echo Scott, "where there is evidence of what seems enduring and unchanging identity, there is a history that needs to be explored" (2001: 304). There are several dimensions to the idea of the fantasy echo that are useful here—first, its emphasis on the psychic processes of identification *echo* feminist film theory's own predominant concerns with identificatory processes as they relate to film viewing. Psychoanalysis reasserts itself here; if not in the frameworks that dominate feminist thinking today, then in an understanding of how to create a lineage within feminist scholarship. Secondly, the processes of identification gesture beyond the filmmakers or texts studied, towards the pleasures of cinema that have drawn many scholars to the field in the first place—the visual pleasures and subject-forming fantasies that have hailed them as thinkers.

Madeline Anderson's film *I Am Somebody* (1970) is a form of fantasy echo that has the power to challenge dominant origin stories about feminist filmmaking. This short film (29 minutes), which charts a 1969 strike of mostly black female hospital workers in Charleston, was commissioned by the hospital workers union. Anderson, herself a black woman, used media coverage to reconstruct a history of the event, with careful framing and retrospective narration from one of the women involved. The film emphasizes that black women's lives and work matter—a concept that resonates today with current issues around police violence against African-American citizens. Considering the continuingly sparse involvement of and representation for black women in North American cinema, this film continues to have serious political relevance (see also Bobo, this volume). Theoretically, *I Am Somebody* provides a moment of origin that challenges any account of feminist filmmaking in the 1970s as purely white, purely middle class, and abstractly theoretical. Anderson reveals the impulse to represent women's raced and classed stories even earlier in the decade than the first works of "feminist film theory" proper. In her essay on the film, Shilyh Warren notes that the film was a part of the feminist film movement at the time—receiving a screening at the first Women's International Film Festival in 1972, being shown the previous year alongside other feminist documentaries at the Flaherty seminar, and mentioned in overviews and guides to feminist filmmaking of the period. As Warren writes:

> *I Am Somebody* both disrupts the singularity at work in the notion of "the" feminist film movement and at the same time redefines the term "feminist" in the concept of seventies feminist documentaries … what we find in the late sixties and early seventies is a landscape of activism by diverse groups and organizations of women, impossible to generalize as existing and cooperating within a singular movement. To continue to stress the existence of a hegemonic movement is to continue to neglect the impact felt throughout diverse communities during those years.
>
> (2013)

My invocation of this film is an effort to enable a different sense of the present through shifting our reference points of the past. This desire to identify, and the real differences that it may render invisible, are issues that must be foregrounded in any invocation of the fantasy echo.

The fantasy echo addresses the potentially problematic nature of combining figures as diverse as Madeline Anderson, B. Ruby Rich, Laura Mulvey, and Sally Potter all in one fell swoop. The invocation of these figures should be subject to historical scrutiny—my interest in them now says more about what it means to be a woman or a feminist at this moment than anything about the past. And I would suggest this impulse is at work in our desire to find female silent film pioneers (see Hennefeld and Gaines in this volume), to unearth female editors or scriptwriters who played key roles during the studio era (see Smyth in this volume), and to seek a less Western-centric account of women's involvement in filmmaking around the world (see Ponzanesi, Wang, Atakav, Jaikumar, and Ciecko, for example, in this volume).

Finally, I want to gesture towards the connected concepts of the catachresis and the future anterior as they are modeled in Tani Barlow's writing on Chinese feminism. Catachreses indicate a kind of epistemological incompatibility between the signifier and referent. As David L. Eng writes,

> historical catachresis works to dislodge a particular version of history as the "way it really was" by denying the possibility of a singular historical context in which the past has transpired and reemerges in the present as a reified object of investigation.
>
> *(2008: 1483)*

The catachresis opens up the past to the future and asks questions about the omissions that have produced the reified history we receive. As Barlow writes,

> If feminism is just a word in North American English ... for a much longer effort to put sexual difference and gendered inequality at the center of social theory, then feminism is itself catachrestic, a concept in search of an adequate referent.
>
> *(2004: 14)*

Thinking about feminist film and theory specifically as catachreses can open up the inaccessible referent of history for new narratives or imaginings in the present. Barlow is interested in the "what will have been" of the past—the future anterior. I am invested in what *will have been* feminist film theory in the present—what is invoked now when feminist film theorists call on their subject in this moment of historicity and how does it shape what they hope "will have been" feminist media scholarship in the future? These concerns cannot be separated from narratives of origins, be they located in the 1970s, the days of silent film, or otherwise.

What is particularly fascinating is that these issues seem to permeate the objects of study themselves. As I have suggested earlier, feminist filmmaking has always also been feminist theory. Sally Potter's first film *Thriller* (1979)—already a canonical feminist film theory film—figures in both Mellencamp and Rich's books. For Rich, *Thriller* "ingeniously connects" representations of women with their realities: "it shows how smoothly male artists manipulating woman's image naturalize and obscure the manipulation in women's lives ... [*Thriller*] not only rereads the official history in terms of the present, but also dares to imagine the future" (1998: 228). Mellencamp discusses the film *as* feminist theory. She writes, "In fact, *Thriller* was way ahead in 1979, including race, lesbianism, local politics, and history, along with a critique of narrative romance. And it raised issues that feminist film theory is only beginning to notice—work, money, and age" (1996: 156). Potter's concerns in *Thriller* complicate the reduction of cinefeminism to any one paradigm. The film revisits Puccini's *La Bohème* to explore the silenced story of the woman (Mimi), whose death in the opera becomes an occasion for male heroism and noble sentiment. Potter casts a black actress as Mimi, highlighting the whiteness of the female lead in the opera and evoking global flows of bodies and capital—all while deconstructing dominant narratives and the positions they offer women. The film foregrounds the classed dimensions of Mimi's character—a seamstress who dies of tuberculosis—as opposed to the heroic "poverty" of the white male artists, and opens up the possibility of lesbian desire between Mimi and her foil,

Musetta. Mimi becomes both a figure of identification (a fantasy echo) and a catachresis—an invocation of woman where there is no woman there. Potter attempts to fill in that absent trace but does so from her own historical moment.

The absence of the referent—at least as far as meaningful historical documentation is concerned—is evident in another video made almost twenty years later. Cheryl Dunye's *The Watermelon Woman* (1996) reveals the queer fantasy echo at work in her creation of an archive that can only point to the absence of the referent. Here we have another instance of a filmmaker enacting what theory can perhaps only gesture towards. The film documents the need—politically and emotionally—to create figures of identification—here queer, female, and black—that do not exist in any (even feminist or lesbian) archives, and their relation to affects and possibilities in the present.

At one point in Petro's writing on nostalgia for the 1970s she describes her thoughts at a panel on (feminist) film and media theories. She wonders,

> why not shift the emphasis from what feminist film theory is (or seems to be) now in an effort to recall and redeem its failed opportunities and unrealized promises? Why not name and thus call into existence that which otherwise might be lost to history and to contemporary thought?
>
> *(2002: 160)*

This project, I submit, requires that history itself become an object of theorization and that feminist theory become a historical object. Petro finishes her essay with a call to a "community of the question," which would, among other things, be "dedicated to a shared sense of what matters, of what questions need to be asked, of what issues need to be thought, of what battles remain to fought" (ibid. 172). The history of feminist film and theory itself needs to be part of the question—one that refuses a clear answer but understands that its exploration in the present will shape the future anterior of the field. Feminist historiography encourages us to take our emotions seriously as objects of critical inquiry and to revisit the old films and texts that carry affective charges across time and start our inquiries there. It also suggests that we create figures of identification where only a trace may be in evidence. This involves not only how we think about what feminist film theory will have been in the future, but also how we can be more accountable to a liberated past.

Related topics

Jacqueline Bobo, "Black women filmmakers: a brief history"
Jane Gaines, "What was 'women's work' in the silent film era?"
Patrice Petro, "Classical feminist film theory: then and (mostly) now"
J. E. Smyth, "Female editors in studio-era Hollywood: rethinking feminist 'frontiers' and the constraints of the archives"

References

Barlow, Tani. (2004) *The Question of Women in Chinese Feminism*. Durham, NC: Duke University Press.
Callahan, Vicky, ed. (2010) *Reclaiming the Archive: Feminism and Film History*. Detroit: Wayne State University Press.
Eng, David L. (2008) "The End(s) of Race" *PMLA* 123.5: 1479–93.

Haskell, Molly. (1974) *From Reverence to Rape: The Treatment of Women in the Movies.* Chicago: University of Chicago Press.

Hesford, Victoria. (2013) *Feeling Women's Liberation.* Durham, NC: Duke University Press.

Juhasz, Alexandra. (2001) *Women of Vision: Histories in Feminist Film and Video.* Minneapolis: University of Minnesota Press.

Mellencamp, Patricia. (1996) *A Fine Romance: Five Ages of Film Feminism.* Philadelphia: Temple University Press.

Mulvey, Laura. (1975) "Visual Pleasure and Narrative Cinema." *Screen* 16.3: 6–18.

Petro, Patrice. (2002) *Aftershocks of the New: Feminism and Film History.* New Brunswick, NJ: Rutgers University Press.

Rich, B. Ruby. (1998) *Chick Flicks: Theories and Memories of the Feminist Film Movement.* Durham, NC: Duke University Press.

Rodowick, David. (2007) "An Elegy for Theory." *October* 122: 91–109.

Rosenberg, Jan. (1983) *Women's Reflections: The Feminist Film Movement.* Ann Arbor: UMI Research Press.

Scott, Joan W. (2001) "Fantasy Echo: History and the Construction of Identity." *Critical Inquiry* 27.2: 284–304.

Signs (2004) Special Issue: *Beyond the Gaze: Recent Approaches to Film Feminisms.*

Warren, Shilyh. (2013) "Recognition on the Surface of Madeline Anderson's *I am Somebody*." *Signs* 33.2: 353–78.

Williams, Linda (2004) "Why I Did Not Want to Write This Essay." *Signs: Journal of Women in Culture and Society* 30.1: 1264–71.

INDEX